Lubrication, Maintenance and Tune-up

Chapter Four
Engine Top End

Chapter Five
Engine Lower End

Chapter Six
Clutch and External Shift Mechanism

Chapter Seven
Transmission and Internal Shift Mechanism

Chapter Eight
Fuel, Emission Control and Exhaust Systems

Chapter Nine
Electrical System

Chapter Ten
Front Suspension and Steering

Chapter Eleven
Rear Suspension

Chapter Twelve
Brakes

Chapter Thirteen
Frame

Index

Wiring Diagrams

CLYMER®

Publisher Shawn Etheridge

EDITORIAL

Managing Editor
James Grooms

Associate Editor
Lee Buell

Technical Writers
Jay Bogart
Michael Morlan
George Parise
Mark Rolling
Ed Scott
Ron Wright

Editorial Production Manager
Dylan Goodwin

Senior Production Editor
Greg Araujo

Production Editors
Holly Messinger
Darin Watson

Associate Production Editor
Susan Hartington
Julie Jantzer
Justin Marciniak

Technical Illustrators
Steve Amos
Errol McCarthy
Mitzi McCarthy
Bob Meyer
Mike Rose

MARKETING/SALES AND ADMINISTRATION

Advertising & Promotions Manager
Elda Starke

Advertising & Promotions Coordinators
Melissa Abbott
Wendy Stringfellow

Art Director
Chris Paxton

Sales Managers
Ted Metzger, Manuals
Dutch Sadler, Marine
Matt Tusken, Motorcycles

Business Manager
Ron Rogers

Customer Service Manager
Terri Cannon

Customer Service Representatives
Shawna Davis
Courtney Hollars
Susan Kohlmeyer
April LeBlond
Jennifer Lassiter
Ernesto Suarez

Warehouse & Inventory Manager
Leah Hicks

PRIMEDIA
Business Magazines & Media
P.O. Box 12901, Overland Park, KS 66282-2901 • 800-262-1954 • 913-967-1719

The following books and guides are published by PRIMEDIA Business Directories & Books.

More information available at *primediabooks.com*

CLYMER® YAMAHA
V-STAR 650 • 1998-2004

The world's finest publisher of mechanical how-to manuals

PRIMEDIA
Business Magazines & Media
P.O. Box 12901, Overland Park, Kansas 66282-2901

Copyright ©2004 PRIMEDIA Business Magazines & Media Inc.

FIRST EDITION
First Printing February, 2001

SECOND EDITION
Updated by James Grooms to include 2001-2003 models
First Printing July, 2003

THIRD EDITION
First Printing July, 2004

Printed in U.S.A.

CLYMER and colophon are registered trademarks of PRIMEDIA Business Magazines & Media Inc.

ISBN: 0-89287-912-2

Library of Congress: 2004094975

TECHNICAL PHOTOGRAPHY: *Ron Wright.*

TECHNICAL ILLUSTRATIONS: *Mitzi McCarthy.*

TOOLS AND EQUIPMENT: *K & L Supply Company at www.klsupply.com.*

PRODUCTION: *Susan Hartington.*

EDITOR: *James Grooms.*

COVER: *Mark Clifford Photography at www.markclifford.com. Yamaha XVS650 provided by JMG Motorsports, Newhall, California.*

All rights reserved. Reproduction or use, without express permission, of editorial or pictorial content, in any manner, is prohibited. No patent liability is assumed with respect to the use of the information contained herein. While every precaution has been taken in the preparation of this book, the publisher assumes no responsibility for errors or omissions. Neither is any liability assumed for damages resulting from use of the information contained herein. Publication of the servicing information in this manual does not imply approval of the manufacturers of the products covered.

All instructions and diagrams have been checked for accuracy and ease of application; however, success and safety in working with tools depend to a great extent upon individual accuracy, skill and caution. For this reason, the publishers are not able to guarantee the result of any procedure contained herein. Nor can they assume responsibility for any damage to property or injury to persons occasioned from the procedures. Persons engaging in the procedure do so entirely at their own risk.

CONTENTS

QUICK REFERENCE DATA IX

CHAPTER ONE
GENERAL INFORMATION 1

Manual organization
Notes, cautions and warnings
Safety first
Service hints
Washing the bike
Special tips
Torque specifications
Fasteners
Lubricants
RTV gasket sealant
Gasket remover
Threadlocking compound

Expendable supplies
Serial numbers
Warning and information labels
Basic hand tools
Precision measuring tools
Special tools
Fabricating tools
Mechanic's tips
Ball bearing replacement
Seals
Riding safety
Storage

CHAPTER TWO
TROUBLESHOOTING 43

- Operating requirements
- Troubleshooting instruments
- Starting the engine
- Starting difficulties
- Engine starting troubleshooting
- Engine performance
- Engine noises
- Engine lubrication
- Cylinder leakdown test
- Clutch
- Gearshift linkage
- Transmission
- Electrical troubleshooting
- Test equipment
- Basic test procedures
- Electrical problems
- Carburetor troubleshooting
- Excessive vibration
- Front suspension and steering
- Brake problems

CHAPTER THREE
LUBRICATION, MAINTENANCE AND TUNE-UP 59

- Pre-ride checks
- Maintenance intervals
- Tires
- Battery
- New battery installation
- Battery electrical cable connectors
- Periodic lubrication
- Periodic maintenance
- Tune-up

CHAPTER FOUR
ENGINE TOP END 94

- Engine principles
- Servicing engine in the frame
- Cylinder head covers
- Cylinder head
- Rocker arms
- Camshaft
- Cam chain and chain guides
- Valves and valve components
- Cylinder block
- Pistons and piston rings

CHAPTER FIVE
ENGINE LOWER END 138

- Servicing engine in the frame
- Engine
- Alternator cover
- Stator and pickup coils
- Alternator rotor and starter gears
- Starter clutch
- Middle driven gear assembly
- Middle drive pinion gear
- Primary drive gear
- Oil pump
- Oil strainer
- Crankcase
- Crankshaft
- Connecting rods
- Break-in

CHAPTER SIX
CLUTCH AND EXTERNAL SHIFT MECHANISM 173

Clutch cover
Clutch
Clutch release mechanism
Clutch cable replacement
Primary drive gear and
 oil pump spur gear
External shift mechanism

CHAPTER SEVEN
TRANSMISSION AND INTERNAL SHIFT MECHANISM 190

Transmission
Internal shift mechanism
Shift pedal/footpeg assembly

CHAPTER EIGHT
FUEL, EMISSION CONTROL AND EXHAUST SYSTEMS. 201

Air filter housing
Surge tank assembly
Carburetor operation
Carburetor
Throttle position sensor
Carburetor heater system
Fuel level
Throttle cable
Choke cable
Fuel tank
Fuel valve
Fuel filter
Fuel pump bracket
Air induction system
Evaporative emission control
Exhaust system

CHAPTER NINE
ELECTRICAL SYSTEM 229

Charging system
Stator
Voltage regulator/rectifier
Ignition system
Ignition coil
Pickup coil
Relay unit
Spark plug
Igniter unit
Starting system
Starter motor
Starting circuit cut-off relay
Starting system diode
Starter relay
Lighting system
Headlight
Meter assembly
Taillight
Signal system
Brake light
Neutral indicator light
Turn signals
Horn
Fuel pump system
Carburetor heater system
 throttle position sensor (TPS)
Switches
Wiring connectors
Fuses

CHAPTER TEN
FRONT SUSPENSION AND STEERING............ 280

    Bike stand
    Front wheel
    Front hub
    Rim and spoke service
    Wheel balance
    Tire changing
    Handlebar
    Steering head
    Front fork

CHAPTER ELEVEN
REAR SUSPENSION............ 310

    Rear wheel
    Rear hub
    Final gearcase and drive shaft
    Shock absorber
    Swing arm

CHAPTER TWELVE
BRAKES............ 324

    Disc brakes
    Front brake pad replacement
    Front caliper
    Front master cylinder
    Front brake hose replacement
    Brake disc
    Bleeding the system
    Rear drum brake
    Brake pedal/footpeg assembly
    Brake rod assembly

CHAPTER THIRTEEN
FRAME............ 347

    Seat
    Front fender
    Rear fender
    Frame neck cover
    Battery box cover
    Right side cover
    Tool box cover
    Left side cover
    Sidestand
    Footpeg
    Frame

INDEX............ 356

WIRING DIAGRAMS............ 361

QUICK REFERENCE DATA

MOTORCYCLE INFORMATION

MODEL:_____ YEAR:_____

VIN NUMBER:_____

ENGINE SERIAL NUMBER:_____

CARBURETOR SERIAL NUMBER OR I.D. MARK:_____

TIRE SPECIFICATIONS

Model	Front	Rear
XVS650		
Tire type	Tube-type	Tube-type
Size	100/90-19 57S	170/80-15M/C 77S
Manufacturer	Bridgestone L309 / Dunlop F24	Bridgestone G546 / Dunlop K555
Minimum tread depth	1.0 mm (0.04 in.)	1.0 mm (0.04 in.)
Inflation pressure (cold)[1]		
Up to 90 kg (198 lb.) load[2]	200 kPa (29 psi)	225 kPa (32.6 psi)
90 kg (198 lb.)-maximum load[2]	200 kPa (29 psi)	250 kPa (36.3 psi)
XVS650A		
Tire type	Tube-type	Tube-type
Size	130/90-16 67S	170/80-15M/C 77S
Manufacturer	Bridgestone G703 / Dunlop D404F	Bridgestone G702 / Dunlop D404
Minimum tread depth	1.0 mm (0.04 in.)	1.0 mm (0.04 in.)
Inflation pressure (cold)[1]		
Up to 90 kg (198 lb.) load[2]	225 kPa (32.6 psi)	225 kPa (32.6 psi)
90 kg (198 lb.)-maximum load[2]	225 kPa (32.6 psi)	250 kPa (36.3 psi)

1. Tire inflation pressure for original equipment tires. Aftermarket tires may require different inflation pressures; refer to the aftermarket manufacturer's specifications.
2. Load equals the total weight of the cargo, rider, passenger, and acessories.

RECOMMENDED LUBRICANTS AND FLUIDS

Fuel	Regular unleaded
Octane	86 [(R + M)/2 method] or research octane of 91 or higher
Capacity	16.0 L (4.2 US gal [3.5 Imp. gal])
Reserve amount	3.0 L (0.79 US gal [0.66 Imp. gal])
Engine oil	
Grade	API SF, SG
Viscosity	
40° F (5° C) or above	SAE 20W40
60° F (15° C) or below	SAE 10W30
Capacity	
Oil change only	2.6 L (2.7 US qt. [2.3 Imp. qt.])
Oil and filter change	2.8 L (3.0 US qt. [2.5 Imp. qt.])
When engine completely dry	3.2 L (3.4 US qt. [2.8 Imp. qt.])

(continued)

RECOMMENDED LUBRICANTS AND FLUIDS (continued)

Final gear oil	
Viscosity	SAE 80 hypoid gear oil
Grade	API GL-4 (GL-5 or GL-6 may also be used)
Capacity	190 cc (6.42 US oz. [6.68 Imp. oz.])
Brake fluid	DOT 4
Battery	Maintenance free
Fork oil	
Viscosity	SAE 10W fork oil
Capacity per leg	
XVS650	454 cc (15.35 U.S. oz [15.98 Imp. oz.])
XV650A	507 cc (17.14 U.S. oz [17.84 Imp. oz.])
Oil level each leg*	
XVS650	114 mm (4.49 in.)
XVS650A	95 mm (3.74 in.)

*Measured from top of the fully compressed fork tube, without spring.

MAINTENANCE AND TUNE-UP SPECIFICATIONS

Recommended spark plug	NGK DPR7EA-9, Denso X22EPR-U9
Spark plug gap	0.8-0.9 mm (0.031-0.035 in.)
Idle Speed	1150-1250 rpm
Pilot screw	2 1/2 turns out
Valve clearance	
Intake	0.07-0.12 mm (0.0028-0.0047 in.)
Exhaust	0.12-0.17 mm (0.0047-0.0067 in.)
Compression pressure (at sea level)	
Standard	1100 kPa (160 psi)
Minimum	1000 kPa (145 psi)
Maximum	1200 kPa (174 psi)
Ignition timing	12° at 1200 rpm
Vacuum pressure (at idle)	29.0 kPa (8.7 in. Hg)
Engine oil pressure (hot)	10 kPa (1.5 psi) at 1200 rpm
Front brake pad wear limit	0.8 mm (0.03 in.)
Rear brake lining wear limit	2 mm (0.08 in.)
Brake pedal height	85 mm (3.35 in.) above top of footpeg
Brake pedal free play	20-30 mm (0.79-1.18 in.)
Throttle cable free play	4-6 mm (0.16-0.24 in.)
Brake lever free play	
At lever end	10-15 mm (0.39-0.59 in.)
Clutch lever free play	
At lever end	10-15 mm (0.39-0.59 in.)
Shift-pedal rod length	188 mm (7.4 in.)
Rim runout	
Radial	
New	1.0 mm (0.04 in)
Limit	2.0 mm (0.08 in.)
Lateral	
New	0.5 mm (0.02 in.)
Limit	2.0 mm (0.08 in.)

MAINTENANCE AND TUNE UP TIGHTENING TORQUES

Item	N·m	ft.-lb.	in.-lb.
Oil filter cover bolt	10	–	88
Oil filter cover plate bolt	10	–	88
Oil drain bolt	43	32	–
Oil gallery bolt	8	–	71
Front brake caliper mounting bolts	40	29.5	–
Front axle	59	43.5	–
Front axle clamp bolt	20	15	–
Upper fork bridge clamp bolts	23	17	–
Lower fork bridge clamp bolt	23	17	–
Front fork bottom Allen bolt	30	22	–
Front fork cap	23	17	–
Steering stem head nut	110	81	–
Torque arm nut	20	15	–
Rear axle nut	97	72	–
Brake pedal height adjuster locknut	7	–	62
Valve adjuster locknut	14	10	–
Camshaft sprocket cover bolt	10	–	88
Valve cover bolt	10	–	88
Spark plugs	18	13	–
Sidestand nut	56	41	–
Final-gear oil filler bolt	23	17	–
Final-gear drain bolt	23	17	–

REPLACEMENT BULBS

Item	Voltage/wattage
Headlight (high/low beam)	12 V 60/55 W
Tail/brake light	12 V 8/27 W
Turn signal	12 V 27 W
License light	12 V 5 W
Meter light	12 V 1.7 W
Neutral indicator light	12 V 1.7 W
High beam indicator light	12 V 1.7 W
Turn signal indicator light	12 V 1.7 W

CHAPTER ONE

GENERAL INFORMATION

This detailed, comprehensive manual covers the Yamaha V-Star Custom (XVS650) and V-Star Classic (XVS650A) from 1998-on. The book includes all you need to know to keep your Yamaha running right. The expert text gives complete information on maintenance, tune-up, repair and overhaul. Hundreds of photos and drawings provide a guide through every step.

A shop manual is a reference source. As in all Clymer books, this one is designed to find information quickly. All chapters are thumb tabbed. Important items are extensively indexed at the rear of the book. All procedures, tables, photos, etc. in this manual are for the reader who may be working on the bike for the first time or using this manual for the first time. All the most frequently used specifications and capacities are summarized in the *Quick Reference Data* pages at the front of the book.

Keep the book handy in a tool box. The book will help you understand how your bike runs, lower repair costs and generally improve your satisfaction with the bike.

Tables 1-8 appear at the end of this chapter.

Table 1 lists VIN and primary identification numbers for V-Star Custom models.

Table 2 lists VIN and primary identification numbers for V-Star Classic models.

Table 3 lists vehicle weight.

Table 4 lists decimal and metric equivalents.

Table 5 lists general torque specifications.

Table 6 lists conversion tables.

Table 7 lists technical abbreviations.

Table 8 lists metric tap and drill sizes.

MANUAL ORGANIZATION

This chapter provides general information and discusses the tools and equipment used for preventive maintenance and troubleshooting.

Chapter Two provides methods and suggestions for quick and accurate diagnosis and repair of problems. Troubleshooting procedures discuss typical symptoms and logical methods to pinpoint a problem.

Chapter Three explains all periodic lubrication and routine maintenance procedures necessary to keep the motorcycle running well. Chapter Three also includes recommended tune-up procedures, eliminating the need to constantly consult chapters on the various assemblies.

Subsequent chapters describe specific systems such as the top end, lower end, clutch, transmission, fuel, suspension and brakes. Each chapter provides disassembly, repair and assembly procedures in simple step-by-step form.

If a repair is impractical for a home mechanic, it is so indicated. It is usually faster and less expensive to take such repairs to a dealer or competent repair shop. Specifications concerning a particular system are included at the end of the appropriate chapter. All dimensions and capacities are expressed in U.S standard units and metric units.

Some of the procedures in this manual require special tools. In most cases, the tool is illustrated either in actual use or alone. Well equipped mechanics may find they can substitute similar tools already on hand or can fabricate their own.

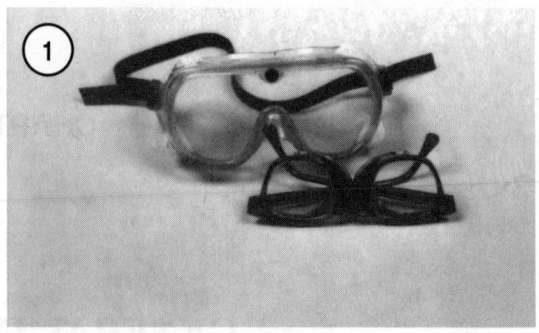

NOTES, CAUTIONS AND WARNINGS

The terms NOTE, CAUTION and WARNING have specific meanings in this manual. A NOTE provides additional information to make a step or procedure easier or clearer. Disregarding a NOTE could cause inconvenience but would not cause equipment damage or injury.

A CAUTION emphasizes areas where equipment damage could result. Disregarding a CAUTION could cause permanent mechanical damage; however, injury is unlikely.

A WARNING emphasizes areas where injury or even death could result from negligence. Mechanical damage may also occur. WARNINGS *should be taken seriously*. In some cases, serious injury or death has resulted from disregarding similar warnings.

SAFETY FIRST

Professional mechanics can work for years and never sustain a serious injury. By observing a few rules of common sense and safety, you can enjoy many safe hours servicing your machine. If you ignore these rules you can hurt yourself or damage the equipment.

1. Never use gasoline as a cleaning solvent.
2. Never smoke or use a torch in the vicinity of flammable liquids, such as cleaning solvent, in open containers.
3. If welding or brazing is required, remove the fuel tank and shock to a safe distance, at least 50 ft. (15 m) away.
4. Use the proper size wrenches to avoid damaging fasteners and injuring yourself.
5. When loosening a tight or stuck nut, be guided by what would happen if the wrench should slip. Be careful. Protect yourself accordingly.
6. When replacing a fastener, use one with the same dimensions and strength as the old fastener. Incorrect or mismatched fasteners might damage the bike and cause possible injury. Avoid fastener kits filled with poorly made nuts, bolts, washers and cotter pins. Refer to this chapter for additional information on hardware.
7. Keep all hand tools and power tools in good condition. Wipe greasy and oily tools after using them. They are difficult to hold and can cause injury. Replace or repair worn or damaged tools.
8. Keep the work area clean and uncluttered.
9. Wear safety goggles (**Figure 1**) during all operations involving drilling, grinding, using a cold chisel or anytime you are feeling unsure about the safety of your eyes. Wear safety goggles when cleaning parts with solvent and compressed air.
10. Keep an approved fire extinguisher nearby. It must be rated for gasoline (Class B) and electrical (Class C) fires.
11. When drying bearings or other rotating parts with compressed air, never allow the air jet to rotate the bearing or part. Compressed air can rotate a bearing at speeds greater than the bearing was designed to withstand. The bearing or rotating part might disintegrate and cause serious injury and damage. To prevent bearing damage when using compressed air, hold both the inner and outer bearing races by hand (**Figure 2**).

SERVICE HINTS

Most of the service procedures covered are straightforward and can be performed by anyone reasonably handy with tools. However, consider your capabilities carefully before attempting any

GENERAL INFORMATION

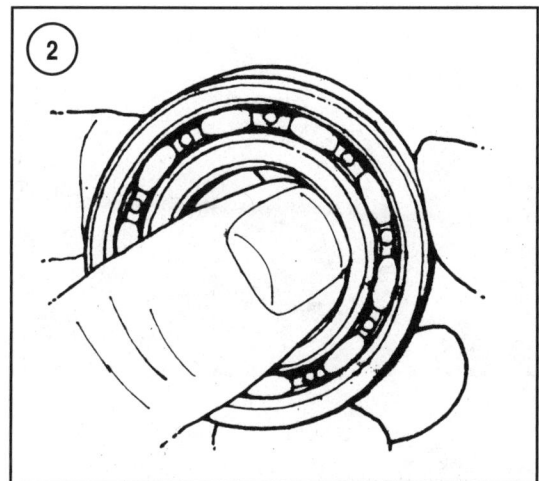

operation involving major disassembly of the engine.

Take the time and do the job right. Do not forget that a newly rebuilt engine must be broken-in the same way as a new one; refer to Chapter Five.

1. *Front*, as used in this manual, refers to the front of the bike. The front of any component is the end closest to the front of the bike. *Left* and *right* refer to the position of the parts as viewed by a rider sitting on the seat facing forward. For example, the throttle control is on the right side. These rules are simple, but confusion can cause a major inconvenience during service.

2. Whenever servicing the engine or clutch, or when removing a suspension component, secure the bike in a safe manner.

3. Disconnect the negative battery cable (**Figure 3**) before disconnecting any electrical wires or when working on or near the electrical, clutch or starter systems. On most batteries, the negative terminal is marked with a minus (–) sign and the positive terminal is marked with a plus (+) sign.

4. Tag all similar internal parts for location and mark all mating parts for position. Record shim quantity, thickness and alignment when removed. Identify and store small parts in plastic sandwich bags. Seal and label them with masking tape.

5. Place parts from a specific area of the engine like the cylinder head, cylinder, clutch, shift mechanism into plastic boxes to keep them separated.

6. When disassembling transmission shaft assemblies, use an egg flat (the type that restaurants get their eggs in). Set the parts from a shaft in one of the depressions in the same order in which they are removed.

7. Label all electrical wiring and connectors before disconnecting them. Again, do not rely on memory alone.

8. Protect finished surfaces from physical damage or corrosion. Keep gasoline, brake fluid and clutch fluid off painted surfaces.

9. Use penetrating oil on frozen or tight bolts, and strike the bolt head a few times with a hammer and punch (use a screwdriver on screws). Avoid the use of heat where possible. The heat can warp, melt or affect the temper of parts. Heat also damages finishes, especially paints and plastics.

10. Unless specified in the procedure, parts should not require unusual force during disassembly or assembly. If a part is difficult to remove or install, find out why before continuing.

11. To prevent small objects and abrasive dust from falling into the engine, cover all openings after exposing them.

12. Read each procedure *completely* while looking at the actual parts before starting a job. Make sure you thoroughly understand each step and then follow the procedure, step by step.

13. Recommendations are occasionally made to refer service or maintenance to a Yamaha dealership or a specialist in a particular field. In these cases, the work is done more quickly and economically than performing the job yourself.

14. In procedural steps, the term *replace* means to discard a defective part and replace it with a new or exchange unit. *Overhaul* means to remove, disassemble, inspect, and then replace defective parts as required.

15. Some operations require the use of a hydraulic press. Have these operations performed by a shop

equipped for such work. Performing these jobs yourself with makeshift equipment may damage the machine.

16. Repairs go much faster and easier if the machine is clean before beginning work. There are many special cleaners on the market, like Bel-Ray Degreaser, for washing the engine and related parts. Follow the manufacturer's directions on the container for the best results. Clean all oily or greasy parts with cleaning solvent after removing them.

WARNING
***Never** use gasoline as a cleaning agent. It presents an extreme fire hazard. Make sure to work in a well-ventilated area when using cleaning solvent. Keep a fire extinguisher, rated for gasoline fires, on hand.*

CAUTION
*If using a car wash to clean the bike, do **not** direct the high pressure water at steering bearings, carburetor hoses, suspension components, wheel bearings or electrical components. High-pressure water flushes grease out of the bearings or damages the seals.*

17. A significant amount of a dealership's labor charge is for the time spent removing, disassembling, assembling and reinstalling parts to reach the defective part. It is frequently possible to perform the preliminary operations yourself and then take the defective unit to the dealership for repair at considerable savings.

18. When special tools are required, have them available before starting. It is frustrating and time-consuming to start a job and then be unable to complete it.

19. Make diagrams (or take a Polaroid photo) wherever similar-appearing parts are found. For instance, crankcase bolts are often not the same lengths. It is difficult to remember where everything came from, but mistakes are costly. There is also the possibility that the procedure may not be completed for days or even weeks in which time carefully laid out parts may have become disturbed.

20. When assembling parts, make sure all shims and washers are replaced exactly as they came out.

21. Whenever a rotating part contacts a stationary part, look for a shim or washer. Use new gaskets, seals and O-rings during assembly. A thin coating of oil on non-pressure type gaskets may help them seal more effectively.

22. A baby bottle graduated in fluid ounces and cubic centimeters makes a good measuring tool for adding oil to the front fork. After it has been used, there will always be oil residue in it. Do **not** use it to drink out of.

CAUTION
When purchasing gasket material to make a gasket, measure the thickness of the old gasket. Purchase material with the same approximate thickness.

23. If it is necessary to make a clutch cover or ignition cover gasket without the old gasket as a guide, use the outline of the cover as a template. Apply engine oil to the cover gasket surface. Place the cover on the new gasket material, and apply pressure by hand. The oil will leave a very accurate outline on the gasket material.

24. Use heavy grease to hold small parts in place if they tend to fall out during assembly. However, keep grease and oil away from electrical and brake components.

25. The carburetor is best cleaned by disassembling it and soaking the parts in a commercial carburetor cleaner. Never soak gaskets and rubber parts in these cleaners. Never use wire to clean out jets and air passages. They will damage easily. Use compressed air to blow out the carburetor only if the float has been removed first.

GENERAL INFORMATION

WASHING THE BIKE

Regular cleaning of the bike is an important part of its overall maintenance. After riding the bike in extremely dirty areas, clean it thoroughly. Doing this makes maintenance and service procedures quick and easy. More important, proper cleaning prevents dirt from falling into critical areas undetected. Failing to clean the bike or cleaning it incorrectly will add to the maintenance costs and shop time because dirty parts wear out prematurely. It is unlikely that the bike will break because of improper cleaning, but it can happen. When cleaning the Yamaha, have a few tools, shop rags, scrub brush, bucket, liquid cleaner and access to water on hand. Many riders use a coin-operated car wash. Coin-operated car washes are convenient and quick, but with improper use the high water pressures can do more damage than good to the bike.

NOTE
Simple Green is a safe biodegradable, non-toxic and non-flammable liquid cleaner that works well for washing the bike as well as for removing grease and oil from the engine and suspension parts. Simple Green can be purchased at some supermarkets, hardware and garden stores, and discount supply houses. Follow the directions on the container for recommended mixing ratios.

When cleaning the bike, and especially when using a spray type degreaser, remember that what goes on the bike will rinse off and drip onto the driveway or into the yard. If possible, use a degreaser at a coin-operated car wash. If cleaning the bike at home, place thick cardboard or newspapers underneath the bike to catch the oil and grease deposits as they are rinsed off.

CAUTION
Some of the steps in this procedure relate to a bike that has been subjected to extremely dirty conditions, like mud or severe road dirt. To avoid surface damage, carefully scrub the frame plastic side covers with a soft sponge or towel—do not use a brush on these covers because the surfaces will scratch.

1. Place the bike on level ground on a sidestand.
2. Check the following before washing the bike:
   a. Make sure the gas filler cap (**Figure 4**) is closed and locked.
   b. Make sure the engine oil filler cap (**Figure 5**) is on tight.
   c. Cover the muffler openings.
   d. Cover the air box air inlet opening(s).
3. Wash the bike from top to bottom with soapy water. Use the scrub brush to get excess dirt out of the wheel rims and engine crannies. Concentrate on the upper controls, engine, side panels, and gas tank during this wash cycle. Do not forget to wash dirt and mud from underneath the fenders, suspension and engine crankcase.
4. Concentrate the second wash cycle on the frame tube members and suspension.
5. Direct the hose underneath the engine and swing arm. Wash this area thoroughly.
6. The final wash is the rinse. Use cold water without soap, and spray the entire bike again. Use as much time and care when rinsing the bike as when washing it. Built up soap deposits quickly corrode electrical connections and remove the natural oils from tires, causing premature cracks and wear. Make sure to thoroughly rinse off the bike.
7. Tip the bike from side to side to allow any water that has collected on horizontal surfaces to drain off.
8. Remove the cover from the air box air inlet(s).
9. Remove the muffler covers.
10. Start the engine and let it idle so the engine will burn off any internal moisture.
11. Before taking the bike into the garage, wipe it dry with a soft terry cloth or chamois. Inspect the machine while drying it for further signs of dirt and grime. Make a quick visual inspection of the clear

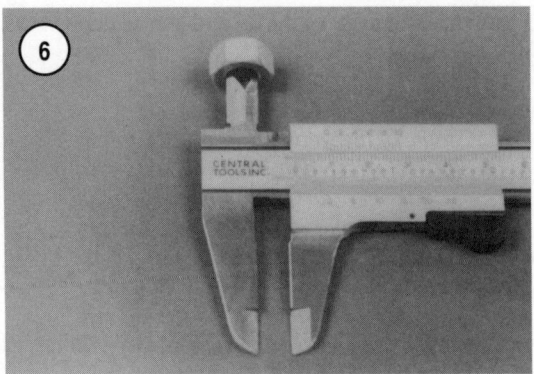

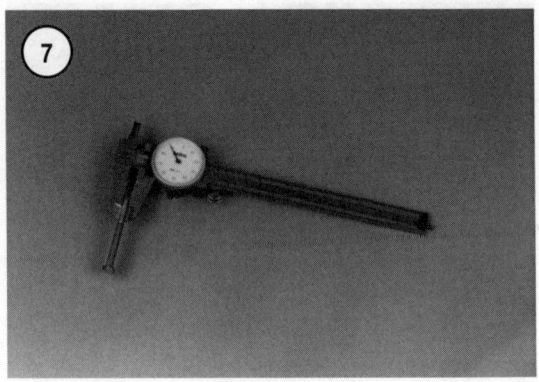

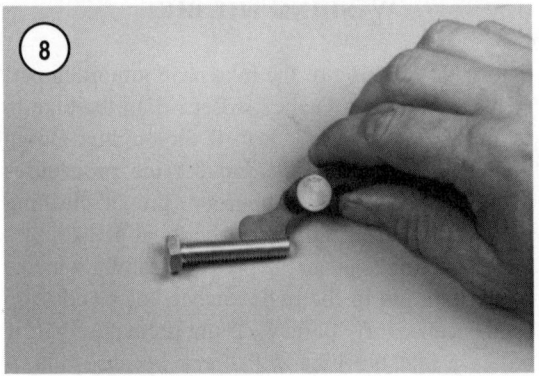

coat and other painted pieces on the frame, swing arm and front fork. Repaint any bare areas with touch-up paint (clear or color).

SPECIAL TIPS

Because of the extreme demands placed on a bike, keep several points in mind when performing service and repair. The following items are general suggestions that may improve the overall life of the machine and help avoid costly failures.

1. Use a threadlocking compound such as ThreeBond No. TB1342 (blue) or Loctite No. 242 (blue) on all bolts and nuts, even if they are secured with lockwashers. This type of locking compound does not harden completely and allows easy removal of the bolt or nut. A screw or bolt lost from an engine cover or bearing retainer could easily cause serious and expensive damage before its loss is noticed. Make sure the threads are clean and free of grease and oil. Clean with contact cleaner before applying the locking compound. When applying the locking compound, use a small amount. If too much is used, it can work its way down the threads and stick parts together not meant to be stuck. Keep a tube of the various locking compounds in a tool box. When used properly it is good insurance.

2. Use a hammer-driven impact tool to remove and install all bolts, particularly engine cover screws. This tool helps prevent the rounding off of bolt and screw heads.

3. When replacing missing or broken fasteners (bolts, nuts and screws), especially on the engine or frame components, always use Yamaha replacement parts. They are specially hardened for each application. The wrong 50-cent bolt could easily cause serious and expensive damage, not to mention rider injury.

4. When installing gaskets in the engine, always use Yamaha replacement gaskets *without* sealer, unless designated. These gaskets are designed to swell when they come in contact with oil. Gasket sealer prevents the gaskets from swelling as intended, which can result in oil leaks. These Yamaha gaskets are cut from material of the precise thickness needed. Installation of a too-thick or too-thin gasket in a critical area could cause engine damage.

TORQUE SPECIFICATIONS

The materials used in the manufacture of the Yamaha may be subjected to uneven stresses if the fasteners used to hold the subassemblies are not installed and tightened correctly. Improper bolt tightening can cause cylinder head warpage, crankcase leaks, premature bearing and seal failure, and suspension failure from loose or missing fasteners. An accurate torque wrench (described in this chapter) should be used together with the torque specifications listed at the end of most chapters.

GENERAL INFORMATION

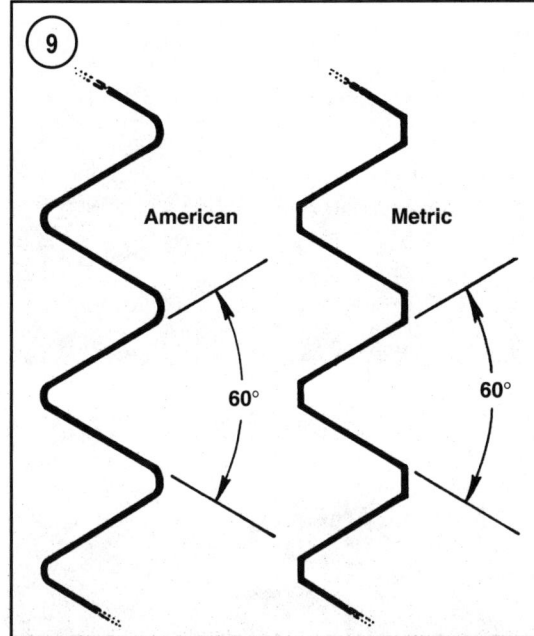

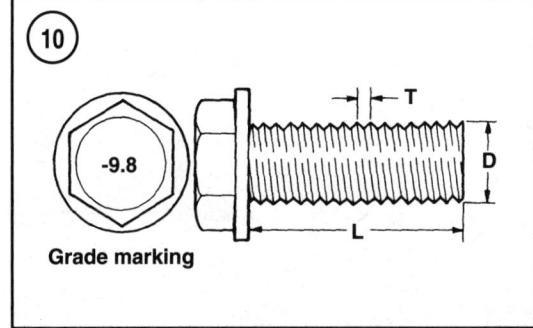

Torque specifications throughout this manual are given in Newton-meters (N•m) and foot-pounds (ft.-lb.).

Torque wrenches calibrated in meter kilograms can be used by performing a simple mathematical conversion. Move the decimal point in the Newton-meter specification one place to the left; for example, 35 N•m = 3.5 m-kg. The exact mathematical conversion is 35 N•m = 3.57 m-kg.

To mathematically convert foot-pounds to Newton meters, multiply the foot pounds specification by 1.3558 to achieve a N•m equivalent. For example 150 ft.-lb. × 1.3558 = 203 N•m.

Refer to **Table 5** for general torque specifications for various size screws, bolts and nuts not listed in the respective chapter tables. To use the table, first determine the size of the bolt or nut. Use a vernier caliper and measure the inside dimension of the threads of the nut (**Figure 6**) and across the threads for a bolt (**Figure 7**).

FASTENERS

Fastener material and design is not arrived at by chance. Fasteners are carefully selected to prevent physical failure. The type of tool required to work a fastener is determined by its design.

Nuts, bolts and screws are manufactured in a wide range of thread patterns. To join a nut and bolt, the diameter of the bolt and the diameter of the hole in the nut must be the same.

The best way to tell if two threads match is to turn the nut onto the bolt (or turn the bolt into the threaded hole in a piece of equipment) by hand. Make sure both pieces are clean. If excessive force is required, check the thread condition on each fastener. If the thread condition is good but the fasteners jam, the threads are not compatible. Use a thread pitch gauge (**Figure 8**) to determine pitch. Yamaha motorcycles are manufactured with ISO (International Organization for Standardization) metric fasteners. The threads are not the same as those of American fasteners (**Figure 9**).

Most fasteners must be turned clockwise to tighten it. These are called right-hand threads. Some fasteners have left-hand threads; they must be turned counterclockwise to be tightened. Left-hand threads are used in locations where normal rotation of the equipment might loosen a right-hand threaded fastener.

ISO Metric Screw Threads
(Bolts, Nuts and Screws)

ISO (International Organization for Standardization) metric threads come in three standard thread sizes: coarse, fine and constant pitch. The ISO coarse pitch is used for almost all common fastener applications. The fine pitch thread is used on certain precision tools and instruments. The constant pitch thread is used mainly on machine parts and not for fasteners. The constant pitch thread, however, is used on all metric spark plugs.

Metric screws and bolts are classified by length (L, **Figure 10**), nominal diameter (D) and distance between thread crests (T). A typical bolt might be identified by the numbers 8—1.25 × 130, which in-

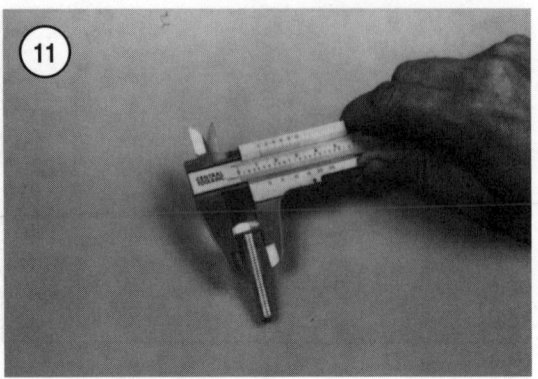

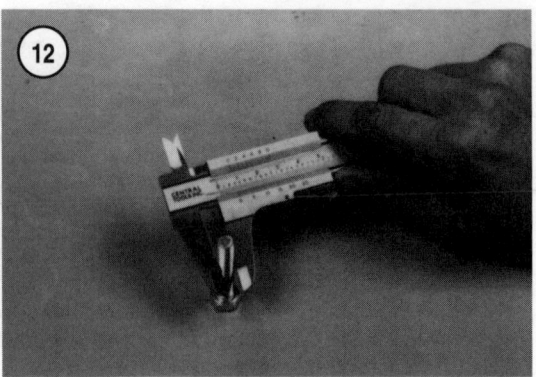

dicates that the bolt has a nominal diameter of 8 mm, the distance between thread crests is 1.25 mm and bolt length is 130 mm.

CAUTION
*Do **not** install screws or bolts with a lower strength grade classification than installed originally by the manufacturer. Doing so may cause engine or equipment failure and possible injury.*

The measurement across two flats on the head of the bolt (**Figure 11**) indicates the proper wrench size to use. **Figure 12** shows how to determine bolt diameter. When buying a bolt from a dealer or parts store, it is important to know how to specify bolt length. The correct way to measure bolt length is by measuring the distance from underneath the bolt head to the end of the bolt (**Figure 13**). Always measure bolt length in this manner to avoid buying bolts that are too long.

Machine Screws

There are many different types of machine screws. **Figure 14** shows a number of screw heads requiring different types of turning tools. Heads are also designed to protrude above the metal (round) or slightly recessed in the metal (flat).

Nuts

Nuts are manufactured in a variety of types and sizes. Most are hexagonal (6-sided) and fit on bolts, screws and studs with the same diameter and pitch. **Figure 15** shows several types of nuts. The common nut is generally used with a lockwasher.

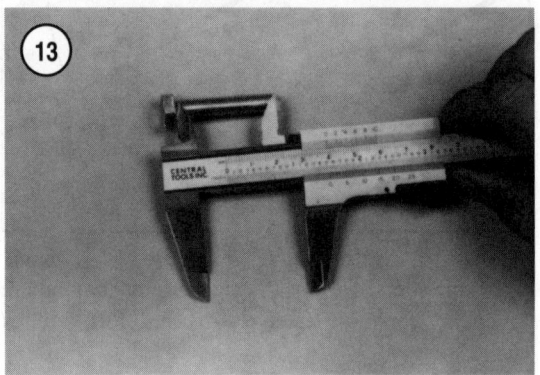

Self-locking nuts have a nylon insert that prevents the nut from loosening. No lockwasher is required. Wing nuts are designed for fast removal by hand. Wing nuts are used for convenience in non-critical locations.

To indicate the size of a metric nut, manufacturers specify the diameter of the opening and the thread pitch. This is similar to bolt specifications, but without the length dimension. The measurement across two flats on the nut indicates the proper wrench size to be used (**Figure 16**).

Self-Locking Fasteners

Several types of bolts, screws and nuts incorporate a system that develops an interference between the bolt, screw, nut or tapped hole threads. Interference is achieved in various ways. For example, distorting threads, coating threads with dry adhesive or nylon, distorting the top of an all-metal nut, and using a nylon insert in the center or at the top of a nut.

Self-locking fasteners offer greater holding strength and better vibration resistance. Some self-locking fasteners can be reused if in good con-

GENERAL INFORMATION

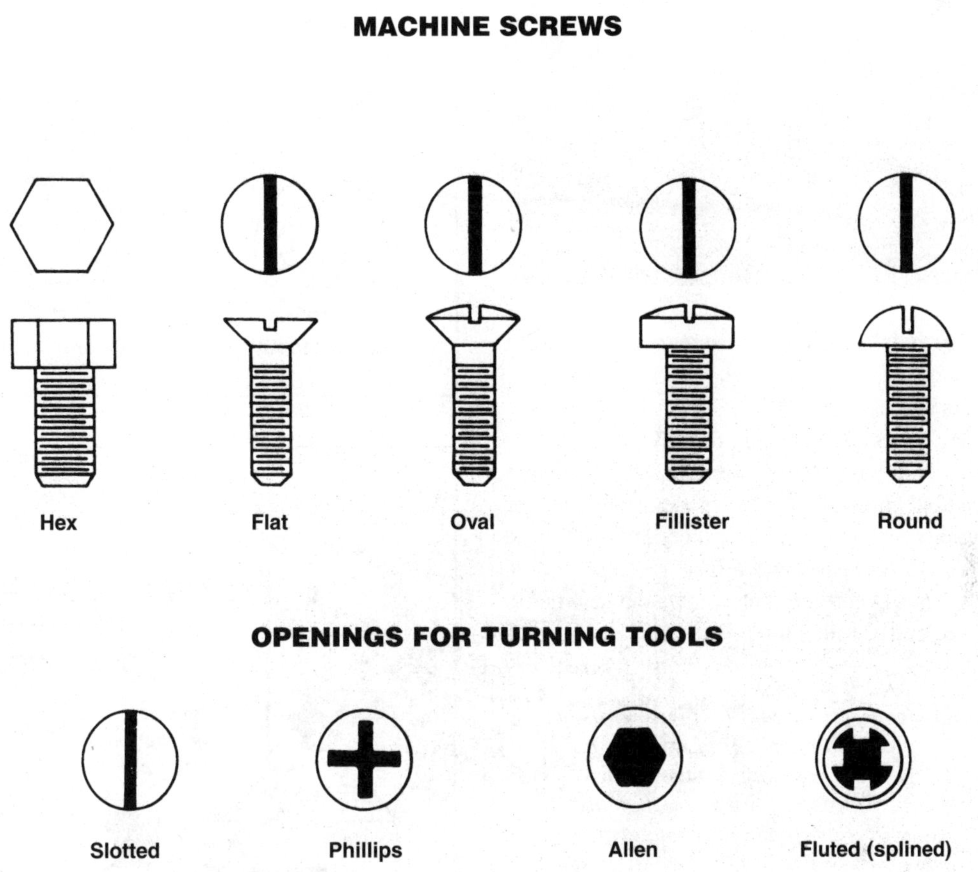

MACHINE SCREWS

Hex | Flat | Oval | Fillister | Round

OPENINGS FOR TURNING TOOLS

Slotted | Phillips | Allen | Fluted (splined)

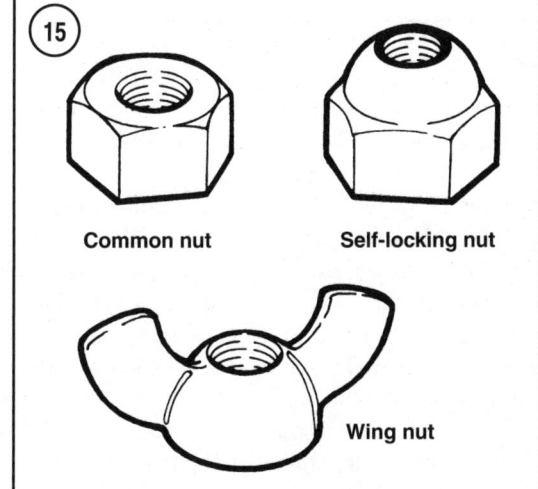

Common nut | Self-locking nut | Wing nut

dition. Others, like the nylon insert nut, form an initial locking condition when the nut is first installed. The nylon forms closely to the bolt thread pattern, thus reducing any tendency for the nut to loosen. To be safe, *always discard* used self-locking fasteners and install new ones during reassembly.

Washers

There are two basic types of washers: flat washers and lockwashers. Flat washers are simple discs with a hole to fit a screw or bolt. Washers can be used in the following functions:

a. As spacers.
b. To prevent galling or damage of the equipment by the fastener.

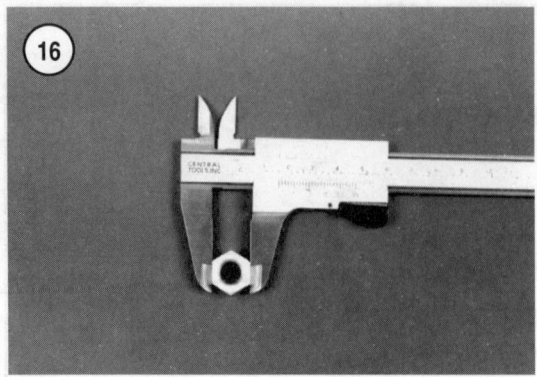

c. To help distribute fastener load during torquing.
d. As seals.

Lockwashers are designed to prevent a fastener from working loose due to vibration, expansion and contraction. **Figure 17** shows several types of lockwashers. Note that flat washers are often used between a lockwasher and a fastener to provide a smooth bearing surface. This allows the fastener to be turned easily with a tool.

> *NOTE*
> *As much care should be given to the selection and purchase of washers as that given to bolts, nuts and other fasteners. Beware of washers that are made of thin and weak materials. These will deform and crush the first time they are used in a high torque application.*

Cotter Pins

Cotter pins (**Figure 18**) are used to secure special kinds of fasteners. The threaded stud, bolt or axle must have a hole in it. A nut or nut lock piece has castellations around which the cotter pin ends wrap. Do not reuse cotter pins.

Circlips

Circlips can be internal or external design. They are used to retain items on shafts (external type) or within tubes (internal type). In some applications, circlips of varying thickness control the end play of assemblies. These are often called selective circlips. Replace circlips during installation because removal weakens and deforms them.

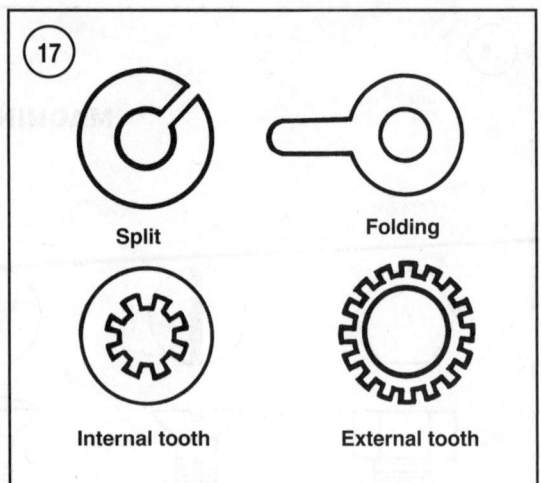

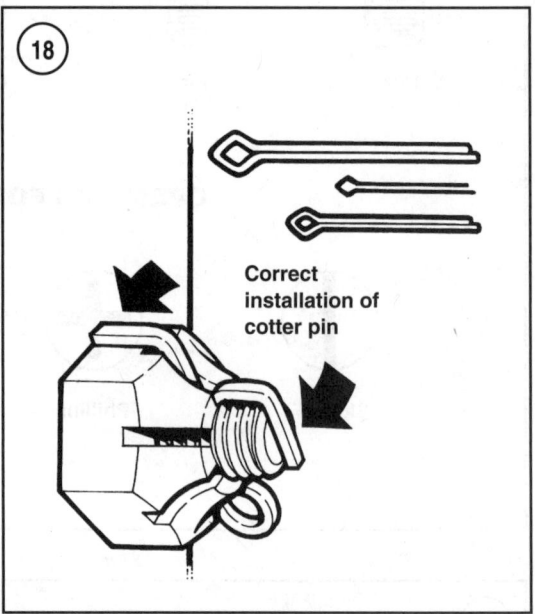

Two basic styles of circlips are available: machined and stamped circlips. Machined circlips (**Figure 19**) can be installed in either direction (shaft or housing) because both faces are machined, thus creating two sharp edges. Stamped circlips (**Figure 20**) are manufactured with one sharp edge and one rounded edge. When installing stamped circlips in a thrust situation (transmission shafts, fork tubes, etc.), the sharp edge must face away from the part producing the thrust. When installing circlips, observe the following:

a. Compress or expand circlips only enough to install them.

GENERAL INFORMATION

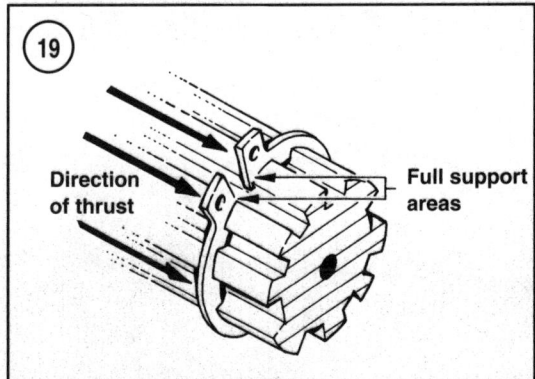

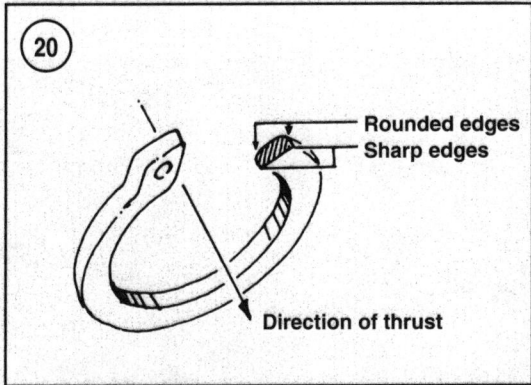

b. After the circlip is installed, make sure it is completely seated in its groove.

c. Transmission circlips become worn with use and increase side play. For this reason, always use new circlips whenever a transmission is reassembled.

LUBRICANTS

Periodic lubrication ensures long life for any type of equipment. The type of lubricant used is just as important as the lubrication service itself, although in an emergency the wrong type of lubricant is better than none at all. The following paragraphs describe the types of lubricants most often used on motorcycle equipment. Be sure to follow the manufacturer's recommendations for lubricant types.

Generally all liquid lubricants are called oil. They may be mineral-based (including petroleum bases), natural-based (vegetable and animal bases), synthetic-based or emulsions (mixtures). Grease is an oil to which a thickening base has been added. Grease is often classified by the type of thickener added; lithium soap is commonly used.

Engine Oil

Four-stroke oil for motorcycles is classified by the American Petroleum Institute (API) and the Society of Automotive Engineers (SAE). Oil containers display these classifications on the label. API oil classification is indicated by letters; oils for gasoline engines are identified by an *S*. Yamaha models described in this manual require SE, SF or SG oil.

Viscosity is an indication of the oil's thickness. The SAE uses numbers to indicate viscosity. Thin oils have low numbers while thick oils have high numbers. A *W* after the number indicates that the viscosity testing was done at a low temperature to simulate cold-weather operation. Engine oils fall into the 5 to 50 range.

Multi-grade oils (for example 10W-40) are less viscous (thinner) at low temperatures and more viscous (thicker) at high temperatures. This allows the oil to perform efficiently across a wide range of engine operating conditions. The lower the number, the better the engine will start in cold climates. Higher numbers are usually recommended when operating an engine in hot weather.

Grease

Greases are graded by the National Lubricating Grease Institute (NLGI). Greases are graded by number according to the consistency of the grease; these range from No. 000 to No. 6, with No. 6 being the most solid. A typical multipurpose grease is NLGI No. 2. For specific applications, equipment manufacturers may require grease with an additive such as molybdenum disulfide (MOS_2).

RTV GASTET SEALANT

Room temperature vulcanizing (RTV) sealant is used on some pre-formed gaskets and some components. RTV is a silicone gel supplied in tubes and can be purchased in a number of different colors.

Moisture in the air causes RTV to cure. RTV has a shelf life of one year and will not cure properly when the shelf life has expired. Check the expiration date on an RTV tube before using it. Always replace the cap on the tube as soon as possible and keep partially used tubes tightly sealed.

Applying RTV Sealant

Clean all gasket residue and oil from mating surfaces. Remove all RTV gasket material from blind attaching holes. If left in place, it can influence bolt torque.

Apply RTV sealant in a continuous bead. Circle all mounting holes unless otherwise specified. Torque mating parts within 10 minutes of application.

GASKET REMOVER

Stubborn gaskets can present a problem during engine service. They can take a long time to remove, and the incorrect use of gasket scraping tools can damage the gasket mating surfaces. To quickly and safely remove stubborn gaskets, use a spray gasket remover. Spray gasket remover can be purchased through automotive parts houses. Follow the manufacturer's directions for use.

THREADLOCKING COMPOUND

Threadlocking compound locks fasteners against vibration loosening and seals against leaks. The following threadlocking compounds are recommended for many threadlock requirements described in this manual.
 a. ThreeBond No. 1342 (blue): low strength, frequent repair.
 b. Loctite No. 242 (blue): low strength, frequent repair.
 c. ThreeBond No. 1360 (green): medium strength, high temperature.
 d. ThreeBond No. 1333B (red): medium strength, bearing and stud lock.
 e. ThreeBond No. 1303 (orange): high strength, frequent repair.
 f. Loctite No. 271 (red): high strength, frequent repair.

There are other quality threadlock brands on the market.

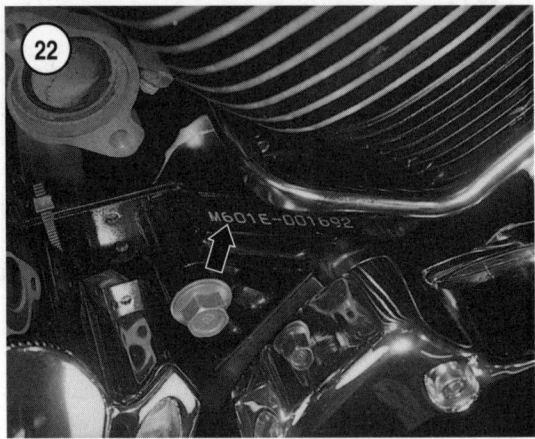

EXPENDABLE SUPPLIES

Certain expendable supplies are required during maintenance and repair work. These include grease, oil, gasket cement, wiping rags and cleaning solvent. Ask the dealership for the special locking compounds, silicone lubricants and other products that make bike maintenance simpler and easier. Cleaning solvent or kerosene is available at some service stations, paint or hardware stores.

Be sure to follow the manufacturer's instructions and warnings listed on the label of these products. Some cleaning supplies are very caustic and are dangerous if not used properly.

WARNING
Store solvent and oil soaked rags in a sealed metal container until they can be washed or properly discarded.

GENERAL INFORMATION 13

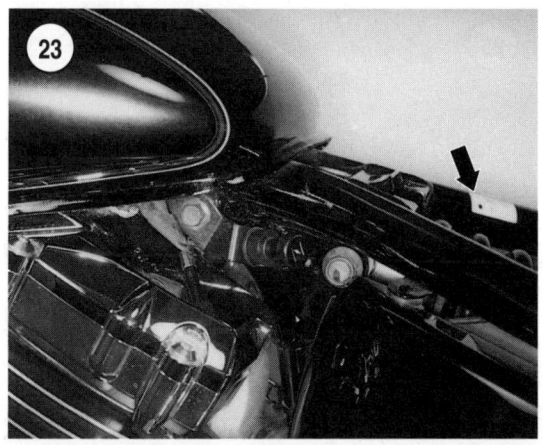

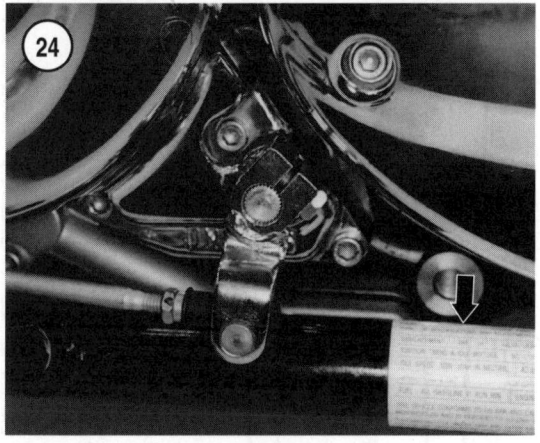

NOTE
To prevent solvent and other chemicals from being absorbed into your skin, wear a pair of petroleum-resistance gloves when cleaning parts. These can be bought through industrial supply houses or well-equipped hardware stores.

SERIAL NUMBERS

Yamaha makes frequent changes during a model year, some minor, some relatively major. When ordering parts from the dealership or other parts distributor, always order by VIN (vehicle identification number) number, engine number, and model number. The VIN is stamped on the right side of the steering head (**Figure 21**). The engine number is stamped on the right side of the crankcase (**Figure 22**). The model number is printed on a label that is affixed to the ride side of the frame beneath the passenger seat (**Figure 23**).

Record these numbers and have them available when purchasing replacement parts. Compare old parts to new and have the parts manager explain the reason for any difference. **Table 1** lists VIN and engine serial numbers for the models covered in this manual.

WARNING AND INFORMATION LABELS

Several warning labels have been attached to the Yamaha. These labels contain information on operation, transportation and storage safety. Refer to information labels (**Figure 24**) at various places on the motorcycle. Refer to the Owner's Manual for a description and location of each label. If a label is missing, order a replacement label.

BASIC HAND TOOLS

Many of the procedures in this manual can be carried out with simple hand tools and test equipment familiar to the average home mechanic. Keep tools clean and organized in a tool box. After using a tool, wipe off dirt and grease with a clean cloth and return the tool to its correct place.

High quality tools are essential; they are also more economical in the long run. Stay away from the advertised specials featured at some stores. They are usually made of inferior materials and are thick, heavy and clumsy. Their rough finish makes them difficult to clean and they usually do not last very long.

Quality tools are made of alloy steel and are heat treated for greater strength. They are lighter and better balanced than poorly made ones. Their surface is smooth, making them a pleasure to work with and easy to clean. The initial cost of quality tools may be more, but they are less expensive in the long run.

Screwdrivers

The screwdriver is a very basic tool, but improper use may cause damage. The slot on a screw has a particular dimension and shape. A screwdriver must be selected to conform to that shape. Use a

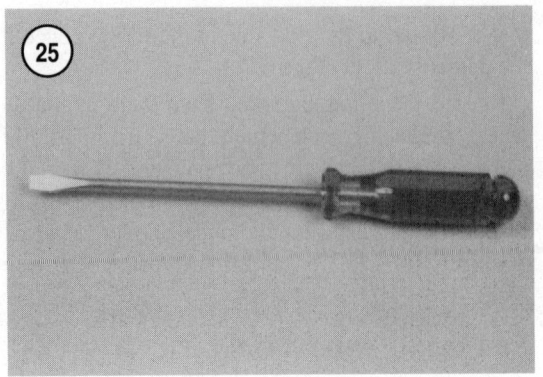
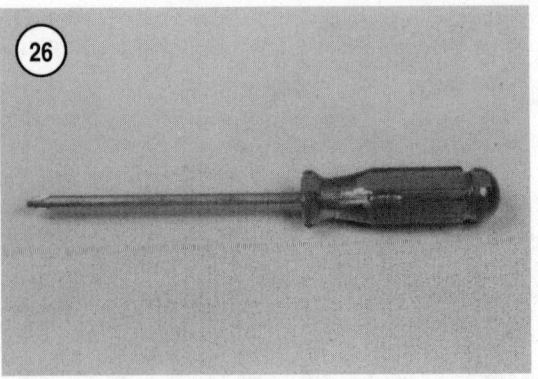

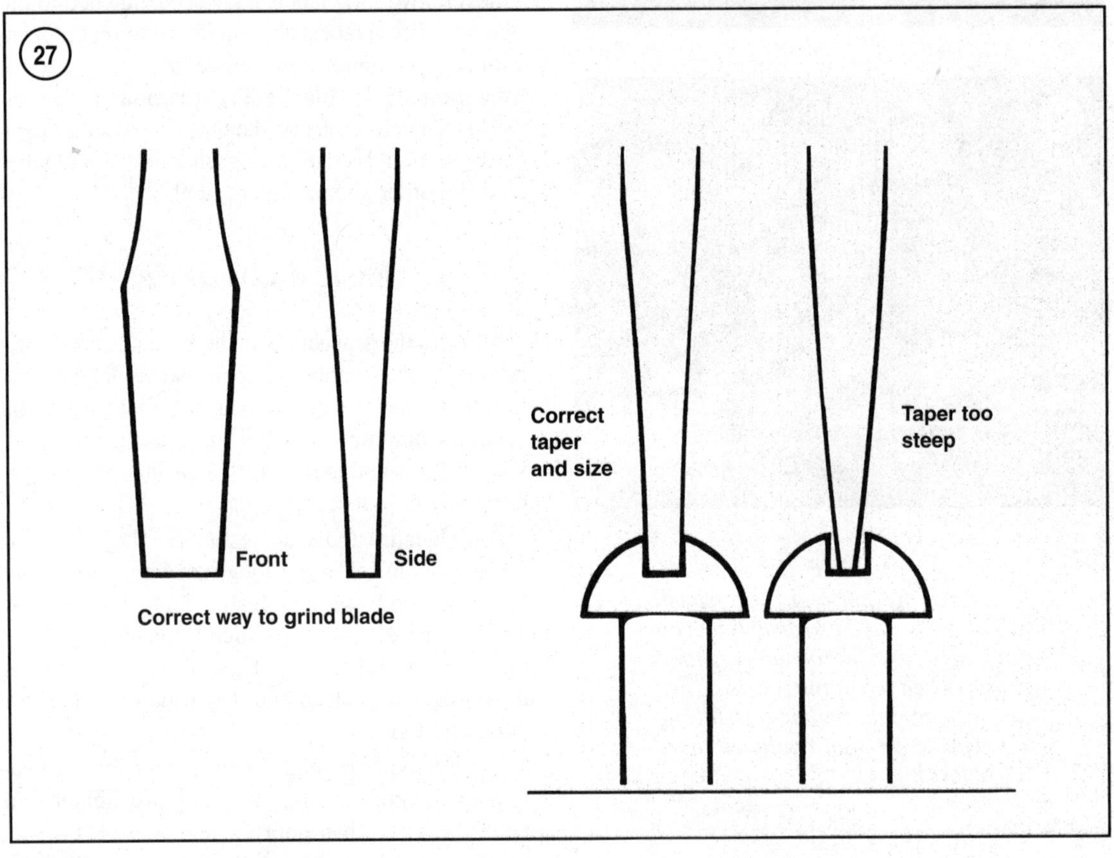

27 Correct way to grind blade — Front, Side. Correct taper and size. Taper too steep.

small screwdriver for small screws and a large one for large screws or the screw head will be damaged.

Two basic types of screwdrivers are required: common (flat-blade) screwdrivers (**Figure 25**) and Phillips screwdrivers (**Figure 26**).

Screwdrivers are available in sets, which often include an assortment of common and Phillips blades. When purchasing them individually, buy at least the following:

a. Common screwdriver—5/16 × 6 in. blade.
b. Common screwdriver—3/8 × 12 in. blade.
c. Phillips screwdriver—size 2 tip, 6 in. blade.
d. Phillips screwdriver—size 3 tip, 6 and 10 in. blade.

Use screwdrivers only for driving screws. Never use a screwdriver for prying or chiseling metal. Do not try to remove a Phillips or Allen head screw with a common screwdriver (unless the screw has a combination head that will accept either type); this will damage the head so that the proper tool will be

GENERAL INFORMATION

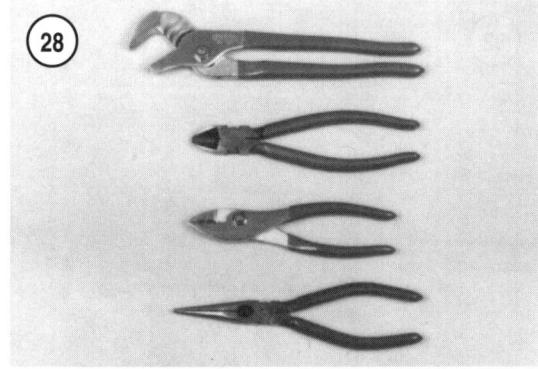

28

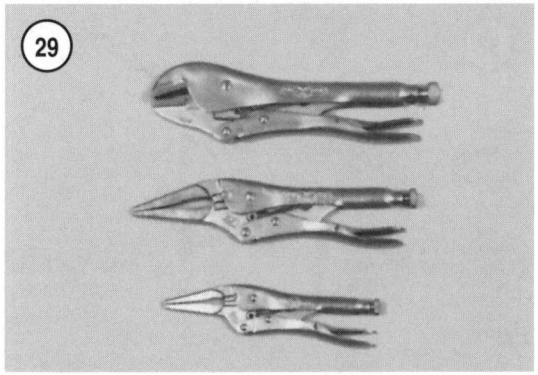

29

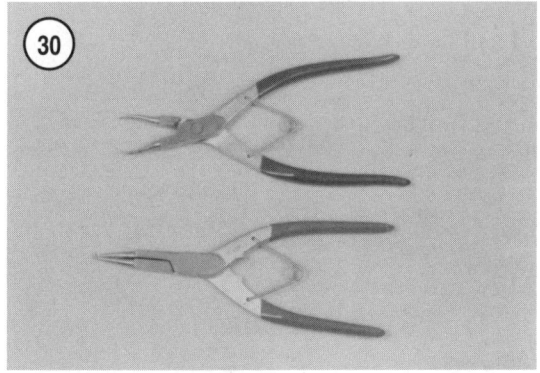

30

unable to remove it. Keeping screwdrivers in the proper condition assures they last longer and perform better. Always keep the tip of a common screwdriver in good condition. **Figure 27** shows how to grind the tip to the proper shape if it becomes damaged. Note the symmetrical sides of the tip.

Pliers

Pliers come in a wide range of types and sizes. Pliers are useful for cutting, bending and crimping.

Do not use them to cut hardened objects or to turn bolts or nuts. **Figure 28** shows several pliers useful in motorcycle repair. Each type of pliers has a specialized function. Slip-joint pliers are general purpose pliers. These are used mainly for holding things and for bending.

Needlenose pliers are used to hold or bend small objects. Adjustable pliers can be adjusted to hold various sizes of objects. The jaws remain parallel to grip around objects such as pipe or tubing. There are many more types of pliers. The ones described here are most suitable for bike repairs.

Locking Pliers

Locking pliers (**Figure 29**) are used to hold objects very tightly like a vise. Avoid using them unless necessary since their sharp jaws permanently scar any objects they hold. Locking pliers are available in many types for more specific tasks.

Circlip Pliers

Circlip pliers (**Figure 30**) are made for removing and installing circlips. External pliers (spreading) are used to remove circlips that fit on the outside of a shaft. Internal pliers (squeezing) are used to remove circlips which fit inside a gear or housing.

> *WARNING*
> *Because circlips can sometimes slip and fly off, always wear safety glasses when removing and installing them.*

Box-end, Open-end and Combination Wrenches

Box-end, open-end and combination wrenches are available in sets or separately in a variety of sizes. On open- and box-end wrenches, the number stamped near the end refers to the distance between two parallel flats on the hex head bolt or nut. On combination wrenches, the number is stamped near the center.

Box-end wrenches require clear overhead access to the fastener but can work well in situations where the fastener head is close to another part. They grip on all six edges of a fastener for a very secure grip. They are available in either 6-point or 12-point. The 6-point gives superior holding power and durability,

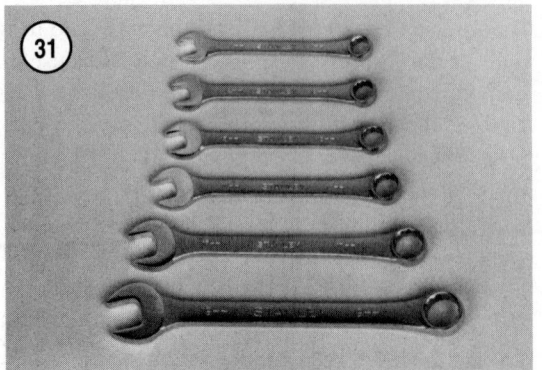

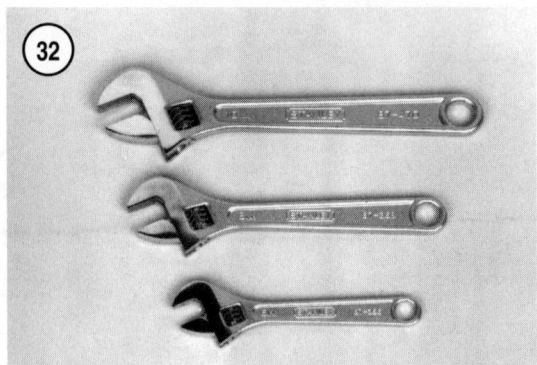

but it requires a greater swinging radius. The 12-point works better in situations where the swinging radius is limited.

Open-end wrenches are speedy and work best in areas with limited overhead access. Their wide flat jaws make them unstable for situations where the bolt or nut is sunken in a well or close to the edge of a casting. These wrenches grip only two flats of a fastener so if either the fastener head or the wrench jaws are worn, the wrench may slip off.

Combination wrenches (**Figure 31**) have open-end on one side and box-end on the other with both ends being the same size. Professional mechanics favor these wrenches because of their versatility.

Adjustable Wrenches

An adjustable wrench (sometimes called a Crescent wrench) can be adjusted to fit nearly any nut or bolt head that has clear access around its entire perimeter. An adjustable wrench (**Figure 32**) is best used as a backup wrench to keep a large nut or bolt from turning while the other end is being loosened or tightened with a proper wrench.

Adjustable wrenches have only two gripping surfaces which make them more subject to slipping off the fastener and damaging the part and causing possible injury. The fact that one jaw is adjustable only aggravates this shortcoming.

These wrenches are directional; the solid jaw must be the one transmitting the force. If the adjustable jaw is used to transmit the force, it will loosen and possibly slip off.

An adjustable wrench in the 10-12 in. range is recommended as an all purpose wrench.

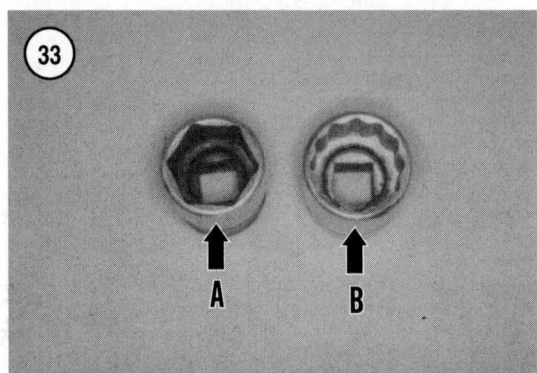

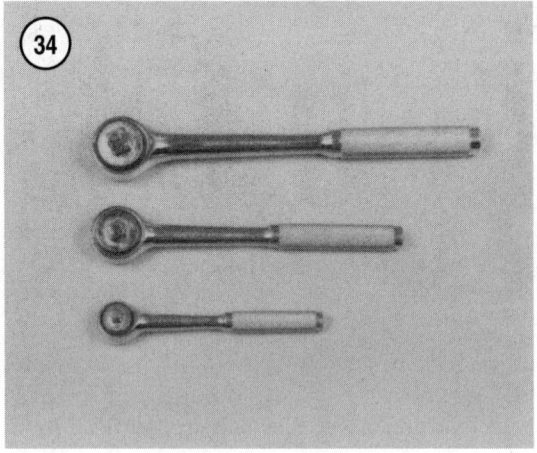

Socket Wrenches

This type is undoubtedly the fastest, safest and most convenient wrench to use. Sockets, which attach to a ratchet handle, are available with 6-point (A, **Figure 33**) or 12-point openings (B, **Figure 33**) and with 1/4, 3/8, 1/2 and 3/4 in. drives. The drive size indicates the size of the square hole which mates with the ratchet handle (**Figure 34**).

GENERAL INFORMATION

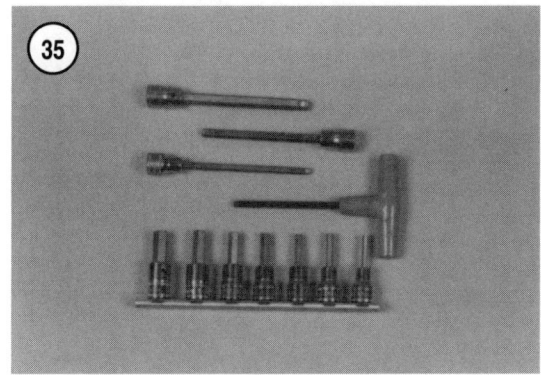

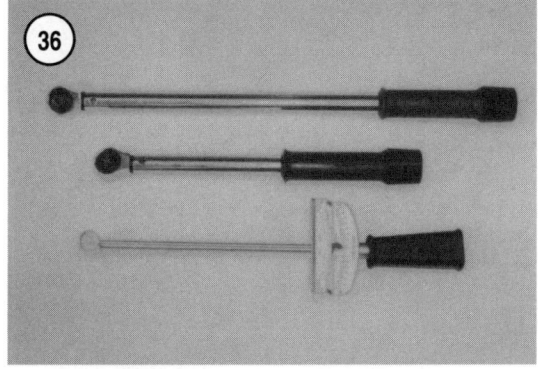

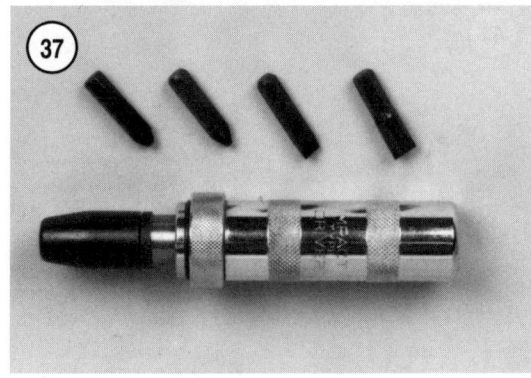

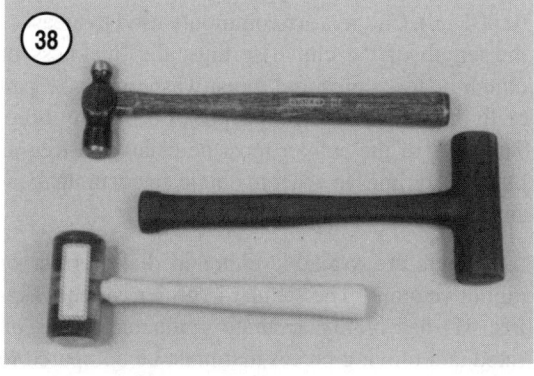

Allen Wrenches

Allen wrenches are available in sets or separately in a variety of sizes. These sets come in U.S. standard and metric sizes. Yamaha motorcycles require a metric set. Allen bolts are sometimes called socket bolts. Since the bolts can be difficult to reach, consider purchasing a variety of Allen wrenches like the socket driven, T-handle and extension type that are shown in **Figure 35**.

Torque Wrench

A torque wrench is used with a socket to measure how tightly a nut or bolt is installed. They come in a wide price range and with either 1/4, 3/8 or 1/2 in. square drive (**Figure 36**). The drive size indicates the size of the square drive that mates with the socket.

Impact Driver

This tool might have been designed with the motorcycle rider in mind. An impact driver makes removal of fasteners easy and eliminates damage to bolts and screw slots. Impact drivers (**Figure 37**) and interchangeable bits are available at most large hardware, motorcycle or auto parts stores. Sockets can also be used with a hand impact driver; however, make sure that the socket is designed for use with an impact driver or air tool. Do not use regular hand sockets. They may shatter during use.

Hammers

The correct hammer (**Figure 38**) is necessary for repairs. A soft-faced hammer (rubber or plastic) or a soft-faced hammer filled with leadshot is sometimes necessary. Never use a metal-faced hammer on engine or suspension parts. Severe damage will result in most cases. The same amount of force can be produced with a soft-faced hammer. The shock of a metal-faced hammer, however, is required for using a hand impact driver.

Support Jacks

The correct support jack is necessary for many routine service or major component replacement procedures on the bike. When it is necessary to raise either the front or rear end of the vehicle, the Centerstand Scissor Jack available through Yamaha dealerships from K&L Supply, Santa Clara, CA (**Figure 39**) is suitable for most service procedures on the series of bikes. It is adjustable and is very stable for use with the frame configuration of this vehicle.

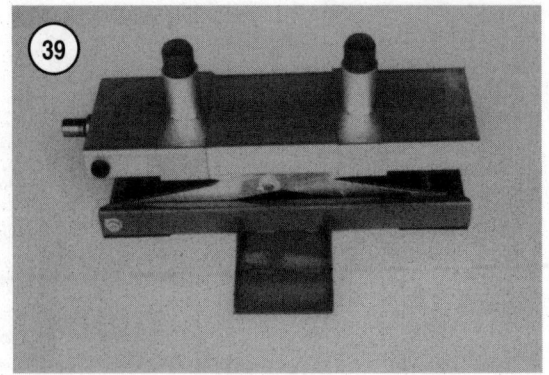

PRECISION MEASURING TOOLS

Measurement is an important part of engine and suspension service. Many of the service procedures in this manual require making a number of measurements. These include basic checks such as engine compression and spark plug gap. As your shop work is expanded into engine disassembly and service, measurements will be required to determine the size and condition of the piston and cylinder bore, crankshaft runout and so on. When making these measurements, the degree of accuracy will dictate which tool is required. Precision measuring tools are expensive. It may be worthwhile to have the checks and measurements made at a Yamaha dealership, a competent independent motorcycle repair shop or a machine shop. The following is a description of the measuring tools required to perform the various service procedures described in this manual.

Feeler Gauge

Feeler gauges come in assorted sets and types (**Figure 40**). The feeler gauge is made of either a piece of a flat or round hardened steel of a specified thickness. Wire gauges are used to measure spark plug gap. Flat gauges are used for other measurements. Feeler gauges are also designed for specialized uses. For example, the end of a gauge is usually small and angled to facilitate checking valve clearances.

Vernier Caliper, Dial Caliper and Digital Electronic Caliper

These are valuable tools for reading inside, outside and depth measurements with semi-close precision. Although this type of tool is not as precise as a micrometer, they allow reasonable, non-close tol-

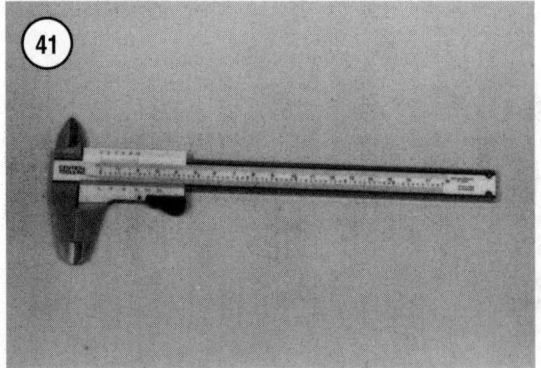

erance measurements, typically to within 0.025 mm (0.001 in.). Calipers are commonly used to measure the length of the clutch springs; the thickness of clutch plates, shims and thrust washers; brake pad or lining thickness or the depth of a bearing bore. The jaws of the caliper must be clean and free of burrs at all times in order to obtain an accurate measurement.

Calipers are available either in dial, vernier or digital versions. The standard vernier caliper (**Figure 41**) has highly accurate graduated scales on fixed and moving pieces that must be compared to

GENERAL INFORMATION

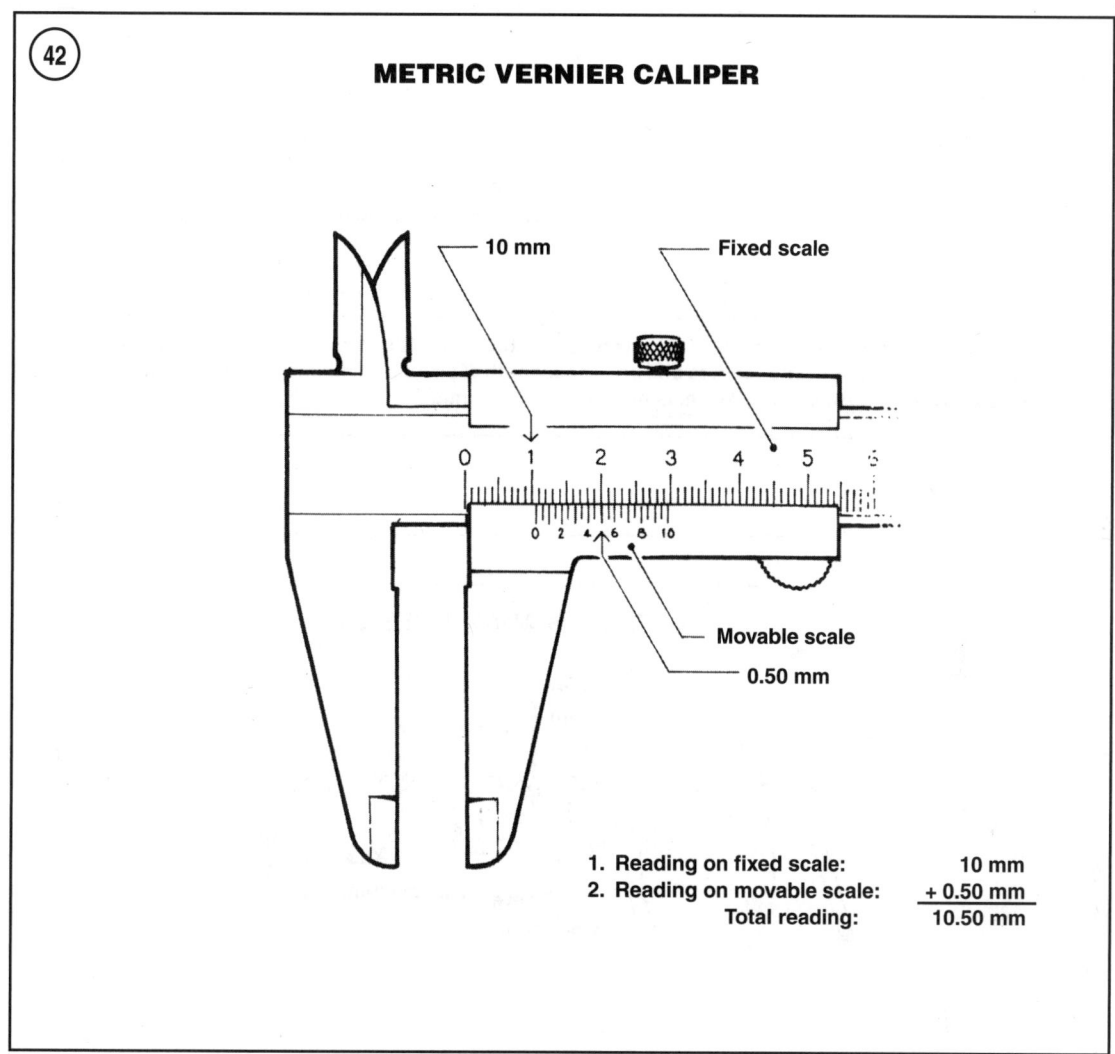

determine the reading. A dial indicator caliper is equipped with a small dial and needle that indicates the measurement reading. The digital electronic type, however, uses an LCD display that shows the measurement on the small display screen. Some calipers must be zeroed before making a measurement to ensure an accurate measurement. Refer to the manufacturer's instructions for this procedure.

Figure 42 shows a measurement taken with a metric vernier caliper. To read the measurement, note that the scale on the fixed piece is graduated in centimeters, which is indicated by the whole numbers 1, 2, 3 and so on. Each centimeter is then divided into millimeters, which are indicated by the small line between the whole numbers. (1 centimeter equals 10 millimeters). The movable scale is marked in increments representing 0.05 mm. The value of a measurement equals the reading on the fixed scale plus the reading on the movable scale.

To determine the reading on the fixed scale, look for the line on the fixed scale immediately to the left of the 0-line on the movable scale. The value of this fixed-scale line equals the fixed scale reading. In the example in **Figure 42**, the fixed scale reading is 1 centimeter (or 10 millimeters)

To determine the reading on the movable scale, note the one line on the movable scale that precisely aligns with a line on the fixed scale. A number of lines will seem close, but only one aligns precisely with a line on the fixed scale. The value of this movable-scale line (measured in hundredths of a millimeter) equals the movable scale reading. In the

DECIMAL PLACE VALUES*

0.1	Indicates 1/10 (one tenth of an inch or millimeter)
0.010	Indicates 1/100 (one one-hundreth of an inch or millimeter)
0.001	Indicates 1/1,000 (one one-thousandth of an inch or millimeter)

*This chart represents the values of figures placed to the right of the decimal point. Use it when reading decimals from one-tenth to one one-thousandth of an inch or millimeter. It is not a conversion chart (for example: 0.001 in. is not equal to 0.001 mm).

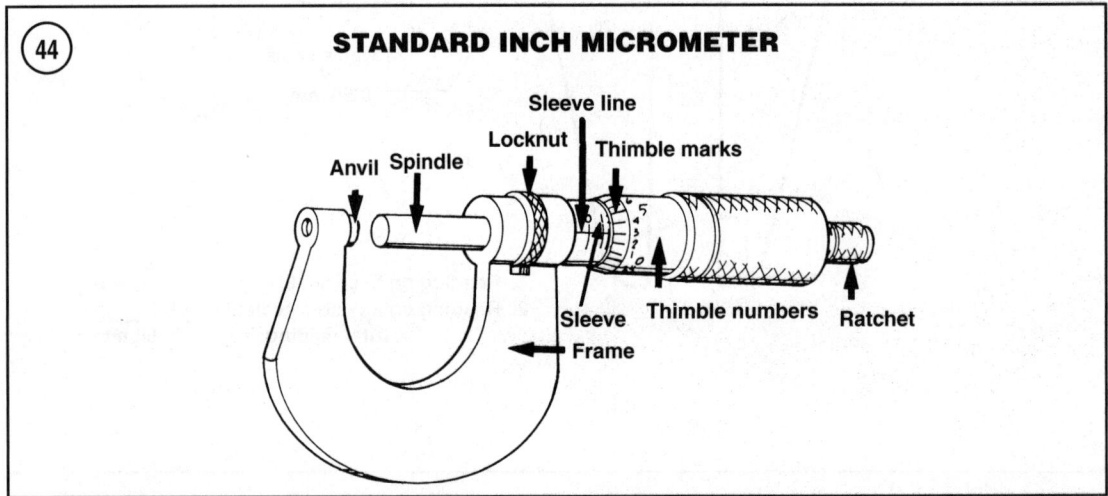

example (**Figure 42**), the movable scale reading is 0.50 mm.

To calculate the measurement, add the fixed scale reading (10 mm) to the movable scale reading (0.50 mm) for a value of 10.50 mm.

Outside Micrometers

An outside micrometer is a precision tool used to accurately measure parts using the decimal divisions of the inch or meter (**Figure 43**). While there are many types and styles of micrometers, this section describes steps on how to use the outside micrometer. The outside micrometer is the most common type of micrometer used when servicing a motorcycle. It accurately measures the outside diameter, length and thickness of parts used on these vehicles. These parts include pistons, piston pins, crankshaft, piston rings, transmission shafts and various shims. The outside micrometer is also used to measure the dimension taken by a small hole gauge or a telescoping gauge described later in this section. After the small hole gauge or telescoping gauge has been carefully expanded within the bore of the component, carefully remove the gauge and measure the outer dimension of the gauge with the outside micrometer.

Other types of micrometers include the depth micrometer and screw thread micrometer. **Figure 44** identifies the various parts of the outside micrometer.

GENERAL INFORMATION

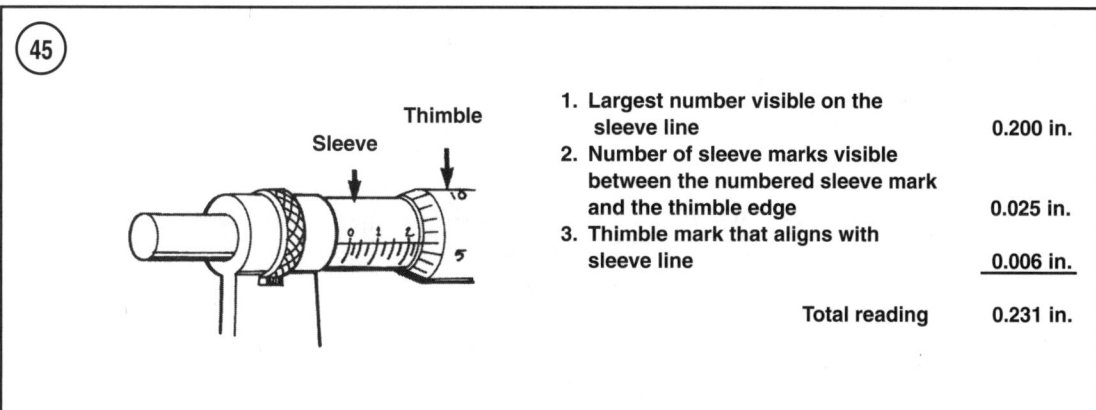

1. Largest number visible on the sleeve line	0.200 in.
2. Number of sleeve marks visible between the numbered sleeve mark and the thimble edge	0.025 in.
3. Thimble mark that aligns with sleeve line	0.006 in.
Total reading	0.231 in.

Micrometer Range

A micrometer's size indicates the minimum and maximum size of a part that it can measure. The usual sizes are: 0-1 in. (0-25 mm), 1-2 in. (25-50 mm), 2-3 in. (50-75 mm) and 3-4 in. (75-100 mm). These micrometers use fixed anvils.

Some micrometers use the same frame with interchangeable anvils. This allows the installation of the correct length anvil for a particular job. For example, a 0-4 in. interchangeable micrometer is equipped with four different length anvils. While purchasing one or two micrometers to cover a range from 0-4 in. or 0-6 in. is less expensive, its overall frame size makes it less convenient to use.

How To Read a Micrometer

When reading a micrometer, numbers are taken from different scales and then added together. The following sections describe how to read the standard inch micrometer, the vernier inch micrometer, the standard metric micrometer and the metric vernier micrometer.

Standard inch micrometer

The standard inch micrometer is accurate up to one-thousand of an inch (0.001 in.). The heart of the micrometer is its spindle screw with 40 threads per inch. Every turn of the thimble moves the spindle 1/40 of an inch or 0.025 in.

Before learning how to read a micrometer, study the markings and part names in **Figure 44**. Turn the micrometer's thimble until its zero mark aligns with the zero mark on the sleeve line. Now turn the thimble counterclockwise and align the next thimble mark with the sleeve line. The micrometer now reads 0.001 in. (one one-thousandths of an inch). Thus, each thimble mark is equal to 0.001 in. Every fifth thimble mark is numbered to assist reading: 0, 5, 15 and 20.

Reset the micrometer so the thimble and sleeve-line zero marks align. Then turn the thimble counterclockwise one complete revolution and align the thimble zero mark with the first line in the sleeve line. The micrometer now reads 0.025 in. (twenty-five thousandths of an inch). Thus each sleeve line represents 0.025 in.

Now turn the thimble counterclockwise while counting the sleeve line marks. Every fourth mark on the sleeve line is marked with a number ranging from 1 through 9. Manufacturers usually mark the last mark on the sleeve with a 0. This is the end of the micrometer's measuring range. Each sleeve number represents 0.100 in. For example, the number 1 represents 0.100 in. and the number 9 represents 0.900 in.

When reading a standard micrometer, read the following three measurements described below and add them together. The sum of the three readings gives the final measurement in a thousandth of an inch (0.001 in.).

To read a micrometer, perform the following steps and refer to the example in **Figure 45**.

1. Read the sleeve line to find the largest number visible—each sleeve number mark equals 0.100 in.

2. Count the number of sleeve marks visible between the numbered sleeve mark and the thimble edge—each sleeve mark equals 0.025 in. If there is no visible sleeve mark, continue to Step 3.

CHAPTER ONE

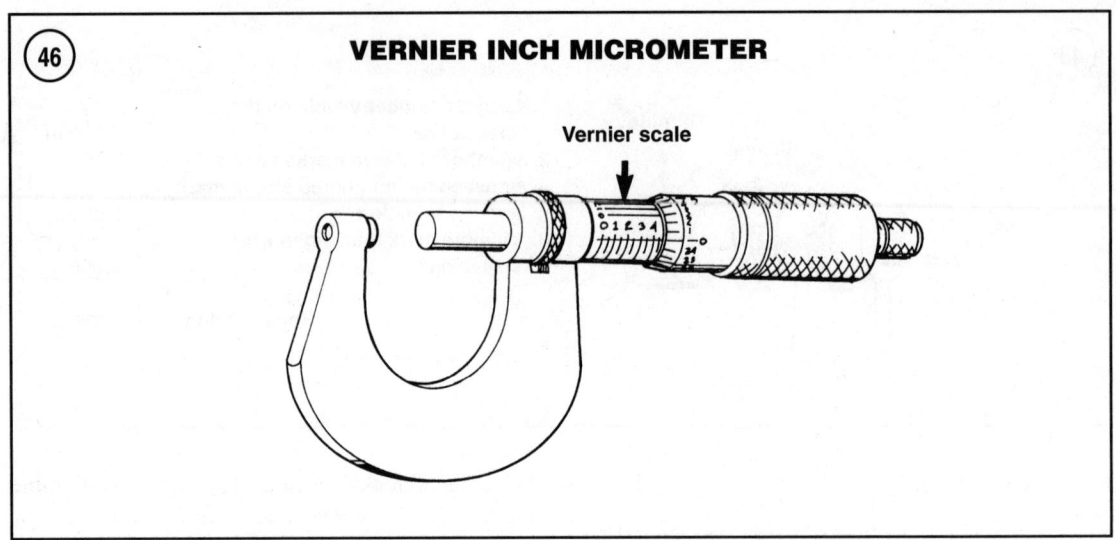

VERNIER INCH MICROMETER

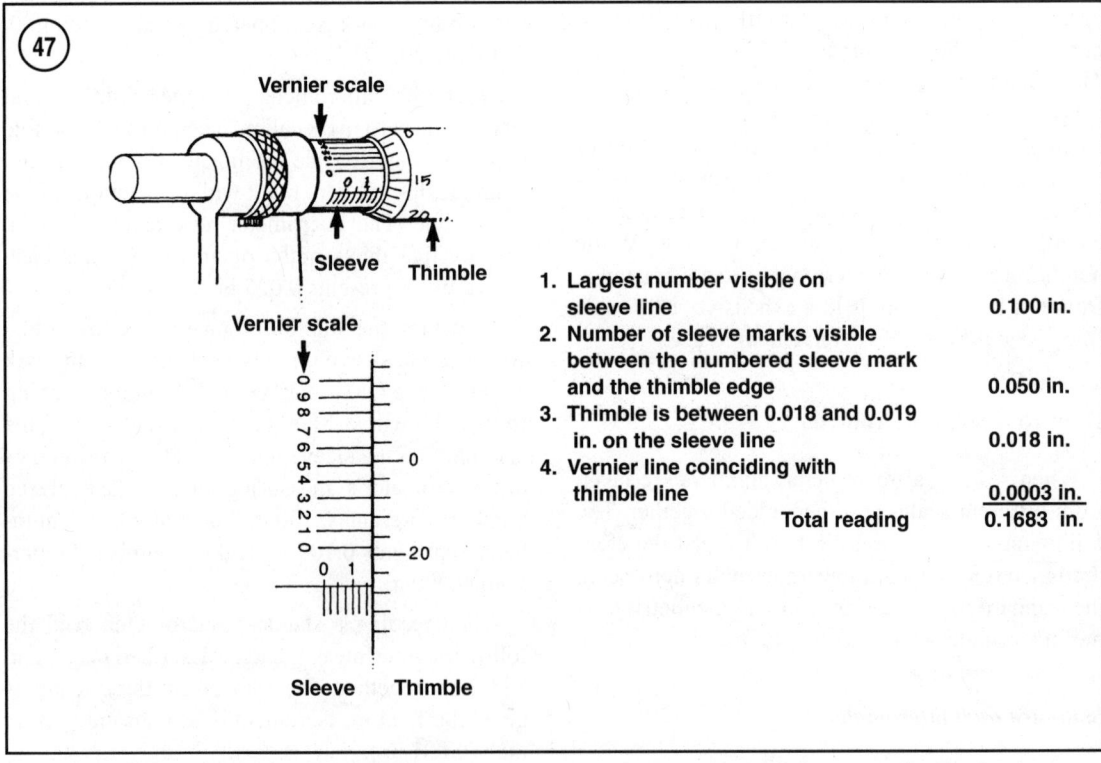

1. Largest number visible on sleeve line	0.100 in.
2. Number of sleeve marks visible between the numbered sleeve mark and the thimble edge	0.050 in.
3. Thimble is between 0.018 and 0.019 in. on the sleeve line	0.018 in.
4. Vernier line coinciding with thimble line	0.0003 in.
Total reading	0.1683 in.

3. Read the thimble mark that aligns with the sleeve line—each thimble mark equals 0.001 in.

NOTE
If a thimble mark does not align exactly with the sleeve line but falls between two lines, estimate the fraction of decimal amount between the lines.

4. Adding the micrometer readings in Steps 1, 2 and 3 gives the actual measurement.

Vernier inch micrometer

A vernier micrometer can accurately measure in ten-thousandths of an inch (0.0001 in.). While it has

GENERAL INFORMATION

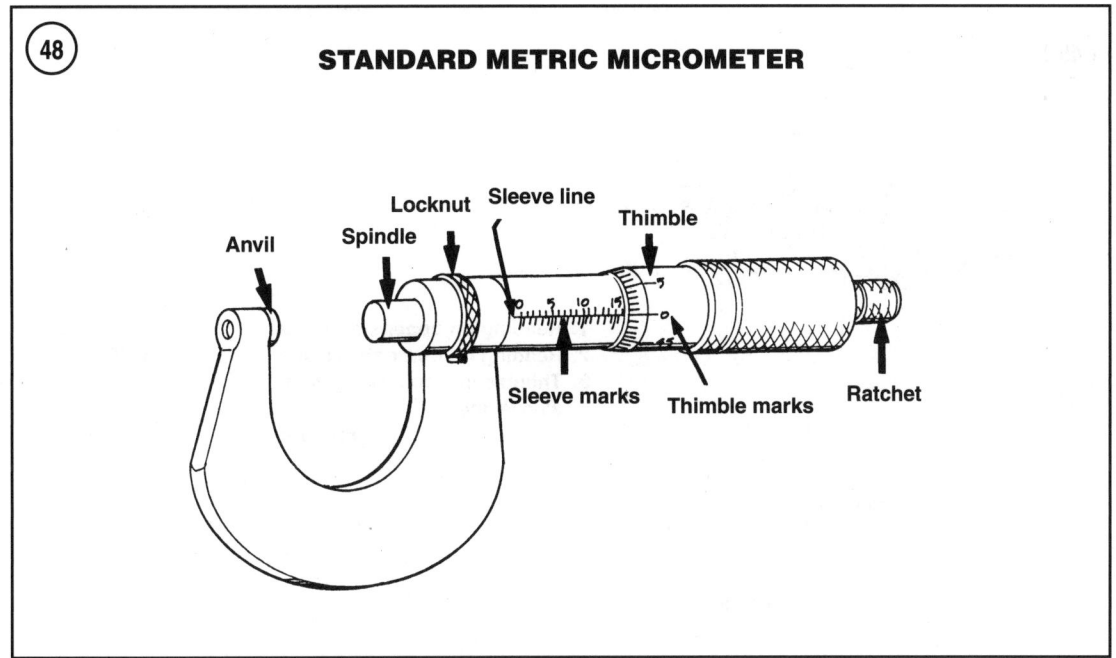

STANDARD METRIC MICROMETER

the same markings as the standard inch micrometer, a vernier scale scribed on the sleeve (**Figure 46**) makes it unique. The vernier scale consists of eleven equally spaced lines marked 0-9 with a 0 on each end. These lines run parallel on the top of the sleeve where each line is equal to 0.0001 in. Thus, the vernier scale divides a thousandth of an inch (0.001 in.) into ten-thousandths of an inch (0.0001 in.).

To read the vernier micrometer, perform the following steps and refer to the example in **Figure 47**:

1. Read the micrometer in the same way as on the standard inch micrometer. This is the initial reading.

2. If a thimble mark aligns exactly with the sleeve line, reading the vernier scale is not necessary. If a thimble mark does not align exactly with the sleeve line, read the vernier scale in Step 3.

3. Read the vernier scale to find the one vernier mark that aligns with a thimble mark. The number of that vernier mark is the number of ten-thousandths of an inch to add to the initial reading taken in Step 1.

Metric micrometer

The metric micrometer is very similar to the standard inch micrometer. The differences are the graduations on the thimble and sleeve as shown in **Figure 48**.

The standard metric micrometer accurately measures to one one-hundredths of a millimeter (0.01 mm). On the metric micrometer, the spindle screw is ground with a thread pitch of one-half millimeter (0.5 mm). Thus, every turn of the thimble moves the spindle 0.5 mm.

The sleeve line is graduated in millimeters and half millimeters. The marks on the upper side of the sleeve line are equal to 1.00 mm. Every fifth mark above the sleeve line is marked with a number. The actual numbers depends on the size of the micrometer. For example, on a 0-25 mm micrometer, the sleeve marks are numbered 0, 5, 10, 15, 20 and 25. On a 25-50 mm micrometer, the sleeve marks are numbered 25, 30, 35, 40, 45 and 50. This numbering sequence continues with larger micrometers (50-75 and 75-100). Each mark on the lower side of the sleeve line is equal to 0.5 mm.

The thimble scale is divided into fifty graduations where one graduation is equal to 0.01 mm. Every fifth graduation is numbered to help with reading from 0-45. The thimble edge is used to indicate which sleeve markings to read.

To read the metric micrometer add the number of millimeters and half-millimeters on the sleeve line to the number of one one-hundredth millimeters on

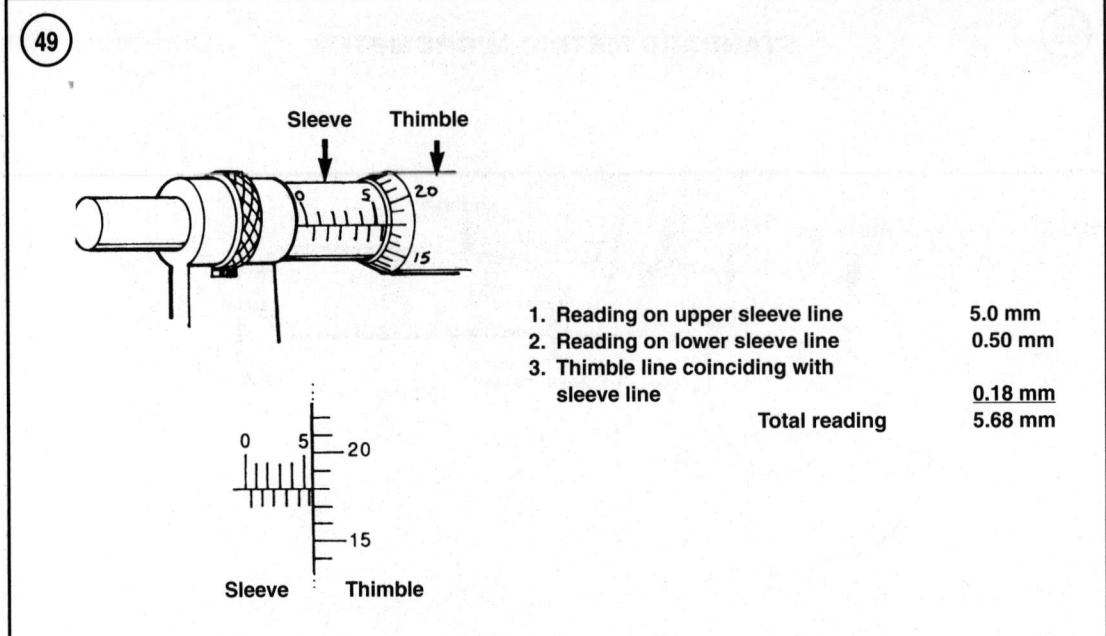

1. Reading on upper sleeve line	5.0 mm
2. Reading on lower sleeve line	0.50 mm
3. Thimble line coinciding with sleeve line	0.18 mm
Total reading	5.68 mm

the thimble. To do so, perform the following steps and refer to the example in **Figure 49**:

1. Take the first reading by counting the number of marks visible on the upper sleeve line. Record the reading.
2. Look below the sleeve line to see if a lower mark is visible directly past the upper line mark. If so, add 0.50 to the first reading.
3. Now read the thimble mark that aligns with the sleeve line. Record this reading.

> *NOTE*
> *If a thimble mark does not align exactly with the sleeve line but falls between the two lines, estimate the decimal amount between the lines. For a more accurate reading, use a metric vernier micrometer.*

4. Adding the micrometer readings in Steps 1, 2 and 3 gives the actual measurement.

Metric vernier micrometer

A metric micrometer can accurately measure to two thousandths of a millimeter (0.002 mm). While it has the same markings as the standard metric micrometer, a vernier scale scribed on the sleeve (**Figure 50**) makes it unique. The vernier scale consists of five equally spaced lines 0, 2, 4, 6 and 8. These lines run parallel on the top of the sleeve where each line is equal to 0.002 mm.

To read the metric vernier micrometer, perform the following steps and refer to the example in **Figure 51**:

1. Read the metric vernier micrometer the same way as with the metric standard micrometer. This is the initial reading.
2. If a thimble mark aligns exactly with the sleeve line, reading the vernier scale is not necessary. If a thimble line does not align exactly with the sleeve line, read the vernier scale in Step 3.
3. Read the vernier scale to find which mark aligns with one thimble mark. The number of the vernier mark is the number of thousands of a millimeter to add to the initial reading taken in Step 1.

Micrometer Accuracy Check

The micrometer must be checked frequently to ensure accuracy as follows:

1. Make sure the anvil and spindle faces (**Figure 48**) are clean and dry.
2. To check a 0-1 in. (0-25 mm) micrometer, perform the following:
  a. Turn the spindle until the spindle contacts the anvil. If the micrometer has a ratchet stop, use

GENERAL INFORMATION

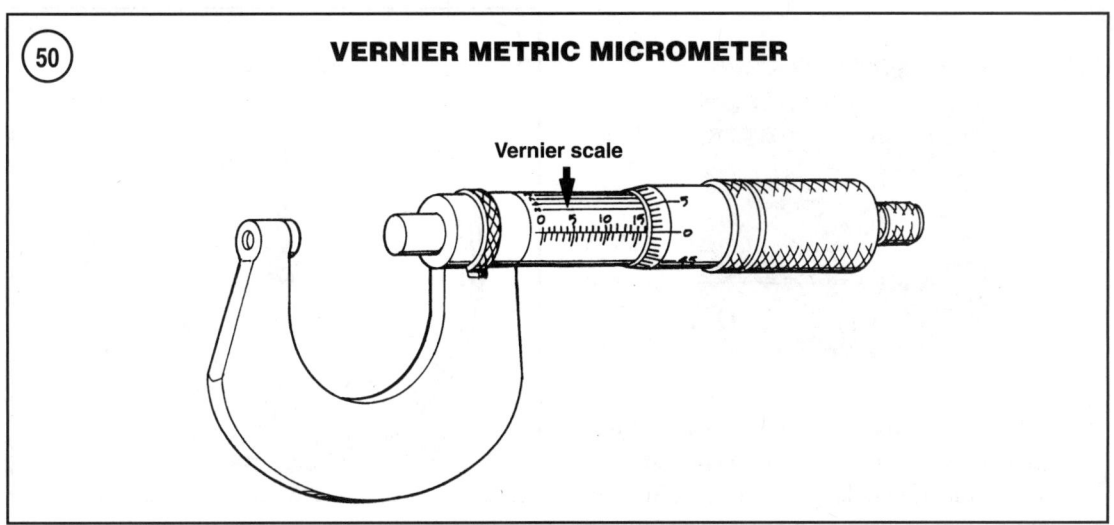

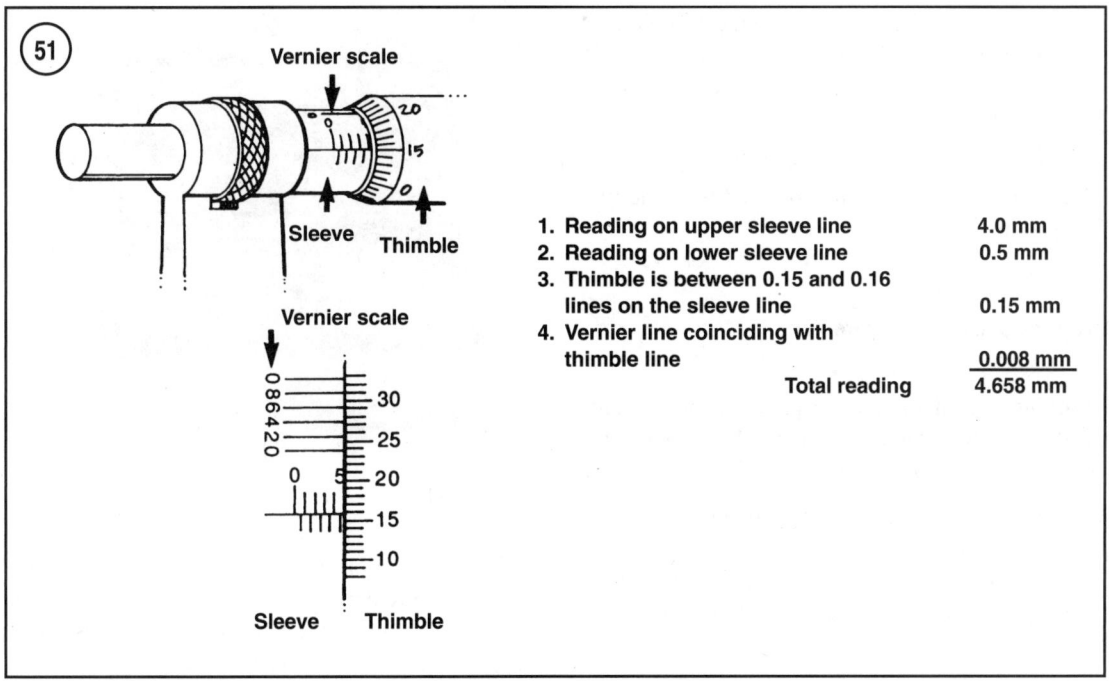

1. Reading on upper sleeve line	4.0 mm
2. Reading on lower sleeve line	0.5 mm
3. Thimble is between 0.15 and 0.16 lines on the sleeve line	0.15 mm
4. Vernier line coinciding with thimble line	0.008 mm
Total reading	4.658 mm

it to ensure that the proper amount of pressure is applied against the contact surfaces.

b. Read the micrometer. If the adjustment is correct, the 0 mark on the thimble will be aligned exactly with the 0 mark on the sleeve line. If the 0 marks do not align, the micrometer is out of adjustment.

c. To adjust the micrometer, follow the manufacturer's instructions provided with the micrometer.

3. To check the accuracy of a micrometer above the 1 in. (25 mm) size, perform the following:

a. Manufacturers usually supply a standard gauge with their micrometers. A standard is a steel block, disc or rod that is ground to an exact size to check the accuracy of the micrometer. For example, a 1-2 inch micrometer is equipped with a 1 inch standard gauge. A 25-50 mm micrometer is equipped with a 25 mm standard gauge.

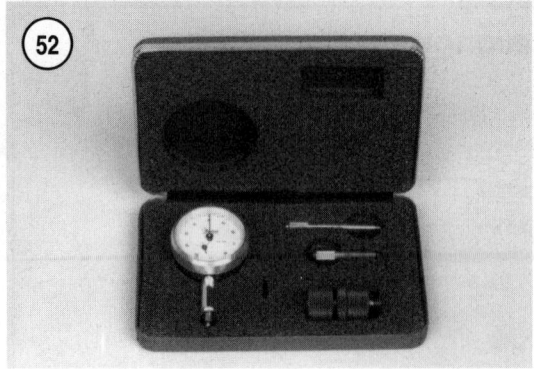

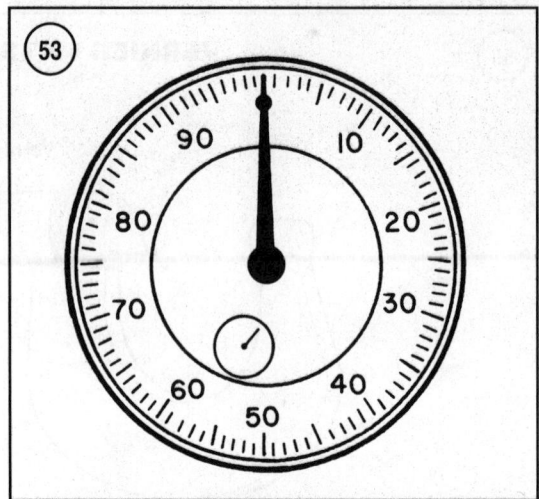

b. Place the standard gauge between the micrometer's spindle and anvil, and measure the outside diameter or length in the same manner as you would measure a component from a vehicle. Read the micrometer. If the adjustment is correct, the 0 mark on the thimble will be aligned exactly with the sleeve line. If the 0 marks do not align, the micrometer is out of alignment.

c. To adjust the micrometer, follow the manufacturer's instructions provided with the micrometer.

Proper Care of a Micrometer

Because the micrometer is a precision instrument, use it correctly and with great care. When using and storing a micrometer, refer to the following:

1. Store a micrometer in its box or in a protected place where dust, oil and other debris cannot come in contact with it. Do not store micrometers in a drawer with other tools nor hang them on a tool board.

2. When storing a 0-1 in. (0-25 mm) micrometer, the spindle and anvil must not contact each other. If they do, rust may form on the contact ends or the spindle may be damaged from temperature changes.

3. Do not clean a micrometer with compressed air. Dirt forced under pressure into the tool can cause premature damage.

4. Occasionally lubricate the micrometer with light weight oil to prevent rust and corrosion.

5. Before using a micrometer, check its accuracy as previously described in this section.

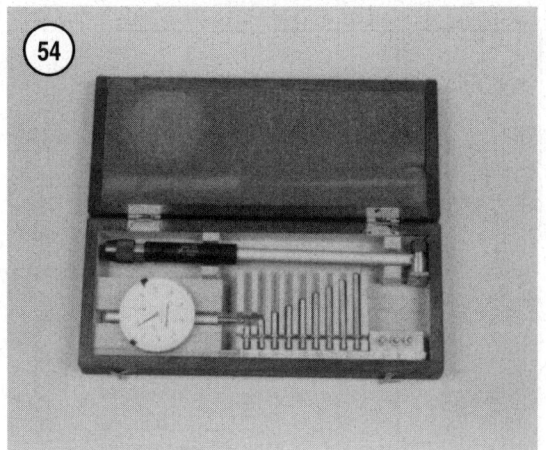

Dial Indicator

A dial indicator (**Figure 52**) is a precision tool used to check dimensional variations, both radial and lateral runout, of machined parts such as transmission shafts and to check crankshaft runout and end play. A dial indicator may also be used to locate the piston at a specific position when checking ignition timing. For motorcycle service procedures, select a dial indicator with a continuous dial (**Figure 53**). Several different mounting types are available, including magnetic stands that attach to iron or steel surfaces, a clamp that can be attached to various components and a spark plug adapter that locates the probe of the dial indicator through the spark plug hole. See *Magnetic Stand* in this chapter. The measurement being taken determines the type of mount needed.

GENERAL INFORMATION

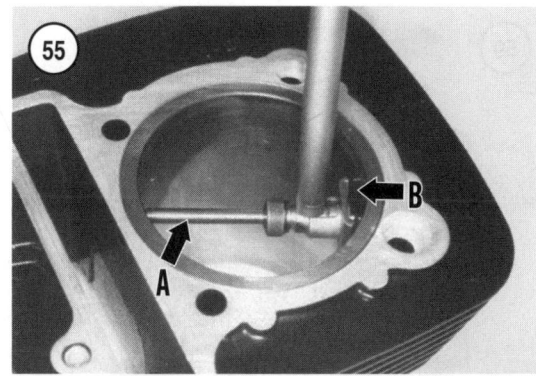

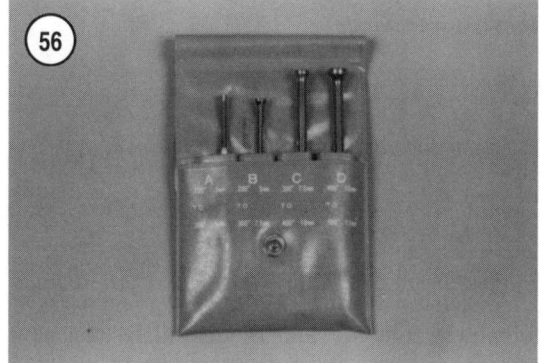

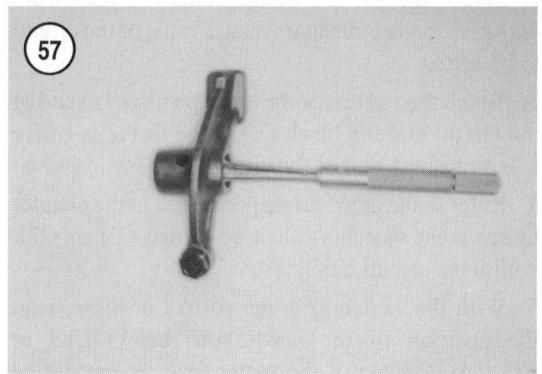

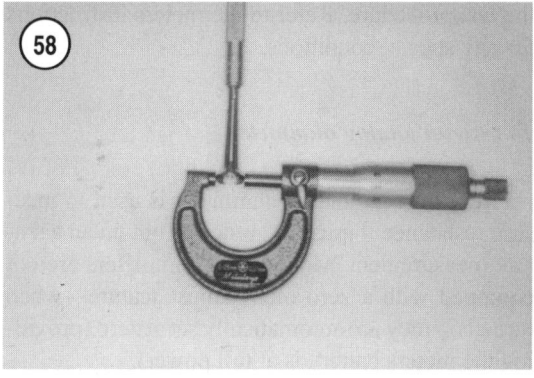

Cylinder Bore Gauge

The cylinder bore gauge is a specialized precision tool. The gauge set shown in **Figure 54** consists of a dial indicator, handle and a number of different length adapters for different bore sizes. The bore gauge is used to make cylinder bore measurements such as bore size, taper and out-of-round. Depending on the bore gauge, it can sometimes be used to measure brake caliper and master cylinder bore sizes. In some cases, an outside micrometer must be used together with the bore gauge to determine bore dimensions.

Select the correct length adapter (A, **Figure 55**) for the size of the bore to be measured. Zero the bore gauge according to the manufacturer's instructions, and insert the bore gauge into the cylinder. Carefully move the gauge around in the bore to make sure it is centered and the gauge foot (B, **Figure 55**) is sitting correctly on the bore surface. This is necessary in order to obtain a correct reading. Refer to the manufacturer's instructions for reading the actual measurement obtained.

Small Hole Gauges

A set of small hole gauges (**Figure 56**) is used to measure a hole, groove or slot. A small hole gauge measures the smallest holes. A telescoping gauge, on the other hand, measures slightly larger holes (see below). A small hole gauge is required to measure rocker arm bore and brake master cylinder bore diameters. The small hole gauge does not have a scale for direct readings. Use an outside micrometer together with the small hole gauge to determine the bore dimension.

Carefully insert the small hole gauge into the bore of the component to be measured. Tighten the knurled end of the gauge to carefully expand the gauge fingers to the limit within the bore (**Figure 57**). *Do not overtighten* the gauge as there is no built-in release feature. If tightened too much, the gauge fingers can damage the bore surface. Carefully remove the gauge, and measure the outside dimension of the gauge with a micrometer (**Figure 58**), as described in this chapter.

CHAPTER ONE

Telescoping Gauges

A telescoping gauge (**Figure 59**) is used to measure hole diameters from approximately 8 mm (5/16 in.) to 150 mm (6 in.). For example, it could be used to measure brake caliper bore and cylinder bore diameters. Like the small hole gauge, the telescoping gauge does not have a scale for direct reading. Use an outside micrometer together with the telescoping gauge to determine the bore dimension.

Select the correct size telescoping gauge for the bore to be measured. Compress the movable side of the gauge post. Carefully install the gauge into the bore, and release the movable post against the bore. Center the gauge by carefully moving it around in the bore. Tighten the knurled end of the gauge to hold the movable gauge post in this position. Carefully remove the gauge and measure the outside dimension of the gauge posts with a micrometer as described in this chapter.

Compression Gauge

An engine with low compression cannot be properly tuned and will not develop full power. A compression gauge (**Figure 60**) measures engine compression. The one shown has a flexible stem with an extension that allows it to be held while the engine is being turned over. Open the throttle all the way when checking engine compression as described in Chapter Three.

Multimeter

A mulitimeter is a valuable tool for all electrical system troubleshooting (**Figure 61**). The voltage application is used to indicate the voltage applied or available to various electrical components. The ohmmeter portion of the meter is used to check for continuity and to measure the resistance of a component. Some tests are easily accomplished using a meter with a sweeping needle (analog), but other tests require a digital multimeter.

In some electrical tests, the internal design of a meter affects the test readings. In these instances, the vehicle's manufacturer instructs the use of their specific meter because another meter may produce inaccurate results. The text in this book notes when a particular meter is required to perform a test.

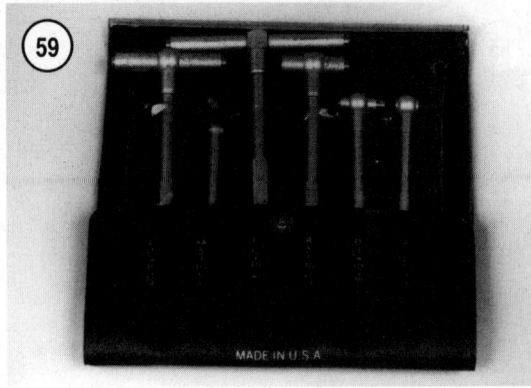

To measure voltage

NOTE
Make sure the negative (–) or ground surface that will be used is clean and free of paint and/or grease. If possible, use a non-painted bolt that is attached directly to the frame.

1. Make sure the meter battery power source is at full power. If its condition is doubtful, install a new battery(s).
2. Select the meter voltage range to *one scale higher* than the indicated voltage value of the circuit to be tested.
3. Touch the red test probe to the *positive* (+) end of the circuit and the black test probe to the *negative* (–), or ground, end of the circuit.
4. Refer to the appropriate procedure in the chapter to see what switch(s) must be turned ON or OFF within the circuit being tested.
5. With the switch(s) in the correct position, read the position of the needle on the VOLTS or VOLTAGE scale of the meter face, or the digital readout, and refer to the specified voltage listed in the test procedure. Refer to the meters instructions for any special conditions.

To zero an analog ohmmeter

Every time an analog ohmmeter is used to measure resistance it must be zeroed to obtain an accurate measurement. Most digital ohmmeters are not equipped with a zero ohms adjust feature—when turned on they are automatically set at zero (providing the meters battery is at full power).

GENERAL INFORMATION

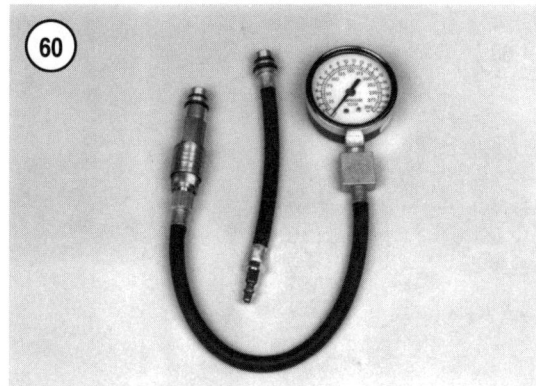

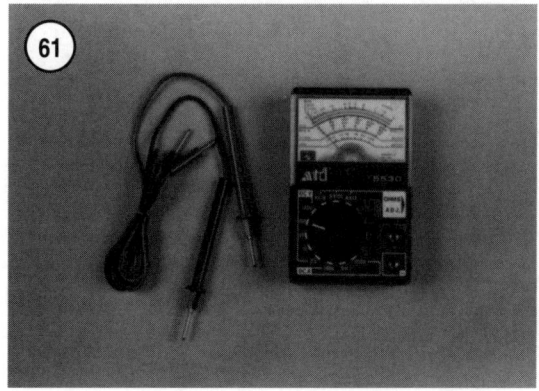

1. Make sure the meter's battery power source is at full power. If its condition is doubtful, install a new battery(s).
2. Make sure the test probes are clean and free of corrosion.
3. Touch the two test probes together and observe the meter needle location on the OHMS scale on the meter face. The needle must be on the 0 mark at the end of the scale.
4. If necessary, rotate the ohms adjust knob on the meter, in either direction, until the needle is directly on the 0 mark on the scale. The meter is now ready for use.

To measure resistance

1. Zero the analog meter as previously described.
2. Disconnect the component from the circuit.

NOTE
Polarity is not important when measuring the resistance of a component. Either test probe can be placed at either terminal of the component.

3. Place the test probes at each end of the component, read the position of the needle on the OHMS scale of the meter face, or the digital readout, and refer to the specified resistance in the test procedure.
4. If the component is not within specification, replace it.
5. If the component is within specification, reinstall it in the circuit.

Continuity test

A continuity test is used to determine the integrity of a circuit, wire or component. Continuity is indicated by a low resistance reading, usually zero ohms, on the meter. No continuity is indicated by an infinity reading. A broken or open circuit has no continuity, while a complete circuit has continuity. A continuity test is also useful to check components for a short to ground. A shorted component has a complete circuit (continuity) between the component and ground.

NOTE
Every time an analog ohmmeter is used for a continuity check, it must be zeroed to obtain an accurate reading.

1. Zero the analog meter as previously described.

NOTE
Polarity is not important when making a continuity check on a component or circuit. Either test probe can be placed at either terminal of the component or circuit.

2. Place the test probes at each end of the component or circuit, and read the position of the needle on the OHMS scale of the meter face or digital readout.
3. If there is *continuity (low resistance)*, the meter will read zero or very low resistance. In this test the resistance value is not important—the goal is to determine if the circuit is complete or not.
4. If there is *no continuity (infinite resistance)*, the meter needle will not move and will stay at the infinity symbol or the digital readout will indicate infinity.
5. If the component is not within specification, replace it.
6. If the component is within specification, reinstall it in the circuit.

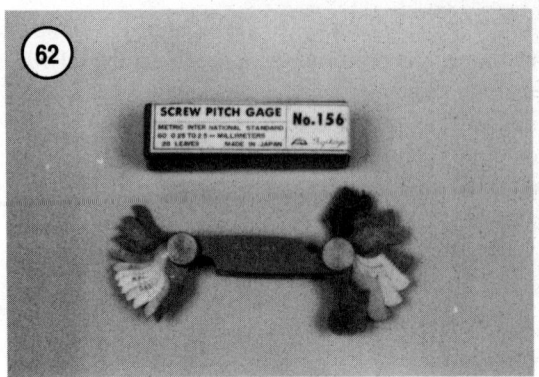

Screw Pitch Gauge

A screw pitch gauge (**Figure 62**) determines the thread pitch of fasteners. The gauge is made up of a number of thin plates. Each plate has a thread shape cut on one edge to match one thread pitch. When using a screw pitch gauge to determine a thread pitch size, try to fit different blade sizes onto the bolt thread until both threads match.

Magnetic Stand

A magnetic stand (**Figure 63**) is used to hold a dial indicator securely when checking the runout of a round object or when checking the end play of a shaft.

V-Blocks

V-blocks (**Figure 64**) are precision ground blocks used to hold a round object when checking its runout or condition. In motorcycle repair, V-blocks can be used for checking transmission shafts, crankshaft, wheel axles and other shafts and collars.

Surface Plate

A surface plate (**Figure 65**) is used to check the flatness of parts. While industrial quality surface plates are quite expensive, the home mechanic can improvise. A piece of thick, flat metal or plate glass can sometimes be used as a surface plate. The quality of the surface plate will affect the accuracy of the measurement being taken. The surface plate can have a piece of fine grit paper mounted on its surface to assist in cleaning and smoothing a flat sur-

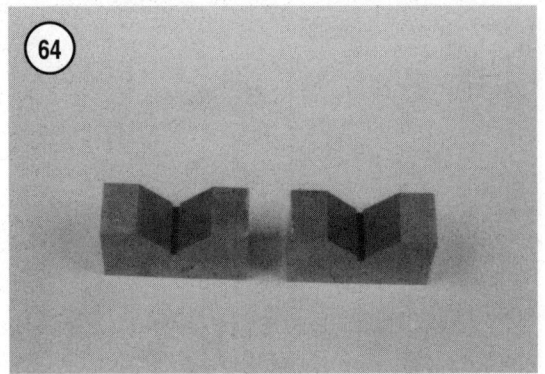

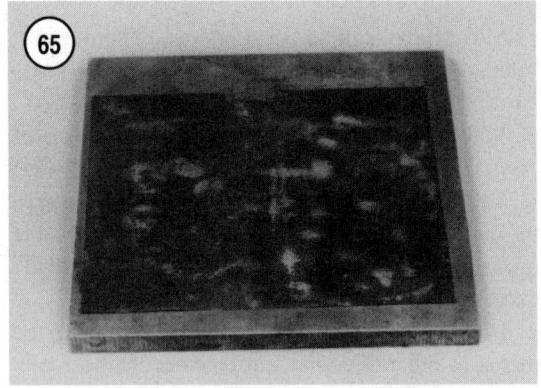

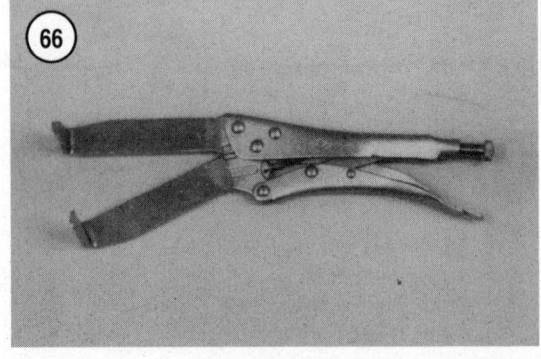

GENERAL INFORMATION

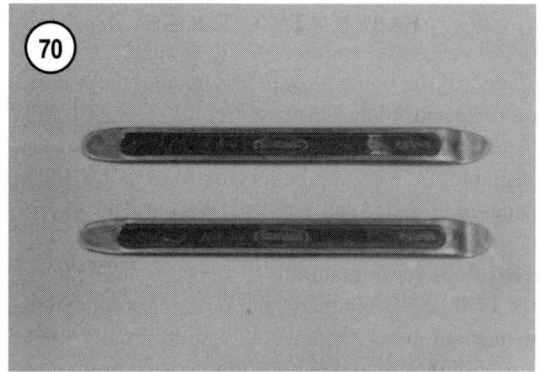

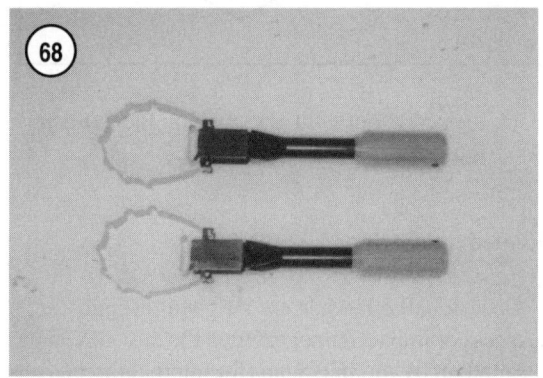

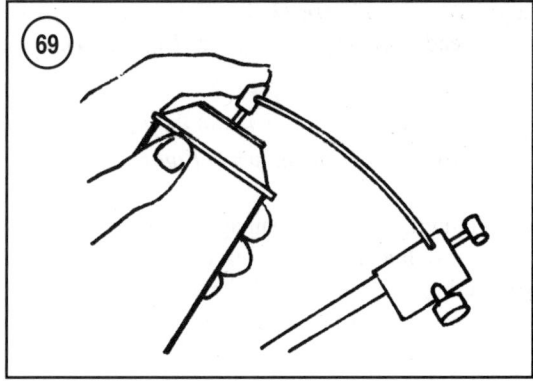

face of a part. The machined surfaces of the cylinder head, cylinder, crankcase and other close fitting parts may require a very good quality surface plate to smooth nicked or damaged surfaces.

SPECIAL TOOLS

A few special tools may be required for major service. These are described in the appropriate chapters and are available either from a Yamaha dealership or other manufacturer as indicated.

This section describes special tools unique to this type of bike's service and repair.

Clutch Holding Tool

The clutch holding tool (**Figure 66**) (Yamaha part No. 90890-04086) is a special tool used to hold various parts, like the clutch hub, sprockets and gears, when loosening and tightening fasteners.

Piston Ring Compressor Tools

The piston ring compressor tool (**Figure 67** or **Figure 68**) is used to compress the piston rings during cylinder installation to prevent piston ring damage.

Pressure Cable Lube Tool

A cable lube tool is used to force cable lubricant throughout a control cable.

This tool (**Figure 69**) is clamped to one end of a control cable. It has a tube fitting that allows pressurized cable lubricant to be forced throughout the entire length of the cable.

Tire Levers

When changing tires, use a good set of tire levers (**Figure 70**). Never use a screwdriver in place of a tire lever; refer to Chapter Ten for its use. Before using a tire lever, check the working end of the tool and remove any burrs with a file. Do not use a tire lever for prying anything but tires.

CHAPTER ONE

FABRICATING TOOLS

Some of the procedures in this manual require the use of special tools. The resourceful mechanic can, in many cases, think of acceptable substitutes for special tools. This can be as simple as using a few pieces of threaded rod, some washers and nuts to remove or install a bearing. A tool can also be fabricated from scrap material. If a special tool can be designed and safely made, but it requires some type of machine work, contact a local community college or high school that has a machine shop curriculum. Some shop teachers welcome outside work as practical shop applications for students.

MECHANIC'S TIPS

Removing Frozen Nuts and Screws

When a fastener rusts and cannot be removed, several methods may be used to loosen it. First, apply penetrating oil such as Liquid Wrench or WD-40 (available at hardware or auto supply stores). Apply it liberally and let it penetrate for 10-15 minutes. Rap the fastener several times with a small hammer; do not hit it hard enough to cause damage. Reapply the penetrating oil if necessary.

For frozen screws, apply penetrating oil as described, then insert a screwdriver in the slot and rap the top of the screwdriver with a hammer. This loosens the rust so the screw can be removed in the normal way. If the screw head is too chewed up to use this method, grip the head with locking pliers and twist the screw out.

Avoid applying heat unless specifically instructed. The heat may melt, warp or remove the temper from parts.

Removing Broken Screws or Bolts

When the head breaks off a screw or bolt, several methods are available for removing the remaining portion. If a large portion of the remainder projects out, try gripping it with locking pliers. If the projecting portion is too small, file it to fit a wrench or cut a slot in it to fit a screwdriver. See **Figure 71**.

If the head breaks off flush, use a screw extractor. To do this, centerpunch the exact center of the remaining portion of the screw or bolt. Drill a small hole in the screw and tap the extractor into the hole.

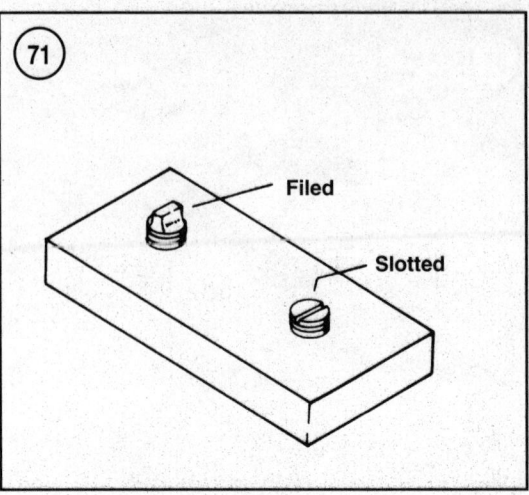

Back the screw out with a wrench on the extractor. See **Figure 72**.

Remedying Stripped Threads

Occasionally, threads are stripped through carelessness or impact damage. Often the threads can be cleaned up by running a tap (for internal threads on nuts) or die (for external threads on bolts) through the threads. See **Figure 73**. To clean or repair spark plug threads, use a spark plug tap (**Figure 74**).

NOTE
*Tap and dies can be bought individually or in a set as shown in **Figure 75**.*

If an internal thread is damaged, it may be necessary to install a Helicoil (**Figure 76**) or some other type of thread insert. Follow the manufacturer's instructions when installing the insert.

If it is necessary to drill and tap a hole, refer to **Table 8** for metric tap and drill sizes.

BALL BEARING REPLACEMENT

Bearings (**Figure 77**) are used throughout the engine and drive assembly to reduce power loss, heat and noise resulting from friction. Because bearings are precision-made parts, they must be properly lubricated and maintained. When a bearing is damaged, replace it immediately. However, when installing a new bearing, take care not to damage the new bearing. While bearing replacement is de-

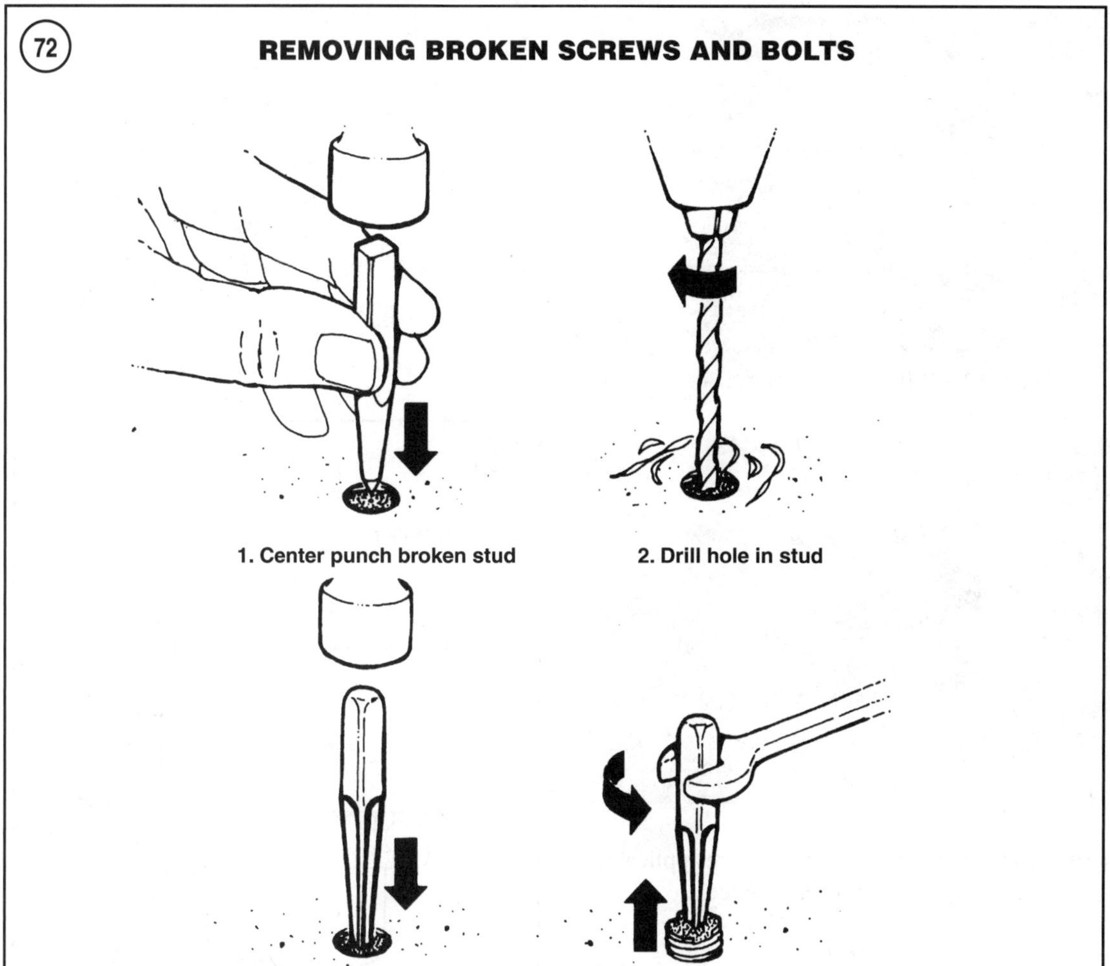
72
REMOVING BROKEN SCREWS AND BOLTS
1. Center punch broken stud
2. Drill hole in stud
3. Tap in screw extractor
4. Remove broken stud

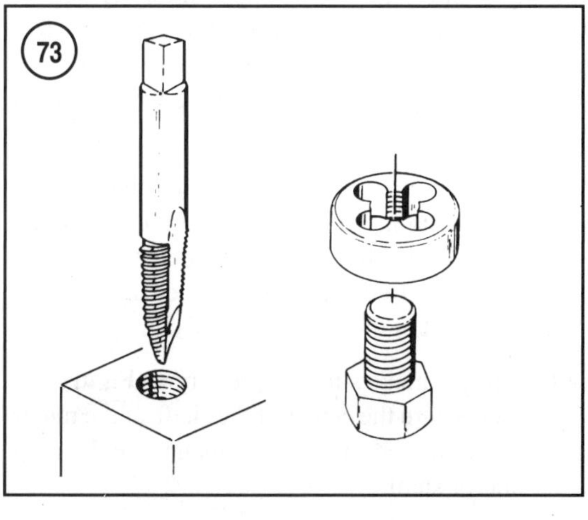
73

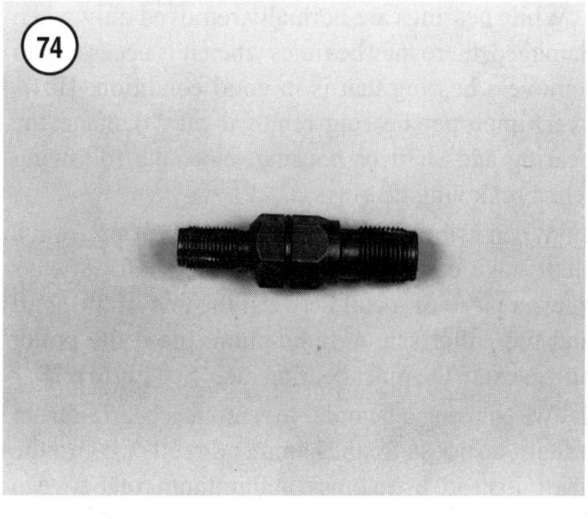
74

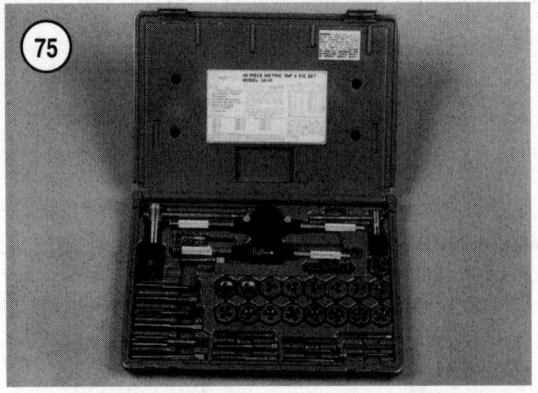

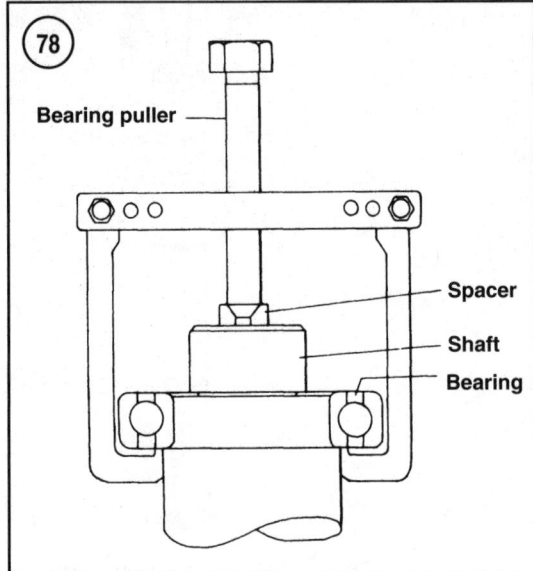

scribed in the individual chapters where applicable, the following should be used as a guideline.

NOTE
Unless otherwise specified, install bearings with the manufacturer's mark or number facing outward.

Bearing Removal

While bearings are normally removed only when damaged, there may be times when it is necessary to remove a bearing that is in good condition. However, improper bearing removal may damage the bearing and shaft or housing. Note the following when removing bearings.

1. When using a puller to remove a bearing from a shaft, take care not to damage the shaft. Always place a piece of metal between the end of the shaft and the puller screw. In addition, place the puller arms next to the inner bearing race. See **Figure 78**.

2. When using a hammer to remove a bearing from a shaft, do not strike the hammer directly against the shaft. Instead, use a brass or aluminum rod between the hammer and shaft (**Figure 79**). Make sure to support both bearing races with wooden blocks as shown.

3. A hydraulic press is the ideal tool for bearing removal. However, certain procedures must be followed or damage may occur to the bearing, shaft or bearing housing. Note the following when using a press:

   a. Always support the inner and outer bearing races with a suitable size wood or aluminum ring (**Figure 80**). If only the outer race is being supported, pressure applied against the balls and/or the inner race will damage them.

   b. Always make sure the press ram (**Figure 80**) aligns with the center of the shaft. If the ram is not centered, it may damage the bearing and/or shaft.

GENERAL INFORMATION

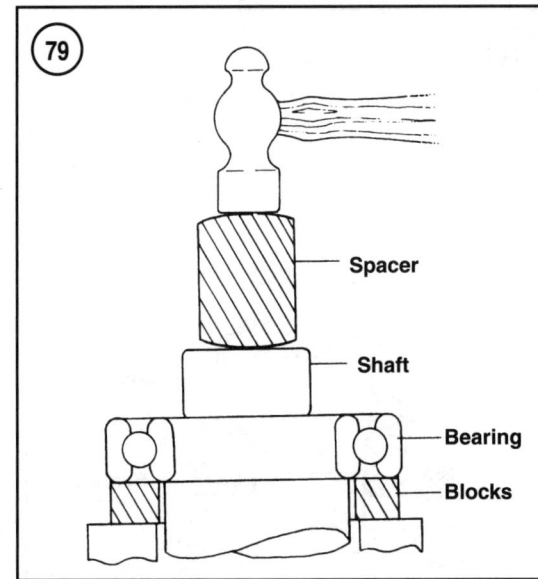

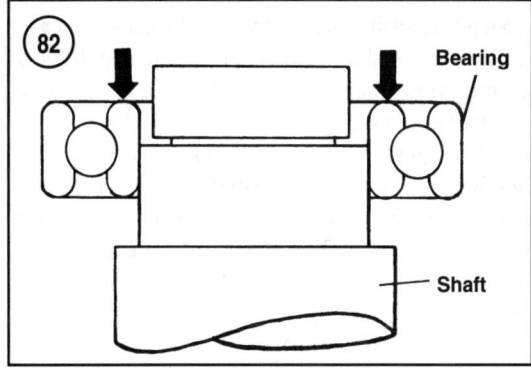

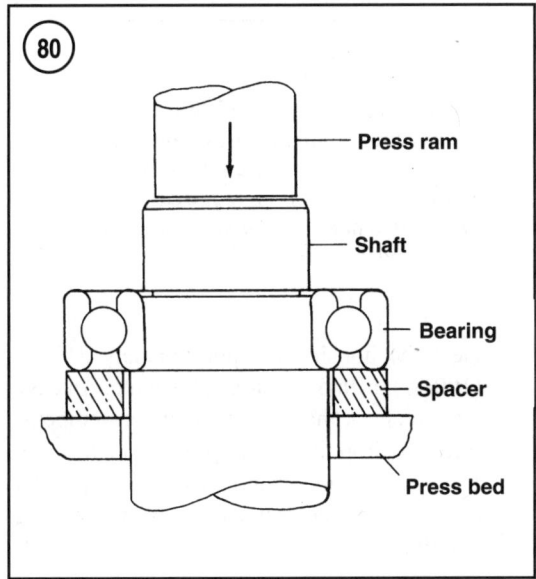

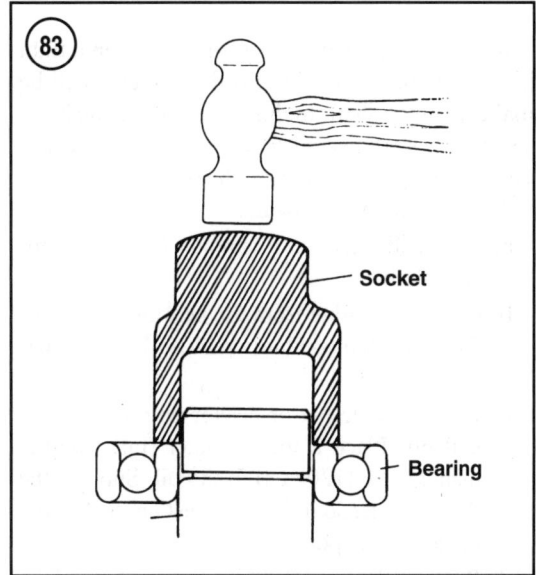

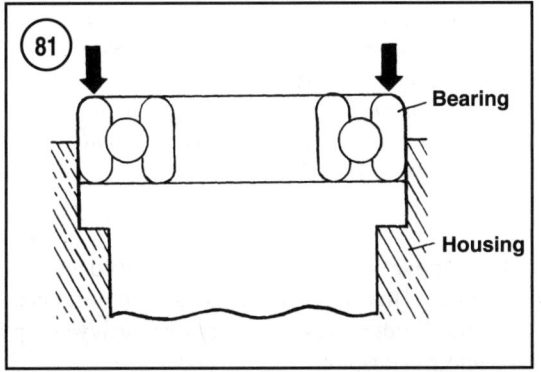

c. The moment the shaft is free of the bearing, it will drop to the floor. Secure or hold the shaft to prevent it from falling.

Bearing Installation

1. When installing a bearing in a housing, pressure must be applied to the *outer* bearing race (**Figure 81**). When installing a bearing on a shaft, pressure must be applied to the *inner* bearing race (**Figure 82**).

2. When installing a bearing as described in Step 1, use some type of driver. Never strike the bearing directly with a hammer or the bearing will be damaged. When installing a bearing, use a piece of pipe or a socket with a diameter that matches the bearing race. **Figure 83** shows the correct way to use a socket and hammer when installing a bearing.

3. Step 1 describes how to install a bearing in a case half or over a shaft. However, when installing a bearing over a shaft and into a housing at the same time, make sure there is a snug fit for both outer and inner bearing races. In this situation, install a spacer underneath the driver tool so that pressure is applied evenly across both races. See **Figure 84**. If the outer race is not supported as shown in **Figure 84**, the balls will push against the outer bearing track and damage it.

Shrink Fit

1. *Installing a bearing over a shaft*—When a tight fit is required, the bearing inside diameter will be smaller than the shaft. In this case, driving the bearing onto the shaft using normal methods may cause bearing damage. Instead, heat the bearing before installation. Note the following:
   a. Secure the shaft so it is ready for bearing installation.
   b. Clean all residue from the bearing surface of the shaft. Remove burrs with a file or sandpaper.
   c. Fill a suitable pot or beaker with clean mineral oil. Place a thermometer (rated higher than 248° F [120° C]) in the oil. Support the thermometer so it does not rest on the bottom or side of the pot.
   d. Remove the bearing from its wrapper and secure it with a piece of heavy wire bent to hold it in the pot. Hang the bearing in the pot so that it does not touch the bottom or sides of the pot.
   e. Turn the heat on and monitor the thermometer. When the oil temperature rises to approximately 248° F (120° C), remove the bearing from the pot and quickly install it. If necessary, place a socket on the inner bearing race and tap the bearing into place. As the bearing chills, it will tighten on the shaft so work quickly to install it. Make sure the bearing is installed all the way.

2. *Installing a bearing into a housing*—Bearings are generally installed into a housing with a slight interference fit. Driving the bearing into the housing using normal methods may damage the housing or cause bearing damage. Instead, heat the housing before the bearing is installed. Note the following:

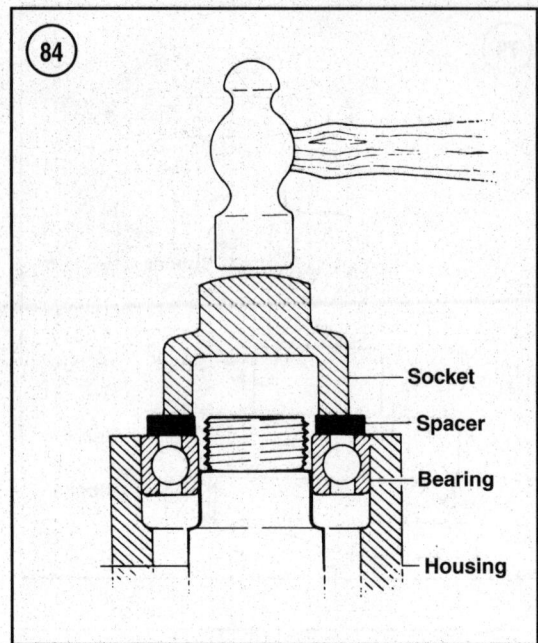

CAUTION
Before heating the crankcases in this procedure, wash the cases thoroughly with detergent and water. Rinse and rewash the cases as required to remove all traces of oil and other chemical deposits.

a. Heat the housing to approximately 212° F (100° C) in an oven or on a hot plate. An easy way to check that it is at the proper temperature is to drop tiny drops of water on the case; if they sizzle and evaporate immediately, the temperature is correct. Heat only one housing at a time.

CAUTION
Do not heat the housing with a torch (propane or acetylene)—never bring a flame into contact with the bearing or housing. Direct heat destroys the case hardening of the bearing and warps the housing.

b. Remove the housing from the oven or hot plate. Hold onto the housing with a kitchen pot holder, heavy gloves, or heavy shop cloth—it is hot.

GENERAL INFORMATION

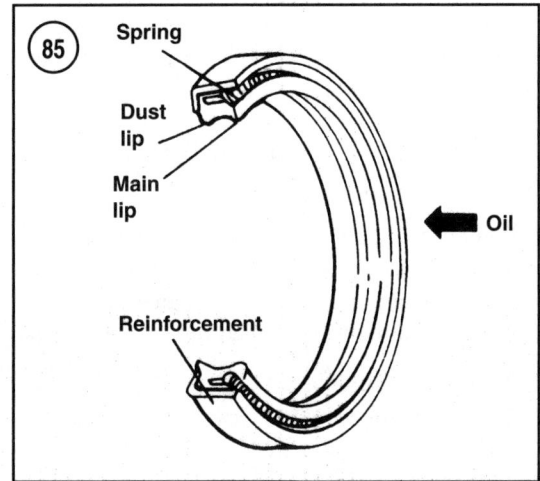

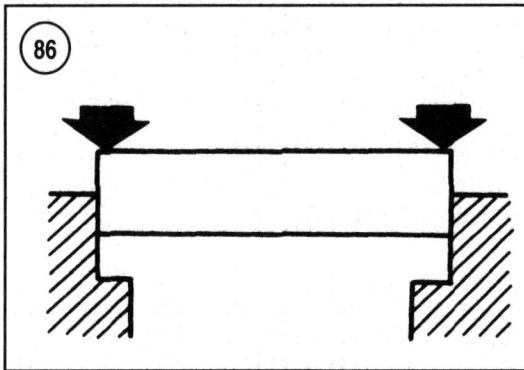

NOTE
A suitable size socket and extension works well for removing and installing bearings.

c. Hold the housing with the bearing side down and tap the bearing out. Repeat for all bearings in the housing.
d. Before heating the bearing housing, place the new bearing in a freezer, if possible. Chilling a bearing slightly reduces its outside diameter while the heated bearing housing assembly is slightly larger due to heat expansion. This makes bearing installation much easier.

NOTE
Always install bearings with the manufacturer's mark or number facing outward.

e. While the housing is still hot, install the new bearing(s) into the housing. Install the bearings by hand, if possible. If necessary, lightly tap the bearing(s) into the housing with a socket placed on the outer bearing race. Do not install new bearings by driving on the inner bearing race. Install the bearing(s) until it seats completely in the housing.

SEALS

Seals (**Figure 85**) are used to contain oil, water, grease or combustion gasses in a housing or shaft. Improper removal of a seal can damage the housing or shaft. Improper installation of the seal can damage the seal. Note the following:
1. Prying is generally the easiest and most effective method of removing a seal from a housing. However, always place a rag underneath the pry tool to prevent damage to the housing.
2. Pack waterproof grease in the seal lips before the seal is installed.
3. Always install oil seals so that the manufacturer's numbers or marks face out.
4. Install oil seals with a socket placed on the outside of the seal as shown in **Figure 86**. Make sure the seal is driven squarely into the housing. Never install a seal by hitting against the top of the seal with a hammer.

RIDING SAFETY

General Tips

1. Read the owner's manual and know the machine.
2. Check the throttle and brake controls before starting the engine.
3. Know how to make an emergency stop.
4. Never add fuel while anyone is smoking in the area or when the engine is running.
5. Never wear loose scarves, belts or boot laces that could catch on moving parts.
6. Always wear eye protection, head protection and protective clothing to protect your entire body.
7. Never allow anyone to operate the bike without proper instruction. This is for their bodily protection and to keep your machine from damage or destruction.
8. Never attempt to repair the machine with the engine running except when necessary for certain tune-up procedures.

9. Check all of the machine components and hardware frequently, especially the wheels and the steering.

STORAGE

Several months of inactivity can cause serious problems and general deterioration of the bike. This is especially important in areas with extreme temperature variations.

Selecting a Storage Area

When selecting a storage area, consider the following points.
1. The area must be dry. A heated area is not necessary, but it should be insulated to minimize extreme temperature variations.
2. Avoid buildings with large window areas. If this is not possible, mask the window to keep direct sunlight off the bike.
3. Avoid buildings in industrial areas where factories are liable to emit corrosive fumes. Also avoid buildings near bodies of salt water.
4. Select an area where there is minimum risk of fire, theft or vandalism. Check with your insurance agent to make sure that your insurance covers the motorcycle where it is stored.

Preparing Motorcycle for Storage

Careful preparation minimizes deterioration and makes it easier to restore the bike to service. Use the following procedure.
1. Wash the bike thoroughly. Make certain to remove all the dirt and mud which may have accumulated during the season. Thoroughly clean all plastic and metal components. Apply a plastic preservative such as Armor-All to all the plastic parts as well as the tires. Make sure to follow the manufacturer's instructions when applying the preservative.
2. Run the engine until it reaches operating temperature. Drain the engine oil regardless of the riding time since the last change. Fill the engine with the recommended type and quantity of fresh oil.
3. Drain all the gasoline from the fuel tank, fuel line and carburetor. Run the engine at idle speed until all the fuel in the carburetor is consumed.

4. Remove the fuel tank as described in Chapter Eight. Pour about 250 ml (1/2 pint) of engine oil into the fuel tank. Move the tank around to distribute the oil within interior surfaces of the tank, then pour out the excess oil. Reinstall the tank and close the filler cap.

5. Remove the spark plugs and add a small quantity of engine oil into each cylinder. Place a rag over the cylinder head and slowly roll the engine over a few times to distribute the oil, then reinstall the spark plugs.

6. Check the tire pressures, reduce the normal inflation pressure by 20 percent, and move the machine to the storage area.

7. Place the bike securely on a stand, or wooden blocks, so both wheels are off the ground. If not possible, place a piece of wood (plywood) under the tires to keep moisture from the tire rubber.

Returning Motorcycle to Service

1. Thoroughly check all fasteners, suspension components and brake components. Move the front suspension through several complete strokes and check the fork seals for leakage.

2. Pour out any remaining engine oil from the fuel tank, then fill the fuel tank with fresh gasoline.

3. Check all controls and cables. Replace any cables that are frayed or kinked.

4. Make sure both brakes, the clutch and the throttle operate smoothly. Adjust the controls if necessary.

5. Make sure all the wiring is correctly routed and all connections are tight and corrosion-free. Check that the ENGINE STOP SWITCH stops the engine. Check the horn operation with the horn button. Make sure none of the wires are positioned against the exhaust pipes.

6. Before starting the engine, remove the spark plugs and turn the engine over a few times to blow out the storage oil. Place a rag over the cylinder head to keep the oil off the engine. Install new spark plugs and connect the spark plug leads.

GENERAL INFORMATION

Table 1 V-STAR CUSTOM SERIAL NUMBERS

Year/model	VIN number	Primary ID number	Model code
1998			
XVS650K (USA)	JYAVM01E*WA002150-on	VM01E-002150-on	5FB1, 4
XVS650KC (Ca)	JYAVM01Y*WA000611-on	VM01Y-000611-on	5FB2, 5
XV650K (Cdn)	JYAVM01N*WA000210-on	VM01N-000210-on	5FB3
1999			
XVS650L (USA)	JYAVM01E*XA005204-on	VM01E-005204-on	5FB7
XVS650LC (Ca)	JYAVM01Y*XA000937-on	VM01Y-000937-on	5FB8
XVS650L (Cdn)	JYAVM01N*XA001110-on	VM01N-001110-on	5FB9
2000			
XVS650M (USA)	JYAVM01E*YA012938-on	VM01E-012938-on	5FBA
XVS650MC (Ca)	JYAVM01Y*YA002146-on	VM01Y-002146-on	5FBB
XVS650AM (Cdn)	JYAVM01N*YA002810-on	VM01N-002810-on	5FBC
2001-on	NA	NA	NA

USA = 49-state model   Ca = California model   Cdn = Canadian model

Table 2 V-STAR CLASSIC SERIAL NUMBERS

Year/model	VIN number	Primary ID number	Model code
1998			
XVS650AK (USA)	JYAVM01E*WA000014-on	VM01E-000014-on	5BN1
XVS650AKC (Ca)	JYAVM01Y*WA000011-on	VM01Y-000011-on	5BN2
XVS650AK (Cdn)	JYAVM01N*WA000010-on	VM01N-000010-on	5BN3
1999			
XVS650AL (USA)	JYAVM01E*XA005207-on	VM01E-005207-on	5BNE
XVS650ALC (Ca)	JYAVM01Y*XA000736-on	VM01Y-000736-on	5BNF
XVS650AL (Cdn)	JYAVM01N*XA000910-on	VM01N-000910-on	5BNG
2000			
XVS650AM (USA)	JYAVM01E*YA012938-on	VM01E-012938-on	5BNJ
XVS650AMC (Ca)	JYAVM01Y*YA002196-on	VM01Y-002196-on	5BNK
XVS650AM (Cdn)	JYAVM01N*YA002010-on	VM01N-002010-on	5BNR
2001-on	NA	NA	NA

USA = 49-state model   Ca = California model   Cdn = Canadian model

Table 3 VEHICLE DIMENSIONS AND WEIGHT

Dimension	XVS650	XVS650A
Overall length	2295 mm (90.4 in.)	2450 mm (96.5 in.)
Overall width	880 mm (34.6 in.)	930 mm (36.6 in.)
Overall height	1065 mm (41.9 in.)	1135 mm (44.7 in.)
Seat height	695 mm (27.4 in.)	710 mm (28.0 in.)
Wheelbase	1610 mm (63.4 in.)	1625 mm (64.0 in.)
Minimum ground clearance	140 mm (5.5 in.)	145 mm (5.7 in.)
Minimum turning radius	3100 mm (122 in.)	3400 mm (133.9 in.)
Curb weight (with oil and full tank)	227 kg (501 lb.)	243 kg (535.7 lb.)
Maximum load (Total weight rider, passenger, cargo and accessories)	180 kg (397 lb.)	200 kg (441 lb.)

Table 4 DECIMAL AND METRIC EQUIVALENTS

Fractions	Decimal in.	Metric mm	Fractions	Decimal in.	Metric mm
1/64	0.015625	0.39688	33/64	0.515625	13.09687
1/32	0.03125	0.79375	17/32	0.53125	13.49375
3/64	0.046875	1.19062	35/64	0.546875	13.89062
1/16	0.0625	1.58750	9/16	0.5625	14.28750
5/64	0.078125	1.98437	37/64	0.578125	14.68437
3/32	0.09375	2.38125	19/32	0.59375	15.08125
7/64	0.109375	2.77812	39/64	0.609375	15.47812
1/8	0.125	3.1750	5/8	0.625	15.87500
9/64	0.140625	3.57187	41/64	0.640625	16.27187
5/32	0.15625	3.96875	21/32	0.65625	16.66875
11/64	0.171875	4.36562	43/64	0.671875	17.06562
3/16	0.1875	4.76250	11/16	0.6875	17.46250
13/64	0.203125	5.15937	45/64	0.703125	17.85937
7/32	0.21875	5.55625	23/32	0.71875	18.25625
15/64	0.234375	5.95312	47/64	0.734375	18.65312
1/4	0.250	6.35000	3/4	0.750	19.05000
17/64	0.265625	6.74687	49/64	0.765625	19.44687
9/32	0.28125	7.14375	25/32	0.78125	19.84375
19/64	0.296875	7.54062	51/64	0.796875	20.24062
5/16	0.3125	7.93750	13/16	0.8125	20.63750
21/64	0.328125	8.33437	53/64	0.828125	21.03437
11/32	0.34375	8.73125	27/32	0.84375	21.43125
23/64	0.359375	9.12812	55/64	0.859375	22.82812
3/8	0.375	9.52500	7/8	0.875	22.22500
25/64	0.390625	9.92187	57/64	0.890625	22.62187
13/32	0.40625	10.31875	29/32	0.90625	23.01875
27/64	0.421875	10.71562	59/64	0.921875	23.41562
7/16	0.4375	11.11250	15/16	0.9375	23.81250
29/64	0.453125	11.50937	61/64	0.953125	24.20937
15/32	0.46875	11.90625	31/32	0.96875	24.60625
31/64	0.484375	12.30312	63/64	0.984375	25.00312
1/2	0.500	12.70000	1	1.00	25.40000

Table 5 GENERAL TIGHTENING TORQUES

Fastener size or type	N•m	in.-lb.	ft.-lb.
5 mm screw	4	35	–
5 mm bolt and nut	5	44	–
6 mm screw	9	80	–
6 mm bolt and nut	10	88	–
6 mm flange bolt (8 mm head, small flange)	9	80	–
6 mm flange bolt (10 mm head) and nut	12	106	–
8 mm bolt and nut	22	–	16
8 mm flange bolt and nut	27	–	20
10 mm bolt and nut	35	–	26
10 mm flange bolt and nut	40	–	29
12 mm bolt and nut	55	–	41

GENERAL INFORMATION

Table 6 CONVERSION TABLES

Multiply	By	To get equivalent of
Length		
Inches	25.4	Millimeter
Inches	2.54	Centimeter
Miles	1.609	Kilometer
Feet	0.3048	Meter
Millimeter	0.03937	Inches
Centimeter	0.3937	Inches
Kilometer	0.6214	Mile
Meter	0.0006214	Mile
Fluid volume		
U.S. quarts	0.9463	Liters
U.S. gallons	3.785	Liters
U.S. ounces	29.573529	Milliliters
Imperial gallons	4.54609	Liters
Imperial quarts	1.1365	Liters
Liters	0.2641721	U.S. gallons
Liters	1.0566882	U.S. quarts
Liters	33.814023	U.S. ounces
Liters	0.22	Imperial gallons
Liters	0.8799	Imperial quarts
Milliliters	0.033814	U.S. ounces
Milliliters	1.0	Cubic centimeters
Milliliters	0.001	Liters
Torque		
Foot-pounds	1.3558	Newton-meters
Foot-pounds	0.138255	Meter-kilograms
Inch-pounds	0.11299	Newton-meters
Newton-meters	0.7375622	Foot-pounds
Newton-meters	8.8507	Inch-pounds
Meters-kilograms	7.2330139	Foot-pounds
Volume		
Cubic inches	16.387064	Cubic centimeters
Cubic centimeters	0.0610237	Cubic inches
Temperature		
Fahrenheit	$(F - 32°) \times 0.556$	Centigrade
Centigrade	$(C \times 1.8) + 32$	Fahrenheit
Weight		
Ounces	28.3495	Grams
Pounds	0.4535924	Kilograms
Weight (continued)		
Grams	0.035274	Ounces
Kilograms	2.2046224	Pounds
Pressure		
Pounds per square inch	0.070307	Kilograms per square centimeter
Kilograms per square centimeter	14.223343	Pounds per square inch
Kilopascals	0.1450	Pounds per square inch
Pounds per square inch	6.895	Kilopascals
Speed		
Miles per hour	1.609344	Kilometers per hour
Kilometers per hour	0.6213712	Miles per hour

Table 7 TECHNICAL ABBREVIATIONS

AIS	Air induction system
ABDC	After bottom dead center
ATDC	After top dead center
BBDC	Before bottom dead center
(continued)	

Table 7 TECHNICAL ABBREVIATIONS (continued)

BDC	Bottom dead center
BTDC	Before top dead center
C	Celsius (Centigrade)
cc	Cubic centimeters
cid	Cubic inch displacement
CDI	Capacitor discharge ignition
cu. in.	Cubic inches
DOHC	Dual overhead camshaft
F	Fahrenheit
ft.	Feet
ft.-lb.	Foot-pounds
gal.	Gallons
H/A	High altitude
hp	Horsepower
in.	Inches
in.-lb.	Inch-pounds
I.D.	Inside diameter
kg	Kilograms
kgm	Kilogram meters
km	Kilometer
kPa	Kilopascals
L	Liter
m	Meter
MAG	Magneto
ml	Milliliter
mm	Millimeter
N•m	Newton-meters
O.D.	Outside diameter
oz.	Ounces
psi	Pounds per square inch
PTO	Power take off
pt.	Pint
qt.	Quart
rpm	Revolutions per minute
TPS	Throttle position sensor

Table 8 METRIC TAP EQUIVALENT DRILL SIZE

Metric tap (mm)	Drill size	Decimal equivalent	Nearest fraction
3 × 0.50	No. 39	0.0995	3/32
3 × 0.60	3/32	0.0937	3/32
4 × 0.70	No. 30	0.1285	1/8
4 × 0.75	1/8	0.125	1/8
5 × 0.80	No. 19	0.166	11/64
5 × 0.90	No. 20	0.161	5/32
6 × 1.00	No. 9	0.196	13/64
7 × 1.00	16/64	0.234	15/64
8 × 1.00	J	0.277	9/32
8 × 1.25	17/64	0.265	17/64
9 × 1.00	5/16	0.3125	5/16
9 × 1.25	5/16	0.3125	5/16
10 × 1.25	11/32	0.3437	11/32
0 × 1.50	R	0.339	11/32
11 × 1.50	3/8	0.375	3/8
12 × 1.50	13/32	0.406	13/32
12 × 1.75	13/32	0.406	13/32

CHAPTER TWO

TROUBLESHOOTING

By observing orderly procedures and basic principles, diagnosing electrical and mechanical problems is relatively simple. The first step in any troubleshooting procedure is to define the symptoms closely and then to localize the problem. Subsequent steps involve testing and analyzing those areas that could cause the symptoms until the problem is isolated to a particular component.

Proper lubrication, maintenance and periodic tune-ups as described in Chapter Three will reduce the necessity for troubleshooting. Even with the best of care, however, a motorcycle may develop problems that require troubleshooting.

The troubleshooting procedures in this chapter analyze typical symptoms and show logical methods for isolating their causes. These are not the only adequate troubleshooting methods. There may be several ways to solve a problem, but only a systematic approach can guarantee success.

Never assume anything. Do not overlook the obvious. Check the easiest, most accessible possibilities first. Is there gasoline in the tank? Has a spark plug wire fallen off?

If nothing obvious turns up after a quick check, look a little further. Learning to recognize and describe symptoms will make repairs easier. Describe problems accurately and fully, if deciding to have a repair shop perform the diagnostics.

Gather as much information as possible to aid in diagnosis. Note whether the engine lost power gradually or all at once, what color smoke (if any) came from the exhaust and other clues.

After the symptoms are defined, test and analyze the areas that could cause those symptoms. Guessing at the cause of a problem may provide the solution, but it can easily lead to frustration, wasted time and a series of expensive, unnecessary part replacements.

Expensive equipment or complicated test gear is not necessary to determine whether to attempt repairs at home. A few simple checks could save a large repair bill and lost time while the bike sits in a dealership's service department. On the other hand, be realistic and do not attempt repairs beyond your abilities. Service departments tend to charge heavily for reassembling an engine that someone else has disassembled or damaged. Some shops will not take on such work, so use common sense when deciding on a course of action.

OPERATING REQUIREMENTS

An engine needs three basic elements (**Figure 1**) to run properly: correct air/fuel mixture, compression and a spark at the correct time. If one basic requirement is missing, the engine will not run. Four-stroke engine operating principles are described in Chapter Four.

If the machine has been sitting for any length of time and refuses to start, check and clean the spark plugs and then look at the gasoline delivery system. This includes the fuel tank, fuel valve, fuel pump and fuel lines to the carburetors. Gasoline deposits may have gummed up the carburetor jets and air passages. Gasoline tends to lose its potency after standing for long periods. Condensation may contaminate the fuel with water. Drain the old fuel (fuel tank, fuel lines and carburetor) and try starting with a tank of fresh fuel.

TROUBLESHOOTING INSTRUMENTS

Refer to Chapter One for a list of the instruments needed for troubleshooting.

STARTING THE ENGINE

When experiencing engine starting troubles, it is easy to work out of sequence and forget basic engine starting procedures. The following sections are a guide of basic starting procedures. In all cases, make sure there is an adequate supply of fuel in the tank.

Starting Notes

1. A sidestand ignition cut-off system is used on all models covered in this manual. The position of the sidestand does affect engine starting. Note the following:
    a. The engine cannot start when the sidestand is down and the transmission is in gear.
    b. The engine can start when the sidestand is down and the transmission is in NEUTRAL. The engine will stop, however, if the transmission is put in gear while the sidestand is down.
    c. The engine can start when the sidestand is up and the transmission is in NEUTRAL. If the

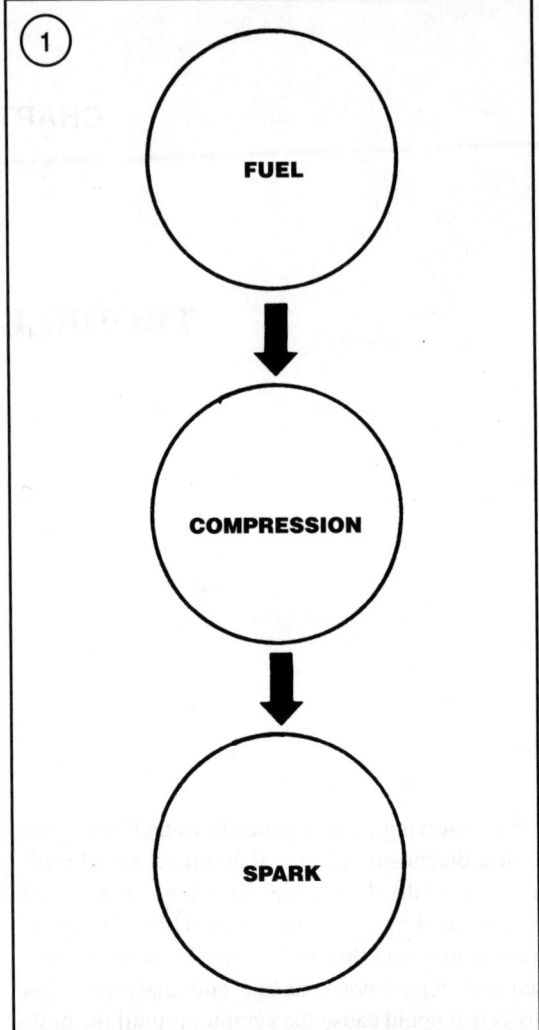

sidestand is up, the engine will also start if the transmission is in gear and the clutch lever is pulled in.

2. Before starting the engine, shift the transmission into NEUTRAL and confirm that the engine stop switch is set to RUN.

3. Make sure the fuel valve is in the ON position.

4. Turn the ignition switch to ON. The neutral indicator light should be ON (when transmission is in NEUTRAL).

5. The engine is now ready to start. Refer to the starting procedure in this section that best meets the air temperature and engine condition.

6. If the engine idles at a fast speed for more than 5 minutes or if the throttle is repeatedly snapped on

TROUBLESHOOTING

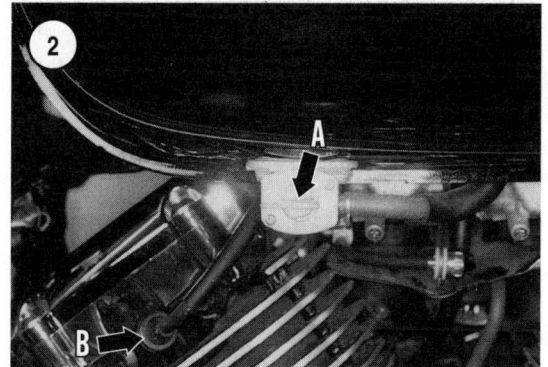

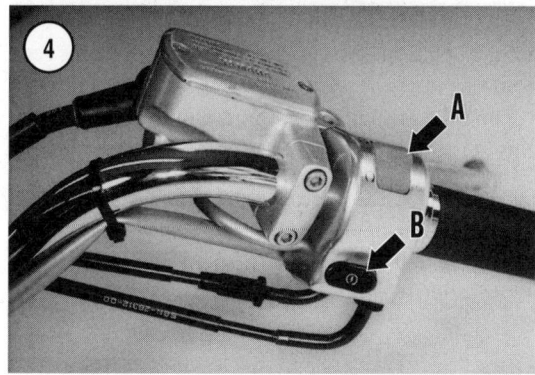

Starting a Cold Engine

1. Shift the transmission into NEUTRAL.
2. Turn the fuel valve to the ON position (A, **Figure 2**).
3. Turn the ignition switch to ON.
4. Pull the choke knob (**Figure 3**) to the fully ON position.
5. Make sure the engine stop switch (A, **Figure 4**) is in the RUN position.

NOTE
Starting a cold engine with the throttle open and the choke ON results in a lean mixture and causes hard starting.

6. Depress the starter button (B, **Figure 4**) and start the engine. Do not open the throttle when pressing the starter button.
7. Once the engine is running, open the throttle slightly to help warm the engine. Continue warming the engine until the choke can be turned to the fully OFF position and the engine responds to the throttle cleanly.

Starting a Warm or Hot Engine

1. Shift the transmission into NEUTRAL.
2. Turn the fuel valve to the ON position (A, **Figure 2**).
3. Turn the ignition switch to ON.
4. Make sure the engine stop switch (A, **Figure 4**) is in the RUN position.
5. Make sure the choke knob (**Figure 3**) is in the fully OFF position.
6. Open the throttle slightly and depress the starter button (B, **Figure 4**).

and off at normal air temperatures, the exhaust pipes may discolor.

7. Excessive choke use can cause an excessively rich fuel mixture. This condition can wash oil off the piston and cylinder walls causing piston and cylinder scuffing.

NOTE
Do not operate the starter motor for more than 5 seconds at a time. Wait approximately 10 seconds between starting attempts.

Starting a Flooded Engine

If the engine does not start and there is a strong gasoline smell, the engine is probably flooded. To start a flooded engine, open the throttle all the way and operate the starter. Do not open the choke. Holding the throttle completely open allows more air to reach the engine.

NOTE
If the engine refuses to start, check the carburetor overflow hose attached to the bottom of the float bowl. If fuel

runs out the end of the hose, the fuel inlet valve is stuck open, allowing the carburetor to overfill. Remove the carburetor and correct the problem. Refer to Chapter Eight.

STARTING DIFFICULTIES

If the engine cranks but is difficult to start or does not start at all, check for obvious problems before proceeding. Go down the following list step by step. Perform each check. If the bike still does not start, refer to the appropriate troubleshooting procedure in this chapter.

WARNING
Do not use an open flame to check in the fuel tank. A serious explosion is certain to result.

1. Make sure there is fuel in the tank. Open the filler cap and rock the bike.
2. Make sure the fuel valve (A, **Figure 2**) in the ON position. Turn the valve to the ON position or the RES position.
3. Make sure the choke knob (**Figure 3**) is in the correct position. The choke should be OFF for a warm engine and ON for a cold engine.
4. Set the engine stop switch in the run position. The engine should start and operate when the switch (A, **Figure 4**) is in the RUN position. Also make sure the switch is not shorted. If necessary, test the engine stop switch as described in Chapter Nine.
5. Make sure spark plug caps on tight. Push the spark plug cap (B, **Figure 2**) on each plug. Slightly rotate each cap to clean the electrical connection between the plug and the connector.
6. Perform the ignition spark test described in Chapter Nine. If there is a strong spark, perform Step 7. If there is no spark or if the spark is very weak, test the ignition system as described in Chapter Nine.
7. Check the cylinder compression by performing the following:
   a. Turn the fuel valve to the OFF position.

CAUTION
The ignition system can be permanently damaged if the spark plugs are not grounded when performing this test.

   b. Remove each spark plug. Reconnect the spark plug cap and ground the spark plug against the engine.
   c. Put a finger over one of the spark plug holes.
   d. Press the START button. When the piston rises on the compression stroke, increasing pressure in the cylinder should force your finger off the spark plug hole. If it does, the cylinder probably has sufficient compression to start the engine.
   e. Repeat for the other cylinder.

NOTE
There may still be a compression problem even though the engine passed this test. Check cylinder compression with a compression gauge as described in Chapter Three.

ENGINE STARTING TROUBLESHOOTING

An engine that refuses to start or is difficult to start can be very frustrating. More often than not, the problem is very minor and can be found with a simple and logical troubleshooting approach.

First, review the engine starting procedures in this chapter. If the engine does not start by following the engine starting steps, continue with this section.

The following are beginning points to isolate engine starting problems.

NOTE
Do not operate the starter motor for more than 5 seconds at a time. Wait approximately 10 seconds between starting attempts.

Engine Fails to Start

1. Test the integrity of the ignition system by performing the ignition spark test described in Chapter Nine.
2. If the test produces a good spark, proceed with Step 3. If the spark is weak or if there is no spark, perform Step 5.
3. Check engine compression as described in Chapter Three. If the compression is good, perform Steps 5-9. If the compression is low, check for one or more of the following:
   a. Leaking cylinder head gasket(s).

TROUBLESHOOTING

b. Cracked or warped cylinder head(s).
c. Worn piston rings, pistons and cylinders.
d. Valve stuck open.
e. Worn or damaged valve seat(s).
f. Incorrect valve timing.
4. Turn the fuel valve (A, **Figure 2**) to the OFF position. Disconnect the fuel line from the fuel valve and connect a spare line to the fuel valve.
5. Insert the open end of the spare fuel line into a clear container.
6. Turn the fuel valve to ON. A steady flow of fuel should be observed with the valve in the ON or RES positions. The fuel flow should stop when the valve is turned to the OFF position.
7. If the fuel flow is good, check for one or more of the following:
   a. Clogged fuel line.
   b. Stuck or clogged carburetor float valve.
8. If there is no fuel flow or if the flow is slow and intermittent, check for one or more of the following conditions:
   a. Empty fuel tank.
   b. Plugged fuel tank cap vent.
   c. Clogged fuel filter.
   d. Clogged fuel valve.
9. If the spark was weak or if there was no spark at one or both plugs, note the following:
   a. If there is no spark at both plugs, there may be a problem in the input side of the ignition system. Test the igniter unit, pickup coil, sidestand switch or neutral switch as described in Chapter Nine.
   b. If there is no spark at one of the spark plugs, the spark plug is probably defective or there is a problem with that spark plug wire or plug cap. Replace the spark plug and retest. If there is still no spark at that one plug, test the spark plug wire and plug cap as described in Chapter Nine. If those test good, test the ignition coil and the igniter unit as described in Chapter Nine.

Engine is Difficult to Start

Check for one or more of the following possible malfunctions:
1. Fouled spark plug(s).
2. Improperly adjusted choke.
3. Intake manifold air leak.
4. Contaminated fuel system.
5. Improperly adjusted carburetor(s).
6. Ignition system malfunction.
7. Weak ignition coil(s).
8. Poor compression.
9. Engine oil too heavy.

Engine Will Not Crank

Check for one or more of the following possible malfunctions:
1. Blown fuse.
2. Discharged battery.
3. Defective starter motor, starter relay or start switch.
4. Seized piston(s).
5. Seized crankshaft bearings.
6. Broken connecting rod(s).
7. Locked-up transmission or clutch assembly.
8. Defective starter clutch.

ENGINE PERFORMANCE

In the following checklist, it is assumed that the engine runs, but is not operating at peak performance. This serves as a starting point to isolate a performance malfunction. Where ignition timing is mentioned as a problem, remember that there is no method for adjusting the ignition timing. Ignition timing is a troubleshooting tool. If the timing is incorrect, there is a defective part within the ignition system. Check individual parts, and replace them as necessary.

Engine Will Not Start or Is Hard to Start

1. Fuel tank empty.
2. Obstructed fuel line, fuel valve or fuel filter.
3. Sticking float valve in carburetor(s).
4. Carburetor(s) incorrectly adjusted.
5. Improper starter valve (choke) operation.
6. Improper throttle operation.
7. Fouled or improperly gapped spark plug(s).
8. Ignition timing incorrect.
9. Broken or shorted ignition coil(s).
10. Weak or defective igniter unit or pickup coil.
11. Improper valve timing.
12. Clogged air filter element.
13. Contaminated fuel.
14. Engine flooded with fuel.

Engine Starts but Then Stops

1. Incorrect choke adjustment.
2. Incorrect carburetor adjustment.
3. Incorrect ignition timing.
4. Contaminated fuel.
5. Intake manifold air leak.

Engine Will Not Idle

1. Carburetor(s) incorrectly adjusted (too lean or too rich).
2. Fouled or improperly gapped spark plug(s).
3. Leaking head gasket(s) or vacuum leak.
4. Ignition timing incorrect.
5. Improper valve timing.
6. Obstructed fuel line or fuel valve.
7. Low engine compression.
8. Starter valve (choke) stuck in the open position.
9. Incorrect pilot screw adjustment.
10. Clogged pilot jet in the carburetor(s).
11. Clogged air filter element.
12. Valve(s) and valve seat(s) require service.

Poor High Speed Performance

1. Check the ignition timing as described in Chapter Three. If the ignition timing is correct, perform Step 2. If the timing is incorrect, test the following ignition system components as described in Chapter Nine:
    a. Pickup coil.
    b. Ignition coils.
    c. Igniter unit.
2. Turn the fuel valve (A, **Figure 2**) to the OFF position. Disconnect the fuel line from the fuel valve and connect a spare line to the fuel valve.
3. Insert the open end of the spare fuel line into a clear container. Turn the fuel valve to ON. A steady flow of fuel should be observed with the fuel valve in the ON or RES positions. The fuel flow should stop when the valve is turned to the OFF.
4. If the fuel flow is good, check for one or more of the following:
    a. Clogged fuel line.
    b. Stuck or clogged carburetor float valve.
5. If there is no fuel flow or if the flow is slow and intermittent, check for one or more of the following conditions:
    a. Empty fuel tank.
    b. Plugged fuel tank cap vent.
    c. Clogged fuel filter.
    d. Clogged fuel valve.
6. Check for a damaged fuel pump.
7. Remove the carburetor assembly as described in Chapter Eight. Then remove the float bowl(s) and check for contamination and plugged jets. If any contamination is found, disassemble and clean the carburetor(s). Also pour out and discard the remaining fuel in the fuel tank and flush the fuel tank thoroughly. If no contamination was found and the jets were not plugged, perform Step 8.
8. Incorrect valve timing and worn or damaged valve springs can cause poor high speed performance. If the valve timing was set just before the onset of this type of problem, the valve timing may be incorrect. If the valve timing was not set or changed, and all the other inspection procedures in this section were performed without locating the problem area, remove the cylinder head and inspect the valve train assembly.

Low or Poor Engine Power

1. Support the bike with the rear wheel off the ground, and then spin the rear wheel by hand. If the wheel spins freely, perform Step 2. If the wheel does not spin freely, check for the following conditions:
    a. Dragging rear brake.
    b. Excessive rear axle tightening torque.
    c. Worn or damaged rear wheel bearings.
    d. Final drive gear bearing damage.
    e. Damaged drive shaft assembly.
2. Check the clutch adjustment and operation. If the clutch slips, refer to *Clutch* in this chapter.
3. If Steps 1 and 2 did not locate the problem, test ride the bike and accelerate lightly. If the engine speed increased according to throttle position, perform Step 4. If the engine speed did not increase, check for one or more of the following problems:
    a. Clogged or damaged air filter.
    b. Restricted fuel flow.
    c. Clogged fuel tank vent.
    d. Incorrect choke adjustment or operation.
    e. Clogged or damaged muffler.
4. Check for one or more of the following problems:
    a. Low engine compression.
    b. Fouled spark plug(s).
    c. Clogged carburetor jet(s).

TROUBLESHOOTING

    d. Incorrect ignition timing.
    e. Incorrect oil level (too high or too low).
    f. Contaminated oil.
    g. Worn or damaged valve train assembly.
    h. Engine overheating.

Engine Overheating

1. Incorrect carburetor adjustment or jet selection.
2. Ignition timing retarded due to defective ignition component(s).
3. Improper spark plug heat range.
4. Clogged cooling fins.
5. Oil level low.
6. Oil not circulating properly.
7. Valves leaking.
8. Heavy engine carbon deposits.
9. Dragging brake(s).
10. Clutch slipping.

Engine Runs Roughly

1. Clogged air filter element.
2. Carburetor adjustment incorrect; mixture too rich.
3. Choke not operating correctly.
4. Water or other contaminants in fuel.
5. Clogged fuel line.
6. Spark plugs fouled.
7. Ignition coil defective.
8. Igniter unit or pickup coil defective.
9. Loose or defective ignition circuit wire.
10. Short circuit from damaged wire insulation.
11. Loose battery cable connection(s).
12. Valve timing incorrect.

Engine Lacks Acceleration

1. Carburetor mixture too lean.
2. Clogged fuel line.
3. Improper ignition timing.
4. Dragging brake(s).
5. Slipping clutch.

Engine Backfires

1. Improper ignition timing.
2. Carburetor(s) improperly adjusted.
3. Lean fuel mixture.

Engine Misfires During Acceleration

1. Improper ignition timing.
2. Lean fuel mixture.
3. Excessively worn or defective spark plug(s).
4. Ignition system malfunction.
5. Incorrect carburetor adjustment.

ENGINE NOISES

Often the first evidence of an internal engine problem is a strange noise. That knocking, clicking or tapping sound that has never been heard before may be a warning of impending trouble. While engine noises can indicate problems, they are difficult to interpret correctly. They can seriously mislead inexperienced mechanics.

Professional mechanics often use a special stethoscope (which looks like a doctor's stethoscope) for isolating engine noises. A sounding stick, which can be an ordinary piece of doweling or a section of small hose can do nearly as well. By placing one end in contact with the area in question and the other end to the front of your ear (not directly on your ear), sounds emanating from that area can be heard. The first time this is done, there may be confusion about the strange sounds coming from even a normal engine. If possible, have an experienced friend or mechanic help you sort out the noises.

Consider the following when troubleshooting engine noises:

1. *Knocking or pinging during acceleration*—Caused by using a lower octane fuel than recommended. May also be caused by poor fuel, a spark plug of the wrong heat range or carbon buildup in the combustion chamber. Check the spark plugs and engine compression as described Chapter Three.

2. *Slapping or rattling noises at low speed or during acceleration*—May be caused by excessive piston-to-cylinder wall clearance.

NOTE
Piston slap is easier to detect when the engine is cold and before the pistons have expanded. Once the engine has warmed up, piston expansion reduces piston-to-cylinder clearance.

3. *Knocking or rapping while decelerating*—Usually caused by excessive rod bearing clearance.

4. *Persistent knocking and vibration on every crankshaft rotation*—Usually caused by worn rod or main bearing(s). Can also be caused by broken piston rings or damaged piston pins.
5. *Rapid on-off squeal*—Compression leak around cylinder head gasket(s) or spark plug(s).
6. *Valve train noise*—Check for the following:
   a. Valve sticking in guide.
   b. Broken valve spring.
   c. Low oil pressure.
   d. Clogged oil passage.
   e. Excessively worn or damaged cam chain.
7. *Cylinder head noise (other than valve train noise)*—Check the following:
   a. Excessively worn or damaged cam chain tensioner.
   b. Excessively worn or damaged cam chain.
   c. Excessively worn or damaged cam sprocket.
   d. Damaged rocker arm follower or valve stem end.
   e. Damaged rocker arm or rocker shaft.
   f. Excessively worn or damaged camshaft.

ENGINE LUBRICATION

An improperly operating engine lubrication system quickly leads to engine seizure. Check and top off the engine oil level as described in Chapter Three. Oil pump service is described in Chapter Five.

Oil Consumption High or Engine Smokes Excessively

1. Worn valve guides.
2. Worn or damaged piston rings.

Excessive Engine Oil Leaks

1. Clogged air filter breather hose.
2. Loose engine parts.
3. Damaged gasket sealing surfaces.

Black Smoke

1. Clogged air filter.
2. Incorrect carburetor fuel level (too high).
3. Choke stuck closed.
4. Incorrect main jet (too large).

White Smoke

1. Worn valve guide.
2. Worn valve seal.
3. Worn piston ring oil ring.
4. Excessive cylinder and/or piston wear.

Oil Pressure Too High

1. Clogged oil filter.
2. Clogged oil gallery or metering orifices.
3. Pressure relief valve stuck closed.
4. Incorrect type of engine oil.

Low Oil Pressure

1. Low oil level.
2. Damaged oil pump.
3. Clogged oil screen.
4. Clogged oil filter.
5. Internal oil leakage.
6. Pressure relief valve stuck open.
7. Incorrect type of engine oil.

No Oil Pressure

1. Damaged oil pump.
2. Excessively low oil level.
3. Internal oil leakage.
4. Damaged oil pump drive gear.
5. Damaged oil pump drive shaft.

Oil Level Too Low

1. Oil level not maintained at correct level.
2. Worn piston rings.
3. Worn cylinder(s).
4. Worn valve guides.
5. Worn valve seals.
6. Piston rings incorrectly installed during engine overhaul.
7. External oil leakage.

CYLINDER LEAKDOWN TEST

A cylinder leakdown test can isolate engine problems caused by leaking valves, a blown head gasket, or broken, worn or stuck piston rings. A cylinder leakdown test is performed by applying compressed

TROUBLESHOOTING

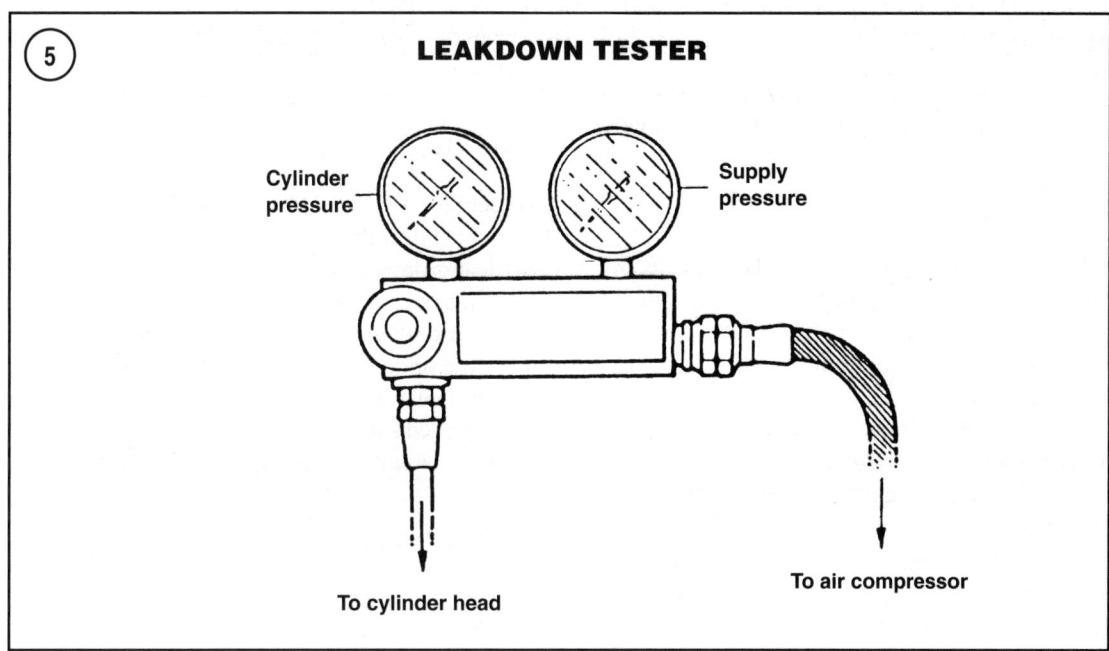

LEAKDOWN TESTER

air to a cylinder, and then measuring the percentage of leakage. A cylinder leakdown tester (**Figure 5**) and an air compressor is needed to perform this test.

Follow the manufacturer's instructions along with the following when performing a cylinder leakdown test.

1. Run the engine until it reaches normal operating temperature. Then turn off the engine.

2. Remove the air filter assembly. Secure the throttle in its wide open position.

3. Set the piston for the cylinder being tested to TDC on the compression stroke as described in Chapter Three.

4. Remove the spark plug.

5. Install the leakdown tester into the cylinder spark plug hole. Connect a compressed-air hose to the tester fitting.

NOTE
The engine may turn over when air pressure is applied to the cylinder. To prevent this from happening, shift the transmission into fifth gear.

6. Shift the transmission into fifth gear and have an assistant apply the brake.

7. Perform a cylinder leakdown test following the manufacturer's instructions. Listen for air leaking while noting the following:

a. Air leaking through the exhaust pipe indicates a leaking exhaust valve.

b. Air leaking through the carburetor points to a leaking intake valve.

c. Air leaking through the crankcase breather tube indicates worn piston rings.

8. Repeat Steps 3-7 for the other cylinder.

9. For a used engine, any cylinder with 10 percent or more cylinder leakage requires further service. For a new or rebuilt engine, a leakage rate of 2 to 4 percent is desirable.

CLUTCH

The basic clutch troubles and causes are listed in this section.

Excessive Clutch Lever Operation

If the clutch lever is too hard to pull in, check the following:

1. Clutch cable not properly adjusted.
2. Clutch cable requires lubrication.
3. Clutch cable improperly routed or bent.
4. Damaged clutch lifter bearing.

Rough Clutch Operation

This condition can be caused by excessively worn, grooved or damaged clutch housing slots.

Clutch Slipping

If the engine speed increases without accelerating the bike, the clutch is probably slipping. Some of the main causes of clutch slipping are:
1. Incorrect clutch cable adjustment.
2. Weak clutch springs.
3. Worn clutch or friction plates.
4. Damaged pressure plate.
5. Clutch release mechanism wear or damage.
6. Incorrectly assembled clutch.
7. Loose clutch nut.
8. Improper oil level.
9. Improper oil viscosity.
10. Engine oil additive being used (clutch plates contaminated).

Clutch Drag

If the clutch does not disengage or if the bike creeps with the transmission in gear and the clutch disengaged, the clutch is dragging. Some of the main causes of clutch drag are:
1. Incorrect clutch adjustment.
2. Uneven clutch spring compression.
3. Warped clutch plate or friction discs.
4. Bent push rod.
5. Excessive clutch lever free play.
6. Damaged clutch release mechanism.
7. Clutch housing/hub splines damaged.
8. Friction discs incorrectly installed.
9. Engine oil level too high.
10. Incorrect oil viscosity.
11. Engine oil additive being used.

GEARSHIFT LINKAGE

The gearshift linkage assembly connects the gearshift pedal to the shift drum (internal shift mechanism). The external shift mechanism can be examined after the clutch has been removed. The internal shift mechanism can only be examined once the engine has been removed and the crankcase separated.

Common gearshift linkage troubles and their checks are listed below.

Transmission Jumps out of Gear

1. Bent or worn shift fork.
2. Bent shift fork shaft.
3. Gear groove worn.
4. Damaged stopper bolt.
5. Weak or damaged stopper arm spring.
6. Loose or damaged shift cam.
7. Worn gear dogs or slots.
8. Damaged shift drum grooves.
9. Weak or damaged gearshift linkage springs.

Difficult Shifting

1. Incorrect clutch cable adjustment.
2. Incorrect oil viscosity.
3. Bent shift fork shaft(s).
4. Bent or damaged shift fork(s).
5. Worn gear dogs or slots.
6. Damaged shift drum grooves.
7. Weak or damaged gearshift linkage springs.

TRANSMISSION

Transmission symptoms are sometimes hard to distinguish from clutch symptoms. Common transmission troubles are listed below. Refer to Chapter Seven for transmission service procedures. Before working on the transmission, make sure the clutch and gearshift linkage assemblies are not causing the trouble.

Difficult Shifting

1. Incorrect clutch adjustment.
2. Incorrect clutch operation.
3. Bent shift fork shaft.
4. Damaged shift-fork guide pin(s).
5. Bent or damaged shift fork.
6. Worn gear dogs or slots.
7. Damaged shift drum grooves.

Jumps Out of Gear

1. Loose or damaged shift drum stopper arm.
2. Bent or damaged shift fork(s).

TROUBLESHOOTING

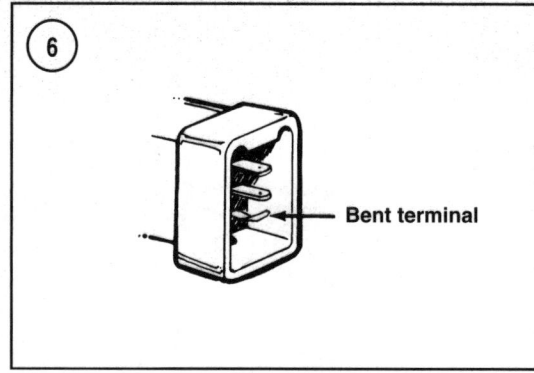

Bent terminal

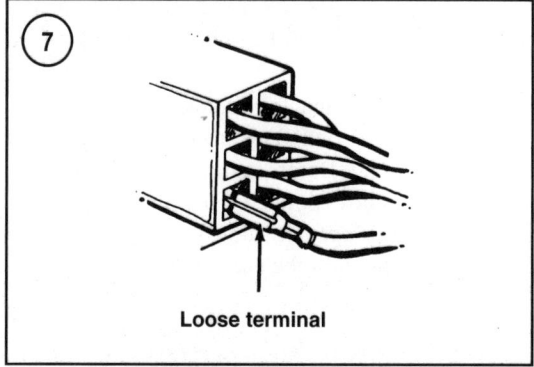

Loose terminal

3. Bent shift fork shaft(s).
4. Damaged shift drum grooves.
5. Worn gear dogs or slots.
6. Broken shift linkage return spring.
7. Improperly adjusted shift lever position.

Incorrect Shift Lever Operation

1. Bent shift lever.
2. Stripped shift lever splines.
3. Damaged shift lever linkage.
4. Improperly adjusted shift pedal rod.

Excessive Gear Noise

1. Worn bearings.
2. Worn or damaged gears.
3. Excessive gear backlash.

ELECTRICAL TROUBLESHOOTING

This section describes basic electrical troubleshooting and how to use test equipment in various test procedures.

Electrical troubleshooting can be very time-consuming and frustrating without proper knowledge and a suitable plan. Refer to the wiring diagram at the end of the book and the individual system diagrams included in Chapter Nine. Wiring diagrams help determine how the circuit works by tracing the current paths from the power source through the circuit components to ground. Also check any circuits that share the same fuse, ground or switch, etc. If the other circuits work properly, the shared wiring is good and the cause must be in the wiring used only by the suspect circuit. If all related circuits are faulty at the same time the probable cause is a poor ground connection or a blown fuse(s).

As with all troubleshooting procedures, analyze typical symptoms in a systematic manner. Never assume anything, and do not overlook the obvious, like a blown fuse or a separated electrical connector. Test the simplest and most obvious items first, and try to make tests at easily accessible points on the bike.

Preliminary Checks and Precautions

Before starting any electrical troubleshooting procedure, perform the following:
1. Check the main fuse. Replace it if necessary.
2. Check the individual fuse(s) for each circuit. Replace any blown fuse.
3. Inspect the battery. Make sure it is fully charged and the battery leads are clean and securely attached to the battery terminals as described in Chapter Three.
4. Disconnect each electrical connector in the suspect circuit, and check that there are no bent terminals on either side of the electrical connector (**Figure 6**). A bent terminal will not connect to its mate in the other connector, causing an open circuit.
5. Check each end of the connector. Make sure that the metal terminals on the end of each wire (**Figure 7**) are pushed all the way into the plastic connector. If not, carefully push them in with a narrow blade screwdriver.
6. Check all electrical wires where they join the individual terminals in both the male and female sides of the plastic connectors.
7. Make sure all electrical terminals within the plastic connector are clean and free of corrosion.

Clean, if necessary, and pack the connectors with dielectric grease.

8. Push the connectors together and make sure they are fully engaged and locked together (**Figure 8**).

9. Never pull the electrical wires when disconnecting an electrical connector. Only pull the connector's plastic housing.

10. Never use a self-powered test light on circuits that contain solid-state devices. The solid-state devices may be damaged.

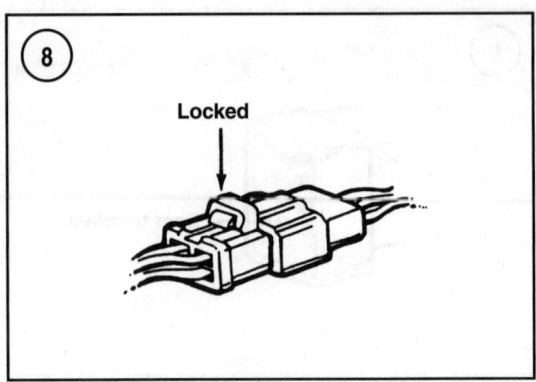

TEST EQUIPMENT

Test Light or Voltmeter

A test light can be purchased or constructed from a 12-volt light bulb and a pair of test leads soldered to the bulb. To check for battery voltage (12 volts) in a circuit, attach one lead to ground and the other lead to various points along the circuit. The test light will come on when battery voltage is present.

A voltmeter can also be used to test for battery voltage in any given circuit. The voltmeter, unlike the test light, also indicates how much voltage is present at each test point. When using a voltmeter, attach the red lead (+) to the component or wire to be checked and the negative (–) lead to a good ground.

Self-powered Test Light and Ohmmeter

A self-powered test light can be constructed from a 12-volt light bulb, a pair of test leads and a 12-volt battery. When the test leads are touched together the light bulb goes on.

Use a self-powered test light as follows:
1. Touch the test leads together to make sure the light bulb goes on. If not, correct the problem before using it in a test procedure.
2. Disconnect the bike's battery or remove the fuse(s) that protects the circuit to be tested.
3. Select two points within the circuit where there should be continuity.
4. Attach one lead of the self-powered test light to each point.
5. If there is continuity, the self-powered test light will come on.
6. If there is no continuity, the self-powered test light will not come on indicating an open circuit.

An ohmmeter can be used in place of the self-powered test light. The ohmmeter, unlike the test light, also indicates how much resistance is present between each test point. Low resistance (zero or near-zero ohms) means good continuity in a complete circuit. Before using an analog ohmmeter, it must first be calibrated. This is done by touching the leads together and turning the ohms calibration knob until the meter reads zero.

CAUTION
An ohmmeter must never be connected to any circuit that has power applied to it. Always disconnect the battery negative lead before using the ohmmeter.

Jumper Wire

When using a jumper wire always install an inline fuse/fuse holder (available at most auto supply stores or electronic supply stores) to the jumper wire. Never use a jumper wire across any load (a component that is connected and turned on). This results in a direct short and will blow the fuse(s) and/or damage components and wiring in that circuit.

BASIC TEST PROCEDURES

Voltage Testing

Unless otherwise specified, all voltage tests are made with the electrical connector still connected. Insert the test leads into the backside of the connector and make sure the test lead touches the electrical wire or metal terminal within the plastic connector.

TROUBLESHOOTING

If the test lead only touches the wire insulation, there will be a false reading.

Always check both sides of the connector as one side may be loose or corroded thus preventing electrical flow through the connector. This type of test can be performed with a test light or a voltmeter. A voltmeter will give the best results.

NOTE
When using a test light, either test lead can be attached to ground.

1. Attach the negative test lead (if using a voltmeter) to a good ground (bare metal). Make sure the part used for ground is not insulated with a rubber gasket or a rubber grommet.
2. Attach the positive test lead (if using a voltmeter) to the point being checked.
3. Turn the ignition switch on. If using a test light, the test light will come on if voltage is present. If using a voltmeter, note the voltage reading. The reading should be within 1 volt of battery voltage. If the voltage is less then there is a problem in the circuit.

Voltage Drop Test

A voltage drop of 1 or more volts means there is a problem in the circuit. All components within the circuit are designed for low resistance to conduct electricity with a minimum loss of voltage.
1. Connect the voltmeter positive test lead to the end of the wire or switch closest to the battery.
2. Connect the voltmeter negative test lead to the other end of the wire or switch.
3. Turn the components on in the circuit.
4. The voltmeter should indicate zero volts. If it reads 1 volt or more, voltage drop is excessive. A problem exists within the circuit.
5. Check the circuit for loose or dirty connections within an electrical connector(s).

Continuity Test

A continuity test determines the integrity of a circuit. A circuit has continuity if the circuit is complete with no opens in either the electrical wires or components within that circuit.

Unless otherwise specified, all continuity tests are made with the electrical connector still connected. Insert the test leads into the backside of the connector. Make sure the test lead touches the electrical wire or metal terminals within the connector. If the test lead only touches the wire insulation, there will be a false reading.

Always check both sides of the connectors as one side may be loose or corroded thus preventing electrical flow through the connector. This type of test can be performed with a self-powered test light or an ohmmeter. An ohmmeter gives the best results.

If using an analog ohmmeter, calibrate the meter by touching the leads together and turning the ohms calibration knob until the meter reads zero. This is necessary in order to get accurate results.
1. Disconnect the battery negative lead as described in Chapter Three.
2. Attach one test lead (test light or ohmmeter) to one end of the part or circuit to be tested.
3. Attach the other test lead to the other end of the part or circuit to be tested.
4. The self-powered test light comes on if there is continuity. The ohmmeter will indicate low or no resistance or it will indicate infinite resistance. No resistance indicates the circuit has continuity; the circuit is complete. Infinity indicates no continuity. There is an open in the circuit.

Testing for a Short with a Self-powered Test Light or Ohmmeter

This test can be performed with either a self-powered test light or an ohmmeter.
1. Disconnect the battery negative lead as described in Chapter Three.
2. Remove the blown fuse from the fuse panel.
3. Connect one test lead of the test light or ohmmeter to the load side (battery side) of the fuse terminal in the fuse panel.
4. Connect the other test lead to a good ground (bare metal). Make sure the part used for a ground is not insulated with a rubber gasket or a rubber grommet.
5. With the self-powered test light or ohmmeter attached to the fuse terminal and to ground, wiggle the wiring harness relating to the suspect circuit at 6 in. (15.2 cm) intervals. Start next to the fuse panel and work away from the fuse panel while watching the self-powered test light or ohmmeter.
6. If the test light blinks or the needle on the ohmmeter moves, there is a short-to-ground at that point in the harness.

Testing For a Short with a Test Light or Voltmeter

This test can be performed with either a test light or voltmeter.
1. Remove the blown fuse from the fuse panel.
2. Connect the test light or voltmeter across the fuse terminals in the fuse panel. Turn the ignition switch on and check for battery voltage (12 volts).
3. With the test light or voltmeter attached to the fuse terminals, wiggle the wiring harness relating to the suspect circuit at 6 in. (15.2 cm) intervals. Start next to the fuse panel and work away from the fuse panel while watching the test light or voltmeter.
4. If the test light blinks or the voltmeter indicates battery voltage, there is a short-to-ground at that point in the harness.

ELECTRICAL PROBLEMS

If light bulbs burn out frequently, the cause may be excessive vibration, a loose connection that permits sudden current surges, or the wrong type of bulb is installed in the component.

Most light and ignition problems are caused by loose or corroded ground connections. Check these before replacing a light bulb or electrical component.

Chapter Nine includes a troubleshooting checklist for each of the following systems:
1. Charging system.
2. Ignition system.
3. Starting system.
4. Signal system.
5. Fuel pump system.
6. Carburetor heater system.

If the problem is isolated in one of these systems, refer to the appropriate checklist and perform the indicated tests.

CARBURETOR TROUBLESHOOTING

Engine Will Not Start

If the engine does not start and the problem is not in the electrical and mechanical systems, check the following:
1. If there is no fuel going to the carburetors, check the following:
   a. Clogged fuel tank breather.
   b. Clogged fuel tank-to-carburetor line.
   c. Clogged fuel valve.
   d. Incorrect float adjustment.
   e. Stuck or clogged float valve in carburetor(s).
2. If the engine is flooded (too much fuel), check the following:
   a. Flooded carburetor(s). Float valve in carburetor(s) stuck open.
   b. Clogged air filter element.
3. A defective emission control system (if equipped) can cause fuel problems. Check the following:
   a. Faulty air induction system (AIS).
   b. Loose, disconnected or plugged emission control system hoses.
4. If steps 1-3 failed to locate the problem, check for the following:
   a. Contaminated or deteriorated fuel.
   b. Intake manifold air leak.
   c. Clogged pilot or choke circuit.

Engine Starts but Idles and Runs Poorly or Stalls Frequently

An engine that idles roughly or stalls may have one or more of the following problems:
1. Clogged air cleaner.
2. Contaminated fuel.
3. Incorrect pilot screw adjustment.
4. Incorrect idle speed.
5. Loose, disconnected or damaged fuel and emission control vacuum hoses.
6. Intake air leak.
7. Incorrect air/fuel mixture.
8. Plugged carburetor jets.
9. Partially plugged fuel tank breather hose.

Incorrect Fast Idle Speed

A fast idle speed can be due to one of the following problems:
1. Idle adjust screw incorrectly set.
2. Incorrect choke cable free play.
3. Incorrect carburetor synchronization.
4. Stuck choke valve.

TROUBLESHOOTING

Poor Gas Mileage and Engine Performance

Poor gas mileage and engine performance can be caused by infrequent engine tune-ups. Check the service records against the recommended tune-up intervals in Chapter Three. If the last tune-up was within the specified service intervals, check for one or more of the following problems:
1. Clogged air filter.
2. Clogged fuel system.
3. Loose, disconnected or damaged fuel and emission control vacuum hoses.
4. Ignition system malfunctions.

Rich Fuel Mixture

A rich carburetor fuel mixture can be caused by one or more of the following conditions:
1. Clogged or dirty air filter.
2. Worn or damaged fuel valve and seat.
3. Clogged air jets.
4. Incorrect float level (too high).
5. Flooded carburetor(s).
6. Damaged vacuum piston.

Lean Fuel Mixture

A lean carburetor fuel mixture can be caused by one or more of the following conditions:
1. Clogged carburetor jet(s).
2. Clogged fuel filter.
3. Restricted fuel line.
4. Intake air leak.
5. Incorrect float level (too low).
6. Worn or damaged float valve.
7. Defective throttle valve.
8. Defective vacuum piston.

Engine Backfires

Check for the following:
1. Lean fuel mixture.
2. Incorrect carburetor adjustment.

Engine Misses During Acceleration

When there is a pause before the engine responds to the throttle, there is a miss in the engine. An engine miss can occur when starting from a dead stop or at any speed. An engine miss may be due to one of the following:
1. Lean fuel mixture.
2. Defective ignition coil secondary wires; check for cracking, hardening or bad connections.
3. Defective vacuum hoses; check for kinks, splits or bad connections.
4. Vacuum leaks at the carburetor(s) and/or intake manifold(s).
5. Fouled spark plug(s).
6. Low engine compression, especially at one cylinder only. Check engine compression as described in Chapter Three. Low compression can be caused by worn engine components.

EXCESSIVE VIBRATION

Usually this is caused by loose engine mounting hardware. If the mounting hardware is acceptable, vibration can be difficult to find without disassembling the engine.

FRONT SUSPENSION AND STEERING

Poor handling may be caused by improper tire pressure, a damaged frame or front steering components, a worn front fork assembly, worn wheel bearings or dragging brakes.

Bike Steers to One Side

1. Bent axle.
2. Bent frame.
3. Worn or damaged front wheel bearings.
4. Worn or damaged swing arm pivot bearings.
5. Damaged steering head bearings.
6. Uneven front fork adjustment.
7. Incorrectly installed wheels.
8. Front and rear wheels not aligned.

Suspension Noise

1. Loose mounting fasteners.
2. Damaged fork or rear shock absorber.
3. Incorrect front fork oil.

Wobble/Vibration

1. Loose front or rear axle.

2. Loose or damaged wheel bearing(s).
3. Damaged wheel rim(s).
4. Damaged tire(s).
5. Loose swing arm pivot bolt.
6. Unbalanced tire and wheel.

Hard Suspension (Front Fork)

1. Insufficient tire pressure.
2. Damaged steering head bearings.
3. Incorrect steering head bearing adjustment.
4. Bent fork tubes.
5. Binding slider.
6. Incorrect fork oil.
7. Plugged fork oil hydraulic passage.

Hard Suspension (Rear Shock Absorbers)

1. Excessive tire pressure.
2. Bent damper rod.
3. Incorrect shock adjustment.
4. Damaged shock absorber bushing(s).
5. Damaged shock absorber bearing.
6. Damaged swing arm pivot bearing.

Soft Suspension (Front Fork)

1. Insufficient tire pressure.
2. Insufficient fork oil level or fluid capacity.
3. Incorrect oil viscosity.
4. Weak or damaged fork springs.

Soft Suspension (Rear Shock Absorbers)

1. Insufficient tire pressure.
2. Weak or damaged shock absorber spring.
3. Damaged shock absorber.
4. Incorrect shock absorber adjustment.
5. Leaking damper unit.

BRAKE PROBLEMS

Sticking disc brakes may be caused by a stuck piston(s) in a caliper assembly or warped pad shim(s) or improper rear brake adjustment.

Brake Drag

1. Clogged brake hydraulic system.
2. Sticking caliper pistons.
3. Sticking master cylinder piston.
4. Incorrectly installed brake caliper.
5. Warped brake disc.
6. Sticking caliper slide pin.
7. Incorrect wheel alignment.
8. Worn or weak drum return springs.

Brakes Grab

1. Contaminated brake pads or linings.
2. Incorrect wheel alignment.
3. Warped brake disc.
4. Glazed pads or linings.

Brake Squeal or Chatter

1. Contaminated brake pads or linings.
2. Incorrectly installed brake caliper.
3. Warped brake disc.
4. Incorrect wheel alignment.
5. Anti-rattle spring missing in caliper.

Soft or Spongy Front Brake Lever

1. Low brake fluid level.
2. Air in brake hydraulic system.
3. Leaking brake hydraulic system.

Hard Front Brake Lever Operation

1. Clogged brake hydraulic system.
2. Sticking caliper pistons.
3. Sticking master cylinder piston.
4. Glazed or worn brake pads.

CHAPTER THREE

LUBRICATION, MAINTENANCE AND TUNE-UP

A motorcycle, even in normal use, is subjected to tremendous heat, stress and vibration. When neglected, any bike becomes unreliable and actually dangerous to ride.

To gain the utmost in safety, performance and useful life from the Yamaha V-Star, it is necessary to make periodic inspections and adjustments. Frequently, minor problems that are found during these inspections are simple and inexpensive to correct. If they are not corrected at this time, however, they could lead to major and more expensive problems later on.

When properly maintained, a Yamaha will give many miles and years of dependable and safe riding. By maintaining a routine service schedule as described in this chapter, costly mechanical problems and unexpected breakdowns can be prevented.

Tables 1-6 are at the end of this chapter.

PRE-RIDE CHECKS

Perform the following checks before the first ride of the day. Most of the following checks are described in this chapter. If a component requires service, refer to the appropriate chapter.

1. Examine the engine for signs of oil or fuel leaks.
2. Check the engine oil level at the oil level window (**Figure 1**) on the left side of the motorcycle.
3. Inspect all fuel lines and fittings for wetness.
4. Make sure the fuel tank is full of fresh gasoline.
5. Check the operation of the front and rear brakes. Add hydraulic fluid to the brake master cylinder or adjust the rear drum brake as necessary.
6. Check the operation of the clutch. If necessary, adjust the clutch free play as described in this chapter.
7. Inspect the front and rear suspension; make sure they have a good solid feel with no looseness.
8. Check tire pressure. Refer to **Table 2**.
9. Check the tires for imbedded stones. Pry them out with a suitable tool.
10. Check the exhaust system for damage or leaks.

11. Check the tightness of all fittings and fasteners, especially engine mounting hardware.

12. Start the engine and check the throttle. While the engine idles, sit on the bike with the rear brake applied and the transmission in neutral. Move the handlebars from side to side and check the engine speed. It must not increase or decrease as the handlebars are moved. Make sure the throttle moves smoothly in all steering positions.

13. With the engine running, check the lights and horn by performing the following:

   a. Pull the front brake lever and check that the brake light turns on.

   b. Press the rear brake pedal and check that the brake light turns on soon after depressing the pedal.

   c. Check to see that the headlight and taillight are on.

   d. Move the dimmer switch between the high and low positions, and check to see that both headlight elements are working.

   e. Push the turn signal switch to the left position and the right position. Make sure that all four turn signal lights are working.

   f. Push the horn button and note that the horn blows loudly.

14. Operate the engine stop switch. The engine should stop running when the switch is turned to the OFF position.

MAINTENANCE INTERVALS

Table 1 lists the recommended maintenance schedule for the V-Star Custom and Classic. Strict adherence to these recommendations ensures long life from the Yamaha. If the bike is run in an area of high humidity, perform the lubrication services more frequently to prevent possible rust damage.

For convenience, most of the services shown in **Table 1** are described in this chapter. Those procedures that require more than minor disassembly or adjustment are covered elsewhere in the appropriate chapter. Use the *Table of Contents* and *Index* to locate a particular service procedure.

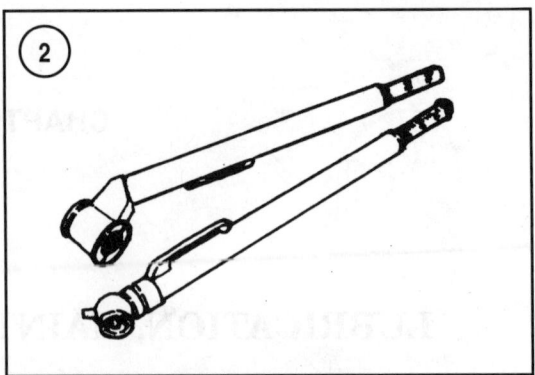

TIRES

Tire Pressure

Check and adjust tire pressure to accommodate the rider and luggage weight. Purchase a simple, accurate tire-pressure gauge (**Figure 2**) and carry it in a motorcycle tool kit. The appropriate tire pressures are listed in **Table 2**.

NOTE
*After checking and adjusting the tire pressure, make sure to reinstall the air valve cap (A, **Figure 3**). The cap prevents small pebbles and/or dirt from collecting in the valve stem. A dirty valve stem could allow air leakage or result in incorrect tire pressure readings.*

Tire Inspection

The likelihood of tire failure increases with tread wear. It is estimated that the majority of all tire failures occur during the last 10 percent of usable tread wear. Check tire tread for excessive wear, deep cuts,

LUBRICATION, MAINTENANCE AND TUNE-UP

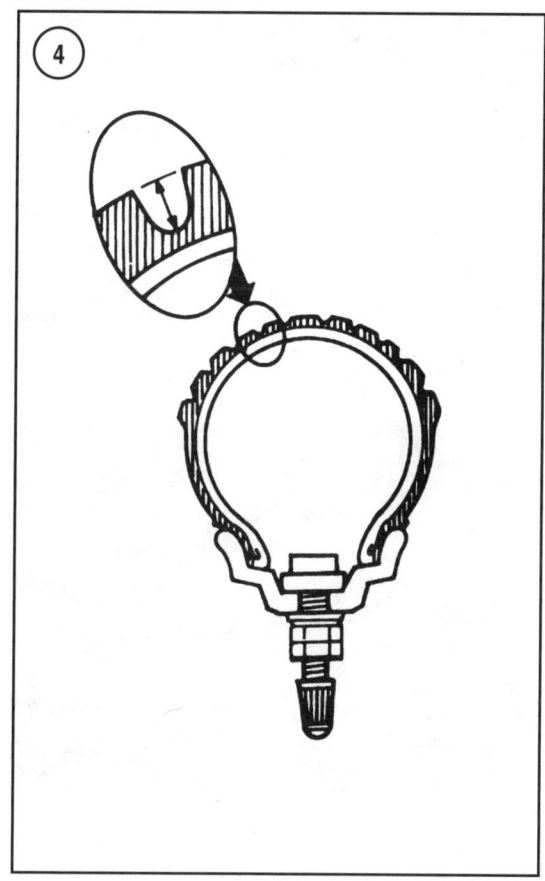

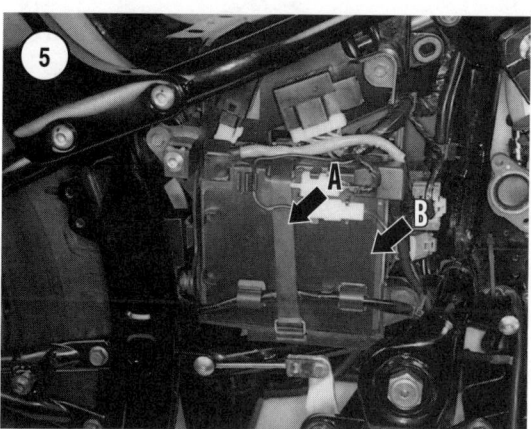

embedded objects such as stones, nails, etc. Check also for high spots that indicate internal tire damage. Replace tires that show high spots or swelling. If there is a nail in a tire, mark its location with a light crayon before pulling it out. This will help locate the hole for repair. Refer to Chapter Ten for tire changing procedures.

Measure tread wear (**Figure 4**) at the center of the tire tread with a tread depth gauge or small ruler. Because tires sometimes wear unevenly, measure wear at several points. Replace the original equipment tires if any tread depth measurement is less than the value specified in **Table 2**.

Rim Inspection and Runout

Frequently inspect the wheel rims (B, **Figure 3**) for cracks, warping, or dents. A damaged rim may cause an air leak.

Wheel rim runout is the amount of wobble a wheel shows as it rotates. Quickly check runout with the wheel on the bike by simply supporting the bike with the wheel off the ground. Slowly turn the wheel while holding a pointer solidly against a fork leg or the swing arm with the other end against the rim. If there is a suspicion that either lateral runout (side-to-side movement) or radial runout (up-and-down movement) exceeds the specification in **Table 5**, measure both the lateral and radial runout as described in Chapter Ten or Chapter Eleven.

BATTERY

The battery is an important component in the electrical system. It is also the one most frequently neglected. Clean and inspect the battery at regular intervals. All models are equipped with a maintenance-free sealed battery. Electrolyte level cannot be checked.

Removal/Installation

The battery in the V-Star is negative grounded. During battery removal, always disconnect the negative (–) cable first and then the positive (+) cable. This minimizes the chance of a tool shorting to ground when disconnecting the positive cable.

1. Securely support the bike on level ground.

2. Remove the rider's seat and the battery box cover as described in Chapter Thirteen.

3. Remove the battery hold-down strap (A, **Figure 5**).

4. Release the wires and connectors from their holders on the protective cover (B, **Figure 5**) and remove the cover.

5. Disconnect the negative (–) cable (A, **Figure 6**) from the battery.

6. Pull back the boot (B, **Figure 6**) and disconnect the positive (+) cable.

7. Remove the battery by carefully pulling it straight up and out of the battery box.

8. Set the battery on some newspapers or shop cloths to protect the workbench surface.

9. After the battery has been recharged or replaced, install it by reversing these removal steps. Note the following:

   a. Make sure the back of the battery box (**Figure 7**) is in place and that the foam side faces out.
   b. Properly secure the wires and connectors to their holders on the protective cover (B, **Figure 5**).

Inspection and Testing

The battery used in the Yamaha is a maintenance-free battery. Battery state of charge is checked by measuring terminal voltage.

The battery does not require periodic electrolyte inspection or refilling. Never attempt to remove the sealing bar cap from the top of the battery. This cap was removed for initial filling of electrolyte prior to delivery of the bike or battery. It is not to be removed thereafter.

> *WARNING*
> *Always wear safety glasses while servicing the battery. Even though this is a sealed battery, electrolyte could leak from a cracked battery case. Protect eyes, skin and clothing. Electrolyte is corrosive and can cause severe burns as well as permanent injury. If electrolyte gets into your eyes, flush your eyes thoroughly with clean, running water, and get immediate medical attention.*

1. Remove the battery from the motorcycle as described in this chapter. Do not clean the battery while it is mounted in the bike.

2. Clean the battery case with warm water and baking soda. Rinse it thoroughly with clean water.

3. Inspect the physical condition of the battery. Look for bulges, corrosion buildup, cracks in the case, or leaking electrolyte.

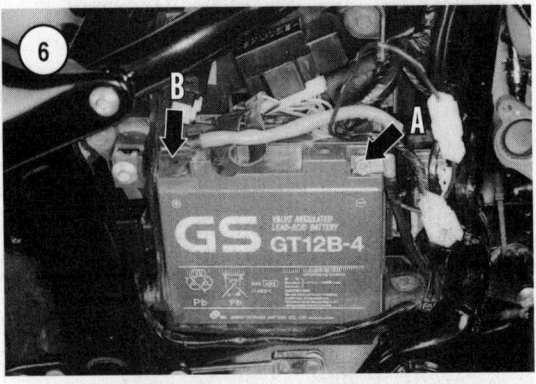

4. Clean the battery terminals, bolts and cable ends with a wire brush, and then rinse with water.

5. Check the cables for signs of chafing, deterioration or other damage.

> *NOTE*
> *Use a digital voltmeter when checking the battery's voltage. The precision of a digital meter will help accurately determine the battery's state of charge.*

6. Check the state of charge by connecting a digital voltmeter between the battery negative and positive leads (**Figure 8**).

   a. If the battery voltage is greater than 12.8 volts (at 68° F [20° C]), the battery is fully charged.
   b. If the battery voltage is 12.0-12.7 volts (at 68° F [20° C]), the battery is undercharged and requires charging.
   c. If battery voltage is less than 12.0 volts, replace the battery.

LUBRICATION, MAINTENANCE AND TUNE-UP

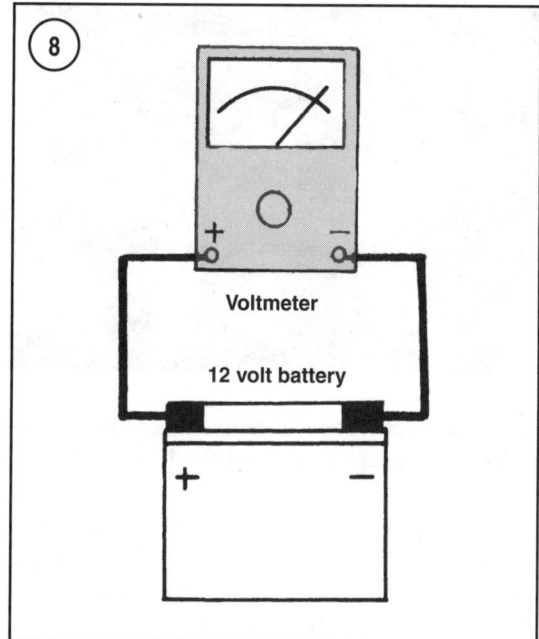

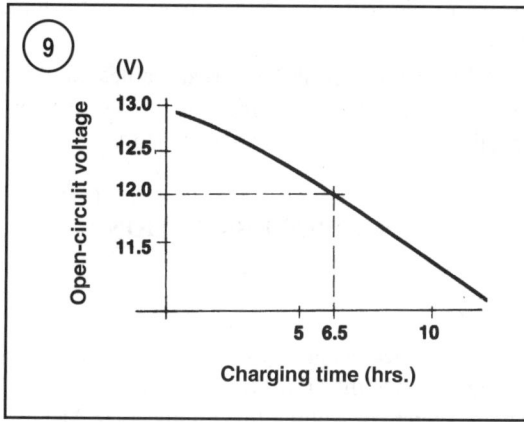

the charge by arcing (connecting pliers or other metal objects) across the terminals. The resulting spark can ignite the hydrogen gas.

CAUTION
*Do **NOT** use an automotive-type battery charger; the battery might overheat and cause internal plate damage. Use only a small trickle charger designed specifically for motorcycle batteries.*

CAUTION
Always disconnect the cables from the battery and remove the battery from the motorcycle before charging. The charger could destroy the diodes within the voltage regulator/rectifier if the cables are left connected.

1. Remove the battery from the bike as described in this chapter.
2. Connect the positive (+) charger lead to the positive (+) battery terminal and the negative (–) charger lead to the negative (–) battery terminal. Also connect an ammeter between the charger and the battery.
3. Set the charger to 12 volts. If using a variable output charger, it is best to select the low setting.

CAUTION
Never set the battery charger to exceed 4 amps. If the charge rate exceeds 4 amps, the battery could be damaged.

4. The charging time depends upon the condition of the battery. Refer to the chart in **Figure 9** to determine approximate charge time. Normally, a battery should be charged at a slow rate of one-tenth its given amp-hour rating.
5. Turn the charger on. If using a variable charger, adjust the amperage so the current is at the charge rate listed in **Table 3**.

NOTE
*If charging takes longer than five hours, check the charge current after five hours. Adjust the amperage as necessary so the charge current remains at the standard level listed in **Table 3**.*

Charging

Use a variable output charger to charge a maintenance free battery. If one is not available, take the battery to a Yamaha dealership or other qualified shop for charging to avoid damaging the battery.

WARNING
During the charging process, a small amount of highly explosive hydrogen gas is released from the battery. Charge the battery only in a well-ventilated area away from any open flames (including pilot lights on home gas appliances). Do not allow any smoking in the area. Never check

6. After the battery has charged for the specified amount of time, turn the charger off, and disconnect the charger leads from the battery.

7. Check the charge by connecting a voltmeter across the battery's negative and positive terminals. A fully charged battery should read 12.8 or more volts. If the voltage is 12.7 or less, the battery is undercharged.

8. If the battery remains stable at the specified voltage for one hour, the battery is fully charged.

9. Clean the battery terminals and the surrounding case. Coat the terminals with a thin layer of dielectric grease to retard corrosion.

10. To ensure good electrical contact, cables must be clean and tight on the battery's terminals as described in this chapter.

11. Reinstall the battery as described in this chapter.

NEW BATTERY INSTALLATION

Always replace a maintenance free battery with another maintenance-free battery. Also charge the battery completely before installing it. Failure to do so will reduce the life of the battery. Check with the dealership on the type of pre-service that the battery received.

NOTE
Recycle the old battery. The lead plates and the plastic case can be recycled. Most motorcycle dealerships will accept the old battery in trade when you purchase a new one. If they will not, many automotive supply stores certainly will. Never place an old battery in the household trash. It is illegal in most states to place any acid or lead (heavy metal) contents in landfills. There is also the danger of the battery being crushed in the trash truck and spraying acid on the truck operator.

BATTERY ELECTRICAL CABLE CONNECTORS

To ensure good electrical contact between the battery and the electrical cables, the cables must be clean and free of corrosion.

1. If the electrical cable terminals are badly corroded, disconnect them from the bike's electrical system.

2. Thoroughly clean each connector with a wire brush and then with a baking soda solution. Rinse thoroughly with clean water and wipe the connector dry with a clean cloth.

3. After cleaning, apply a thin layer of dielectric grease to the battery terminals before reattaching the cables.

4. After connecting the electrical cables, apply a light coating of dielectric grease to the electrical terminals of the battery to retard corrosion.

PERIODIC LUBRICATION

Oil

Oil is graded according to its viscosity, which is an indication of the oil's thickness. The system used by the Society of Automotive Engineers (SAE) distinguishes oil viscosity by numbers. Thick oils have higher viscosity numbers than thin oils. For example, an SAE 5 oil is a thin oil while an SAE 90 oil is relatively thick.

Grease

Use a good-quality grease (preferably waterproof). Water does not wash grease off parts as easily as it washes off oil. In addition, grease maintains its lubricating qualities better than oil on long and strenuous rides. Always use the recommended lubricant. In an emergency, though, the wrong lubricant is better than none at all. Correct the situation as soon as possible.

LUBRICATION, MAINTENANCE AND TUNE-UP

Engine Oil Level Check

Check the engine oil level through the inspection window (**Figure 1**) on the left side of the engine.
1. Start the engine, and allow it reach normal operating temperature.
2. Stop the engine, and allow the oil to settle.
3. Have an assistant hold the bike so it is *straight up and level*.

> *CAUTION*
> *If the bike is not parked correctly, an incorrect oil level reading will be observed.*

4. The oil level should be between the maximum and minimum window marks. If necessary, remove the oil filler cap (**Figure 10**) from the top of the alternator cover and add enough of the recommended oil (see **Table 4**) to raise the oil to the proper level. Do not overfill.
5. Reinstall the oil filler cap, and tighten it securely.

Engine Oil and Filter Change

The recommended oil and filter change interval is specified in **Table 1**. This assumes that the motorcycle is operated in moderate climates. The time interval is more important than the mileage interval because combustion acids, formed by gasoline and water vapor, will contaminate the oil even if the motorcycle is not run for several months. If a motorcycle is operated under dusty conditions, the oil will get dirty more quickly and should be changed more frequently than recommended.

Use only a high-quality detergent motor oil with an API classification of SF or SG. The classification is printed on the label. Try to use the same brand of oil at each oil change, and avoid the use of oil additives. They may cause clutch slippage. Refer to **Table 4** and select the correct oil viscosity for the anticipated ambient temperatures (not engine oil temperature).

To change the engine oil and filter obtain the following:
1. Drain pan.
2. Funnel.
3. Wrench or sockets.
4. Quantity of oil.
5. Oil filter element.

> *NOTE*
> *Never dispose of engine oil in the trash, on the ground, or down a storm drain. Many service stations accept used engine oil and waste haulers provide curbside used engine oil collection. Do not combine other fluids with oil to be recycled. To locate a recycler, contact the American Petroleum Institute (API) at www.recycleoil.org.*

1. Run the engine until it is at normal operating temperature, then turn the engine off.
2. Securely support the bike on level ground.
3. Place a drain pan under the crankcase and remove the oil drain bolt (**Figure 11**) from the left side of the crankcase.
4. Allow the oil drain for at least 15-20 minutes.
5. Inspect the sealing washer on the crankcase drain plug. Replace the washer if its condition is in doubt.
6. Install the oil drain bolt and washer. Tighten the bolt to the torque specification listed in **Table 6**.

> *CAUTION*
> *The exhaust pipes will be **HOT**. Wear thick work gloves when removing the exhaust pipes.*

7. Remove the exhaust pipes as described in Chapter Eight.
8. Replace the oil filter by performing the following:

a. Remove the three mounting bolts (A, **Figure 12**) and the oil filter cover plate (B, **Figure 12**).
b. Remove the five mounting bolts (A, **Figure 13**) and the oil filter cover (B, **Figure 13**) from the clutch cover.
c. Remove the oil filter from the oil filter cavity in the clutch cover.
d. Remove the O-ring (**Figure 14**) from the back of the oil filter cover. Lubricate the new O-ring with fresh engine oil, and install it onto the back of the oil filter cover.
e. Apply fresh oil to the grommet on a new oil filter, and install the filter so the end with the grommet faces out as shown in **Figure 15**.
f. Install the oil filter cover and then the oil filter cover plate. Torque the oil-filter-cover bolts and the oil-filter-cover-plate bolts to the specification in **Table 6**.

9. Remove the oil filler cap (**Figure 10**), and insert a funnel into the oil fill hole. Fill the crankcase with the correct weight and quantity of oil listed in **Table 4**. Screw in the oil filler cap securely.

10. Check the oil pressure by performing the following:
    a. Slightly loosen the intake rocker arm shaft bolt on the rear cylinder.
    b. Start the engine, and let it idle. Oil should seep from the loosened shaft bolt. If it does not within one minute, turn the engine off and inspect the oil lines, oil filter and oil pump damage.
    c. Turn the engine off, and torque the rocker arm shaft bolt to the specification in **Table 6**.

11. Check for oil leaks. Once the oil has settled, check the oil level in the inspection window on the alternator cover. Adjust the oil level if necessary.

12. Reinstall the exhaust pipes as described in Chapter Eight.

Final Gear Oil Check

1. Move the bike to a level surface. Use a suitable stand to support the bike in an upright position.
2. Remove the oil filler bolt (A, **Figure 16**) from the final gear case.
3. The oil level should sit at the bottom on the oil filler brim as shown in **Figure 17**.

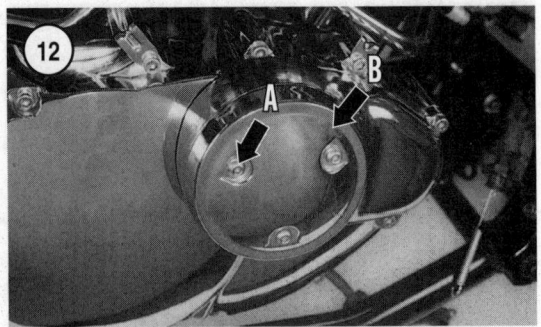

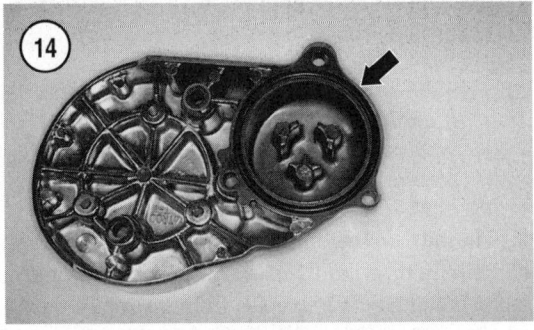

4. If the oil level is low, add final gear oil until the final gear case is full. Refer to **Table 4** for the recommended final gear oil.
5. Reinstall the oil filler bolt, and torque it to the specification in **Table 6**.

Final Gear Oil Change

1. Move the bike to a level surface. Use a suitable stand to support the bike in an upright position.
2. Place a drain pan under the drain bolt (B, **Figure 16**) on the final gear case.
3. Remove the drain bolt, and drain the oil from the final gear case.
4. Reinstall the drain bolt, and torque it to the specification in **Table 6**.

LUBRICATION, MAINTENANCE AND TUNE-UP   67

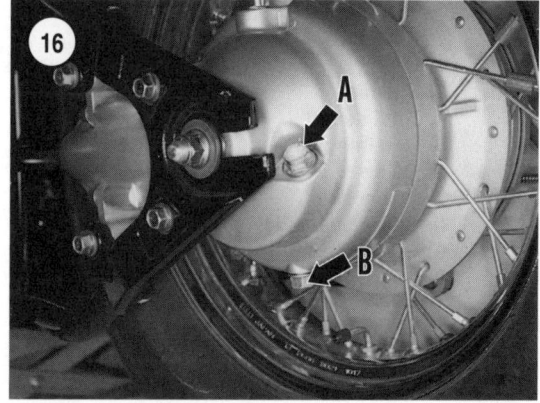

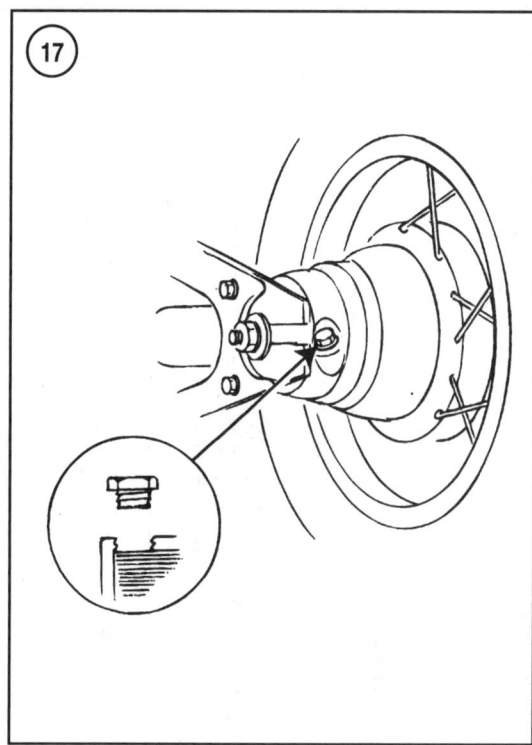

5. Refer to **Table 4** and add the recommended quantity of final gear oil.

6. Check the level of oil in the final gear case. Add oil as necessary.

7. Reinstall the oil filler bolt (A, **Figure 16**), and torque it to the specification in **Table 6**.

Front Fork Oil Change

Yamaha does not provide an oil change interval for the front fork. Nonetheless, it is a good practice to change the fork oil once a year. If the fork oil becomes contaminated with dirt or water, change it immediately.

NOTE
While it is possible to position the bike so the fork is vertical while mounted in place, this requires a suitable jack to prevent the bike from falling over.

Changing the fork oil requires setting the fork oil level. Because the fork must be in a vertical position to accurately measure and set the oil level, it is easier to do so with the fork removed from the bike.

Refer to **Figure 18** when changing the fork oil.

1. Remove the fork leg as described in Chapter Ten.

2. To prevent scratching the fork slider in the vise, make a holder out of a piece of flat metal (**Figure 19**).

CAUTION
The fork cap is under spring pressure. Remove the spring cap carefully.

3. Remove the fork cap (D, **Figure 20**) from the fork tube, and then remove the spacer (C), spring seat (B) and fork spring (A) from the fork tube.

4. Pour the fork oil into a drain pan. Pump the fork several times to expel the last of the oil.

5. Hold the fork assembly upright and fill the fork tube with the correct quantity of SAE 10W fork oil. Refer to **Table 4** for the specified quantity.

6. Hold the fork assembly upright, and slowly pump the fork up and down several times to distribute the oil.

7. Compress the fork completely and measure the fluid level after the fork oil settles. Use an oil level gauge to measure the fluid level from the top of the

CHAPTER THREE

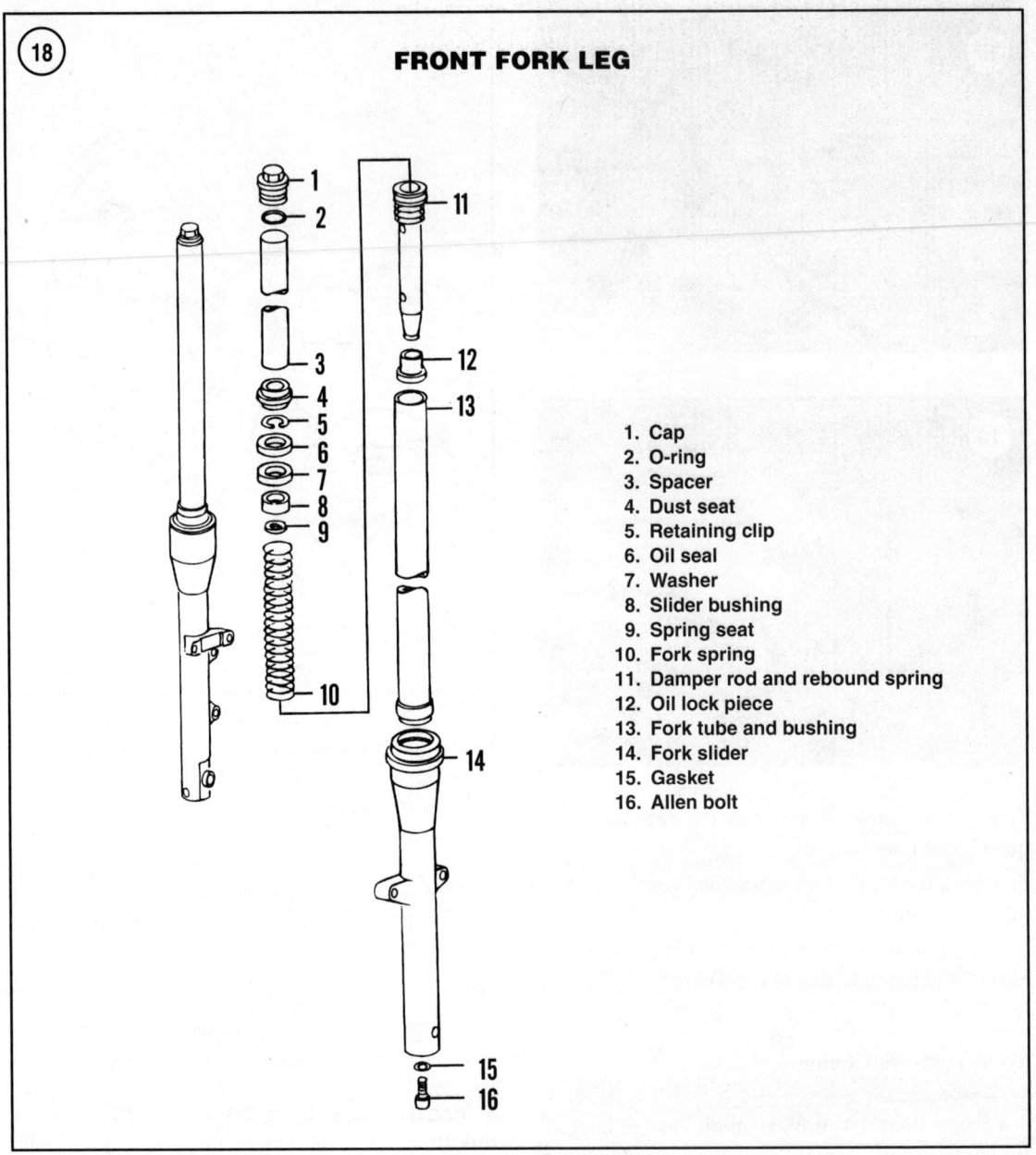

⑱ FRONT FORK LEG

1. Cap
2. O-ring
3. Spacer
4. Dust seat
5. Retaining clip
6. Oil seal
7. Washer
8. Slider bushing
9. Spring seat
10. Fork spring
11. Damper rod and rebound spring
12. Oil lock piece
13. Fork tube and bushing
14. Fork slider
15. Gasket
16. Allen bolt

fork tube as shown in **Figure 21**. If necessary, add or remove oil to set the fluid level to the value specified in **Table 4**.

8. Pull the fork tube out of the slider until it is fully extended.

9. Install the fork spring (A, **Figure 20**) into the fork tube.

10. Install the spring seat (B, **Figure 20**) onto the top of the fork spring. Make sure it is seated correctly.

11. Install the spacer (C, **Figure20**).

12. Lubricate a new O-ring (**Figure 22**) with fork oil and install it onto the fork cap.

13. Install the fork cap (D, **Figure 20**) while pushing down on the spring. Start the bolt slowly, don't cross thread it. Tighten the fork cap as tightly as possible. Once the fork is installed on the motorcycle, tighten the fork cap to the torque specified in **Table 6**.

14. Repeat for the other fork leg.

LUBRICATION, MAINTENANCE AND TUNE-UP

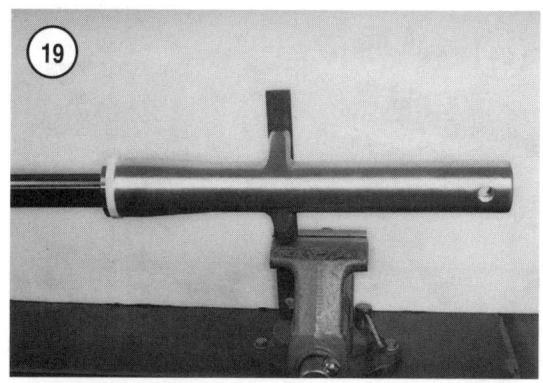

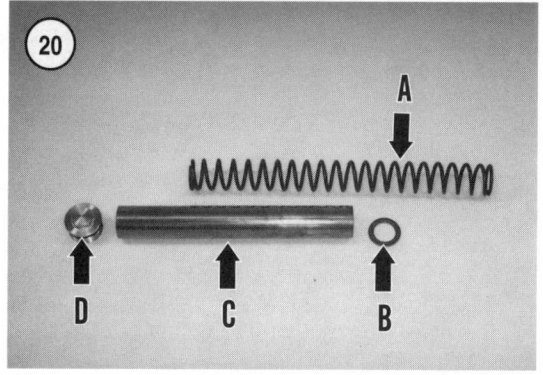

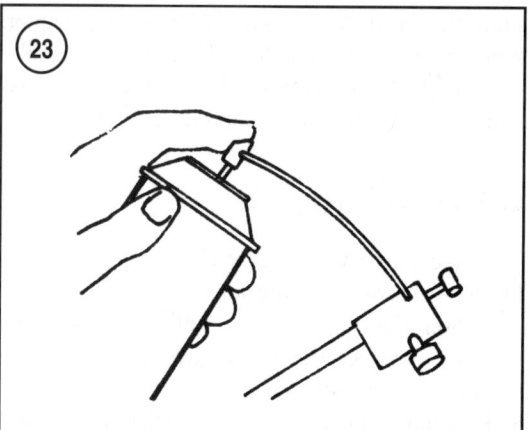

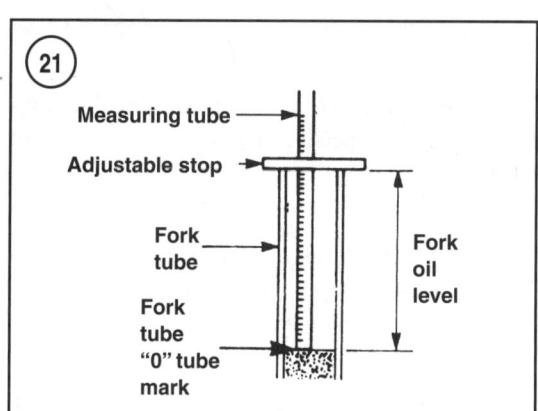

15. Install the fork legs as described in Chapter Ten.

Control Cable Lubrication

Lubricate the control cables at the intervals specified in **Table 1**. When lubricating a cable, also inspect it for fraying, and check the cable sheath for chafing. A cable is relatively inexpensive. Replace it if it is faulty.

Lubricate cables with a cable lubricant and a cable lubricator as shown in **Figure 23**. Do not use chain lube to lubricate the cables.

NOTE
The main cause of cable breakage or cable stiffness is improper lubrication. Maintaining the throttle cable as described in this section ensures a long service life.

Throttle Cable Lubrication

1. Remove the two mounting screws and separate the halves of the right handlebar switch assembly (A, **Figure 24**) as described in Chapter Nine.
2. Disengage the ends (B, **Figure 24**) of the pull and push cables from the throttle grip.
3. Attach a cable lubricator to the cable following the manufacturer's instructions.
4. Insert the nozzle of the lubricant can into the lubricator, press the button on the can and hold it

down until the lubricant begins to flow out of the other end of the cable.

NOTE
Place a shop cloth at the end of the cable to catch all excess lubricant that flows out.

NOTE
If lubricant does not flow out the end of the cable, check the entire cable for fraying, bending or other damage.

5. Remove the lubricator, reconnect the cables, and adjust the throttle cable as described in this chapter. When installing the right handlebar assembly, make sure the projection (**Figure 25**) on the switch assembly aligns with the hole in the handlebar.

Clutch Cable Lubrication

1. At the handlebar, slide the clutch lever boot (A, **Figure 26**) away from the adjuster.
2. Loosen the clutch cable locknut (B, **Figure 26**) and rotate the adjuster (C, **Figure 26**) to provide maximum slack in the cable.
3. Disconnect the cable end from the clutch hand lever.
4. Attach a cable lubricator to the cable following the manufacturer's instructions.
5. Insert the nozzle of the lubricant can into the lubricator, press the button on the can and hold it down until the lubricant begins to flow out of the other end of the cable.

NOTE
Place a shop cloth at the end of the cable to catch all excess lubricant that flows out.

NOTE
If lubricant does not flow out the end of the cable, check the entire cable for fraying, bending or other damage.

6. Remove the lubricator, reconnect, and adjust the throttle cable as described in this chapter.

Speedometer Cable Lubrication

Lubricate the speedometer cable every year or whenever needle operation is erratic.

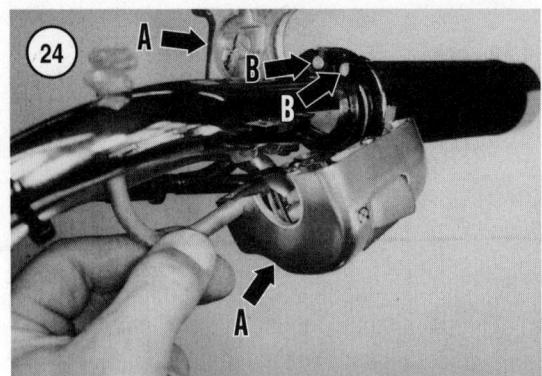

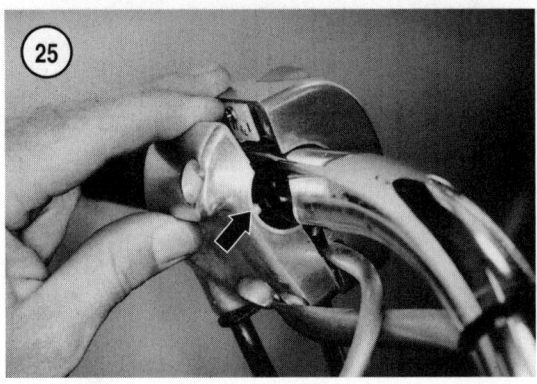

1. Remove the meter assembly as described in *Fuel Tank* in Chapter Eight.

2. Unscrew the end of the speedometer cable (**Figure 27**) from the speedometer drive unit on the front wheel.

NOTE
Use Yamaha Chain and Cable Lube or SAE 10W30 motor oil for lubricating the speedometer cable.

3. Insert the nozzle of the lubricant can into the top (meter) end of the cable, press the button on the can and hold it down until the lubricant begins to flow out of the other end of the cable.

NOTE
Place a shop cloth at the end of the cable to catch all excess lubricant that flows out.

4. Reinstall the speedometer cable. Make sure the cable is properly installed in the meter and the speedometer housing.

LUBRICATION, MAINTENANCE AND TUNE-UP

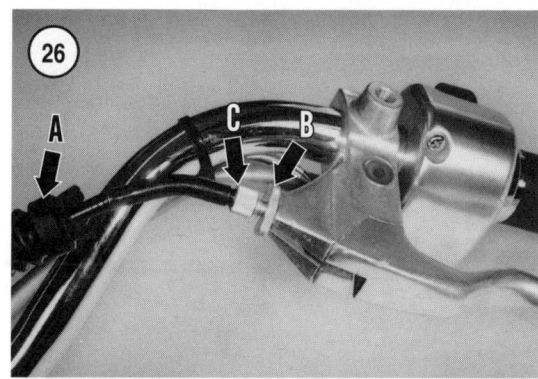

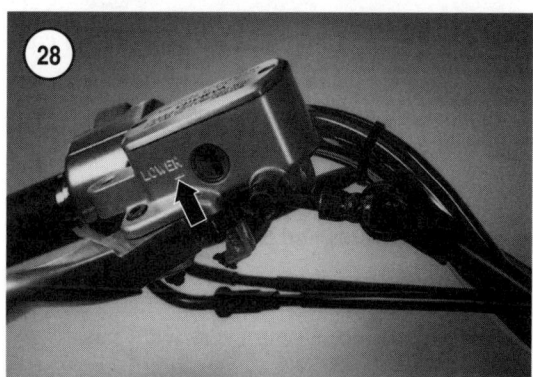

Swing Arm Bearings Lubrication

Frequent lubrication of the swing arm bearings keeps the rear suspension in peak condition. Clean the swing arm bearings in solvent and pack them with molybdenum disulfide grease at the intervals specified in **Table 1**. The swing arm must be removed to service the bearings. Refer to Chapter Eleven.

Steering Stem Bearings Lubrication

Remove, clean and lubricate the steering stem bearings with lithium grease at the interval specified in **Table 1**. Refer to the procedure in Chapter Ten.

Wheel Bearings Inspection/Lubrication

Worn wheel bearings cause excessive wheel play that results in vibration and other steering troubles. Inspect and lubricate the wheel bearings at the intervals specified in **Table 1**. Refer to Chapter Ten for the front hub; Chapter Eleven for the rear hub.

Miscellaneous Lubrication Points

Lubricate the clutch lever, front brake lever, sidestand pivot point and the footpeg pivot points with lithium grease.

PERIODIC MAINTENANCE

Front Brake Fluid Level

Keep the fluid level above the lower mark on the reservoir. If the brake fluid level reaches the lower level mark on the front master cylinder (**Figure 28**), correct the fluid level by adding fresh brake fluid.

1. Place the bike on level ground and position the handlebars so the front master cylinder reservoir is level.
2. Clean any dirt from the area around the top cover before removing the cover.
3. Remove the screws securing the front master-cylinder top cover. Remove the top cover and the diaphragm.

WARNING
Use brake fluid from a sealed container and clearly marked DOT 4 only (specified for disc brakes). Others may vaporize and cause brake failure. Do not mix different brands or types of brake fluid as they may not be compatible.

CAUTION
Be careful when handling brake fluid. Do not spill it on painted, plated or plastic parts as it will destroy the surface. If it does spill, wash the area immediately with soapy water and thoroughly rinse it off.

4. Add brake fluid from a sealed brake fluid container.

5. Reinstall the diaphragm and the top cover. Tighten the screws securely.

Front Brake Hoses and Seals

Replace the disc brake hose every four years; replace the brake piston seals every two years.

Check the brake hose between the master cylinder and the brake caliper. If there is any leakage, tighten the connections and bleed the brakes as described in Chapter Twelve. If this does not stop the leak or if a line is obviously damaged, cracked, or chafed, replace the hose and seals, and then bleed the brake.

Front Brake Pad Inspection

Inspect the brake pads for excessive or uneven wear, scoring, and oil or grease on the friction surface.

1. Remove the caliper as described in Chapter Twelve.
2. Look into the caliper assembly, and inspect the wear indicators (**Figure 29**).
3. Replace both pads in the caliper if either pad is worn to the wear limit. Refer to Chapter Twelve for brake pad replacement.

Front Brake Fluid Change

Every time the reservoir cap is removed, a small amount of dirt and moisture enters the brake fluid. The same thing happens if a leak occurs or when any part of the hydraulic system is loosened or disconnected. Dirt can clog the system and cause unnecessary wear. Water in the fluid vaporizes at high temperatures, impairing the hydraulic action and reducing brake performance.

To change brake fluid, drain the master cylinders as described in Chapter Twelve. Add new fluid to the master cylinders, and bleed at the caliper until the fluid leaving the caliper is clean and free of contaminants and air bubbles. Refer to brake bleeding procedure in Chapter Twelve.

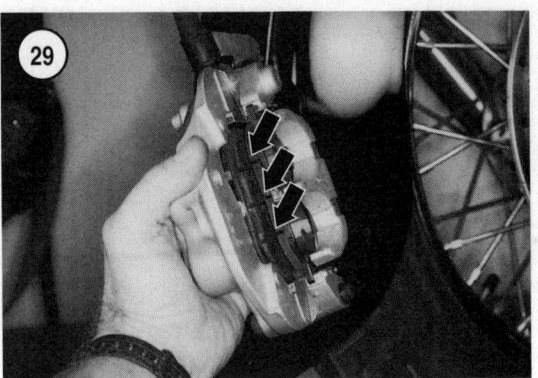

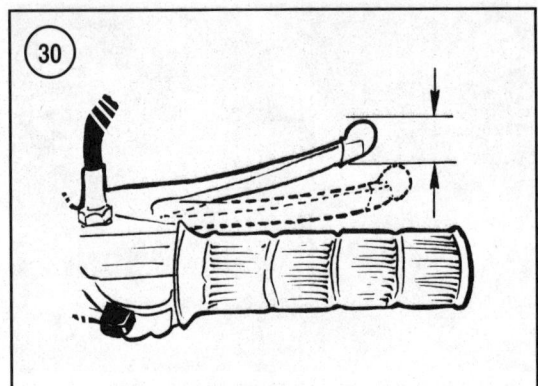

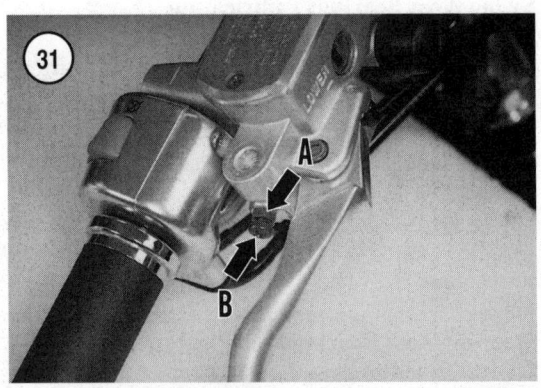

WARNING
Use brake fluid clearly marked DOT 4 only. Others may vaporize and cause brake failure.

Front Brake Lever Free Play

The front brake lever free play is the distance the brake lever moves before the master piston starts moving. Brake lever free play is measured at the end of the hand lever (**Figure 30**).

LUBRICATION, MAINTENANCE AND TUNE-UP

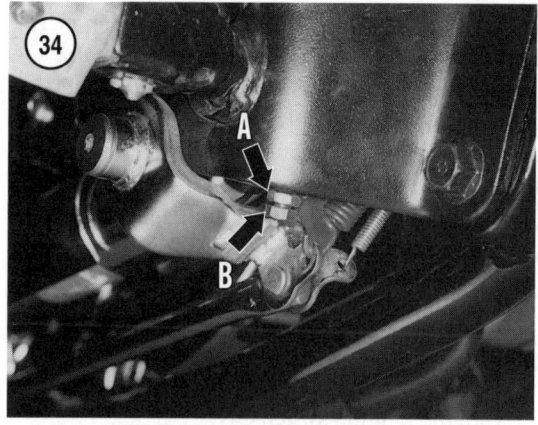

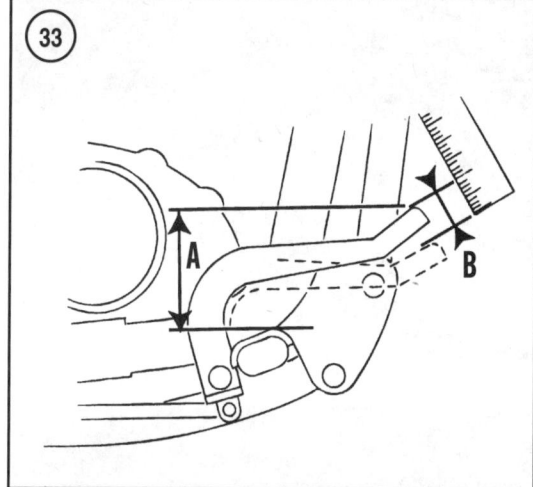

1. Push the brake lever forward, away from the handle grip.
2. Pull the lever and measure free play.
3. If free play is outside the range specified in **Table 5**, perform the following:
   a. Loosen the brake adjuster locknut (A, **Figure 31**).
   b. Turn the adjuster (B, **Figure 31**) in or out until free play is within the specification in **Table 5**. Turning the adjuster in decreases free play; turning it out increases free play.
4. After adjusting free play, spin the wheel and check for brake drag. Readjust free play as necessary.

Rear Brake Shoe Inspection

1. Apply the rear brake several times.
2. Inspect the wear indicator on the brake panel.

3. Replace the brake shoes if the indicator points to the wear limit line (**Figure 32**).

Rear Brake Pedal Height Adjustment

Rear brake pedal height is the distance from the top of the footpeg to the top of the brake pedal (A, **Figure 33**).

1. Support the bike so it sits straight up.
2. Make sure the brake pedal is in the at-rest position.
3. Measure the distance from the top of the brake pedal to the top of the footpeg. If the pedal height is not within the specification in **Table 5**, adjust the pedal height by performing the following:
   a. Loosen the adjuster locknut (A, **Figure 34**) and turn the adjuster (B, **Figure 34**) until the pedal height is within the specification listed in **Table 5**. Turning the adjuster in lowers the brake pedal; turning the adjuster out, raises the pedal.
   b. Tighten the locknut to the specification in **Table 6**.
   c. After adjusting the brake pedal height, check the brake pedal free play. If necessary, adjust the free play as described below.

Rear Brake Pedal Free Play

Brake pedal free play is the distance the brake pedal moves before the rear brake is activated (B, **Figure 33**).

1. Operate the brake pedal and measure the free play.

2. If free play is not within the specification in **Table 5**, adjust it by turning the rear brake free play adjuster on the end of the brake rod (**Figure 35**). Turning the adjuster in (clockwise) decreases free play; turning it out (counterclockwise) increases free play.

3. After adjusting free play, spin the wheel and check for any brake drag. Readjust free play as necessary.

Rear Brake Light Switch Adjustment

1. Turn the ignition switch ON.
2. Depress the brake pedal. The brake light should come on after the brake pedal is depressed but just before the rear brake is applied. If necessary, adjust as follows.
3. Hold the rear brake light switch body (A, **Figure 36**), and turn the adjuster (B, **Figure 36**) in or out until the brake light operates properly.

WARNING
Do not ride the bike until the rear brake light operates properly.

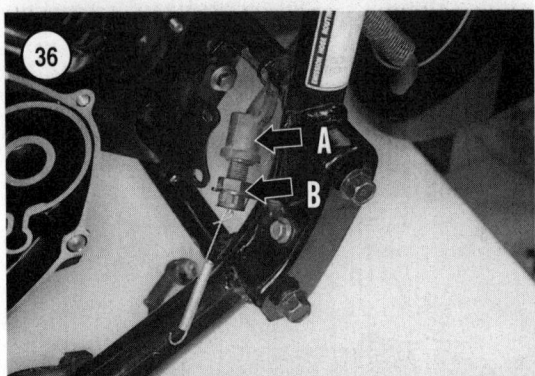

Shift Pedal Adjustment

Measure the length of the shift rod on the shift pedal assembly. The shift rod length equals the distance from the edge of the linkage at the shift pedal (A, **Figure 37**) to the edge of the linkage at the shift lever (B, **Figure 37**). If the length does not equal the value specified in **Table 5**, adjust the length by performing the following:
1. Loosen the locknut at each end of the shift rod.
2. Turn the shift rod (C, **Figure 37**) to attain the desired length.
3. Tighten each locknut securely.

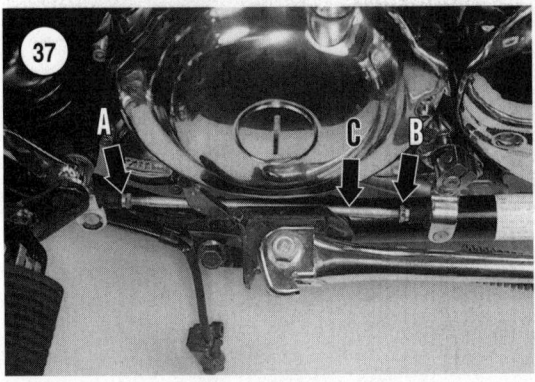

Clutch Adjustment

Adjust the clutch at the interval indicated in **Table 1**. For the clutch to engage and disengage properly, the clutch cable free play must be maintained at the specification listed in **Table 5**. If there is no clutch free play, the clutch cannot disengage completely. This causes clutch slippage and rapid clutch plate wear.

Clutch lever free play is measured at the end of the hand lever (**Figure 30**). If the clutch lever free play is outside the range specified in **Table 5**, adjust free play by performing the following:

1. At the clutch hand lever, pull the rubber boot (A, **Figure 26**) back from the adjuster.
2. Loosen the clutch cable locknut (B, **Figure 26**).
3. Turn the adjuster (C, **Figure 26**) in or out to attain the amount of free play specified in **Table 5**.
4. Tighten the locknut, and reinstall the rubber boot.
5. If the proper free play cannot be achieved at the hand lever adjuster, additional adjustment can be

LUBRICATION, MAINTENANCE AND TUNE-UP

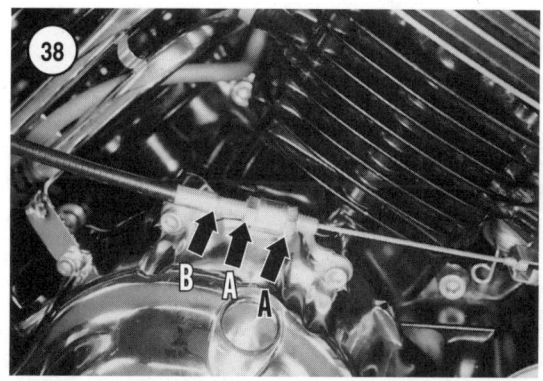

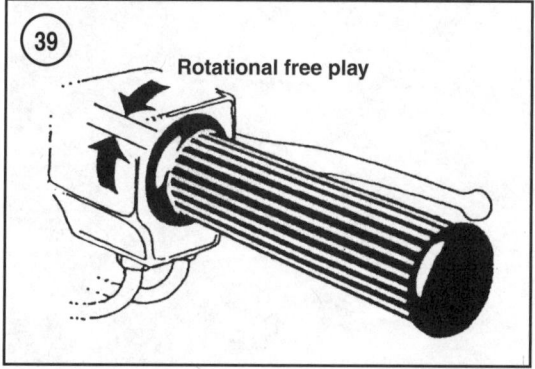

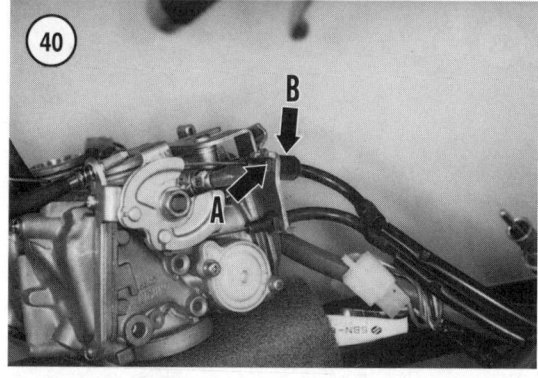

Throttle Cable Adjustment

Always check the throttle cables before making any carburetor adjustments. Excessive free play causes delayed throttle response; too little free play causes unstable idling.

Check the throttle cables from the throttle grip to the carburetors. Make sure they are not kinked or chafed. Replace the cables if necessary.

Make sure the throttle grip rotates smoothly from fully closed to fully open. Check free play with the handlebars at the center, full-left, and full-right steering positions.

Check free play at the throttle grip flange (**Figure 39**). Free play range is specified in **Table 5**. If adjustment is necessary, perform the following:

1. Remove the fuel tank as described in Chapter Eight.
2. Remove the seat as described in Chapter Thirteen.
3. At the handlebar, make sure the throttle cable locknut and adjuster are tight.

NOTE
The carburetor assembly is shown removed for clarity. The carburetor assembly does not have to be removed to adjust throttle cable free play.

4. At the carburetor assembly, loosen the pull cable locknut (A, **Figure 40**).
5. Rotate the pull cable adjuster (B, **Figure 40**) until the specified free play is achieved. Tighten the locknut securely.

NOTE
If the specified free play cannot be achieved at the carburetor, additional adjustment can be made at the handlebar adjuster.

6. At the handlebar, loosen the throttle cable locknut (A, **Figure 41**).
7. Rotate the adjuster (B, **Figure 41**) in either direction to adjust the amount of free play. Tighten the adjuster locknut.

WARNING
If idle speed increases when the handlebar is turned to right or left, check the throttle cable routing. Do not ride the motorcycle in this unsafe condition.

made at the lower clutch cable adjuster located on the alternator cover. Perform the following:

   a. Loosen the locknuts (A, **Figure 38**) at the lower clutch cable adjuster.

   b. Turn the adjuster (B, **Figure 38**) until the proper free play is obtained at the clutch hand lever, and then tighten the locknuts.

6. Recheck the amount of free play at the hand lever and perform any minor adjustments at the hand lever if necessary.

8. Start the engine and let it idle in neutral. Observe the engine speed while turning the handlebar from steering lock to steering lock. If the idle speed changes while turning the handlebar, the throttle cable is routed incorrectly or there is insufficient cable free play. Make the necessary corrections.

Fuel Line Inspection

Inspect the condition of all the fuel lines for cracks or deterioration; replace if necessary. Make sure the hose clamps are in place and secure.

Fuel Filter

Replace the fuel filter when it is dirty or at the interval specified in **Table 1**. Refer to the procedure in Chapter Eight.

Exhaust System

Check for leakage at all fittings. Tighten all bolts and nuts; replace any gaskets as necessary. Refer to Chapter Eight.

Air Filter Removal/Installation

Remove and clean the air filter element at the interval listed in **Table 1**. Replace the air filter if it is soiled, excessively clogged or broken in any area.

The air filter removes dust and abrasive particles from the incoming air before the air enters the carburetors and the engine. Without the air filter, very fine particles would enter into the engine and cause rapid wear of the piston rings, cylinders and bearings. These particles may also clog small passages in the carburetors. Never operate the motorcycle without the air filter element installed.

Proper air filter servicing can do more to ensure long service from the engine than almost any other single item.

The air filter is a dry-element type; no oiling is required.

1. Check that the ignition switch is OFF.
2. Securely support the motorcycle on level ground with a scissors jack or jack stands.
3. Remove the air filter cover (**Figure 42**), and the air filter element.

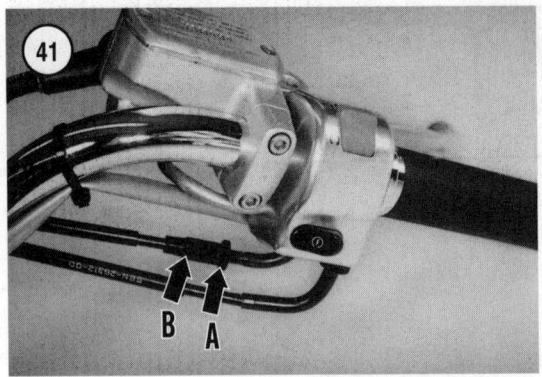

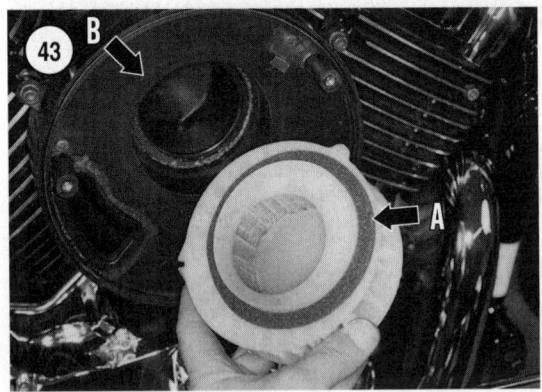

4. Wipe the interior of the air box with a shop rag dampened with cleaning solvent. Remove any foreign matter that may have passed through the element.

5. Inspect the air filter element for tears or other damage that would allow unfiltered air to pass into the engine. Also check the element gasket (A, **Figure 43**) for tears. Replace the element if necessary.

6. Gently tap the air filter element to loosen the dust.

LUBRICATION, MAINTENANCE AND TUNE-UP

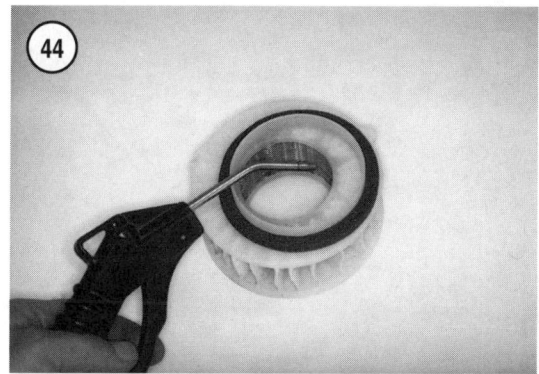

CAUTION
In the next step, do not direct compressed air toward the outside surface of the element. This forces the dirt and dust into the pores of the element, thus restricting air flow.

7. Apply compressed air toward the *inside surface* of the element (**Figure 44**) to remove all loosened dirt and dust.

8. Installation is the reverse of removal. Note the following:

   a. Install the air filter so the notch on the filter (**Figure 45**) engages the post on the air filter housing.
   b. Make sure the filter gasket (A, **Figure 43**) is properly seated against the sealing surface (B, **Figure 43**) in the housing so there are no air leaks.
   c. Tighten the three air filter cover screws securely.

Emission Control System (California Models)

At the service intervals in **Table 1**, Check all the emission control lines and the EVAP canister for loose connections or damage. Refer to Chapter Eight.

Sidestand

Check the operation of the sidestand and the sidestand switch at the service interval listed in **Table 1**. Perform the following:

1. Use a suitable stand to support the bike on a level surface.
2. Operate the sidestand and check its movement and spring tension. Replace the spring if it is weak or damaged.
3. Lubricate the sidestand pivot surfaces with lithium grease.
4. Check the sidestand switch operation by performing the following:

   a. Park the bike so both wheels are on the ground.
   b. Sit on the motorcycle and raise the sidestand.
   c. Shift the transmission in to NEUTRAL.
   d. Start the engine, pull in the clutch lever, and shift the transmission into gear.
   e. Move the sidestand down. The engine should stop.
   f. If the engine does not stop, inspect the sidestand switch as described in Chapter Nine.

5. If loosened, tighten the sidestand nut to the specification in **Table 6**.

Steering Play

Check the steering head for looseness at the intervals specified in **Table 1** or whenever the following symptoms or conditions exist:

1. The handlebar vibrates more than normal.
2. The front fork makes a clicking or clunking noise when the front brake is applied.
3. The steering feels tight or slow.
4. The motorcycle does not want to steer straight on level road surfaces.

CHAPTER THREE

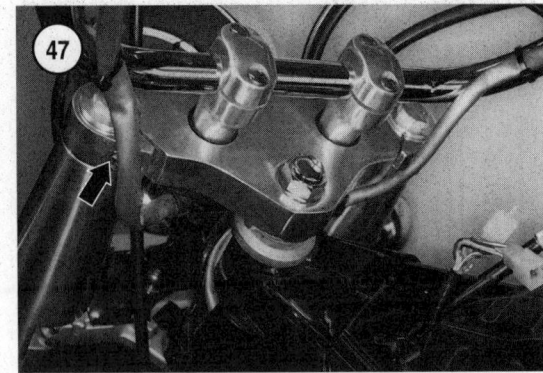

Inspection

1. Securely support the motorcycle so the front tire clears the ground.

2. Center the front wheel. Push lightly against the left handlebar grip to start the wheel turning to the right, then let go. The wheel should continue turning under its own momentum until the fork hits the stop.

3. Center the wheel, and push lightly against the right handlebar grip.

4. If the front wheel does not turn all the way to the stop when lightly pushing a handlebar grip, the steering is too tight. Adjust the steering head bearings as described in Chapter Ten.

5. Center the front wheel and kneel in front of it. Grasp the bottom of the front fork sliders. Try to pull the legs forward, and then try to push them toward the engine. If play is felt, the steering adjustment is loose. Adjust the steering head bearings as described in Chapter Ten.

Front Suspension Check

1. Apply the front brake and pump the fork up and down as vigorously as possible. Check for smooth fork operation and any oil leakage.

NOTE
Figure 46 shows the two lower fork bridge clamp bolts for the V-Star Classic. V-Star Custom models only use one lower fork bridge clamp bolt.

2. Make sure the upper (**Figure 47**) and lower (**Figure 46**) fork bridge clamp bolts are secure.

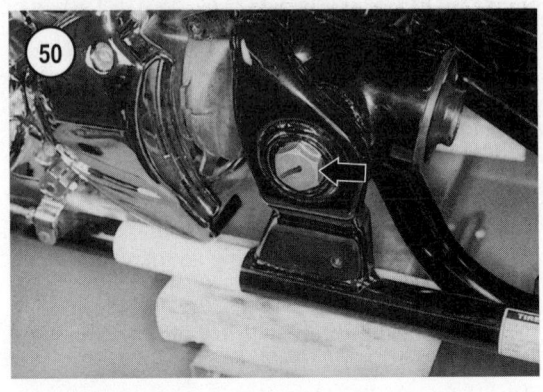

LUBRICATION, MAINTENANCE AND TUNE-UP

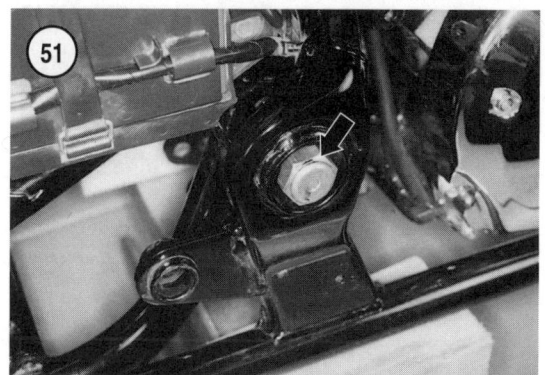

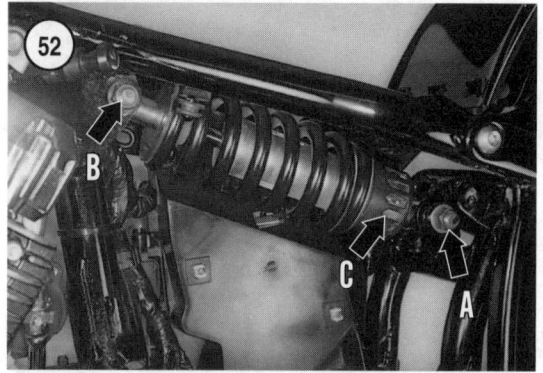

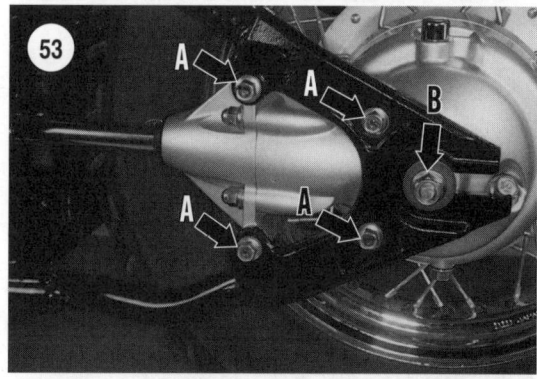

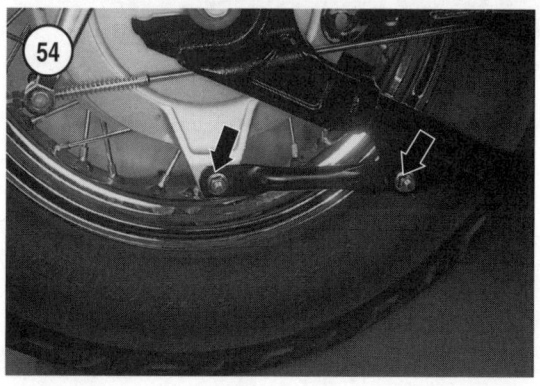

3. Make sure the Allen bolts (**Figure 48**) on each handlebar holder are secure, and that the handlebar is securely held in place.
4. Make sure the front axle clamp bolt (A, **Figure 49**) and axle (B, **Figure 49**) are secure.

WARNING
If any of the previously mentioned bolts and nuts are loose, refer to Chapter Ten for correct tightening procedures and torque specifications.

Rear Suspension Check

1. Use jack stands or a scissors jack to support the bike securely with the rear wheel off the ground.
2. Push the rear wheel sideways to check for side play in the swing arm bearings.
3. Remove the rider and passenger seats as described in Chapter Thirteen.
4. Remove the following items as described in Chapter Thirteen:
   a. Battery box cover.
   b. Right side cover.
   c. Tool box cover.
   d. Tool box.
   e. Left side cover.
5. Make sure the left swing arm pivot shaft (**Figure 50**) and right swing arm pivot nut (**Figure 51**) are secure.
6. Check the tightness of the shock absorber's lower (A, **Figure 52**) and upper (B) mounting bolts and nuts.
7. Make sure the four final gearcase bolts (A, **Figure 53**), the axle nut (B, **Figure 53**) and rear brake torque arm nuts (**Figure 54**) are secure.

WARNING
If any of the previously mentioned nuts or bolts are loose, refer to Chapter Eleven for correct tightening procedures and torque specifications.

Shock Absorber Spring Preload Adjustment

CAUTION
Never turn the cam ring beyond the maximum or minimum position.

The spring preload can be adjusted to seven different positions to suit riding, load and speed condi-

tions. The third position is the original equipment setting. The adjuster ranges are as follows:
  a. Soft: No. 1 and No. 2.
  b. Standard: No. 3.
  c. Hard: No. 4, 5, 6 and 7.

1. Remove the rider and passenger seats as described in Chapter Thirteen.
2. Use the spanner wrench and extension from the tool kit to adjust the preload by rotating the cam ring (C, **Figure 52**) at the base of the shock absorber. Turning the cam ring clockwise to a higher numbered setting increases the preload. Turning the ring counterclockwise to a lower numbered setting decreases preload.

Nuts, Bolts and Other Fasteners

Constant vibration can loosen many fasteners on a motorcycle. Check the tightness of all fasteners, especially those on:
1. Engine mounting hardware.
2. Engine crankcase covers.
3. Handlebar and front fork.
4. Gearshift lever.
5. Drive shaft components.
6. Brake pedal and lever.
7. Exhaust system.
8. Lighting equipment.

TUNE-UP

A tune-up is general adjustment and maintenance to ensure peak engine performance. The following procedures discuss each phase of a proper tune-up.

To perform a tune-up on the V-Star, use the following tools and equipment:
  a. Spark plug wrench.
  b. Socket wrench and assorted sockets.
  c. Compression gauge.
  d. Spark plug feeler gauges and gap adjusting tool.
  e. Ignition timing light.
  f. Portable tachometer.
  g. Carburetor synchronization tool.

Have the necessary tools and parts on hand before beginning.

Because the different systems in an engine interact, perform the procedures in the following order:
  a. Clean or replace the air filter element.

  b. Check and adjust valve clearances.
  c. Perform a cylinder compression test.
  d. Check or replace the spark plugs.
  e. Check the ignition timing.
  f. Synchronize carburetors and set the idle speed.

Table 5 provides tune-up specifications.

LUBRICATION, MAINTENANCE AND TUNE-UP

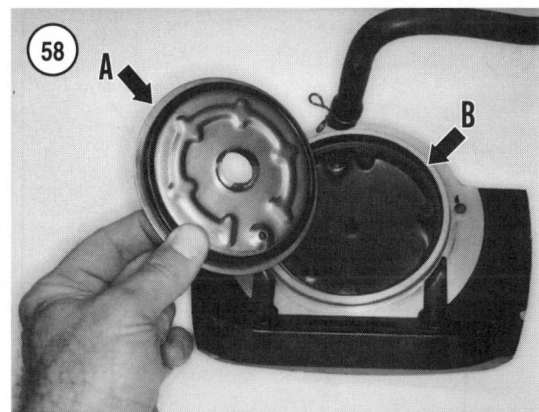

Air Filter Element

Clean or replace the air filter element as described earlier in this chapter.

Valve Clearance Measurement

Valve clearance measurement and adjustment must be performed with the engine cool, at a temperature below 95° F (35° C).

The exhaust valve is located on the rear side of the rear cylinder and on the front side of the front cylinder.

NOTE
This procedure is shown with the engine removed from the frame for clarity. The valves can be adjusted with the engine in the frame.

1. Remove the cylinder head covers as described in Chapter Four.

2. Remove both valve covers (**Figure 55**) from each cylinder head.

3. Remove the timing plug (A, **Figure 56**) and rotor bolt plug (B, **Figure 56**) from the alternator cover.

NOTE
A breather plate is not used in the front cylinder head.

4. Remove the two mounting screws (A, **Figure 57**) and the cam sprocket cover (B, **Figure 57**) and its O-ring from each cylinder head.

When working on the rear cylinder, make sure the breather plate (A, **Figure 58**) and its O-ring come out with the cam-sprocket cover (B, **Figure 58**).

5. Remove both spark plugs. This makes it easier to rotate the engine.

6. Use the alternator rotor bolt to turn the crankshaft clockwise until a cylinder is at top dead center on the compression stroke.

  a. The *rear cylinder* is at TDC on the compression stroke when the T-mark on the rotor aligns with the cutout in the alternator cover (see **Figure 59**) and when the timing mark on the rear cam sprocket aligns with the pointer on the rear cylinder head (see **Figure 60**).

NOTE
When the front cylinder is set to TDC on the compression stroke, the timing mark on the front cam sprocket may not precisely align with the pointer on the front cylinder head. On some models, the mark could be off by as much as a half tooth.

b. The *front cylinder* is at TDC on the compression stroke when the I-mark (A, **Figure 61**) on the rotor aligns with the cutout in the alternator cover (B, **Figure 61**) and when the timing mark on the front cam sprocket aligns with the pointer on the front cylinder head (see **Figure 60**).

NOTE
A cylinder at TDC on the compression stroke has free play in both rocker arms, which indicates that both valves are closed.

7. Check that the cylinder is at TDC by pressing each rocker arm. There should be free play at both the intake and exhaust rocker arms. If both rocker arms do not have free play, rotate the engine an additional 360° until they do.
8. Check the clearance of both the intake and exhaust valves by performing the following:
    a. Insert a feeler gauge (A, **Figure 62**) between the valve stem and the adjuster end.
    b. The clearance is correct if there is a slight drag on the feeler gauge when it is inserted and withdrawn. The correct valve clearances for the intake and exhaust valves are listed in **Table 5**.
    c. If necessary, adjust the valve clearance as described below.
9. Use the alternator rotor bolt to turn the crankshaft clockwise until the other cylinder is at top dead center on the compression stroke, and then check the valve clearances as described in Step 8.
10. When the clearance of each valve is within specification, reinstall the removed parts by reversing the removal procedure. Pay attention to the following:
    a. Before installing the rear-cylinder cam sprocket cover, fit a new O-ring onto the breather plate (A, **Figure 58**) and set the breather plate in place in the cam sprocket cover (B, **Figure 58**).

NOTE
A breather plate is not used on the front cylinder cam sprocket cover.

    b. Use a new O-ring when installing each cam sprocket cover onto the cylinder head. Torque the cam sprocket cover bolts to the specification in **Table 6**.

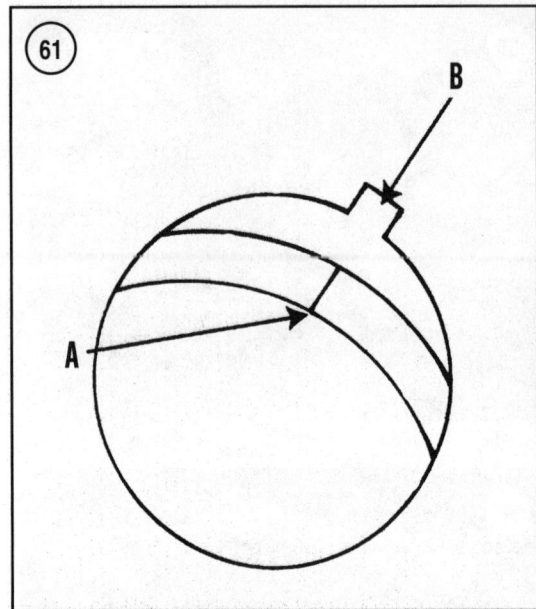

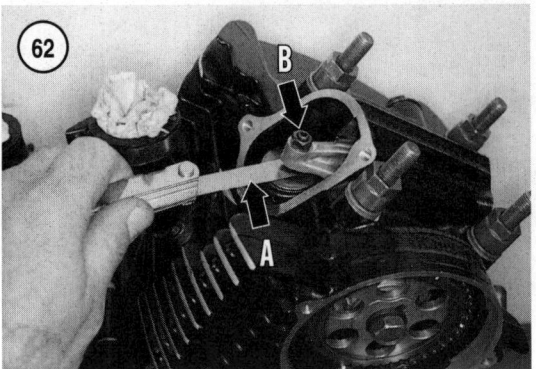

    c. Torque the valve cover bolts and the spark plugs to the specification in **Table 6**.
    d. Install the cylinder head covers as described in Chapter Four.

Valve Clearance Adjustment

For best performance, adjust the valve clearance to the smaller dimension listed in **Table 5**.

1. Set a cylinder to top dead center on the compression stroke as described above.
2. Loosen the locknut (B, **Figure 62**) on the valve adjuster.
3. With the feeler gauge between the valve stem and the adjuster end, turn the valve adjuster to obtain the specified clearance.

LUBRICATION, MAINTENANCE AND TUNE-UP

4. Hold the adjuster to prevent it from turning, and tighten the locknut to the specification in **Table 6**.
5. Recheck the valve clearance. If the clearance changes when the locknut is tightened, loosen the nut and repeat the adjustment procedure.

Cylinder Compression

A cylinder compression test is a quick way to check the conditions of the pistons, rings, valves, cylinders, and head gasket. Check the cylinder compression at every tune-up. Record the results of each cylinder, and compare them to the readings at the next check. A running record helps spot any developing problems.

Use a screw-in type compression tester for this procedure.

Before starting the test, confirm that:
 a. The cylinder head bolts are tightened to the specified torque. Refer to Chapter Four.
 b. The valves are properly adjusted as described in this chapter.
 c. The battery is fully charged to ensure proper cranking speed.

1. Warm the engine to normal operating temperature, and turn the engine off.
2. Remove the spark plugs as described in this chapter.
3. Insert each spark plug into its spark plug cap, and ground the spark plug against the cylinder head.
4. Connect the compression tester to one cylinder following the manufacturer's instructions. Make sure the gauge is properly seated in the cylinder head.
5. Completely open the throttle, and crank the engine until there is no further rise in pressure (**Figure 63**). Remove the tester, and record the reading.
6. Repeat Steps 3-5 for the other cylinder.
7. Standard compression pressure is specified in **Table 5**. When interpreting the results, actual readings are not as important as the difference between the readings. Large differences indicate worn or broken rings, leaky or sticky valves, a blown head gasket or a combination of the above.

If the compression reading between cylinders does not differ by more than 10 percent, the rings and valves are in good condition.

If a low reading (10 percent or more) is obtained on one of the cylinders, it indicates valve or ring trouble. To determine which, pour about a teaspoon of engine oil through the spark plug hole onto the top of the piston. Turn the engine over once to clear some of the excess oil, then take another compression test and record the reading. If the compression increases significantly, the rings are worn or defective. If compression does not increase, the valves are leaking.

NOTE
If the compression is low, the engine cannot be tuned to maximum performance. Replace the worn parts and rebuild the engine.

Correct Spark Plug Heat Range

Spark plugs are available in various heat ranges that are hotter or colder than the original equipment spark plugs.

Select plugs in a heat range designed for the loads and temperature conditions under which the engine will operate. Using plugs with an incorrect heat range can cause piston seizure, scored cylinder walls or damaged piston crowns.

In general, use a hotter plug for low speeds, low loads and low temperatures. Use a colder plug for high speeds, high engine loads and high temperatures. The plug must operate hot enough to burn off unwanted deposits, but not so hot that it causes preignition. A spark plug of the correct heat range shows a light tan color on the insulator after the plug has been in service.

The reach (**Figure 64**) of a plug is also important. A longer than normal plug could interfere with the valves and pistons, causing permanent and severe damage. The standard heat range spark plugs are listed in **Table 5**.

Spark Plug Removal/Cleaning

1. Grasp the spark plug lead (A, **Figure 65**) as near to the plug as possible and pull the lead off the plug.

> *CAUTION*
> *Dirt could fall into the cylinders when the plugs are removed, causing serious engine damage.*

2. Blow away any dirt in the spark plug well.

> *NOTE*
> *If a plug is difficult to remove, apply penetrating oil, like WD-40 or Liquid Wrench, around the base of the plug and let it soak in for about 10-20 minutes.*

3. Remove each spark plug with an 18 mm spark plug socket. Label plugs in order to tell which cylinder they came from.
4. Inspect the spark plugs carefully. Look for a broken center porcelain, excessively eroded electrodes and excessive carbon or oil fouling. Replace such a plug. If deposits are light, regap the plug as explained in this chapter.

> *NOTE*
> *Do not use a sand-blast type device to clean spark plugs. While this cleaning is thorough, the plug must be perfectly free of all abrasive cleaning material when done. If not, it is possible for the cleaning material to fall into the engine during operation and cause damage.*

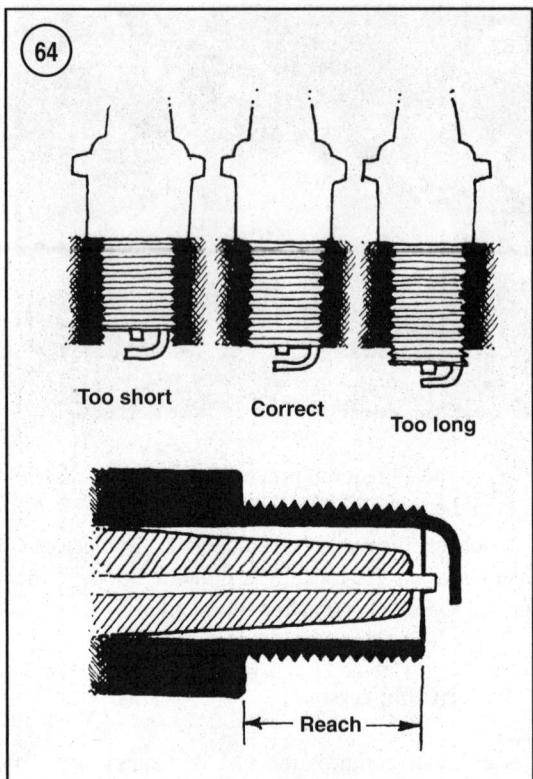

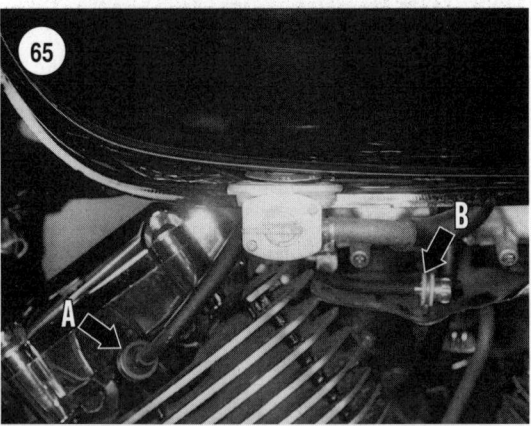

Spark Plug Gapping and Installation

Carefully gap new plugs to ensure a reliable, consistent spark. Use a special spark plug gapping tool with a wire gauge.
1. Remove the new plugs from the box. Do *not* screw in the small terminal cap that is loose in each box (**Figure 66**). It is not used.
2. Insert a wire gauge between the center and the side electrode of each plug (**Figure 67**). If the gap is correct, there will be a slight drag as the wire is pulled through. If there is no drag or if the gauge will not pass through, bend the side electrode *with the gapping tool* (**Figure 68**) to set the proper gap.

3. Apply a *small* amount of anti-seize compound onto the threads of the spark plug.

4. Screw each spark plug in by hand until it seats. Very little effort is required. If force is necessary, the plug is cross-threaded; unscrew it and try again.

LUBRICATION, MAINTENANCE AND TUNE-UP

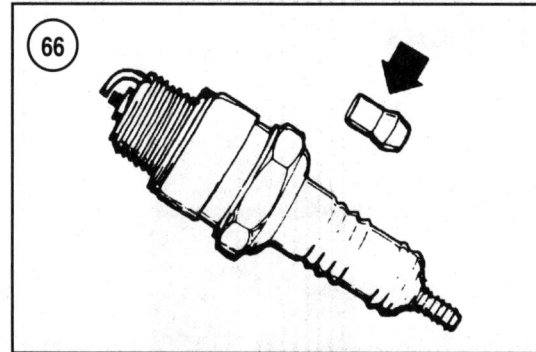

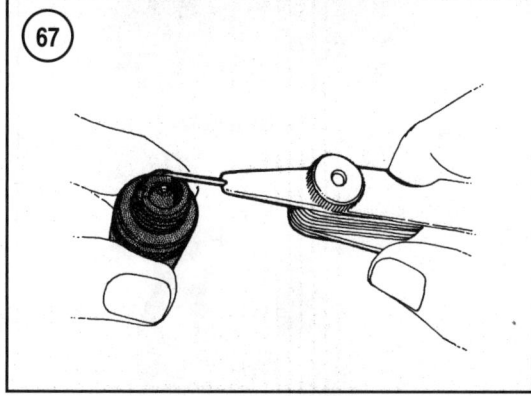

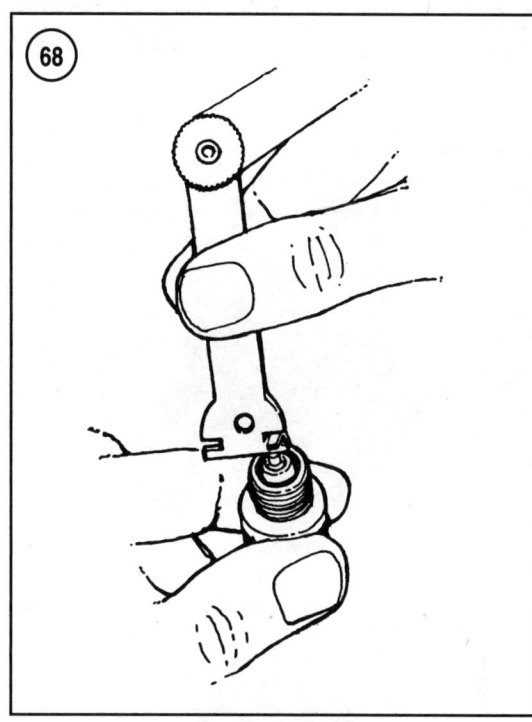

NOTE
If a spark plug is difficult to install, the cylinder head threads may be dirty or slightly damaged. To clean the threads, apply grease to the threads of a spark plug tap and screw it carefully into the cylinder head. Turn the tap slowly until it is completely installed. If the tap cannot be installed, the threads are severely damaged.

5. Tighten the spark plugs to the torque listed in **Table 6**. If a torque wrench is not available, turn the plug an additional quarter to a half turn after the gasket makes contact with the head. If reinstalling old, regapped plugs and reusing the old gasket, only tighten the plug an additional quarter turn.

CAUTION
Do not overtighten the spark plugs. Besides making the plug difficult to remove, the excessive torque will squash the gasket and destroy its sealing ability.

6. Install each spark plug wire. Make sure it goes onto the correct spark plug and is completely seated on the plug.
7. Repeat this procedure for the other spark plug.

Reading Spark Plugs

A careful examination of the spark plugs can reveal a significant amount of information regarding engine and spark plug performance.

Remove the spark plugs as described in this chapter and compare them to the plugs in **Figure 69**.

If the insulator tip is white or burned, the plug is too hot. Replace it with a colder one. A plug that is too cold will have sooty deposits ranging in color from dark brown to black. Replace with a hotter plug, and check for rich carburetion or evidence of oil blow-by at the piston rings.

If any one plug is found unsatisfactory, replace both spark plugs.

Normal condition

If the plug has a light tan- or gray-colored deposit and no abnormal gap wear or erosion, good engine, air/fuel mixture and ignition conditions are indi-

CHAPTER THREE

SPARK PLUG CONDITIONS

NORMAL

GAP BRIDGED

CARBON FOULED

OVERHEATED

OIL FOULED

SUSTAINED PREIGNITION

LUBRICATION, MAINTENANCE AND TUNE-UP

cated. The plug is in the proper heat range and may be serviced and returned to use.

Carbon fouled

Soft, dry, sooty deposits covering the entire firing end of the plug are evidence of incomplete combustion. Even though the firing end of the plug is dry, the plug's insulation decreases. An electrical path is formed that lowers the voltage from the ignition system. Engine misfiring is a sign of carbon fouling. Carbon fouling can be caused by one or more of the following:
1. Fuel mixture too rich.
2. Spark plug heat range too cold.
3. Clogged air filter.
4. Over-retarded ignition timing.
5. Ignition component failure.
6. Low engine compression.
7. Prolonged idling.

Oil fouled

The tip of an oil fouled plug has a black insulator, a damp oily film over the firing end and a carbon layer over the entire nose. The electrodes will not be worn. Common causes for this condition are:
1. Incorrect carburetor jetting.
2. Low idle speed or prolonged idling.
3. Ignition component failure.
4. Spark plug heat range too cold.
5. Engine still being broken in.
6. Valve guides worn.
7. Piston rings worn or broken.

Oil fouled spark plugs may be cleaned in an emergency, but it is better to replace them. It is important to correct the cause of fouling before the engine is returned to service.

Gap bridging

Plugs in this condition have combustion deposits bridging the gap between the electrodes, creating an electrical short. If this condition is encountered, check for an improper oil type or excessive carbon in the combustion chamber. Make sure to locate and correct the cause of this condition.

Overheating

Badly worn electrodes and premature gap wear are signs of overheating, along with a gray or white blistered porcelain insulator surface. Using a spark plug of the wrong heat range (too hot) commonly causes this condition. Consider the following causes:
1. Lean fuel mixture.
2. Ignition timing too advanced.
3. Engine lubrication system malfunction.
4. Engine air leak.
5. Improper spark plug installation (overtightening).
6. No spark plug gasket.
7. Incorrect spark plug heat range.

Worn out

Corrosive gases formed by combustion and high voltage sparks have eroded the electrodes. A spark plug in this condition requires more voltage to fire under hard acceleration. Replace with a new spark plug.

Preignition

If the electrodes are melted, preignition is usually the cause. Check for carburetor mounting or intake manifold leaks and over-advanced ignition timing. It is also possible that a plug of the wrong heat range (too hot) is being used. Find the cause of the preignition before returning the engine into service.

Ignition Timing

The V-Star is equipped with a digital controlled ignition system. This system uses no breaker points and is non-adjustable. Check the timing to make sure all ignition components are operating correctly. The ignition timing cannot be adjusted.
1. Start the engine and let it reach normal operating temperature. Shut the engine off.
2. Remove the timing plug (A, **Figure 56**) from the alternator cover.
3. Connect a portable tachometer following the manufacturer's instructions.
4. Connect a timing light to the No. 1 spark plug wire (rear cylinder) following the manufacturer's instructions.

5. Start the engine, and make sure the idle speed is set to the specification in **Table 5**.

6. Aim the timing light at the timing window. The timing is correct if the timing mark on the rotor (B, **Figure 70**) aligns with the cutout in the timing window (A, **Figure 70**).

7. If the timing is incorrect, refer to the ignition system section in Chapter Nine for probable causes. The ignition timing cannot be adjusted.

8. Shut off the engine, and disconnect the timing light and portable tachometer. Install the timing plug.

Carburetor Synchronization

Synchronizing the carburetors ensures that one cylinder does not try to run faster than the other, reducing power and gas mileage. The only accurate way to synchronize the carburetors is to use a gauge set that measures the intake vacuum of both cylinders at the same time.

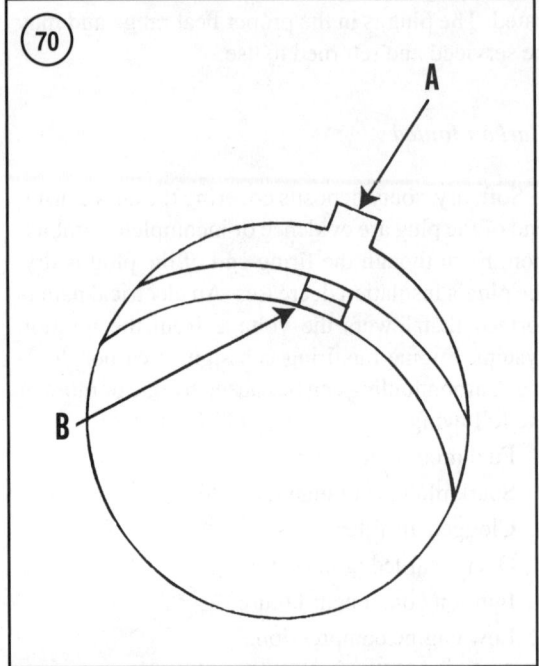

> *NOTE*
> *Before synchronizing the carburetors, check the ignition timing and valve clearance. Both must be within specification.*

1. Start the engine and warm it up to operating temperature.
2. Attach a portable tachometer to the rear cylinder (No.1) spark plug lead, following the manufacturer's instructions.
3. Remove the plug (A, **Figure 71**) from the vacuum fitting on the rear-cylinder inlet pipe, and remove the AIS hose (B, **Figure 71**) from the vacuum fitting on the front-cylinder inlet pipe.
4. Connect the vacuum lines from the vacuum gauge to the fitting on each inlet pipe (**Figure 72**), following the manufacturer's instructions. Make sure to route the vacuum lines to the correct cylinder.
5. Start the engine, and let it run at the idle speed listed in **Table 5**.
6. Check the gauge readings. If the vacuum in the two cylinders differs by 1.33 kPa, (10 mm Hg [0.4 in. Hg]) or less, the carburetors are synchronized.
7. If the difference between the vacuum readings in the two cylinders is greater than 1.33 kPa, (10 mm Hg [0.4 in. Hg]) synchronize the No. 1 carburetor to the No. 2 carburetor by adjusting the synchronizing

screw (**Figure 73**). Turn the screw until the vacuum readings in the two cylinders are equal or as close as possible.

> *NOTE*
> *To gain the utmost in performance and efficiency from the engine, adjust the carburetors so that the gauge readings are as close to each other as possible.*

8. Check the idle speed. If necessary, adjust it as described below.
9. Stop the engine and detach the equipment.
10. Reinstall the plug (A, **Figure 71**) onto the rear cylinder vacuum fitting, and reconnect the AIS hose

LUBRICATION, MAINTENANCE AND TUNE-UP

(B, **Figure 71**) to the fitting on the front cylinder inlet pipe.

Idle Speed Adjustment

Before adjusting the idle speed, clean or replace the air filter, test the cylinder compression and synchronize the carburetors. Idle speed cannot be properly adjusted if these items are not within specification. Refer to the procedures described earlier in this chapter.

1. Attach a portable tachometer to the rear cylinder (No.1) spark plug lead following the manufacturer's instructions.
2. Start the engine and warm it to normal operating temperature.
3. Sit on the seat while the engine is idling and adjust your weight to remove as much weight as possible from the front wheel. Turn the front wheel from side to side without touching the throttle grip. If the engine speed increases when the wheel is turned, the throttle cable may be damaged or incorrectly adjusted. Adjust the throttle cable as described in this chapter.
4. Turn the throttle stop screw (B, **Figure 72**) to set the idle speed to the specification in **Table 5**. Turning the screw *clockwise* increases idle speed. Turning it *counterclockwise* decreases idle speed.
5. Open and close the throttle a few times. Make sure the speed returns to idle. Readjust, if necessary.
6. Shut off the engine and disconnect the portable tachometer.

Table 1 MAINTENANCE SCHEDULE *

Odometer reading	Procedure
Initial 600 miles (1,000 km) or 1 month:	Check the valve clearance; adjust as necessary.
	Check carburetor synchronization; adjust as necessary.
	Change engine oil and filter
	Check clutch operation; adjust the cable free play or replace the cable as necessary.
	Check the front brake operation; replace the pads if necessary.
	Check brake fluid level in the master cylinder; adjust as necessary.
	Check rear brake operation. Adjust the free play or replace the brake shoes as necessary.
	(continued)

Table 1 MAINTENANCE SCHEDULE* (continued)

Odometer reading	Procedure
Initial 600 miles (1,000 km) or 1 month: (continued)	Check the steering bearings for smoothness or excessive play. Adjust as necessary. Check the operation of the sidestand. Lightly lubricate the pivot and contact surfaces with lithium grease. Check the operation of the sidestand switch; replace if necessary. Lubricate all control and meter cables. Check all fasteners. Tighten them as necessary. Replace the final gear oil.
4,400 miles (7,000 km) or 7 months:	Check the valve clearance; adjust as necessary. Check carburetor synchronization; adjust as necessary. Check the condition of the spark plugs; clean and adjust the gap as necessary. Check the crankcase ventilation hose for cracks or damage: replace as necessary. Check the fuel line for cracks or damage; replace as necessary. Check the exhaust system for leaks. Retighten hardware and/or replace gaskets as necessary. Check the engine idle speed and throttle free play; adjust either as necessary. Change engine oil and filter. Check clutch operation; adjust the cable free play or replace the cable as necessary. Check the front brake operation; replace the pads if necessary. Check brake fluid level in the master cylinder; adjust as necessary. Check rear brake operation. Adjust the free play or replace the brake shoes as necessary. Check the operation of the sidestand. Lightly lubricate the pivot and contact surfaces with lithium grease. Check the operation of the sidestand switch; replace if necessary. Lubricate all control and meter cables. Check all fasteners. Tighten them as necessary Check the level of the final gear oil; add oil as necessary. Check the wheels for runout and balance; adjust as necessary. Check the spoke tightness; adjust as necessary. Check tire tread for wear or damage; replace as necessary. Check the wheel bearings for wear or damage. Replace if necessary. Check the operation of the front fork, and check for leaks. Check the operation of the shock absorber, and check for leaks. Lubricate the brake and clutch lever pivot shafts with lithium grease. Lubricate the brake pedal and shift pedal pivot shafts with lithium grease. Clean the air filter; replace if damaged.

(continued)

LUBRICATION, MAINTENANCE AND TUNE-UP

Table 1 MAINTENANCE SCHEDULE* (continued)

Odometer reading	Procedure
8,200 miles (13,000 km) or 13 months:	Perform the 4,400 mile (7,000 km) checks. Replace the spark plugs. Check the swing arm pivot operation. Adjust the play as necessary. Check the steering bearings for smoothness or excessive play. Adjust as necessary.
12,000 miles (19,000 km) or 19 months:	Perform the 4,400 mile (7,000 km) checks. On California models, check the evaporative emission control system for damage. Replace as necessary
15,800 miles (25,000 km) or 25 months:	Perform the 8,200 mile (13,000 km) checks. Repack the swing arm pivot with molybdenum disulfide grease. Repack the steering bearings with lithium grease. Replace the final gear oil.
19,600 miles (31,000 km) or 31 months:	Perform the 4,400 mile (7,000 km) checks. Replace the fuel filter. Check the steering bearings for smoothness or excessive play. Adjust as necessary. On California models, check the evaporative emission control system for damage. Replace as necessary.

*Use this maintenance schedule as a guide for general maintenance and lubrication intervals. Sustained severe or high speed operation under adverse conditions may require more frequent attention to most maintenance items.

Table 2 TIRE SPECIFICATIONS

Model	Front	Rear
XVS650		
Tire type	Tube-type	Tube-type
Size	100/90-19 57S	170/80-15M/C 77S
Manufacturer	Bridgestone L309/Dunlop F24	Bridgestone G546/Dunlop K555
Minimum tread depth	1.0 mm (0.04 in.)	1.0 mm (0.04 in.)
Inflation pressure (cold)[1]		
Up to 90 kg (198 lb.) load[2]	200 kPa (29 psi)	225 kPa (32.6 psi)
90 kg (198 lb.)-maximum load[2]	200 kPa (29 psi)	250 kPa (36.3 psi)
XVS650A		
Tire type	Tube-type	Tube-type
Size	130/90-16 67S	170/80-15M/C 77S
Manufacturer	Bridgestone G703/Dunlop D404F	Bridgestone G702/Dunlop D404
Minimum tread depth	1.0 mm (0.04 in.)	1.0 mm (0.04 in.)
Inflation pressure (cold)[1]		
Up to 90 kg (198 lb.) load[2]	225 kPa (32.6 psi)	225 kPa (32.6 psi)
90 kg (198 lb.)-maximum load[2]	225 kPa (32.6 psi)	250 kPa (36.3 psi)

1. Tire inflation pressure for original equipment tires. Aftermarket tires may require different inflation pressures; refer to the aftermarket manufacturer's specifications.
2. Load equals the total weight of the cargo, rider, passenger, and acessories.

Table 3 BATTERY

Battery type	Maintenance free (sealed)
Capacity	12 V 10 AH
Charge rate	1.0 amp
Terminal voltage at 68° F (20° C)	
Fully-charged	12.8 volts
Requires charging	12.0-12.7 volts
Replace the battery	Less than 12.0 volts

Table 4 RECOMMENDED LUBRICANTS, FLUIDS AND FLUID CAPACITIES

Fuel	Regular unleaded
Octane	86 [(R + M)/2 method] or research octane of 91 or higher
Capacity	16.0 L (4.2 US gal [3.5 Imp. gal])
Reserve amount	3.0 L (0.79 US gal [0.66 Imp. Gal])
Engine oil	
Grade	API SF or SG
Viscosity	
40° F (5° C) or above	SAE 20W40
60° F (15° C) or below	SAE 10W30
Capacity	
Oil change only	2.6 L (2.7 US qt. [2.3 Imp. qt.])
Oil and filter change	2.8 L (3.0 US qt. [2.5 Imp. qt.])
When engine completely dry	3.2 L (3.4 US qt. [2.8 Imp. qt.])
Final gear oil	
Viscosity	SAE 80 hypoid gear oil
Grade	API GL-4 (GL-5 or GL-6 may also be used)
Capacity	190 cc (6.42 US oz. [6.68 Imp. oz.])
Brake fluid	DOT 4
Battery	Maintenance free
Fork oil	
Viscosity	10W fork oil
Capacity per leg	
XVS650	454 cc (15.35 U.S. oz [15.98 Imp. oz.])
XV650A	507 cc (17.14 U.S. oz [17.84 Imp. oz.])
Oil level each leg*	
XVS650	114 mm (4.49 in.)
XVS650A	95 mm (3.74 in.)

*Measured from top of the fully compressed fork tube, without spring.

Table 5 MAINTENANCE AND TUNE-UP SPECIFICATIONS

Recommended spark plug	NGK DPR7EA-9, Denso X22EPR-U9
Spark plug gap	0.8-0.9 mm (0.031-0.035 in.)
Idle speed	1150-1250 rpm
Pilot screw	2 ½ turns out
Valve clearance	
Intake	0.07-0.12 mm (0.0028-0.0047 in.)
Exhaust	0.12-0.17 mm (0.0047-0.0067 in.)
Compression pressure (at sea level)	
Standard	1100 kPa (160 psi)
Minimum	1000 kPa (145 psi)
Maximum	1200 kPa (174 psi)
Ignition timing	12° B.T.D.C. at 1200 rpm

(continued)

LUBRICATION, MAINTENANCE AND TUNE-UP

Table 5 MAINTENANCE AND TUNE-UP SPECIFICATIONS (continued)

Vacuum pressure (at idle)	29.0 kPa (8.7 in. Hg)
Engine oil pressure (hot)	10 kPa (1.5 psi) at 1,200 rpm
Front brake pad wear limit	0.8 mm (0.03 in.)
Rear brake lining wear limit	2 mm (0.08 in.)
Brake pedal height	85 mm (3.35 in.) above top of footpeg
Brake pedal free play	20-30 mm (0.79-1.18 in.)
Throttle cable free play	4-6 mm (0.16-0.24 in.)
Brake lever free play	
at lever end	10-15 mm (0.39-0.59 in.)
Clutch lever free play	
at lever end	10-15 mm (0.39-0.59 in.)
Shift-pedal rod length	188 mm (7.4 in.)
Rim runout	
Radial	
New	1.0 mm (0.04 in)
Limit	2.0 mm (0.08 in.)
Lateral	
New	0.5 mm (0.02 in.)
Limit	2.0 mm (0.08 in.)

Table 6 MAINTENANCE AND TUNE UP TIGHTENING TORQUES

Item	N•m	ft.-lb.	in.-lb.
Brake pedal height adjuster locknut	7	–	62
Camshaft sprocket cover bolt	10	–	88
Final-gear drain bolt	23	17	–
Final-gear oil filler bolt	23	17	–
Fork bottom Allen bolt	30	22	
Front brake caliper mounting bolts	40	29.5	–
Fork bridge lower clamp bolt	23	17	–
Fork bridge upper clamp bolts	23	17	–
Fork cap	23	17	–
Front axle	59	43.5	–
Front axle clamp bolt	20	15	–
Oil drain bolt	43	32	–
Oil filter cover bolt	10	–	88
Oil filter cover plate bolt	10	–	88
Oil gallery bolt	8	–	71
Rear axle nut	97	72	–
Rocker arm shaft bolt	38	28	–
Sidestand nut	56	41	–
Spark plugs	18	13	–
Steering stem head nut	110	81	–
Torque arm nut	20	15	–
Valve adjuster locknut	14	10	–
Valve cover bolt	10	–	88

CHAPTER FOUR

ENGINE TOP END

The V-Star engine is an air-cooled, 4-stroke, single overhead camshaft (SOHC) V-twin. The crankshaft is supported by two main bearings in a vertically split crankcase.

The camshaft in each cylinder is chain-driven from the crankshaft with the chain tension being controlled by an automatic, spring–loaded tensioner. This tensioner bears against the rear run of the cam chain.

The engine and transmission share a common case and the same wet-sump oil supply. The wet-plate clutch is located on the right side of the engine. Refer to Chapter Six for clutch service procedures; refer to Chapter Seven for transmission procedures.

This chapter provides complete service and overhaul procedures for engine top end components. This includes the camshafts, valves, cylinder heads, pistons, piston rings and the cylinder blocks. Refer to Chapter Three for valve adjustment procedures.

Before starting any work, read the service hints in Chapter One.

Tables 1-3 are at the end of this chapter. **Table 1** lists general engine specifications, **Table 2** upper end specifications, and **Table 3** lists upper end torque specifications.

ENGINE PRINCIPLES

Figure 1 explains basic 4-stroke engine operation. This information is helpful when troubleshooting or repairing the engine.

SERVICING ENGINE IN THE FRAME

The following components can be serviced while the engine is in the frame:

1. External gearshift mechanism.
2. Clutch.
3. Carburetors.
4. Starter motor.
5. Alternator and electrical system.
6. Oil pump.

CYLINDER HEAD COVERS

Each cylinder head has two chrome covers. **Figure 2** shows the cylinder head covers for the front cylinder. **Figure 3** shows them for the rear cylinder.

ENGINE TOP END

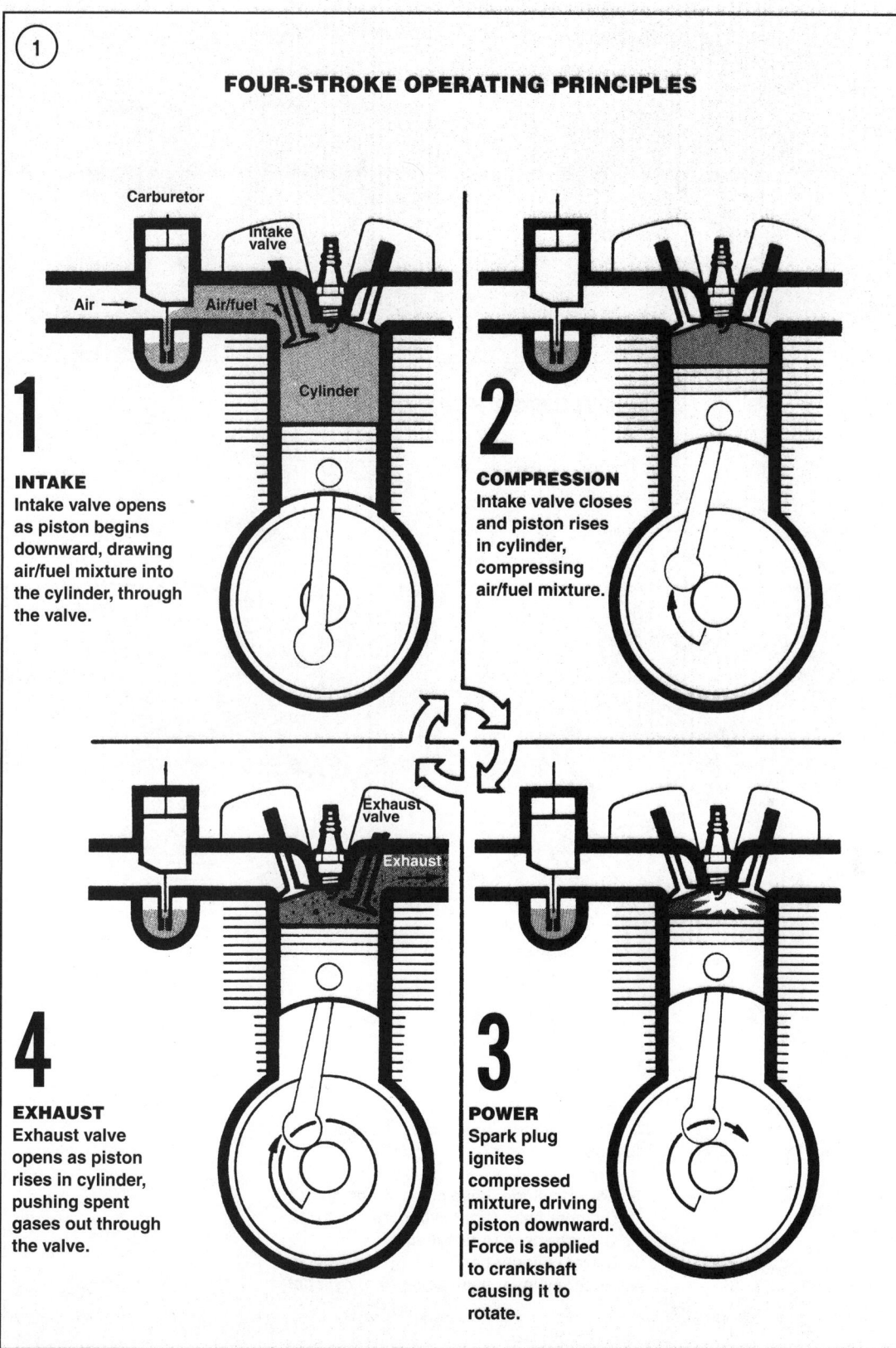

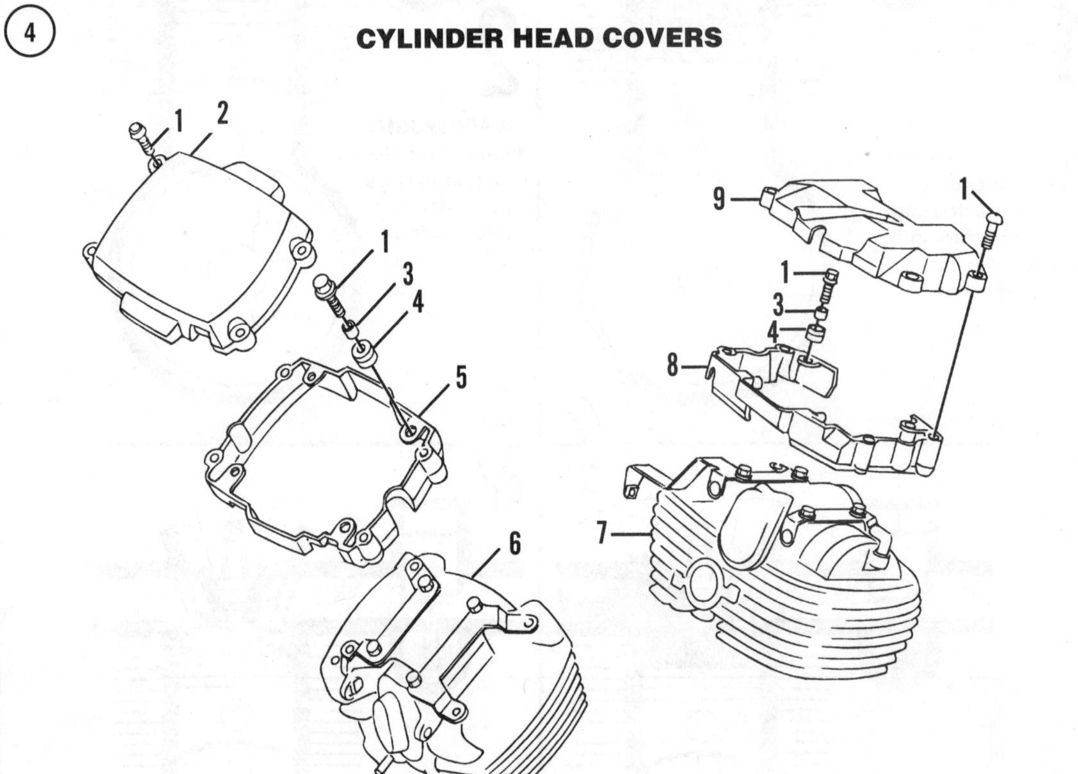

CHAPTER FOUR

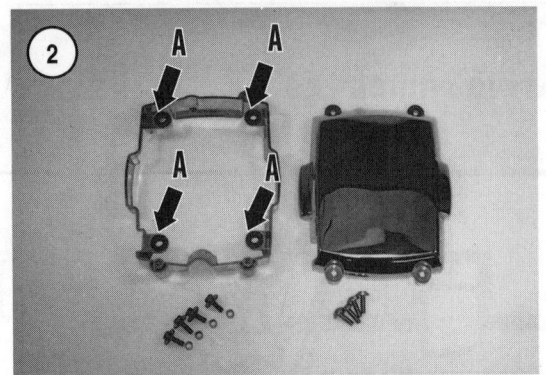

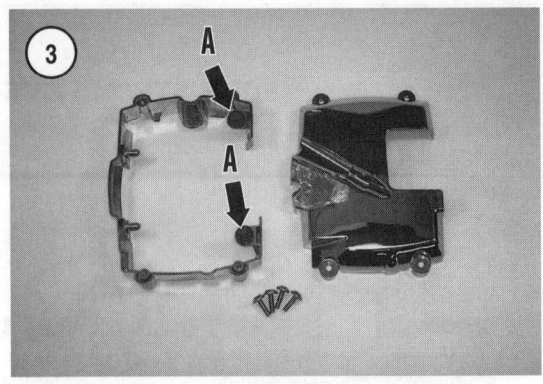

CYLINDER HEAD COVERS

1. Bolt
2. Upper cylinder head cover (front cylinder)
3. Collar
4. Grommet
5. Lower cylinder head cover (front cylinder)
6. Cylinder head (front cylinder)
7. Cylinder head (rear cylinder)
8. Lower cylinder head cover (rear cylinder)
9. Upper cylinder head cover (rear cylinder)

ENGINE TOP END

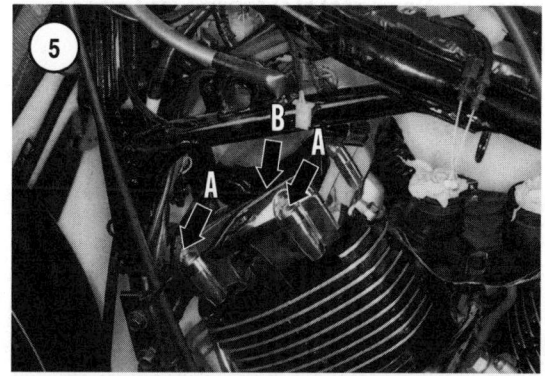

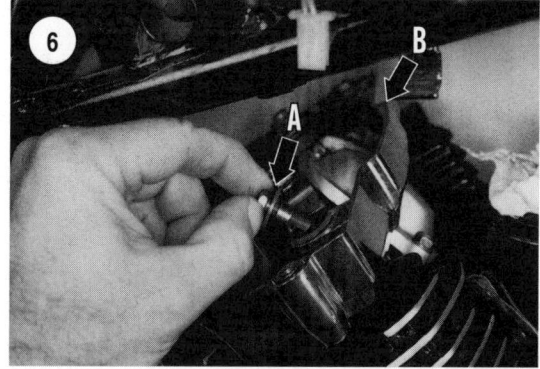

Removal/Installation

Refer to **Figure 4** when servicing the cylinder head covers.

1. Use a suitable jack or jack stands to securely support the bike on level ground.

2. Remove the fuel tank and carburetor assembly as described in Chapter Eight.

3. Remove the cylinder head covers from the front cylinder by performing the following:

  a. Remove the four mounting bolts (A, **Figure 5**) and the upper cover (B, **Figure 5**) from the cylinder head.

  NOTE
  When removing the lower cover from the front cylinder, make sure the spark plug is installed in the head so a collar cannot fall into the spark plug hole.

  b. Remove the four lower cover mounting bolts. A washer and collar should come out with each bolt as shown in A, **Figure 6**.

  c. Remove the lower cover (B, **Figure 6**) from the cylinder head.

4. Remove the cylinder head covers from the rear cylinder by performing the following.

  a. Remove the four upper cover mounting bolts (A, **Figure 7**) and the upper cover (B, **Figure 7**) from the cylinder head.

  b. Remove the two lower cover mounting bolts (A, **Figure 8**). A washer and collar should come out with each bolt as shown in A, **Figure 6**.

  c. Remove the lower cover (B, **Figure 8**) from the cylinder head.

5. Installation is the reverse of removal.

  a. Make sure a grommet is in place in each mounting hole on the lower cylinder head cover. See A, **Figure 2** for the mounts on the front cylinder head cover. See A, **Figure 3** for the mounts in the rear cover.

  b. Fit a collar onto each lower cylinder head cover mounting bolt.

  c. Torque the upper and lower cover bolts to the specification in **Table 3**.

CHAPTER FOUR

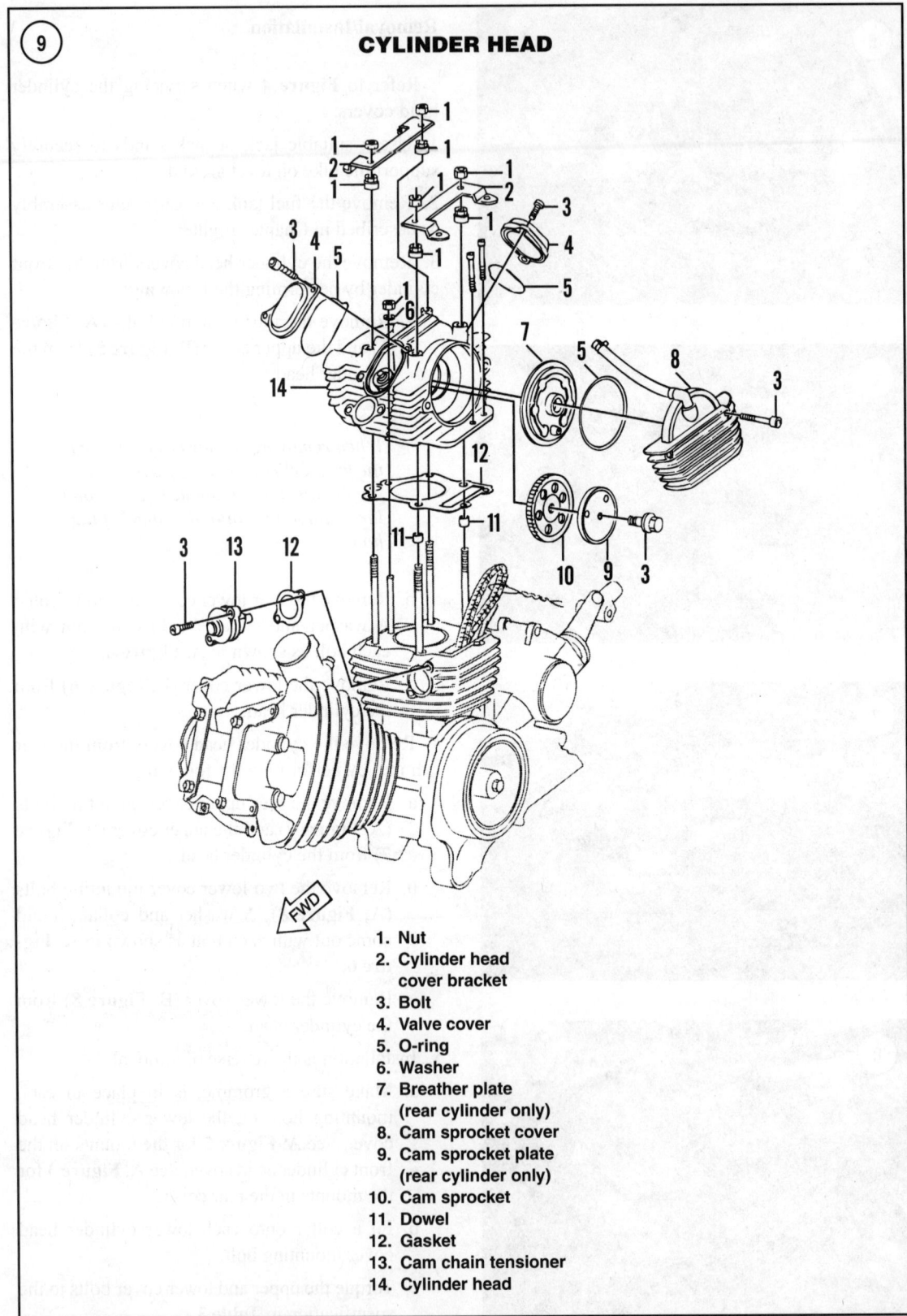

CYLINDER HEAD

1. Nut
2. Cylinder head cover bracket
3. Bolt
4. Valve cover
5. O-ring
6. Washer
7. Breather plate (rear cylinder only)
8. Cam sprocket cover
9. Cam sprocket plate (rear cylinder only)
10. Cam sprocket
11. Dowel
12. Gasket
13. Cam chain tensioner
14. Cylinder head

ENGINE TOP END

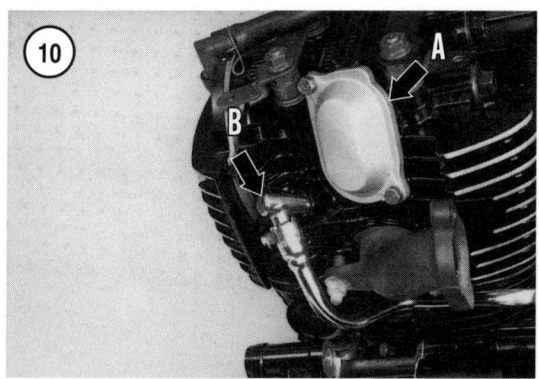

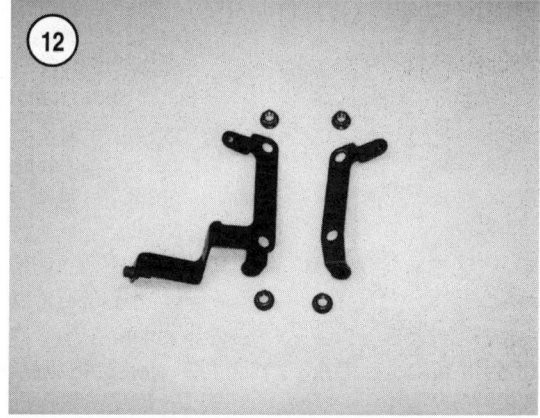

NOTE
Examine the position of the cam timing marks for each cylinder before removing the engine. Make a drawing of each cam sprocket and pointer in order to help correctly time the camshafts during assembly. Note how the timing marks align as described in Steps 8a and 8b.

1. Use a suitable jack or jack stands to securely support the bike on level ground.
2. Remove the engine from the frame as described in Chapter Five.

NOTE
The exhaust valve cover on the front cylinder head is held in place by two silver mounting bolts. Each of the other valve covers is held in place by two green bolts.

3. Remove the intake and exhaust valve covers (A, **Figure 10**) from the cylinder head.
4A. When removing the rear cylinder head, remove the four bracket nuts (**Figure 11**) and lift the two cylinder head cover brackets (**Figure 12**) from the cylinder studs.
4B. When removing the front cylinder head, remove the four bracket nuts (**Figure 13**) and lift the three cylinder head cover brackets (**Figure 14**) from the cylinder studs.
5. Remove the two mounting screws. (A, **Figure 15**) the cam sprocket cover, (B, **Figure 15**) and its O-ring from the cylinder head.

NOTE
A breather plate is not used in the front cylinder head.

CYLINDER HEAD

Removal

The procedure for removing the front and rear cylinder heads are similar. The few differences are noted. If removing both cylinder heads, remove the rear head first.

Refer to **Figure 9** while removing the cylinder heads.

6. When working on the rear cylinder, remove the breather plate (A, **Figure 16**) and its O-ring from the cam-sprocket cover (B, **Figure 16**).

7. Remove both spark plugs. This makes it easier to rotate the engine.

8. Use the alternator rotor bolt to turn the crankshaft clockwise until the cylinder is at TDC on the compression stroke.

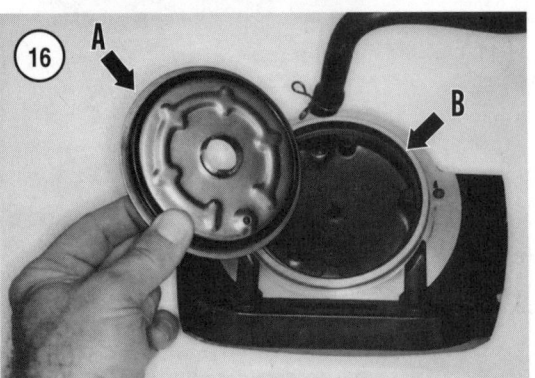

  a. The *rear cylinder* is at TDC on the compression stroke when the T-mark on the rotor aligns with the cutout in the alternator cover (see **Figure 17**) and when the timing mark on the rear cam sprocket aligns with the pointer on the rear cylinder head (see A, **Figure 18**).

> *NOTE*
> *When the front cylinder is set to TDC on the compression stroke, the timing mark on the front cam sprocket may not precisely align with the pointer on the front cylinder head. On some models, the mark could be off by as much as half a tooth.*

  b. The *front cylinder* is at TDC on the compression stroke when the I-mark (A, **Figure 19**) on the rotor aligns with the cutout in the alternator cover (B, **Figure 19**) and when the timing mark on the front cam sprocket aligns with the pointer on the front cylinder head (see A, **Figure 18**).

> *NOTE*
> *A cylinder at TDC on the compression stroke has free play in both rocker arms, which indicates that both valves are closed.*

9. Check that the cylinder is at TDC by pressing each rocker arm. There should be free play at both

ENGINE TOP END

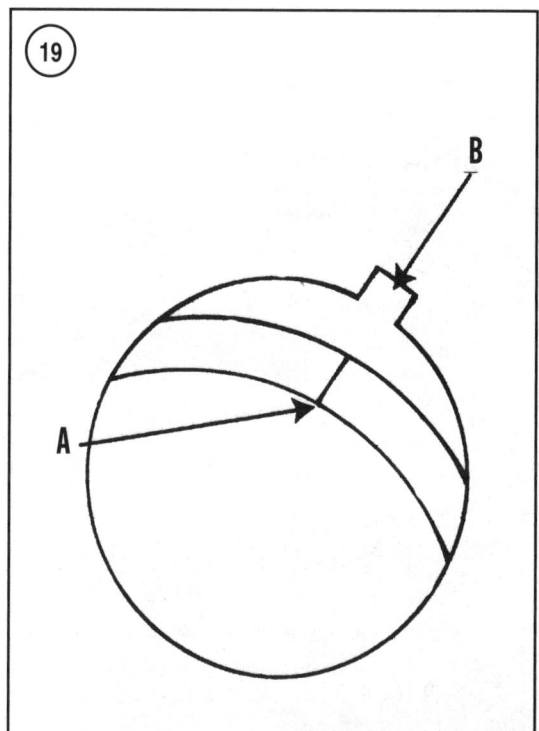

the intake and exhaust rocker arms. If both rocker arms do not have free play, rotate the engine an additional 360° until they do.

10. Remove the chain tensioner center bolt and spring (**Figure 20**) from the tensioner body.

11. Remove the two mounting bolts (A, **Figure 21**), and then remove the chain tensioner (B, **Figure 21**) and gasket from the cylinder.

12. Hold the alternator rotor with a sheave holder, Yamaha part No. YS-01880 (**Figure 22**) or equivalent, and loosen the cam sprocket bolt (A, **Figure 23**). Remove the bolt along with its washer.

NOTE
A cam sprocket plate is not used on the front cylinder.

13. When working on the rear cylinder, remove the cam sprocket plate (B, **Figure 23**) from the cylinder head.

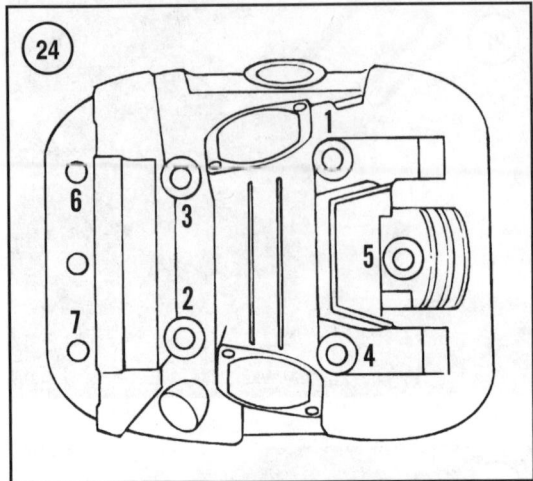

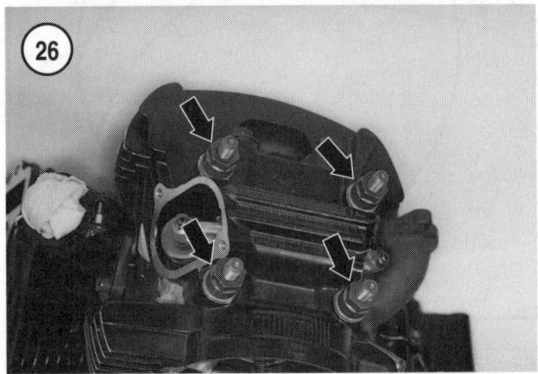

14. Slide the cam sprocket (B, **Figure 18**) from the camshaft and remove the sprocket from the drive chain.

CAUTION
If the crankshaft must be rotated with the cam sprocket removed, pull up on the cam chain and keep it taut so the chain remains meshed with the crankshaft timing sprocket. If the chain is not held taut, the chain may kink and damage the crankcase, the cam chain, and the timing sprocket on the crankshaft.

15. Tie a safety wire around the cam chain and secure the wire to the engine so the chain does not fall into the crankcase.

16. Disconnect the AIS line from its fitting (B, **Figure 10**) on the cylinder head. Remove and discard the gasket.

17. Loosen the cylinder head fasteners a quarter turn at a time, by reversing the tightening sequence shown in **Figure 24**.

18. Once all the fasteners are loose, remove the two bolts (**Figure 25**), remove the four nuts from the cylinder studs (**Figure 26**) and remove the nut next to the spark plug opening (**Figure 27**). Make sure a washer comes out with each nut.

CAUTION
The cooling fins are fragile and easily damaged. Never use a metal hammer to loosen the cylinder head.

19. Loosen the head by tapping around its perimeter with a plastic mallet.

20. Remove the cylinder head by pulling it straight up and off the cylinder studs. Untie the cam chain from the engine while removing the head, and then retie the chain.

21. Remove the two dowels (A, **Figure 28**) from the cylinder studs, and remove the cylinder head gasket (B, **Figure 28**).

ENGINE TOP END

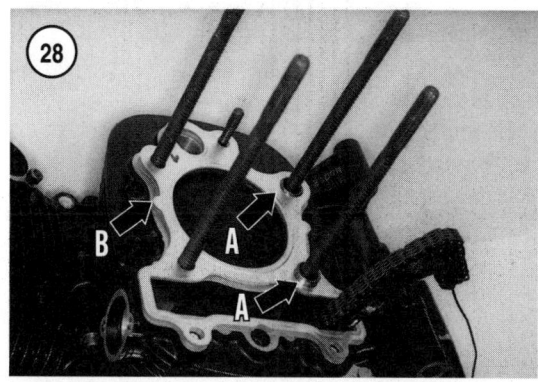

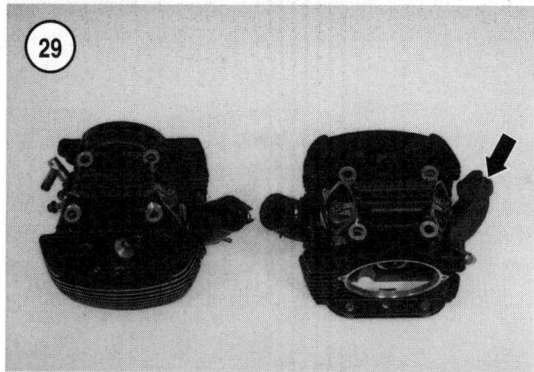

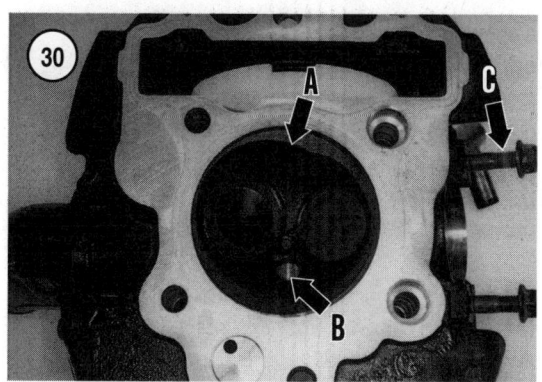

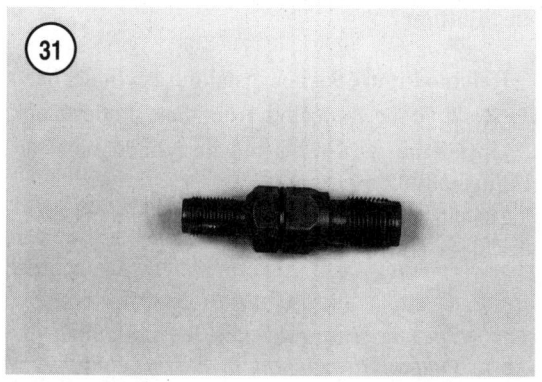

22. Place a clean shop rag in the cam chain tunnel in the cylinder block to keep debris out of the crankcase.

NOTE
An exhaust manifold is not used on the front cylinder.

23. If necessary, remove the two nuts and the exhaust manifold (**Figure 29**) from the rear cylinder. Also remove and discard the exhaust gasket. Use a new gasket during assembly.
24. Inspect the cylinder head as described below.

Inspection

1. Remove all gasket material from the mating surfaces on the cylinder head and cylinder block.

CAUTION
Cleaning the combustion chamber with the valves removed can damage the valve seat surfaces. A damaged or even slightly scratched valve seat causes poor valve sealing.

2. Without removing the valves, remove all carbon deposits from the combustion chambers (A, **Figure 30**). Use a fine wire brush dipped in solvent or make a scraper from hardwood. Take care not to damage the head, valves or spark plug threads.
3. Examine the spark plug threads (B, **Figure 30**) in the cylinder head for damage. If damage is minor or if the threads are dirty or clogged with carbon, use a spark plug thread tap to clean the threads (**Figure 31**). If the damage is excessive, restore the threads by installing a steel thread insert. Purchase thread insert kits at an automotive supply store or have it installed at a Yamaha dealership.
4. After all carbon is removed from the combustion chambers and valve ports, clean the entire head in solvent.
5. Clean away all carbon on the piston crowns. Do not remove the carbon ridge at the top of the cylinder bore.

NOTE
The intake manifolds are not interchangeable. Mark each manifold before removal so it will be reinstalled on the correct cylinder head during assembly.

6. Inspect the intake manifolds (**Figure 32**) for cracks or other damage that would allow unfiltered air into the engine. If necessary, remove the manifolds and discard the O-rings. Reinstall the manifolds with new O-rings. Install each manifold in its original location, and tighten the mounting screws securely.

7. Check for cracks in the combustion chambers and exhaust ports. If necessary, remove the exhaust manifold from the rear cylinder. Replace a cracked head.

8. Inspect the threads on the exhaust pipe mounting studs (C, **Figure 30**). Clean the threads with an appropriate size metric die. Replace a stud if damage is excessive.

9. After thoroughly cleaning the head, place a straightedge across the gasket surface at several points. Measure the warp by inserting a feeler gauge between the straightedge and the cylinder head at each location (**Figure 33**). If warp exceeds the wear limit listed in **Table 1**, replace or resurface the cylinder head. Consult a Yamaha dealership or machine shop experienced in this type of work.

10. Inspect the cam chain tensioner by performing the following:

   a. Visually inspect the cam chain tensioner assembly (**Figure 34**) for wear or damage. If any part is damaged, replace the chain tensioner assembly.

   b. Check the operation of the tensioner by pressing the one-way cam (A, **Figure 35**) and pushing the tensioner rod (B, **Figure 35**) into the body. The rod should move smoothly. If it does not, replace the chain tensioner assembly.

11. Inspect the cam sprocket for wear or missing teeth (**Figure 36**). Replace the sprocket if necessary.

> *NOTE*
> *If a cam sprocket is worn, also inspect the cam chain, chain guides and the timing sprocket on the crankshaft. Refer to Chapter Five.*

12. Check the sliding surfaces of the rear chain guide (the free-standing guide, **Figure 37**) and the bolted chain guide (the front guide) for wear or damage. Use a flashlight to inspect the bolted chain guide. Replace the chain guide(s) as necessary.

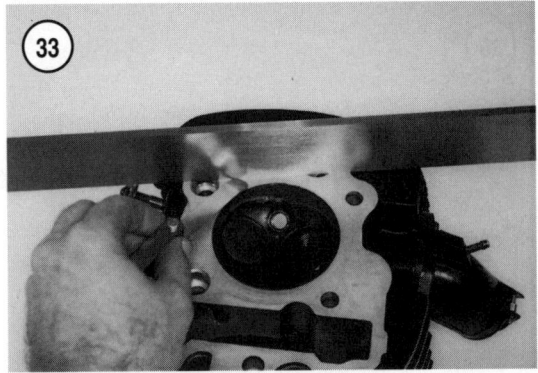

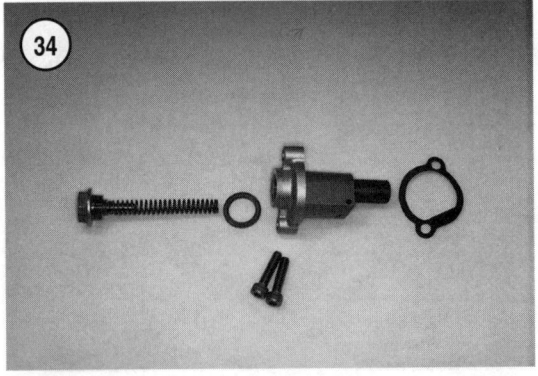

Installation

Refer to **Figure 9** when installing a cylinder head.

1. Remove the shop cloth from the cylinder block.
2. Install the two dowels into the cylinder block (A, **Figure 28**).
3. Install a new cylinder head gasket onto the cylinder block (B, **Figure 28**).

> *NOTE*
> *The rear chain guide (the free-standing guide) is directional. Install this guide*

ENGINE TOP END

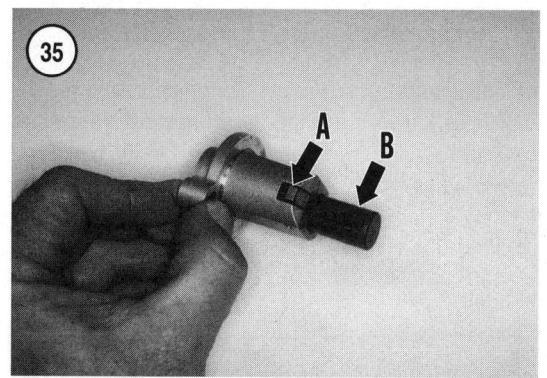

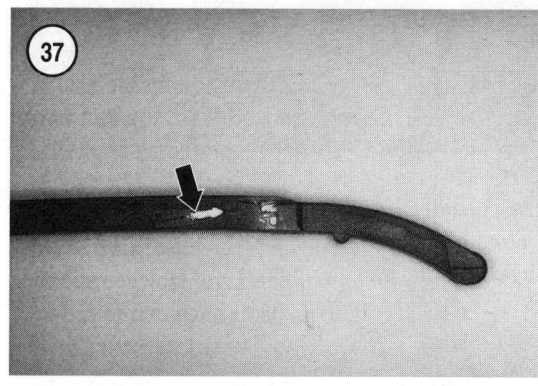

with the arrow (**Figure 37**) pointing up.

4. If removed, install the rear chain guide (the free-standing guide). Lower the chain guide through the cam chain tunnel in the cylinder block and fit the lower end of the guide into the seat in the crankcase. See **Figure 38**. Make sure the chain guide is installed with the arrow (**Figure 37**) pointing up.

5. Lower the cylinder head partially down the cylinder studs, and feed the cam chain and safety wire up through the cam chain tunnel in the cylinder head. Secure the cam chain to the frame.

6. Carefully lower the cylinder head until it is seated on the cylinder block. While lowering the head into place, note the following:

   a. The top of the rear chain guide (the free-standing guide) must be captured by the cavity in the cylinder head. If it is not, remove the cylinder head and reinstall it properly. The rear chain guide cannot be installed once the cylinder head is in place.

   b. Make sure the two locating dowels engage the cylinder head.

7. Pull the cam chain taut and make sure it still properly engages the timing sprocket on the crankshaft.

8. Install and finger-tighten the two cylinder head bolts (**Figure 25**), the four 10 mm cylinder-head nuts (**Figure 26**) and the 8 mm cylinder-head nut (**Figure 27**). Install a washer with each nut.

CAUTION
The cylinder head fasteners must be evenly tightened in sequence as described below. The head could be damaged if it is not tightened properly.

9. Evenly tighten all the cylinder head fasteners in quarter-turn increments. Follow the tightening sequence shown in **Figure 24**. Torque the fasteners to the specifications listed in **Table 3**.

10. Connect the AIS line to its fitting (B, **Figure 10**) on the cylinder head. Install a new gasket between the hose and the fitting, and tighten the clamp bolt securely.

11. If removed, install the locating dowel (**Figure 39**) into the camshaft.

> *CAUTION*
> *When rotating the crankshaft with the cam sprocket removed, pull up on the cam chain and keep it taut so the chain remains meshed with the crankshaft timing sprocket. If the chain is not held taut, the chain may kink and damage the crankcase, the cam chain, and the timing sprocket on the crankshaft.*

12. Use the alternator rotor bolt to turn the crankshaft clockwise until the cylinder is at top dead center on the compression stroke.

   a. The *rear cylinder* is at TDC on the compression stroke when the T-mark on the rotor aligns with the cutout in the alternator cover (**Figure 17**) and when the locator pin on the camshaft aligns (A, **Figure 40**) with the pointer on the cylinder head (B, **Figure 40**).

> *NOTE*
> *When the front cylinder is set to TDC on the compression stroke, the timing mark on the front cam sprocket may not precisely align with the pointer on the front cylinder head. On some models, the mark could be off by as much as half a tooth.*

   b. The *front cylinder* is at TDC on the compression stroke when the I-mark (A, **Figure 19**) on the rotor aligns with the cutout in the alternator cover (B, **Figure 19**) and when the locator pin on the camshaft (A, **Figure 40**) aligns with the pointer on the cylinder head (B, **Figure 40**).

> *NOTE*
> *A cylinder at TDC on the compression stroke has free play in both rocker arms, which indicates that both valves are closed.*

13. Check that the cylinder is at TDC by pressing each rocker arm. There should be free play at both the intake and exhaust rocker arms. If both rocker arms do not have free play, rotate the engine an additional 360° until they do.

14. Install the cam sprocket. Fit the sprocket onto the cam shaft so the camshaft's locating pin (C, **Figure 18**) fits into the cutout in the cam sprocket. Make sure the timing mark on the cam sprocket faces out.

15. Rotate the camshaft to remove any slack from the rear side of the cam chain. Insert a finger into the chain tensioner mounting hole in the cylinder and push the front chain guide (the bolted guide) inward. See **Figure 41**.

> *NOTE*
> *When the front cylinder is set to TDC on the compression stroke, the timing mark on the front cam sprocket may not precisely align with the pointer on the front cylinder head. On some models, the mark could be off by as much as half a tooth.*

ENGINE UPPER END

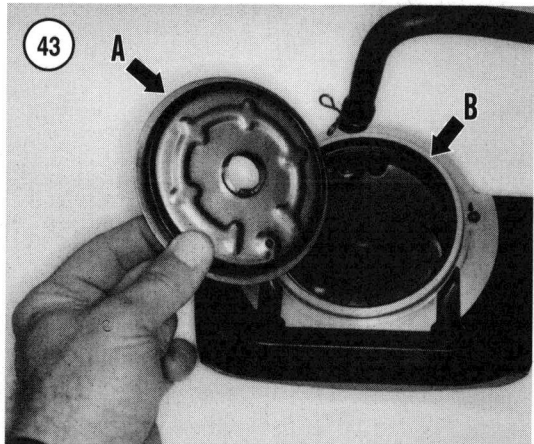

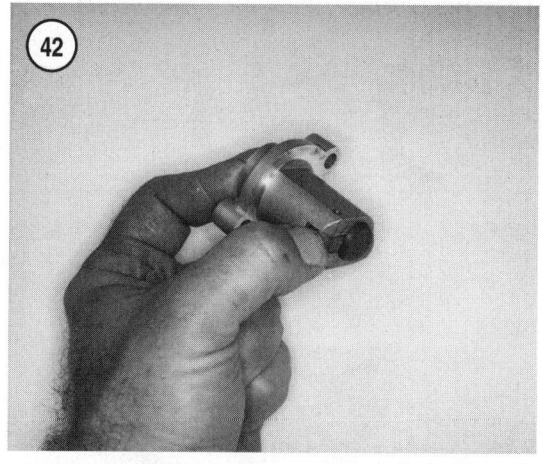

16. While pushing on the chain guide note the position of the timing mark on the cam sprocket. It should align with the pointer on the cylinder head as shown in A, **Figure 18**. If the timing marks do not align, remove the sprocket, use a screwdriver to walk the cam chain one way or the other and reinstall the cam sprocket. Repeat this as necessary until the timing mark on the cam sprocket aligns with the pointer on the cylinder head (A, **Figure 18**) while pressing the front chain guide inward.

17. Install the cam chain tensioner and new gasket by performing the following:

   a. If necessary, press the one-way cam on the chain tensioner and push the tensioner rod all the way into the body as shown in **Figure 42**.

   b. Slide a new gasket onto the tensioner body and install the chain tensioner (B, **Figure 21**) into the cylinder. Torque the cam-chain-tensioner mounting bolts (A, **Figure 21**) to the specification in **Table 3**.

   c. Install the chain tensioner center bolt, washer and spring (**Figure 20**). Torque the cap bolt to the specification in **Table 3**.

NOTE
A cam sprocket plate is not used on the front cylinder.

18. When working on the rear cylinder, fit the cam sprocket plate (B, **Figure 23**) onto the camshaft. Make sure the dimple in the sprocket plate engages the timing mark on the cam sprocket.

19. Install the cam sprocket bolt (A, **Figure 23**) and washer.

20. Hold the alternator rotor with a sheave holder (**Figure 22**, Yamaha part No YS-01880) or equivalent, and tighten the cam sprocket bolt (A, **Figure 23**). Torque the bolt to the specification in **Table 3**.

NOTE
A breather plate is not used in the front cylinder head.

21. When working on the rear cylinder, fit a new O-ring onto the breather plate (A, **Figure 43**) and set the breather plate in place in the cam sprocket cover (B, **Figure 43**).

22. Use a new O-ring and set the cam sprocket cover (B, **Figure 44**) onto the cylinder head. Install the two mounting bolts (A, **Figure 44**) and torque the bolts to the specification in **Table 3**.

23A. When installing the rear cylinder head, place the two cylinder head cover brackets (**Figure 45**) on the cylinder studs, and secure the brackets in place

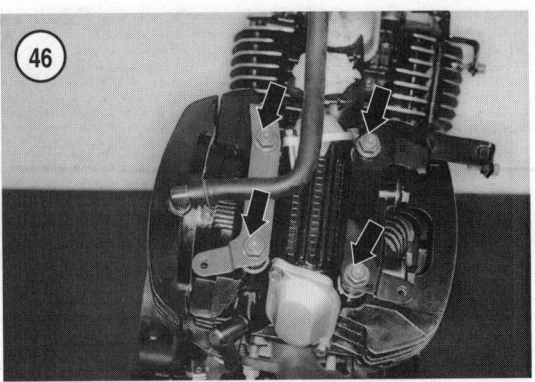

with the four bracket nuts (**Figure 46**). Torque the cylinder-head-cover bracket nuts to the specification in **Table 3**.

23B. When installing the front cylinder head, place the three cylinder head cover brackets (**Figure 47**) on the cylinder studs and secure the brackets in place with the four bracket nuts (**Figure 48**). Torque the cylinder-head-cover bracket nuts to the specification in **Table 3**.

NOTE
The exhaust valve cover on the front cylinder is secured in place by two silver bolts. The remaining valve covers each use two green bolts. Use the proper bolts when installing a valve cover.

24. Install the valve covers (A, **Figure 10**) onto the cylinder head.
25. Install the spark plugs.
26. Install the engine into the frame as described in Chapter Five.

ROCKER ARMS

Removal

Mark the rocker arms and shafts (intake or exhaust) during removal, so they can be reinstalled in their original locations.

Refer to **Figure 49** when servicing the rocker arms.

1. Remove the cylinder head as described in this chapter.

ENGINE TOP END

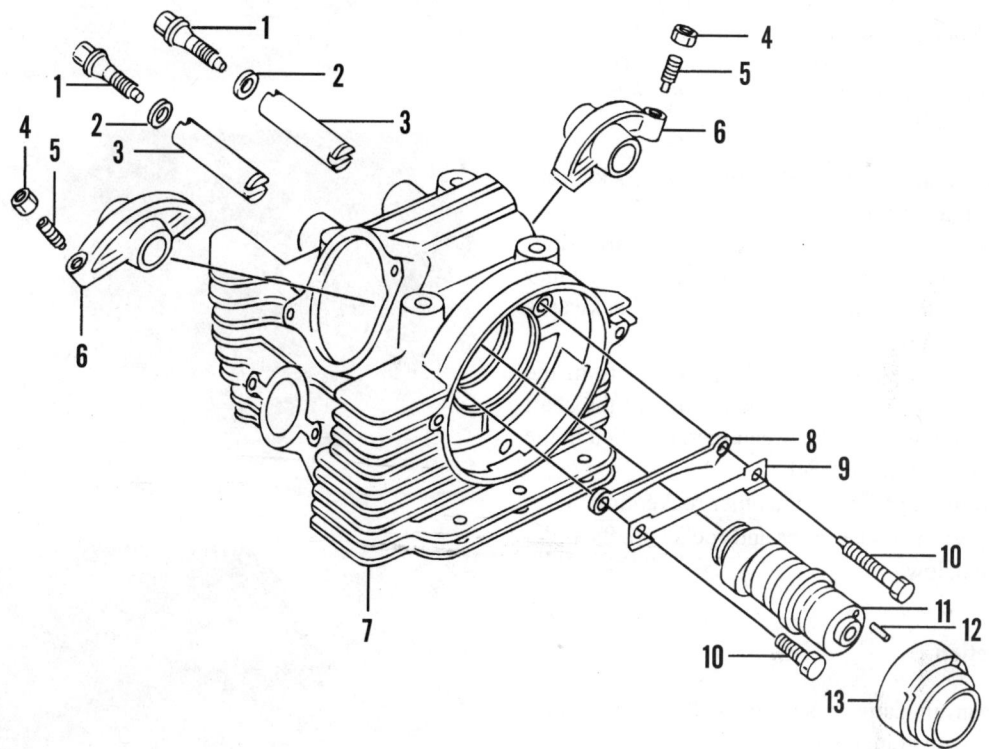

CAMSHAFT AND ROCKER ARMS

1. Rocker arm shaft bolt
2. Washer
3. Rocker arm shaft
4. Valve adjuster locknut
5. Valve adjuster
6. Rocker arm
7. Cylinder head
8. Bushing retainer
9. Lockplate
10. Camshaft bushing retainer bolt
11. Camshaft
12. Locating pin
13. Camshaft bushing

2. Remove each rocker arm shaft bolt (**Figure 50**) from the cylinder head.

NOTE
Yamaha recommends using a slide hammer to remove the rocker arm shafts. However, use an 8 mm bolt with a 1.25 mm thread pitch if a slide hammer is not available. This method is described below. Note that a slide hammer may be required to remove the rocker arm shafts from some engines, particularly those with heat damage.

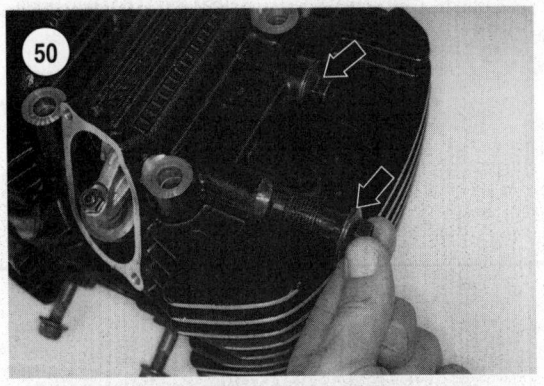

3. Thread an 8 — 1.25 mm bolt into a rocker arm shaft (**Figure 51**).
4. Pull the bolt and remove the rocker arm shaft from the cylinder head. Keep the bolt threaded into the shaft so the shaft will not be installed backwards during assembly.
5. Remove the rocker arm (**Figure 52**) from the cylinder head. Label the rocker arm and the shaft (intake or exhaust) so they can be reinstalled in the same location in the head.
6. Repeat Steps 3-5 for the other rocker arm.
7. Inspect the rocker arms and rocker shafts as described below.

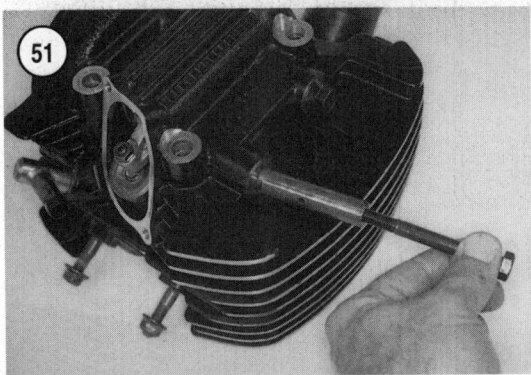

Inspection

1. Clean all parts in solvent and dry them thoroughly with compressed air.
2. Inspect the rocker arm pad (A, **Figure 53**) where it contacts the cam lobe. Replace the rocker arm if the pad surface is scratched, unevenly worn or shows signs of blue discoloration. If the rocker arm pad is worn or damaged, also inspect the cam lobe for scoring, chipping or flat spots.
3. Inspect the valve adjuster (B, **Figure 53**) where it contacts the valve stem. Replace the adjuster if it is scratched, pitted, or if shows signs of blue discoloration.
4. Measure the diameter of the rocker arm bore (C, **Figure 53**). Replace the rocker arm if the bore is outside the specification listed in **Table 2**.
5. Measure the diameter of the rocker arm shaft (**Figure 54**). Replace the rocker arm shaft if its diameter is outside the specification listed in **Table 2**.
6. Calculate the rocker-arm-to-shaft clearance by subtracting the shaft diameter from the

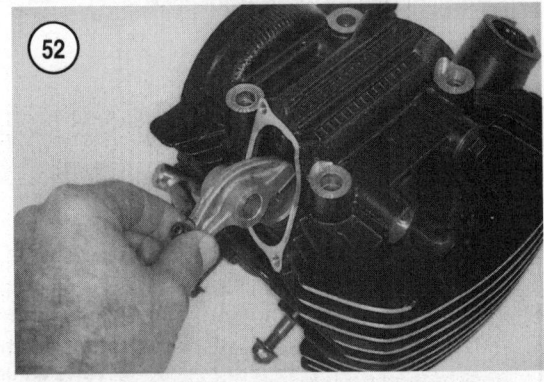

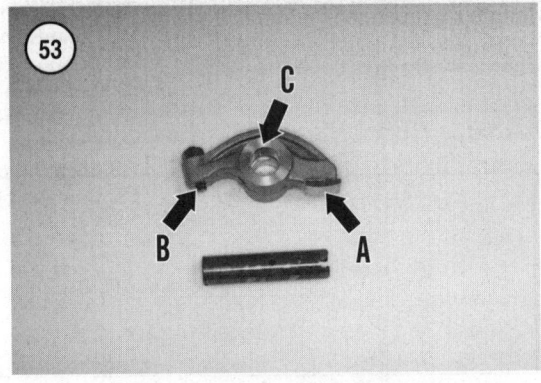

ENGINE TOP END

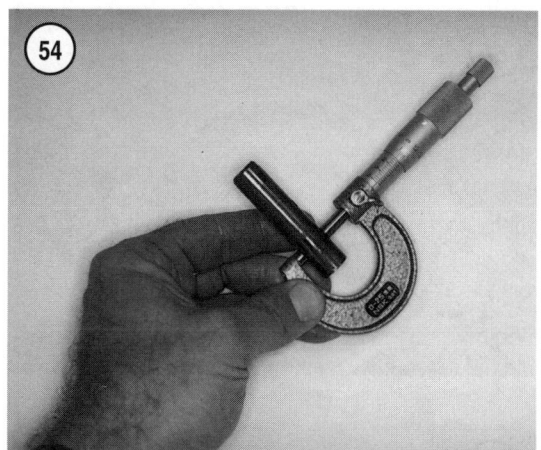

rocker-arm-bore diameter. If the clearance is outside the range specified in **Table 2**, replace the defective part.

7. Inspect the threads of the rocker arm shaft bolt (**Figure 55**) for stretching or other signs of damage. Blow the passages clear with compressed air. Replace the bolt as necessary.

Installation

NOTE
Install each rocker arm with its original rocker shaft, and install them in their original locations (intake or exhaust side) in the cylinder head.

1. Apply engine oil to the rocker arm bore and the rocker shaft.

CAUTION
The rocker shaft is directional. The non-threaded end of the shaft is the inboard side. The slot on the inboard side of the rocker shaft must be parallel to the cooling fins. The rocker shaft will not be properly seated in the head if the inboard slot is not properly aligned.

2. Position the rocker arm into its original place in the cylinder head (**Figure 52**). Rotate the rocker shaft so the slot on the inboard side of the shaft parallels the cooling fins on the head (**Figure 51**), and install the shaft through the rocker arm bore.
3. If an 8 — 1.25 mm bolt was used to install the shaft, the bolt must be removed.
4. Slide a new washer on the rocker arm shaft bolt, and install the bolt (**Figure 50**) into the cylinder head. Torque the bolt to the specification in **Table 3**.
5. Repeat Steps 1-3 for the other rocker arm.
6. Reinstall the cylinder head as described in this chapter.

CAMSHAFT

Removal

Refer to **Figure 49** when servicing the camshaft.
1. Remove the cylinder head and the rocker arms as described in this chapter.
2. Use a punch to bend the lock tab (A, **Figure 56**) away from the flat on each camshaft bushing retainer bolt (B, **Figure 56**).
3. Remove the two camshaft bushing retainer bolts and the lockplate (C, **Figure 56**) from the cylinder head.
4. Remove the bushing retainer (**Figure 57**) from the cylinder head.

CHAPTER FOUR

5. Remove the locating pin (A, **Figure 58**) from the camshaft.
6. Thread the 10 mm camshaft sprocket bolt into the camshaft, and pull the camshaft assembly from the cylinder head (**Figure 59**).
7. Remove the camshaft bushing from the camshaft.

Inspection

1. Clean all parts in solvent, and blow them dry with compressed air.
2. Visually inspect the camshaft bearing journals (A, **Figure 60**) for wear and scoring. Replace if necessary.
3. Visually inspect the inside diameter and the outside diameter of the camshaft bushing (B, **Figure 60**). Replace it if necessary. If the camshaft bushing is excessively worn, inspect the bushing bore in the cylinder head. The surface should be smooth with no visible marks. Replace the cylinder head if this surface is worn.
4. Check the camshaft lobes (C, **Figure 60**) for wear. The lobes should not be scored, and the edges should be square. Remove any slight damage with silicon carbide oil stone. Use No. 100-120 grit initially, and then polish the lobe with No. 280-320 grit.
5. Even if the cam lobe surface is satisfactory, measure the cam lobe height (**Figure 61**) and width (**Figure 62**) with a micrometer. Replace the camshaft if a lobe is worn beyond the service limit in **Table 2**.
6. Measure the camshaft runout with a dial indicator and V-blocks. Replace the camshaft if the runout exceeds the service limit in **Table 2**.
7. Measure the camshaft journal outside diameter (**Figure 63**) and the inside diameter of the camshaft bushing (B, **Figure 60**). Calculate the camshaft-to-bushing clearance by subtracting the camshaft outside diameter from the bushing inside diameter. If the clearance exceeds the specification in **Table 2**, replace the worn camshaft and/or bushing.

Installation

NOTE
The camshafts in this engine are not interchangeable. Each camshaft is

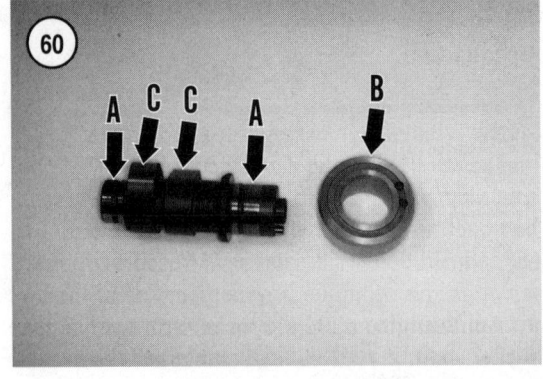

ENGINE TOP END

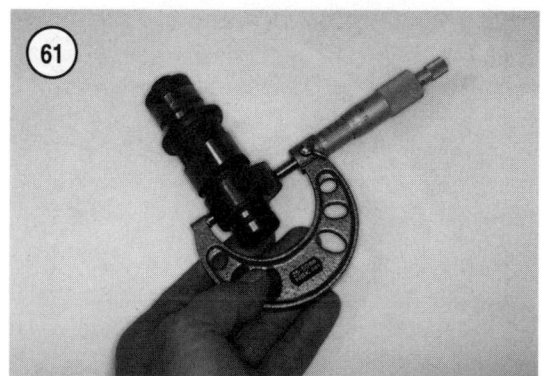

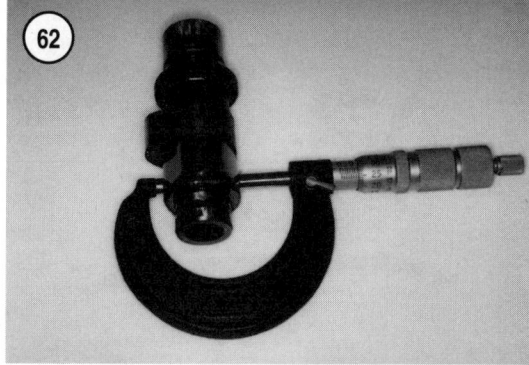

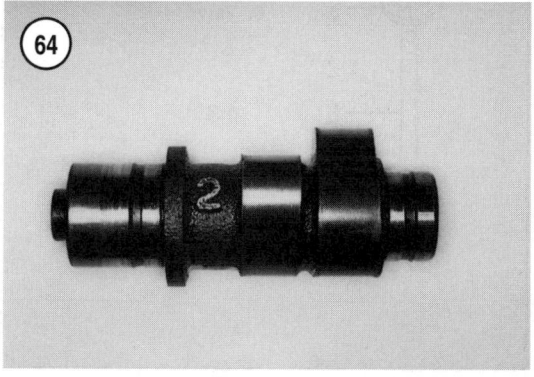

*identified by a No. 1 or a No. 2 cast into it (**Figure 64**). The No. 1 camshaft goes in the rear cylinder head; the No. 2 camshaft in the front. Make sure each camshaft is installed in the correct cylinder head.*

1. Apply molybdenum disulfide oil to the bearing surfaces of the camshaft, and install the camshaft into the cylinder head.
2. Install the locating pin (A, **Figure 58**) into the camshaft, and rotate the camshaft so the locating pin aligns with the pointer (B, **Figure 58**) on the top of the cylinder head.
3. Apply molybdenum disulfide oil to the inside of the camshaft bushing, and install the bushing (C, **Figure 58**) onto the camshaft. Position the bushing so the cutout faces up.
4. Install the bushing retainer into the cutout in the bushing. Rotate the bushing as necessary so the retainer's mounting holes align with the holes in the cylinder head. See **Figure 57**.
5. Install a new lockplate (C, **Figure 56**) over the bushing retainer, and install the two camshaft bushing retainer bolts (B, **Figure 56**). Torque the bolts to the specification in **Table 3**.
6. Lock each bolt in place, by bending the lock tab (A, **Figure 56**) against a bolt flat.
7. Reinstall the rocker arms as described in this chapter.

CAM CHAIN AND CHAIN GUIDES

Removal/Installation

1. Remove the cylinder head as described in this chapter.
2. Remove the rear chain guide (the free-standing guide) by lifting it from its seat in the crankcase and pulling it from the cam chain tunnel in the cylinder.
3A. When servicing the rear cylinder, remove the alternator rotor as described in Chapter Five.
3B. When servicing the front cylinder, remove the primary drive gear as described in Chapter Five.
4. Remove the two mounting bolts (rear cylinder: **Figure 65**, front cylinder: **Figure 66**) and the front chain guide.
5. Disengage the cam chain from the timing sprocket on the crankshaft, and remove the cam chain.

CHAPTER FOUR

6. Inspect the cam chain and chain guides as described in this chapter.
7. Installation is the reverse of the removal. Note the following:
   a. Torque the front cam chain guide bolts to the specification in **Table 3**.
   b. The rear chain guide (the free-standing guide) is directional. Install the rear guide so its arrow (**Figure 37**) points up.
   c. Make sure the rear chain guide bottoms in its seat (**Figure 38**) in the crankcase.

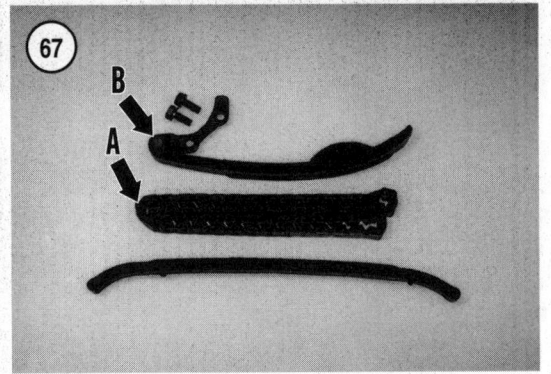

Inspection

1. Inspect the cam chain (A, **Figure 67**) for wear, stretching or link damage. Replace the cam chain if necessary.
2. Inspect the sliding surface of each chain guide. Replace the guide if it is damaged or excessively worn.
3. Inspect the pivot point (B, **Figure 67**) on the front chain guide (the bolted guide). Make sure the pivot moves freely. Replace the chain guide if necessary.

VALVES AND VALVE COMPONENTS

Complete valve service requires a number of special tools. The following procedures describe how to check for valve component wear and to determine what type of service is required. Use a valve spring compressor to remove and install the valves.

Valve Removal

Refer to **Figure 68** for this procedure.

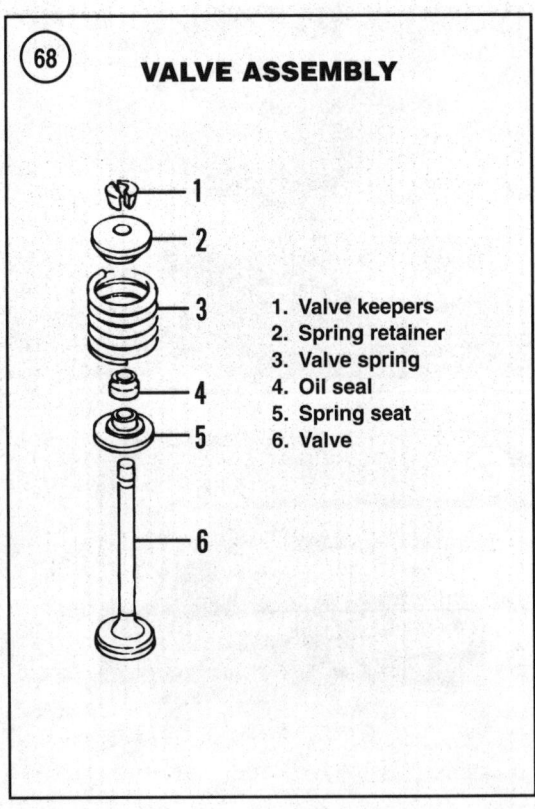

VALVE ASSEMBLY

1. Valve keepers
2. Spring retainer
3. Valve spring
4. Oil seal
5. Spring seat
6. Valve

ENGINE TOP END

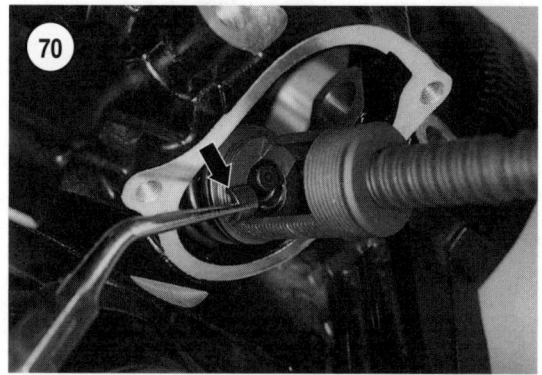

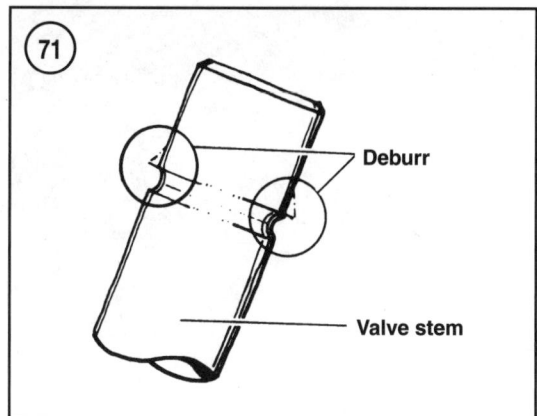

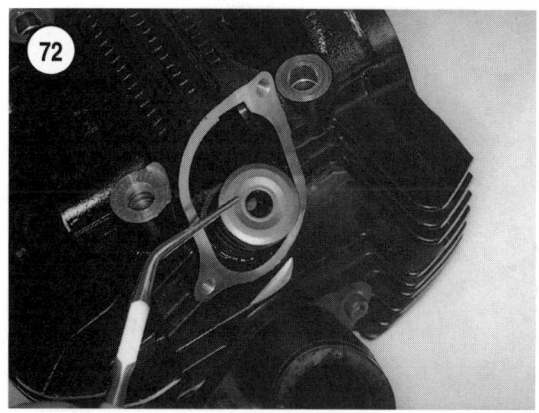

NOTE
A bore protector can be made from a plastic 35-mm film canister. Cut out the bottom of the canister and part of its side. Cut away enough of the canister so it slides between the valve assembly and the side of the bore. The plastic canister will prevent the valve spring compressor from damaging the bore during valve spring removal and installation.

3. Fit a bore protector between the valve assembly and the bore.
4. Install a valve spring compressor (Yamaha part No. YM-04019) squarely over the valve retainer. Make sure the opposite end of the compressor is against the valve head. See **Figure 69**.

CAUTION
To avoid loss of spring tension, do not compress the spring any more than necessary to remove the valve keepers.

5. Tighten the compressor until the valve keepers separate from the valve stem. Remove both valve keepers with a magnet, tweezers or needlenose pliers (**Figure 70**).
6. Carefully remove the valve spring compressor.

CAUTION
*Remove any burrs (**Figure 71**) from the valve stem grooves before removing the valve. Burrs on the valve stem damage the valve guide when the stem passes through it.*

7. Remove the spring retainer (**Figure 72**).

CAUTION
Keep the component parts of each particular valve assembly together. Do not mix components from different valve assemblies. Excessive wear may result.

1. Remove the cylinder head as described in this chapter.
2. Remove the rocker arms and camshaft as described in this chapter.

8. Remove the valve spring (**Figure 73**).

9. Remove the valve seal (**Figure 74**) from the valve guide. Discard the valve seal.

10. Remove the spring seat (**Figure 75**).

11. Remove the valve (**Figure 76**) from the cylinder head while rotating it slightly.

CAUTION
*All the components of each valve assembly must be kept together (**Figure 77**). Place each set in a divided carton or into separate small boxes. Do not mix components from different valve assemblies; excessive wear may result.*

12. Repeat Steps 3-11 for the remaining valve assembly. Keep the parts from each valve assembly separate.

Valve Inspection

NOTE
Whenever a valve needs replacing also replace its valve guide. Do not install a new valve into an old valve guide. Excessive wear results.

1. Clean the valve in solvent. Do not gouge or damage the valve-seating surface.

2. Inspect the contact surface of each valve for burning (**Figure 78**). Remove minor roughness or pitting by lapping the valve as described in this chapter. Excessive unevenness indicates that the valve is not serviceable. Replace the valve and the valve guide.

3. Inspect the valve stem for wear and roughness. Measure the runout as shown in **Figure 79**. Replace

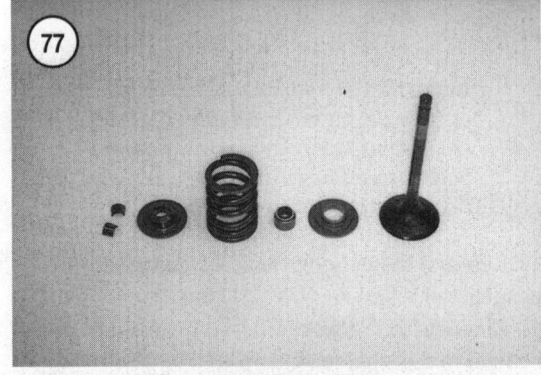

ENGINE TOP END

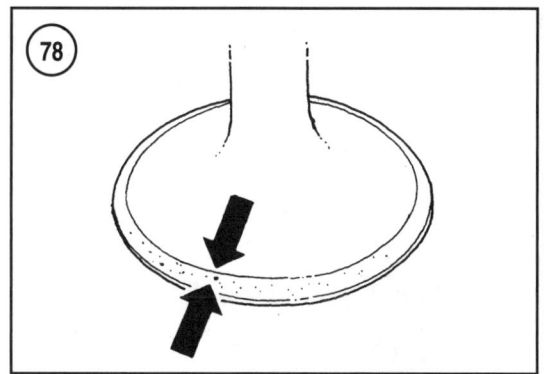

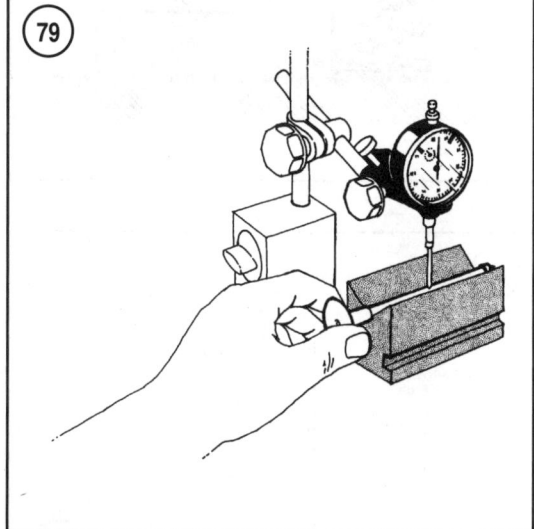

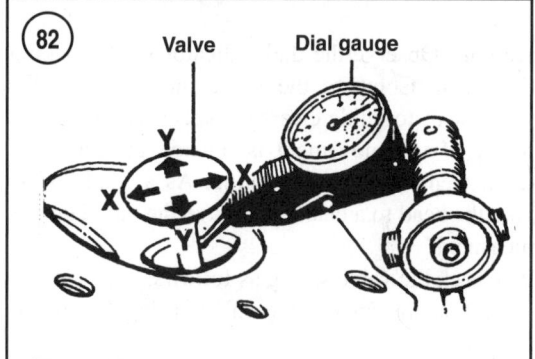

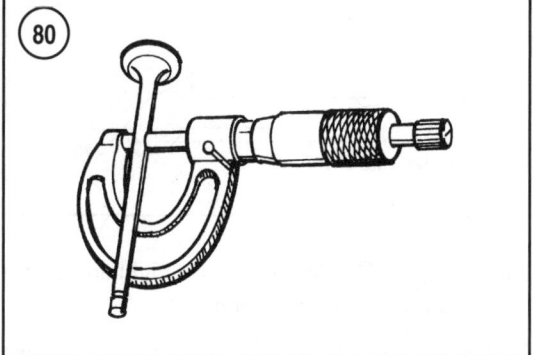

the valve and valve guide if runout exceeds the wear limit in **Table 2**.

4. Measure the diameter of the valve stem using a micrometer (**Figure 80**). Replace the valve and valve guide if the diameter of the valve stem is worn past the wear limit listed in **Table 2**.

5. Remove all carbon and varnish from the valve guides with a stiff spiral wire brush.

6. Measure the inside diameter of the valve guide with a small hole gauge (**Figure 81**), and then measure the gauge with a micrometer. Measure at the top, middle, and bottom of the guide. Replace the valve guide if any measurement exceeds the wear limit listed in **Table 2**.

7. Subtract the valve stem diameter (Step 4) from the valve guide inside diameter (Step 6). The difference is the valve stem-to-guide clearance. If the clearance is outside the range specified in **Table 2**, replace the valve and valve guide.

NOTE
If measuring tools to calculate valve stem-to guide clearance are not available, perform Step 8. However, measure the valve stem diameter before performing this test. This test is only accurate if the valve stem is within specification.

8. Insert the valve into its guide, and attach a dial indicator as shown in **Figure 82**. Hold the valve slightly off its seat and rock it sideways in two di-

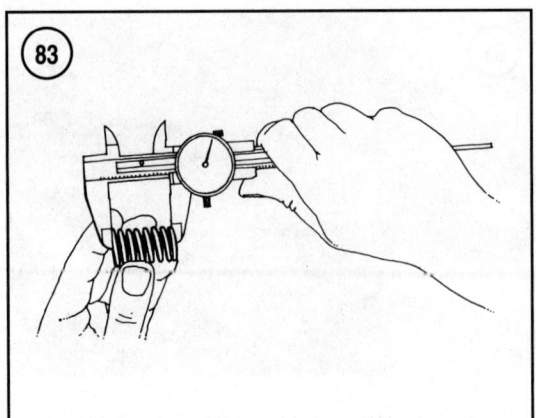

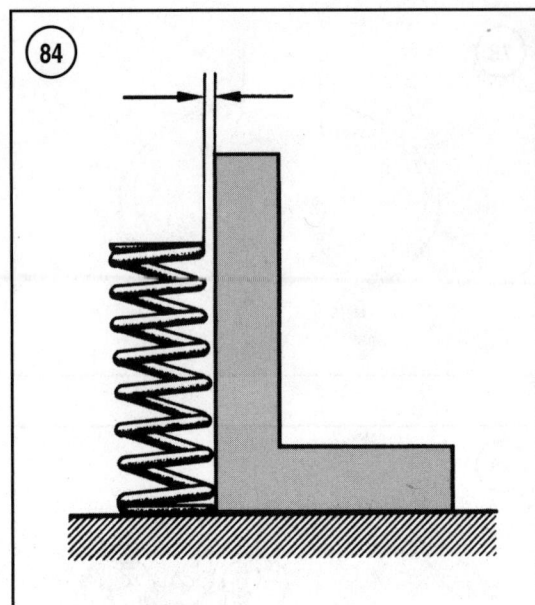

rections. Observe the dial indicator while rocking the valve. Compare the valve movement to the valve stem-to-guide clearance specification in **Table 2**. If the movement is outside the specified range, replace the valve guide. As a final check, take the head to a dealer and have the valve guides measured.

9. Check the valve spring as follows.
   a. Visually inspect the valve spring for distortion.
   b. Measure each valve spring free length with a vernier caliper (**Figure 83**). Replace the spring if the free length is not within the specification in **Table 2**.
   c. Use a square to measure the tilt of each spring (**Figure 84**). Replace the spring if the tilt is not within the specification in **Table 2**.

10. Measure the valve margin thickness (**Figure 85**) with a vernier caliper. Replace the valve and valve guide if the margin thickness is outside the range specified in **Table 2**.

11. Check the spring seat, spring retainer and valve keepers for cracks or other damage.

12. Inspect each valve seat (**Figure 86**) in the cylinder head. If a seat is burned or worn, recondition it. This should be performed by the dealership or local machine shop. Seats and valves in near-perfect condition can be reconditioned by lapping with fine carborendum paste. However, lapping is inferior to precision grinding.

Valve Installation

1. Clean the end of the valve guide.
2. Apply molybdenum disulfide oil to a new valve seal, and install the seal over the end of the valve

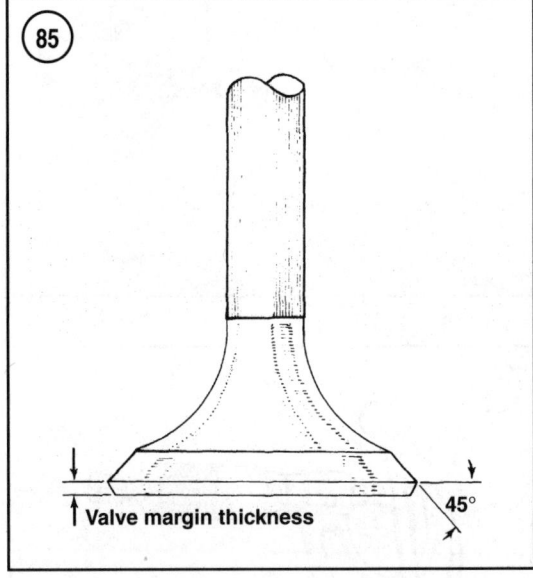

guide (**Figure 74**). Push the seal straight down onto the valve guide until the seal bottoms.

3. Apply molybdenum disulfide oil to the valve stem. Install the valve partially into the guide (**Figure 76**). Slowly turn the valve as it enters the seal, and continue turning the valve until it is completely installed.

4. Install the spring seat (**Figure 75**) over the valve seal. Make sure the spring seat is completely seated in the cylinder head.

ENGINE TOP END 119

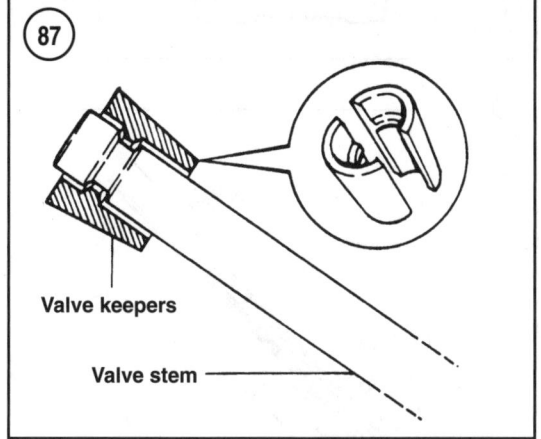

5. Install the valve spring (**Figure 73**) so the end with the closer wound coils faces in toward the cylinder head.
6. Install the spring retainer (**Figure 72**) on top of the spring.
7. Fit a bore protector between the valve assembly and the bore.
8. Install a valve spring compressor squarely over the valve retainer. Make sure the opposite end of the compressor is against the valve head (**Figure 69**).

CAUTION
To avoid loss of spring tension, do not compress the springs any more than necessary to install the valve keepers.

9. Compress the valve springs with a valve spring compressor, and install the valve keepers (**Figure 87**).
10. When both valve keepers are seated around the valve stem, slowly release the compressor. Remove the compressor, and inspect the keepers (**Figure 88**). Tap the end of the valve stem with a soft-faced mallet to ensure that the keepers are properly seated.
11. Repeat Steps 1-10 for the remaining valve.
12. Install the rocker arms and camshaft as described in this chapter.
13. Install the cylinder head as described in this chapter.
14. Adjust the valve clearance as described in Chapter Three.

Valve Guide Replacement

When valve stem-to-guide clearance is excessive, replace the valve guides. This job requires a number of special tools and should be entrusted to a Yamaha dealership or other qualified specialist. If a valve guide is replaced, also replace its respective valve.

The following procedure is provided if choosing to perform this task yourself. The required special tools along with the Yamaha part numbers are listed below.

  a. 7 mm (0.28 in.) Valve guide remover (YM-01225-A).
  b. 7 mm (0.28 in.) Valve guide installer (YM-04017).
  c. 7 mm (0.28 in.) Valve guide reamer (YM-0127).

NOTE
The valve guides have a slight interference fit. Cooling the guides and heating the head makes installation easier.

1. Install new circlips onto the new valve guides, and place the valve guides in a freezer.
2. Remove the intake manifold and O-ring from the cylinder head. Discard the O-ring.

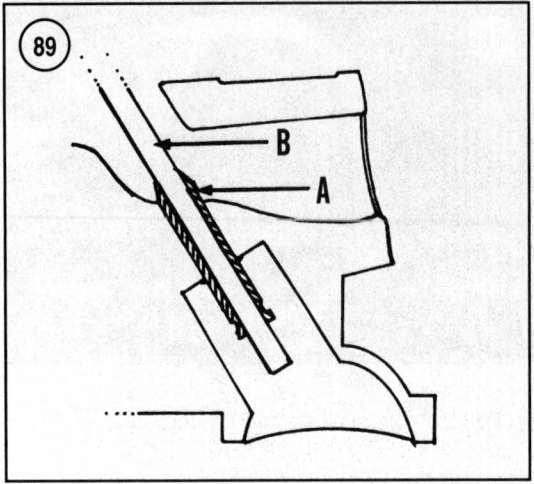

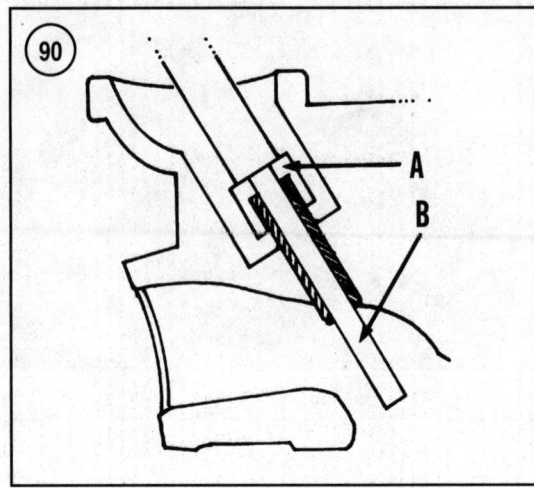

CAUTION
Do not heat the cylinder head with a torch. Never bring a flame into contact with the cylinder head. Direct flame can warp the cylinder head.

3. Place the cylinder head in a heated oven and warm it to 100° C (212° F). To check the temperature of the cylinder head, place tiny drops of water onto the head. The cylinder head is heated to the proper temperature if the drops sizzle and evaporate immediately.

WARNING
Wear heavy gloves when performing this procedure. The cylinder head will be very hot.

4. Using heavy gloves or kitchen pot holders, remove the cylinder head from the oven and place it onto wooden blocks with the combustion chamber facing up.

5. From the combustion side of the head, drive the old valve guide (A, **Figure 89**) out of the cylinder head with the 7 mm valve guide remover (B, **Figure 89**) and a hammer.

6. Remove and discard the valve guide and circlip. *Never* reinstall a valve guide or circlip. They are no longer true or within tolerance.

7. After the cylinder head cools, check the guide bore for carbon or other contamination. Clean the bore thoroughly.

8. Reheat the cylinder head as described in step 3.

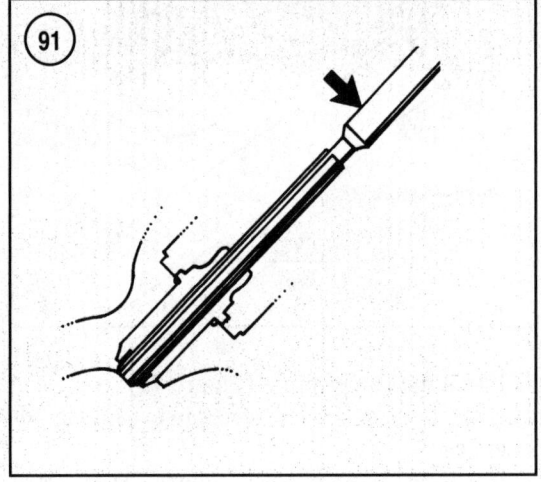

WARNING
Wear heavy gloves when performing this procedure. The cylinder head will be very hot.

9. Using heavy gloves or kitchen pot holders, remove the cylinder head form the oven and place it onto wooden blocks with the combustion chamber facing down.

10. Remove the valve guide from the freezer.

CAUTION
Failure to lubricate the new valve guide and guide bore will result in damage to the cylinder head and/or valve guide.

11. Apply clean engine oil to the new valve guide and the valve guide bore in the cylinder head.

ENGINE TOP END

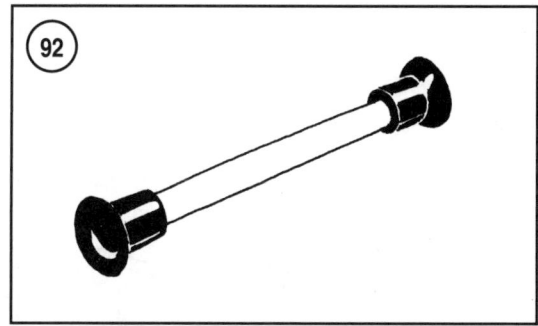

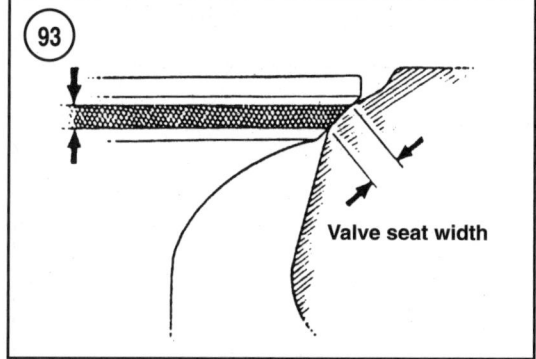

Valve seat width

12. From the top side of the cylinder head (camshaft side), drive the new valve guide into the cylinder head with a hammer, the 7 mm (0.28 in.) valve guide installer (A, **Figure 90**) and the valve guide remover. (B, **Figure 90**). Drive the valve guide into the bore until the circlip is completely seated against the cylinder head.

13. After the cylinder head has cooled down, ream the new valve guides as follows:

　a. Apply cutting oil to both the new valve guide and to the valve guide reamer.

CAUTION
Always rotate the valve guide reamer clockwise. The valve guide will be damaged if the reamer is rotated counterclockwise.

　b. Insert the 7 mm (0.28 in.) valve guide reamer from the top side (**Figure 91**), and rotate the reamer *clockwise*. Continue to rotate the reamer and work it down through the entire length of the new valve guide. Continue to apply additional cutting oil during this procedure.

　c. Rotate the reamer *clockwise* until it has traveled all the way through the new valve guide.

　d. Rotate the reamer *clockwise*, and completely withdraw the reamer from the valve guide.

　e. Measure the inside diameter of the valve guide with a small hole gauge. Measure the gauge with a micrometer, and compare the measurement to the specification in **Table 2**. Replace the valve guide if it is not within specification.

14. If necessary, repeat Steps 1-13 for any other valve guide.

15. Thoroughly clean the cylinder head and valve guides with solvent to wash out all metal particles. Dry the head with compressed air.

16. Lightly oil the valve guides to prevent rust.

17. Reface the valve seats as described in this chapter.

18. Install the intake manifold. Use a new O-ring.

Valve Seat Inspection

1. Remove the valves as described in this chapter.
2. Thoroughly clean the valve seat and valve mating areas with contact cleaner.
3. Spread a thin layer of Prussian Blue or machinist's dye evenly on the valve face.
4. Apply molybdenum disulfide oil to the valve stem, and install the valve into its guide. Using the valve lapping tool (**Figure 92**), rotate the valve in the valve seat.
5. Remove the valve and measure the seat width (**Figure 93**) with a vernier caliper.
6. The seat width must be within the range specified in **Table 2** all the way around the seat. If the seat width is outside the specified range, recondition the valve seat as described in this chapter.

Valve Seat Reconditioning

Special valve cutting tools and considerable expertise are required to properly recondition the valve seats in the cylinder head. Considerable expense can be avoided by removing the cylinder head and having a Yamaha dealership or machine shop perform the service.

The following procedure is provided for those who choose to perform this task.

Have on hand a valve seat cutting set consisting of 30°, 45° and 60° cutters and the appropriate handle. These tool sets are available from a Yamaha

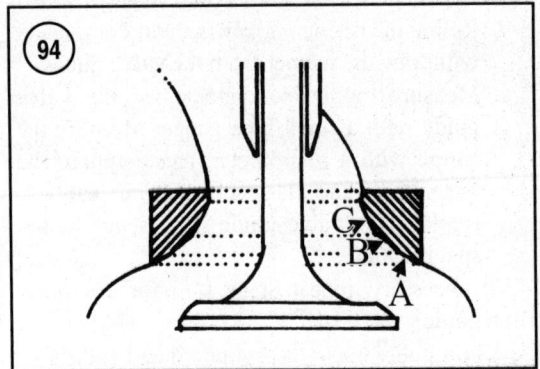

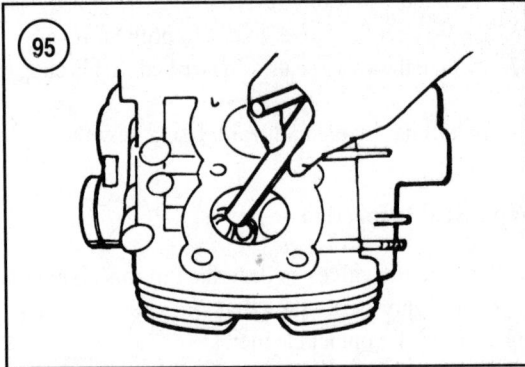

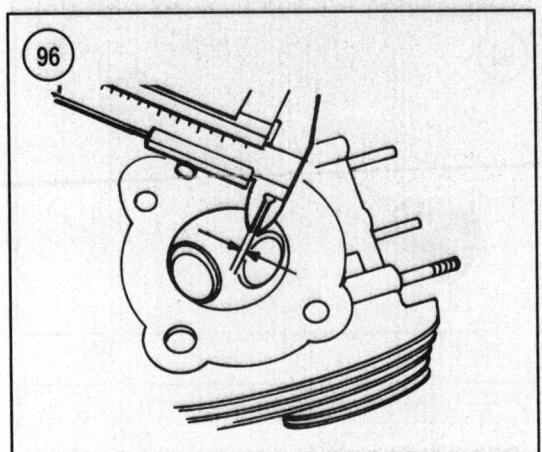

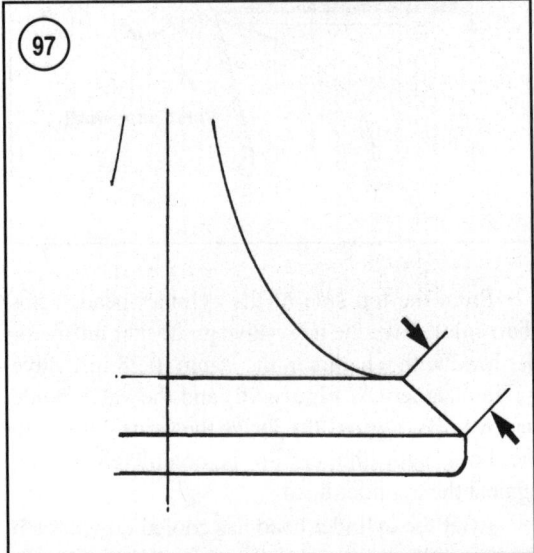

dealership or from machine shop supply outlets. Follow the manufacturer's instructions when using the cutters.

The valve seats for both the intake valves and exhaust valves are machined to the same angles as follows:

a. The area below the contact surface (closest to the combustion chamber) is cut to a 30° angle (A, **Figure 94**).
b. The valve contact surface is cut to a 45° angle (B, **Figure 94**).
c. The area above the contact surface (closest to the valve guide) is cut to a 60° angle (C, **Figure 94**).

1. Using the 45° cutter, descale and clean the valve seat with one or two turns (**Figure 95**).

NOTE

CAUTION
Measure the valve seat contact area in the cylinder head after each cut to make sure the contact area is correct and to prevent removing too much material. If too much material is removed, the cylinder head must be replaced.

2. If the seat is still pitted or burned, turn the 45° cutter until the surface is clean. Refer to the previous CAUTION.
3. Remove the valve cutter and T-handle from the cylinder head.
4. Inspect the valve seat-to-valve face impression as follows:

   a. Spread a thin layer of Prussian Blue or machinist's dye evenly on the valve face.
   b. Moisten the end of a suction cup valve tool and attach it to the valve. Insert the valve into the guide.
   c. Using the suction cup tool, rotate the valve in the valve seat.
   d. Remove the valve and examine the impression.

ENGINE TOP END

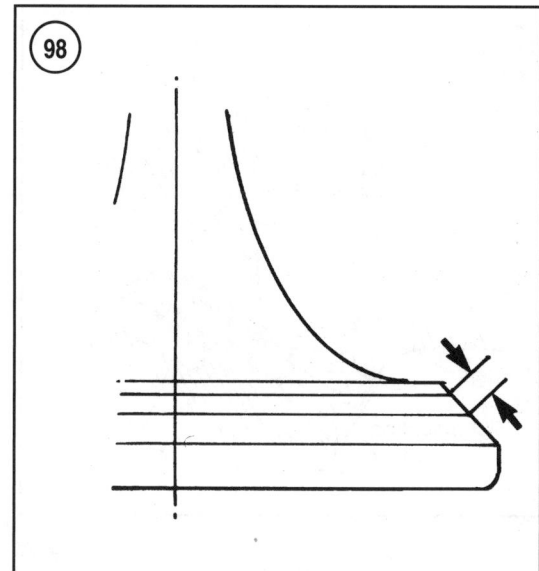

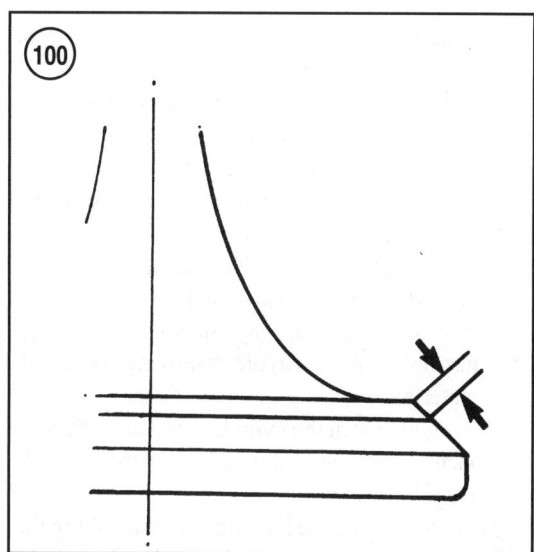

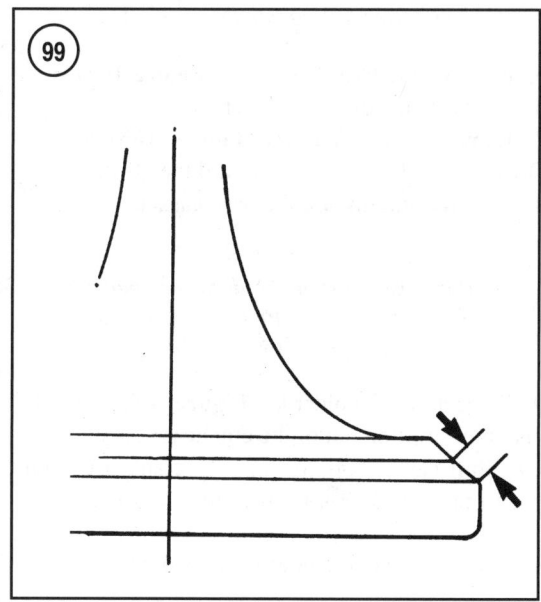

7. If the contact area is too narrow and up close to the valve head (**Figure 99**), first use the 30° cutter and then use the 45° cutter to center the contact area.

8. If the contact area is too narrow and down away from the valve head (**Figure 100**), first use the 60° cutter and then use the 45° cutter to center the contact area.

9. After obtaining the desired valve seat position and width, use the 45° side of the cutter and T-handle and *very lightly* clean away any burrs made by the previous cuts—remove only enough material as necessary.

10. Check that the finish has a smooth and velvety surface. It should *not* be shiny or highly polished.

11. Repeat Steps 1-10 for all remaining valve seats.

12. After the valve seat has been reconditioned, lap the seat and valve as described in this chapter.

e. Measure the valve seat width as shown in **Figure 96**. Refer to **Table 1** for the seat width specifications.

5. If the contact area is centered on the valve face but is too wide (**Figure 97**), use either the 30° or the 60° cutter and remove a portion of the valve seat material to narrow the contact area.

6. If the contact area is centered on the valve face but is too narrow (**Figure 98**), use the 45° cutter and remove a portion of the valve seat material to increase the contact area.

Valve Seat Lapping

Valve lapping is a simple operation that can restore the valve seat without machining if the amount of wear or distortion is not excessive. Lapping is also recommended after the valve seat has been refaced or when a new valve and valve guide have been installed.

1. Smear a light coating of fine grade valve lapping compound such as Carborendum or Clover Brand on the seating surface of the valve.

2. Apply molybdenum disulfide oil to the valve stem, and insert the valve into the cylinder head.

3. Wet the suction cup of the valve lapping tool (**Figure 92**) and stick it onto the valve head.
4. Lap the valve to the valve seat as follows:
   a. Lap the valve by rotating the lapping stick between your hands in both directions.
   b. Every 5 to 10 seconds, *stop* and rotate the valve 180° in the valve seat.
   c. Continue lapping until the contact surfaces of the valve and the valve seat in the cylinder head are a uniform gray. Stop as soon as they turn this color to avoid removing too much material.
5. Thoroughly clean the cylinder head and all valve components in solvent, followed by a wash with detergent and hot water.
6. After completing the lapping and reinstalling the valve assemblies into the cylinder head, test the valve seat. Check the seat of each valve by pouring solvent or kerosene into each of the intake and exhaust ports (**Figure 101**). The solvent should not flow past the valve head and the valve seat. Perform this test on all valves. If the fluid leaks past any of the seats, disassemble that valve assembly and repeat the lapping procedure until there are no leaks.
7. Clean the cylinder head and valve components in detergent and hot water, then apply a light coat of engine oil to all bare metal surfaces to prevent rust.

CYLINDER BLOCK

The alloy cylinder block has pressed-in cylinder sleeves, which can be bored 0.5 mm (0.020 in.) or 1 mm (0.040 in.) oversized.

Refer to **Figure 102** when servicing the cylinder block.

Removal

1. Remove the cylinder head and head gasket as described in this chapter.
2. If still installed, remove the rear cam-chain guide (the free-standing guide) from the cylinder (**Figure 103**).
3. Remove the cylinder bolt (**Figure 104**) from the cam-chain side of the cylinder.
4. Loosen the cylinder block by tapping around the perimeter with a rubber or plastic mallet.
5. Pull the cylinder block straight up and off the pistons and cylinder studs.

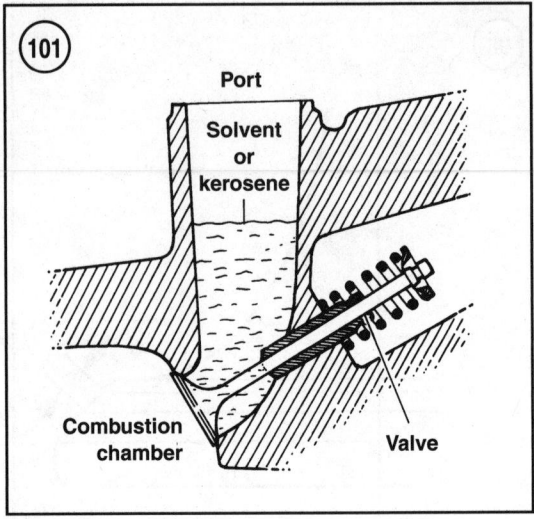

NOTE
Keep the cam chain wired up to prevent it from falling into the crankcase.

6. Remove the two dowels (A, **Figure 105**) from the exhaust side of the cylinder.
7. Remove the collar (B, **Figure 105**) and its O-ring from the cylinder. Discard the O-ring.
8. Remove and discard the base gasket.

NOTE
Purchase piston holders or make them from wood to the dimensions shown in Figure 106.

9. Place a piston holder (C, **Figure 105**) under the piston protruding out of the crankcase opening.
10. Stuff clean shop rags into the crankcase opening to prevent debris from falling into the crankcase.
11. Inspect the cylinder as described below.

Inspection

The following procedure requires highly specialized and expensive measuring instruments. If such equipment is not available, have a dealership or qualified machine shop perform the measurements.

If a cylinder requires reboring or replacing, also replace the piston and rings.

1. Remove all gasket residue from the top and bottom gasket surfaces on the cylinder block. Apply a gasket remover or use solvent and soak any old gasket material stuck to the cylinder block. If neces-

ENGINE TOP END

CYLINDER AND PISTON

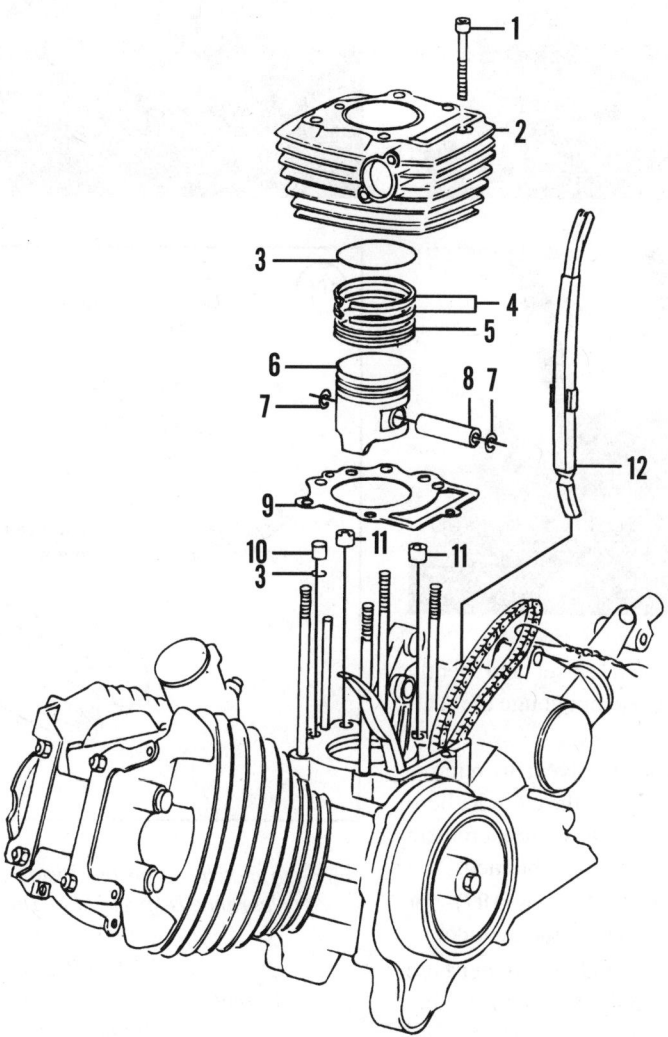

1. Bolt
2. Cylinder
3. O-ring
4. Compression rings
5. Oil ring assembly
6. Piston
7. Piston pin circlip
8. Piston pin
9. Gasket
10. Collar
11. Dowel
12. Rear cam chain guide

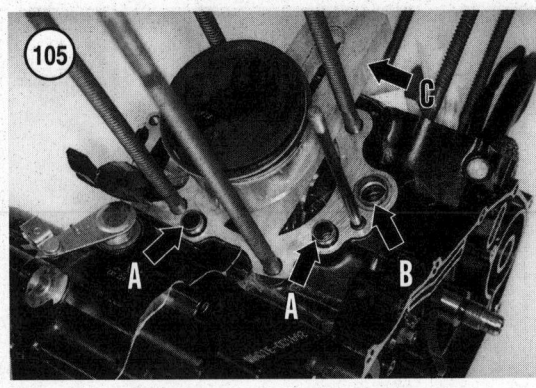

sary, use a broad-tipped, *dull* chisel and gently scrape off all gasket residue. Do not gouge the sealing surface.

2. Wash the cylinder block in solvent to remove any oil and carbon particles. Clean the cylinder bore thoroughly before attempting any measurement otherwise incorrect readings may be obtained.

3. Check the cylinder wall (**Figure 107**) for scratches. If any are evident, rebore the cylinder.

4. Measure the cylinder bore with a cylinder bore gauge (**Figure 108**) at a point 40 mm (1.57 in.) below the top of the cylinder block. Measure the cylinder bore in two axes: in-line with the piston pin and at 90° to the pin.

5. Calculate the average of these two cylinder bore measurements. If the average is outside the range specified in **Table 2**, rebore the cylinder and replace the piston and rings. If the average exceeds the wear limit in **Table 2**, replace the cylinder, piston and rings.

NOTE
*Obtain the new piston before the cylinder is bored so that the piston can be measured. The cylinder must be bored to match the piston. Piston-to-cylinder clearance is specified in **Table 2**.*

CAUTION
A combination of soap and water is the only solution that completely cleans cylinder walls. Solvent and kerosene cannot wash fine grit out of cylinder crevices. Grit left in the cylinder acts as a grinding compound and causes premature wear to the new rings.

6. After the cylinder has been serviced, wash the cylinder bore in hot soapy water. This is the only way to remove the fine grit material left from the bore or honing job. After washing the cylinder walls, run a clean white cloth through each wall; it should show no traces of grit or other debris. If the

ENGINE TOP END

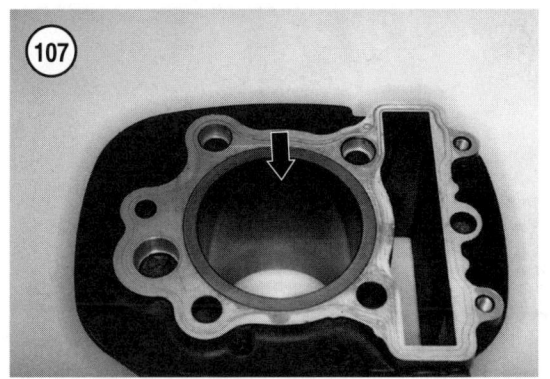

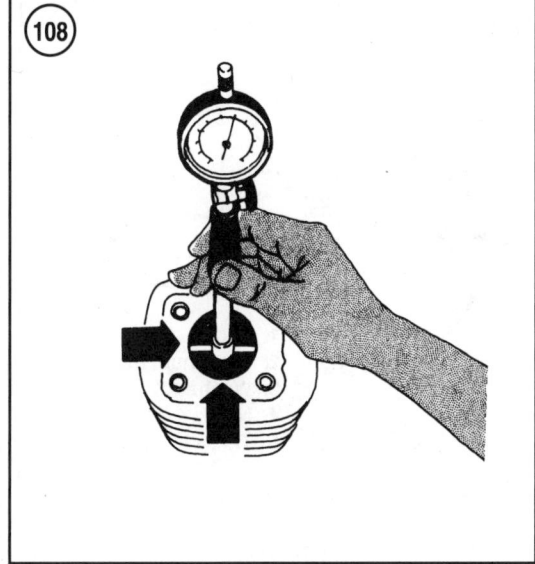

rag is dirty, the wall is not thoroughly clean and must be rewashed. After the cylinder is cleaned, lubricate the cylinder walls with clean engine oil.

7. Replace the cylinder's O-ring (**Figure 109**).

Installation

1. Check that the top and bottom cylinder surfaces are clean of all gasket residue.

2. Install the collar (B, **Figure 105**) and a new O-ring into the crankcase.

3. Install the two dowels (A, **Figure 105**) into the crankcase.

4. Install a new base gasket.

5. Lubricate the cylinder and piston liberally with engine oil prior to installation.

6. Rotate the crankshaft so the piston is at top dead center, and place a piston holder (C, **Figure 105**) under the piston.

7. Carefully install the cylinder block onto the crankcase studs. Make sure the front cam chain guide (the bolted chain guide) passes through the cam chain tunnel in the cylinder block.

8. Slowly lower the cylinder until the piston rings are within the cylinder sleeves. Compress each ring as it enters the cylinder by hand or with a piston ring compressor (**Figure 110**). Take the time to carefully compress each ring individually if necessary.

9. Remove the piston holders, and carefully lower the cylinder block all the way down onto the crankcase, and install the cylinder bolt (**Figure 104**) into the cam-chain side of the cylinder. Torque the cylinder bolt to the specification in **Table 3**.

10. Run the cam chain and safety wire up through the cam chain tunnel in the cylinder block, and secure the safety wire to the outside of the engine.

11. Install the cylinder head as described in this chapter.

12. Follow the break-in procedure in this Chapter Five if the cylinder block was rebored or honed or a new piston or piston rings were installed.

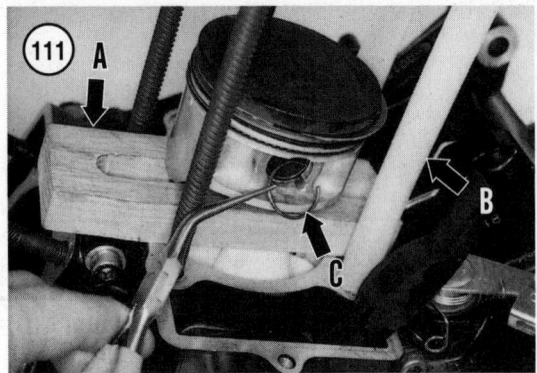

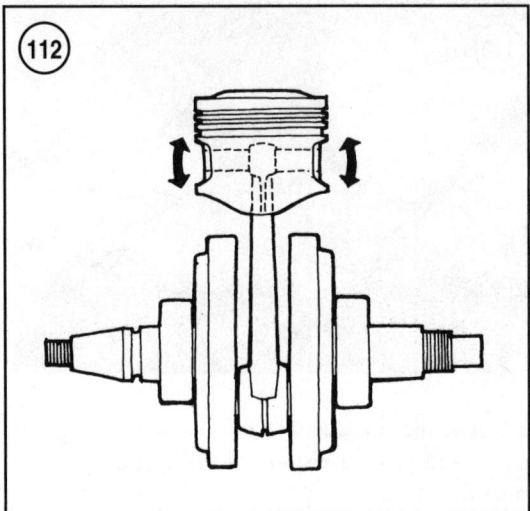

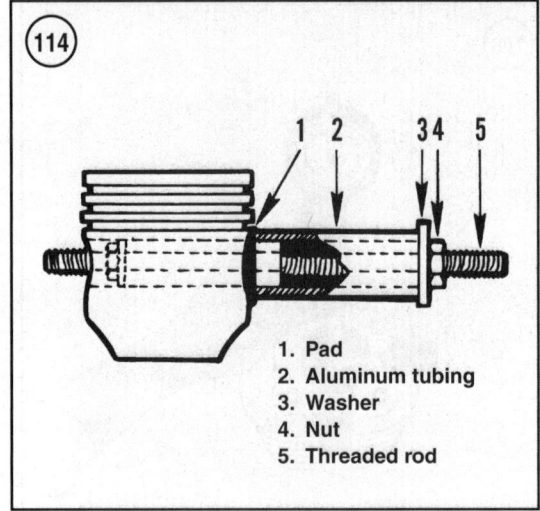

1. Pad
2. Aluminum tubing
3. Washer
4. Nut
5. Threaded rod

PISTONS AND PISTON RINGS

The pistons are made of an aluminum alloy. The piston pins are made of steel and are a precision fit. The piston pin is held in place by a clip at each end.

Refer to **Figure 102** when servicing the piston and rings.

Piston Removal

1. Remove the cylinder head and cylinder block as described in this chapter.
2. Lightly mark the top of the piston (front or rear) so it can be installed in the correct cylinder during installation.
3. Install plastic hoses (B, **Figure 111**) over the two crankcase studs that the piston leans against. The threads on the studs could damage the piston during removal and installation.

WARNING
The edges of all piston rings are very sharp. Be careful when handling them to avoid cutting fingers.

4. Before removing the piston, hold the connecting rod tightly and rock the piston (**Figure 112**). Any rocking motion (do not confuse with the normal sliding motion) indicates wear on the piston pin, piston pin bore or connecting rod bore (more likely a combination of these). If necessary, replace the piston and piston pin as a set.

NOTE
Wrap a clean shop cloth under the piston so the piston pin clip does not fall into the crankcase.

5. The piston pin circlip may be difficult to remove. Support the piston with a piston holder (A, **Figure 111**) to relieve any stress on the piston pin.

ENGINE TOP END

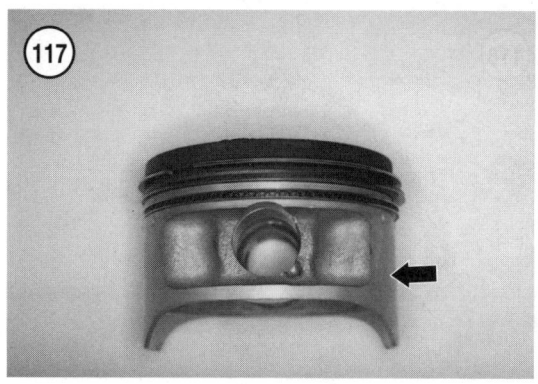

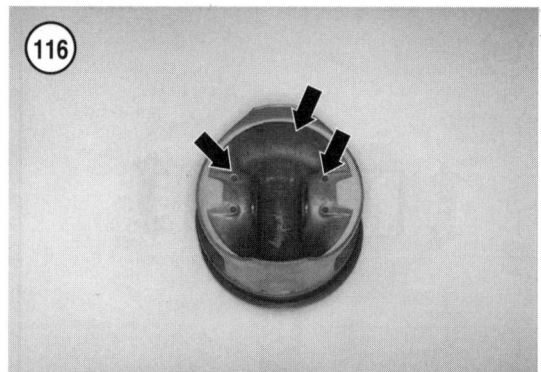

6. Remove a circlip (C, **Figure 111**) from one side of the piston pin bore with a small screwdriver or scribe. Hold a thumb over one edge of the clip when removing it to prevent the clip from springing out. Deburr the piston pin and the circlip groove as necessary.

NOTE
Discard the piston pin circlip. Install new circlips during assembly.

7. From the other side, push the piston pin out of the piston by hand (**Figure 113**). If the pin is tight, remove it with the homemade tool shown in **Figure 114**. Do not drive out the piston pin. This could damage the piston pin, connecting rod, or piston.
8. Remove the piston from the connecting rod and the remaining circlip from the piston. Discard both piston pin circlips.
9. Mark the piston pin in relation to the piston so they will be reassembled as a set.
10. If the piston is going to be left off for some time, place a piece of foam insulation tube over the end of the connecting rod to protect it.

Inspection

1. Carefully clean the carbon from the piston crown (**Figure 115**) with a chemical remover or with a soft scraper. Remark the piston as soon as it is cleaned. Do not remove or damage the carbon ridge around the circumference of the piston above the top ring. If the piston, rings and cylinder are found to be dimensionally correct and can be reused, removal of the carbon ring from the top of the piston or the carbon ridge from the top of the cylinder block wall promotes excessive oil consumption in this cylinder.

CAUTION
Do not wire brush the piston skirts.

2. After cleaning the piston, examine the crown. It should show no signs of wear or damage.
3. Examine each ring groove for burrs, dented edges and wide wear. Pay particular attention to the top compression ring groove. It usually wears more than the other grooves. Since the oil rings are constantly bathed in oil, these rings and grooves wear little compared to compression rings and their grooves. If the oil ring groove shows signs of wear, or if the oil ring assembly is tight and difficult to remove, the piston skirt may have collapsed. If so, replace the piston.
4. Check the oil control holes (**Figure 116**) in the piston for carbon or oil sludge buildup. If necessary, clean the holes and blow them out with compressed air.
5. Check the piston skirt (**Figure 117**) for galling and abrasion which may have been caused by piston seizure. If a piston shows signs of partial seizure (bits of aluminum buildup on the piston skirt), replace the piston and bore the cylinder (if necessary)

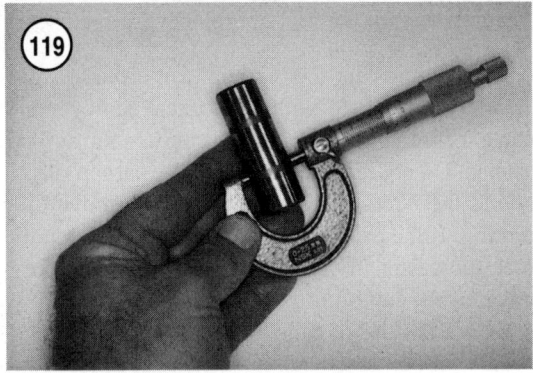

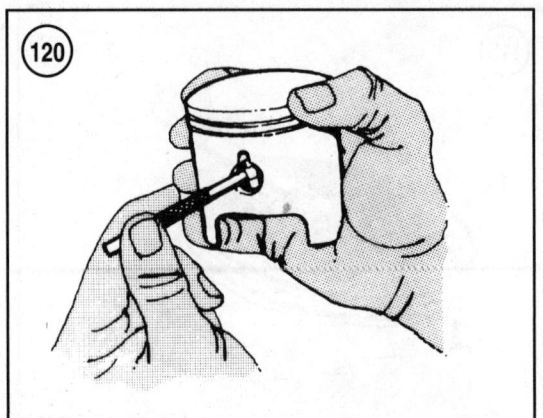

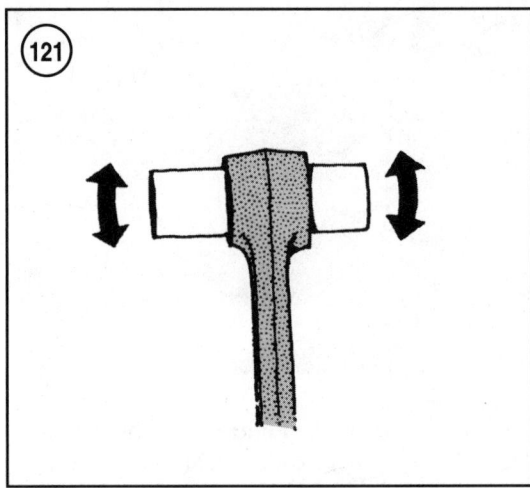

to reduce the possibility of engine noise and further piston seizure.

NOTE
If the piston skirt is worn or scuffed unevenly from side-to-side, the connecting rod may be bent or twisted.

6. Check the circlip groove (**Figure 118**) on each side of the piston for wear or other damage. Install a new circlip into each piston circlip groove and try to move the clip from side to side. If the circlip has any side play, the groove is worn and the piston must be replaced.

7. Measure the piston-to-cylinder clearance as described in *Piston Clearance* in this chapter.

8. If damage or wear indicates piston replacement, select a new piston as described in *Piston Clearance* in this chapter.

Piston Pin Inspection

1. Clean the piston pin in solvent, and dry it thoroughly.

2. Inspect the piston pin for chrome flaking or cracks. Replace the pin if necessary.

3. Measure the diameter of the piston pin with a micrometer (**Figure 119**). If the measurement is outside the range specified in **Table 2**, replace the piston pin.

4. Measure the diameter of the piston pin bore in the piston with a small bore gauge (**Figure 120**).

5. Calculate piston pin-to-piston clearance by subtracting the piston pin diameter from the piston pin bore diameter. If the clearance is outside the range specified in **Table 2**, replace the piston (providing that the piston pin diameter is within specification).

6. Oil the piston pin, and install it in the connecting rod. Slowly rotate the piston pin and check for radial and lateral play (**Figure 121**). If any play exists, replace the connecting rod (providing the piston pin diameter is within specification). Inspect the connecting rod as described in Chapter Five.

ENGINE TOP END

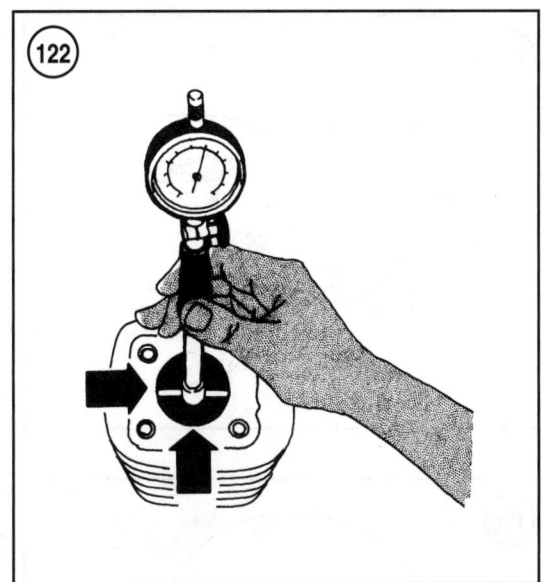

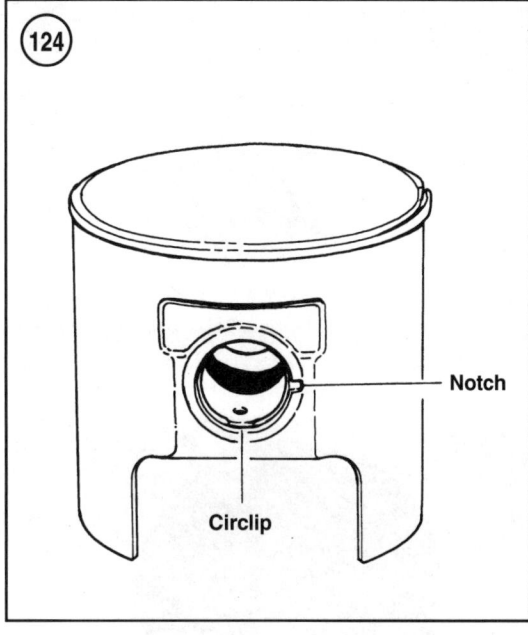

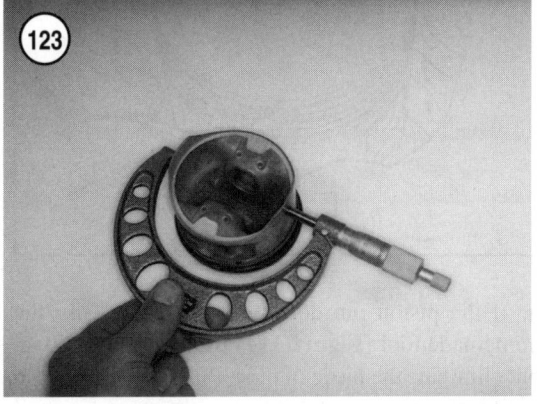

Piston Clearance

1. Make sure the pistons and cylinder walls are clean and dry.

2. Measure the cylinder bore with a cylinder bore gauge (**Figure 122**) at a point 40 mm (1.57 in.) below the top of the cylinder block. Measure the cylinder bore in two axes: in-line with the piston pin and at 90° to the pin. Calculate the average of the two measurements. This average is the cylinder bore diameter.

3. Measure the diameter of the piston across the skirt at right angles to the piston pin. Measure the piston at a point 6 mm (0.24 in.) up from the bottom of the piston skirt (**Figure 123**).

4. Piston-to-cylinder clearance is the difference between the piston diameter and the cylinder bore diameter. Subtract the diameter of the piston from the cylinder bore diameter calculated in Step 2. If this value is outside the range specified in **Table 2**, rebore the cylinder to the next oversize and install a new piston and rings. If the clearance exceeds the wear limit specified in **Table 2**, replace the cylinder, piston, and rings.

5. To establish a final overbore dimension, purchase the new piston first. Measure the piston diameter and add the specified piston clearance to determine the proper finished cylinder bore diameter. Remember, do not exceed the cylinder bore service limit indicated in **Table 2**.

Piston Installation

1. Apply fresh engine oil to the inside surface of the connecting rods.

> **NOTE**
> *Install new piston pin circlips during assembly. Install the circlips with the gap away from the cutout in the piston.*

2. Install a new piston pin circlip into one side of the piston. Make sure the circlip end gap does **not** align with the notch in the piston (**Figure 124**).

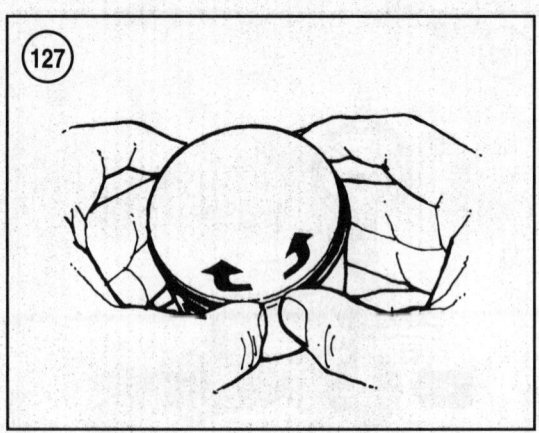

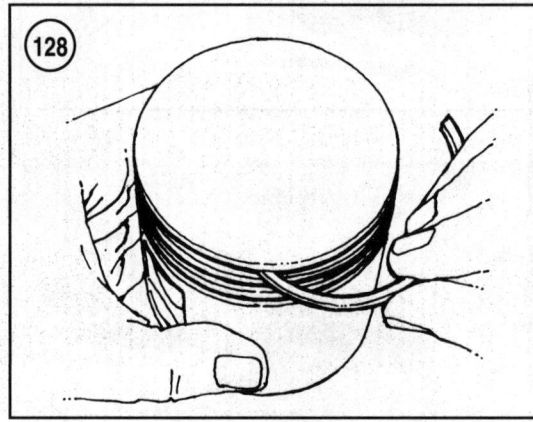

3. Apply fresh engine oil to the piston pin, and install the piston pin in the piston until it is flush with the inside of the piston-pin boss (**Figure 125**).

4. Place the piston over the connecting rod (**Figure 113**). Be sure the *EX* on the piston crown (**Figure 126**) faces the exhaust side of the cylinder. This is the front side on the front cylinder and the rear side on the rear cylinder.

CAUTION
When installing the piston pin in Step 5, do not push the pin in too far, or the piston pin circlip installed in Step 2 will be forced into the piston metal, destroying the clip groove and loosening the clip.

5. Align the piston pin with the hole in the connecting rod. Push the piston pin through the connecting rod and into the piston boss on the other side of the piston. It may be necessary to move the piston around until the piston pin enters the connecting rod. Do not use force during installation or damage may occur. Push the piston pin in until it bottoms against the pin clip on the other side of the piston.

6. If the piston pin does not slide easily, use the homemade tool (**Figure 114**) used during removal but eliminate the piece of pipe. Pull the piston pin in until it stops.

7. After the piston is installed, recheck and make sure that the *EX* on top of the piston faces the exhaust side of the cylinder.

NOTE
In the next step, install the second circlip with the gap away from the cut-out in the piston.

8. Install the second piston pin circlip (C, **Figure 111**) into the groove in the piston. Make sure the circlip's end gap does *not* align with the notch in the piston (**Figure 124**). Also, make sure both piston pin circlips are seated in their grooves in the piston.

9. Check the installation by rocking the piston back and forth around the pin axis and from side to side along the axis. It should rotate freely back and forth but not from side to side.

ENGINE TOP END

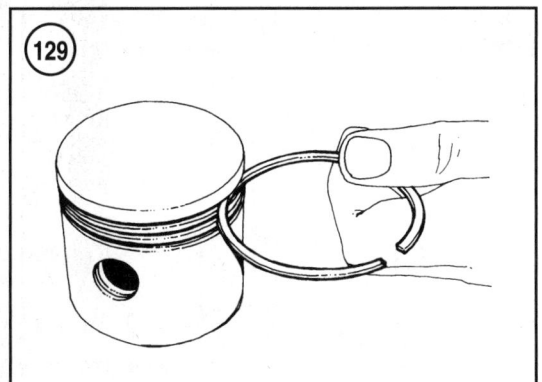

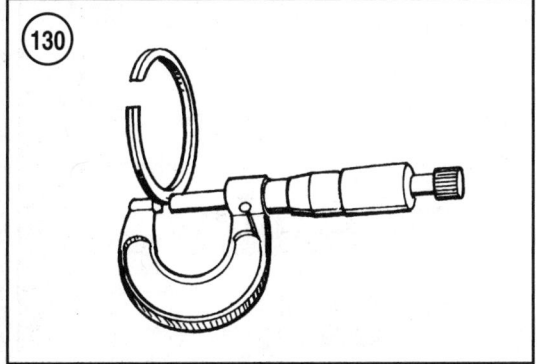

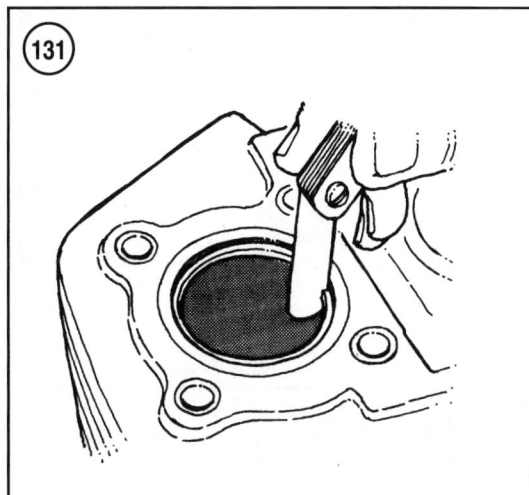

3. Inspect the grooves carefully for burrs, nicks or broken and cracked lands. Recondition or replace the piston if necessary.
4. Roll each ring around its piston groove as shown in **Figure 129** to check for binding. Remove the cause of minor binding with a fine-cut file.
5. Measure the thickness of each ring with a micrometer (**Figure 130**). If the thickness is less than the value specified in **Table 2**, replace the ring(s).

NOTE
When checking the oil control ring assembly, measure the end gap of each ring rail. The end gap of the expander spacer cannot be measured. If either ring rail has excessive end gap, replace the entire oil ring assembly.

6. Place each ring, one at a time, into the cylinder. Push the ring with the crown of the piston to a point 40 mm (1.57 in.) below the top of the cylinder. Measure the ring end gap with a flat feeler gauge (**Figure 131**). If the gap is outside the range specified in **Table 2**, replace the rings.
7. Install the piston rings as described below and measure the side clearance of each ring in its groove with a flat feeler gauge (**Figure 132**). If the clearance is greater than specified, replace the rings. If the side clearance of the new rings is still excessive, replace the piston.
8. When installing new rings, measure their end gaps as described in Step 5, and compare the measurements to the dimensions given in **Table 2**. If the end gap is greater than specified, return the rings for another set(s). If the end gap is smaller than speci-

10. If necessary, install the piston rings as described in this chapter.
11. Install the cylinder and cylinder head as described in this chapter.

Piston Ring Removal and Inspection

A 3-ring assembly is used. The top and second rings are compression rings. The lower ring is an oil control ring assembly consisting of two ring rails and an expander spacer.

WARNING
The edges of all piston rings are very sharp. Be careful when handling them to avoid cutting fingers.

1. Remove the compression rings with a ring expander tool or spread the ends by hand just enough to slide the ring up over the piston (**Figure 127**). Repeat for the remaining rings.
2. Carefully remove all carbon buildup from the ring grooves with a broken piston ring (**Figure 128**). Do not remove aluminum material from the ring grooves. This increases ring side clearance.

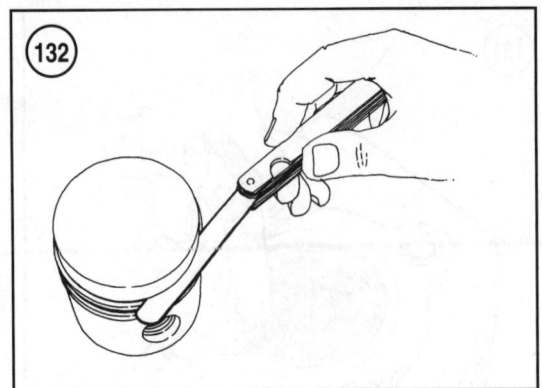

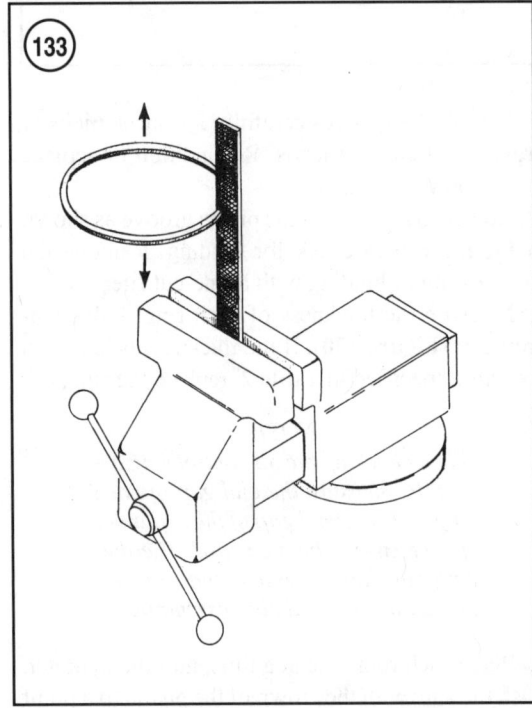

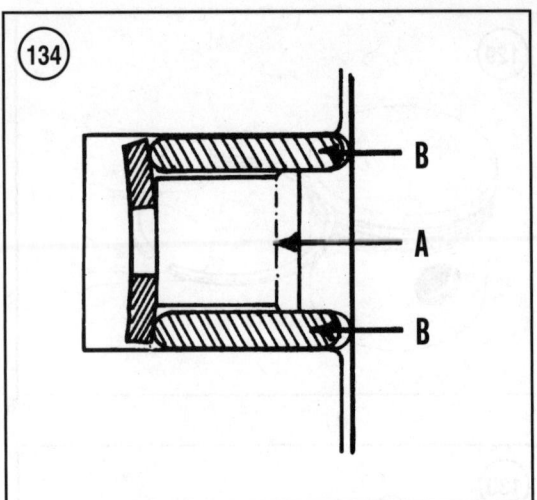

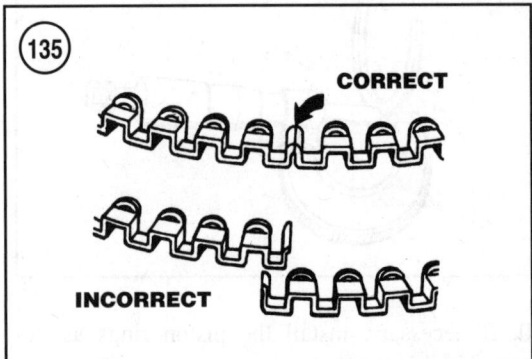

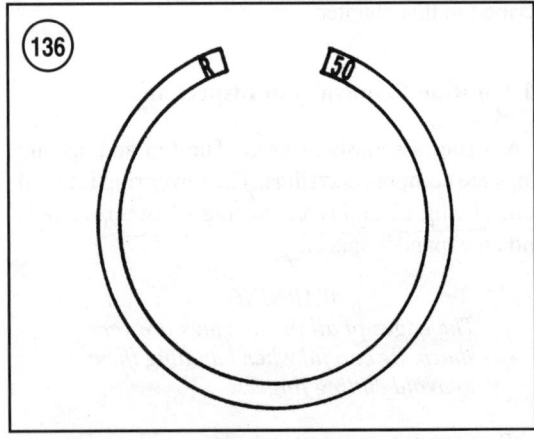

fied, secure a small file in a vise, grip the ring by hand, and enlarge the gap (**Figure 133**).

Piston Ring Installation

NOTE
When installing rings, liberally lubricate the ring and piston groove with clean engine oil.

1. Install the oil control ring assembly into the bottom ring groove. Install the oil ring expander spacer first (A, **Figure 134**), and then install each ring rail (B, **Figure 134**). Make sure the ends of the expander spacer butt together (**Figure 135**). They should not overlap. If reassembling used parts, install the ring rails as they were removed.

NOTE
Oversize compression rings (top and second rings) are stamped with a .50

ENGINE TOP END

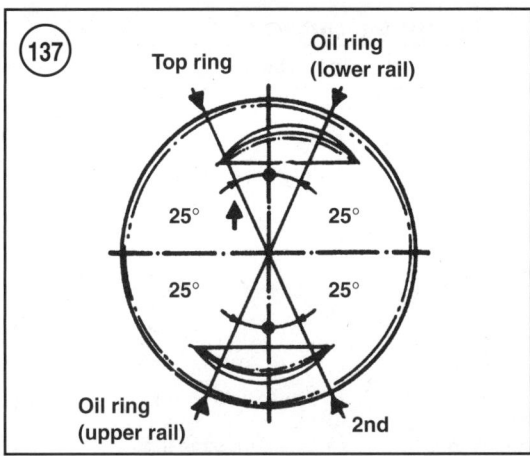

(Figure 136) or 1.00 to indicate the oversize.

2. Install the second compression ring, and then install the top ring. Carefully spread the ends of each ring by hand and slip the ring over the top of the piston (**Figure 127**). Install each compression ring with its manufacturing marks (**Figure 136**) facing up. Install the ring marked *RN* in the top groove; install the ring marked *R* in the second groove.

3. Make sure the rings are seated completely in their grooves all the way around the piston and the ends are distributed around the piston.

4. Check the side clearance of each ring as shown in **Figure 132**. If side clearance is not within the specification shown in **Table 2**, re-examine the condition of the piston and rings.

5. Distribute the ring gaps around the piston as shown in **Figure 137**.

6. Follow the break-in procedure in Chapter Five if a new piston or new piston rings have been installed or if the cylinder was rebored or honed.

Table 1 GENERAL ENGINE SPECIFICATIONS

Item	Specification
Engine type	4-stroke, air-cooled, SOHC, V-twin
Bore x stroke	81 x 63 mm (3.19 x 2.48 in.)
Displacement	649 cc (39.60 cu. in.)
Compression ratio	9:1
Compression pressure	1000 kPa (145 psi) at 300 rpm
Ignition timing	12° B.T.D.C. at 1200 rpm

Table 2 ENGINE UPPER END SPECIFICATIONS

Item	Specification	Wear limit
Cylinder head warp	–	0.03 mm (0.0012 in.)
Camshaft		
Cam lobe height		
Intake	39.733 mm (1.5643 in.)	39.63 mm (1.5602 in.)
Exhaust	39.772 mm (1.5658 in.)	39.67 mm (1.5618 in.)
Cam lobe width		
Intake	32.217 mm (1.2684 in.)	32.12 mm (1.2646 in.)
Exhaust	32.302 mm (1.2717 in.)	32.20 mm (1.2677 in.)
Cam bushing inside diameter	28.000-28.021 mm (1.1024-1.1032 in.)	–
Camshaft journal outside		
diameter	27.96-27.98 mm (1.1008-1.1016 in.)	–
Camshaft–to–cam bushing		
clearance	0.020-0.061 mm (0.0008-0.0024) in.	–
Camshaft runout	–	0.03 mm (0.0012 in.)
(continued)		

Table 2 ENGINE UPPER END SPECIFICATIONS (continued)

Item	Specification	Wear limit
Rocker arm		
Rocker arm bore inside diameter	14.000-14.018 mm (0.5512-0.5519 in.)	–
Rocker arm shaft outside diameter	13.980-13.991 mm (0.5504-0.5508 in.)	
Rocker-arm-to-rocker shaft clearance	0.009-0.038 mm (0.0035-0.0015 in.)	
Valves and valve springs		
Valve clearance		
Intake	0.07-0.12 mm (0.0028-0.0047 in.)	–
Exhaust	0.12-0.17 mm (0.0047-0.0067 in.)	–
Valve stem runout	–	0.03 mm (0.0012 in.)
Valve stem diameter		
Intake	6.975-6.990 mm (0.2746-0.2752 in.)	6.955 mm (0.2738 in.)
Exhaust	6.960-6.975 mm (0.2740-0.2746 in.)	6.935 mm (0.2730 in.)
Valve guide inside diameter (intake and exhaust)	7.000-7.012 mm (0.2756-0.2761 in.)	7.042 mm (0.2772 in.)
Valve stem-to-guide clearance		
Intake	0.010-0.037 mm (0.0004-0.0015 in.)	0.08 mm (0.003 in.)
Exhaust	0.025-0.052 mm (0.001-0.002 in.)	0.10 mm (0.004 in.)
Valve head diameter		
Intake	36.9-37.1 mm (1.4528-1.4606 in.)	–
Exhaust	31.9-32.1 mm (1.2559-1.2638 in.)	–
Valve face width (intake and exhaust)	2.3 mm (0.09 in.)	–
Valve seat width (intake and exhaust)	1.0-1.2 mm (0.039-0.047 in.)	1.8 mm (0.07 in.)
Valve margin thickness (intake and exhaust)	1.0-1.4 mm (0.039-0.055 in.)	0.8 mm (0.03 in.)
Valve seat cutting angle	30, 45, 60°	
Valve spring free length	43.2 mm (1.7 in.)	42.0 mm (1.65 in.)
Valve spring tilt		2.5°/1.9 mm (0.075 in.)
Cylinders		
Bore*	80.945-80.995 mm (3.1868-3.1889 in.)	81.1 mm (3.1929 in.)
Oversize pistons and rings	+ 0.5 mm or + 1.0 mm	
Pistons		
Outside diameter		
Standard	80.90-80.95 mm (3.185-3.187 in.)	–
Oversize 1st	81.5 mm (32.1 in.)	
Oversize 2nd	82 mm (32.28 in.)	
Piston-to-cylinder clearance	0.035-0.055 mm (0.0014-0.0022 in.)	0.15 mm (0.0059 in.)
Piston off-set	0	–
Piston-pin bore inside diameter	20.004-20.015 mm (0.7876-0.7880 in.)	–
Piston pin outside diameter	19.995-20.000 mm (0.7872-0.7874 in.)	–
Piston pin-to-piston clearance	0.004-0.020 mm (0.00016-0.00079 in.)	–
Piston rings		
Side clearance (ring-to groove clearance)		
Top	0.03-0.07 mm (0.0012-0.003 in.)	0.12 mm (0.005 in.)
Second	0.02-0.06 mm (0.0008-0.0024 in.)	0.12 mm (0.005 in.)
Ring thickness		
Top	1.2 mm (0.047 in.)	–
Second	1.5 mm (0.059 in.)	–
Oil ring	2.5 mm (0.098 in.)	–

(continued)

ENGINE UPPER END

Table 2 ENGINE UPPER END SPECIFICATIONS (continued)

Item	Specification	Wear limit
Piston rings (continued)		
Ring end gap		
Top	0.15-0.30 mm (0.006-0.012 in.)	0.55 mm (0.022 in.)
Second	0.30-0.045 mm (0.012-0.018 in.)	0.8 mm (0.031 in.)
Oil ring	0.2-0.7 mm (0.008-0.028 in.)	–

*Measured 40 mm (1.58 in.) from top of cylinder.

Table 3 UPPER END TIGHTENING TORQUES

Item	N•m	ft.-lb.	in.-lb.
Air filter housing bolt	12	–	106
Air filter housing bracket bolt	12	–	106
Cam chain guide bolt	10	–	88
Cam chain tensioner cap bolt	20	15	–
Cam chain tensioner mounting bolt	12	–	106
Cam sprocket bolt	55	41	–
Cam sprocket cover bolt	10	–	88
Camshaft bushing retainer bolt	20	15	–
Cylinder bolt	10	–	88
Cylinder head 8 mm nut	20	15	–
Cylinder head 10 mm nuts	35	26	–
Cylinder head bolts	20	15	–
Cylinder head cover bolt (lower)	10	–	88
Cylinder head cover bracket	35	26	–
Cylinder head cover screw (upper)	5	–	44
Exhaust pipe nut			
Front	25	18	–
Rear	20	15	–
Exhaust pipe stud	15	11	–
Exhaust pipe-to-muffler screw	20	15	–
Intake manifold bolts			
Muffler bolt	25	18	–
Primary drive gear bolt	70	52	–
Rocker arm shaft bolt	38	28	–
Rotor bolt	80	59	–
Spark plug	18	13	–
Valve adjuster locknut	14	10	–
Valve cover bolt	10	–	88

CHAPTER FIVE

ENGINE LOWER END

This chapter describes the service procedures for the following lower end components:
1. Crankcase assembly.
2. Crankshaft.
3. Connecting rods.
4. Alternator rotor and starter clutch.
5. Oil pump.
6. Middle gear.
7. Transmission removal and installation.

Before removing and disassembling the crankcase, clean the engine and frame with a commercial degreaser, like Gunk or Bel-Ray Degreaser. It is easier to work on a clean engine. Also make sure the work area is clean.

Make certain all the necessary tools are on hand. Proper preparation is one of the more important aspects of engine overhaul. Always identify parts before removal. Use boxes, plastic bags, and containers for storing parts. Also have masking tape and a permanent, waterproof marking pen to label parts as required.

The text makes frequent references to the left and right side of the engine. This refers to the engine as installed in the frame, not as it sits on the workbench.

Tables 1-4 are at the end of this chapter. **Table 1** lists engine lower end specifications, **Table 2** rod bearing selection specifications, **Table 3** main bearing selection specifications, and **Table 4** lists lower end tightening torques.

SERVICING ENGINE IN THE FRAME

The following components can be serviced while the engine is in the frame:
1. External gearshift mechanism.
2. Clutch.
3. Carburetors.
4. Starter motor.
5. Alternator and starter clutch.
6. Oil pump.

ENGINE

Removal

Refer to **Figure 1** when removing the engine from the frame.

1. Use a suitable jack or jack stands to securely support the motorcycle in an upright position with the rear wheel off the ground.
2. Drain the engine oil and remove the oil filter as described in Chapter Three.

ENGINE LOWER END

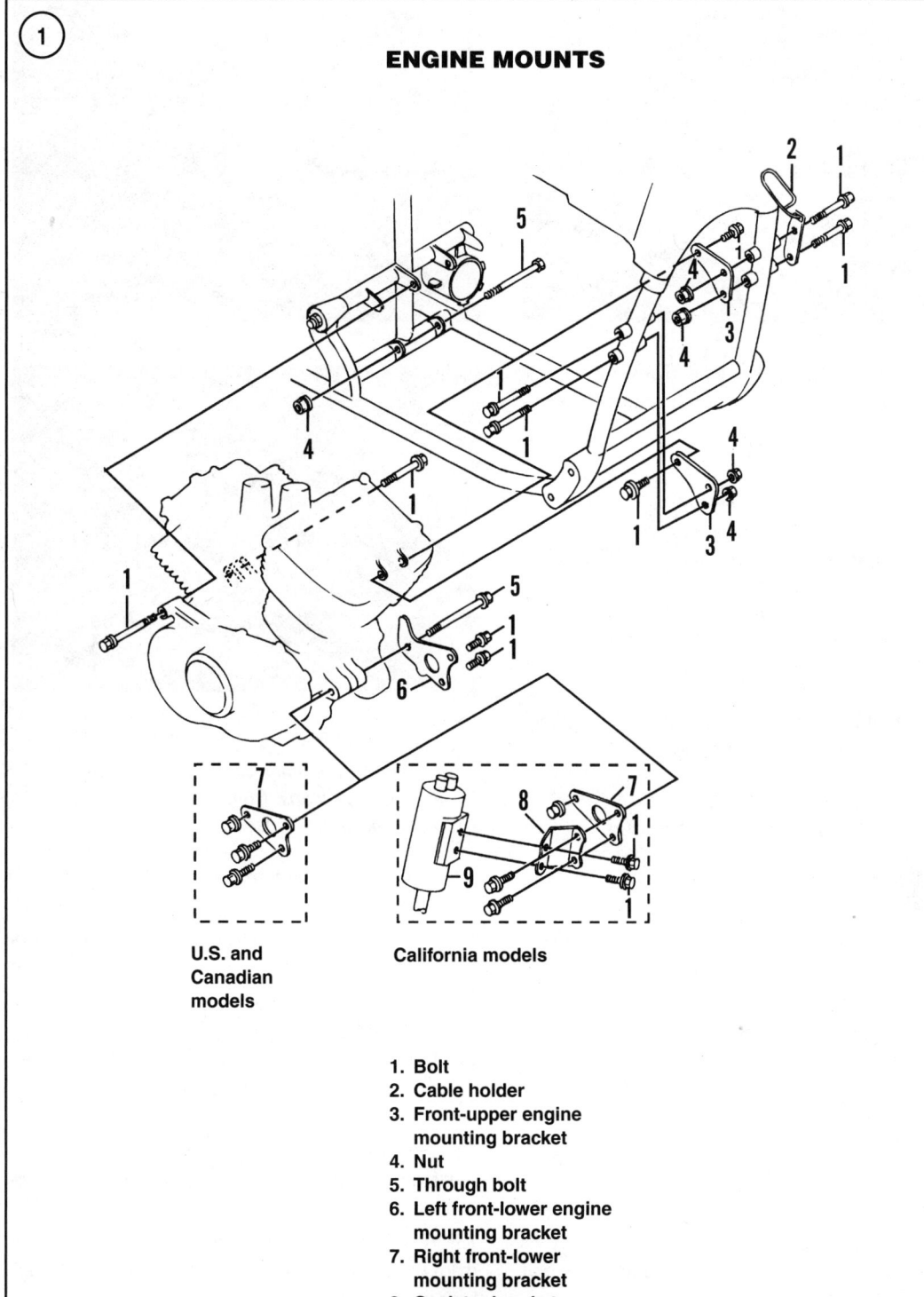

①

ENGINE MOUNTS

U.S. and Canadian models

California models

1. Bolt
2. Cable holder
3. Front-upper engine mounting bracket
4. Nut
5. Through bolt
6. Left front-lower engine mounting bracket
7. Right front-lower mounting bracket
8. Canister bracket
9. EVAP canister

3. Disconnect the negative lead from the battery (**Figure 2**) and then disconnect the positive lead.

NOTE
Before removing the engine, examine the position of the cam timing marks for each cylinder. If necessary, make a drawing of each cam sprocket and pointer in order to help correctly time the camshafts during assembly. Refer to Cylinder Head Removal in Chapter Four.

4. Remove the starter motor and the regulator/rectifier as described in Chapter Nine.

CAUTION
Cover the intake manifold openings to prevent debris from entering the intake tubes and cylinder head.

5. Refer to Chapter Eight and remove the following:
   a. Exhaust pipes.
   b. Fuel tank.
   c. Fuel pump assembly.
   d. Air filter housing.
   e. Carburetor assembly.
   f. AIS assembly.
   g. EVAP canister (California models only).

6. Remove the brake pedal/footpeg assembly as described in Chapter Twelve, and remove the rear brake switch as described in Chapter Nine.

7. Remove the right and left side covers as described in Chapter Thirteen.

8. Remove the shift pedal/footpeg assembly as described in Chapter Seven.

NOTE
Before removing the spark plug caps, twist the caps from side to side to break them loose. Also label each spark plug wire if the original equipment labels are no longer in place.

9. Disconnect the spark plug cap from each spark plug.

10. Remove the ignition coil for the rear cylinder as described in Chapter Nine.

11. Remove the upper and lower cylinder head covers from each cylinder as described in Chapter Four.

12. Remove the middle gearcase cover from the left side, and remove the alternator cover as described in this chapter.

13. If still installed, disconnect the clutch cable from the clutch release lever as described in Chapter Six.

14. Disconnect the electrical lead (**Figure 3**) from the neutral switch.

15. Disconnect the engine ground lead (**Figure 4**) from the right side of the crankcase.

ENGINE LOWER END

16. Remove the swing arm as described in Chapter Eleven.

17. Remove the middle driven gear assembly as described in this chapter.

NOTE
*If the clutch plates have been removed, hold both the alternator rotor and the clutch boss (**Figure 5**) when removing the middle-drive-pinion-gear nut.*

18. If the crankcase will be disassembled, perform the following:
    a. Remove the middle-drive pinion gear as described in this chapter.
    b. Loosen the cam sprocket bolt in each cylinder head, the alternator rotor bolt, the primary-drive gear nut, and the clutch nut at this time. It is easier to break these fasteners loose now while the engine is in the frame than when it is on the bench. Hold the clutch or the alternator rotor with the appropriate tool when breaking loose a particular nut or bolt.
    c. Once all the fasteners are loose, remove the clutch, primary drive gear, and alternator rotor. This reduces the weight of the engine, which facilitates engine removal.

19. Place a jack under the crankcase to support the engine once the mounting bolts are removed. (See **Figure 6**).

NOTE
Note that each front upper engine mounting bracket is located on the inboard side of the frame downtube. Make sure to install each bracket in the same location during assembly.

20. Remove the right front upper engine mounting bracket (C, **Figure 7**) by performing the following:
    a. Remove the nuts and bolts (A, **Figure 7**) securing the mounting bracket to the frame.
    b. Remove the bolt (B, **Figure 7**) securing the bracket to the engine, and remove the bracket.

21. Remove the left front upper engine mounting bracket (D, **Figure 8**) by performing the following:
    a. Remove the nuts and bolts (A, **Figure 8**) securing the mounting bracket to the frame.
    b. Remove the cable holder (B, **Figure 8**) from the outboard side of the frame.

c. Remove the bolt (C, **Figure 8**) securing the bracket to the engine, and remove the bracket.

22. Remove the left (C, **Figure 9**) and right (C, **Figure 10**) front lower engine mounting brackets by performing the following:

    a. Remove the bolts (A, **Figure 9**) securing the left mounting bracket to the frame and the bolts (A, **Figure 10**) securing the right mounting bracket to the frame.

    b. From the right side of the motorcycle, remove the engine mounting nut (B, **Figure 10**).

    c. From the left side of the motorcycle, pull the front lower engine mounting through bolt (B, **Figure 9**) from the engine and remove both lower mounting brackets.

23. Remove the left rear upper mounting bolt (A, **Figure 11**) and the right rear upper mounting bolt (A, **Figure 12**).

24. From the right side of the motorcycle, remove the nut (B, **Figure 12**) from the rear lower mount, and pull the through bolt (B, **Figure 11**) out from the left side.

25. Make sure all cables, wires, and hoses are disconnected from the engine and safely moved out of the way.

> *WARNING*
> *The engine is heavy and has many sharp edges. It may shift or drop suddenly once the mounting bolts are removed. Never place your hands or any other part of your body where the engine could drop and crush your hands or arms. Have one or more assistants help remove the engine from the frame. Do not attempt engine removal by yourself.*

26. With an assistant, lift the engine off the jack and remove it from the right side of the frame.

27. While the engine is removed for service, check all the frame engine mounts for cracks or other damage. If any cracks are detected, take the chassis assembly to a Yamaha dealership for further examination.

Installation

Refer to **Figure 1** when installing the engine.

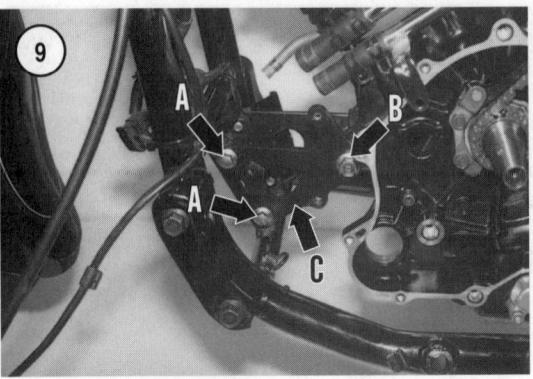

> *NOTE*
> *Install the cylinder heads before installing the engine in the frame. When installing the cylinder heads, temporarily install the alternator rotor onto the crankshaft taper, time the camshafts as described in Chapter Four, and then remove the alternator rotor. The reduced weight makes engine installation easier.*

1. Before installing the engine, protect the frame with shop rags so it will not be scratched.

2. Fit the engine through bolt (B, **Figure 11**) into place in the rear lower mounting boss on the left side of the frame.

> *WARNING*
> *The engine is very heavy and has many sharp edges. Never place your hands or any other part of your body where the engine could drop and crush your hands or arms. Have one or more assistants help install the engine into the frame. Do not attempt engine removal by yourself.*

ENGINE LOWER END 143

7. Install the front lower engine mounting brackets by performing the following:
   a. Set the left mounting bracket (C, **Figure 9**) in place on the frame, and install the two mounting bolts (A, **Figure 9**).
   b. Set the right front lower mounting bracket (C, **Figure 10**) on the frame, and install the two mounting bolts (A, **Figure 10**).
   c. From the left side of the motorcycle, install the front lower engine mounting bolt (B, **Figure 9**) through the engine and both lower mounting brackets.
   d. From the right side, install the nut (B, **Figure 10**) onto the front lower engine mounting bolt.
8. Install the left front upper engine mounting bracket (D, **Figure 8**) by performing the following:
   a. Set the bracket in place in the inboard side of the frame downtube.
   b. Set the cable holder (B, **Figure 8**) in place on the outboard side of the downtube.
   c. Install the bolts (A, **Figure 8**) through the cable holder, downtube, and out of the bracket.
   d. Install a nut onto each bolt.
   e. Install the bolt (C, **Figure 8**) through the left front upper engine mounting bracket and thread it into the mount on the engine.
9. Install the right front upper engine mounting bracket (C, **Figure 7**) by performing the following:
   a. Set the bracket in place in the inboard side of the frame downtube.
   b. Install the bolts (A, **Figure 7**) into the downtube and out through the bracket.
   c. Install a nut onto each bolt.
   d. Install the bolt (B, **Figure 7**) through the bracket and thread it into the mount in the engine.
10. Torque the engine mounting hardware to the specification in **Table 4**. Tighten the hardware in the following sequence.
    a. Rear lower through bolt and nut.
    b. The left and right rear upper bolts.
    c. Right front lower engine mounting bracket hardware.
    d. Left front lower engine mounting bracket hardware.
    e. Left front upper engine mounting bracket hardware.
    f. Right front upper engine mounting bracket hardware.

3. With the aid of an assistant, lift the engine and fit it into the frame from the right side. Lower the rear of the engine between the rear lower mounting bosses so the through bolt can be installed.

4. While the assistant holds the engine, place a suitable jack under the crankcase to support the engine.

5. Loosely install the nut (B, **Figure 12**) onto the through bolt where it emerges from the right side of the frame.

NOTE
Install the engine-mounting hardware finger-tight during Steps 6-9. They will be torqued after all the hardware has been installed.

6. Install the left rear upper mounting bolt (A, **Figure 11**) and the right rear upper mounting bolt (A, **Figure 12**).

NOTE
*The front lower engine mounting brackets are not interchangeable. The left bracket (C, **Figure 9**) has a tang that is not on the right bracket.*

144

11. Complete the installation procedure by reversing removal steps 1-18. Note the following:
    a. When the engine is completely assembled, fill the crankcase with the recommended type and quantity of oil as described in Chapter Three.
    b. Adjust the throttle cable and clutch cable as described in Chapter Three.
    c. Start the engine and check for oil and exhaust leaks.

ALTERNATOR COVER

Removal/Installation

1. Drain the engine oil as described in Chapter Three.
2. Disconnect the electrical lead from the negative battery terminal (**Figure 2**).
3. Disconnect the shift lever from the shift shaft. See **Figure 13**.
4. Remove the sidestand (A, **Figure 14**) and the left side cover (B, **Figure 14**) as described in Chapter Thirteen.
5. Remove the middle gearcase cover (C, **Figure 14**).
6. Open the cable clamp (**Figure 15**) and release the stator and pickup-coil wires.
7. Trace the wires to the connectors, and disconnect the 3-pin stator connector and the 2-pin pickup coil connector.
8. Pull the stator- and pickup-coil wires from the frame. Note how the wires are routed along the frame. Make sure to reroute these wires along the same path during installation.
9. Disconnect the clutch cable from the clutch release lever (A, **Figure 16**) as described in Chapter Six.
10. Remove the 11 mounting bolts and remove the alternator cover and gasket.

> *NOTE*
> *Five different length bolts secure the alternator cover to the crankcase. Note the location of these bolts. They must be reinstalled in the same location during assembly. See **Figure 17**. Also notice the location of the two bolts (C, **Figure 16**) that hold the clutch cable bracket in place and the bolt (B, **Figure 16**) that holds the*

CHAPTER FIVE

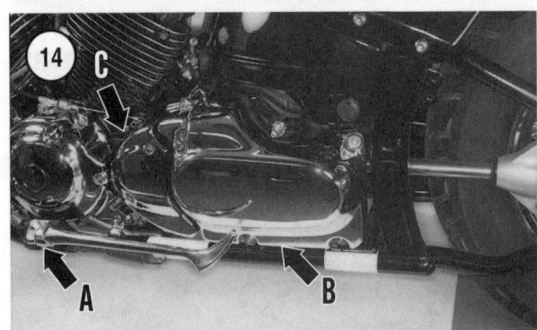

AIS-hose bracket in place. Install the brackets behind these bolts during assembly.

11. If still installed, remove the alternator cover gasket (A, **Figure 18**) and the two dowels (B, **Figure 18**) from the crankcase.
12. Installation is the reverse of removal. Note the following:
    a. Make sure the two dowels (B, **Figure 18**) are in place in the crankcase.
    b. Install a new alternator cover gasket (A, **Figure 18**).
    c. Install the clutch cable bracket and the AIS-hose bracket in their original locations on the alternator cover.

ENGINE LOWER END

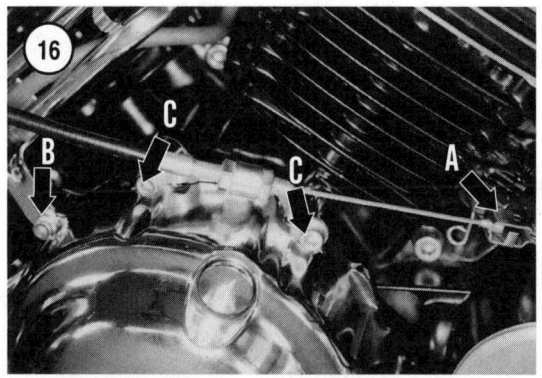

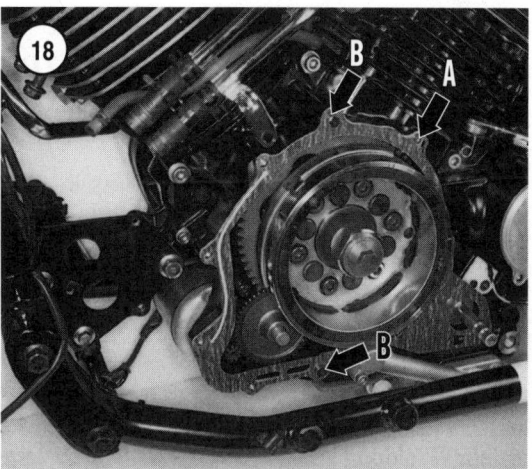

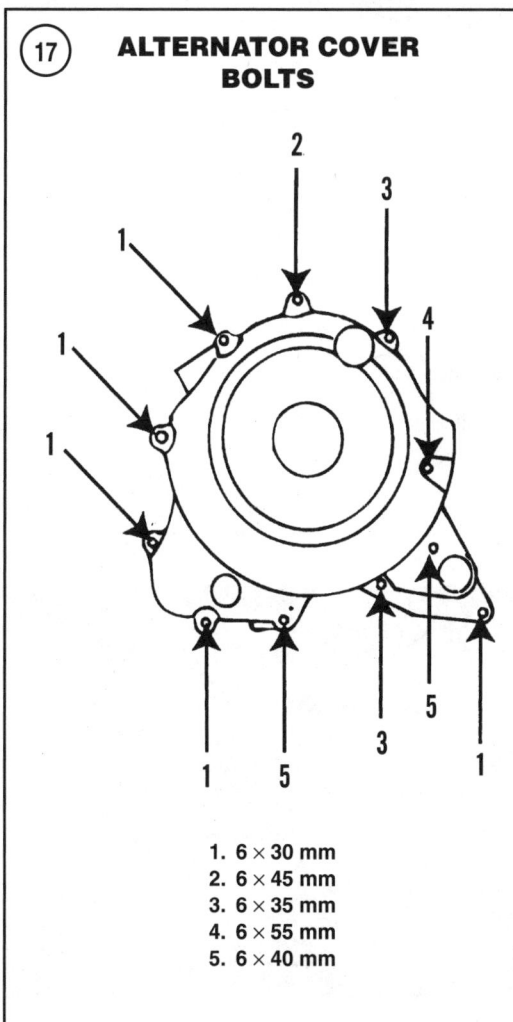

ALTERNATOR COVER BOLTS

1. 6 × 30 mm
2. 6 × 45 mm
3. 6 × 35 mm
4. 6 × 55 mm
5. 6 × 40 mm

d. Torque the alternator cover bolts to the specification in **Table 4**.

e. Install the shift lever so the index mark on the shift shaft (A, **Figure 13**) aligns with the slot in the shift lever. Tighten the shift lever clamp bolt (B, **Figure 13**) to the specification in **Table 4**.

STATOR AND PICKUP COILS

Stator and pickup coil removal and inspection procedures appear in Chapter Nine.

ALTERNATOR ROTOR AND STARTER GEARS

Refer to **Figure 19** when servicing the rotor and starter gears.

Removal

1. Remove the alternator cover as described in this chapter.
2. Remove the starter idler gear shaft (A, **Figure 20**) and the starter idler gear (B, **Figure 20**) from the crankcase.
3. Hold the rotor with the Yamaha sheave holder (part No. YS-01880) or equivalent.
4A. If the starter clutch will not be serviced, loosen the rotor bolt (A, **Figure 21**) and every other starter clutch bolt (B, **Figure 21**).
4B. If the starter clutch will be serviced, loosen the rotor bolt (A, **Figure 21**) and the six starter clutch bolts (B, **Figure 21**).
5. Remove the rotor bolt and washer, and remove every other starter clutch bolt.
6. Fit the adapter (part No. YU-33282) and the flywheel puller (part No. YU-33270) onto the rotor.

CHAPTER FIVE

ALTERNATOR ROTOR AND STARTER CLUTCH

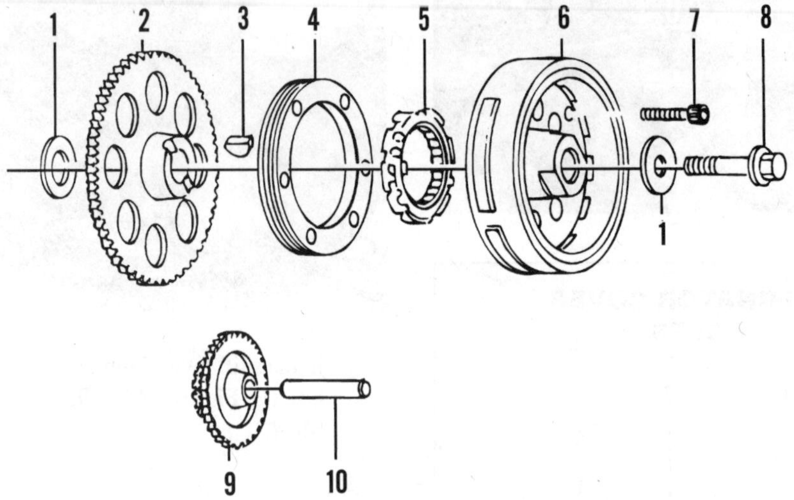

1. Washer
2. Starter wheel gear
3. Woodruff key
4. Starter clutch housing
5. Sprague clutch
6. Rotor
7. Bolt
8. Rotor bolt
9. Starter idler gear
10. Shaft

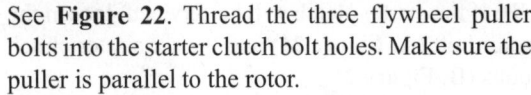

See **Figure 22**. Thread the three flywheel puller bolts into the starter clutch bolt holes. Make sure the puller is parallel to the rotor.

7. Turn the puller's center screw and drive the rotor off the crankshaft. If necessary, adjust a puller screw to keep the puller parallel to the rotor.

8. Remove the Woodruff key (A, **Figure 23**) and the starter wheel gear (B, **Figure 23**) from the crankshaft.

9. Remove the washer (**Figure 24**) from the crankshaft.

ENGINE LOWER END

Inspection

1. Clean the parts in solvent and dry them with compressed air.

WARNING
Replace a cracked or chipped rotor. A damaged rotor can fly apart at high speed, throwing metal fragments into the engine. Do not attempt to repair a damaged rotor.

2. Inspect the rotor for cracks or breaks. Make sure the magnet is free of all metal debris.

3. Check the rotor tapered bore and the crankshaft taper for damage. Replace damaged parts as necessary

4. Inspect the threads of the rotor bolt. Replace the bolt if the threads are stretched or damaged.

5. Inspect the inner and outer teeth of the starter idler gear (A, **Figure 25**). Replace the gear if any teeth are worn, broken or missing.

6. Inspect the idler gear shaft (B, **Figure 25**) and the bearing surface of the starter idler gear for nicks or other signs of damage. Replace either if worn or damaged.

7. Inspect the teeth of the starter wheel gear (A, **Figure 26**). Replace the gear if any teeth are worn, broken or missing.

8. Inspect the bearing surface of the starter wheel gear for nicks or scratches. Replace the wheel gear if it shows signs of wear.

NOTE
The starter clutch is sold as an assembly. The sprague clutch and starter clutch housing are not available separately.

CHAPTER FIVE

9. Inspect the rollers in the sprague clutch (B, **Figure 26**) for wear or damage. All the rollers should rotate freely. If there is damage or wear, replace the starter clutch.

10. Check the operation of the starter clutch as described in this chapter.

Installation

1. Install the washer (**Figure 24**) onto the crankshaft.

2. Install the starter wheel gear (B, **Figure 23**), and insert the Woodruff key (A, **Figure 23**) into the crankshaft.

3. Install the rotor by performing the following:
   a. Align the keyway in the rotor with the Woodruff key in the crankshaft.
   b. Slide the rotor over the crankshaft until the sprague clutch pushes against the starter wheel gear.
   c. Turn the starter wheel gear counterclockwise while gently pushing the rotor onto the crankshaft until the wheel gear bottoms within the sprague clutch.
   d. Install the rotor bolt and washer (**Figure 27**). Make sure the convex side of the washer faces the bolt head.
   e. Hold the rotor with the sheave holder and torque the rotor bolt to the specification in **Table 4**.

4. Set the starter idler gear (B, **Figure 20**) onto the boss in the crankcase. Make sure the inner gear teeth (A, **Figure 28**) engage the starter wheel gear (B, **Figure 28**) behind the rotor, and the outer gear teeth (C, **Figure 28**) engage the starter motor.

5. Install the shaft (A, **Figure 20**) through the starter idler gear and into the boss in the crankcase.

6. Install the alternator cover as described in this chapter.

STARTER CLUTCH

Removal/Installation

Refer to **Figure 19** when servicing the starter clutch.

1. Remove the alternator as described in this chapter.

ENGINE LOWER END

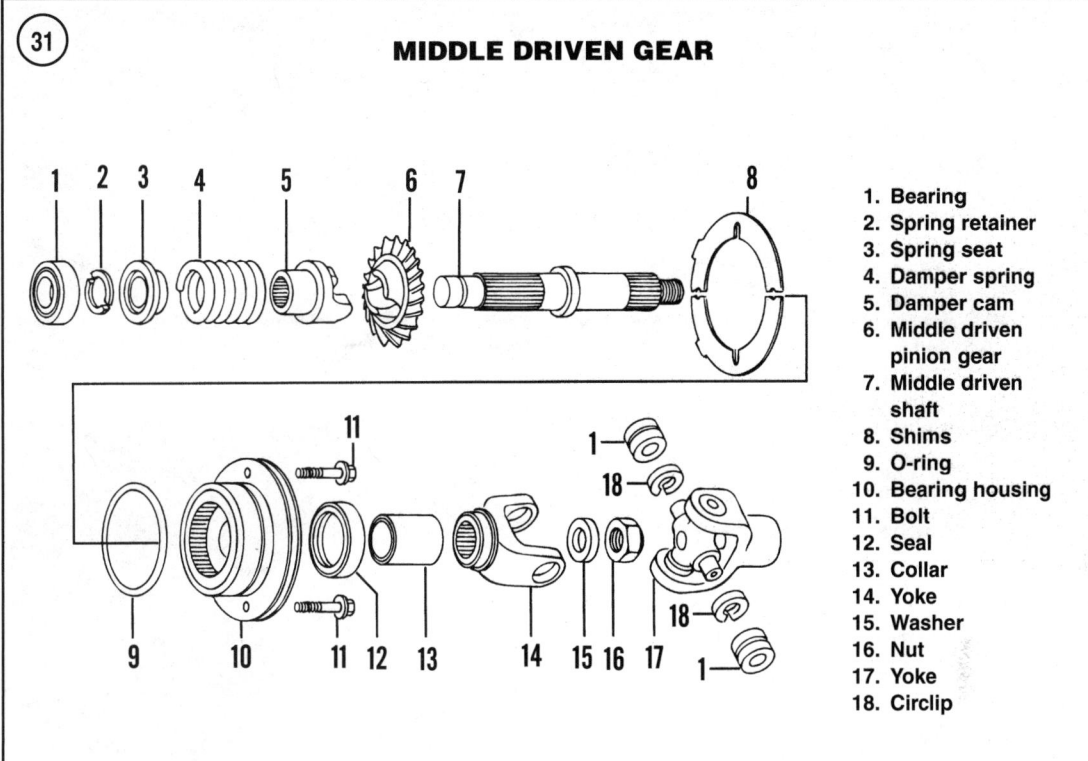

31 MIDDLE DRIVEN GEAR

1. Bearing
2. Spring retainer
3. Spring seat
4. Damper spring
5. Damper cam
6. Middle driven pinion gear
7. Middle driven shaft
8. Shims
9. O-ring
10. Bearing housing
11. Bolt
12. Seal
13. Collar
14. Yoke
15. Washer
16. Nut
17. Yoke
18. Circlip

2. If necessary, hold the alternator rotor with the sheave holder or equivalent and remove the three remaining starter clutch bolts (**Figure 29**).

3. Remove the starter clutch (**Figure 30**) from the back of the rotor.

4. Installation is the reverse of removal. Note the following:
   a. Apply Loctite 242 (blue) to the threads of each starter clutch bolt, and install the bolts.
   b. Hold the rotor with the sheave holder and torque all six starter clutch bolts to the specification in **Table 4**.

Inspection

1. Install the starter wheel gear into the starter clutch by performing the following:
   a. Set the rotor assembly face down on the bench.
   b. Set the bearing surface of the starter wheel gear between rollers in the sprague clutch.
   c. Press the starter wheel gear down while rotating it clockwise. Gently press the gear until it bottoms within the sprague clutch.

2. Hold the rotor, and turn the starter wheel gear clockwise. The wheel gear should turn freely within the starter clutch.

3. Hold the rotor, and turn the starter wheel gear counterclockwise. It should not turn in this direction.

NOTE
The starter clutch is sold as an assembly. The sprague clutch and starter clutch housing are not available separately.

4. The starter clutch is defective if it fails either test. Replace the starter clutch assembly as described above.

MIDDLE DRIVEN GEAR ASSEMBLY

Removal/Installation

Refer to **Figure 31** when servicing the middle driven gear assembly.

The middle driven gear assembly can be removed with the engine installed in the frame. The procedure is shown with the engine removed for clarity.

1. Remove the swing arm as described in Chapter Eleven.

2. Remove the two mounting bolts (**Figure 32**) and remove the middle gearcase cover.

3. Remove the two bolts securing the middle gear housing cover (**Figure 33**), and then remove the cover and its O-ring.

4. Remove the four bolts (**Figure 34**) from the middle driven gear bearing housing.

5. Remove the two shims from behind the bearing housing. Note how the tab on one shim points at six o'clock (A, **Figure 35**). Reinstall the shims with the same orientation during assembly.

6. Pull the middle driven gear assembly (B, **Figure 35**) from its bearing in the middle gear case, and remove the assembly.

7. Remove the O-ring (C, **Figure 36**) from the bearing housing.

8. Inspect the middle driven gear assembly as described below.

9. Installation is the reverse of removal. Note the following:

   a. Lubricate a *new* O-ring (C, **Figure 36**) with lithium grease, and install the O-ring onto the bearing housing.

   b. Install the middle driven gear assembly into the middle gearcase so the middle driven shaft is seated within the middle gear bearing (**Figure 37**) in the gear case.

   c. Loosely install the four bearing housing bolts, and then install both shims between the bearing housing and the middle-gear case. Install the shim as shown in the inset in **Figure 38**.

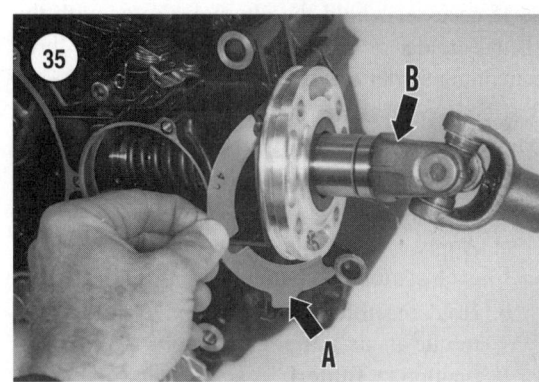

When the shims are properly installed, the tab on the outboard shim should face six o'clock.

   d. Torque the bearing housing bolts to the specification in **Table 4**.

Inspection

A number of special tools are required to disassemble the middle driven gear assembly. Refer this work to a Yamaha dealership or other qualified machine shop.

ENGINE LOWER END

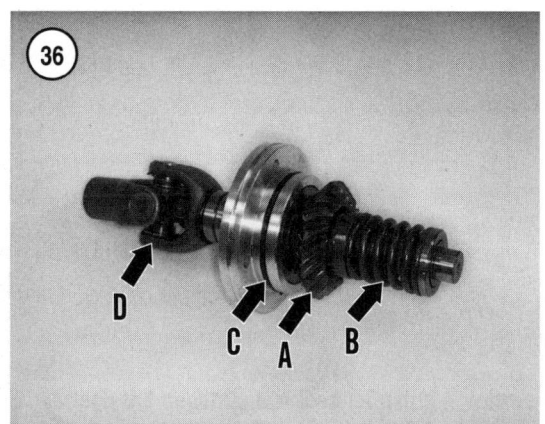

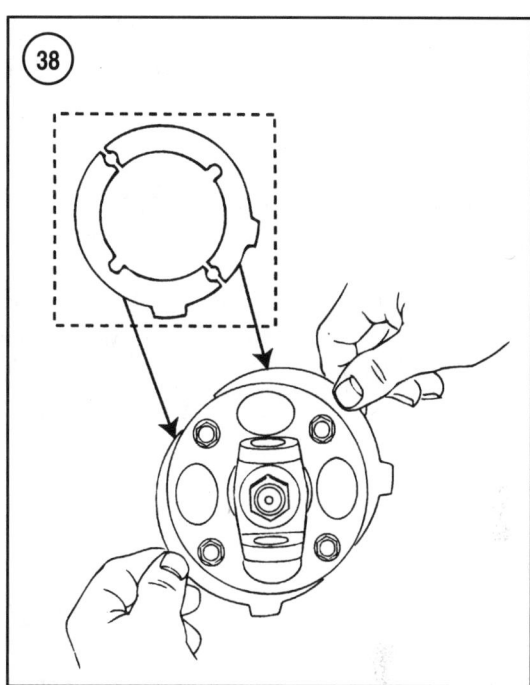

1. Inspect the middle driven pinion gear (A, **Figure 36**) for chipped or missing teeth. If there is any damage replace the middle driven pinion gear and the middle drive pinion gear. Replace both of these gears as a set.

2. Inspect the splines on the middle drive pinion gear. If damaged, replace both the middle drive pinion gear and the middle driven pinion gear. Also inspect the splines on the countershaft for damage.

3. Inspect the damper spring (B, **Figure 36**) for wear, cracks or damage. Replace the spring if necessary.

4. Check the movement of the universal joint (D, **Figure 36**). Replace the universal joint if it is stiff or loose.

5. Inspect the inner splines of the universal joint. If the splines are damaged, replace the universal joint. Also inspect the outer splines on the drive shaft. They may also be damaged.

MIDDLE DRIVE PINION GEAR

Removal

Refer to **Figure 39** when servicing the middle drive pinion gear.

1. Remove the middle driven gear assembly as described in this chapter.
2. Shift the transmission into first gear.
3. Remove the cover (**Figure 33**) and O-ring from the middle gear housing.
4. Use a punch to flatten the lock tab (A, **Figure 40**) on the middle-drive-pinion-gear nut.

NOTE
If the clutch plates have been removed, hold both the alternator rotor and the clutch boss when removing the middle drive pinion gear nut.

5. Hold the clutch with a Grabbit (**Figure 41**) or similar tool, and remove the nut (B, **Figure 40**) from the countershaft. If possible, remove the nut with an air gun and a 30 mm socket.

6. Pull the middle drive pinion gear from the countershaft and remove it from the middle gear housing. Do not lose the shim(s) behind the middle drive pinion gear.

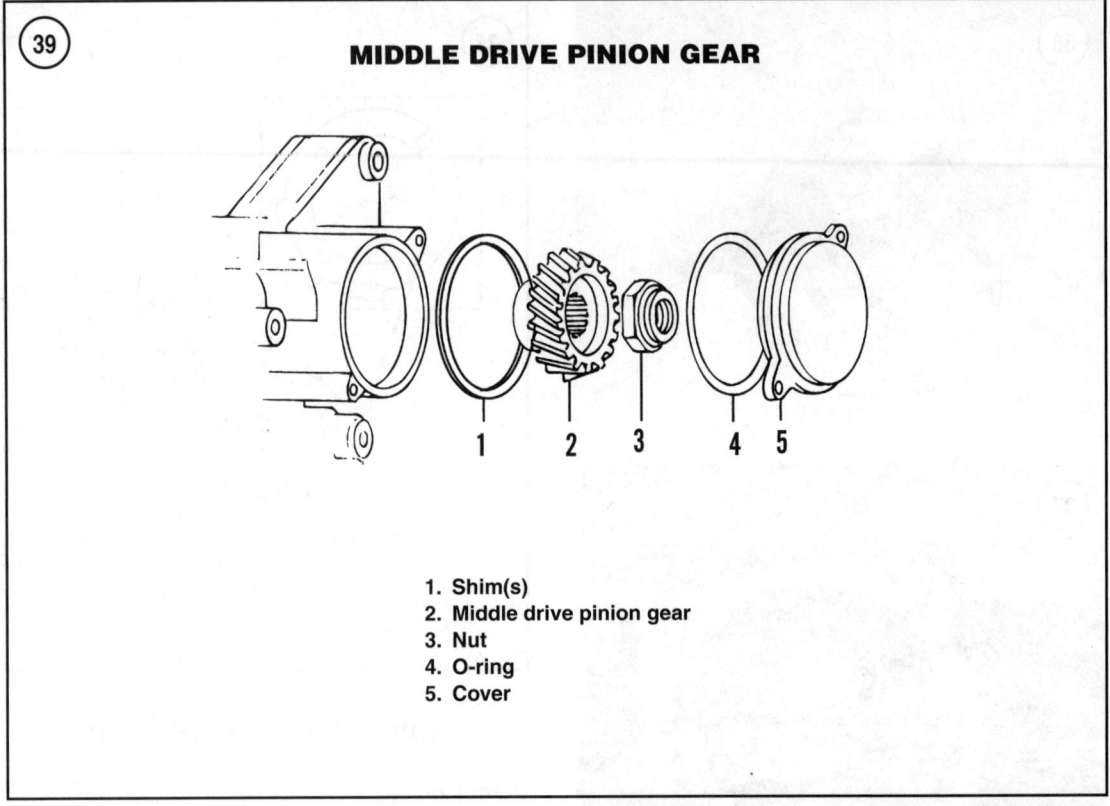

39 MIDDLE DRIVE PINION GEAR

1. Shim(s)
2. Middle drive pinion gear
3. Nut
4. O-ring
5. Cover

7. Inspect the middle drive pinion gear (A, **Figure 42**) for chipped or missing teeth. If there is any damage, replace the middle drive pinion gear and the middle driven pinion gear. Replace both of these gears as a set.

8. Inspect the splines (B, **Figure 42**) on the middle drive pinion gear. If damaged, replace both the middle drive pinion gear and the middle driven pinion gear. Also inspect the splines on the countershaft for damage.

Installation

NOTE
If replacing the crankcase or the middle drive pinion gear, also replace the shim(s). Calculate the middle drive pinion gear shim thickness and select the correct shim(s) as described below.

1. Set the correct shim(s) onto the shoulder of the middle drive pinion gear, and install the gear onto the countershaft.

2. Install a *new* middle drive pinion gear nut onto the countershaft.

3. Hold the clutch with a Grabbit (**Figure 41**) or similar tool, and torque the nut to the specification in **Table 4**.

4. Lock the nut in place by bending the lock tab on the nut (A, **Figure 40**).

5. Lubricate a new O-ring with lithium grease, and install the O-ring on the middle gear case cover.

6. Install the cover (**Figure 33**) onto the middle gear case, and tighten the two screws securely.

Middle Drive Pinion Gear Shim Selection

Calculate the middle drive pinion gear shim thickness by using the following formula:

Shim thickness = A − B.

A = This is the base number 44 plus or minus the number stamped on the middle drive pinion gear (**Figure 43**).

B = This is the number stamped on the left crankcase half (**Figure 44**).

Example:

ENGINE LOWER END

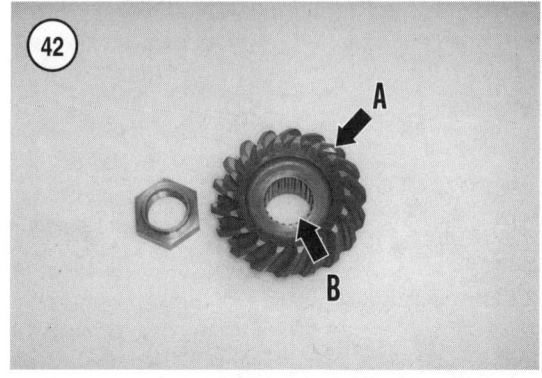

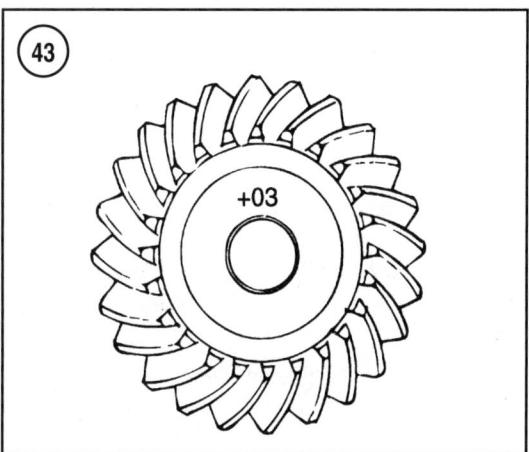

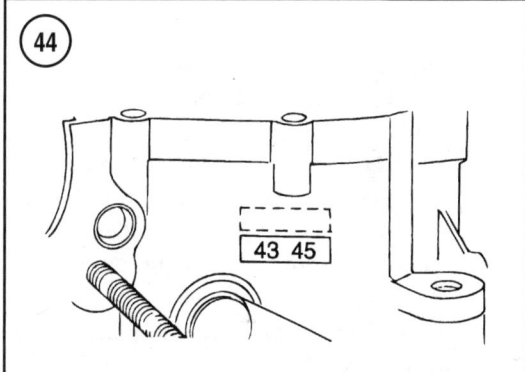

tenths digit. For example if the calculated value is 0.54, round shim thickness down to 0.50 mm.

If the hundredths digit is 5-9, round shim thickness up to the next tenth of a millimeter. For example, if the shim thickness is 0.58 mm (as calculated above) round shim thickness up to 0.60 mm and install two 0.30 mm shims so the total thickness equals 0.60 mm.

If the number on middle drive pinion gear is +03 as in **Figure 43**, A = 44 + 03 or 44.03.

If the number on the crankcase is 43 45 as in **Figure 44**, B = 43.45.

Shim thickness is 0.58mm (44.03 − 43.45 = 0.58 mm).

Middle-pinion-gear shims are available in three sizes (0.20, 0.30 and 0.40 mm), round off the calculated shim thickness to the nearest tenth of a millimeter.

If the hundredths digit in the calculated value is 0-4, round shim thickness down to the existing

PRIMARY DRIVE GEAR

Refer to Chapter Six for primary drive gear removal and installation procedures.

OIL PUMP

Removal/Installation

The oil pump can be removed with the engine mounted in the frame. The procedure is shown with the engine removed for clarity.

1. Drain the oil, and remove the clutch cover as described in Chapter Six.
2. Remove the circlip (A, **Figure 45**) securing the oil pump gear to the pump shaft, and remove the gear (B, **Figure 45**).
3. Remove the three oil pump mounting bolts (**Figure 46**) and the oil pump from the crankcase.
4. Remove the small O-ring (A, **Figure 47**) and then the dowel and O-ring (B, **Figure 47**) from the crankcase.
5. Inspect the oil pump as described in this chapter.
6. Installation is the reverse of removal. Note the following:
    a. Use *new* O-rings. Lubricate each O-ring with grease before installation.
    b. Make sure the ports on the back of the pump engage those on the crankcase (**Figure 48**).
    c. Apply blue Loctite 242 (blue) to the threads of the oil pump mounting bolts, and torque the bolts to the specification in **Table 2**.
    d. Install the oil pump gear so the side with the shoulder faces out. Make sure the oil pump gear meshes with the oil pump spur gear (C, **Figure 45**) on the crankshaft.
    e. Use a new circlip when installing the oil pump gear.

Disassembly/Inspection/Assembly

Except for the oil pump gear, replacement parts are not available for the oil pump. If an inspection reveals any defective part(s), replace the oil pump.

Refer to **Figure 49** when servicing the oil pump.
1. Remove the screw (**Figure 50**) and the spring retainer from the oil pump cover.
2. Remove the spring (**Figure 51**) and relief valve from the oil pump cover.
3. Remove the Phillips screw (**Figure 52**) and separate the pump cover from the pump housing.
4. Remove the oil pump shaft (**Figure 53**) from the pump housing and remove the pin from the shaft.
5. Remove the inner and outer rotors from the pump housing.
6. Clean all parts in solvent and dry them thoroughly with compressed air.
7. Inspect both rotors (**Figure 54**) for wear. Replace the oil pump if either rotor is worn or damaged.

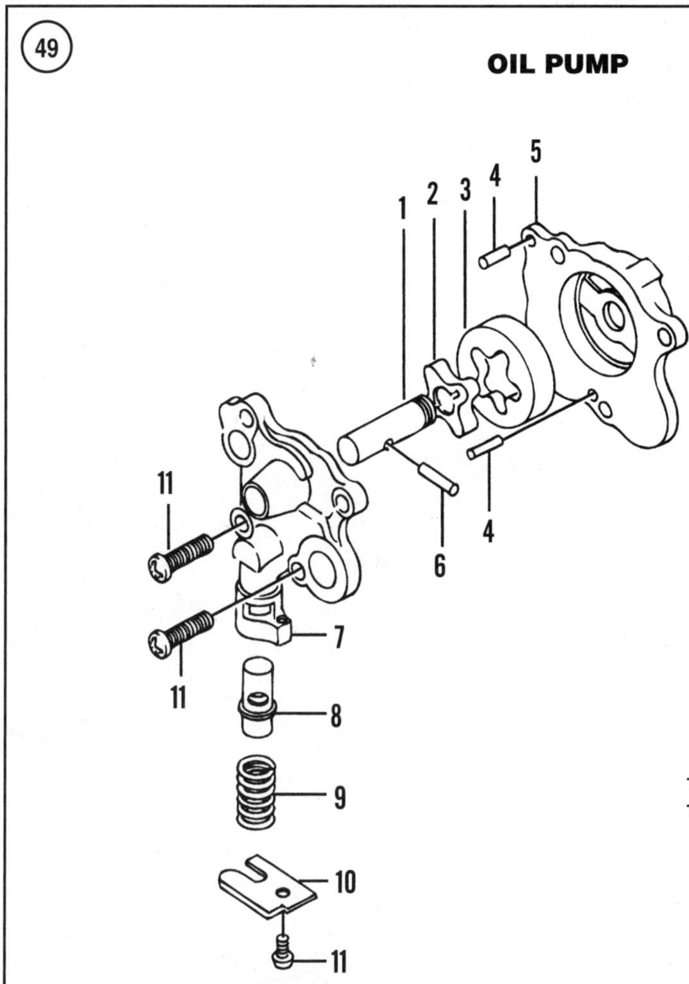

ENGINE LOWER END

⑨ OIL PUMP

1. Oil pump shaft
2. Inner rotor
3. Outer rotor
4. Locating pin
5. Oil pump housing
6. Pin
7. Oil pump cover
8. Relief valve
9. Spring
10. Spring retainer
11. Screw

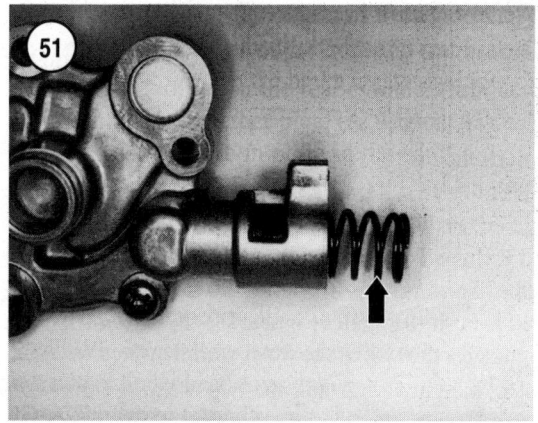

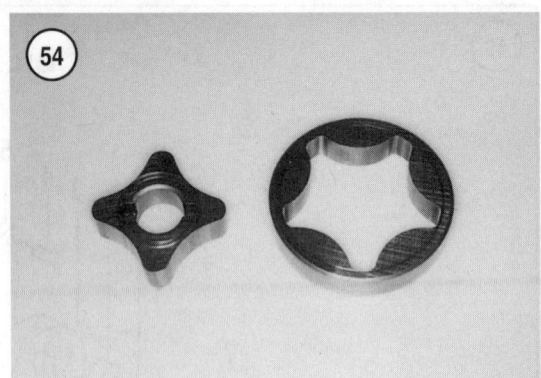

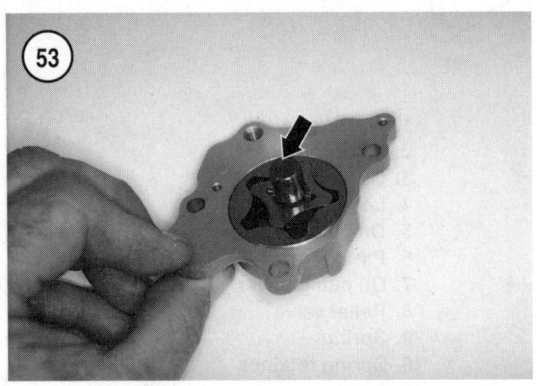

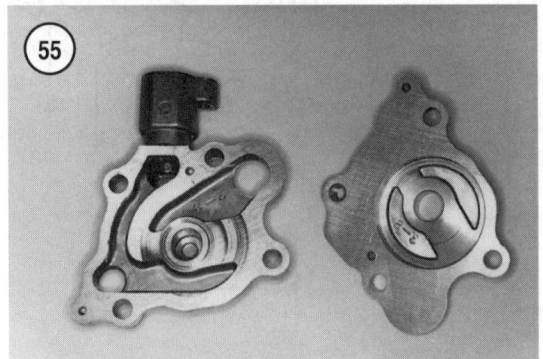

8. Inspect the oil pump body and cover for cracks (**Figure 55**). Replace the oil pump if there is any damage.

9. Inspect the teeth on the oil pump gear (**Figure 56**). Replace the gear if any teeth are worn, broken, or missing. Also inspect the oil pump spur gear.

10. Coat all parts with fresh oil prior to assembly.

11. Install the outer rotor into the oil pump body.

12. Use a flat feeler gauge to measure the clearance between the outer rotor and the oil pump body (**Figure 57**). Replace the oil pump if the clearance exceeds the wear limit in **Table 1**.

13. Install the inner rotor into the outer rotor in the oil pump body.

14. Use a flat feeler gauge to measure the clearance between the tip of the inner rotor and the outer rotor (**Figure 58**). Replace the oil pump if the clearance exceeds the wear limit in **Table 1**.

15. Install the pin into the oil pump shaft and install the shaft into the inner rotor in the oil pump housing. Push the shaft (**Figure 53**) down until the pin engages the slot in the inner rotor.

16. If removed, install the two locating pins (**Figure 59**) into the oil pump housing.

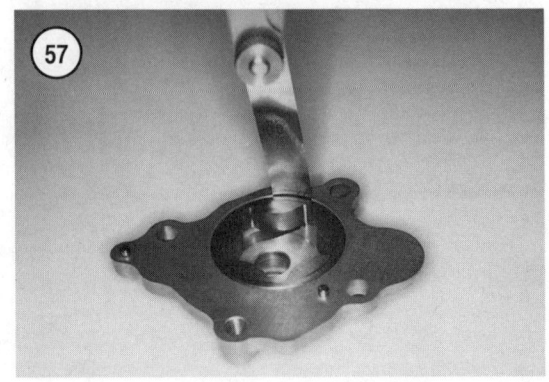

ENGINE LOWER END

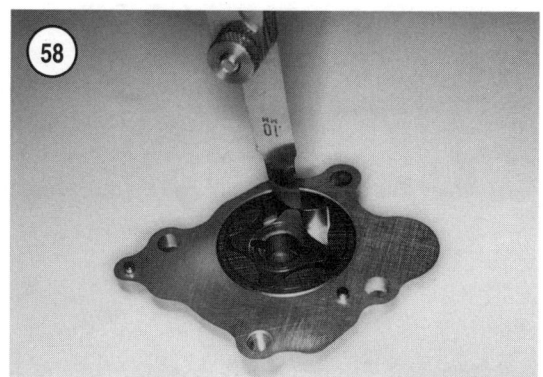

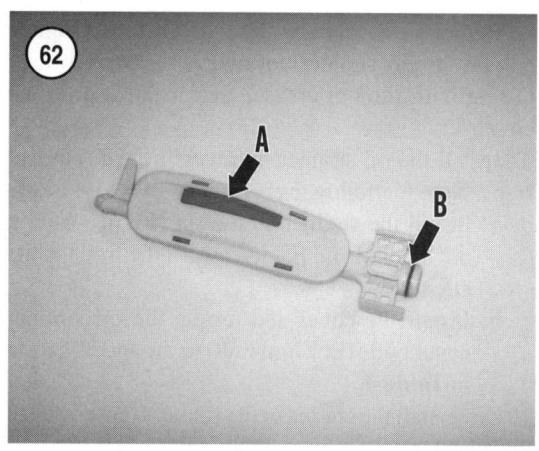

17. Fit the oil pump cover onto the oil pump housing. Make sure the locating pins in the housing engage the holes in the cover.

18. Install the Phillips screw (**Figure 52**) and secure the cover to the housing. Tighten the screw securely.

19. Install the relief valve and the spring (**Figure 51**) into the oil pump cover.

20. Install the spring retainer and secure it in place with the screw (**Figure 50**). Tighten the screw securely.

OIL STRAINER

Removal/Inspection/Installation

1. Remove the engine as described in this chapter.

2. Remove the three mounting bolts and the oil strainer cover (A, **Figure 60**). Note that the bolt (B, **Figure 60**) at the end of the cover extension is longer than the two mounting bolts (C, **Figure 60**) on the housing.

3. Pull the oil strainer (**Figure 61**) from the housing in the crankcase.

4. Clean the strainer and cover in solvent, and dry them with compressed air.

5. Inspect the screen (A, **Figure 62**) in the strainer. Replace the strainer if the screen is damaged.

6. Remove and discard the O-ring (B, **Figure 62**) from the strainer. Lubricate a new O-ring with lithium grease, and install it onto the strainer.

7. Inspect the oil strainer cover for cracks or other signs of damage. Replace the cover as necessary.

CHAPTER FIVE

8. Remove and discard the two O-rings (**Figure 63**) on the oil strainer cover. Lubricate each new O-ring with lithium grease, and install it onto the cover.
9. Install the oil strainer by reversing the removal steps. Note the following:
    a. Install the strainer so the fin (**Figure 64**) on the inboard end points toward the front of the engine.
    b. Install the cover and torque the oil strainer cover bolts (B, **Figure 60**) to the specification in **Table 4**.
10. Reinstall the engine in the frame as described in this chapter.

CRANKCASE

Crankcase Disassembly

This procedure describes the disassembly of the crankcase halves and the removal of the crankshaft, transmission shaft assemblies, and internal shift mechanism. Disassembly and inspection procedures for the transmission shaft assemblies and internal shift mechanism are in Chapter Seven.

1. Remove the engine as described in this chapter. Remove all exterior assemblies from the crankcase as described in this chapter and other related chapters:
    a. Oil filter (Chapter Three).
    b. Cylinder head (Chapter Four).
    c. Cylinder and piston (Chapter Four).
    d. Clutch (Chapter Six).
    e. External shift mechanism (Chapter Six).
    f. Oil pump (this chapter).
    g. Primary drive gear and oil pump spur gear (Chapter Six).
    h. Alternator rotor (this chapter).
    i. Cam chain and chain guides (Chapter Four).
    j. Oil strainer (this chapter).
    k. Middle drive pinion gear (this chapter).
2. Rotate the shift drum so the ramps on the shift cam align with the cutouts in the right crankcase half as shown in **Figure 65**. This is necessary so the shift cam can pass through the right case half when the cases are separated.

NOTE
Crankcase bolts are identified by a number embossed on the crankcase near each bolt hole. These numbers

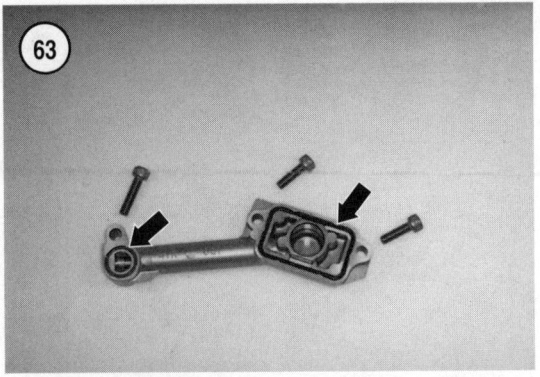

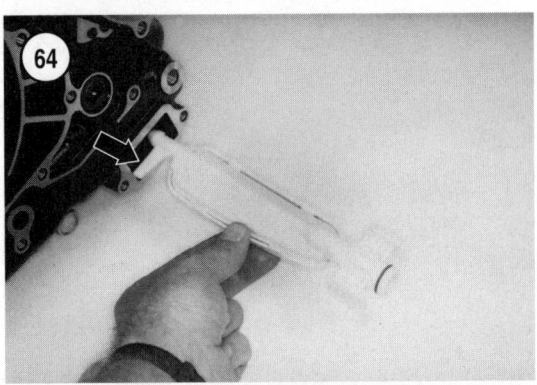

also indicate the crankcase bolt tightening sequence. See **Figure 66**.

3. Before removing the crankcase bolts, draw an outline of each case half on a piece of cardboard. Punch holes along the drawing outline corresponding to the bolt location in each crankcase half shown in **Figure 66**. Insert each bolt in its respective hole in the cardboard after removing it so it can be quickly identified during assembly.

ENGINE LOWER END

66 CRANKCASE BOLT TIGHTENING SEQUENCE

LEFT CASE

RIGHT CASE

CAUTION
If it is necessary to pry apart the case halves, do it very carefully to avoid marring the gasket surfaces. If they do get damaged, the cases will leak and must be replaced as a set. They cannot be repaired.

NOTE
Notice that bolt No. 14 is a chrome bolt while bolt No. 13 is black. Reinstall these bolts in their original locations during assembly.

4. Evenly loosen all the crankcase bolts one-quarter turn at a time. Start with bolt No. 14 and loosen the bolts in descending order. After all bolts are loose, remove them and place them in the corresponding holes in the cardboard templates.

5. Set the crankcase on wooden blocks so the right crankcase half faces up.

6. Separate the crankcase halves by carefully tapping around the crankcase perimeter with a plastic mallet. Do not use a metal hammer. Separate the crankcase halves by lifting the right case half off the left half.

7. Leave the transmission and crankshaft assemblies in the left crankcase.

8. Remove the three dowels (A and B, **Figure 67**) from the crankcase mating surface. Also remove the O-ring from the dowel (A, **Figure 67**) beneath the crankshaft.

9. Remove the mainshaft shift fork shaft (A, **Figure 68**) and the countershaft shift fork shaft (B, **Figure 68**).

160 CHAPTER FIVE

10. Rotate the shift forks away from the shift drum and lift the shift drum from the crankcase half. See **Figure 69**.
11. Each shift fork is identified by a letter embossed on its face. Note the letter on each shift fork to remember the correct location during assembly.
12. Remove the mainshaft shift fork (A, **Figure 70**) and the two countershaft shift forks (B and C, **Figure 70**).
13. Simultaneously lift both the mainshaft assembly (A, **Figure 71**) and the countershaft assembly (B, **Figure 71**) from the left crankcase half.
14. Store each individual shaft assembly (**Figure 72**) in a sealed and labeled plastic bag until service.
15. Lift the crankshaft (**Figure 73**) out of the left crankcase and remove it.
16. Remove the neutral switch (A, **Figure 74**) from the left crankcase half, and then remove and discard the neutral-switch O-ring (**Figure 75**).

Crankcase Inspection

1. Remove all sealer residue from all crankcase mating surfaces.

> *WARNING*
> *When drying the crankcase bearings in Step 2, do not allow the inner bearing race to spin. The bearings lack lubrication and damage will result. When drying the bearings with compressed air, hold both races by hand so the bearing does not rotate. The air jet will force the bearings to turn at speeds that exceed their designed limit. The likelihood of a bearing disintegrating and causing serious injury and damage is very great.*

2. Clean both crankcase halves and all crankcase bearings with cleaning solvent. Thoroughly dry them with compressed air.
3. Clean all crankcase oil passages with compressed air.
4. Lightly oil the crankcase bearings with engine oil before checking the bearings in Step 5.

> *NOTE*
> *When replacing a bearing, also replace its mate in the opposite case half. Crankcase bearings should be replaced as a set.*

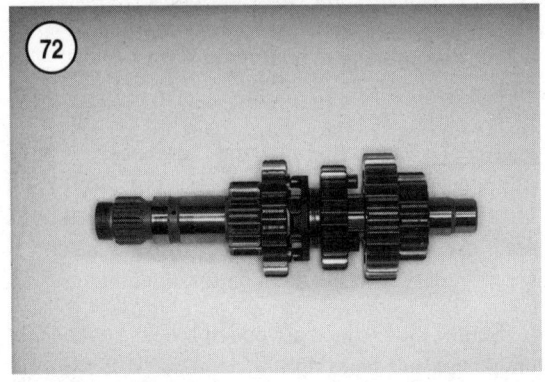

ENGINE LOWER END   161

5. Check the bearings for roughness, pitting, galling and play by rotating them slowly by hand. Replace any bearing that turns roughly or shows excessive play.

6. Replace any worn or damaged bearings as described in this chapter.

7. Inspect the crankcase studs. Make sure they are straight, and their threads are in good condition. Check that they are tightly screwed into the crankcase.

8. Inspect the mating surfaces of both halves. They must be free of gouges, burrs or any damage that causes an oil leak.

9. Inspect the cases for cracks and fractures, especially in the lower areas where they are vulnerable to rock damage.

10. Check the areas around the stiffening ribs, around bearing bosses and threaded holes for damage. Repair or replace damaged cases.

11. Check the threaded holes in both crankcase halves for thread damage, dirt or oil buildup. If necessary, clean or repair the threads with a suitable size metric tap. Coat the tap threads with kerosene or an aluminum tap fluid before use.

12. Check for loose or damaged shift-shaft stopper bolt (**Figure 76**); retighten or replace if necessary. Note the following:
   a. Apply Loctite 242 (blue) to the bolt threads before installing.
   b. Tighten the shift-shaft stopper bolt to the torque specification in **Table 4**.

13. Inspect the mounting bosses (B, **Figure 74**) for cracks or damage.

14. Check the shift shaft seal (C, **Figure 74**). Replace it as necessary. Use a wide blade screwdriver to remove the seal. Use the appropriate size socket or bearing driver to install the new seal.

Crankcase Bearing Replacement

Prior to replacing the crankcase bearings and bushings, note the following:

1. Because of the number of bearings used in the left and right crankcase, make sure to identify each bearing and note its location before removing it. Use the size code markings to identify a bearing.

2. Refer to *Bearing Replacement* in Chapter One for general information on bearing removal and installation.

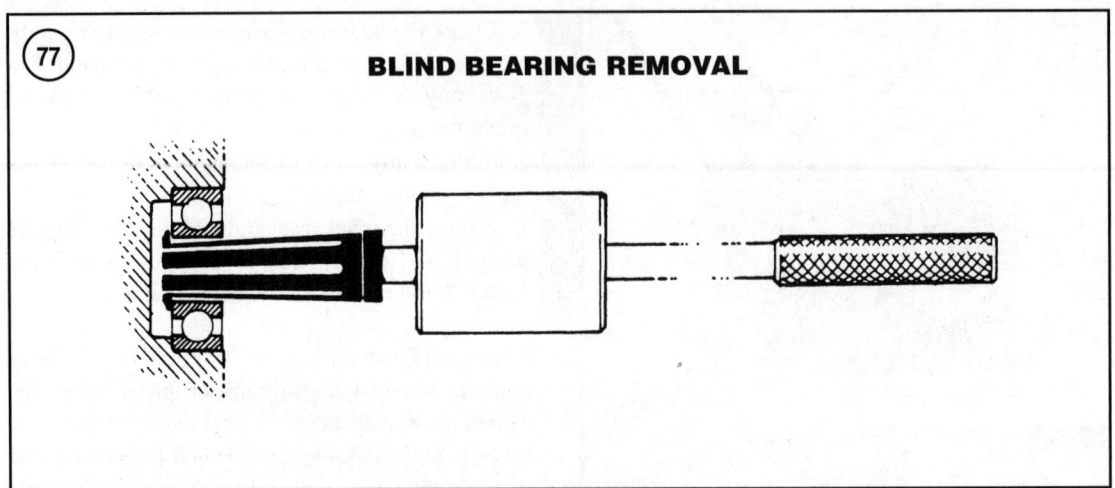

BLIND BEARING REMOVAL

3. Heat the crankcase to approximately 205-257° F (95-125° C) in an oven or on a hot plate. Do not heat the crankcase with a torch. This type of localized heating may warp the cases.
4. Drive the bearing out with a suitable size bearing driver, socket or a drift.
5. After removing the bearings and bushings, clean the crankcase half in solvent and dry it thoroughly.
6. A blind bearing remover (**Figure 77**) is required to remove some of the blind bearings in the following procedures.
7. When installing new bearings, press the outer bearing race only (**Figure 78**).

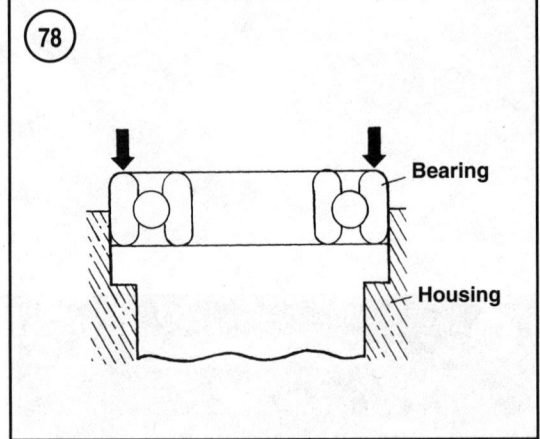

Mainshaft bearing replacement

1. To replace the left mainshaft bearing (A, **Figure 79**):
   a. Remove the clutch release mechanism as described in Chapter Six.
   b. Remove the bearing with a blind bearing remover.
   c. Press the new bearing into place until it bottoms in the crankcase.
2. To replace the right mainshaft bearing (A, **Figure 80**):
   a. Press the bearing from the crankcase.
   b. Press the new bearing into place until it bottoms in the crankcase.

Countershaft bearing replacement

1. To replace the left countershaft bearing (B, **Figure 79**):
   a. Remove the two bearing retainers, and press the bearing from the crankcase.
   b. Press the new bearing into place until it bottoms in the crankcase.
   c. Torque the bearing retainer Torx screws to the specification in **Table 4**. Use a punch to lock the Torx head in place.
2. To replace the right countershaft bearing (B, **Figure 80**):
   a. Remove the bearing with a blind bearing remover.
   b. Press the new bearing into place until it bottoms in the crankcase.

Middle gear bearing replacement

1. To replace the middle gear bearing (**Figure 81**):

ENGINE LOWER END 163

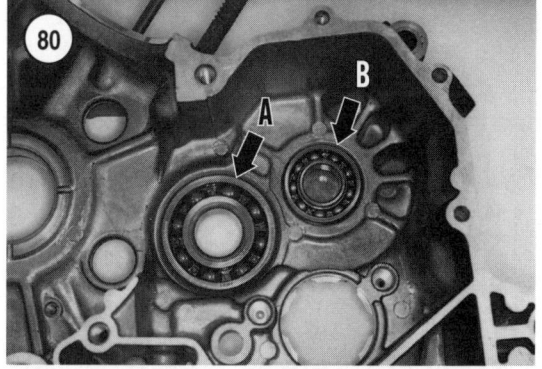

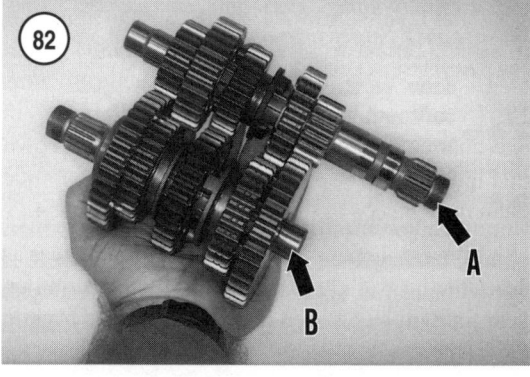

a. Remove the bearing with a blind bearing remover.
b. Press the new bearing into place until it bottoms in the crankcase.

Main bearing replacement

Refer to *Crankshaft Main Bearing Replacement* later in this chapter.

Crankcase Assembly

This procedure describes the installation of the crankshaft, transmission shaft assemblies, and internal shift mechanism as well as the assembly of the crankcase halves.

Coat all parts with engine oil prior to assembly.

1. If removed, install the neutral switch (A, **Figure 74**) into the left crankcase half. Install a new O-ring (**Figure 75**) and tighten the three neutral switch screws securely.
2. Place the left crankcase half on wooden blocks.
3. Install the crankshaft as described below in this chapter. Make sure the connecting rods are positioned correctly within the piston openings. See **Figure 73**.
4. Mesh the mainshaft (A, **Figure 82**) and countershaft (B, **Figure 82**) assemblies together and simultaneously lower both assemblies into place in the left crankcase half (A and B, **Figure 71**). Make sure each shaft slides into its respective bearing.

NOTE
Each shift fork is identified by a letter embossed on its face. The forks must be installed with the letter facing up, toward the right side of the engine.

5. Install the shift forks by performing the following:
   a. Set the fork with the L identification mark into the fork groove in countershaft fifth gear. See C, **Figure 70**.
   b. Set the fork with the R identification mark into the fork groove in countershaft fourth gear. See B, **Figure 70**.
   c. Set the fork with the C identification mark into the fork groove in mainshaft third gear. See A, **Figure 70**.

6. Rotate the shift forks outward as necessary, and lower the shift drum into place (**Figure 69**).

7. Rotate the shift forks toward the shift drum so the guide pin in each fork engages its respective groove in the shift drum.

8. Install the short shift-fork shaft (A, **Figure 68**) through the mainshaft shift fork and into the boss in the case half.

9. Install the long shift-fork shaft (B, **Figure 68**) through both countershaft shift forks, and seat the shaft in the boss in the case half.

10. Spin the transmission shafts and use the shift drum to shift through the gears. Make sure it is possible to shift into all gears. This is the time to find a problem with the transmission not after the engine is assembled and installed in the frame.

11. After confirming that the transmission shifts normally, shift it into NEUTRAL.

12. Install the three dowels (A and B, **Figure 67**) into the crankcase mating surface. Install a new O-ring on the dowel (A, **Figure 67**) beneath the crankshaft.

13. Check the left and right crankcase mating surfaces for old sealant material or other residue. Clean them as necessary.

14. Apply engine oil to the transmission shafts and to the main bearing in the right crankcase half.

15. Apply a light coat of Yamaha Bond No. 1215 (part No. ACC-1100-15-01 or 90890-85505) or equivalent to the sealing surface of the left crankcase half. Make the coating as thin as possible while also completely covering the sealing surface.

16. Lower the right crankcase half onto the left. Note the following:
   a. Align the bearings in the right case half with their respective assemblies in the left case half.
   b. Rotate the shift drum so the ramps on the shift cam align with the cutouts in the right crankcase half as shown in **Figure 65**.
   c. If necessary, reach through the middle gearcase to center the countershaft within the countershaft bearing.

NOTE
The crankcase bolt numbers are embossed on the crankcase near the bolt holes. Bolt No. 14 is a chrome bolt; bolt No. 13 is black.

CRANKCASE BOLTS

Bolt number (embossed on crankcase)	Bolt number (diameter × length)
1, 3, 9-14	M6 × 45 mm
2	M6 × 55 mm
8	M6 × 95 mm
4, 6	M8 × 60 mm
7	M8 × 80 mm
5	M8 × 100 mm

17. Install the fourteen crankcase bolts in the locations noted during removal. Finger-tighten the bolts at this time. **Figure 83** provides the size of each bolt.

CAUTION
Rotate the crankshaft frequently during the tightening process. If there is any binding, stop and correct the cause before proceeding.

18. Evenly tighten the crankcase bolts in one-quarter turn increments in the sequence shown in **Figure 66**. Once all the bolts are tight, torque them *in sequence* to the specification in **Table 4**.

19. Loosely install the middle drive pinion gear as described in this chapter. The middle-drive pinion gear nut will be torqued once the engine is back in the frame.

ENGINE LOWER END

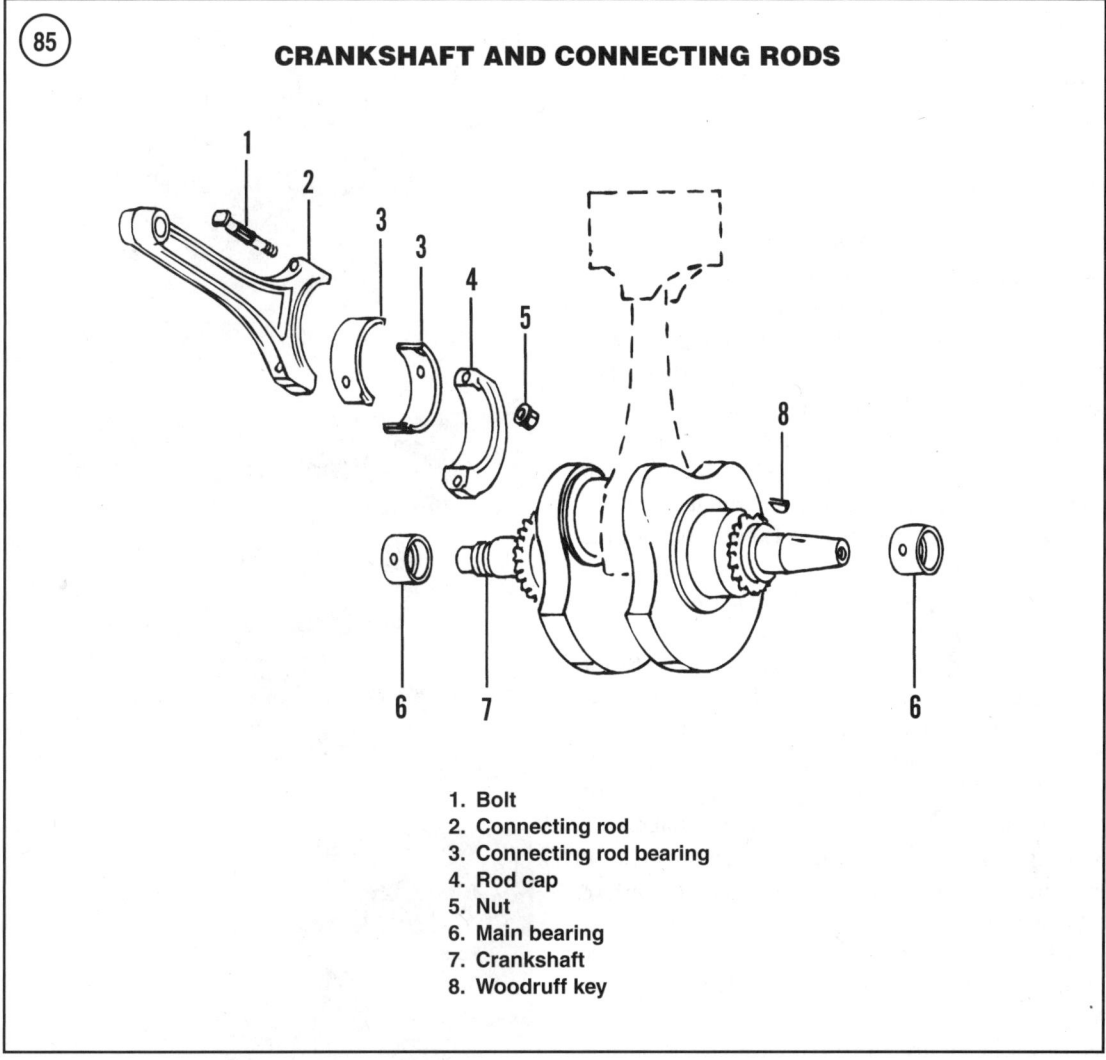

85 CRANKSHAFT AND CONNECTING RODS

1. Bolt
2. Connecting rod
3. Connecting rod bearing
4. Rod cap
5. Nut
6. Main bearing
7. Crankshaft
8. Woodruff key

20. Check the operation of the crankshaft and transmission.

   a. Because the stopper lever is not in place until the shift shaft is reinstalled, place a piece of tape on the crankcase with an arrow indicating the point where the stopper lever operates (**Figure 84**).

   b. Shift the transmission into neutral. The transmission is in neutral when the neutral detent on the shift cam is opposite the arrow as shown in **Figure 84**.

   c. Turn the mainshaft and watch the middle drive pinion gear. When the transmission is in neutral, the mainshaft and countershaft should turn independently of each other.

   d. Shift the transmission into gear and spin the mainshaft. Both shafts should turn when the transmission is in gear.

   e. If the transmission fails either test, disassemble the crankcase and correct the problem.

21. Install all external assemblies that were removed.

22. Install the engine as described in this chapter. Once the engine is installed in the frame, torque the middle drive pinion gear nut to the specification in **Table 4**.

CRANKSHAFT

Refer to **Figure 85** when servicing the crankshaft.

CHAPTER FIVE

Removal/Installation

Remove and install the crankshaft as described in *Crankcase* in this chapter.

Crankshaft Inspection

1. Clean the crankshaft thoroughly with solvent, and dry it with compressed air. Lightly oil the journal surfaces immediately to prevent rust.
2. Blow the oil passages clear with compressed air.
3. Check the main bearing journals (A, **Figure 86**) for scratches, heat discoloration or other defects.
4. Measure the diameter of each main bearing journal with a micrometer (**Figure 87**). Measure each journal at two places. If either measurement is less than the wear limit specified in **Table 1**, replace the crankshaft.
5. Check the flywheel taper (B, **Figure 86**), threads and keyway for damage.
6. Check the timing sprockets (C, **Figure 86**) for excessive wear or tooth damage. If either sprocket is worn or damaged, replace the crankshaft.
7. Check the connecting rod-to-crank pin journal area for evidence of seizure, bearing or thrust washer damage or for connecting rod damage.
8. Check the connecting rod-to-piston pin area for evidence of excessive heat (blue coloration) or other damage.
9. Check the connecting rod-to-crankshaft side clearance. Slide the connecting rods to one side. Measure the side clearance with a flat feeler gauge as shown in **Figure 88**. If the clearance is outside the range specified in **Table 1**, replace the connecting rods and recheck the clearance. If the side clearance is still outside the specified range, replace the crankshaft.
10. Use V-blocks and a dial gauge to check the crankshaft runout (**Figure 89**). If the runout exceeds the specification in **Table 1**, replace the crankshaft.

Crankshaft Main Bearing Clearance Inspection

The crankshaft main bearing (A, **Figure 90**) is installed within a steel sleeve that is part of each crankcase half.

1. Check the inside of each bearing for wear, bluish tint (burned), flaking abrasion and scoring. If either bearing is questionable, replace them both. The main bearings must be replaced as a set.

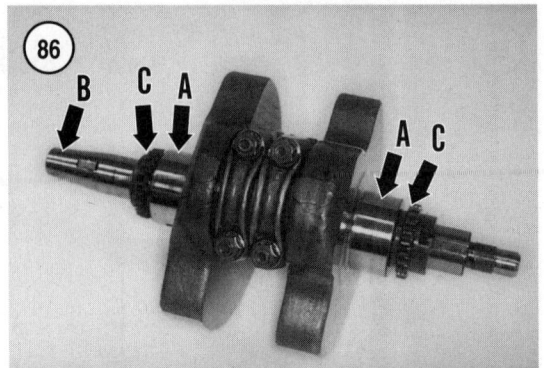

2. Measure the inside diameter of the bearing with a bore gauge or an inside micrometer. Measure the diameter at two places and take the average of the two measurements.

3. Measure the outside diameter of the crankshaft main bearing journal with a micrometer (**Figure 87**). Measure that journal at two places. Use the smaller of the two measurements as the main bearing journal outside diameter.

4. Calculate the main bearing clearance by subtracting the crankshaft main bearing journal outside

ENGINE LOWER END

diameter (measured in Step 3) from the inside diameter of the main bearings (measured in Step 2).

5. Repeat Steps 2 and 3 for the other bearing and bearing journal.

6. If either main bearing clearance is outside the range specified in **Table 1**, replace both main bearings as described below.

Crankshaft Main Bearing Replacement

Use a plain bearing installer/remover (part No. YM-28898) and the middle driven shaft bearing driver (part No. YM-04058) when replacing the main bearings. Consider entrusting this task to a Yamaha dealership or a shop experienced in this work. Perform the following procedure if choosing to do this yourself.

1. From the inside of the case half, drive the main bearing (**Figure 91**) from the sleeve in the case half. Use the plain bearing installer/remover and the middle driven shaft bearing driver.

2. Clean the bearing sleeve with solvent and dry it with compressed air.

3. Measure the inside diameter of the main bearing sleeve in the crankcase half. Using a bore gauge or an inside micrometer, measure the inside diameter at two places that are 90° apart. Take the average of these two measurements. This average is the bearing sleeve inside diameter for that case half.

4. Repeat Step 3 for the bearing sleeve in the other crankcase half.

5A. If the bearing sleeve inside diameter of either case half exceeds the wear limit in **Table 1**, replace both crankcase halves.

5B. If the bearing sleeve inside diameter is less than the wear limit, use the chart in **Table 3** to select the correct size bearing.

6. Install new bearings by performing the following:

 a. Apply engine oil to a new bearing and the bearing sleeve in the crankcase half.

 b. Fit the bearing onto the middle driven shaft bearing driver so the notch on the bearing aligns with the slot in the driver.

 c. From the outside of the case, align the slot on the bearing driver with the cutout on the sleeve in the crankcase, and drive the bearing until it bottoms in the crankcase. The bearing is properly installed when the notch on the bearing aligns with the cutout in the crankcase sleeve as shown in B, **Figure 90**.

7. Repeat Step 7 for the bearing in the other case half.

CONNECTING RODS

Removal/Installation

1. Split the crankcase as described in this chapter and remove the crankshaft as described in this chapter.
2. Check the connecting rod-to-crankshaft side clearance as described in *Crankshaft Inspection*.

> **NOTE**
> *Prior to disassembly, mark the rods and caps with an F (front) and R (rear) in order to install them in their original locations.*

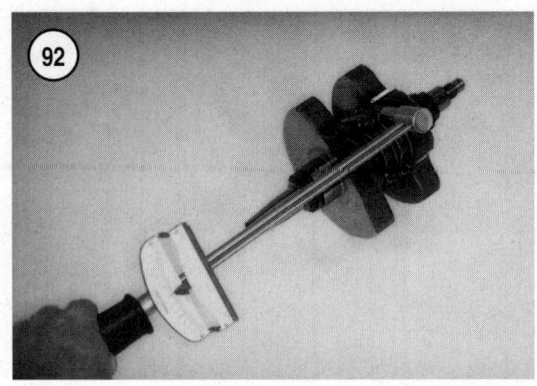

3. Remove the connecting rod cap nuts (**Figure 92**) and separate the rods from the crankshaft.

> **NOTE**
> *Keep each bearing insert in its original place in the rod or rod cap. If assembling the engine with the original inserts, install them in their original locations, or they will rapidly wear.*

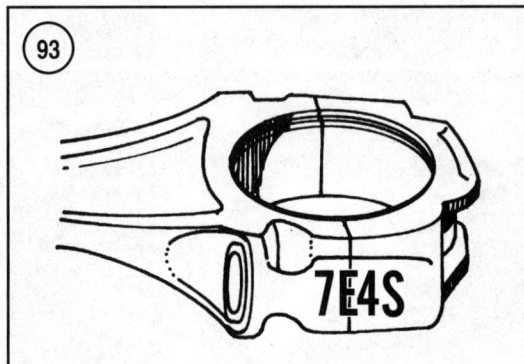

4. Mark each rod cap and bearing insert in order to reinstall them in their original location. Make sure the weight mark on the end of the cap matches the mark on the rod (**Figure 93**).
5. Install by reversing these removal steps, while noting the following:
   a. Install the bearing insert (**Figure 94**) into each connecting rod and cap. Make sure the bearing inserts are locked in place correctly (**Figure 95**).

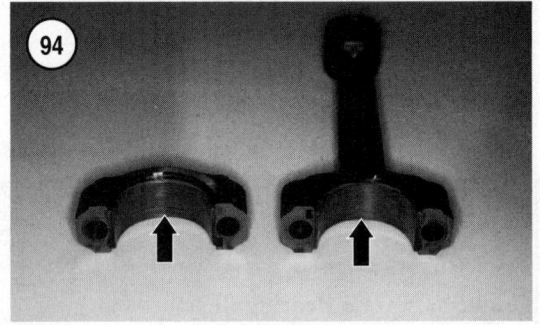

> **NOTE**
> *Each connecting rod has a Y embossed on one side. (**Figure 96**). Install the connecting rod so this side faces the left crankshaft end (the tapered end).*

   b. Apply engine oil to the bearing inserts.
   c. If installing new bearing inserts, check the bearing clearance as described in this chapter.
   d. Install the bearing caps so the numbers on the rod and cap align with each other (**Figure 93**).
   e. Apply a light-grade molybdenum disulfide grease to the threads of the connecting rod bolts.
   f. Tighten the connecting rod nuts evenly.

> **CAUTION**
> *When tightening the connecting rod nuts to the torque specification of 36 N•m (22 ft.-lb.), do not stop the tightening motion after the torque of 30 N•m (22 ft.-lb.) is achieved. If tightening is interrupted after 30 N•m (22 ft.-lb.), loosen the nut too less than 30 N•m (22 ft.-lb.) and tighten it to the specification in one continues motion.*

   g. Using a beam-type torque wrench (**Figure 92**), tighten each connecting rod nut to 36

ENGINE LOWER END

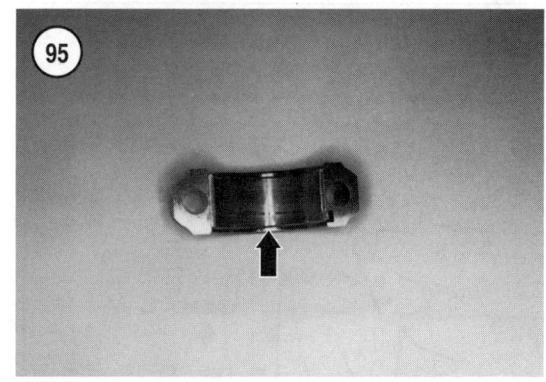

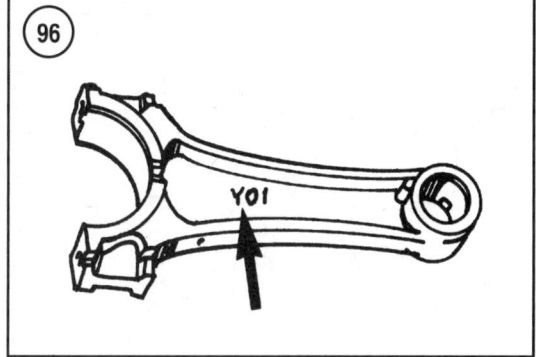

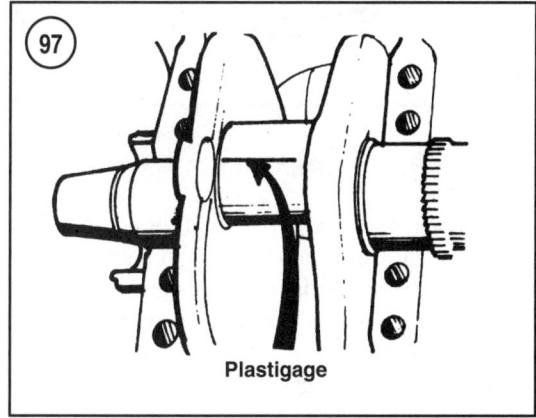

Plastigage

N•m (26.5 ft.-lb.). Apply continuous torque when tightening the nut from 30 N•m (22 ft-lb.) to 36 N•m (26.5 ft.-lb.). Do not stop tightening the nut until the final torque specification is reached.

Connecting Rod Inspection

1. Check each rod for obvious damage such as cracks and burns.

2. Check the piston pin bushing for wear or scoring.

3. Have a machine shop inspect them for twisting and bending.

4. Examine the bearing inserts (**Figure 95**) for wear, scoring or burning. They are reusable if in good condition. If replacing the bearings, make a note of any number or color identification on the back of the old inserts. A previous owner may have used undersize bearings.

5. Remove the connecting rod bolts, and check them for cracks or twisting. Replace any bolts as required.

6. Check bearing clearance as described in this chapter.

Connecting Rod Bearing Radial Clearance Measurement

CAUTION
If reusing the old bearings, make sure they are installed in their original locations.

1. Wipe the bearing inserts and crankpins clean. Install the bearing inserts into the connecting rod and cap (**Figure 94**).

2. Place a piece of Plastigage on the crankpin parallel to the crankshaft (**Figure 97**).

NOTE
*Each connecting rod has a Y embossed on one side (**Figure 96**). Install the connecting rod so this side faces the left crankshaft end (the tapered end).*

3. Install the rod and cap. Make sure the weight marks (**Figure 93**) on the side of the rod and cap align.

CAUTION
When tightening the connecting rod nuts to the torque specification of 36 N•m (22 ft.-lb.), do not stop the tightening motion after the torque of 30 N•m (22 ft.-lb.) is achieved. If tightening is interrupted after 30 N•m (22 ft.-lb.), loosen the nut too less than 30 N•m (22 ft.-lb.) and tighten it to the specification in one continues motion.

4. Using a beam-type torque wrench (**Figure 92**), tighten each connecting rod nut to 36 N•m (26.5 ft.-lb.). You must apply continuous torque when tightening the nut from 30 N•m (22 ft-lb.) to 36 N•m (26.5 ft.-lb.). Do not stop tightening the nut until the final torque specification is reached.

CAUTION
Do not rotate the crankshaft while Plastigage is in place.

5. Remove the rod cap.
6. Determine the clearance by measuring the width of flattened Plastigage according to the manufacturer's instructions (**Figure 98**). Replace the bearings if the connecting rod clearance is outside the range specified in **Table 1**.
7. To select new bearings, perform the following.
   a. The connecting rods and caps are marked with a No. 4 or No. 5 (**Figure 93**). The crankweb is marked with a number (**Figure 99**) that relates to the connecting rod bearing journals.
   b. To select the proper bearing insert number, subtract the crankshaft connecting rod journal number from the number on the connecting rod and cap. For example, if the connecting rod is marked with a *4* and the matching connecting rod journal is a *2*, 4 - 2 = 2. The new bearing insert is a No. 2.
   c. The connecting rod bearings are then identified by number and color; refer to **Table 2**.

NOTE
Determine the bearing insert number for both connecting rods. Then use the insert numbers and colors to purchase bearings from a Yamaha dealership.

8. Repeat Steps 1-7 for the other connecting rod.
9. After selecting new bearings, recheck clearance as described in Steps 2-6. If clearance is still out of specification, take the crankshaft and connecting rods to a Yamaha dealership for further service. Yamaha does not provide connecting rod or connecting-rod bearing journal wear specifications.
10. Clean all Plastigage from the crankshaft and bearing inserts. Install the connecting rods as described in this chapter.

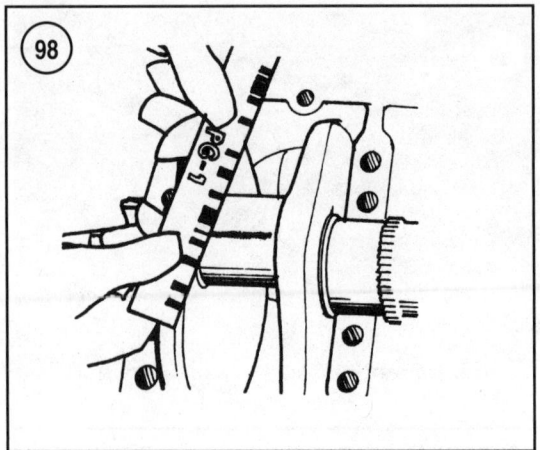

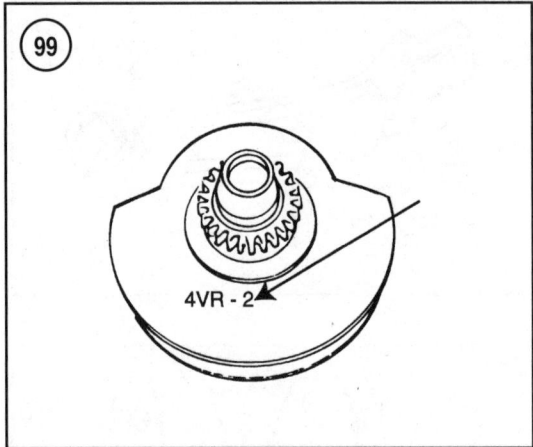

BREAK-IN

Following cylinder servicing (boring, honing, new rings, etc.) and major lower end work, the engine should be broken in just as though it were new. The performance and service life of the engine greatly depends upon a careful and sensible break-in. Stop the engine after every hour of operation and let it cool for five to ten minutes. Periodically vary the speed of the motorcycle. Avoid prolonged steady running at one speed, no matter how moderate, and avoid hard acceleration.

For the first 600 miles (1000 km), avoid operating the motorcycle above one-third throttle.

Replace the engine oil, oil filter and final gear oil after completing this initial break-in period. This ensures that all of the particles produced during break-in are removed from the engine.

Between 600 to 1000 miles (1000 and 1600 km), avoid prolonged operation above one-half throttle.

ENGINE LOWER END

Table 1 ENGINE LOWER END SPECIFICATIONS

Item	Specification	Wear limit
Connecting rods		
Oil clearance	0.026-0.050 mm (0.001-0.002 in.)	–
Side clearance	0.270-0.424 mm (0.0106-0.0167 in.)	–
Radial clearance	0.026-0.050 mm (0.001-0.002 in.)	–
Crankshaft		
Main bearing clearance	0.020-0.052 mm (0.0008-0.002 in.)	–
Main bearing journal runout	–	0.02 mm (0.0008 in.)
Main bearing journal diameter	–	44.95 mm (1.77 in.)
Main bearing inside diameter	45.000-45.012 mm (1.7717-1.7721 in.)	
Main bearing sleeve inside diameter		49.02 mm (1.9299 in.)
Oil pump		
Inner-to-outer rotor tip clearance	0.12 mm (0.005 in.)	0.2 mm (0.008 in.)
Outer rotor to housing clearance	0.03-0.08 mm (0.001-0.003 in.)	0.15 mm (0.006 in.)
Relief valve operating pressure	440-540 kPa (63.8-78.3 psi)	–
Oil pressure (hot)*	10 kPa (1.5 psi) at 1200 rpm	–
Middle gear backlash	0.05-0.10 mm (0.002-0.004 in.)	–

*Measured at the rocker arm shaft bolt.

Table 2 CONNECTING ROD BEARING SELECTION

Connecting rod bearing number	Bearing insert color
1	Blue
2	Black
3	Brown
4	Green

The connecting rod bearing number equals the number on the connecting rod minus the number on the crankweb.

Table 3 MAIN BEARING SELECTION

Bearing sleeve inside diameter average	Bearing color
49.000-49.010 mm (1.9291-1.9295 in.)	Blue
49.011-49.020 mm (1.9296-1.9299 in.)	Green

Table 4 LOWER END TIGHTENING TORQUES

Item	N•m	ft.-lb.	in.-lb.
Engine mounts			
Frame–to–bracket			
Front upper nut	40	29.5	–
Front lower bolt	30	22	–
Engine–to–bracket			
Front upper bolt	40	29.5	–
Front lower through bolt and nut	40	29.5	–
Engine–to–frame			
Rear upper bolt	40	29.5	–
Rear lower through bolt and nut	74	55	–
(continued)			

Table 4 LOWER END TIGHTENING TORQUES (continued)

Item	N•m	ft.-lb.	in.-lb.
Alternator cover bolt	10	–	88
Alternator rotor bolt	80	59	–
Bearing retainer Torx screw	25	18	–
Crankcase bolt			
Clutch cover bolt	10	–	88
Clutch nut	70	52	–
Connecting rod nut	36	26.5	–
Crankcase stud			
8 mm	13	–	115
10 mm	20	15	–
Crankcase bolt			
6 mm	10	–	88
8 mm	24	18	–
Middle gear			
Middle drive pinion gear nut	120	89	–
Bearing housing bolt	25	18	–
Oil drain bolt	43	32	–
Oil filter cover bolt	10	–	88
Oil gallery bolt	8	–	71
Oil pump mounting bolt	7	–	62
Oil strainer cover bolt	10	–	88
Pickup coil mounting screw	7	–	62
Primary drive gear nut	70	52	–
Shift-lever clamp bolt	10	–	88
Shift-shaft stopper bolt	22	16	–
Shock absorber mount			
(upper and lower)	62	46	–
Stator mounting screw	7	–	62
Starter clutch bolt	20	15	–

CHAPTER SIX

CLUTCH AND EXTERNAL SHIFT MECHANISM

This chapter includes the service procedures for the clutch, primary gear, oil pump spur gear, and the external shift mechanism.

Table 1 and **Table 2** are at the end of the chapter. Clutch specifications are listed in **Table 1**; clutch torque specifications in **Table 2**.

CLUTCH COVER

Removal/Installation

Refer to **Figure 1** when servicing the clutch cover.

1. Place the motorcycle on level ground, and support it with wooden blocks or a jack.
2. Remove the brake pedal/footpeg assembly as described in Chapter Twelve.
3. Remove the exhaust pipe as described in Chapter Eight.
4. Drain the engine oil and remove the oil filter as described in Chapter Three.
5. Before removing the clutch cover bolts, note how the AIS hose brackets are secured behind two clutch cover bolts (**Figure 2**). Each bracket must be installed behind the same bolt during installation.

Also notice how the clamps (**Figure 3**) behind the four lower bolts secure the rear brake switch wire to the crankcase. The wire must be rerouted in the same manner during installation.

6. Remove the eleven clutch cover bolts and remove the clutch cover. Four different length bolts secure the clutch cover to the crankcase. Note the location of these bolts. They must be reinstalled in the same location during assembly. See **Figure 4**.
7. Remove the clutch cover from the crankcase.
8. Remove and discard the clutch cover gasket.
9. Remove the two dowels (**Figure 5**) from the crankcase.
10. Inspect the clutch cover for cracks and other signs of wear. Replace the cover if necessary.
11. Inspect the seal (A, **Figure 6**) in the cover. Replace the seal as necessary. Use a new circlip (B, **Figure 6**) when replacing the seal.
12. Installation is the reverse of removal. Note the following:

CHAPTER SIX

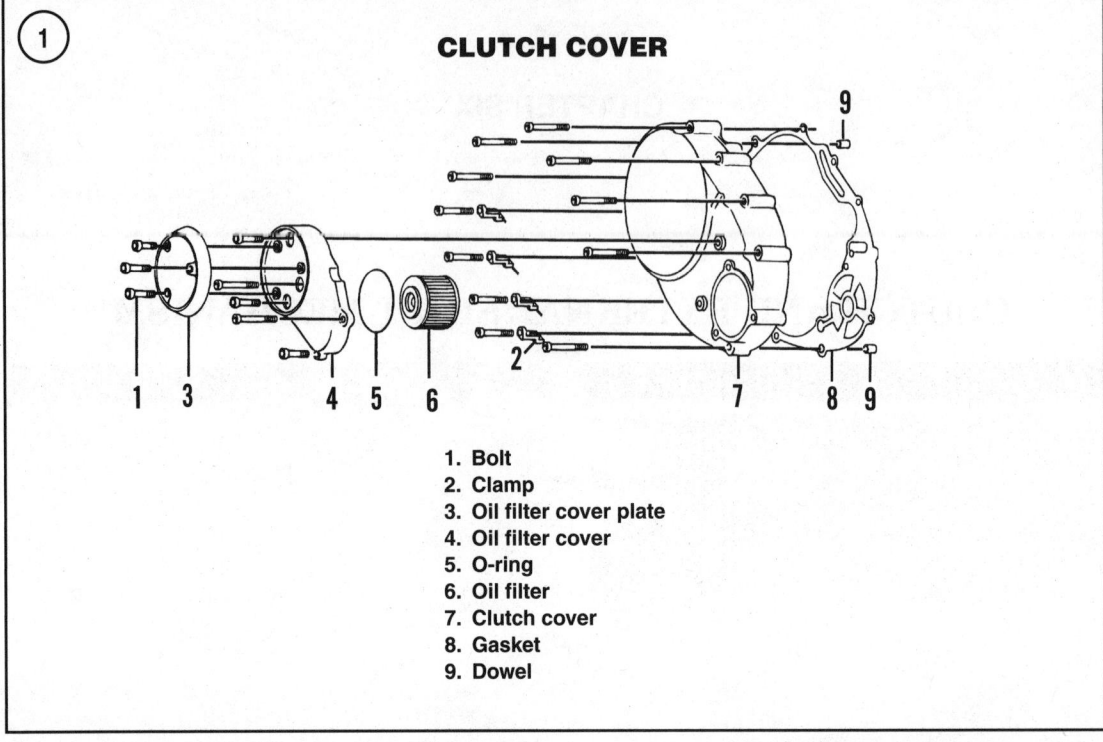

CLUTCH COVER

1. Bolt
2. Clamp
3. Oil filter cover plate
4. Oil filter cover
5. O-ring
6. Oil filter
7. Clutch cover
8. Gasket
9. Dowel

a. Install the two dowels (**Figure 5**) in the crankcase.
b. Install a new clutch cover gasket (**Figure 7**).
c. Secure the clutch cover with the eleven clutch cover bolts. Install each bolt in its original location. Torque the bolts to the specification in **Table 2**.
d. Make sure the rear-brake-switch wire is secured in the four clamps (**Figure 3**) and the AIS hose brackets are mounted in their original locations (**Figure 2**).
e. Install the oil filter and add engine oil as described in Chapter Three.

CLUTCH

The clutch is a wet, multi-plate type which operates immersed in engine oil. It is mounted on the right side of the transmission mainshaft. The clutch can be serviced with the engine in the frame.

The clutch release mechanism is mounted in the left side of the crankcase and is cable operated by

CLUTCH AND EXTERNAL SHIFT MECHANISM

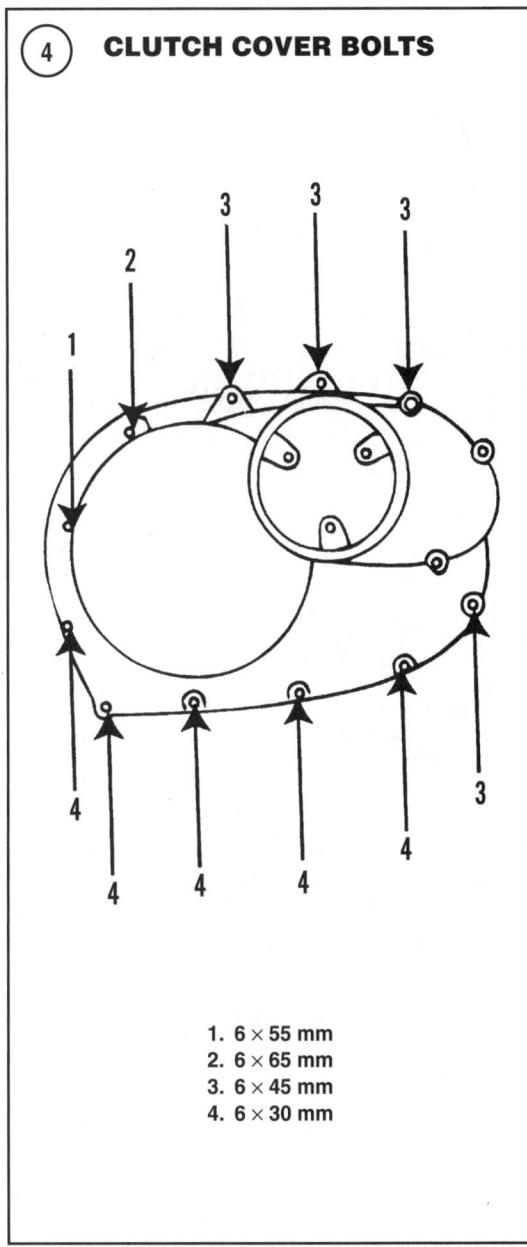

CLUTCH COVER BOLTS

1. 6 × 55 mm
2. 6 × 65 mm
3. 6 × 45 mm
4. 6 × 30 mm

the clutch hand lever on the left side of the handlebar.

Removal

Refer to **Figure 8** for this procedure.
1. Place the motorcycle on level ground, and support it with wooden blocks or a jack.
2. At the handlebar, slide the clutch lever boot (A, **Figure 9**) away from the adjuster. Loosen the clutch cable locknut (B, **Figure 9**) and rotate the adjuster (C, **Figure 9**) to provide maximum slack in the cable.
3. At the clutch cable lower adjuster, loosen the locknuts (A, **Figure 10**) and rotate the adjuster (B, **Figure 10**) to provide maximum slack in the cable.
4. Disconnect the clutch cable from the clutch release lever (C, **Figure 10**).
5. Remove the clutch cover as described in this chapter. Do not lose the two dowels (**Figure 5**) behind the cover.

CHAPTER SIX

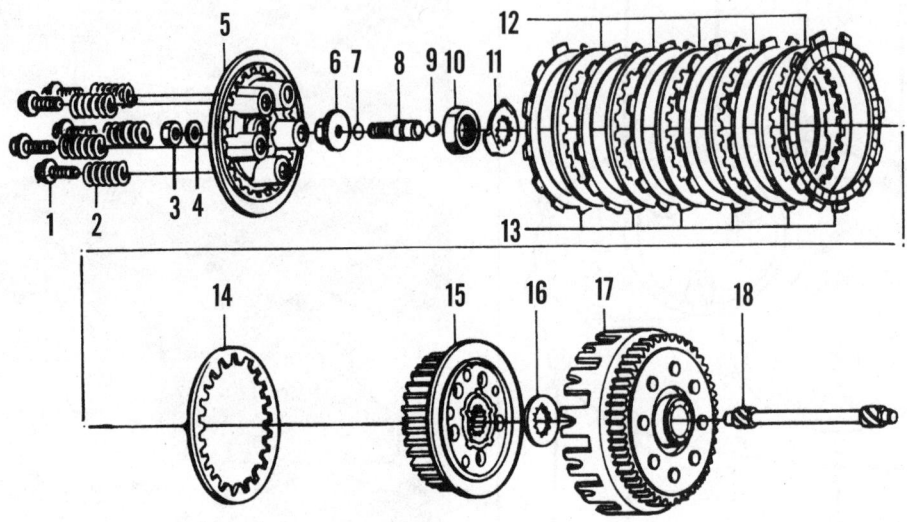

CLUTCH

1. Bolt
2. Spring
3. Locknut
4. Washer
5. Pressure plate
6. Push plate
7. O-ring
8. Pushrod No. 1
9. Steel ball
10. Clutch nut
11. Lockwasher
12. Clutch plates
13. Friction discs
14. Clutch plate No. 1
15. Clutch boss
16. Splined thrust washer
17. Clutch housing
18. Pushrod No. 2

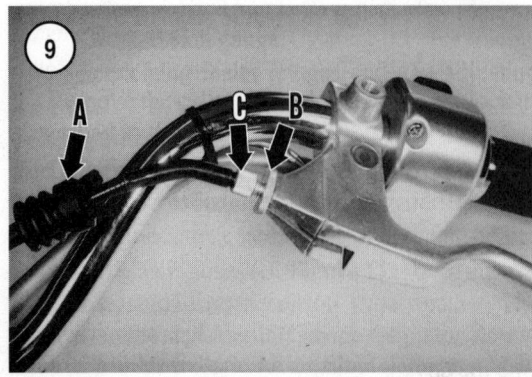

CLUTCH AND EXTERNAL SHIFT MECHANISM

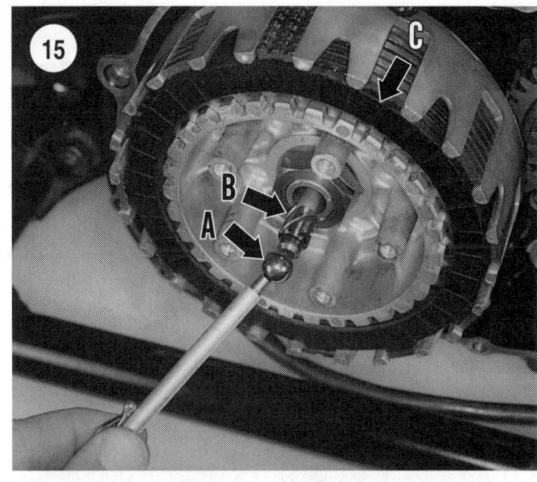

6. Remove the circlip (A, **Figure 11**) and remove the oil pump gear (B, **Figure 11**).

7. Evenly loosen the pressure plate bolts (A, **Figure 12**) in a crisscross pattern. Then remove the bolts and clutch springs (**Figure 13**).

8. Remove the pressure plate (A, **Figure 14**). Pushrod No. 1 (B, **Figure 14**) will come out with the pressure plate.

9. Use a magnetic tool to remove the steel ball (A, **Figure 15**) from the center of the mainshaft, and then remove pushrod No. 2 (B, **Figure 15**).

> *NOTE*
> *Clutch plate No. 1 (the plate closest to the clutch boss) is thicker than the other clutch plates.*

10. Remove all the friction discs (C, **Figure 15**) and clutch plates, including clutch plate No 1. Stack the disc and plates in the order of removal.

11. Straighten both ears of the lockwasher (**Figure 16**) away from the flats on the clutch nut.

> *NOTE*
> *To prevent the clutch housing from turning when removing the clutch nut, use the Yamaha clutch holding tool (part No. YM-91042), or equivalent special tool, available from motorcycle dealerships.*

> *CAUTION*
> *Do not clamp the clutch holder too tightly. The tool could damage the grooves in the clutch boss.*

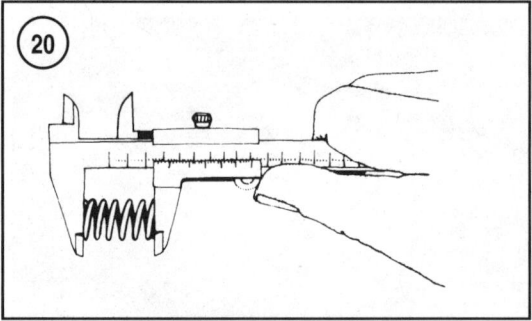

12A. Hold the clutch boss with a clutch holder (**Figure 17**), and loosen the clutch nut.

12B. If a clutch holder is not available, stuff a shop cloth, copper penny, or brass washer between the clutch outer housing gear and the primary drive gear. This prevents the clutch from rotating while loosening the nut.

CAUTION
*Any soft metal washer (copper, brass, or aluminum) works in the above step. However, **do not** use a steel washer. Steel damages the gear teeth.*

13. Remove the clutch nut (A, **Figure 18**) and discard the lockwasher (B, **Figure 18**).

14. Remove the clutch boss (C, **Figure 18**).

15. Remove the thrust washer (A, **Figure 19**) and the clutch housing (B, **Figure 19**) from the mainshaft.

Inspection

1. Clean all clutch parts in a petroleum-based solvent such as a commercial solvent or kerosene. Thoroughly dry the parts with compressed air.

2. Measure the free length of each clutch spring as shown in **Figure 20**. Compare to the specification listed in **Table 1**. If any spring has sagged to the service limit or less, replace all the springs as a set.

3. Measure the thickness of each friction disc (**Figure 21**) at several places around the disc. Compare the measurements to the specification listed in **Table 1**. If any disc is worn to the service limit, replace all the friction discs as a set.

CLUTCH AND EXTERNAL SHIFT MECHANISM

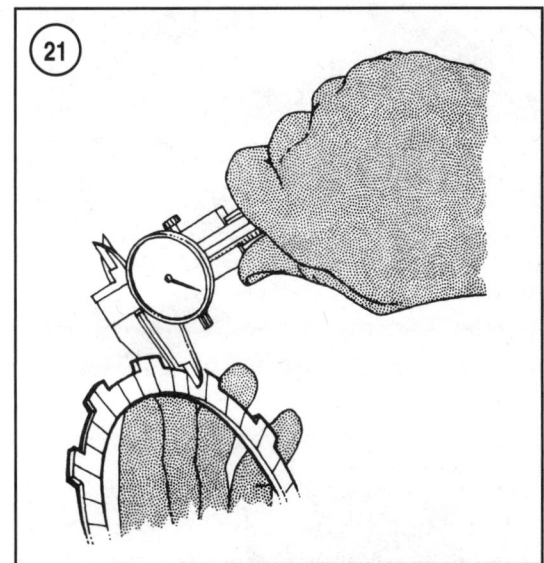

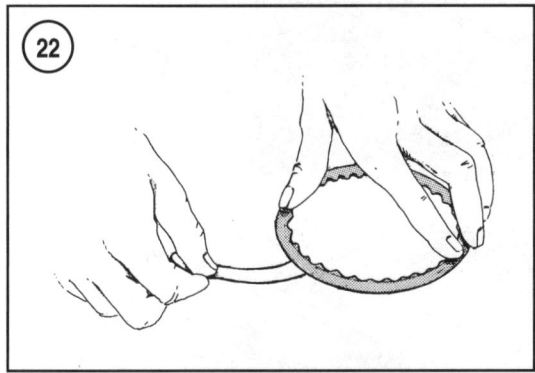

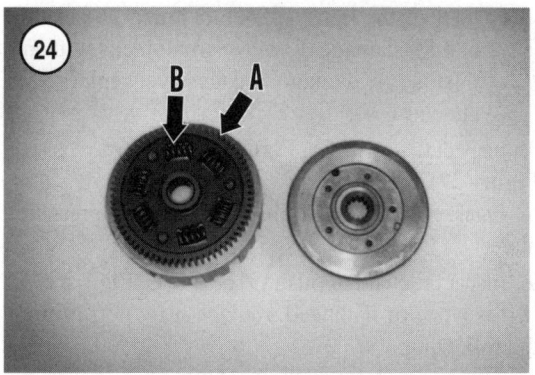

NOTE
*The clutch plate thickness specified in **Table 1** does not apply to clutch plate No. 1. Clutch plate No. 1 is thicker than the six standard clutch plates.*

4. Measure the thickness of each clutch plate at several places around the plate. Compare the measurements to the specification listed in **Table 1**. If any plate is worn to the service limit, replace all the clutch plates as a set.

5. Check the clutch plates and clutch plate No. 1 for warp on a surface plate or a piece of plate glass (**Figure 22**). Replace all the clutch plates as a set if the warp of any plate is equal to or greater than the wear limit in **Table 1**.

6. Inspect the clutch housing by performing the following:

a. Check the fingers (**Figure 23**) for cracks, nicks or galling where they come in contact with the friction disc tabs. They must be smooth for chatter-free operation. If any damage is evident, replace the clutch housing and inspect the friction disc tabs for excessive wear.

b. Check the primary driven gear (A, **Figure 24**) on the clutch housing for tooth wear, damage or cracks. Replace the clutch housing if necessary.

c. If the primary driven gear is worn or damaged, also inspect the primary drive gear as described later in this chapter.

d. Inspect the damping springs (B, **Figure 24**) for breakage or wear. Replace the clutch housing if necessary.

7. Inspect the clutch boss for the following:

a. Check the grooves (**Figure 25**) for cracks, nicks or galling where they contact the clutch plate tabs. They must be smooth for chatter-free operation. If any damage is evident, the components must be replaced.

b. Inspect the posts for wear or galling. If any damage is evident, replace the clutch boss.

c. Inspect the inner splines (**Figure 26**) in the hub for damage. Remove small nicks with an oilstone. If damage is excessive, replace the clutch boss.

8. Inspect the posts (A, **Figure 27**) and grooves (B, **Figure 27**) in the pressure plate. If they show signs of cracks, wear or galling, replace the pressure plate.

9. Inspect the end of pushrod No. 1 (C, **Figure 27**). If it is worn or damaged, replace it by performing the following:

   a. Remove the nut (**Figure 28**) and washer from the front of the pressure plate, and remove the push plate (D, **Figure 27**) and pushrod No. 1 from the pressure plate.

   b. Install the threaded end of the new pushrod No. 1 through the push plate and then through the pressure plate.

   c. Install the washer and nut (**Figure 28**) onto the pushrod threads. Finger-tighten the nut. It will be tightened after the clutch is installed and adjusted.

10. Inspect pushrod No. 2 (**Figure 29**) by rolling it along a surface plate or a piece of glass. Replace the rod if any clicking noise is heard, it is bent.

11. Inspect the clutch nut for wear or damage. Make sure the threads are in good condition. Replace the nut as necessary.

Installation

Refer to **Figure 8** for this procedure.

1. Install the clutch housing onto the mainshaft by performing the following:

   a. Apply oil to the bushing in the clutch housing hub.

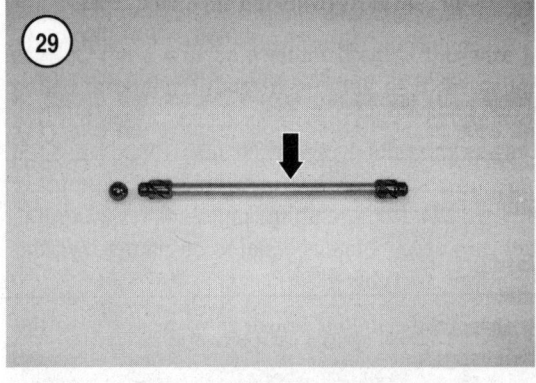

CLUTCH AND EXTERNAL SHIFT MECHANISM

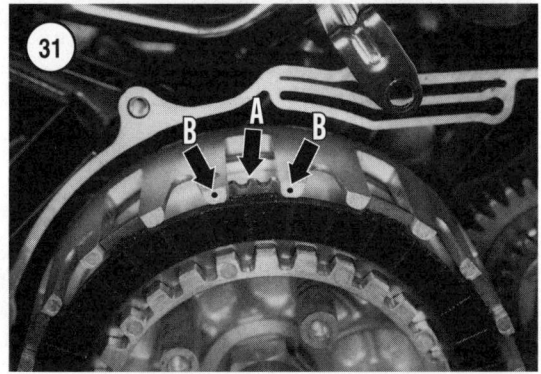

  b. Slide the clutch housing (B, **Figure 19**) onto the mainshaft until the teeth of the primary driven gear on the clutch housing engage the teeth of the primary drive gear (C, **Figure 19**). Gently push the clutch housing onto the mainshaft until it bottoms.

2. Slide the thrust washer (A, **Figure 19**) onto the mainshaft.

3. Install the clutch boss (C, **Figure 18**) onto the mainshaft.

4. Install a new lockwasher (B, **Figure 18**) and thread the clutch nut (A, **Figure 18**) onto the mainshaft. Make sure the concave side of the nut faces in toward the lockwasher.

5. Use the same tool set-up used during removal to hold the clutch boss in place and tighten the clutch nut (**Figure 17**) to the torque specification listed in **Table 2**. Remove the holding tool.

6. Bend each lockwasher ear (**Figure 16**) against one of the flats on the clutch nut.

7. Install clutch plate No. 1 (the thicker clutch plate) so its splines engage the ribs of the clutch boss as shown in **Figure 30**.

NOTE
*Apply fresh engine oil to each friction disc to avoid clutch lock up. Install each friction disc so the tab with the two cutouts (A, **Figure 31**) fits between the clutch-housing fingers with the indexing dots (B, **Figure 31**).*

8. Install the first friction disc so the tabs fit between the fingers of the clutch housing.

9. Install the next clutch plate and then the next friction disc. Continue alternately installing a clutch plate and then a friction disc until all plates and discs are installed. The last item installed should be a friction disc (**Figure 32**).

10. Lubricate pushrod No. 2 (**Figure 29**) and the steel ball with lithium grease.

11. Install pushrod No. 2 (B, **Figure 15**) into the center of the mainshaft, and then install the steel ball (A, **Figure 15**). Push the ball until both the pushrod and ball are seated within the mainshaft (**Figure 33**).

12. Install a *new* O-ring onto pushrod No. 1 (C, **Figure 27**). Lubricate the new O-ring and pushrod No. 1 with lithium grease and seat the O-ring in the pushrod groove.

CHAPTER SIX

13. Align pushrod No. 1 with the center of the mainshaft, and install the pressure plate.
14. Install the clutch springs (**Figure 13**) and loosely install the five pressure plate bolts (A, **Figure 12**).
15. Evenly tighten the pressure plate bolts in a crisscross pattern to the torque specification listed in **Table 2**.
16. Adjust the clutch by performing the following:
    a. Move the clutch release lever (A, **Figure 34**) forward until it stops.
    b. The pointer on the end of the lever should align with the indexing mark (B, **Figure 34**) on the crankcase.
    c. If adjustment is required, loosen the clutch adjuster nut (B, **Figure 12**), and turn pushrod No. 1 (C, **Figure 12**) clockwise or counterclockwise until the pointer on the clutch release lever aligns with the indexing mark while pushing the release lever forward.
    d. Torque the clutch adjuster nut to the specification in **Table 2**.
17. Connect the clutch cable to the clutch release lever, and adjust the clutch lever free play as described in Chapter Three.
18. Install the oil pump gear (B, **Figure 11**) onto the oil pump shaft. Secure the gear in place with a new circlip (A, **Figure 11**).
19. Install the clutch cover as described in this chapter.

CLUTCH RELEASE MECHANISM

Removal/Inspection/Installation

Refer to **Figure 35** when servicing the clutch release mechanism.

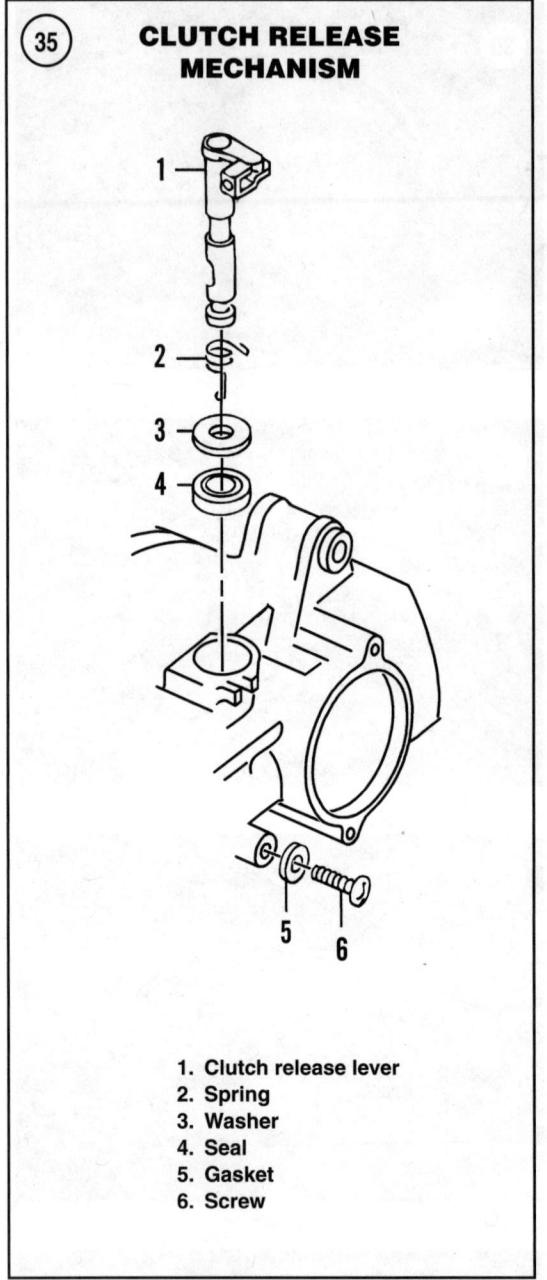

CLUTCH RELEASE MECHANISM

1. Clutch release lever
2. Spring
3. Washer
4. Seal
5. Gasket
6. Screw

1. Remove the rear cylinder as described in Chapter Four.

2. Remove the clutch release shaft screw (A, **Figure 36**) and the gasket from the side of the crankcase.

3. Pull the spring tang (C, **Figure 34**) away from the release lever, and pull the lever shaft up and out of the crankcase.

CLUTCH AND EXTERNAL SHIFT MECHANISM

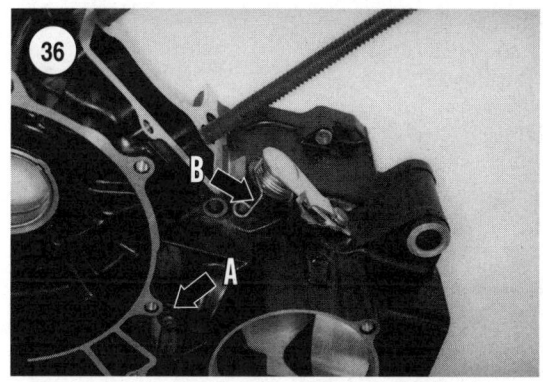

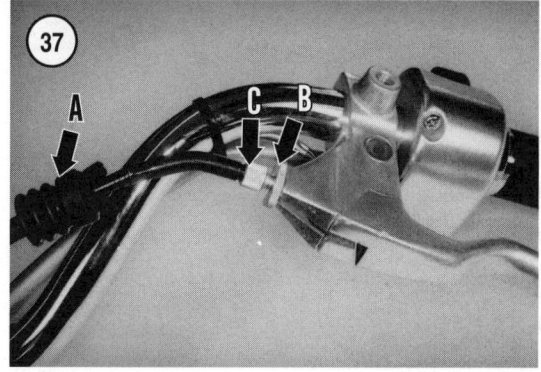

4. Remove the spring and washer from the top of the seal in the crankcase.

5. Inspect the clutch lever shaft for nicks, scratches and other signs of wear. Replace the shaft as necessary.

6. Inspect the spring for cracks, sagging or other signs of fatigue. Replace the spring as necessary.

7. Inspect the seal for signs of leaking. Replace the seal as necessary.

8. Inspect the bearing behind the seal. It should turn smoothly. If there is any roughness or binding, replace the bearing.

9. Assembly is the reverse of disassembly. Note the following:
   a. Apply lithium grease to the clutch release shaft and to the seal in the crankcase.
   b. Install the release shaft so the cutout in the shaft face inboard, toward the mainshaft.
   c. Do not tear the lips of the seal.
   d. Make sure the spring arm (B, **Figure 36**) sits in the cutout in the crankcase.
   e. Use a new gasket behind the clutch release shaft screw (A, **Figure 36**), and tighten the screw to the torque specification in **Table 2**.
   f. Make sure the spring tang engages (C, **Figure 34**) the clutch release lever.

CLUTCH CABLE REPLACEMENT

1. At the handlebar, slide the clutch lever boot (A, **Figure 37**) away from the adjuster. Loosen the clutch cable locknut (B, **Figure 37**) and rotate the adjuster (C, **Figure 37**) to provide maximum slack in the cable.

2. Disconnect the cable end from the clutch hand lever.

3. At the clutch cable lower adjuster, loosen the locknuts (A, **Figure 38**) and rotate the adjuster (B, **Figure 38**) to provide maximum slack in the cable.

4. Bend out the lock tab on the clutch release lever (C, **Figure 38**) and disconnect the cable from the lever.

5. Release the cable from the cable bracket on the alternator cover.

NOTE
Before removing the cable, make a drawing of the cable routing through the frame. The new cable must be rerouted along the same path as the old cable. Avoid any sharp turns.

6. Pull the clutch cable out from behind the steering head area and out of the retaining loop and clips on the frame.

7. Remove the cable and replace it with a new cable.

8. Install by reversing these removal steps. Adjust the clutch as described in Chapter Three.

PRIMARY DRIVE GEAR AND OIL PUMP SPUR GEAR

Removal/Installation

1. Remove the clutch cover as described in this chapter.

2. Remove the circlip (A, **Figure 39**) and the oil pump gear (B, **Figure 39**).

3. Bend the lockwasher away from the flat on the primary gear nut (**Figure 40**).

NOTE
To keep the crankshaft from turning when removing the primary gear nut, hold the clutch with the Yamaha clutch holding tool (part No. YM-91042), or equivalent tool. As an alternative, remove the alternator cover as described in Chapter Five and hold the alternator rotor with the Yamaha sheave holder (YU-01880) or equivalent flywheel holder.

CAUTION
Do not clamp the holding tool too tightly. The tool could damage the grooves in the clutch boss.

4A. Hold the clutch boss with a holding tool (**Figure 17**), and remove the primary drive nut (**Figure 40**).

4B. If a clutch holder is not available, stuff a shop cloth, copper penny, or brass washer between the primary driven gear on the clutch housing and the primary drive gear. This prevents the crankshaft from rotating while removing the primary drive nut (**Figure 40**).

CAUTION
Any soft metal washer (copper, brass, or aluminum) works in the above step. However, (bf ital)do not(bf ital) use a steel washer. Steel will damage the gear teeth.

5. Remove and discard the lockwasher (**Figure 41**).

6. Remove the slotted washer (A, **Figure 42**) from the crankshaft and then remove the oil pump spur gear (B, **Figure 42**).

7. Remove the primary drive gear (A, **Figure 43**) and the key (B, **Figure 43**) from the crankshaft.

8. Inspect the teeth of the primary drive gear (A, **Figure 44**) for broken or missing teeth. If worn, replace the primary drive gear and inspect the primary driven gear on the clutch housing.

9. Inspect the teeth of the oil pump spur gear for broken or missing teeth. If worn, replace the spur gear (B, **Figure 44**) and inspect the oil pump gear.

10. Inspect the key (C, **Figure 44**) for nicks or wear. If worn replace the key and inspect the keyway in each gear, in the crankshaft and in the slotted washer (D, **Figure 44**).

CLUTCH AND EXTERNAL SHIFT MECHANISM

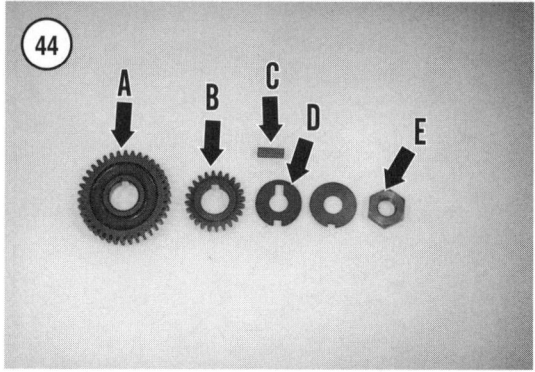

11. Inspect the threads of the primary gear nut (E, **Figure 44**). Replace the nut as necessary.

12. Installation is the reverse of removal. Note the following:

   a. Firmly seat the key (B, **Figure 43**) into the crankshaft keyway.

   b. Install each gear and the slotted washer so their keyways engage the key in the crankshaft. Install the oil pump spur gear so the side with the indexing tab faces out away from the primary drive gear.

   c. Install a new lockwasher so its slot engages the indexing tab (**Figure 41**) on the oil pump spur gear.

   d. Torque the primary gear nut (**Figure 40**) to the specification in **Table 2**.

   e. Bend the lockwasher against a flat of the nut (A, **Figure 40**).

   f. Use a new circlip when installing the oil pump gear onto the oil pump shaft.

EXTERNAL SHIFT MECHANISM

The shift shaft assembly can be removed with the engine in the frame. A portion of this procedure is shown with the engine removed from the frame for clarity.

Removal

Refer to **Figure 45** for this procedure.

1. Securely support the motorcycle on level ground.
2. Remove the alternator cover as described in Chapter Five.
3. Remove the circlip from the end of the shift shaft (A, **Figure 46**) and the washer (B, **Figure 46**) that sits behind the circlip.
4. Remove the clutch as described in this chapter.
5. Remove the shift shaft by performing the following:

   a. Pull the shift arm (A, **Figure 47**) forward and disengage the shift pawls from the shift drum pins, and at the same time press the stopper lever (B, **Figure 47**) down away from the shift cam.

   b. While holding both shift pawls and stopper lever clear of the pins/shift cam, pull the shift shaft assembly from the crankcase. See **Figure 48**.

   c. Make sure the inboard washer (A, **Figure 49**) comes out with the shift shaft.

6. Inspect the external shift mechanism as described in this chapter.

Inspection

If the transmission fails to shift gears, check for a weak shift-arm spring; bent or worn shift arm/shift

CHAPTER SIX

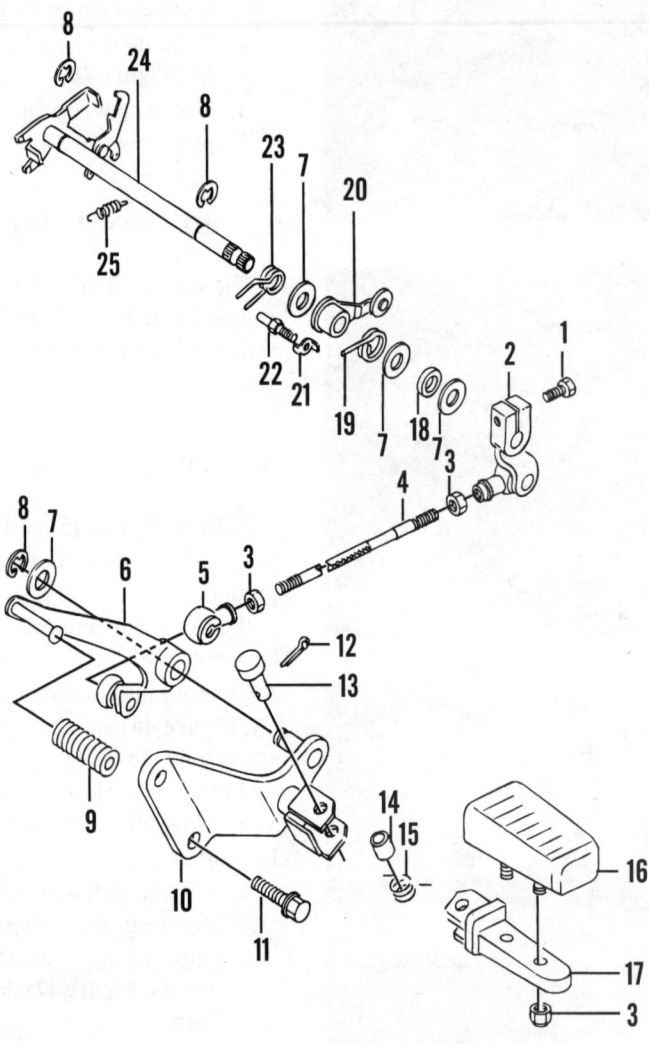

SHIFTER/FOOTPEG ASSEMBLY

1. Clamp bolt
2. Shift lever
3. Nut
4. Linkage rod
5. Boot
6. Shift pedal
7. Washer
8. Circlip
9. Rubber pad
10. Footpeg bracket
11. Bolt
12. Cotter pin
13. Clevis
14. Collar
15. Spring
16. Footpeg pad
17. Footpeg
18. Seal
19. Stopper lever spring
20. Stopper lever
21. Lockwasher
22. Stopper bolt
23. Shift shaft spring
24. Shift shaft
25. Shift arm spring

CLUTCH AND EXTERNAL SHIFT MECHANISM

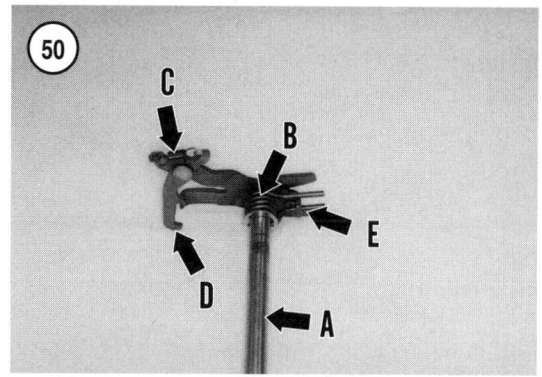

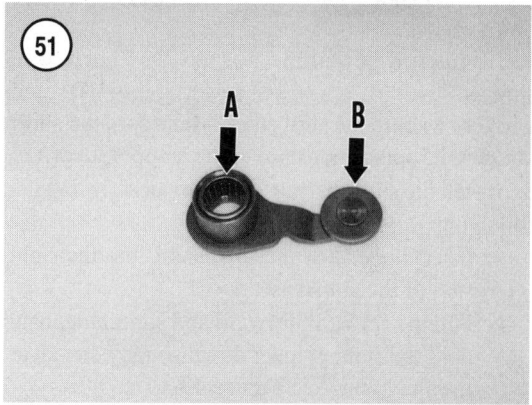

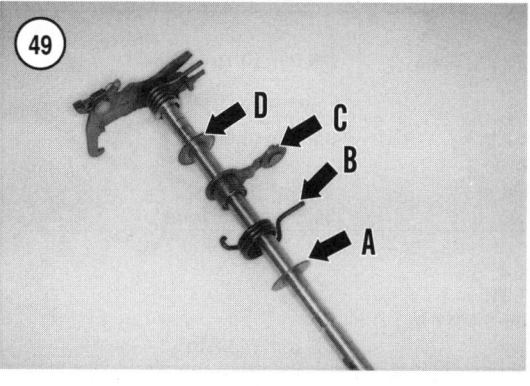

pawls; a broken shift shaft spring; a broken stopper bolt; or worn shift drum pins.

If the transmission undershifts or overshifts, check for a bent or worn shift arm/shift pawls; worn shift drum pins; a loose stopper bolt; a bent or weak shift-shaft spring; or worn stopper-lever spring or roller.

1. Remove the washer (A, **Figure 49**), stopper-lever spring (B), stopper lever (C) and the washer (D) from the shift shaft.

2. Inspect the shift shaft (A, **Figure 50**) for bending, wear or other signs of damage. Replace the shift shaft assembly if there is wear.

3. Inspect the shift shaft spring (B, **Figure 50**), the shift-pawl spring (C, **Figure 50**) and the stopper-lever spring (B, **Figure 49**) for cracks or other signs of fatigue. Replace any worn spring.

4. Inspect the shift pawls (D, **Figure 50**) at the end of the shift arm for wear or other signs of damage. Replace the shift shaft assembly if there is wear.

5. Inspect the needle bearing (A, **Figure 51**) and roller (B, **Figure 51**) in the stopper lever. Replace

the stopper lever if either part is damaged or does not turn freely.

> *NOTE*
> *If the shift drum pins are worn or damaged, replace the pins as described in Chapter Seven.*

Installation

1. If installing a new shift shaft spring (B, **Figure 50**), make sure the spring arms straddle the tab (E, **Figure 50**) on the shift shaft assembly, and install a new circlip.
2. If removed, install the washer (D, **Figure 49**), stopper lever (C), stopper lever spring (B) and washer (A) onto the shift shaft. Make sure the short tang on the spring hooks onto the stopper lever.
3. Install the shift shaft assembly by performing the following:
   a. Insert the end of the shift shaft into the right side of the crankcase.
   b. Pull the shift arm forward and simultaneously hold the stopper lever down so they can clear the shift cam. See **Figure 48**.
   c. Push the shift shaft until it bottoms in the crankcase. The tang on the stopper lever spring should slide down the tapered casting on the crankcase as the shift shaft is seated.
4. The shift shaft is properly installed when:
   a. The shift pawls at the end of the shift arm (A, **Figure 47**) engage the pins on the shift drum.

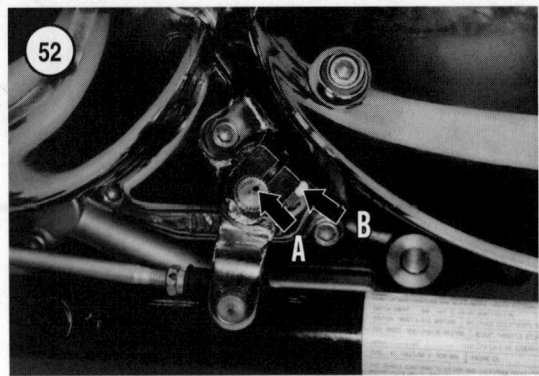

   b. The stopper lever roller (B, **Figure 47**) rests against a detent in the stopper cam.
   c. The long tang on the stopper lever spring (C, **Figure 47**) sits beneath the casting in the crankcase.
   d. The arms of the shift-shaft spring straddle the stopper bolt (D, **Figure 47**) in the crankcase.
5. Install the washer (B, **Figure 46**) onto the end of the shift shaft where it emerges from the left side of the crankcase, and then install a new circlip (A, **Figure 46**). Make sure the circlip is properly seated in the shift shaft groove.
6. Install the alternator cover and shift lever as described in Chapter Five. Make sure the slot in the shift lever aligns with the indexing mark on the shift shaft (A, **Figure 52**). Torque the shift lever clamp bolt (B, **Figure 52**) to the specification in **Table 2**.
7. Install the clutch as described in this chapter.

Table 1 CLUTCH SPECIFICATIONS

Item	Standard	Wear limit
Friction disc		
Thickness	2.9-3.1 mm (0.114-0.122 in.)	2.6 mm (0.102 in.)
Quantity	7	–
Clutch plate		
Thickness	1.5-1.7 mm (0.059-0.067 in.)	0.2 mm (0.008 in.)
Quantity	6, plus clutch plate No. 1	
Clutch plate warp	less than 0.2 mm (0.008 in.)	
Clutch spring free length	39.5 mm (1.555 in.)	38.5 mm (1.516 in.)
Clutch lever free play		
At lever end	10-15 mm (0.39-0.59 in.)	–
Clutch housing thrust clearance	0.10-0.37 mm (0.004-0.015 in.)	–
Clutch housing radial clearance	0.015-0.043 mm (0.0006-0.0017 in.)	–
Push rod bend	–	0.5 mm (0.02 in.)

CLUTCH AND EXTERNAL SHIFT MECHANISM

Table 2 CLUTCH TIGHTENING TORQUES

Item	N•m	ft.-lb.	in.-lb.
Clutch nut	70	52	–
Pressure plate bolts	8	–	71
Clutch cover bolts	10	–	88
Clutch adjuster nut	8	–	71
Clutch release shaft screw	12	–	106
Primary drive gear nut	70	52	–
Shift-lever clamp bolt	10	–	88

CHAPTER SEVEN

TRANSMISSION AND INTERNAL SHIFT MECHANISM

This chapter addresses the service procedures for the transmission shaft assemblies, shift drum and forks. The external shift mechanism is covered in Chapter Six; the middle drive in Chapter Five; and final drive in Chapter Eleven.

It is necessary to remove the engine and separate the crankcase halves to gain access to the transmission and internal shift mechanism.

Table 1 and **Table 2** are at the end of this chapter. Transmission specifications are listed in **Table 1**; torque specifications in **Table 2**.

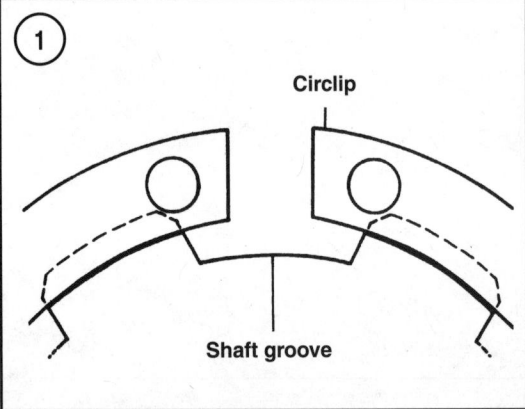

TRANSMISSION

Removal/Installation

Remove and install the transmission shaft assemblies as described in *Crankcase Disassembly* and *Crankcase Assembly* in Chapter Five.

Transmission Service Notes

1. Use a large egg flat (the type that restaurants get their eggs in) to maintain correct alignment and positioning of the parts. After removing each part, set it in one of the depressions in the egg flat in the same position it was on the transmission shaft.

2. The circlips fit tightly on the transmission shafts. They usually become distorted during removal. Replace all circlips during assembly.

3. Circlips turn and fold over, making removal and installation difficult. To ease replacement, open a circlip with a pair of circlip pliers while at the same time holding the back of the circlip with a pair of

TRANSMISSION AND INTERNAL SHIFT MECHANISM

TRANSMISSION

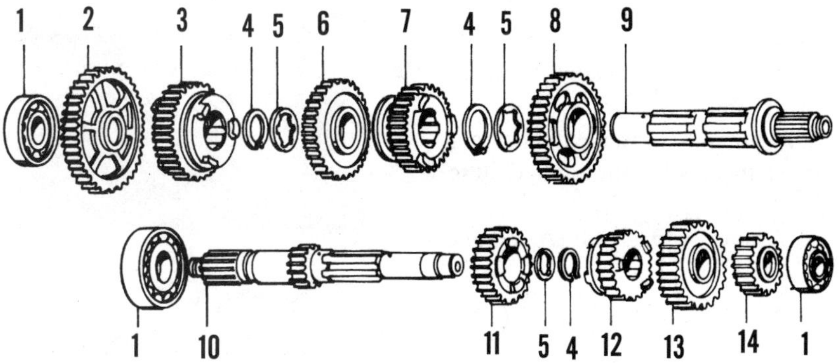

1. Ball bearing
2. Countershaft first gear
3. Countershaft fourth gear
4. Circlip
5. Splined washer
6. Countershaft third gear
7. Countershaft fifth gear
8. Countershaft second gear
9. Countershaft
10. Mainshaft/first gear
11. Mainshaft fourth gear
12. Mainshaft third gear
13. Mainshaft fifth gear
14. Mainshaft second gear

5. Apply molybdenum disulfide oil to the each gear during assembly.

Mainshaft Disassembly

Use a hydraulic press when removing and installing the mainshaft second gear. If a press is not available, have a machine shop remove and install the second gear.

Refer to **Figure 2** when servicing the mainshaft.

1. Clean the assembled shaft in solvent. Dry all components with compressed air or let the assembly sit on rags to drip dry.
2. Before disassembling the mainshaft, use a vernier caliper to measure the overall length of the gear set (**Figure 3**) and measure the clearance between second and fifth gear (**Figure 4**). Record both measurements. They will be needed during assembly.

pliers, and then remove the clip. Repeat the process as necessary for installation.

4. When installing a circlip, position the circlip so its end gap sits above a slot in the transmission shaft as shown in **Figure 1**.

192 CHAPTER SEVEN

3. Install a bearing removal tool (**Figure 5**) beneath second gear and insert the assembly into a hydraulic press.
4. Place a suitable size socket on the end of the mainshaft. This socket must be small enough to pass through the inside diameter of second gear.
5. While holding onto the mainshaft assembly, slowly press second gear off the shaft.
6. Release hydraulic pressure, remove the bearing remover, and remove the shaft from the hydraulic press.
7. If still installed, remove second gear (A, **Figure 6**) from the mainshaft.
8. Slide fifth gear (B, **Figure 6**) from the mainshaft.
9. Remove third gear (C, **Figure 6**).
10. Remove the circlip (A, **Figure 7**) and splined washer (B, **Figure 7**).
11. Remove fourth gear (C, **Figure 7**).
12. Inspect the mainshaft (**Figure 8**) and gears as described in this chapter.

Mainshaft Assembly

Refer to **Figure 2** when servicing the mainshaft.

NOTE
Before installing any component, coat all surfaces with molybdenum disulfide oil.

1. Install fourth gear (**Figure 9**) onto the mainshaft and slide it up against first gear. Make sure the engagement slots on fourth gear face out away from first gear.
2. Install a splined washer onto the mainshaft so the washer's flat side faces fourth gear.
3. Install a new circlip. Make sure the circlip's flat side faces out away from the splined washer and the circlip is completely seated in the shaft groove. Position the circlip so its end gap sits above a slot in the mainshaft as shown in **Figure 1**.
4. Install third gear (B, **Figure 10**) so its shift fork groove faces in toward fourth gear.
5. Install fifth gear (A, **Figure 10**) so the side with the engagement slots faces in toward third gear. See B, **Figure 6**.
6. Apply a light coat of molybdenum disulfide oil to the outer surface of the shaft and to the inner surface of second gear. This minimizes jumping when the gear is pressed onto the shaft.

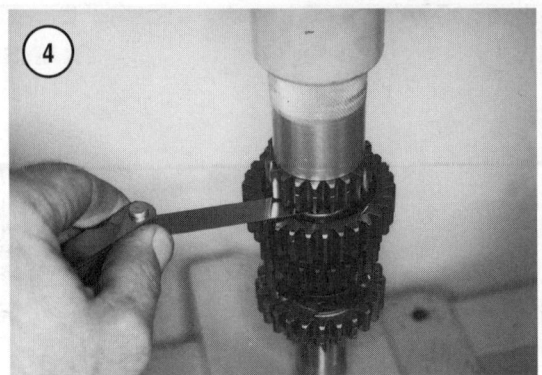

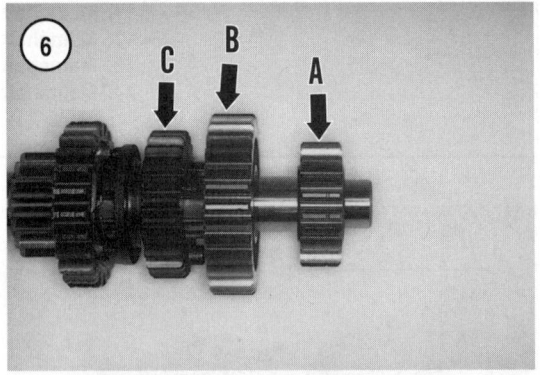

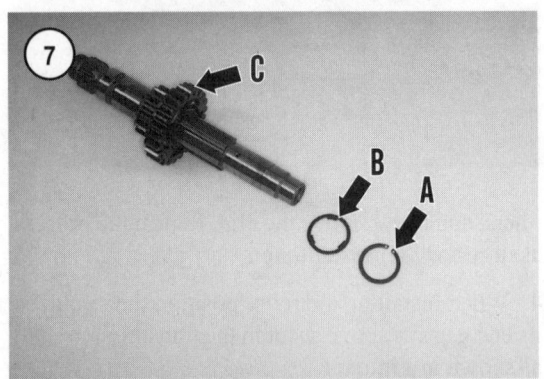

TRANSMISSION AND INTERNAL SHIFT MECHANISM

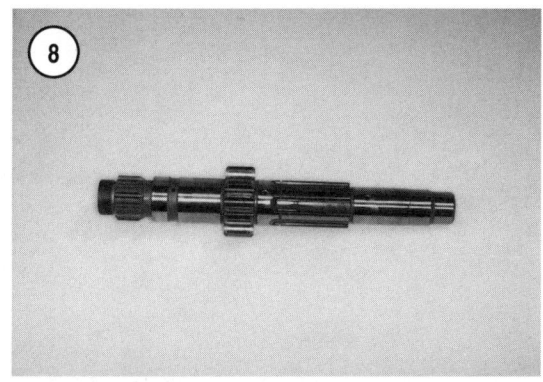

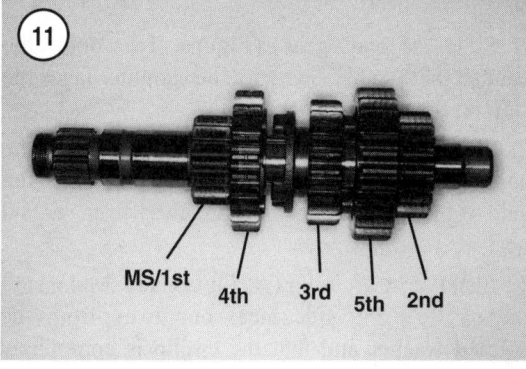

7. Slide second gear (A, **Figure 6**) on the mainshaft as far as it will go without pressure. The side with the groove cut into the teeth must face out away from fifth gear.

8. Set the shaft assembly onto the press plate.

9. Place a suitable size pipe or tubing on top of second gear. The pipe inner diameter must be large enough to pass over the outer diameter of the shaft.

10. Slowly press second gear onto the shaft until it approaches fifth gear, then stop.

11. The gear must be installed so the clearance between second and fifth gear equals the clearance that was measured before disassembling the mainshaft. Select the correct size flat feeler gauge, and insert the feeler gauge (**Figure 4**) between the second and fifth gear.

> **CAUTION**
> Do not press the gear too far onto the shaft. If the clearance between the second and fifth gear is insufficient, fifth gear will not rotate properly. If the gear jumps during the final application of pressure; stop, partially press the second gear back from the fifth gear, and resume pressing the gear onto the shaft. Make sure to maintain the proper clearance between the second and fifth gear.

> **NOTE**
> Initially, second gear will press smoothly onto the mainshaft and then will jump several times, making a loud cracking noise. This is normal during the initial application of the press.

12. Slowly apply hydraulic pressure and check the clearance between the second and fifth gear. Second gear must be pressed onto the shaft until this clearance equals the measurement taken before disassembling the mainshaft.

13. Use a vernier caliper to measure the mainshaft overall gearset length (**Figure 3**). It should be within the range specified in **Table 1**.

14. Release hydraulic pressure, and remove the shaft from the press.

15. Make sure each gear properly engages the adjoining gear where applicable.

16. Refer to **Figure 11** for correct placement of all gears.

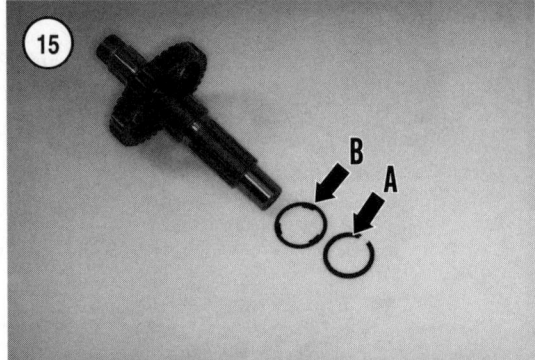

Countershaft Disassembly

Refer to **Figure 2** when servicing the countershaft.

1. Clean the assembled shaft in solvent. Dry all components with compressed air or let the assembly sit on rags to drip dry.
2. Remove first gear (A, **Figure 12**) and fourth gear (B, **Figure 12**) from the countershaft.
3. Remove and discard the circlip (A, **Figure 13**) and then remove the splined washer.
4. Remove third gear (B, **Figure 13**) from the countershaft and then fifth gear (**Figure 14**).
5. Remove the circlip (A, **Figure 15**) and the splined washer (B, **Figure 15**). Discard the circlip.
6. Remove second gear (**Figure 16**) from the countershaft.
7. Inspect the countershaft (**Figure 17**) and gears as described in this chapter.

Countershaft Assembly

Refer to **Figure 2** for this procedure.

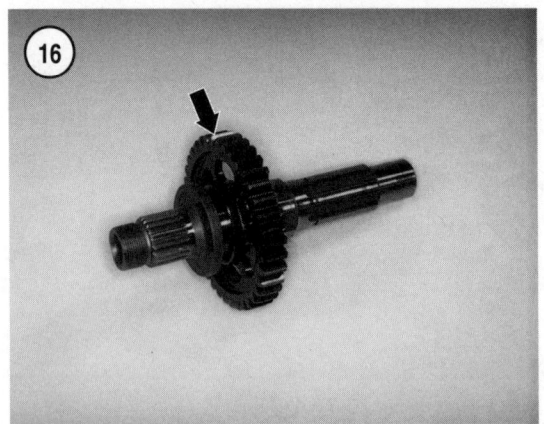

1. Slide second gear (**Figure 16**) onto the countershaft so the side with the shoulder faces the stop on the countershaft.
2. Slide the splined washer (B, **Figure 15**) onto the countershaft and up against second gear. The flat side of the washer must face out away from second gear.
3. Install a new circlip (A, **Figure 15**). Make sure the circlip's flat side faces out away from the splined washer and that the circlip is completely

TRANSMISSION AND INTERNAL SHIFT MECHANISM

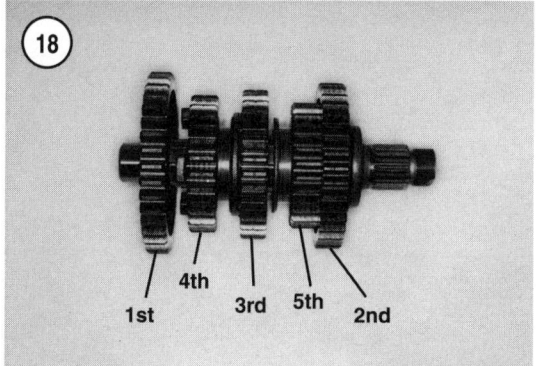

seated in the shaft groove. Position the circlip so its end gap sits above a slot in the countershaft as shown in **Figure 1**.

4. Install fifth gear (**Figure 14**) onto the countershaft so the shift fork groove faces out away from second gear.

5. Install third gear (B, **Figure 13**) onto the countershaft so the side with the engagement slots face out away from fifth gear.

6. Install a splined washer and slide it up against third gear. The flat side of the washer should face out away from third gear.

7. Install a new circlip (A, **Figure 13**). Make sure the circlip's flat side faces out away from the splined washer and that the circlip is completely seated in the shaft groove. Position the circlip so its end gap sits above a slot in the countershaft as shown in **Figure 1**.

8. Install fourth gear (B, **Figure 12**) onto the countershaft so the side with the shift fork groove faces in toward third gear.

9. Install first gear (A, **Figure 12**) onto the countershaft so the side with the engagement slots faces into toward fourth gear.

10. Make sure each gear properly engages the adjoining gear where applicable.

11. Refer to **Figure 18** for the correct placement of gears.

12. Properly mesh both transmission assemblies together (**Figure 19**) to make sure all mating gears align properly.

Inspection

1. Clean all parts in cleaning solvent, and thoroughly dry them.

NOTE
Replace any defective gear. It is recommended to replace the gear's mate from the opposite shaft, even though the mate may not show as much wear or damage. Worn parts usually cause accelerated wear on new parts. Replace gears in sets to ensure proper mating and wear.

2. Inspect the gears visually for cracks or chips as well as for broken or burnt teeth (**Figure 20**).

3. Check the engagement dogs (A, **Figure 21**) and engagement slots. Replace any gear(s) with rounded or damaged edges on the dogs or within the slots.
4. Inspect all gear bearing surfaces (**Figure 22**) for wear, discoloration and galling. Also inspect the respective shaft's bearing surface. If there is any metal flaking or visual damage, replace both parts.
5. Inspect the splines (**Figure 23**) on each shaft for wear or discoloration. Also check the internal splines on the sliding gears (B, **Figure 21**). If there is no damage, install each gear onto its respective shaft and work the gear back and forth to make sure it moves smoothly.
6. Inspect each shift fork groove for wear or damage. Replace the gear(s) if necessary.
7. Replace any washers that show wear.
8. Discard all circlips, and replace them during assembly.
9. If any transmission parts are worn or damaged, make sure to disassemble and inspect the shift drum and shift forks as described in this chapter.

INTERNAL SHIFT MECHANISM

Removal/Installation

Remove and install the shift drum and shift forks as described in *Crankcase Disassembly* and *Crankcase Assembly* in Chapter Five.

Inspection

Refer to **Figure 24** when inspecting the shift drum and shift forks.
1. Inspect each shift fork for wear or cracking. Examine each fork at the points where their fingers (A, **Figure 25**) contact the gears and where the guide post (B, **Figure 25**) contacts the shift drum. These surfaces should be smooth with no signs of wear or damage.
2. Make sure each fork slides smoothly on its shaft (**Figure 26**). If there is any binding, replace the fork shaft and related shift fork(s).
3. Roll each fork shaft along a surface plate or piece of glass. A clicking sound indicates the shaft is bent and requires replacment.
4. Inspect the grooves in the shift drum (A, **Figure 27**) for wear or roughness. Replace the shift drum if any groove is worn.

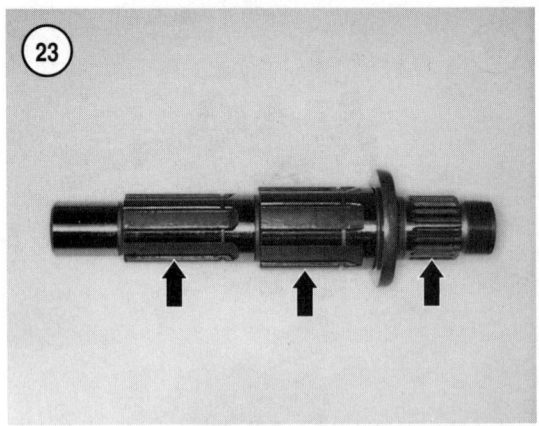

5. Inspect the neutral post (B, **Figure 27**) for wear or damage. If necessary, remove the screw securing the end plate, and replace the neutral post and spring.
6. Spin the drum bearing (A, **Figure 28**), and check for excessive play or roughness.
7. Check the pins (B, **Figure 28**) and ramps (C) in the shift cam for wear. If necessary, remove the shift cam bolt (D) and replace the shift cam, pins, or bearing.

TRANSMISSION AND INTERNAL SHIFT MECHANISM

INTERNAL SHIFT MECHANISM

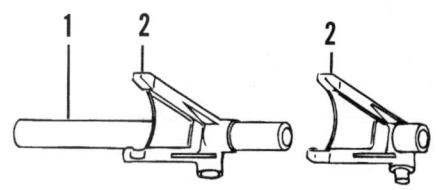
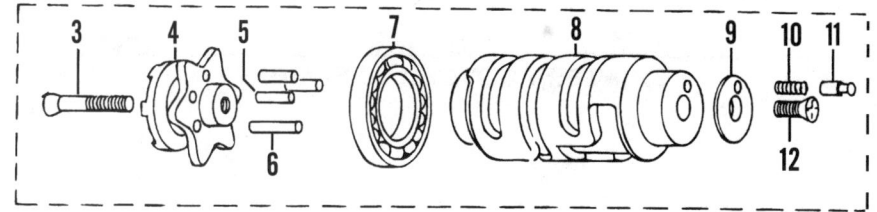
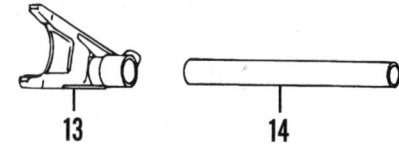

1. Shift fork shaft (countershaft)
2. Countershaft shift fork
3. Shift cam bolt
4. Shift cam
5. Pins
6. Locating pin
7. Bearing
8. Shift drum
9. Plate
10. Spring
11. Neutral post
12. Bolt
13. Mainshaft shift fork
14. Shift fork shaft (mainshaft)

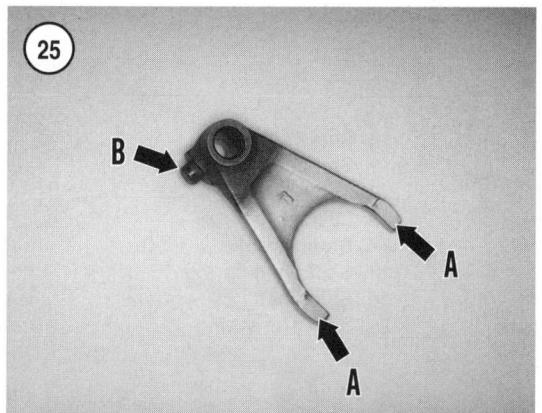
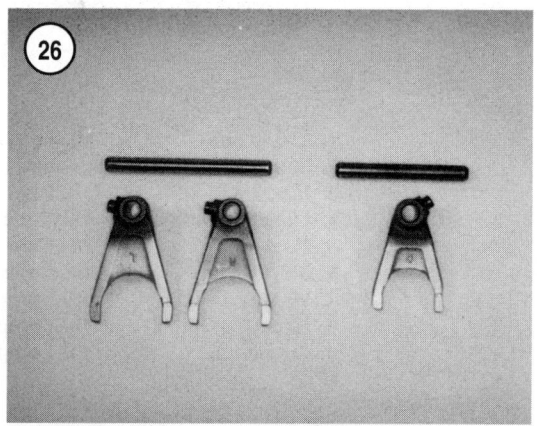

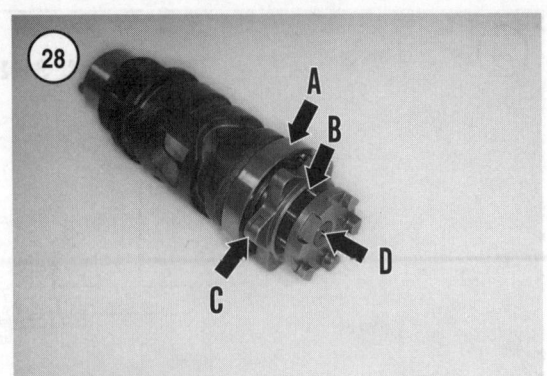

SHIFTER/FOOTPEG ASSEMBLY

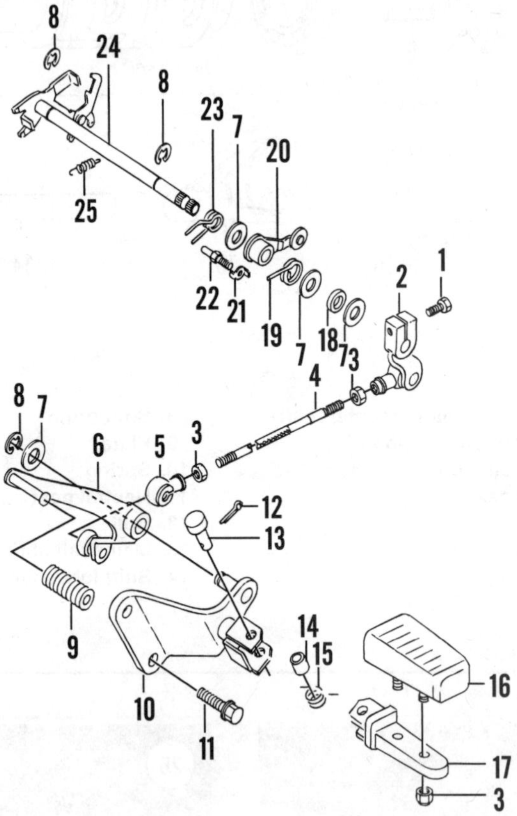

1. Clamp bolt
2. Shift lever
3. Nut
4. Linkage rod
5. Boot
6. Shift pedal
7. Washer
8. Circlip
9. Rubber pad
10. Footpeg bracket
11. Bolt
12. Cotter pin
13. Clevis
14. Collar
15. Spring
16. Footpeg pad
17. Footpeg
18. Seal
19. Stopper lever spring
20. Stopper lever
21. Lockwasher
22. Stopper bolt
23. Shift shaft spring
24. Shift shaft
25. Shift arm spring

TRANSMISSION AND INTERNAL SHIFT MECHANISM

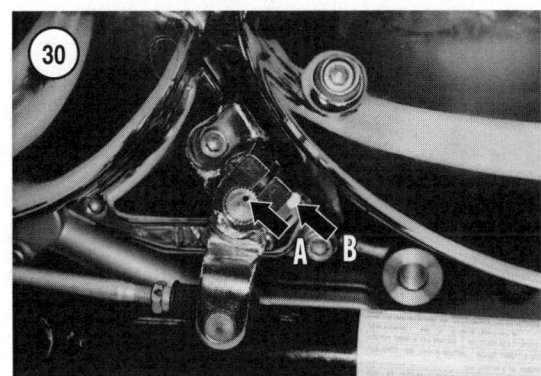

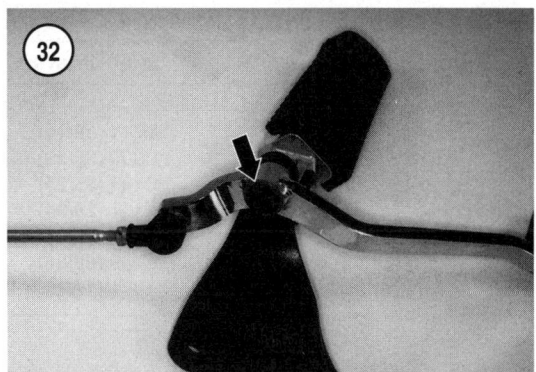

SHIFT PEDAL/FOOTPEG ASSEMBLY

Removal/Installation

Refer to **Figure 29** when servicing the shift pedal/footpeg assembly.

1. Note how the indexing mark on the shift shaft aligns (A, **Figure 30**) with the slot in the shift lever. If necessary, highlight these marks in order to properly align them during installation.

2. Loosen the clamp bolt (B, **Figure 30**) on the shift lever, and remove the lever from the shift shaft.

3. Remove the two footpeg mounting bolts (**Figure 31**), and lower the shift pedal/footpeg assembly from the motorcycle.

4. If necessary, remove the shift pedal from the footpeg bracket by performing the following:

    a. Remove the circlip from the pivot boss (**Figure 32**) on the footpeg bracket.

    b. Remove the washer, and lift the shift pedal from the pivot boss.

5. Installation is the reverse of removal. Note the following:

    a. Lubricate the pivot boss on the footpeg bracket with lithium grease.

    b. Make sure the circlip is properly seated in the groove on the footpeg bracket pivot boss.

    c. Torque the footpeg mounting bolts to the specification in **Table 2**.

    d. Install the shift lever so the indexing mark on the shift shaft aligns with the slot in the shift lever.

    e. Torque the shift lever clamp bolt to the specification in **Table 2**.

    f. Adjust the shift pedal as described in Chapter Three.

Table 1 TRANSMISSION AND GEARSHIFT SPECIFICATIONS

Item	Specification	Wear limit
Mainshaft		
Runout	–	0.06 mm (0.002 in.)
Gearset overall length	103.0-103.2 mm (4.055-4.063 in.)	–
Countershaft runout	–	0.06 mm (0.002 in.)
(continued)		

Table 1 TRANSMISSION AND GEARSHIFT SPECIFICATIONS (continued)

Item	Specification	Wear limit
Transmission gear ratios		
1st gear	2.714 (38/14)	–
2nd gear	1.900 (38/29)	–
3rd gear	1.458 (35/24)	–
4th gear	1.167 (28/24)	–
5th gear	0.967 (29/30)	–
Primary reduction ratio	1.789 (68/38)	–
Secondary reduction ratio	3.071 (19/18 x 32/11)	–

Table 2 TRANSMISSION TIGHTENING TORQUES

Item	N•m	ft.-lb.	in.-lb.
Shift lever clamp bolt	10	–	88
Shift pedal adjuster locknut	7	–	62
Footpeg mounting bolt	30	22	–

CHAPTER EIGHT

FUEL, EMISSION CONTROL AND EXHAUST SYSTEMS

This chapter describes complete procedures for servicing the fuel, emission control and exhaust systems. **Table 1** and **Table 2** are at the end of this chapter. Carburetor specifications are listed in **Table 1**. Torque specifications are in **Table 2**.

AIR FILTER HOUSING

NOTE
Air filter service is described in Chapter Three.

Removal

Refer to **Figure 1** when removing the air filter housing.
1. Use jack stands or a jack to securely support the motorcycle on level ground.
2. Remove the fuel tank as described in this chapter.
3. Remove the three mounting screws and the air filter cover (A, **Figure 2**).
4. Remove the air filter from the air filter housing.
5. Remove the two air filter housing Allen bolts (**Figure 3**) along with their washers.
6. Grasp the bottom of the air filter housing and pull the housing outward until the post (A, **Figure 4**) on the back of the housing is free of the grommet (B, **Figure 4**) on the air filter bracket.
7. Loosen the clamp (B, **Figure 2**) that secures the V-duct to the surge tank duct.
8. Pull the air filter housing down until the V-duct (C, **Figure 4**) pulls free of the surge tank duct (A, **Figure 5**), and remove the housing. The clamp should remain on the surge tank.
9. Cover the surge tank duct to prevent debris from entering the duct while the housing is removed.

Inspection

1. Remove the plug (**Figure 6**) from the drain hose on the V-duct and drain away any accumulated moisture or dirt. If necessary, blow the hose clear with compressed air.
2. Inspect all components of the air filter housing assembly. Look closely for cracks or other damage that would allow unfiltered air into the engine. Replace any part that is damaged or starting to deteriorate.

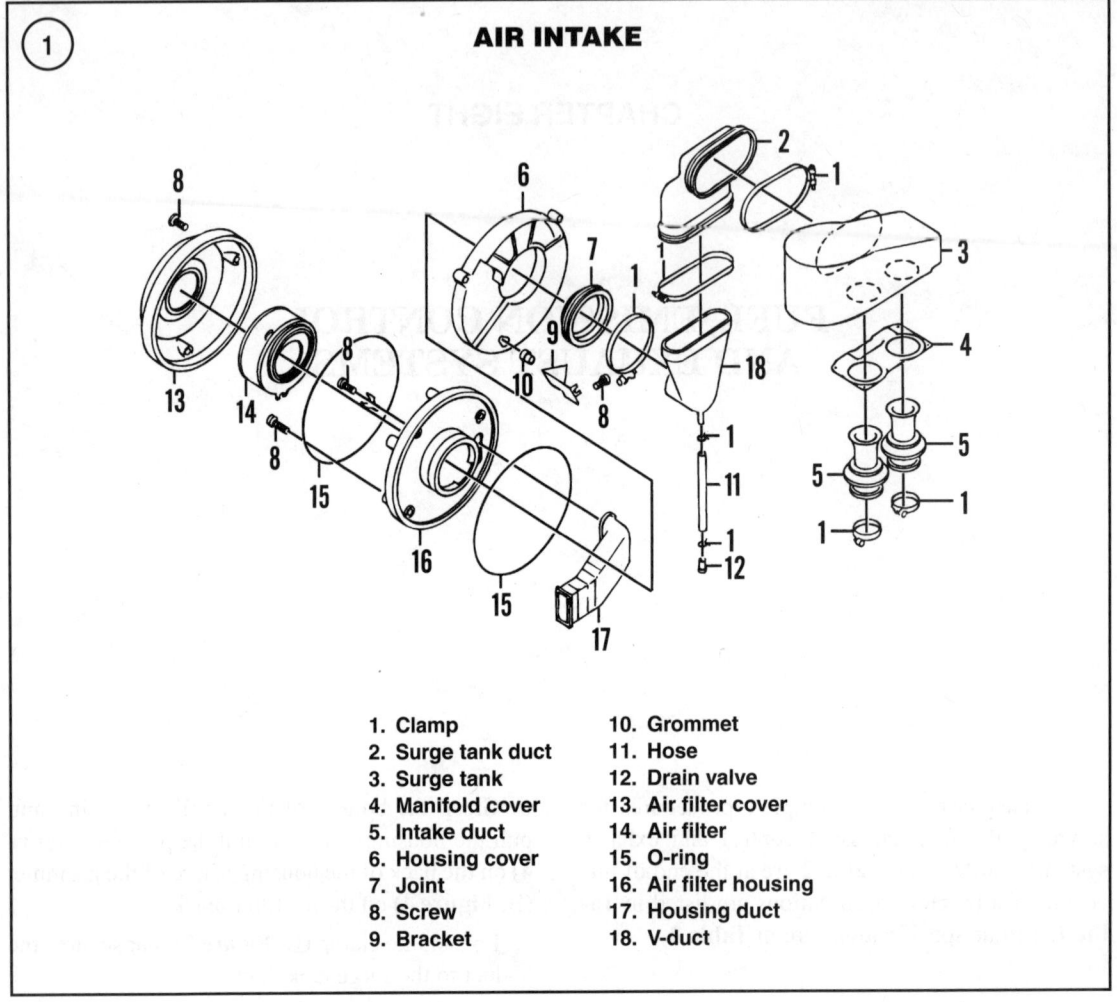

AIR INTAKE

1. Clamp
2. Surge tank duct
3. Surge tank
4. Manifold cover
5. Intake duct
6. Housing cover
7. Joint
8. Screw
9. Bracket
10. Grommet
11. Hose
12. Drain valve
13. Air filter cover
14. Air filter
15. O-ring
16. Air filter housing
17. Housing duct
18. V-duct

3. Wipe out the inside of the air filter housing with a clean rag.

Installation

Refer to **Figure 1** when installing the air filter housing.

1. Make sure the drain hose is in place on the V-duct. See **Figure 6**.
2. Lubricate the lip of the V-duct with a soap solution and insert the V-duct into the surge-tank duct.
3. Tighten the clamp enough to secure the V-duct in place but not too tight, because the seal could deform and leak.
4. Press the housing toward the engine until the housing post (A, **Figure 4**) is seated in the grommet (B, **Figure 4**) on the air filter bracket.

5. Install the two air filter housing Allen bolts (**Figure 3**). Include a washer behind each bolt, and tighten the bolts to the specification in **Table 2**.

6. Install the air filter so the notch on the filter (**Figure 7**) engages the post on the air filter housing.

7. Install the air filter cover and tighten the mounting screws securely.

SURGE TANK ASSEMBLY

Removal/Inspection/Installation

Refer to **Figure 1** when servicing the surge tank assembly.

1. Remove the air filter housing as described in this chapter.

FUEL, EMISSION CONTROL AND EXHAUST SYSTEMS

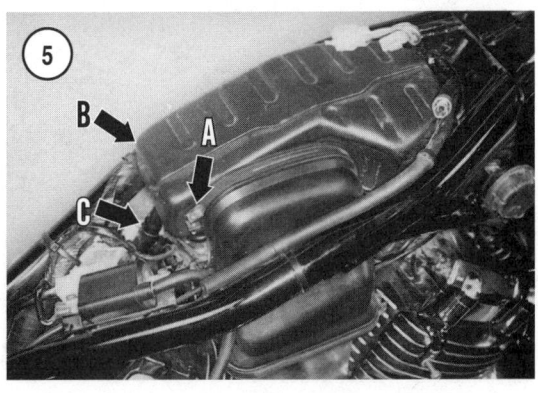

2. Release the clamp and disconnect the cylinder head breather hose (C, **Figure 5**) from the surge tank.

3. Loosen the clamp (A, **Figure 5**) that secures the surge tank duct to the surge tank (B, **Figure 5**).

4. Pull the surge tank duct from the surge tank and remove the duct from the frame.

5. Loosen the clamps that secure each intake duct (**Figure 8**) to its carburetor and lift the surge tank from the carburetors. The intake ducts and clamps should come out with the surge tank.

6. Inspect all components. Look closely for cracks or other damage that would allow unfiltered air into the engine. Replace any part that is damaged or deteriorating.

7. Installation is the reverse of removal. Note the following:

   a. Make sure each intake duct (**Figure 8**) is properly seated on its carburetor intake.
   b. Tighten each intake duct clamp securely.
   c. Make sure the cylinder-head breather hose is secured to the surge tank.
   d. Lubricate the lip on the surge tank with a soap solution, and install the surge tank duct over the lip. Tighten the clamp securely but not so tight that the surge tank or the duct is deformed.

CARBURETOR OPERATION

The carburetor atomizes fuel and mixes it in correct proportions with air that is drawn in through the air intake. At the primary throttle opening (idle), a small amount of fuel is siphoned through the pilot jet by the incoming air. As the throttle is opened further, the air stream begins to siphon fuel through the main jet and needle jet. The tapered needle increases the effective flow capacity of the needle jet as it is lifted, in that it occupies progressively less area in the jet. At full throttle, the carburetor venturi is fully open and the needle is lifted far enough to allow the main jet to flow at full capacity.

The choke circuit is a bystarter system. The choke knob in this system opens a starter valve rather than closing a butterfly in the venturi area as on many other carburetors. When the starter valve is open, an additional stream of fuel discharges into the carburetor venturi, which richens the mixture.

CARBURETOR

Removal/Installation

Remove both carburetors as an assembly.

1. Use jack stands or a jack to securely support the motorcycle on level ground.
2. Remove the fuel tank as described in this chapter.
3. Remove the surge tank as described in this chapter.

FUEL, EMISSION CONTROL AND EXHAUST SYSTEMS

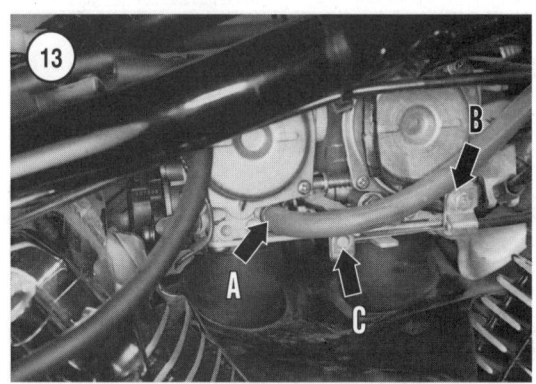

4. Disconnect the carburetor vent hose (**Figure 9**) from the bracket attached to the back of the front cylinder.

NOTE
Do not remove the throttle position sensor (TPS) from the carburetor body. Refer to Throttle Position Sensor in Chapter Nine for TPS inspection and adjustment procedures.

5. Press the tab on the throttle position sensor connector (**Figure 10**) and disconnect the connector from the sensor.

6. Disconnect the thermo switch connector (**Figure 11**).

7. Disconnect the fuel line (**Figure 12**) from the fitting on the rear carburetor.

8. On California models, disconnect the EVAP canister hose (A, **Figure 13**) from the fitting on the rear carburetor.

9. Loosen the clamp screw (B, **Figure 13**) and disconnect the choke cable end (C, **Figure 13**) from the actuator lever.

10. Loosen each carburetor clamp screw (**Figure 14**).

11. Pull the carburetor assembly up until each carburetor disengages from its intake manifold, and remove the carburetors through the top of the frame. Set the carburetor assembly on a frame rail.

12. Loosen the locknut on the pull cable (A, **Figure 15**). Release the cable from the cable bracket (C, **Figure 15**) on the carburetor, and disconnect the cable end from the throttle wheel.

13. Repeat this for the push cable (B, **Figure 15**).

CAUTION
Stuff clean shops rags into each intake manifold to keep debris out of the cylinder head.

14. After removing the carburetor assembly, examine the intake manifold on each cylinder head. Look closely for cracks or other damage that would allow unfiltered air into the engine. Replace any damaged part.

15. Install by reversing these removal steps while noting the following:

CAUTION
The carburetors form an airtight seal with the manifolds. Air leaks can cause excessive engine damage due to the lean mixture and/or unfiltered incoming air.

a. Make sure each carburetor is fully seated on its intake manifold. A solid bottoming should be felt when they are correctly installed. Tighten each carburetor clamp securely.

b. When connecting the throttle cable to the throttle wheel, first attach the push cable (B, **Figure 15**) to the throttle wheel, and then at-

CHAPTER EIGHT

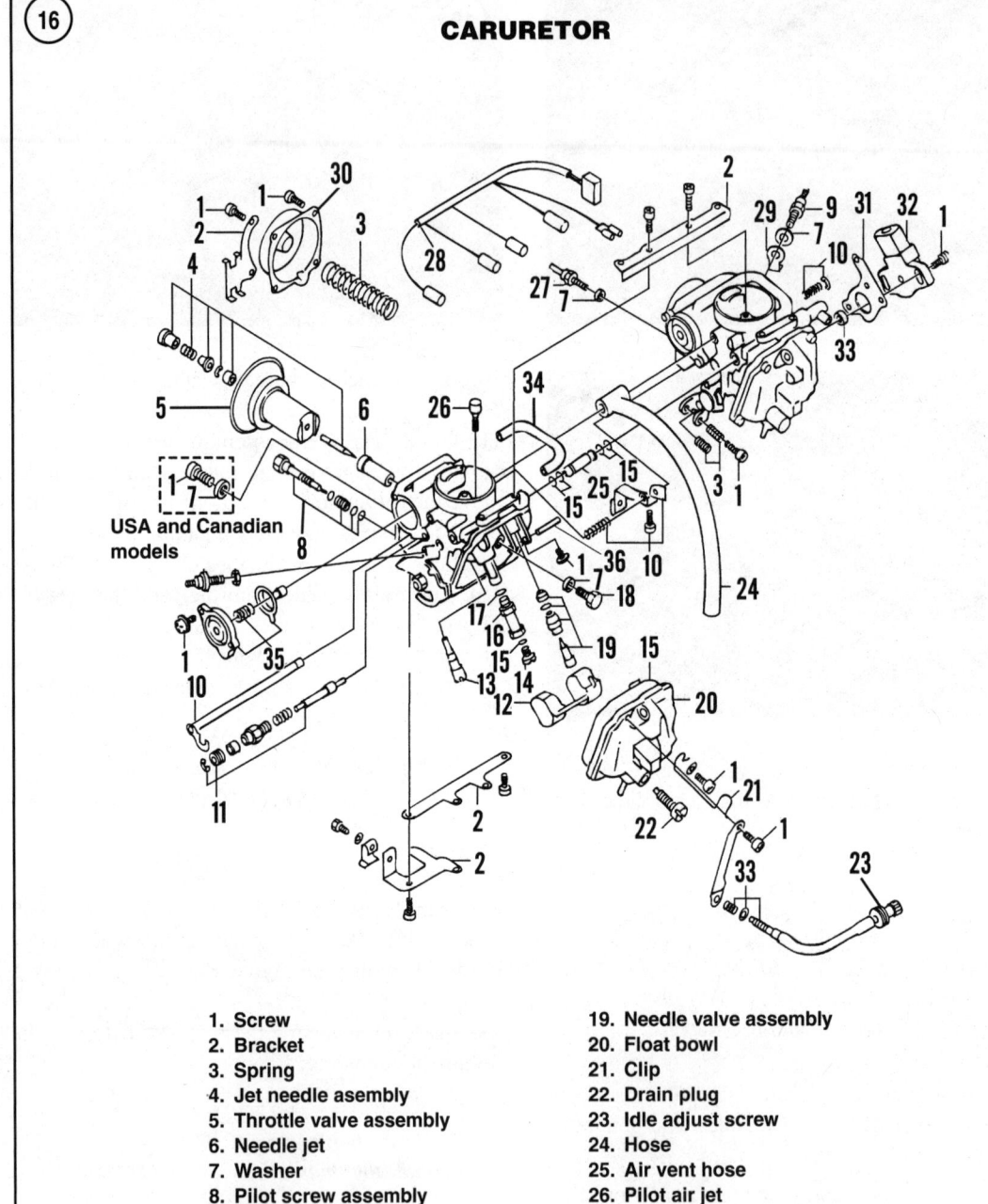

CARURETOR

1. Screw
2. Bracket
3. Spring
4. Jet needle asembly
5. Throttle valve assembly
6. Needle jet
7. Washer
8. Pilot screw assembly
9. Carburetor heater No. 2
10. Starter actuator assembly
11. Starter valve assembly
12. Float
13. Pilot jet
14. Main jet
15. O-ring
16. Main jet holder
17. Gasket
18. Screw
19. Needle valve assembly
20. Float bowl
21. Clip
22. Drain plug
23. Idle adjust screw
24. Hose
25. Air vent hose
26. Pilot air jet
27. Carburetor heater No. 1
28. Carburetor heater lead
29. Terminal
30. Throttle valve cover
31. Gasket
32. Throttle position sensor
33. Seal
34. Pipe
35. Coasting enrichener assembly
36. Float pin

FUEL, EMISSION CONTROL AND EXHAUST SYSTEMS

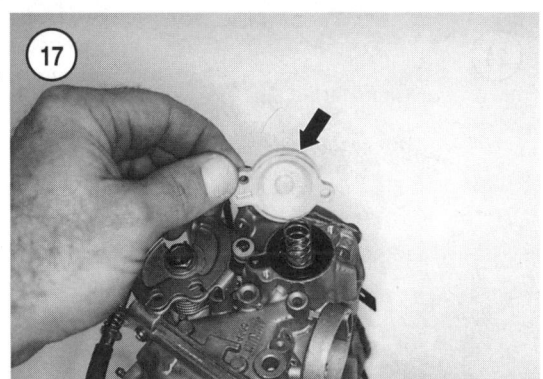

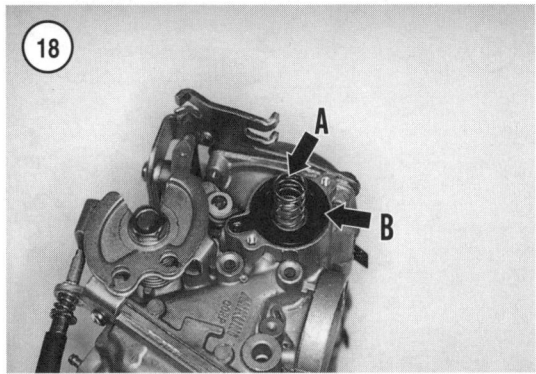

f. On California models, make sure the EVAP canister hose (A, **Figure 13**) is attached to the fitting on the rear carburetor.

16. Reinstall the surge tank and fuel tank as described in this chapter.

Carburetor Disassembly/Assembly

Refer to **Figure 16** for this procedure.

All components that require cleaning can be removed from each carburetor body without separating that body from the other carburetor. *Do not separate a carburetor body from the assembly unless necessary. Service an individual carburetor while it is still attached to the carburetor assembly.*

Disassemble, clean, and reassemble each carburetor separately. This prevents the accidental mixing of parts among carburetor bodies.

CAUTION
When cleaning a carburetor, do not turn the pilot screw. It is preset by the manufacturer and changing this setting will decrease engine performance. Carburetor adjustments are described in Chapter Three.

1. Remove the two mounting screws and lift the coasting enrichener cover (**Figure 17**) from the carburetor body.
2. Remove the spring (A, **Figure 18**) and the coasting enrichener diaphragm (B, **Figure 18**).
3. Loosen the screw (**Figure 19**) on the starter valve actuator lever.
4. Rotate the actuator until its fingers disengage from the starter valve, and remove the starter valve (**Figure 20**).

tach the pull cable (A, **Figure 15**). Make sure each cable is properly secured to the cable bracket (C, **Figure 15**) on the carburetor.

c. Check both the throttle cable and choke cable for correct routing after installation. The cables must not be twisted, kinked or pinched.

d. Adjust the throttle cable as described in Chapter Three.

e. Make sure the carburetor vent hose (**Figure 9**) is attached to the bracket on the front cylinder.

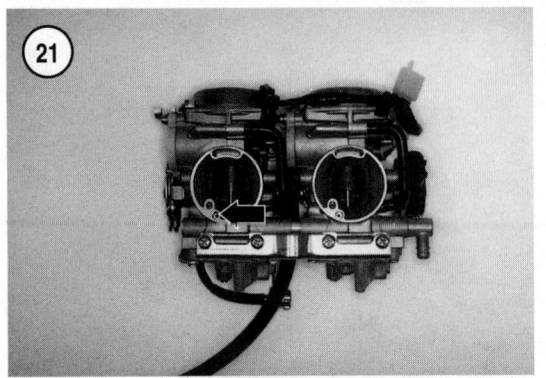
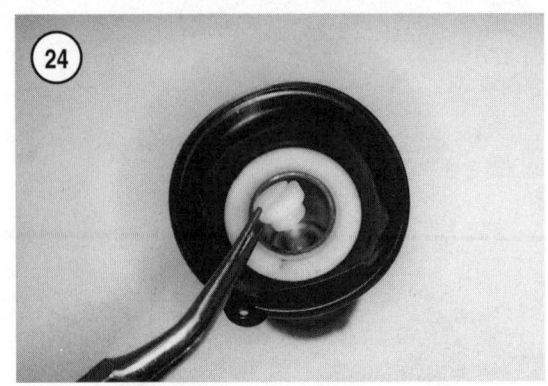

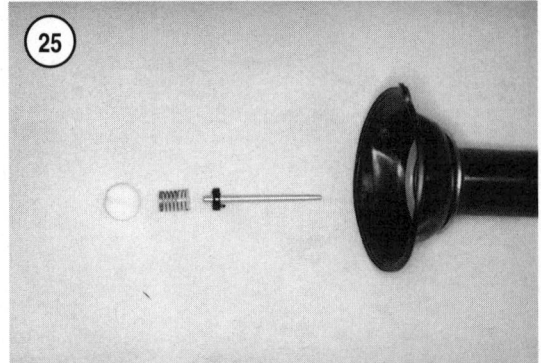

5. Remove the pilot air jet (**Figure 21**).
6. Remove the four mounting screws (**Figure 22**) and the throttle valve cover (A, **Figure 23**).
7. Remove the spring (B, **Figure 23**) and the throttle valve (C, **Figure 23**).
8. Remove the nylon screw (**Figure 24**) from the throttle valve.
9. Remove the spring and then remove the jet needle from the throttle valve. See **Figure 25**.
10. Remove the four screws (**Figure 26**), and remove the float bowl (A, **Figure 27**) from the carburetor body. Remove and discard the float bowl

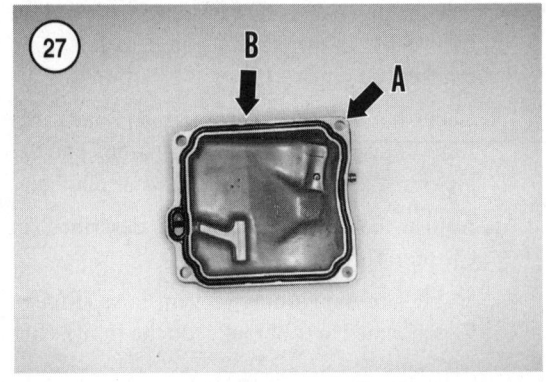

FUEL, EMISSION CONTROL AND EXHAUST SYSTEMS

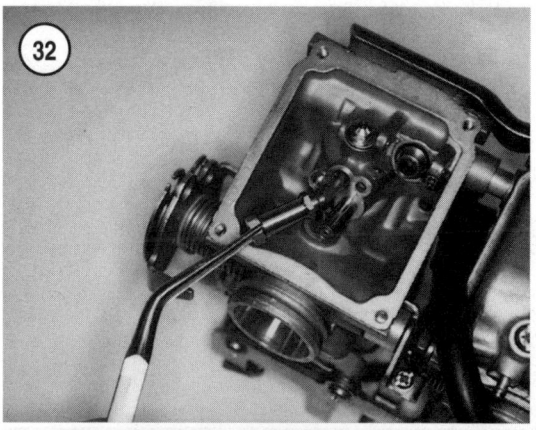

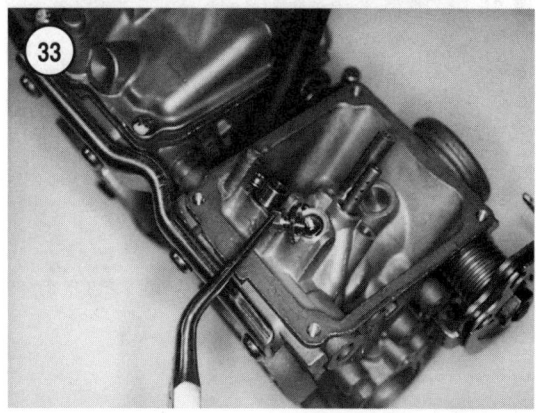

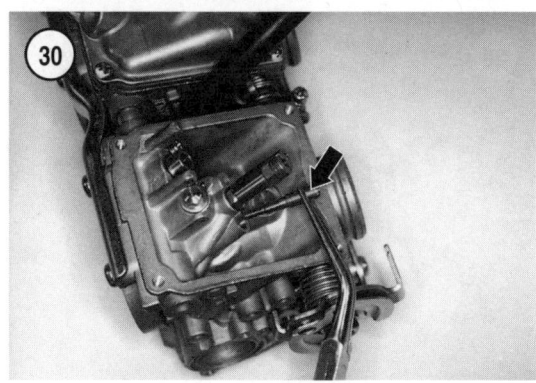

gasket (B, **Figure 27**). Install a new gasket during assembly.

11. Remove the float pin (A, **Figure 28**) from the posts in the carburetor, and remove the float (B, **Figure 28**). Do not lose the needle valve (A, **Figure 29**). It should come out with the float.

12. Remove the pilot jet (**Figure 30**).

13. Remove the main jet (**Figure 31**), and then remove the main jet holder (**Figure 32**). Be sure the gasket comes out with the main jet holder. It could remain behind on the emulsion tube.

14. Remove the needle jet bolt (**Figure 33**) from the float bowl. Make sure to remove the washer behind the bolt.

15. Remove the needle jet (**Figure 34**) from the carburetor bore.

16. Remove the mounting screw (A, **Figure 35**) and the needle valve seat (B, **Figure 35**).

17. Inspect the parts as described in this chapter.

18. Assemble the carburetor by reversing these disassembly steps. Note the following:

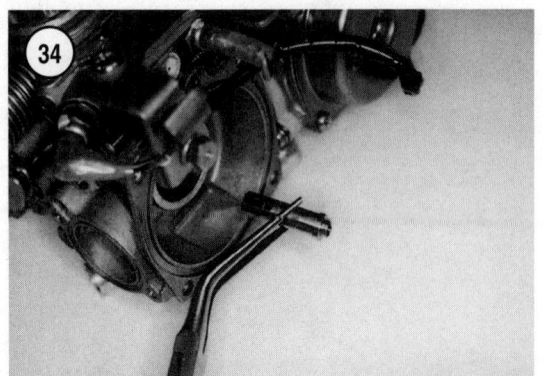

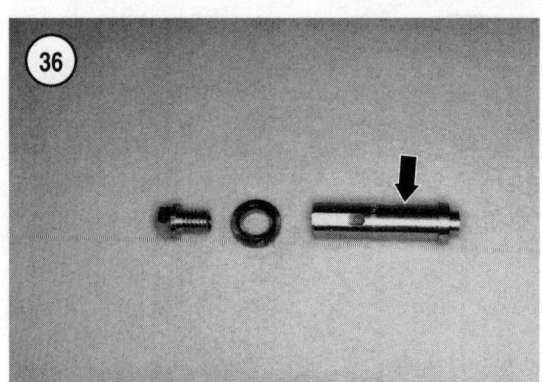

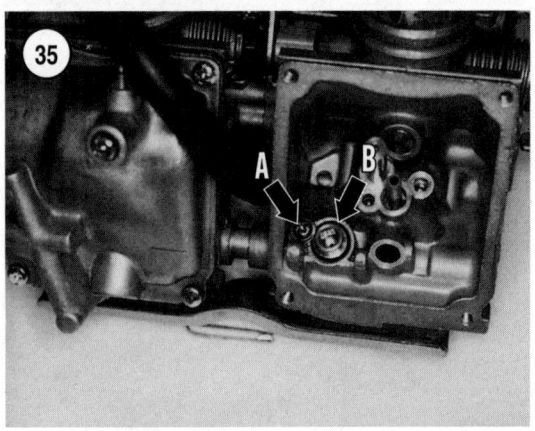

a. Lower the needle jet (**Figure 36**) into the carburetor body. Hold the needle jet with a finger, and secure it in place with the needle jet bolt (**Figure 33**) and washer.
b. Use a new gasket when installing the main jet holder. Set the gasket on the emulsion tube (**Figure 37**), and then install the main jet holder (**Figure 32**).
c. Hook the needle valve onto the float tang (**Figure 38**), and lower the float into the float bowl. Make sure the needle valve (A, **Figure 29**) is seated in the valve seat (B, **Figure 29**).
d. Use a new O-ring (B, **Figure 27**) when installing the float bowl.
e. When installing the jet needle into the throttle valve, make sure the needle properly seats in the throttle valve piston. Rotate the needle as necessary so the tab on the head of the needle (**Figure 39**) drops through the indexing hole in the piston.
f. Install the throttle valve so the tab on the diaphragm fits into the cutout in the carburetor body. See **Figure 40**.

g. When installing the coasting enrichener diaphragm, make sure the tab on the diaphragm seats in the cutout in the carburetor body. See **Figure 18**.

Carburetor Cleaning and Inspection

1. Thoroughly clean and dry all parts. The use of a caustic carburetor cleaning solvent is not recommended. Instead, clean carburetor parts in a petroleum-based solvent. Then rinse in clean water.

FUEL, EMISSION CONTROL AND EXHAUST SYSTEMS

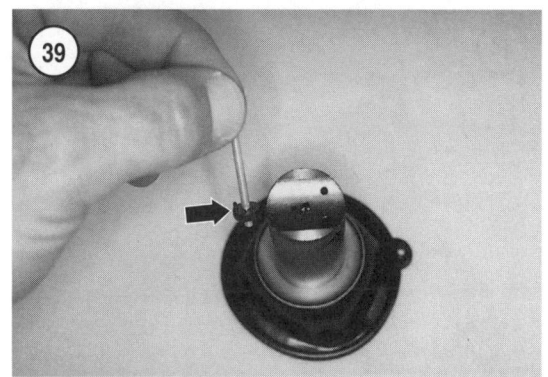

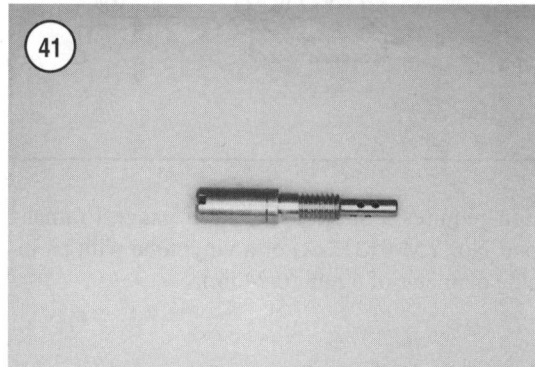

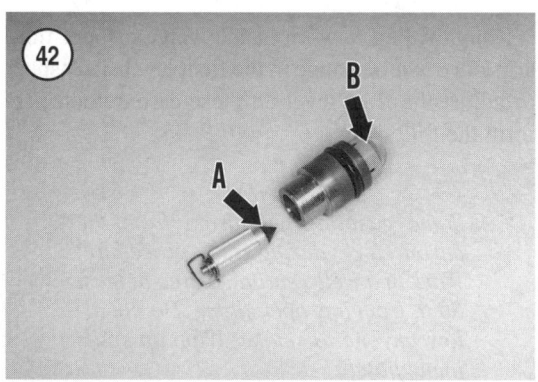

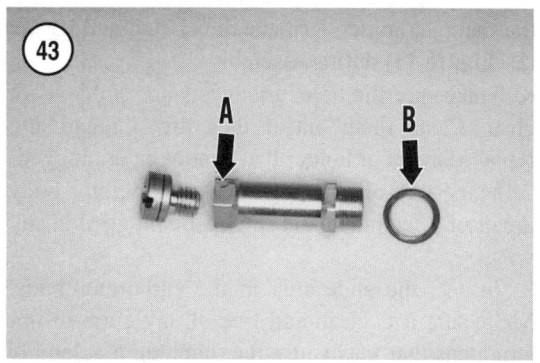

2. Allow the carburetor to dry thoroughly before assembly or blow dry parts with compressed air. Blow out the jets (**Figure 41**) and jet holder with compressed air.

CAUTION
*If compressed air is not available, allow the parts to air dry or dry them with a clean, lint-free cloth. Do **not** use a paper towel to dry carburetor parts. Small paper particles could plug openings in the carburetor body or jets.*

CAUTION
*Do **not** use a piece of wire to clean the jets. Minor gouges in the jet can alter flow rate and change the air/fuel mixture.*

3. Remove the drain screw from the float bowl.
4. Inspect the needle valve assembly by performing the following:
    a. Inspect the end of the needle valve (A, **Figure 42**) for wear or damage.
    b. Check the inside of the needle valve seat. A damaged needle valve or a particle of dirt or grit in the float valve assembly will cause the carburetor to flood and overflow fuel.
    c. Inspect the needle valve filter (B, **Figure 42**). If there are any holes or if the filter starts to deteriorate, replace the needle valve assembly.
    d. Inspect the O-ring on the needle valve seat. If it is torn or beginning to harden, replace the needle valve assembly.
    e. If any part is worn or damaged, replace the entire needle valve assembly as a set.
5. Remove the O-ring from inside the female end of the main jet holder (A, **Figure 43**), and inspect

the main jet holder. Replace the O-ring and gasket (B, **Figure 43**) during assembly.

6. Make sure the holes in all jets and holders are clear. Clean them out if they are plugged and replace any jet or holder that cannot be unplugged.
7. Make sure all openings in the carburetor body are clear. Clean them out if they are plugged in any way.
8. Inspect the slide area in the carburetor body. Make sure it is clean and free of any burrs or obstructions that may cause the diaphragm assembly to hang up during operation.
9. Inspect the throttle valve (**Figure 44**) for scoring and wear. Replace if necessary.
10. Inspect the diaphragm on the throttle valve for tears, cracks or other damage. Replace the throttle valve assembly if the diaphragm is damaged.
11. Inspect the float for deterioration or damage. Place the float in a container of water and push it down. If the float sinks or if bubbles appear (indicating a leak), replace the float.
12. Inspect the coasting enrichener diaphragm (B, **Figure 18**) for tears, cracks or other damage. Replace the diaphragm if it is damaged.

THROTTLE POSITION SENSOR

Refer to Chapter Nine for throttle position sensor inspection and adjustment procedures.

CARBURETOR HEATER SYSTEM

Refer to Chapter Nine for carburetor heater and thermo switch troubleshooting procedures.

FUEL LEVEL

The fuel level in the carburetor float bowls is critical to proper performance. The fuel flow rate depends not only upon the vacuum in the throttle bore and the size of the jets, but also on the fuel level in the float bowl. **Table 1** provides a specification for the actual fuel level, measured from a float line (A, **Figure 45**) on the bottom of the float bowl with the carburetors mounted on the motorcycle.

This measurement is more useful than a simple float height measurement because the actual fuel level can vary from bike to bike, even when the floats are set at the same height. Fuel level inspec-

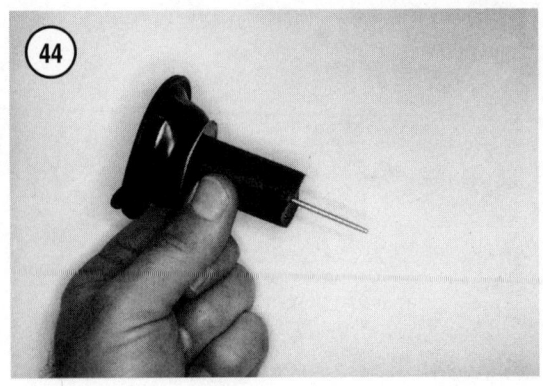

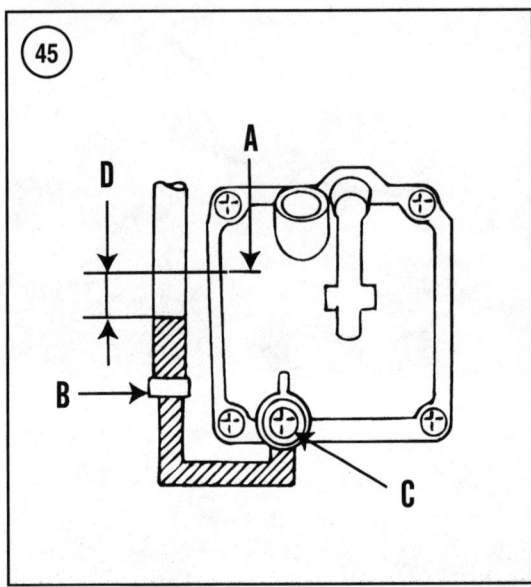

tion requires a special fuel level gauge (Yamaha part No. YM-01312-A) or a vinyl tube with an inside diameter of 6 mm (0.24 in.).

Inspection/Adjustment

Rough riding, a worn needle valve or bent float arm can cause a change in the float level. To inspect or adjust the float level on these carburetors, perform the following.

> *WARNING*
> *Some gasoline will drain from the carburetors during this procedure. Work in a well-ventilated area at least 50 ft. from any open flame. Do not allow anyone to smoke. Wipe up spills immediately.*

FUEL, EMISSION CONTROL AND EXHAUST SYSTEMS

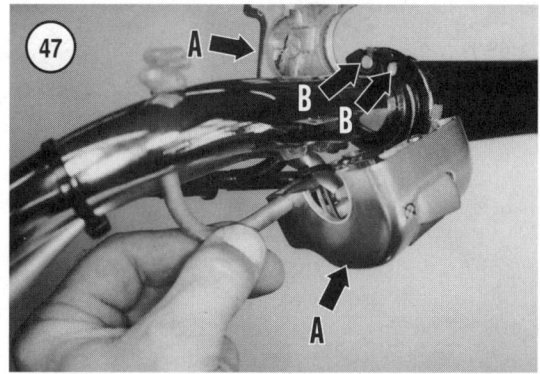

1. Remove the fuel tank and surge tank as described in this chapter.

2. Use a portable jack and/or wooden blocks to level the motorcycle from side-to-side. Make sure the carburetors are level.

3. Connect the fuel level gauge (B, **Figure 45**) to the drain on the carburetor. Secure the gauge so it sits vertically against the float bowl.

4. Loosen the carburetor drain screw (C, **Figure 45**).

5. Wait until the fuel in the gauge settles.

6. Fuel level (D, **Figure 45**) equals the distance between the float line (A, **Figure 45**) on the bottom of the float bowl and the level of the fuel in the gauge. Record the fuel level, and compare the reading to the specification in **Table 1**.

7. Repeat this procedure for the other carburetor.

NOTE
If the float bowls become empty during this procedure, temporarily install the fuel tank and refill the float bowls. Remove the fuel tank, and proceed to the next step.

8. Compare the measurements to the fuel level specification in **Table 1**.

9. If the fuel level in a particular carburetor requires adjustment, adjust the float height by performing the following:
   a. Remove the carburetor assembly as described in this chapter.
   b. Remove the float bowl from the appropriate carburetor.
   c. Remove the float pivot pin (A, **Figure 28**) and the float (B, **Figure 28**).
   d. Remove the needle valve from the float.
   e. Bend the float tang (**Figure 46**) as required to attain the correct fuel level. Install the float bowl.
   f. Reinstall the carburetor assembly, and recheck the fuel level.

THROTTLE CABLE

Replacement

1. Use jack stands or a jack to securely support the motorcycle on level ground.

2. Remove the carburetor assembly as described in this chapter.

3. Remove the two mounting screws and separate the halves of the right handlebar switch assembly (A, **Figure 47**) as described in Chapter Nine.

4. Disengage the ends (B, **Figure 47**) of both the pull and push cables from the throttle grip.

NOTE
The string in the next step is used to pull the new throttle cable through the frame so the cable will be properly routed.

5. Tie a piece of heavy string or cord to the ends of the throttle cable at the carburetor. Wrap this end with tape. Do not use an excessive amount of tape. Too much tape could interfere with the cable's passage through the frame loop on the upper fork bridge during removal. Tie the other end of the string to the frame.

6. Starting at the handlebar, carefully pull the throttle cable out of the frame, through the frame loop, and out from behind the headlight housing. Make sure the attached string follows the same path as the cable through the frame.

7. Untie the string from the old cable, and tie it to the carburetor ends of the new cable.

8. Carefully pull the string back through the frame, routing the new cable through the same path as the old cable.

9. Remove the string, and lubricate the ends of the new cable with lithium grease.

10. Connect the push cable (B, **Figure 48**) to the carburetor wheel.

11. Fit the push cable into the bracket (C, **Figure 48**), and secure it in place with the locknut.

12. Connect the pull cable (A, **Figure 48**) to the carburetor throttle wheel, and secure it to the bracket with its locknut.

13. At the handlebar, lubricate the ends of the new cable with lithium grease. Connect the cable ends (B, **Figure 47**) to the throttle grip.

14. Reinstall the halves of the right handlebar switch assembly as described in Chapter Nine. Make sure the projection (**Figure 49**) on the switch assembly aligns with the hole in the handlebar.

15. Reinstall the carburetor assembly as described in this chapter.

16. Operate the throttle grip. Check that the throttle linkage operates correctly without binding. If necessary, check that the cable is correctly attached and that there are no tight bends in the cable.

17. Adjust the throttle cable as described in Chapter Three.

18. Reinstall the surge tank and the fuel tank as described in this chapter.

19. Start the engine. Turn the handlebar from side to side without operating the throttle. If the engine speed increases while turning the handlebar, the throttle cable is routed incorrectly. Recheck the cable routing.

CHOKE CABLE

NOTE
*The carburetor starter valve is controlled by the choke knob (**Figure 50**) on the left side of the frame by the rear cylinder valve.*

1. Use jack stands or a scissors jack to securely support the motorcycle on level ground.

2. Remove the fuel tank and the surge tank duct as described in this chapter.

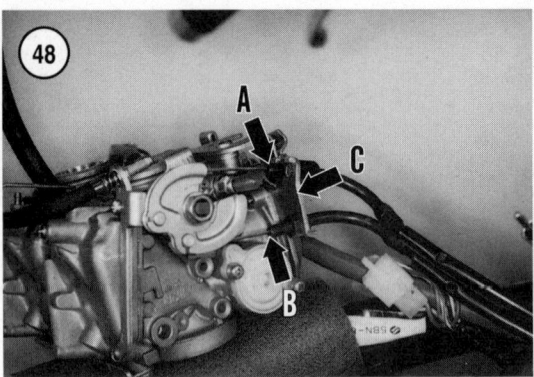

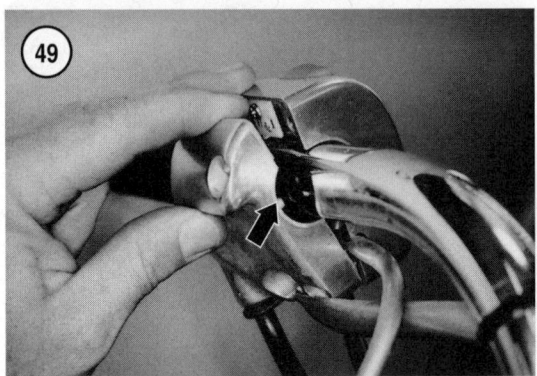

3. Note how the choke cable (A, **Figure 51**) is looped and routed through the frame. The new cable should follow the same path.

4. At the carburetor, loosen the choke cable clamp screw (B, **Figure 51**), and remove the cable end from the actuator lever (C, **Figure 51**).

NOTE
The string in the next step is used to pull the new choke cable through the frame so the cable will be properly routed.

5. Tie a piece of heavy string or cord to the end of the choke cable at the carburetor. Wrap this end with tape. Do not use an excessive amount of tape. Too much tape could interfere with the cable's passage through the frame.

6. If necessary, clip the cable tie (D, **Figure 51**).

7. Starting at the choke knob, carefully pull the cable through the cable tie, across the frame, and out through the choke knob bracket.

8. Lubricate the new cable as described in Chapter Three.

FUEL, EMISSION CONTROL AND EXHAUST SYSTEMS

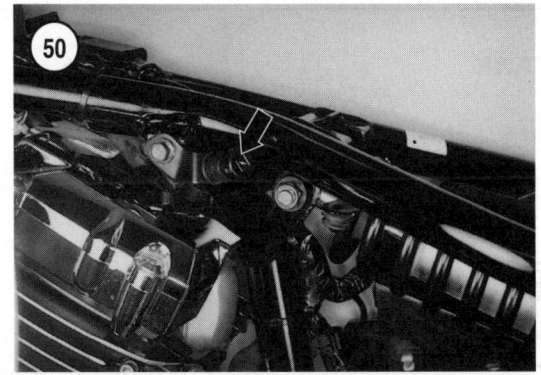

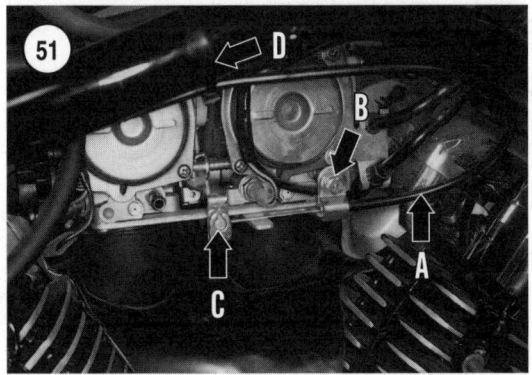

FUEL TANK

WARNING
Some fuel may spill in the following procedure. Work in a well-ventilated area at least 50 ft. from any sparks or flames, including gas appliance pilot lights. Do not allow anyone to smoke in the area. Have a B:C rated fire extinguisher on hand.

Removal/Installation

Refer to **Figure 52** when servicing the fuel tank.

1. Check that the ignition switch is OFF.
2. Use jack stands or a scissors jack to securely support the motorcycle on level ground.
3. Disconnect the lead from the negative battery terminal.
4. Turn the fuel valve (A, **Figure 53**) to the OFF position.
5. Disconnect the fuel hose (B, **Figure 53**) from the fuel valve. Plug the fuel hose to keep out dirt and other contaminants.
6. Remove the meter assembly by performing the following:
   a. Remove the three meter assembly mounting screws.
   b. Lift the meter assembly from the tank and place a rag between the meter assembly and tank so the tank does not get scratched.
   c. Disconnect the speedometer cable (A, **Figure 54**) and the two electrical connectors (B, **Figure 54**) from the meter assembly.
   d. Remove the meter assembly from the motorcycle.
7. *On California models*, remove the EVAP hose (A, **Figure 55**) from the vent stem on the fuel tank. Carefully pull the hose until it is free of the holder (B, **Figure 55**) on the meter bracket. Reroute the hose through this holder during fuel tank installation.
8. Remove the two fuel tank mounting bolts. The left rear tank bolt (**Figure 56**) also secures the choke knob bracket to the frame. Move the choke knob bracket safely out of the way.
9. Lift the rear of the tank, and pull the tank rearward until it is free of the damper (A, **Figure 57**) on each side of the frame.

9. Untie the string from the old cable, and tie it to the carburetor end of the new cable.

10. Carefully pull the string back through the frame, routing the new cable through the same path as the old cable. If the old cable tie (D, **Figure 51**) is still in place, pull the cable through this tie.

11. Remove the string, and lubricate the cable end with lithium grease.

12. Loop the choke cable as shown in A, **Figure 51**.

13. Connect the cable end to the actuator lever (C, **Figure 51**), and secure the cable to the clamp with the clamp screw (B, **Figure 51**).

14. Secure the choke knob to the bracket by tightening the locknut behind the bracket.

15. If necessary, secure the cable to the frame with a new cable tie (D, **Figure 51**).

16. Operate the choke knob, and check the operation of the carburetor starter valve assembly. If it does not operate properly or if there is binding, check that the cable is correctly attached, and check for tight bends in the cable.

17. Reinstall the surge tank duct and fuel tank.

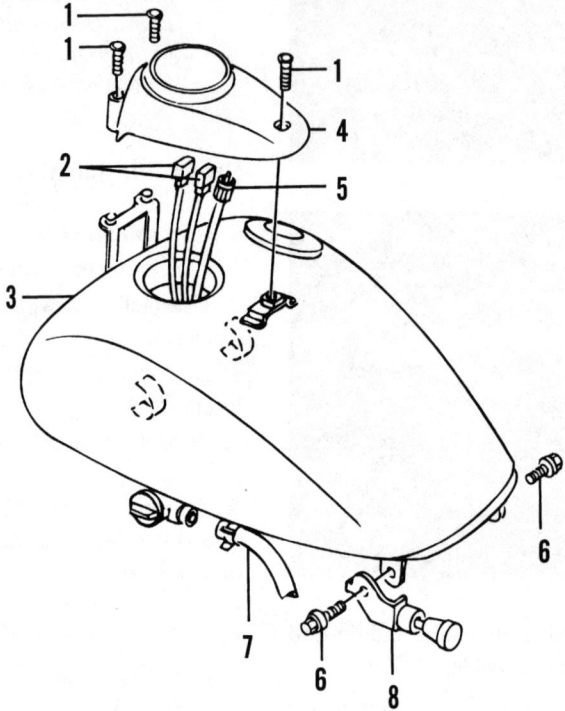

FUEL TANK

1. Meter assembly screw
2. Meter electrical leads
3. Fuel tank
4. Meter assembly
5. Speedometer cable
6. Tank mounting bolt
7. Fuel hose
8. Starter knob bracket

10. Carefully lift the tank until the speedometer cable, electrical leads, and EVAP hose (CA models only) are free of the tank, and remove the tank.

11. Installation is the reverse of removal. Note the following:

    a. Set the tank on the frame and feed the speedometer cable, electrical leads, and EVAP hose (CA models only) through the fuel tank. See **Figure 55**.

    b. Slide the tank forward until the tank engages the damper (A, **Figure 57**) on each side of the frame.

    c. Make sure the left fuel tank mounting bolt also secures the choke knob bracket to the frame.

    d. Torque the fuel tank mounting bolts to the specification in **Table 2**.

FUEL, EMISSION CONTROL AND EXHAUST SYSTEMS

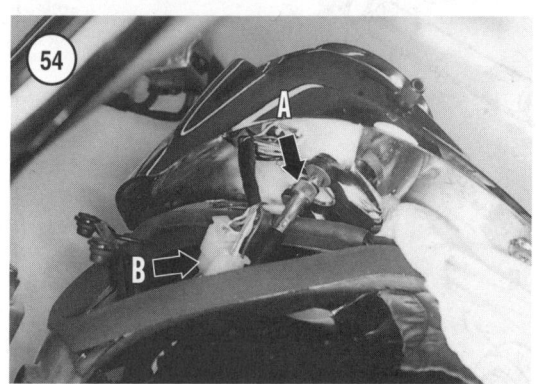

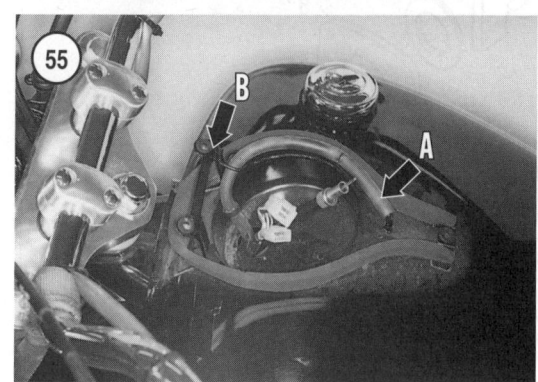

FUEL VALVE

Removal/Installation

WARNING
Some fuel may spill in the following procedure. Work in a well-ventilated area at least 50 ft. from any sparks or flames, including gas appliance pilot lights. Do not allow anyone to smoke in the area. Have a B:C rated fire extinguisher on hand.

Refer to **Figure 58** when servicing the fuel valve.
1. Remove the fuel tank as described in this chapter.
2. Set the fuel tank on a protective pad or blanket.
3. Drain the fuel from the tank into a clean, sealable container.
4. Position the tank so residual fuel does not spill from the tank when the fuel valve is removed.
5. Remove the two screws securing the fuel valve to the fuel tank, and remove the valve and O-ring.
6. The packing and fuel valve seal are the only replaceable parts in the fuel valve. To replace either, perform the following:
   a. Remove the two pan head screws and disassemble the valve as shown in **Figure 58**.
   b. Replace the packing or fuel valve seal.
   c. Assemble the fuel valve by reversing these disassembly steps.
7. Install the fuel valve by reversing these removal steps. Note the following:
   a. Install a new O-ring (1, **Figure 58**) during installation.
   b. After installing the fuel valve, pour a small amount of fuel into the tank and check for

CHAPTER EIGHT

FUEL VALVE

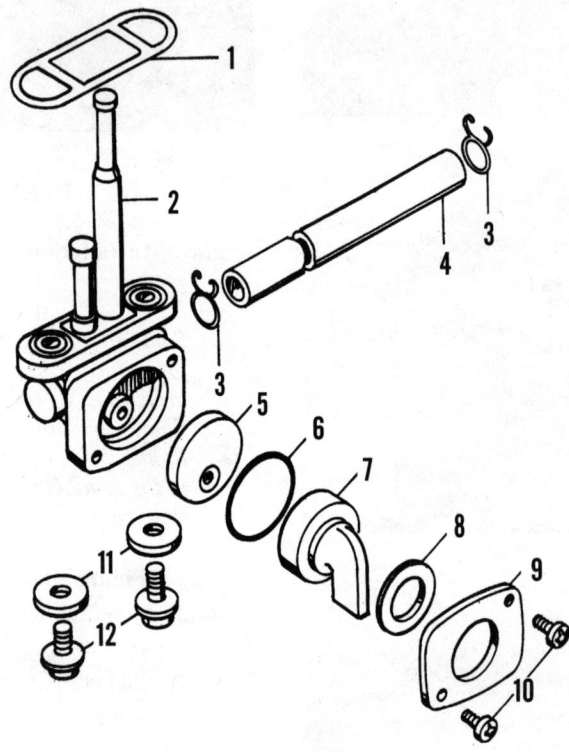

1. O-ring
2. Fuel valve body
3. Clamp
4. Fuel hose
5. Valve packing
6. Valve seal
7. Lever
8. Wave washer
9. Plate
10. Pan head screw
11. Washer
12. Screw

FUEL, EMISSION CONTROL AND EXHAUST SYSTEMS

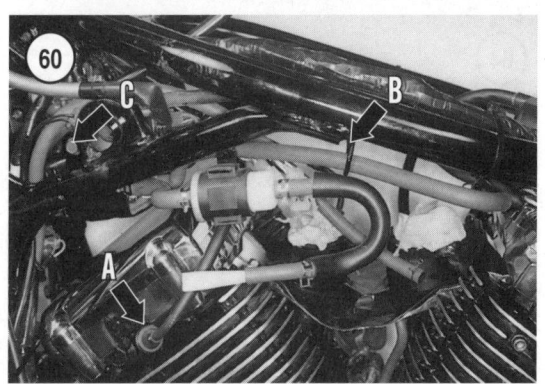

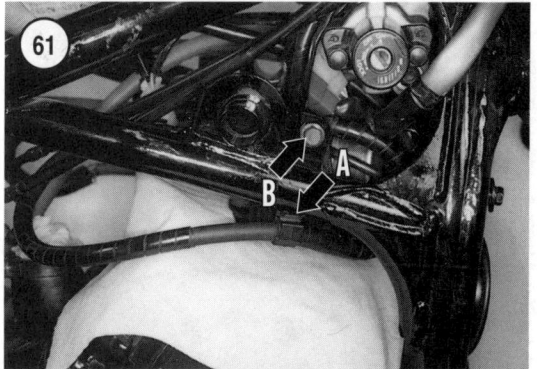

leaks. If a leak is present, solve the problem before installing the fuel tank.

FUEL FILTER

All models are equipped with a separate fuel filter that cannot be cleaned. Replace the fuel filter whenever it is dirty or at the interval specified in Chapter Three.

Removal/Installation

1. Remove the fuel tank as described in this chapter.
2. Remove the inlet and outlet hoses from the fuel filter.
3. Remove the filter from the rubber grommet (B, **Figure 57**).
4. Install by reversing these removal steps while noting the following:
   a. Check the hose clamps for damage; replace if necessary.
   b. After completing installation, thoroughly check for leaks.

FUEL PUMP BRACKET

The fuel pump, front ignition coil, and thermo switch are mounted to the fuel-pump bracket, which sits beneath the fuel tank.

NOTE
The thermo switch is sensitive to shock. Do not drop the bracket or bang the thermo switch when removing and installing the fuel pump bracket.

Removal

1. Remove the fuel tank, the surge tank and carburetors as described in this chapter.
2. Remove the frame neck cover from each side of the frame as described in Chapter Thirteen.
3. Place a rag over the front cylinder head covers to protect the covers while removing the fuel pump/front ignition coil assembly.
4. Disconnect the two primary coil spade connectors (one gray wire and one red/black wire) from the terminals on the ignition coil. See **Figure 59**.
5. Pull the fuel filter rubber grommet (B, **Figure 57**) from the mounting tab on the left side of the frame.
6. Pull the spark plug cap (A, **Figure 60**) from the spark plug in the front cylinder. Note how the front ignition coil secondary wire is routed through the frame. Reroute it along the same path during installation.
7. Release the front ignition coil secondary wire from the plastic cable guide (A, **Figure 61**) on the right side of the frame, and pull the secondary wire from beneath the mounting bracket.

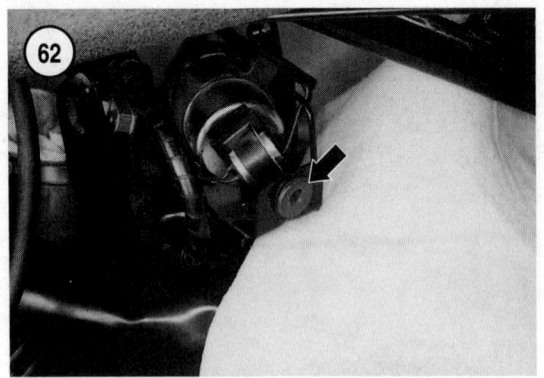
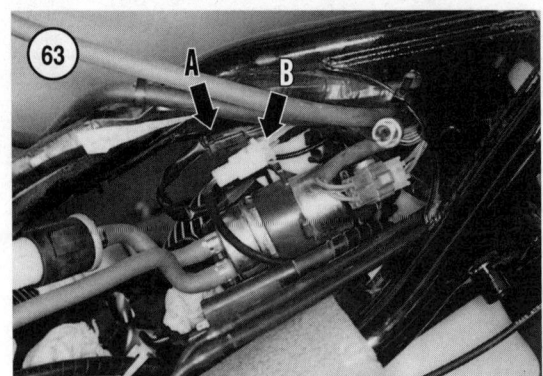

8. Pull the fuel pump supply hose from the hose loop (B, **Figure 60**) on the left frame rail.

9. Remove the assembly mounting bolts from the left (C, **Figure 60**) and right (B, **Figure 61**) sides of the frame.

10. Pull the fuel pump bracket rearward until its grommet (**Figure 62**) at the front of the bracket is free of the mounting pin on the frame.

11. Disconnect the black, 2-pin fuel pump connector (A, **Figure 63**). This connector has a blue/black and a black wire on each side of the connector.

12. Disconnect the white, 2-pin thermo switch connector (B, **Figure 63**). This connector has two brown/yellow wires on the thermo switch side of the connector; a brown/yellow and a brown/black wire on the harness side.

13. Remove the fuel pump/front ignition coil assembly from between the frame rails.

14. Inspect the fuel pump, front ignition coil, or thermo switch as described in Chapter Nine.

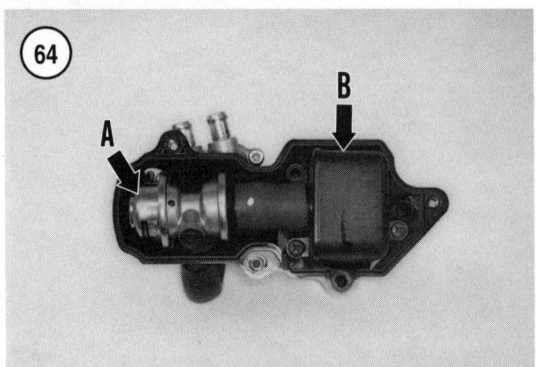

Installation

1. Place a rag on the front cylinder head covers to protect them during installation.

2. Set the fuel pump/front ignition coil assembly between the frame rails. Position the assembly so the fuel pump faces the left side of the motorcycle.

3. Connect the white thermo switch connector (B, **Figure 63**) and the black fuel pump connector (A, **Figure 63**) to their respective mates from the wiring harness.

4. Push the fuel pump bracket forward until the grommet (**Figure 62**) at the front of the bracket engages the mounting pin on the frame.

FUEL, EMISSION CONTROL AND EXHAUST SYSTEMS

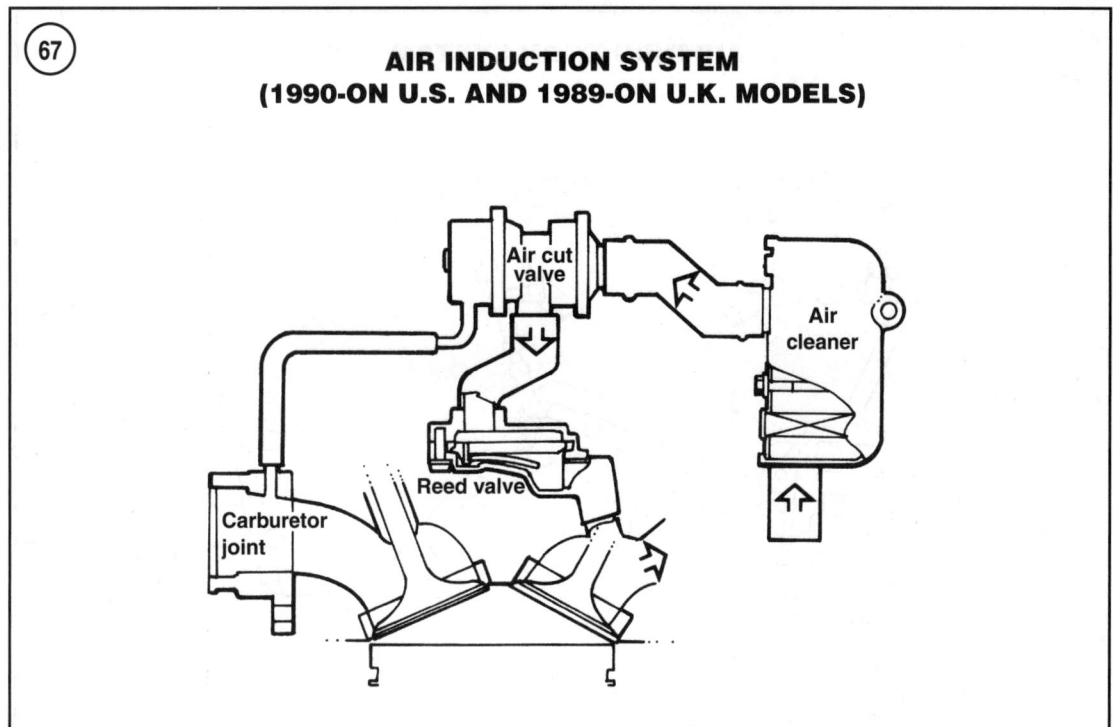

67 AIR INDUCTION SYSTEM (1990-ON U.S. AND 1989-ON U.K. MODELS)

5. Install the mounting bolts into the left (C, **Figure 60**) and right (B, **Figure 61**) sides of the frame. Tighten each bolt securely.

6. Route the fuel pump supply hose through the hose loop (B, **Figure 60**) on the left frame rail.

7. Secure the front ignition coil secondary wire to the plastic cable guide (A, **Figure 61**) on the right side of the frame.

8. Route the ignition coil secondary wire beneath the mounting bracket, and connect the spark plug cap (A, **Figure 60**) to the spark plug in the front cylinder. Make sure the wire is correctly routed along the same path noted during removal.

9. Slide the fuel filter rubber grommet (B, **Figure 57**) onto its mounting tab on the left side of the frame.

10. Connect the two ignition coil primary leads (one gray wire and one red/black wire) to the terminals on the ignition coil. See **Figure 59**.

11. Check the routing and placement of all wires and connectors. Make sure there is no excessive pulling or sharp bends on any wire. If necessary, re-route a wire so it is not excessively stressed.

12. Install the frame neck cover onto each side of the frame as described in Chapter Thirteen.

13. Install the carburetors, surge tank and the fuel tank, as described in this chapter.

AIR INDUCTION SYSTEM

The air induction system reduces hydrocarbon emissions by promoting more complete combustion. The system injects fresh air into each exhaust port so any unburned fuel in the exhaust is burned instead of being released into the atmosphere.

The system consists of an air cut valve (A, **Figure 64**), AIS filter (B, **Figure 64**), a reed valve (**Figure 65**), as well as air and vacuum lines. The AIS uses momentary pressure differentials generated by the exhaust pulses to introduce fresh air into the exhaust ports.

During normal operation, the air cut valve is open so secondary air flows from the AIS filter, through the air cutoff valve, to the reed valve and then into AIS fitting (**Figure 66**) at the exhaust port in each cylinder. See **Figure 67**.

The air cut valve, however, closes during deceleration to prevent backfiring. When the throttle is closed, vacuum from the intake port closes the air cut valve so secondary air cannot flow to the reed valve.

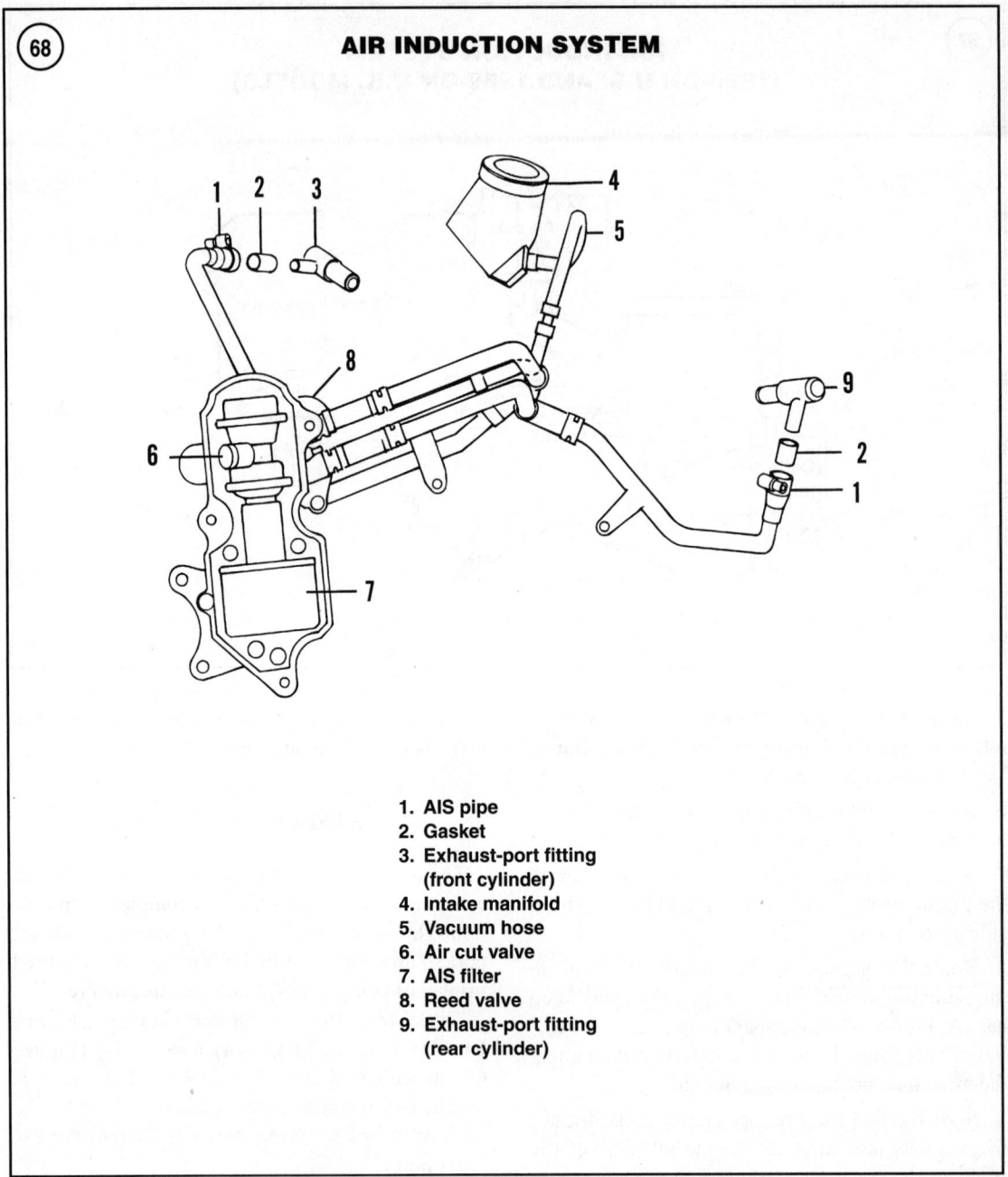

AIR INDUCTION SYSTEM

1. AIS pipe
2. Gasket
3. Exhaust-port fitting (front cylinder)
4. Intake manifold
5. Vacuum hose
6. Air cut valve
7. AIS filter
8. Reed valve
9. Exhaust-port fitting (rear cylinder)

AIS Assembly Removal/Installation

Refer to **Figure 68** when servicing the air induction system.

1. Remove the three AIS assembly cover screws (**Figure 69**) and remove the cover from the AIS assembly.
2. Remove the three AIS assembly mounting screws (**Figure 70**).
3. Release the hose clamps (**Figure 71**) and disconnect the AIS hose from each fitting on the reed valve.
4. Release the clamp and disconnect the vacuum hose from the fitting (**Figure 72**) on the air cut valve.
5. Inspect the AIS assembly as described below.
6. Installation is the reverse of removal. Note the following:

FUEL, EMISSION CONTROL AND EXHAUST SYSTEMS

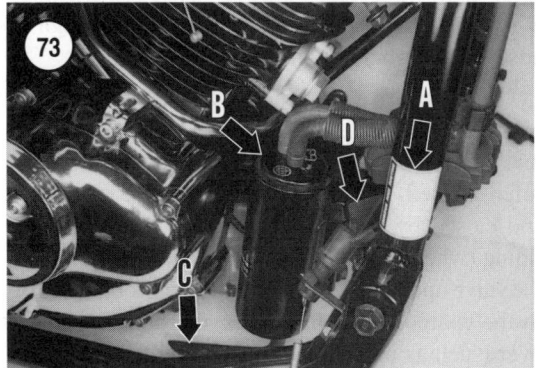

  a. Make sure to correctly route the hoses as shown in **Figure 68**.
  b. Properly secure each hose to its respective fitting.
  c. Torque the AIS assembly mounting screws and cover screws to the specifications in **Table 2**.

AIS Assembly Inspection

1. Inspect the reed valve (**Figure 65**), the air cut valve (A, **Figure 64**) and the AIS filter (B, **Figure 64**) for cracks or other damage. Replace any damaged component.
2. Make sure the ports in the reed valve, air cut valve and AIS filter are unobstructed. Clean them if possible or replace the clogged component.
3. Inspect the air and vacuum lines for cracks or leaks. Replace any hose as necessary.
4. Inspect the hose connections for leaks.

EVAPORATIVE EMISSION CONTROL

All models sold in California are equipped with an evaporative emission control system, which reduces the amount of fuel vapors released into the atmosphere. The system consists of a charcoal canister, roll over valve, vacuum lines, special carburetors and fuel tank. A schematic of the emission control system is on a label (A, **Figure 73**) on the right frame downtube.

The evaporative emission control system captures fumes from the fuel system and stores them in a charcoal canister (**Figure 74**). While the bike is parked or operated at low engine speed, the fuel vapors remain in the charcoal canister. When the bike is ridden at high speed, the vapors pass through a hose to the carburetor and are burned.

The roll over valve, which is installed in line between the fuel tank and charcoal canister, ensures that the fumes remain in the canister until they are safely burned. The gravity operated valve is opened and closed by an internal weight. During normal riding (when the bike is upright), the weight keeps the valve open so fuel vapors can flow from the tank to the charcoal canister. When the bike is leaned over (such as parked on the sidestand), the weight closes the valve so vapors stored in the canister cannot flow back into the fuel tank and escape into the atmosphere.

Service to the emission control system is limited to replacement of damaged parts. Do not attempt to modify or remove the emission control system.

Parts Replacements

When purchasing replacement parts (carburetor and fuel tank), use parts made for California models only. Parts sold for non-California models do not work with the emission control system.

Inspection/Replacement

Maintenance to the evaporative emission control system consists of inspecting the condition and routing of the hoses and checking that the canister is securely mounted to the engine mounting bracket.

> **WARNING**
> *Because the evaporative emission control system stores fuel vapors, make sure the work area is free of flames or sparks before working on the emission system.*

1. Whenever servicing the evaporative system, make sure the ignition switch is turned OFF.

2. Make sure all hoses are attached and they are not damaged or pinched.

3. Replace any worn or damaged parts immediately.

4. Unless the canister is damaged or contaminated no service is required or recommended.

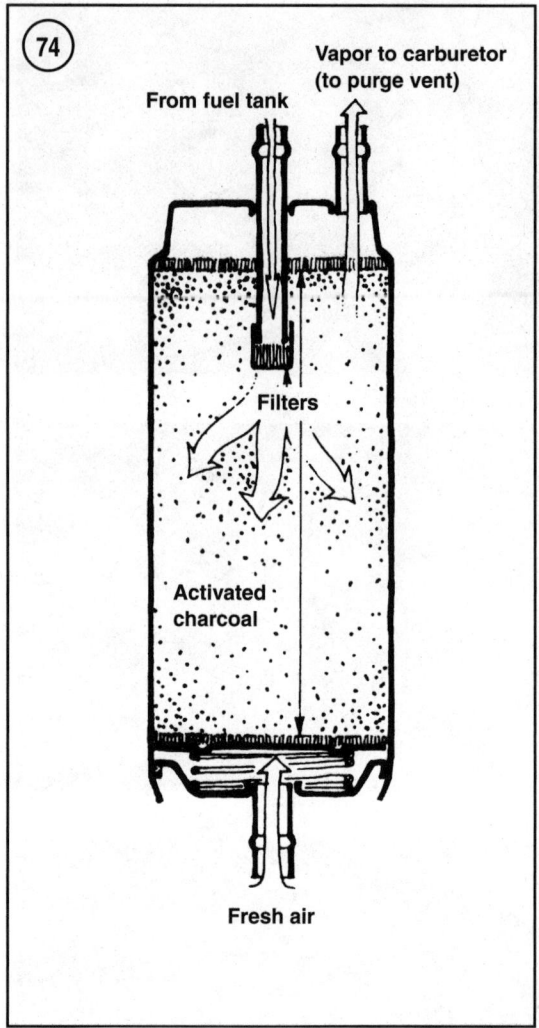

Roll Over Valve Replacement

1. The roll over valve (**Figure 75**) is located in the hose that connects the fuel tank to the EVAP canister.

2. Release the hose clamps and remove the roll over valve.

3. Install by reversing these removal steps. Make sure the hose clamps are tight.

Canister Replacement

> *NOTE*
> *The two ports on the top of the EVAP canister are identified as TANK and CARB. See **Figure 76**. Label each*

FUEL, EMISSION CONTROL AND EXHAUST SYSTEMS

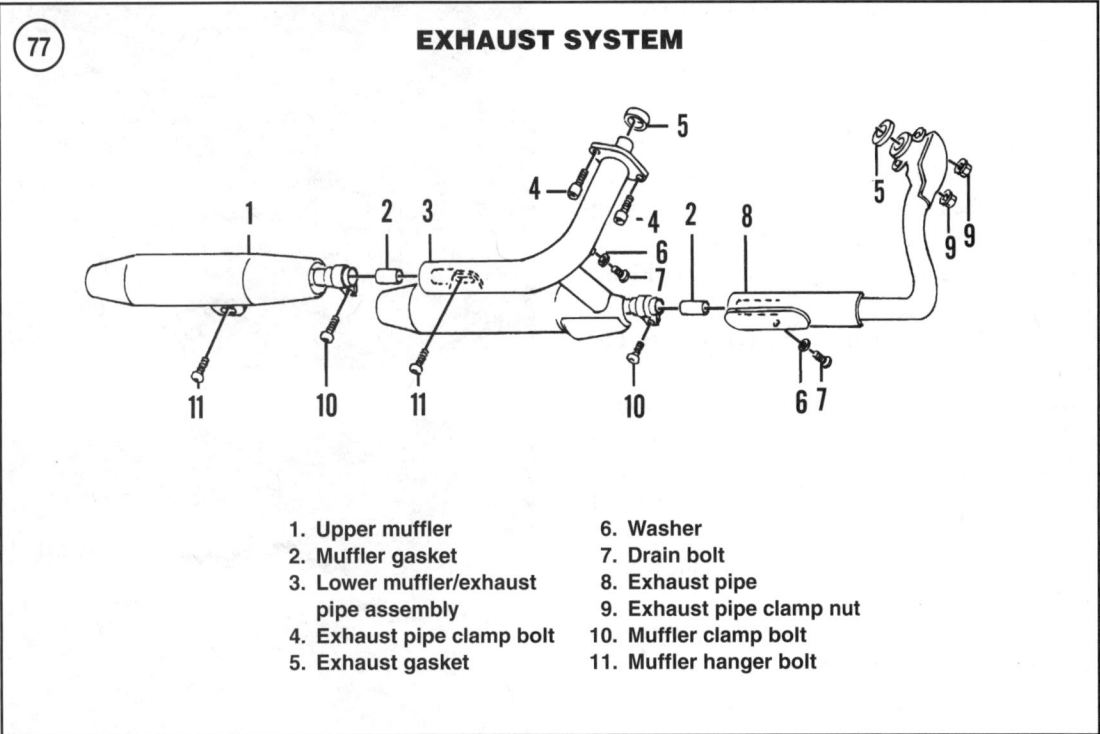

EXHAUST SYSTEM

1. Upper muffler
2. Muffler gasket
3. Lower muffler/exhaust pipe assembly
4. Exhaust pipe clamp bolt
5. Exhaust gasket
6. Washer
7. Drain bolt
8. Exhaust pipe
9. Exhaust pipe clamp nut
10. Muffler clamp bolt
11. Muffler hanger bolt

hose before removal, in order to easily identify them during assembly.

1. Label each hose on top of the canister.

2. Release the hose clamps and disconnect each hose from its port on the EVAP canister (B, **Figure 73**).

3. Make sure the canister vent hose (C, **Figure 73**) is free of the frame member.

4. Remove the two bolts that secure the canister to the engine mounting bracket (D, **Figure 73**) and lift the canister from the frame.

5. Install by reversing these removal steps. Note the following:
   a. Connect each hose to the correct port on the EVAP canister. See **Figure 76**.
   b. Make sure the hose clamps and bolts are tight.

EXHAUST SYSTEM

Removal/Installation

Refer to **Figure 77** for this procedure.

1. Use jack stands or a scissors jack to securely support the bike on level ground.

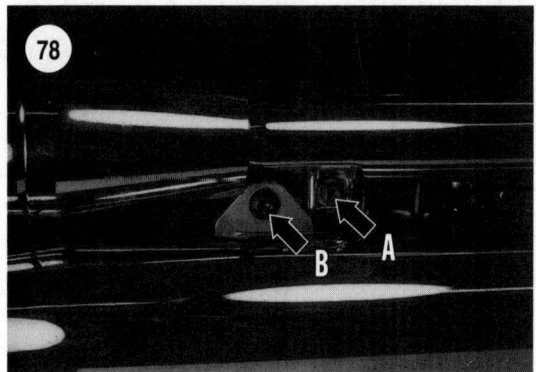

2. Loosen the upper muffler clamp screw (A, **Figure 78**).
3. Remove the upper muffler hanger bolt (**Figure 79**).
4. Pull the muffler from the rear exhaust pipe and remove the muffler.
5. Remove the two exhaust pipe clamp bolts (**Figure 80**) from the rear exhaust manifold.
6. Loosen the lower muffler clamp screw (**Figure 81**).
7. Remove the lower muffler hanger bolt (B, **Figure 78**).
8. Rotate the lower muffler/exhaust pipe assembly until the exhaust pipe clears the rear exhaust manifold, pull the assembly rearward until the muffler is free of the front exhaust pipe, and remove the muffler assembly.
9. Remove the gasket (**Figure 82**) from the rear exhaust manifold.
10. Remove the two exhaust pipe clamp nuts from the front exhaust port and remove the exhaust pipe.
11. Remove the gasket from the exhaust port in the front cylinder.
12. Inspect the system as described below.
13. Installation is the reverse of removal. Note the following:
   a. Install a new exhaust gasket into the rear exhaust manifold (**Figure 82**) and in the exhaust port on the front cylinder.
   b. Install a new muffler gasket in each muffler.
   c. Make sure each exhaust pipe correctly seats in the exhaust port or exhaust manifold.
   d. Loosely install the entire exhaust system and finger-tighten the hardware. Torque the exhaust system hardware to the specifications in **Table 2**. To minimize exhaust leaks, tighten the exhaust pipe clamp nuts first, then the

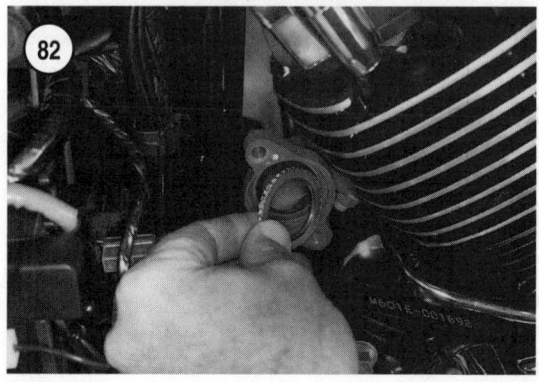

FUEL, EMISSION CONTROL AND EXHAUST SYSTEMS

muffler clamp screws, followed by the hanger bolts.

e. After installation is complete, start the engine and make sure there are no exhaust leaks. Correct any leak prior to riding the bike.

Inspection

1. Check for leakage where each muffler joins an exhaust pipe.
2. Inspect the drain bolts for corrosion or exhaust leakage. Replace the bolts and washers if necessary.
3. Inspect the muffler mounting brackets for wear or damage. Replace the muffler as necessary.

Maintenance

The exhaust system is a vital key to the motorcycle's operation and performance. Periodically inspect, clean and polish (if required) the exhaust system. Special chemical cleaners and preservatives for exhaust systems are available at most motorcycle shops.

Replace damaged parts having excessive dents that cause flow restrictions.

To prevent internal rust buildup, periodically remove the drain bolt from each muffler to drain away any trapped moisture.

Table 1 CARBURETOR SPECIFICATIONS

Carburetor type	Mikuni BDS28
Carburetor I.D.	
USA and Canadian models	5BN 00
California models	5BN 01
Main jet	No. 90
Main air jet	No. 50
Needle jet	O-4
Jet needle	4CT3-1
Needle clip position	1
Pilot jet	No. 20
Pilot outlet size	0.85
Pilot air jet	No. 100
Pilot screw	2 1/2 turns out
Valve seat size	1.0
Starter jet	
GS1	No. 17.5
GS2	0.9
Bypass 1	0.8
Bypass 2	0.8
Bypass 3	0.8
Throttle valve size	No. 140
Fuel level	7.5-8.5 mm (0.3-0.33 in.) below float chamber line
Idle speed	1150-1250 rpm
Intake vacuum	29 kPa (8.66 in Hg)
Fuel pump output pressure	12 kPa (1.7 psi)
Fuel pump amperage	0.8A

Table 2 FUEL AND EXHAUST SYSTEM TIGHTENING TORQUES

Item	N•m	ft.-lb.	in.-lb.
Air filter bracket bolt	12	–	106
Air filter housing bolt	12	–	106
Exhaust pipe clamp nut (front)	25	18	–
(continued)			

Table 2 FUEL AND EXHAUST SYSTEM TIGHTENING TORQUES (continued)

Item	N•m	ft.-lb.	in.-lb.
Exhaust pipe clamp bolt (rear)	20	15	–
Muffler hanger bolt	25	18	–
Muffler clamp screw	20	15	–
AIS-assembly cover screw	10	–	88
AIS-assembly mounting screw	10	–	88
Fuel tank mounting bolt	30	22	–

CHAPTER NINE

ELECTRICAL SYSTEM

This chapter describes service procedures for the following electrical subsystems:
1. Charging system.
2. Ignition system.
3. Starting system.
4. Lighting system.
5. Signal system.
6. Fuel pump system.
7. Carburetor heater system.

It is important to keep all electrical connections securely coupled. Apply dielectric compound (available at motorcycle dealerships or parts houses) to all connectors whenever they are disconnected and reconnected. This helps seal out moisture and prevent corrosion of electrical terminals.

Information regarding the battery and spark plugs is in Chapter Three. **Tables 1 - 3** are at the end of the chapter. **Table 1** lists electrical specifications. **Table 2** bulb specifications, and **Table 3** lists tightening torques.

CHARGING SYSTEM

The charging system consists of the battery, main fuse, main switch, alternator and the regulator/rectifier assembly (**Figure 1**).

Alternating current generated by the alternator is rectified to direct current. The voltage regulator maintains the voltage to the battery and electrical components at a constant voltage regardless of variations in engine speed and load.

Charging System Troubleshooting

Whenever there is a problem with the charging system, follow the troubleshooting procedures listed. Start with the first inspection, and perform the indicated checks. If a test indicates that a component is working properly, reconnect the electrical connections and proceed to the next step. Systematically work through the troubleshooting checklist until the problem is found. Repair or replace defective parts as described in the appropriate section of the manual.

Perform these procedures in the listed sequence. Each test presumes that the components tested in the earlier steps are working properly. The tests can yield invalid results if they are performed out of sequence.
1. Check the main fuse.
2. Check the battery as described in Chapter Three.
3. Perform the battery leakage test.

CHAPTER NINE

CHARGING SYSTEM

(Wiring diagram showing Rectifier/regulator, Main switch, Main fuse, A.C. Magneto, and Battery with color-coded connections: B-Black, W-White, R-Red, L/B-Blue/Black, L/Y-Blue/Yellow, Br/L-Brown/Blue)

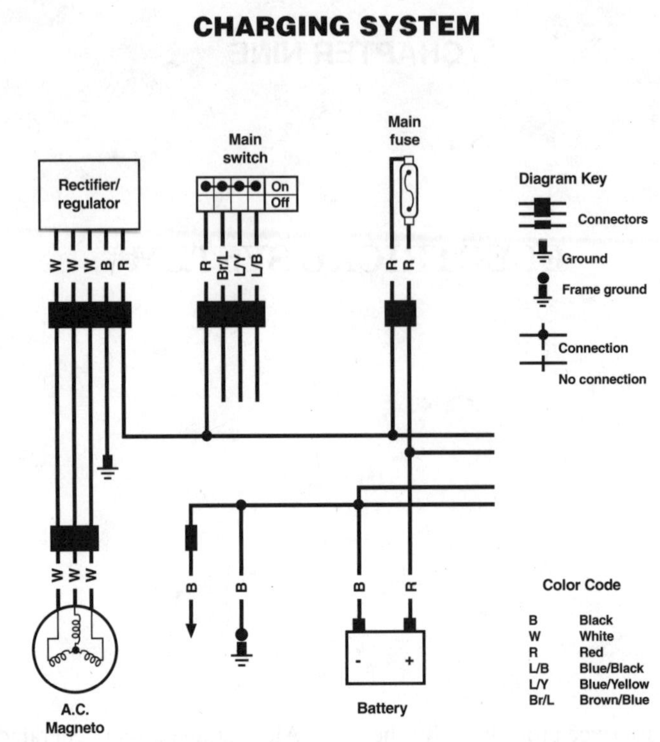

4. Test the charging voltage as described in this chapter.

5. Test the stator coil resistance as described in this chapter.

6. Check the wiring and connections for the entire charging system.

7. Replace the voltage regulator/rectifier.

Battery Leakage Test

1. Turn the ignition switch OFF.

2. Remove the battery box cover and the rider's seat as described in Chapter Thirteen.

3. Disconnect the lead from the battery negative terminal (A, **Figure 2**).

4. Connect an ammeter between the battery negative lead and the negative terminal of the battery.

5. The ammeter should read less than 0.1 mA. If the amperage is greater, there is a voltage drain in the system that will discharge the battery.

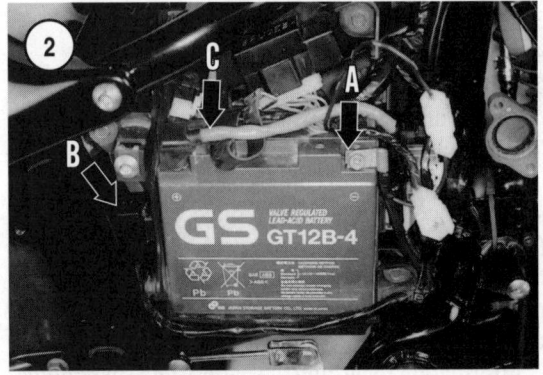

Charging Voltage Test

1. Connect an engine tachometer to the spark plug lead on the rear cylinder.

2. Connect a 0-20 DC voltmeter to the battery terminals as shown in **Figure 3**.

3. Start the engine and increase engine speed to approximately 5,000 rpm. The measured voltage

ELECTRICAL SYSTEM

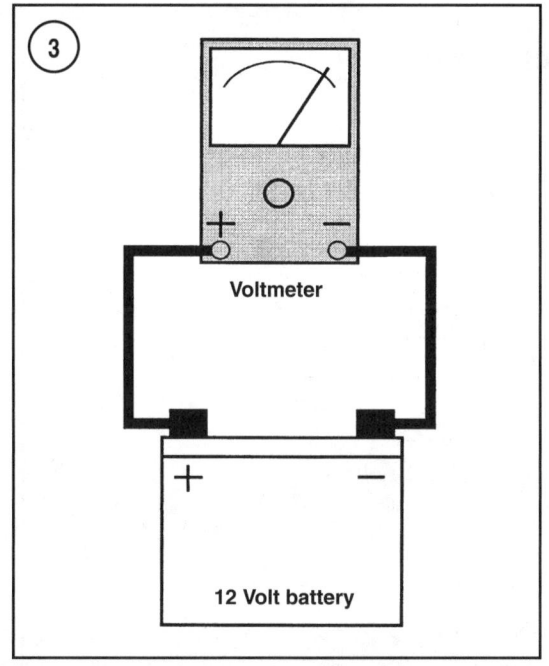

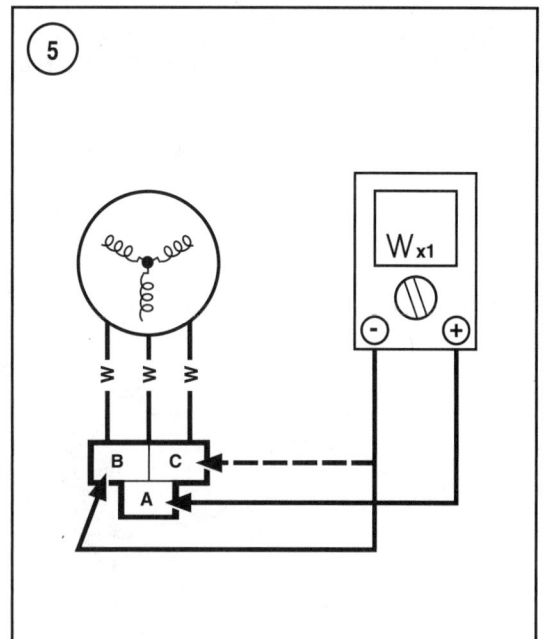

should equal the charging voltage specification in **Table 1**.

4. If the charging voltage is out of specification, check the stator coil resistance as described in this chapter.

STATOR

Resistance Test

To obtain accurate resistance measurements, the stator assembly must be at a minimum temperature of 68° F (20° C).

1. Open the cable clamp (**Figure 4**) and release the stator and pickup coil wires.

2. Follow the wires up to their connectors, and disconnect the 3-pin stator connector (three white wires) from its mate on the wiring harness.

3. Set an ohmmeter to the R × 1 scale, and measure the stator coil resistance.

NOTE
*In each of the following tests, connect the ohmmeter positive lead to the connectors center terminal (A, **Figure 5**) and the ohmmeter negative lead to the other terminal (B or C, **Figure 5**).*

4. Measure the resistance between the center terminal (A, **Figure 5**) and the left terminal (B, **Figure 5**) in the stator side of the connector.

5. Measure the resistance between the center terminal (A, **Figure 5**) and the right terminal (C, **Figure 5**) in the stator side of the connector.

6. Replace the stator assembly if either resistance is not within the range specified in **Table 1**.

7. Check the continuity between each stator wire and ground. There should be no continuity (infinite resistance). Continuity between any stator wire and ground indicates that either the stator or one of the stator wires is shorted to ground. Replace the stator assembly.

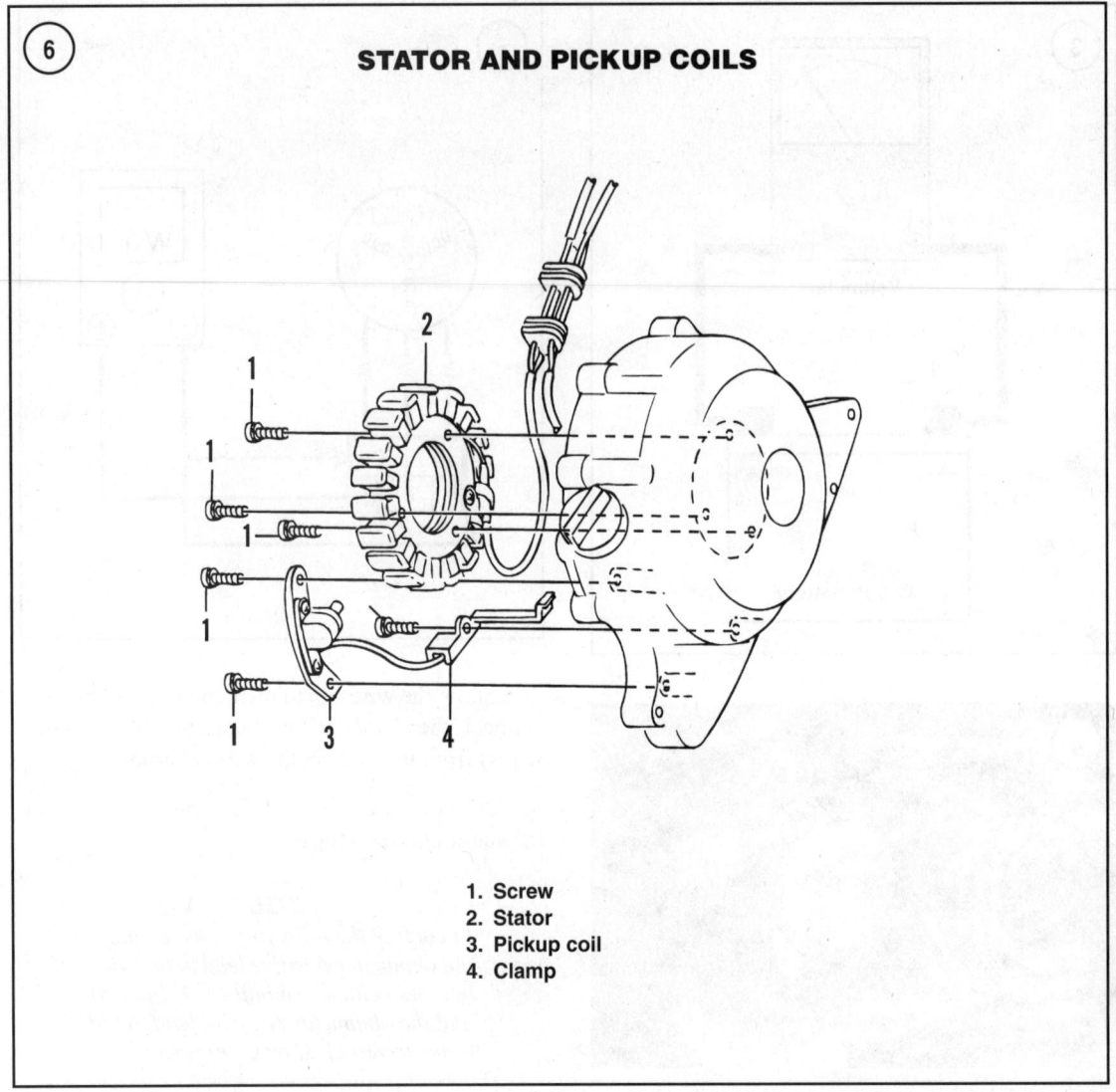

⑥ STATOR AND PICKUP COILS

1. Screw
2. Stator
3. Pickup coil
4. Clamp

Stator Removal/Installation

Refer to **Figure 6** when servicing the stator.

1. Remove the alternator cover as described in Chapter Five.
2. Remove the screw (A, **Figure 7**) securing the clamp to the alternator cover.
3. Remove the three stator mounting screws (C, **Figure 7**).

NOTE
*The stator wire has two rectangular grommets. The pickup coil has two semi-circular grommets. When both wires are properly installed in the alternator cover, the stator coil grommets sit on top of the pickup coil grommets. See B, **Figure 7**.*

4. Pry the two stator grommets (B, **Figure 7**) from the cover.
5. Note how the stator wire is routed through the cover, and remove the stator and wire.
6. Installation is the reverse of removal.

   a. Apply Loctite 242 (blue) to the threads of the stator mounting screws and torque the screws to the specification in **Table 3**.

   b. Make sure the stator grommets are securely seated in the cover. The rectangular stator grommets sit on top of the semi-circular pickup coil grommets.

ELECTRICAL SYSTEM

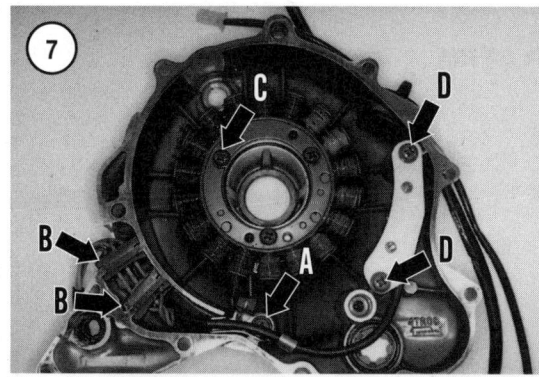

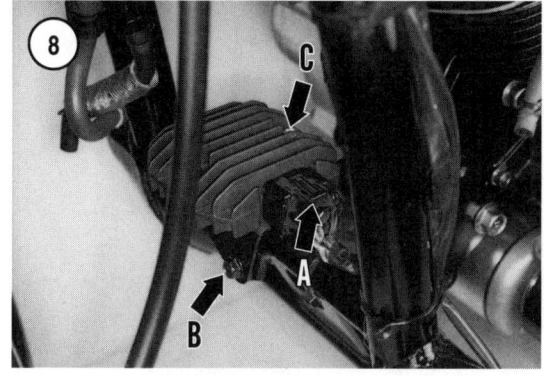

c. Correctly route the stator wire as noted during removal.
d. Make sure the electrical terminals are free of corrosion.
e. To help seal out moisture, pack dielectric grease into the connector and reconnect it securely.

7. Reinstall the alternator cover as described in Chapter Five.

VOLTAGE REGULATOR/RECTIFIER

Removal/Installation

1. Use jack stands or a scissor jack to securely support the bike on level ground.
2. Disconnect the electrical lead from the negative battery terminal (A, **Figure 2**).
3. Press the release tab and disconnect the connector (A, **Figure 8**) from the voltage regulator.
4. Remove the bracket bolt (B, **Figure 8**) and remove the regulator/rectifier and its mounting bracket from the frame.

5. Remove the two regulator/rectifier bolts (C, **Figure 8**) and the regulator/rectifier from the mounting bracket.
6. Install by reversing these removal steps while noting the following:
   a. Torque the regulator/rectifier bolts to the specification in **Table 3**.
   b. Make sure the electrical terminals are free of corrosion.
   c. To help seal out moisture, pack dielectric grease into the connector and reconnect it securely.

IGNITION SYSTEM

All models are equipped with a fully transistorized ignition system. This solid state system provides a long component life and delivers a strong, reliable spark throughout the entire range of engine speed. Ignition timing and advance are maintained without adjustment. Use the ignition timing procedures in Chapter Three to determine if the ignition system is operating properly.

Refer to **Figure 9** for a schematic diagram of the ignition system

When the crankshaft driven rotor (reluctor) passes the pickup coil, an electrical pulse is generated within the pickup coil. This pulse flows to the switching and distribution circuits in the igniter unit. The igniter unit interrupts current flow through the ignition coil, and the magnetic field within the coil collapses. When this occurs, a high voltage is induced in the secondary winding of the ignition coil. This voltage is sufficient to jump the spark plug gap.

Precautions

Take certain measures to protect the transistorized ignition system. Damage to the semiconductors in the system may occur if the following precautions are not observed.

1. Never reverse the battery connections. If the battery polarity is reversed, it will damage the voltage regulator, alternator and igniter unit.
2. Do not disconnect the battery while the engine is running. The resultant voltage surge will damage the voltage regulator and possibly burn out the lights.

CHAPTER NINE

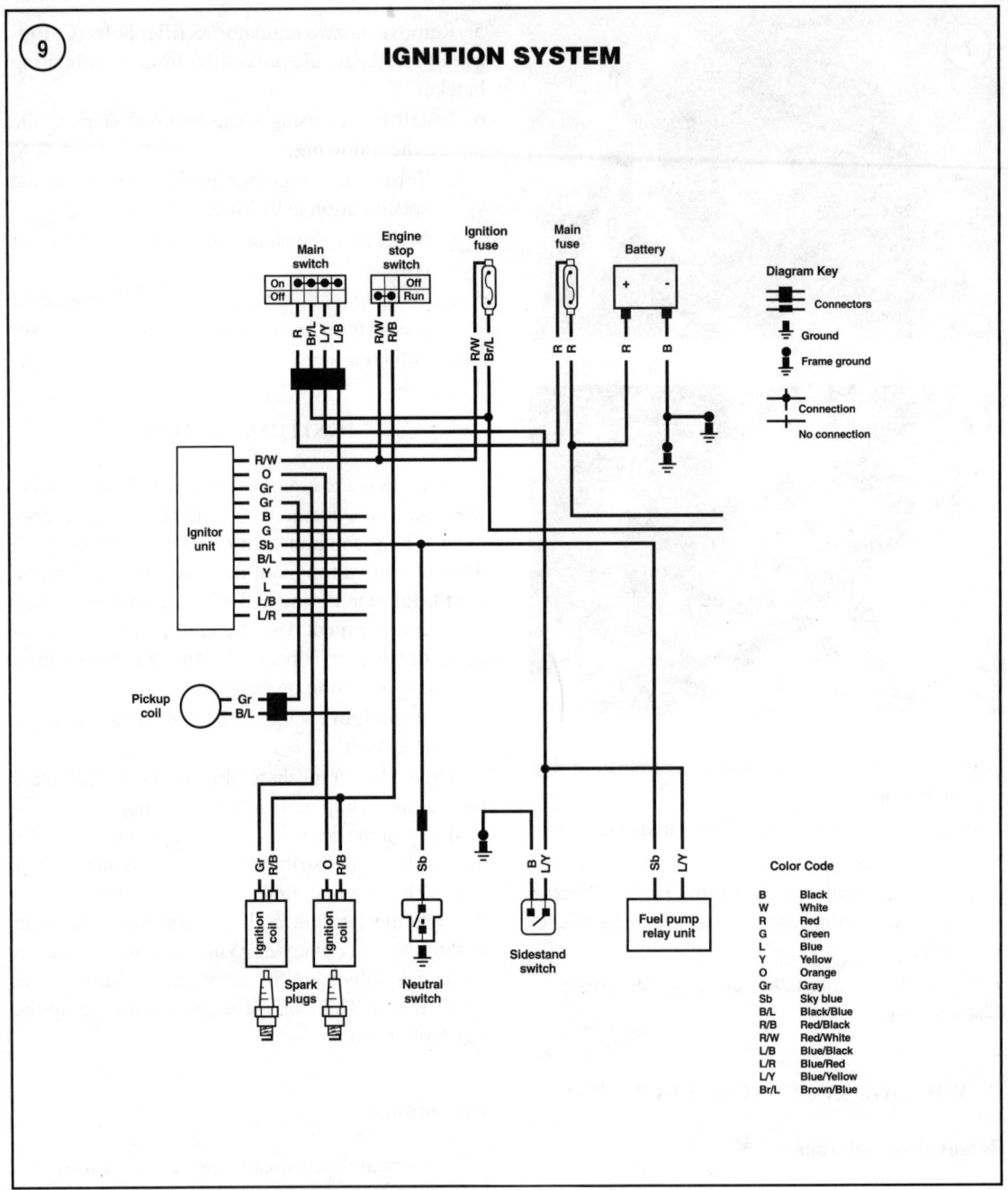

IGNITION SYSTEM

3. Keep all connections between the various units clean and tight. Make sure the wiring connectors are firmly pushed together.

4. Do not substitute another type of ignition coil or battery.

5. Each solid state unit is mounted on a rubber vibration isolator. Make sure the isolators are in place when replacing any units.

Ignition System Troubleshooting

Most problems involving failure to start, poor driveability or rough running are caused by trouble in the ignition system.

Whenever there is a problem with the ignition system, follow the ignition system troubleshooting procedures listed below. Start with the first inspec-

ELECTRICAL SYSTEM

tion, and perform the indicated checks. If a test indicates that a component is working properly, reconnect the electrical connections and proceed to the next step. Systematically work through the troubleshooting checklist until the problem is found. Repair or replace defective parts as described in the appropriate section of the manual.

Perform these procedures in sequence. Each test presumes that the components tested in the earlier steps are working properly. The tests can yield invalid results if they are performed out of sequence.

The ignition system operates only when the sidestand is up or when the transmission is in NEUTRAL. If there is a no-spark problem that cannot be traced to the ignition circuit, check the neutral switch, sidestand switch and sidestand relay as described in this chapter.

1. Inspect the main fuse and the ignition fuse as described in this chapter.
2. Check the battery as described in Chapter Three.
3. Check the condition of each spark plug as described in Chapter Three.
4. Perform the ignition spark test as described in this chapter.
5. Check the resistance of each spark plug cap as described in this chapter.
6. Check the ignition coil as described in this chapter.
7. Check the pickup coil as described in this chapter.
8. Check the continuity of the main switch as described in this chapter.
9. Check the continuity of the engine stop switch as described in this chapter.
10. Check the continuity of the neutral switch as described in this chapter.
11. Check the continuity of the sidestand switch as described in this chapter.
12. Check the ignition system diode (in the relay unit) as described in this chapter.
13. Check the connections in the entire ignition system.
14. Have a dealership check the igniter unit.

Ignition Spark Test

The ignition spark test checks the integrity of the ignition system. The greater the air gap that a spark will jump, the stronger the ignition system. Use the Yamaha Dynamic Spark Tester (part No. YM-34487), the Motion Pro Ignition System Tester (part No. 08-0122), or a similar tool to perform this test. Connect the tester and perform the test as described by the tool manufacturer's instructions. The ignition system is working properly if a spark jumps a gap equal to or greater than the minimum spark plug gap specified in **Table 1**.

1. Remove one of the spark plugs as described in Chapter Three.
2. Insert a new spark plug or a spark tester, into the spark plug cap. Touch the spark plug base or the tester base (**Figure 10**) to a good engine ground. Position the spark plug (or the tester) so the electrode is in view.

WARNING
Make sure the spark plug or the spark tester is away from the spark plug hole in the cylinder so the spark cannot ignite the mixture in the cylinder. If the engine is flooded, do not perform this test. The firing of the spark plug can ignite fuel ejected from the spark plug hole.

WARNING
During the next step, do not hold the spark plug, tester, plug wire or connector by hand. Serious electrical shock may result.

3. Turn the ignition switch ON, and crank the engine over with the starter. A fat blue spark should be evident across the spark plug electrode or across the spark tester terminals. Repeat this test for the other cylinder.

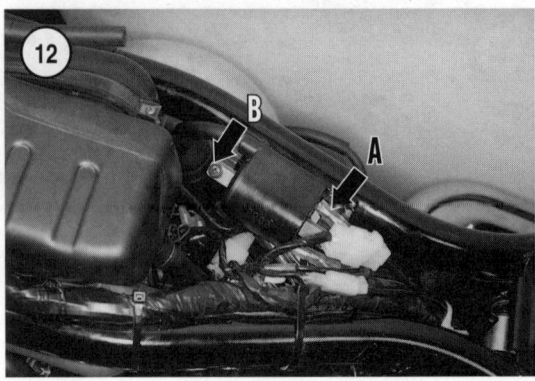

4A. If there is a strong spark in Step 3, the ignition system is working properly. Check the fuel system and spark plugs.

4B. If there is no spark or a weak spark, proceed with the ignition system troubleshooting procedure.

IGNITION COIL

The ignition coil is a form of transformer that develops the high voltage required to jump the spark plug gap. Regular maintenance involves keeping the electrical connections clean and tight. Occasionally check that the coils are mounted securely.

These models have two ignition coils mounted beneath the fuel tank. The front cylinder ignition coil is mounted on the fuel pump bracket, which is in front of the carburetors. The rear cylinder ignition coil is behind the carburetors.

Testing

To obtain accurate results, the ignition coils must be at a minimum temperature of 68° F (20° C). If necessary, start the engine and let it warm up to normal operating temperature.

1. Use jack stands or a scissor jack to securely support the motorcycle on level ground.
2. Remove the fuel tank and surge tank as described in Chapter Eight.
3. Disconnect the electrical lead from the negative battery terminal (A, **Figure 2**).
4. Disconnect the spark plug cap from the respective spark plug.
5. Disconnect the two primary coil spade connectors (Front ignition coil: **Figure 11**; Rear ignition coil: A, **Figure 12**) from the terminals on the ignition coil.

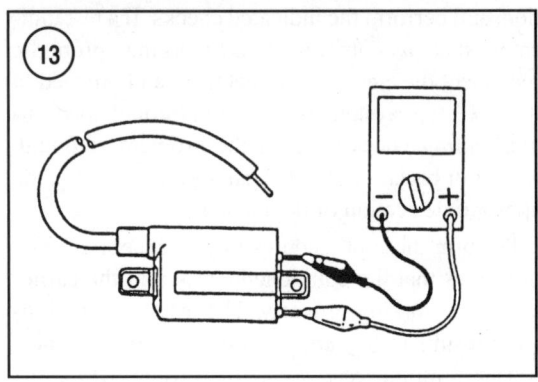

6. Measure the primary coil resistance by performing the following:
   a. Set an ohmmeter to the R × 1 scale.
   b. Measure the resistance across the two primary coil terminals on the ignition coil as shown in **Figure 13**.
   c. Replace the ignition coil if the primary resistance is not within the specification listed in **Table 1**.
7. Measure the secondary coil resistance by performing the following:
   a. Set an ohmmeter to the R × 1,000 scale.
   b. Measure the resistance across the red/black terminal and the spark plug lead as shown in **Figure 14**.
   c. Replace the ignition coil if the secondary coil resistance is not within the specification listed in **Table 1**.
8. Repeat this test for the other ignition coil.

Removal/Installation

1. Use jack stands or a scissor jack to securely support the motorcycle on level ground.

ELECTRICAL SYSTEM

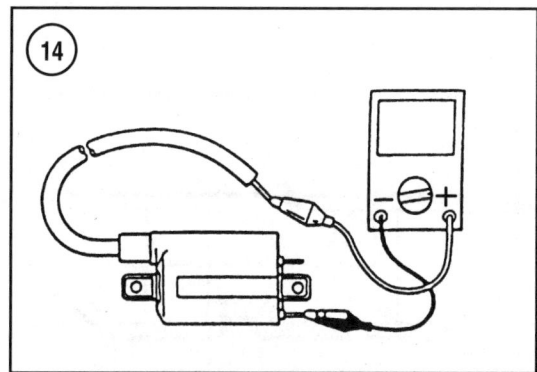

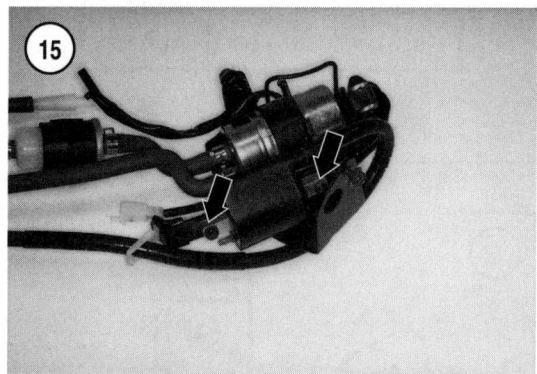

2. Remove the fuel tank and surge tank as described in Chapter Eight.
3. Disconnect the electrical lead from the negative battery terminal (A, **Figure 2**).
4. Disconnect the spark plug cap from the respective spark plug.

> **NOTE**
> *Make a note of how the ignition coil secondary lead is routed through the frame. Make sure to reroute it along the same path during installation.*

5A. If removing the front-cylinder ignition coil, remove the fuel pump bracket as described in Chapter Eight.
5B. If removing the rear-cylinder ignition coil, disconnect the two primary-coil spade connectors (A, **Figure 12**) from the terminals on the ignition coil.
6. Remove the two mounting screws (**Figure 15**, front ignition coil; B, **Figure 12**, rear ignition coil) securing the ignition coil in place, and remove the coil.
7. Install by reversing the removal steps. Pay attention to the following:

a. Make sure the electrical terminals are free of corrosion.
b. To help seal out moisture, pack dielectric grease into the connector and reconnect it securely.
c. Install all removed items.

PICKUP COIL

Resistance Test

To obtain accurate resistance measurements, the pickup coil must be at a minimum temperature of 68° F (20° C). If necessary, start the engine and let it warm up to normal operating temperature.
1. Open the cable clamp (**Figure 4**) and release the stator and pickup coil wires.
2. Trace the wires to the connectors, and disconnect the 2-pin pickup coil connector from the wiring harness.
3. Set an ohmmeter to the $R \times 100$ scale, and measure the resistance across the two terminals at the pickup coil side of the connector.
4. Replace the pickup coil if the resistance is outside the range specified in **Table 1**.

Removal/Installation

Refer to **Figure 6** when servicing the pickup coil.
1. Remove the alternator cover as described in Chapter Five.
2. Remove the screw (A, **Figure 7**) securing the clamp to the alternator cover.
3. Remove the two pickup coil mounting screws (D, **Figure 7**).

> **NOTE**
> *The stator wire has two rectangular grommets. The pickup coil wire has two semi-circular grommets. When both wires are properly installed in the alternator cover, the stator coil grommets sit on top of the pickup coil grommets. See B, **Figure 7**.*

4. Pry the two stator grommets (B, **Figure 7**) from the cover, and then pry out the two pickup coil grommets.
5. Note how the pickup coil wire is routed through the cover, and remove the pickup coil and wire.
6. Installation is the reverse of removal.

a. Apply Loctite 242 (blue) to the threads of the pickup coil mounting screws, and torque the screws to the specification in **Table 3**.
b. Route the pickup coil wire as noted during removal.
c. Install the pickup coil grommets into the cover. Once these semi-circular grommets are seated in the bottom of the cover, install the stator wire grommets (rectangular-shaped). Make sure both sets of grommets are properly seated in the cover as shown in B, **Figure 7**.

7. Reinstall the alternator cover as described in Chapter Five.

RELAY UNIT

The relay unit (B, **Figure 2**) is mounted on the rear side of the battery box. It consists of the fuel pump relay, starting circuit cut-off relay, ignition diode and the the starting system diode.

Removal/Installation

1. Remove the battery box cover from the right side of the motorcycle and remove the rider's seat as described in Chapter Thirteen.
2. Lift the relay unit (B, **Figure 2**) from the holder on the rear of the battery box.
3. Disconnect the harness connector from the relay unit.
4. Installation is the reverse of removal. Make sure the relay properly engages the holder on the rear of the battery box.

Ignition System Diode Testing

1. Remove the relay unit as described in this chapter.
2. Disconnect the harness connector from the relay unit.
3. Set an ohmmeter to the R × 1 scale, and check the continuity as described below.
    a. Connect the positive lead to the blue/yellow terminal (B, **Figure 16**) on the unit, and connect the negative lead to the sky blue terminal (A, **Figure 16**). The meter should show no continuity (infinite resistance).

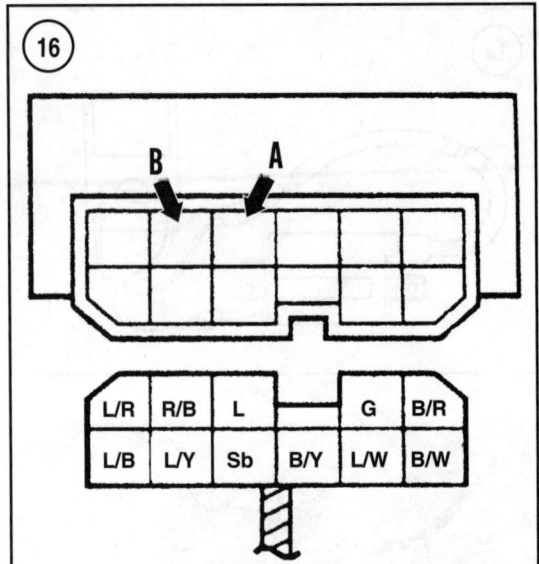

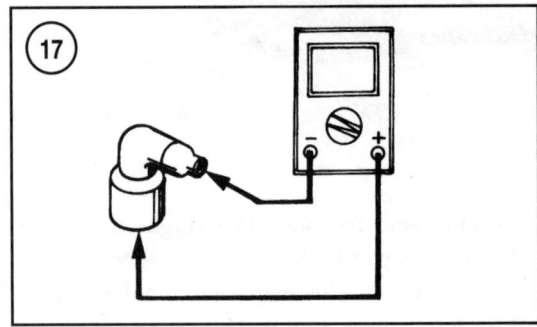

b. Reverse the ohmmeter leads and check the continuity. The meter should show continuity (zero or low resistance).

4. Replace the relay unit if it fails either of the above tests.

SPARK PLUG

Spark Plug Cap Testing

1. Disconnect the spark plug lead from the spark plug.
2. Carefully remove the spark plug cap from the spark plug lead.
3. Set an ohmmeter to the R × 1,000 scale, and measure the resistance between each end of the cap as shown in **Figure 17**.
4. Replace the spark plug cap if the resistance exceeds the specification in **Table 1**.
5. Repeat this test for the other spark plug cap.

ELECTRICAL SYSTEM

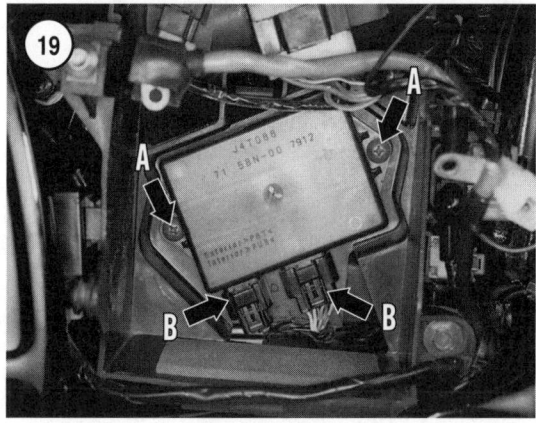

IGNITER UNIT

Testing

There are no test procedures for the igniter unit. Test all of the other ignition system components separately. If a problem or defective part is not found during these tests, the igniter unit is probably defective.

NOTE
The igniter cannot be effectively tested. However, if all other ignition components, wiring and connections are good, consider the igniter unit to be defective by process of elimination.

NOTE
Most dealerships do not accept returns on electrical components; eliminate all other possible faults or have a dealership test the system before purchasing and replacing an electrical component.

Igniter Unit Removal/Installation

1. Remove the battery as described in Chapter Three.

2. Remove the inside cover (**Figure 18**) from the battery case.

3. Remove the two igniter mounting screws (A, **Figure 19**), and pull the igniter unit from the battery box.

4. Carefully disconnect the two electrical connectors (B, **Figure 19**) from the igniter, and remove the igniter.

5. Install by reversing these removal steps while noting the following:

   a. Make sure the electrical terminals are free of corrosion.
   b. To help seal out moisture, pack dielectric grease into the connector and reconnect it securely.
   c. Tighten the bolts securely.
   d. Install all removed items.

STARTING SYSTEM

The starting system circuit diagram is shown in **Figure 20**. When the starter button is pressed under the correct conditions, current flows through the starter relay coil, which energizes the relay. The starter relay contacts close, and current flows from the battery to the starter motor.

The starter only operates when the transmission is in neutral or when the clutch lever is pulled in and the sidestand is up. The starting circuit cut-off relay, which is part of the relay unit, prevents the flow of current to the starter relay unless one of these conditions has been met. The starting circuit cut-off relay is energized and the contacts close only when the neutral switch is closed (the transmission is in neutral) or when both the clutch switch and sidestand switch are closed (when the clutch lever is pulled in and the sidestand is up).

CAUTION
Do not operate the starter for more than five seconds at a time. Let it rest approximately ten seconds, then use it again.

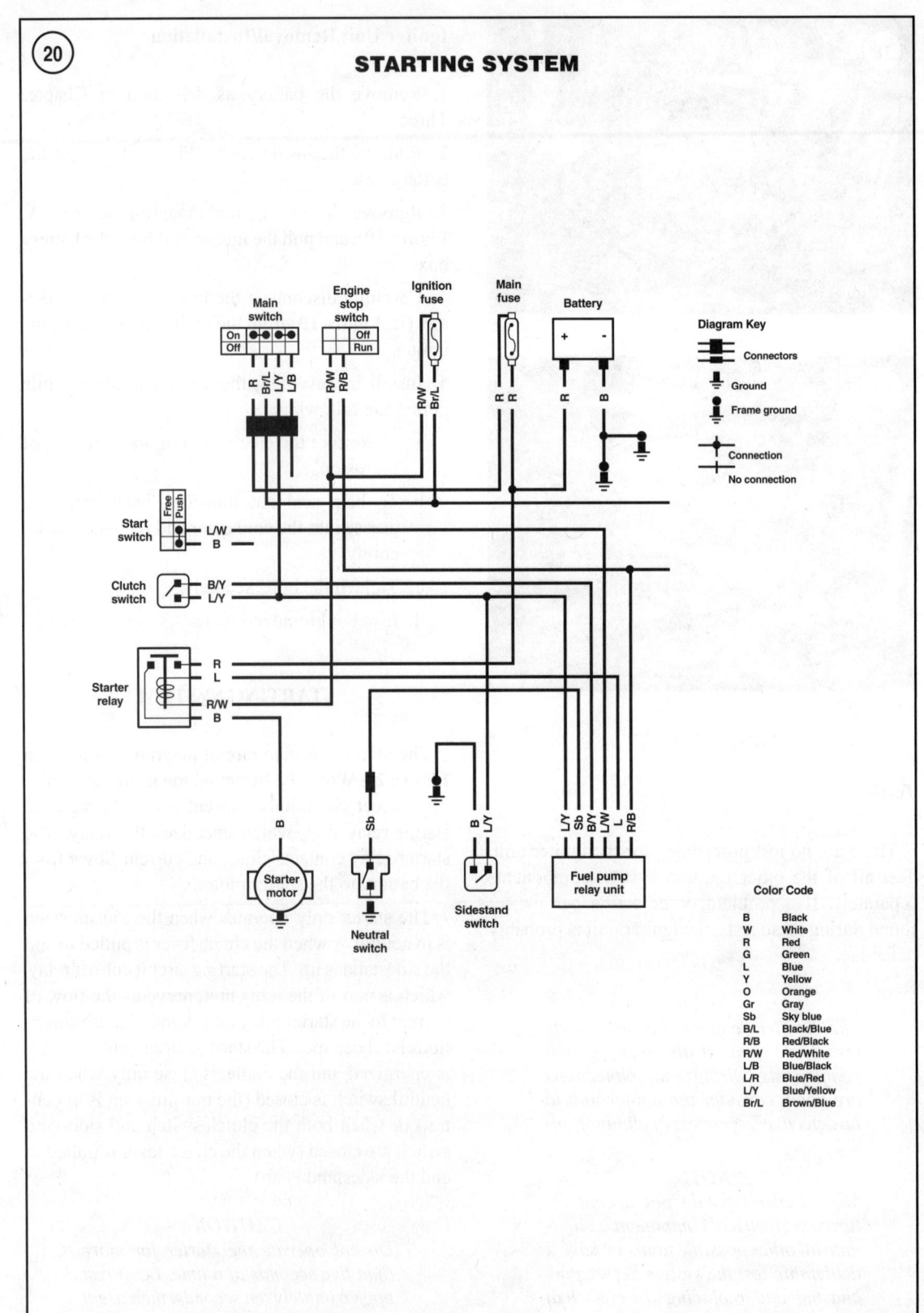

ELECTRICAL SYSTEM

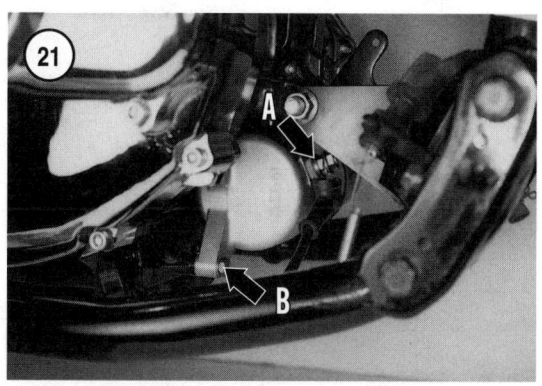

Starting System Troubleshooting

Whenever there is a problem with the starting system, follow the starting system troubleshooting procedures listed below. Start with the first inspection, and perform the indicated checks. If a test indicates that a component is working properly, reconnect the electrical connections and proceed to the next step. Systematically work through the troubleshooting checklist until the problem is found. Repair or replace defective parts as described in the appropriate section of this manual.

Perform these procedures in the indicated sequence. Each test presumes that the components tested in the earlier steps are working properly. The tests can yield invalid results if they are performed out of sequence.

1. Check the main fuse and the ignition fuse.
2. Check the battery as described in Chapter Three.
3. Test the starter motor as described in this chapter.
4. Test the starting circuit cut-off relay (in the relay unit) as described in this chapter.
5. Test the starting system diode (in the relay unit) as described in this chapter.
6. Test the starter relay as described in this chapter.
7. Check the continuity of the main switch as described in this chapter.
8. Check the continuity of the engine stop switch as described in this chapter.
9. Check the continuity of the neutral switch as described in this chapter.
10. Check the continuity of the sidestand switch as described in this chapter.
11. Check the continuity of the clutch switch as described in this chapter.
12. Check the continuity of the start switch as described in this chapter.

13. Check the wiring and each connector in the starting circuit.

STARTER MOTOR

Testing

1. Use jack stands or a scissor jack to securely support the bike on level ground.
2. Make sure the ignition switch is OFF.
3. Drain the engine oil as described in Chapter Three.
4. Remove the fuel tank as described in Chapter Eight.
5. Pull back the rubber boot and disconnect the cable from the starter motor terminal (A, **Figure 21**).
6. Disconnect the battery lead (C, **Figure 2**) from the battery's positive terminal.

> *WARNING*
> *The jumper wire mentioned in the next step must be as large as the battery lead. Make sure the jumper wire is large enough to handle the current flow from the battery. If the wire is too small, it could melt.*

> *WARNING*
> *The test in the next step will probably produce sparks. Make sure no flammable gas or fluid is in the vicinity.*

7. Apply battery voltage directly to the starter motor by connecting a jumper from the battery positive terminal to the starter motor terminal. The motor should operate.
8. If the motor does not operate when applying battery voltage, repair or replace the starter motor.

Removal/Installation

1. Use jack stands or a scissor jack to securely support the bike on level ground.
2. Make sure the ignition switch is OFF.
3. Drain the engine oil as described in Chapter Three.
4. Remove the front cylinder exhaust pipe as described in Chapter Eight.
5. Disconnect the lead from the negative battery terminal (A, **Figure 2**).

6. Pull back the rubber boot and disconnect the cable from the starter motor terminal (A, **Figure 21**).

7. Remove the two starter mounting bolts (B, **Figure 21**). Pull the starter toward the right and remove it.

8. Install by reversing these removal steps while noting the following:
   a. Install a new O-ring (A, **Figure 22**) onto the front cover. Apply lithium grease to the O-ring before assembly.
   b. Tighten the bolts securely.
   c. Make sure the electrical connector is free of corrosion and is tight.

Disassembly

Starter motor repair is generally a job for electrical shops or a Yamaha dealership. The following procedure is provided if choosing to perform this procedure yourself.

Refer to **Figure 23** when servicing the starter motor.

1. Remove and discard the O-ring (A, **Figure 22**) from the front cover.

2. Remove the two case bolts (B, **Figure 22**) from the starter motor.

NOTE
Record the number of shims used on the shaft at each end of the armature. Make sure to install the same number when reassembling the starter.

3. Slide the front cover (A, **Figure 24**) off the armature shaft.

4. Remove the lockwasher (B, **Figure 24**). The washer may remain on the armature shaft or it may come off with the front cover.

NOTE
*The number of shims used in each starter varies. The starter shown in **Figure 24** uses two shims.*

NOTE
Label the washers removed in Step 5, and store them in a plastic bag. Reinstall them in their original locations during assembly.

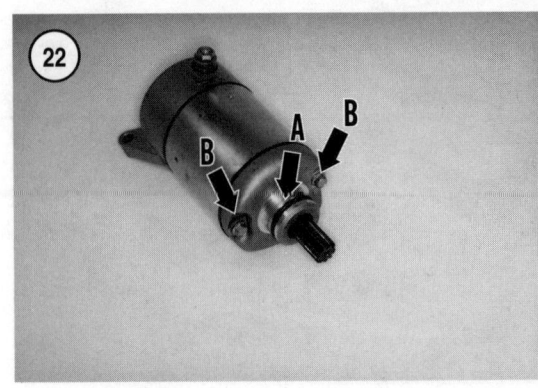

5. Slide the fiber washer (C **Figure 24**) and the steel washer(s) (D, **Figure 24**) from the armature shaft. Store the washers in a marked plastic bag.

6. Slide the end cap (A, **Figure 25**) off the armature.

NOTE
Label the shims removed in Step 7, and store them in a plastic bag. Reinstall them in their original locations during assembly. Do not mix these shims with the washers removed in Step 5.

7. Slide the shims (B, **Figure 25**) off the armature shaft. Record the number of shims and their location. Store the shims in a marked plastic bag.

8. Slide the armature from the housing (C, **Figure 25**).

9. Clean all grease, dirt and carbon from the armature, housing, end cap and cover.

CAUTION
Do not immerse the wire windings in the housing or the armature coil in solvent because this may damage the insulation. Wipe the windings with a cloth lightly moistened with solvent and then thoroughly dry them.

Inspection

NOTE
The O-rings and brush holder assembly are the only starter motor components that can be replaced. If any other starter motor component is defective, replace the starter motor.

ELECTRICAL SYSTEM

STARTER MOTOR

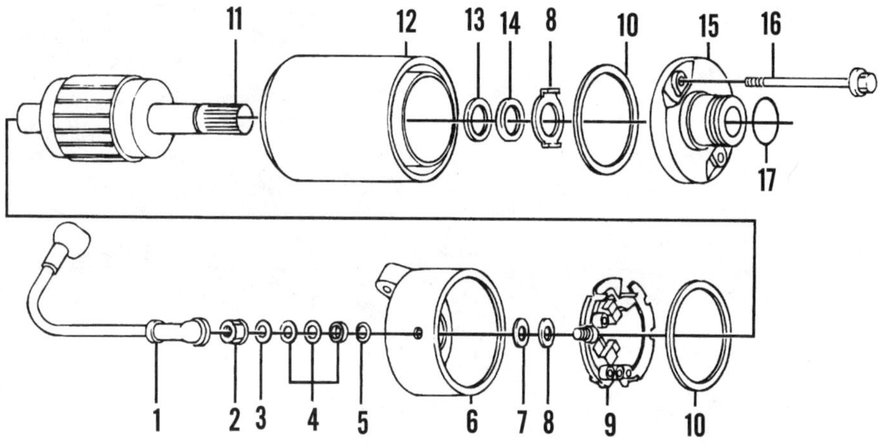

1. Cable
2. Nut
3. Steel washer
4. Fiber washers
5. Terminal O-ring
6. End cap
7. Shim(s)
8. Lockwasher
9. Brush holder assembly
10. Housing O-ring
11. Armature
12. Housing
13. Steel washer(s)
14. Fiber washer
15. Front cover
16. Case bolt
17. Front cover O-ring

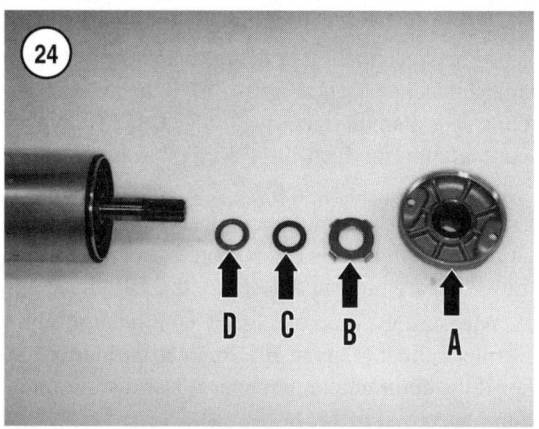

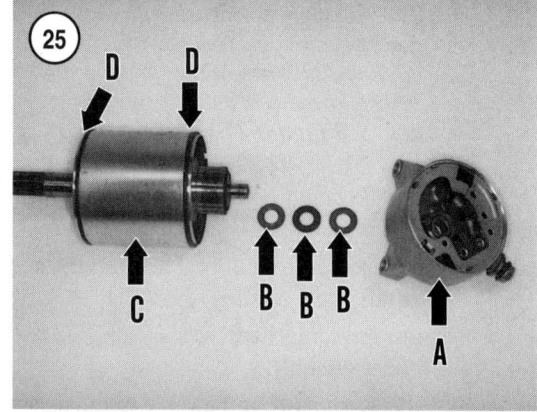

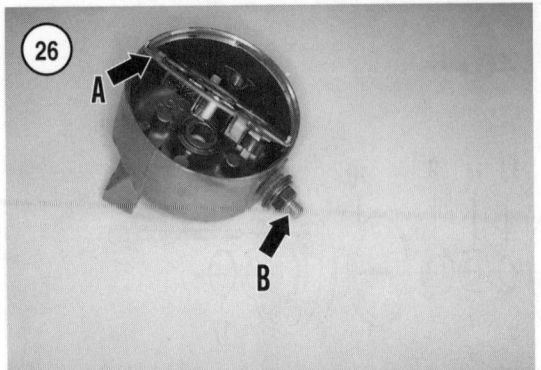

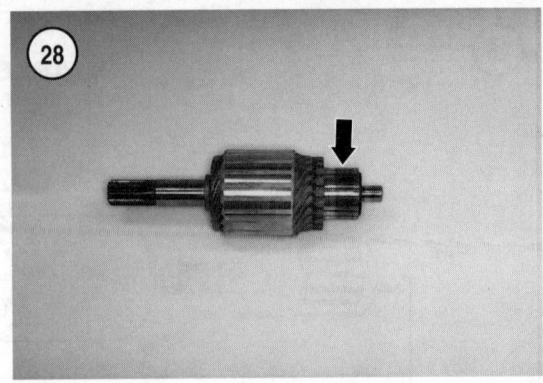

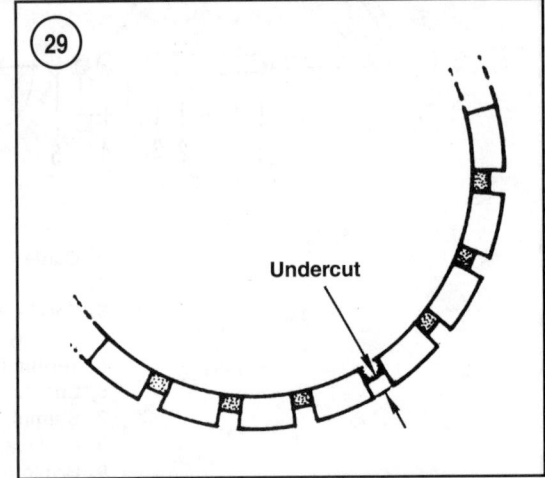

1. Pull the brush holder assembly (A, **Figure 26**) out of the end cap, and carefully turn the holder over to expose the brushes.

2. Pull the spring away from each brush and pull the brush out of its guide. Measure the length of each brush with a vernier caliper. If the length of any brush is less than the wear limit listed in **Table 1**, replace the brush holder assembly. The brushes cannot be replaced individually.

NOTE
The cable terminal assembly (B, Figure 26) consists of four washers and a nut. Label each component when removed. Reinstall them in the same order to insulate the brushes from the housing. See Figure 27.

3. To replace the brush holder assembly, perform the following:
   a. Remove the nut from the cable terminal, and slide off the steel washer.
   b. Remove the large fiber washer and the two small fiber washers.
   c. Slide the O-ring off of the cable terminal.
   d. Push the cable terminal into the end cover, and remove the brush holder assembly.
   e. Install the brush holder assembly by reversing these removal steps. Install a new O-ring, and make sure to install the nut and washers in their original order.

4. Inspect the commutator (**Figure 28**). The mica in a good commutator is below the surface of the copper bars. Measure the mica undercut, the distance between the top of the mica and the top of the adjacent copper bars (**Figure 29**). If the mica undercut is less than the specification in **Table 1** have the commutator serviced by a dealership or electrical repair shop.

5. Inspect the commutator copper bars for discoloration. If a pair of bars is discolored, grounded armature coils are indicated. Replace the starter motor.

6. Measure the diameter of the commutator with a vernier caliper (**Figure 30**). Replace the starter motor if the commutator diameter is less than the wear limit specified in **Table 1**.

ELECTRICAL SYSTEM

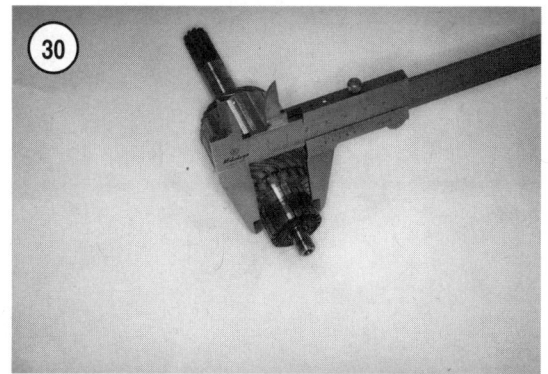

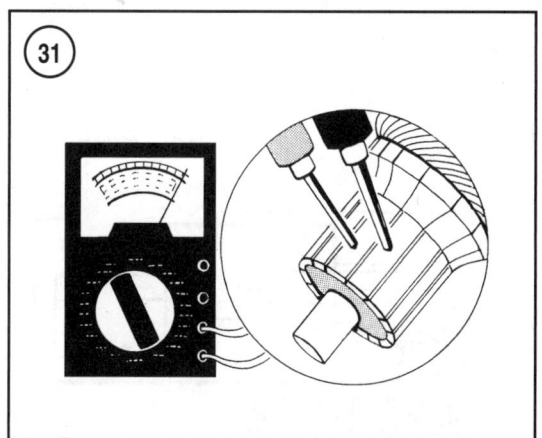

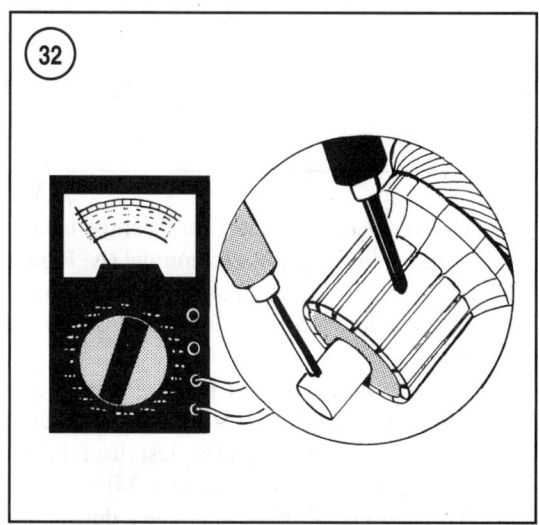

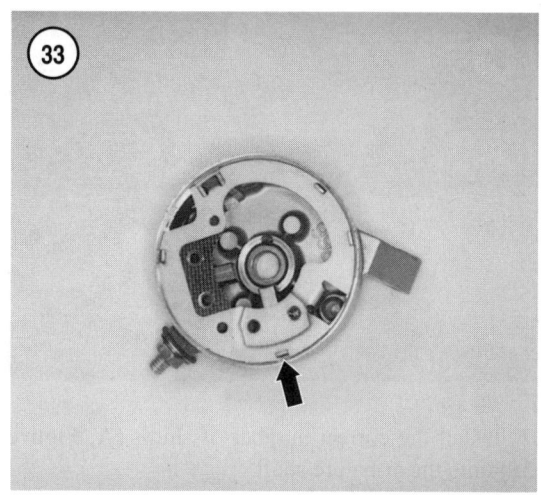

b. Check for continuity between the commutator bars and the armature shaft (**Figure 32**). There should be *no* continuity (infinite resistance).

c. If the unit fails any of these tests, replace the starter motor.

8. Inspect the bearing and seal in the front cover. If either is worn or damaged, replace the starter motor.

9. Inspect the bushing in the end cap for wear or damage. If it is damaged, replace the starter motor.

Assembly

1. If removed, install the brushes into their holders, and secure the brushes with the springs.

2. Install the brush holder assembly in the rear cover. Align the holder locating tab with the notch in the end cap (**Figure 33**).

3. Lubricate two new O-rings with lithium grease, and install an O-ring (D, **Figure 25**) onto either end of the housing.

4. Slide the armature into the housing.

5. Install the correct number of shims (B, **Figure 25**) onto the armature shaft next to the commutator.

6. Install the end cap onto the armature. Hold the end cap over the armature, and turn the armature during installation so the brushes engage the commutator properly. Do not damage the brushes during this step. Also, make sure the armature is not turned upside down so the shims cannot slide off the end of the shaft. Once the end cap is installed, align the marks (A, **Figure 34**) on the housing case and end cover.

7. Use an ohmmeter and perform the following:

  a. Check for continuity between the commutator bars (**Figure 31**). There should be continuity (zero or low resistance) between pairs of bars.

246

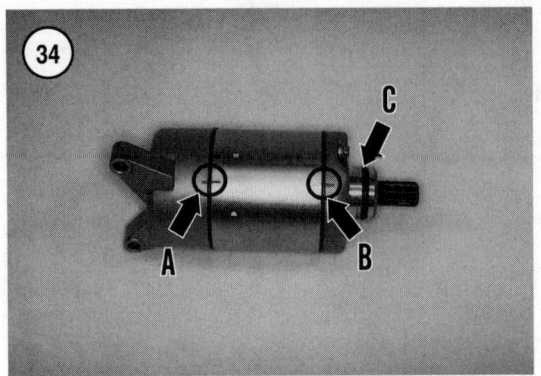

7. Install the correct number of shims (A, **Figure 35**) onto the armature shaft.

8. Install the lockwasher (B, **Figure 35**) into the front cover so the lockwasher tabs engage the slots in the cover.

9. Install the front cover over the armature shaft. Align the marks on the front cover (B, **Figure 34**) with those on the housing and end cap (A, **Figure 34**).

10. Apply blue Loctite (No. 242) to the case bolt threads, and install the bolts, washers and lockwashers. Tighten the bolts securely.

11. Lubricate a new front-cover O-ring with lithium grease, and install it onto the front cover (C, **Figure 34**).

12. Clean the cover mounting lugs of all dirt and other contaminants. The lugs provide the ground for the starter so there must be good contact between them and the crankcase.

STARTING CIRCUIT CUT-OFF RELAY

The starting circuit cut-off relay does not allow current to the starter relay unless the transmission is in neutral or unless the clutch lever is pulled in and the sidestand is up. The starting circuit cut-off relay is part of the relay unit.

Testing

1. Remove the relay unit as described in this chapter.
2. Disconnect the harness connector from the relay unit.
3. Set an ohmmeter to the R × 1 scale.
4. Check the continuity of the starting circuit cutoff relay by performing the following:

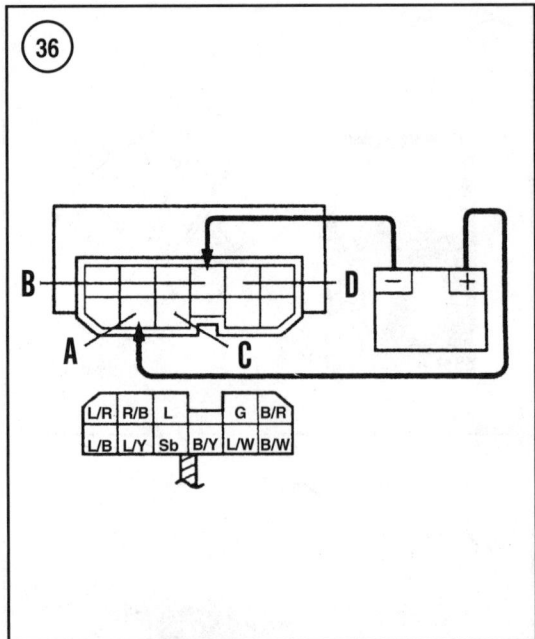

   a. Use jumpers to connect the positive battery terminal to the red/black terminal (A, **Figure 36**) and the negative battery terminal to the black/yellow terminal (B, **Figure 36**) in the relay unit.

   b. Connect the ohmmeter positive test lead to the blue terminal (C, **Figure 36**) in the relay, and connect the negative test lead to the blue/white terminal (D, **Figure 36**).

   c. The unit should have continuity during this test.

5. Replace the relay unit if it has no continuity.

STARTING SYSTEM DIODE

The starting system diode is part of the relay unit.

ELECTRICAL SYSTEM

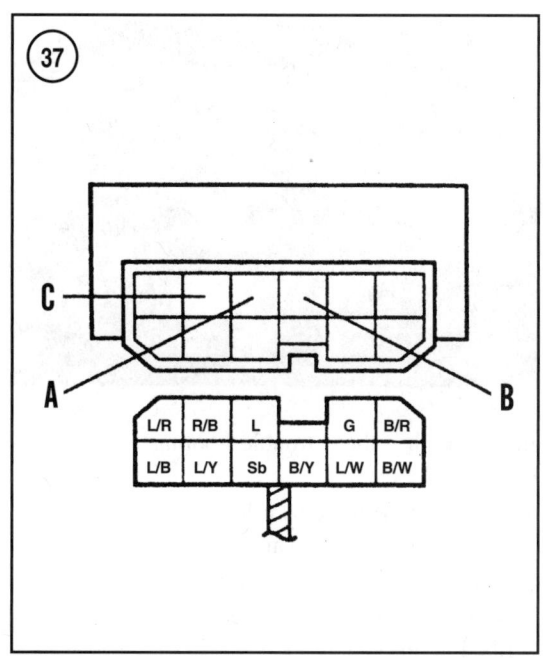

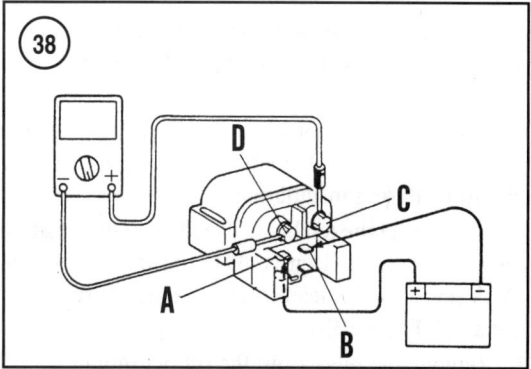

ure 37) and connect the negative test lead to the sky blue terminal (A, **Figure 37**). The diode should have no continuity during this test.

5. Replace the relay unit if the diode fails any of these tests.

STARTER RELAY

Testing

1. Disconnect the connector and electrical leads from the starter relay by performing Steps 1-5 of the starter relay removal/installation procedure.
2. Set an ohmmeter to the R × 1 scale.
3. Check the continuity of the starter relay by performing the following:
   a. Use jumper wires to connect the positive battery terminal to the red/white terminal (A, **Figure 38**) in the relay and to connect the negative battery terminal to the blue terminal (B, **Figure 38**) in the relay.
   b. Check the continuity across the starter relay terminals (C and D, **Figure 38**).
   c. The starter relay should have continuity during this test.
4. Replace the starter relay if it fails this test.

Removal/Installation

1. Remove the battery box cover from the right side of the motorcycle and remove the rider's seat as described in Chapter Thirteen.
2. Make sure the ignition switch is turned OFF. Disconnect the negative terminal (A, **Figure 2**) from the battery.

Testing

1. Remove the relay unit as described in this chapter.
2. Disconnect the harness connector from the relay unit.
3. Set an ohmmeter to the R × 1 scale.
4. Check the continuity of the starting system diode by performing the following:
   a. Connect the ohmmeter positive test lead to the sky blue terminal (A, **Figure 37**) in the relay unit and connect the negative test lead to the black/yellow terminal (B, **Figure 37**). The diode should have continuity during this test.
   b. Reverse the connectors and check the continuity. Connect the positive test lead to the black/yellow terminal in the relay unit (B, **Figure 37**) and connect the negative test lead to the sky blue terminal (A, **Figure 37**). The diode should have no continuity during this test.
   c. Connect the ohmmeters positive test lead to the sky blue terminal (A, **Figure 37**) in the relay unit and connect the negative test lead to the blue/yellow terminal (C, **Figure 37**). The diode should have continuity during this test.
   d. Reverse the connectors and check the continuity. Connect the positive test lead to the blue/yellow terminal in the relay unit (C, **Fig-**

CHAPTER NINE

3. Press the release tab on the electrical connector, and disconnect the connector (A, **Figure 39**) from the starter relay.
4. Pull back the boot on each starter relay cable connector. Label each connector so it can be easily identified during installation.
5. Disconnect the red battery lead from the positive relay terminal (B, **Figure 39**), and disconnect the black starter-motor lead from the negative relay terminal (C, **Figure 39**).
6. Remove the relay from the rubber mount.
7. Installation is the reverse of removal. Note the following:
   a. Install the relay in the rubber mount.
   b. Make sure the nuts securing the electrical connections are free of corrosion and are tight.
   c. Torque the starter relay terminals to the specification in **Table 3**.

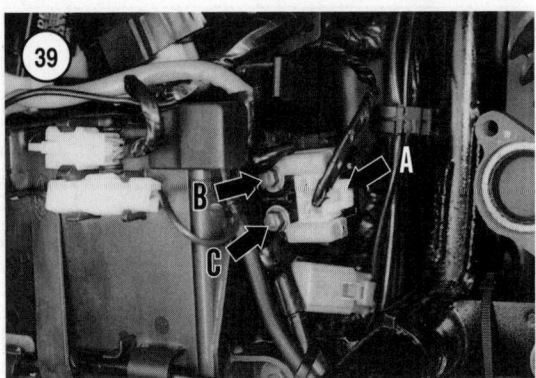

LIGHTING SYSTEM

The lighting system consists of the headlight, taillight/brake light, high beam indicator light and meter illumination light. Whenever there is a problem with a lighting system component, follow the lighting system troubleshooting procedures listed below. Start with the first inspection, and perform the indicated checks. If a test indicates that a component is working properly, reconnect the electrical connections and proceed to the next step. Systematically work through the troubleshooting checklist until the problem is found. Repair or replace the defective part as described in the appropriate section of the manual.

Perform these procedures in the listed sequence. Each test presumes that the components tested in the earlier steps are working properly. The tests can yield invalid results if they are performed out of sequence.

The lighting system circuit diagram is shown in **Figure 40**.

Lighting System Troubleshooting

In the event of trouble with any light, check the bulb in the affected component first. Replacement bulbs are listed in **Table 2**. If the bulb is good, continue with the troubleshooting procedures described below.

1. Check the bulb in the affected unit.
2. Check the main fuse and the headlight fuse.
3. Check the battery as described in Chapter Three.
4. Check the continuity of the main switch as described in this chapter.
5. Check the continuity of the dimmer switch as described in this chapter.
6. Check the wiring and each connector in the lighting circuit.
7. Check the affected part of the circuit by performing the appropriate test described below.

HEADLIGHT

Headlight Voltage Test

If the headlight does not turn on but the bulb is in good working order, check the headlight circuit voltage by performing the following test.

1. Remove the two headlight holding screws (**Figure 41**) and pull the lens assembly from the headlight housing.
2. Unplug the electrical connector (A, **Figure 42**) from the lens assembly.
3. Set a voltmeter to the DC 20 volt range.
4. Turn the dimmer switch to LO, and check the voltage by performing the following:
   a. Connect the voltmeter negative test lead to the black terminal (A, **Figure 43**) in the headlight connector.
   b. Connect the voltmeter positive test lead to the green terminal (B, **Figure 43**).
   c. Turn the main switch ON, and check the voltmeter. It should read battery voltage.

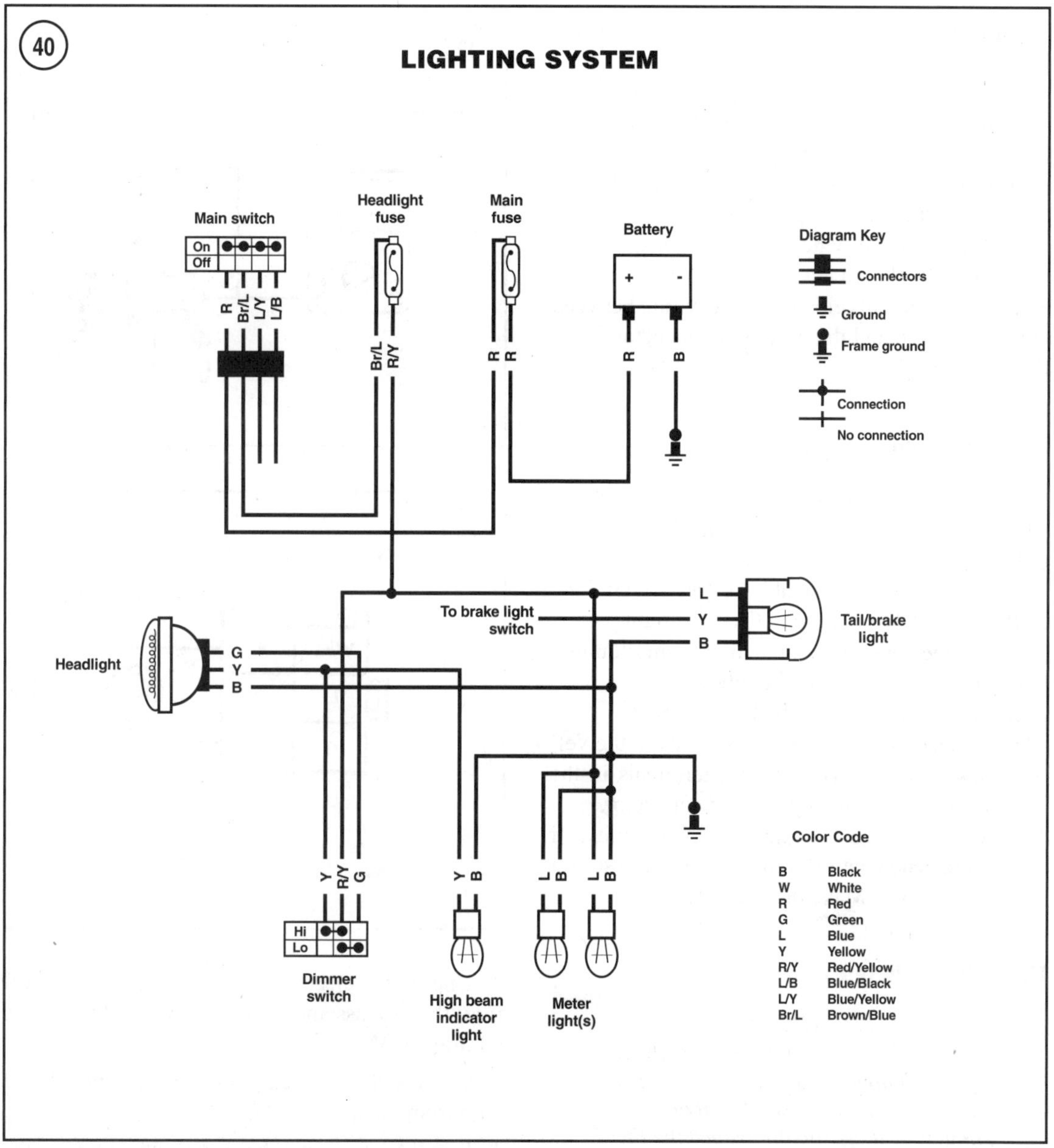

40
LIGHTING SYSTEM
Main switch
On
Off
R
Br/L
L/Y
L/B
Headlight fuse
Br/L
R/Y
Main fuse
R
R
Battery
+
-
R
B
Diagram Key
Connectors
Ground
Frame ground
Connection
No connection
Headlight
G
Y
B
To brake light switch
L
Y
B
Tail/brake light
Y
R/Y
G
Hi
Lo
Dimmer switch
Y
B
High beam indicator light
L
B
L
B
Meter light(s)
Color Code
B Black
W White
R Red
G Green
L Blue
Y Yellow
R/Y Red/Yellow
L/B Blue/Black
L/Y Blue/Yellow
Br/L Brown/Blue

9

41

42
A
B
C

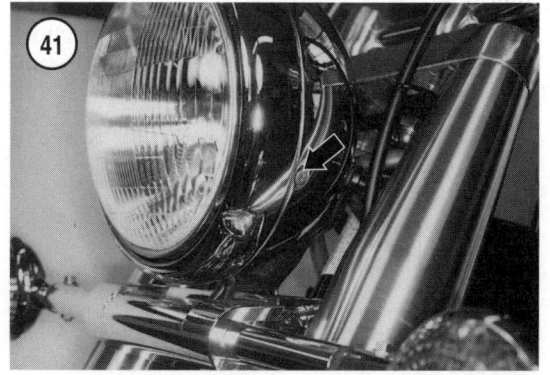

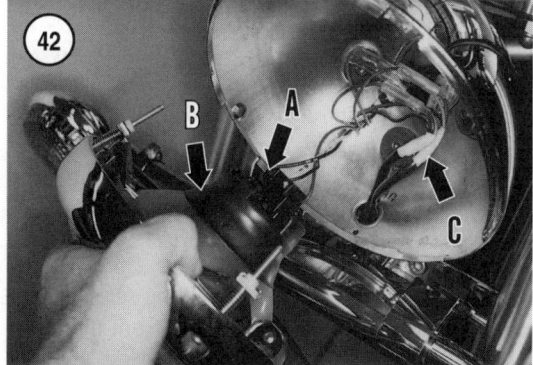

5. Turn the dimmer switch to HI, and check the voltage by performing the following:
   a. Connect the voltmeter negative test lead to the black terminal (A, **Figure 43**) in the headlight connector.
   b. Connect the voltmeter positive lead to the yellow terminal (C, **Figure 43**).
   c. Turn the main switch ON, and check the voltmeter. It should read battery voltage.
6. If the system fails either test, the wiring between the main switch and the headlight connector is defective. Make the necessary repairs.

High Beam Indicator Test

If the high beam indicator light does not turn on when the high beam is on, perform the following test.
1. Remove the meter assembly as described in *Fuel Tank Removal/Installation* in Chapter Eight.
2. Check the continuity of the high beam illumination circuit by performing the following:
   a. Set an ohmmeter to the R × 1 scale.
   b. Connect the ohmmeters test leads to the yellow and black (**Figure 44**) terminals in the meter side of the 6-pin meter connector.
   c. The ohmmeter should show continuity. If there is no continuity, the bulb or bulb socket is defective. Make the necessary repairs.

Headlight Bulb Replacement

> *CAUTION*
> *All models are equipped with a quartz-halogen bulb. Do not touch the bulb glass because the oil on your fingers will drastically reduce the life of the bulb. Clean any traces of oil from the bulb with a cloth moistened in alcohol or lacquer thinner.*

> *WARNING*
> *If the headlight has just burned out or been turned off, the bulb will be **hot**. Do not touch the bulb until it cools off.*

Refer to **Figure 45** for V-Star Classics; refer to **Figure 46** for V-Star Customs.
1. Remove the two headlight holding screws (**Figure 41**) and pull the lens assembly from the headlight housing.

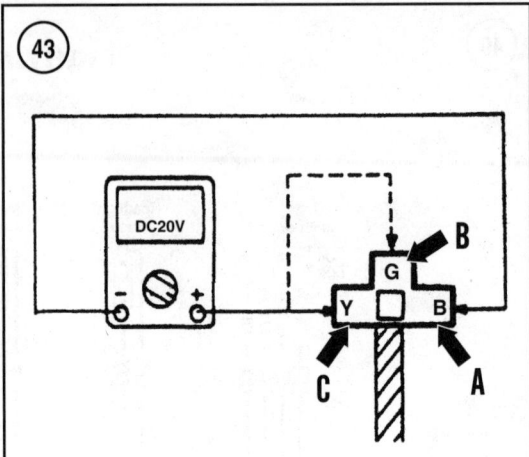

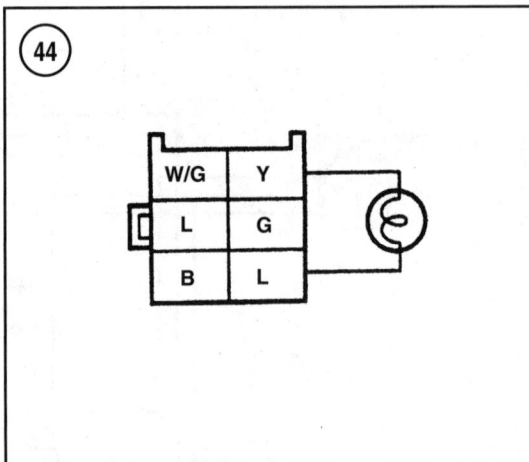

2. Unplug the electrical connector (A, **Figure 42**) from the lens assembly and remove the bulb cover (B, **Figure 42**).
3. Unhook the bulb clip (**Figure 47**) and lift the bulb from the lens.
4. Install by reversing these steps while noting the following:
   a. Install the bulb and make sure the projections on the bulb engage the slots in the lens assembly.
   b. Make sure the electrical connector is free of corrosion and secure.

Headlight Housing Removal/Installation

Refer to **Figure 45** when servicing V-Star Classics; refer to **Figure 46** for V-Star Customs.

ELECTRICAL SYSTEM

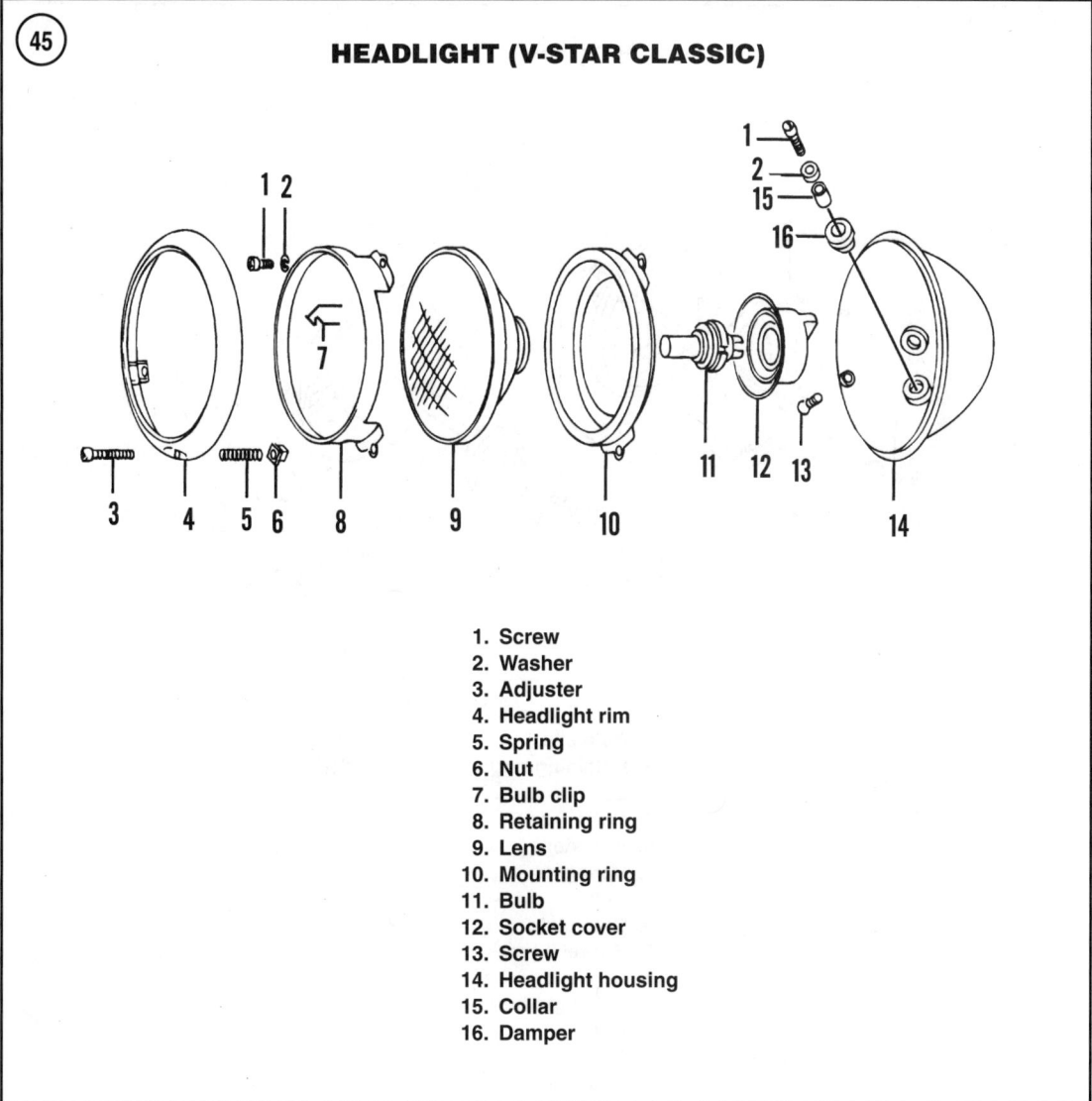

45 HEADLIGHT (V-STAR CLASSIC)

1. Screw
2. Washer
3. Adjuster
4. Headlight rim
5. Spring
6. Nut
7. Bulb clip
8. Retaining ring
9. Lens
10. Mounting ring
11. Bulb
12. Socket cover
13. Screw
14. Headlight housing
15. Collar
16. Damper

1. Remove the headlight lens as described in *Headlight Bulb Replacement*.

2. Disconnect the bullet connectors (C, **Figure 42**) for each front turn signal assembly.

3. Feed the wiring harness lead and the turn signal leads through the openings in the headlight housing.

4A. On V-Star Classics, remove the two mounting bolts that secure the headlight housing to the headlight bracket on the lower fork bridge. Remove the housing. Do not lose the washer and collar on each bolt.

4B. On V-Star Customs, remove the two mounting bolts that secure the headlight housing to the headlight bracket on the lower fork bridge. Remove the housing.

5. Installation is the reverse of removal. Note the following:
 a. Make sure the electrical connectors are free of corrosion and secure.
 b. Adjust the headlight as described in this chapter.

Headlight Adjustment

Adjust the headlight horizontally and vertically according to the Department of Motor Vehicles regulations in your area.

CHAPTER NINE

HEADLIGHT (V-STAR CUSTOM)

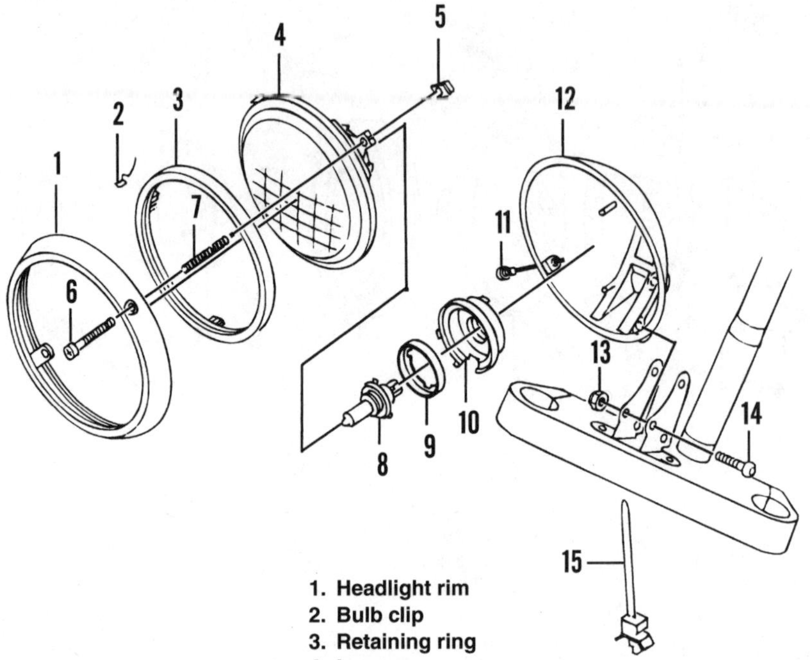

1. Headlight rim
2. Bulb clip
3. Retaining ring
4. Lens
5. Nut
6. Adjuster
7. Spring
8. Bulb
9. Bulb plate
10. Socket cover
11. Screw
12. Headlight housing
13. Nut
14. Bolt
15. Cable tie

ELECTRICAL SYSTEM

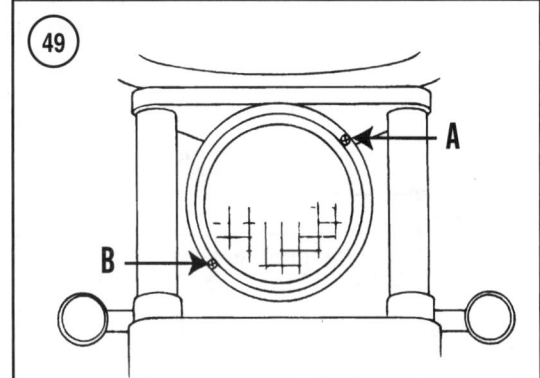

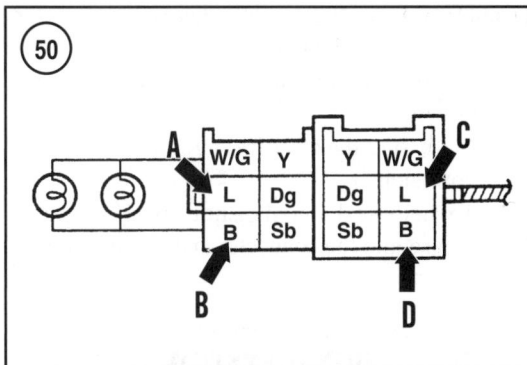

On V-Star Classics, the horizontal adjuster (A, **Figure 48**) is located at 8 o'clock on the headlight rim; the vertical adjuster (B, **Figure 48**) is at 4 o'clock. On V-Star Customs, the horizontal adjuster (A, **Figure 49**) is located at 1 o'clock on the headlight rim; the vertical adjuster (B, **Figure 49**) is at 8 o'clock.

1. Horizontal adjustment: To adjust the beam to the right, turn the horizontal adjuster counterclockwise. To adjust the beam to the left, turn the horizontal adjuster clockwise.

2. Vertical adjustment: To raise the beam, turn the vertical adjuster counterclockwise. To lower the beam, turn the vertical adjuster clockwise.

METER ASSEMBLY

Meter Illumination Light Test

If the meter illumination lights do not operate, perform the following test.
1. Remove the meter assembly as described in *Fuel Tank Removal/Installation* in Chapter Eight.
2. Check the continuity of the meter illumination circuit by performing the following:
   a. Set an ohmmeter to the R × 1 scale.
   b. Connect the ohmmeter test leads to the blue (A, **Figure 50**) and black (B, **Figure 50**) terminals in the meter side of the 6-pin meter connector.
   c. The ohmmeter should show continuity. If there is no continuity, a bulb or bulb socket is defective. Make the necessary repairs.
3. Check the voltage in the illumination light circuit by performing the following:
   a. Set a voltmeter to the DC 20 volt range.
   b. Connect the voltmeter positive test lead to the blue terminal (C, **Figure 50**) in the harness side of the 6-pin meter connector.
   c. Connect the voltmeter negative test lead to the black terminal (D, **Figure 50**) in the harness side of the 6-pin meter connector.
   d. Turn the main switch ON.
   e. The voltmeter should read battery voltage. If it does not, the wiring between the main switch and the meter connector is defective. Make the necessary repairs.

TAILLIGHT

Taillight Test

If a taillight does not operate, check the circuit by performing the following test.
1. Remove the battery box cover as described in Chapter Thirteen
2. Disconnect the 6-pin taillight/brake light connector (**Figure 51**).
3. Check the continuity of the taillight circuit by performing the following:
   a. Set an ohmmeter to the R × 1 scale.

b. Connect the ohmmeter test leads to the blue (A, **Figure 52**) and black (B, **Figure 52**) terminals in the taillight side of the 6-pin taillight connector.
c. The ohmmeter should show continuity. If there is no continuity, the bulb or socket is defective. Make the necessary repairs.

4. Check the voltage in the taillight circuit by performing the following:
   a. Set a voltmeter to the DC 20 volt range.
   b. Connect the voltmeter positive test lead to the blue terminal (D, **Figure 52**) in the harness side of the 6-pin taillight connector.
   c. Connect the voltmeter negative test lead to the black terminal (C, **Figure 52**) in the harness side of the 6-pin taillight connector.
   d. Turn the main switch ON.
   e. The voltmeter should read battery voltage. If it does not, the wiring between the main switch and the taillight socket is defective. Make the necessary repairs.

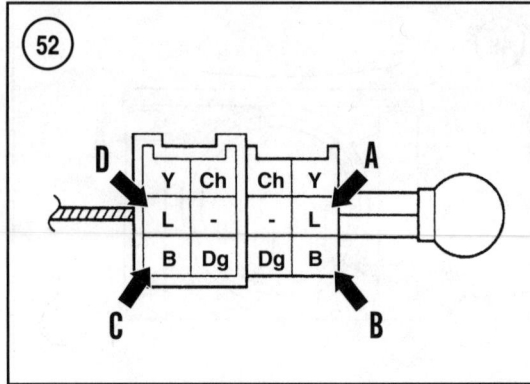

   c. Disconnect the taillight harness connector, and remove the taillight bracket.
3. Install by reversing these removal steps. Note the following.
   a. Make sure the electrical terminals are free of corrosion.
   b. To help seal out moisture, pack dielectric grease into the connector and reconnect it securely.

Taillight/Brake Light Replacement

1. Remove the taillight lens from the taillight assembly.
2. Turn the bulb counterclockwise, and remove it.
3. Push the new bulb into the socket and turn it clockwise to lock it in position.
4. Reinstall the lens.

Taillight/Brake Light Assembly Removal/Installation

Refer to **Figure 53** for V-Star Classics; **Figure 54** for V-Star Customs.
1. Remove the taillight lens and gasket.
2A. On V-Star Classic models, remove the taillight housing by performing the following:
   a. Remove the nut, washer, damper, and collar from each housing bolt.
   b. Pull out the housing and disconnect the taillight/brake light bullet connectors.
   c. Remove the housing and the damper.
2B. On V-Star Custom models, remove the taillight housing by performing the following:
   a. Remove the nut and washer from each housing bolt.
   b. Pull the housing from the taillight bracket.

SIGNAL SYSTEM

The signal system includes the turn signals, brake light, horn and indicator lights. Whenever there is a problem with a signal system component, follow the signal system troubleshooting procedures listed below. Start with the first inspection, and perform the indicated checks. If a test indicates that a component is working properly, reconnect the electrical connections and proceed to the next step. Systematically work through the troubleshooting checklist until the problem is found. Repair or replace the faulty part as described in the appropriate section of the manual.

Perform these procedures in the indicated sequence. Each test presumes that the components tested in the earlier steps are working properly. The tests can yield invalid results if they are performed out of sequence.

The signal system circuit diagram is shown in **Figure 55**.

Signal System Troubleshooting

1. Check the main fuse and the signal fuse.
2. Check the battery as described in Chapter Three.

ELECTRICAL SYSTEM

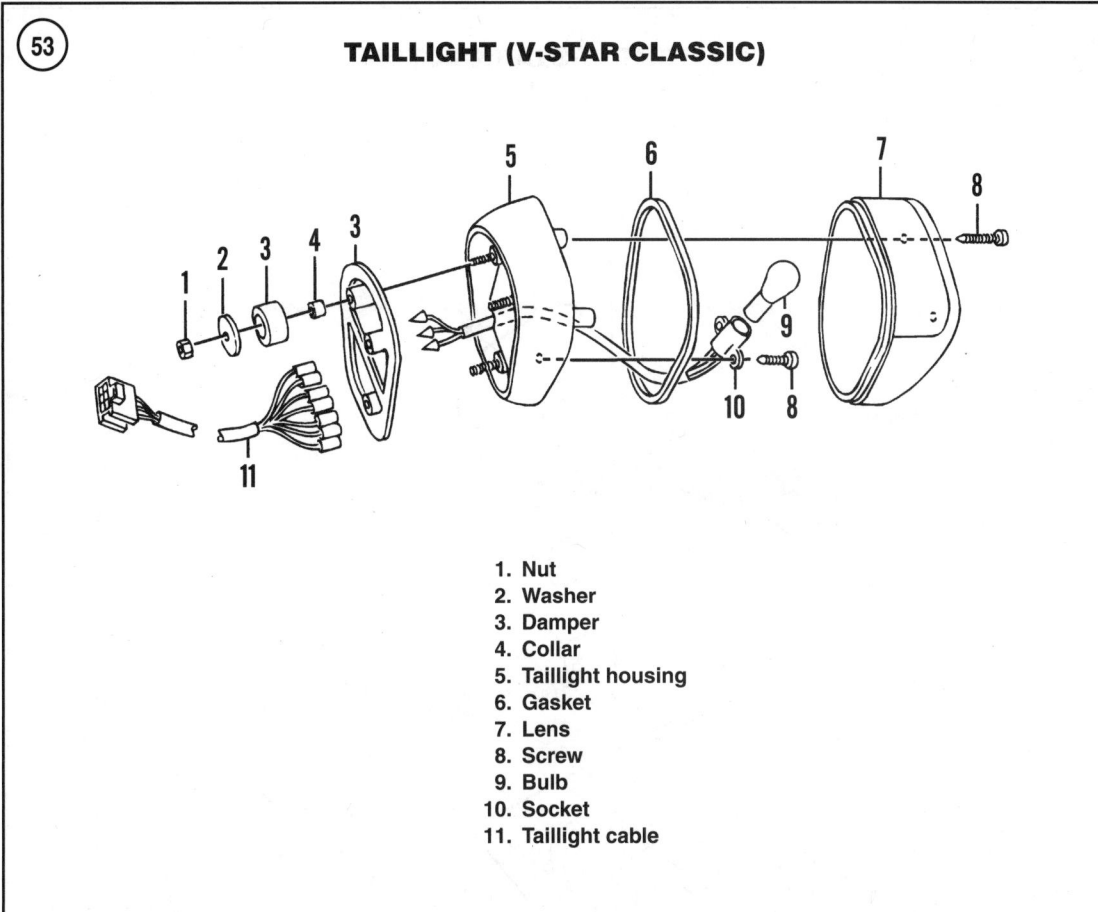

53 TAILLIGHT (V-STAR CLASSIC)

1. Nut
2. Washer
3. Damper
4. Collar
5. Taillight housing
6. Gasket
7. Lens
8. Screw
9. Bulb
10. Socket
11. Taillight cable

3. Check the continuity of the main switch as described in this chapter.
4. Check the wiring and each connector in the signal circuit.
5. Test the affected part of the circuit by performing the appropriate test described below.

BRAKE LIGHT

Brake Light Test

If a brake light does not operate, check the circuit by performing the following test.

1. Check the continuity of the brake light switch (either front or rear) as described in this chapter. Replace the switch if necessary.
2. Remove the battery box cover as described in Chapter Thirteen.
3. Disconnect the 6-pin taillight/brake light connector (**Figure 51**).

4. Set a voltmeter to the DV 20 volt range.
5. Connect the voltmeter positive test lead to the yellow terminal (A, **Figure 56**) in the harness side of the connector, and connect the negative test lead to the black terminal (B, **Figure 56**).
6. Turn the main switch ON, and pull the brake lever or press the brake pedal. The meter should read battery voltage.
7. If it does not, the wiring between the main switch and the bulb socket is defective.

NEUTRAL INDICATOR LIGHT

Neutral Indicator Test

Perform the following test if the neutral indicator lamp fails to illuminate.

1. Check the continuity of the neutral switch as described in this chapter. Replace the neutral switch if necessary.

CHAPTER NINE

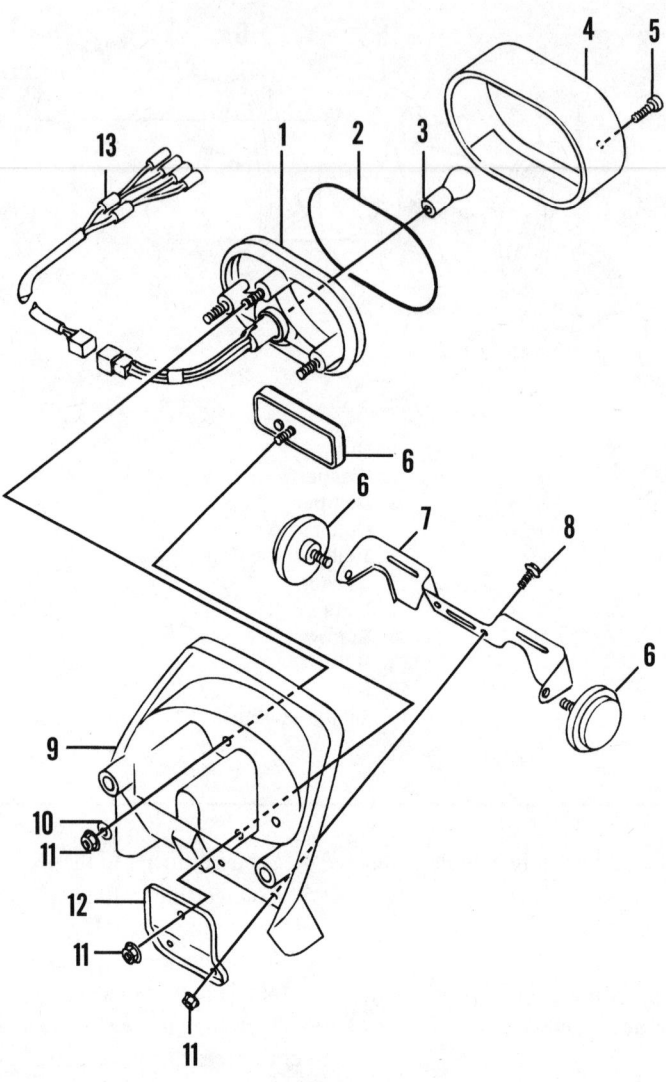

54 TAILLIGHT (V-STAR CUSTOM)

1. Reflector
2. Gasket
3. Bulb
4. Lens
5. Screw
6. Reflector
7. License plate bracket
8. Bolt
9. Taillight housing
10. Washer
11. Nut
12. Fender bracket
13. Taillight cable

55

SIGNAL SYSTEM
Main switch
On
Off
Signal system fuse
Headlight fuse
Rear brake switch
Ignitor unit
Main fuse
Battery
Diagram Key
Connectors
Ground
Frame ground
Connection
No connection
Turn indicator light
Front right turn signal
Front left turn signal
Engine warning light
Neutral indicator light
Horn
Right rear turn signal
Tail/brake light
Left rear turn signal
Horn switch
Front brake switch
Turn switch
Flasher relay
Neutral switch
Color Code
B Black
W White
R Red
G Green
L Blue
Y Yellow
O Orange
P Pink
Gr Gray
Br Brown
Sb Sky blue
B/L Black/Blue
W/G White/Green
R/W Red/White
L/B Blue/Black
L/R Blue/Red
L/Y Blue/Yellow
G/Y Green/Yellow
Y/R Yellow/Red
Br/W Brown/White
Br/L Brown/Blue

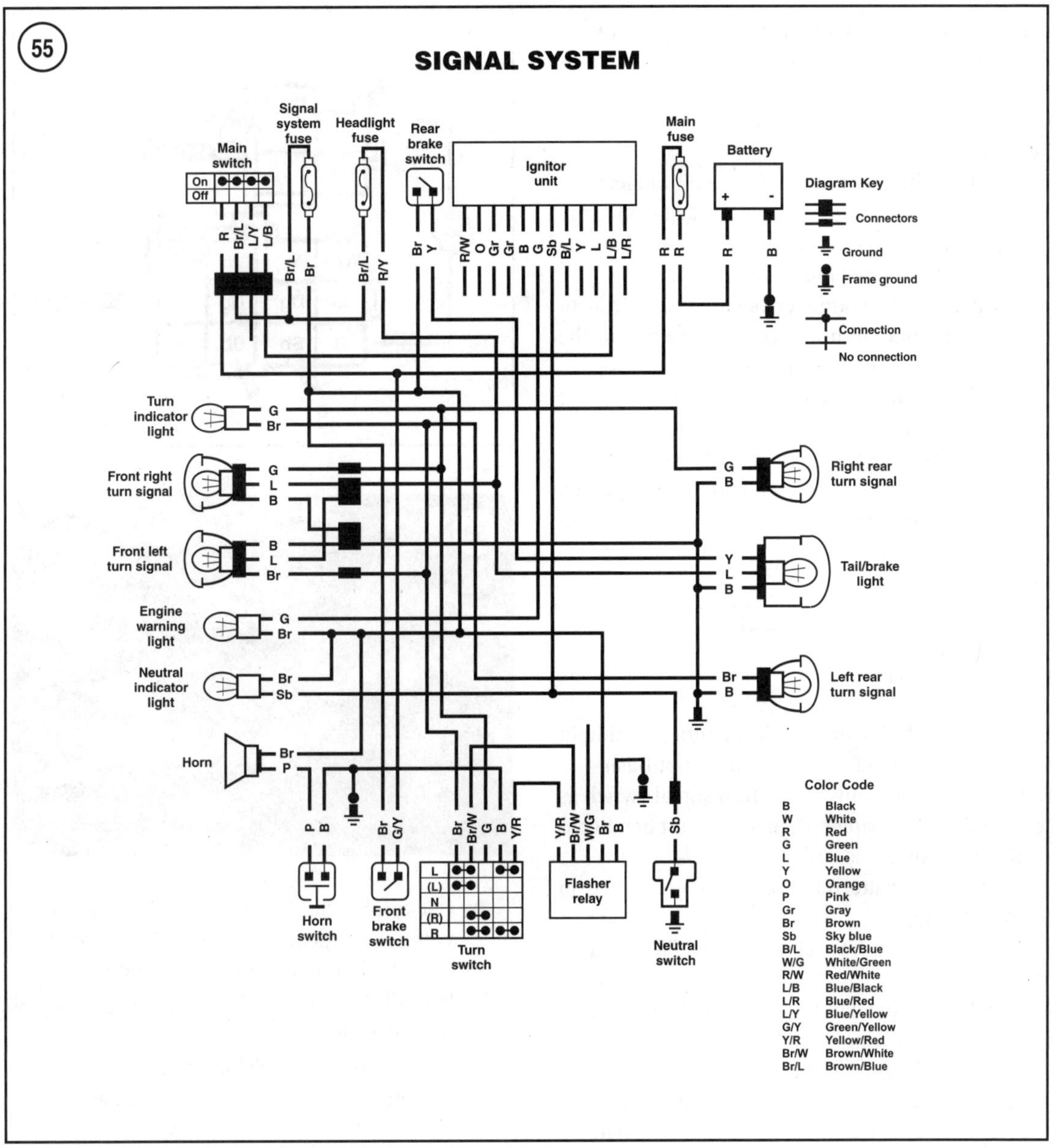

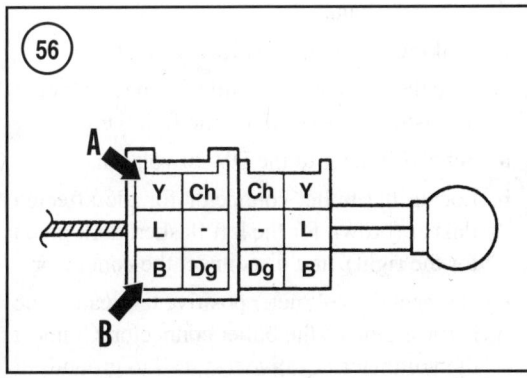

56

A
B
Y
Ch
Ch
Y
L
-
-
L
B
Dg
Dg
B

2. Remove the fuel tank as described in Chapter Eight.

3. Check the continuity of the bulb and socket by performing the following:

   a. Set an ohmmeter to the R × 1 scale.

   b. Connect the ohmmeter leads to the brown terminal (A, **Figure 57**) in the meter side of the 2-pin meter connector and the sky blue terminal (B, **Figure 57**) in the meter side of the 6-pin meter connector. There should be continuity.

c. Replace the bulb or repair the wiring between the socket and connector if there is no continuity.
4. Check the voltage in the circuit by performing the following.
   a. Set a voltmeter to the DC 20 volt range.
   b. Connect the voltmeter positive test lead to the brown terminal (C, **Figure 57**) in the harness side of the 2-pin meter connector.
   c. Connect the voltmeter negative test lead to the sky blue terminal (D, **Figure 57**) in the harness side of the 6-pin meter connector.
   d. Shift the transmission into neutral, turn the main switch to ON, and check the voltage on the meter. It should read battery voltage.
   e. If the reading is less than battery voltage, the wiring between the main switch and the connector is defective.

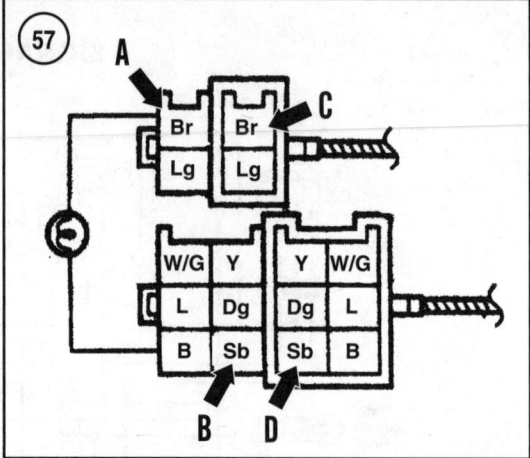

TURN SIGNALS

Turn Signal Test

Perform the following check if a turn signal light or the turn signal indicator light does not flash.
1. Check the continuity of the turn signal switch as described in this chapter. Replace the left handlebar switch if the switch is defective.
2. Remove the battery box cover as described in Chapter Thirteen.
3. Remove the flasher relay (**Figure 58**) from its bracket.
4. Check the input voltage into the relay by performing the following:
   a. Set a voltmeter to the DV 20 volt range.
   b. Disconnect the connector from the relay.
   c. Connect the voltmeter positive test lead to the brown terminal of the connector as shown in **Figure 59**. Connect the voltmeter negative test lead to a good frame ground.
   d. Turn the main switch ON, and check the voltage on the meter. It should read battery voltage. If it does not, the wiring between the main switch and the flasher relay is defective. Repair the wiring if input voltage is less than battery voltage.
   e. Reconnect the connector to the relay.
5. Check the output voltage from the relay by performing the following:
   a. Set a voltmeter to the DV 20 volt range.

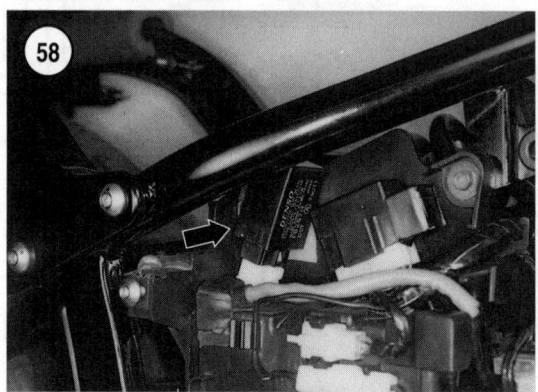

   b. Backprobe the flasher relay and connect the voltmeter positive test lead to the brown/white relay terminal as shown in **Figure 60**. Connect the voltmeter negative test lead to ground.
   c. Turn the main switch ON, and check the voltage on the meter. It should read battery voltage.
   d. Replace the relay if output voltage is less than battery voltage.
   e. Seal the wiring with silicon sealant.
6A. Check the voltage at the bullet connector for the affected flasher by performing the following.
   a. Set a voltmeter to the DV 20 volt range.
   b. Locate the bullet connector for the affected flasher (brown for the left flasher; dark green for the right), and disconnect the connector.
   c. Connect the voltmeter positive test lead to the harness side of the bullet connector. Connect the voltmeter negative test lead to ground.

ELECTRICAL SYSTEM

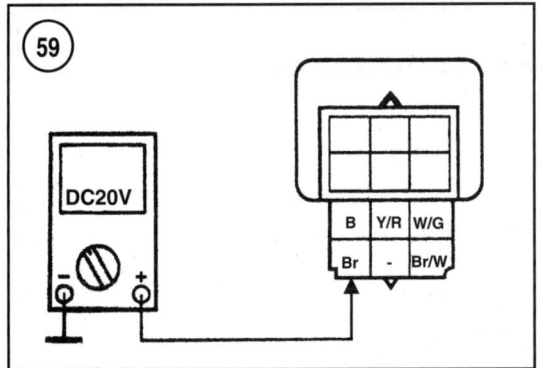

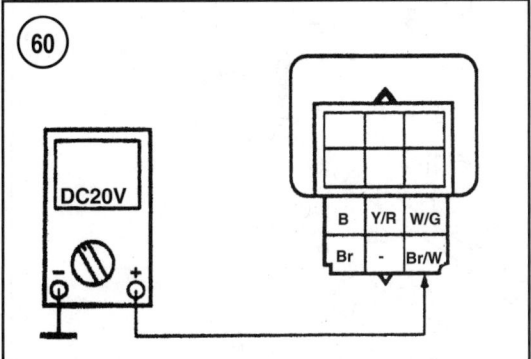

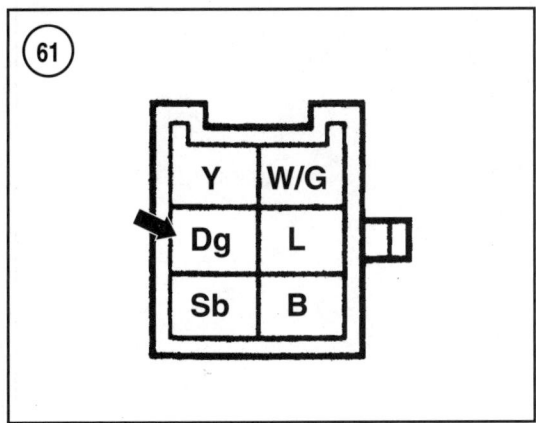

b. Remove the fuel tank as described in Chapter Eight, and locate the meter 6-pin connector.

c. Connect the voltmeter positive test lead to the dark green terminal (**Figure 61**) on the harness side of the connector. Connect the voltmeter negative test lead to ground.

d. Turn the main switch to ON, and turn on the turn signal switch, and check the voltage on the meter. It should read battery voltage.

e. If the reading is less than battery voltage, the wiring between the turn signal switch and the connector is defective.

Turn Signal Light Replacement

Refer to **Figure 62** for V-Star Classics; **Figure 63** for V-Star Customs.

1. Remove the two screws securing the lens assembly.
2. Remove the lens (A, **Figure 64**) and lens ring (B, **Figure 64**).
3. Wash the lens (inside and outside) with a mild detergent.
4. Install a new bulb.
5. Make sure the gasket (C, **Figure 64**) is in place on the housing.
6. Install the lens ring and lens. Do not overtighten the lens screws because this will crack the lens.

Turn Signal Assembly Removal/Installation

Refer to **Figure 62** for V-Star Classics; **Figure 63** for V-Star Customs.

1A. Front turn signals: Perform the following:
  a. Remove the headlight lens as described in *Headlight Bulb Replacement*.
  b. Locate and disconnect the two bullet connectors (C, **Figure 42**) for the particular turn signal assembly. Feed the turn signal leads out through the hole in the headlight housing.
  c. Loosen and remove the nut from the turn-signal clamp bolt (D, **Figure 64**).
  d. Remove the turn signal housing from the mounting bracket.

1B. Rear turn signals: Perform the following:
  a. On V-Star Classic models, remove the license plate holder from the license plate bracket.

d. Turn the main switch ON, turn on the turn signal switch for that side, and check the voltage on the voltmeter. It should read battery voltage.

e. The wiring between the turn signal switch and the bulb socket is defective if voltage is less than battery voltage.

6B. Check the voltage at the turn signal indicator lamp connector by performing the following:
  a. Set the voltmeter to the DV 20 volt range.

CHAPTER NINE

TURN SIGNAL ASSEMBLY (V-STAR CLASSIC)

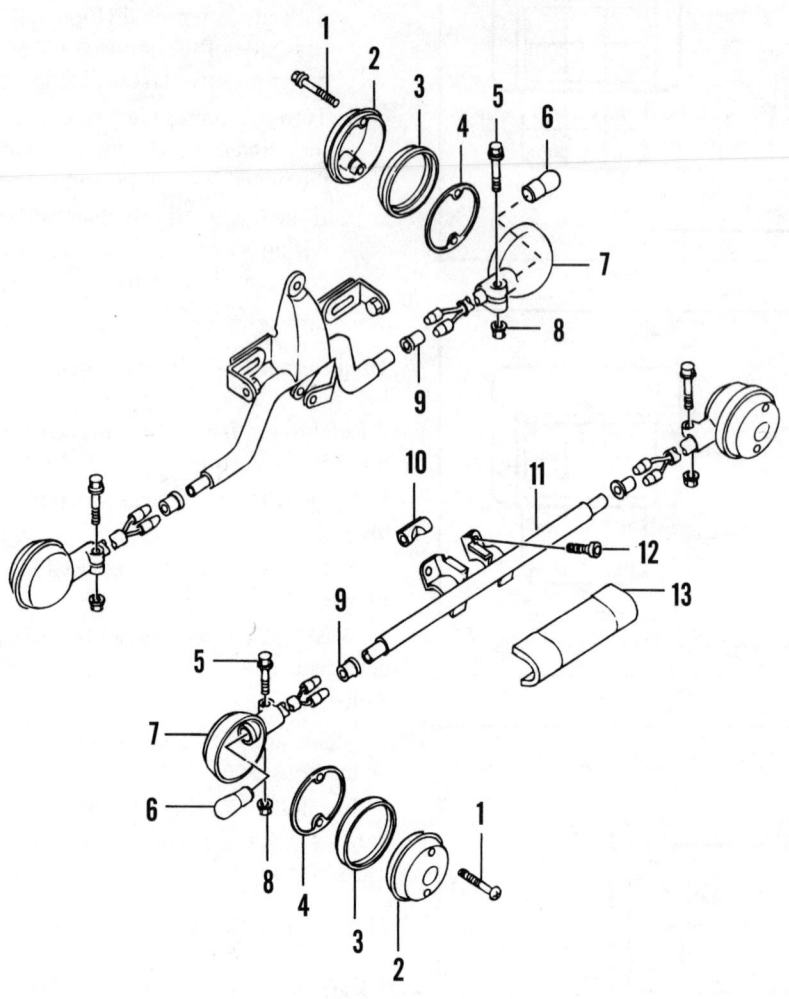

1. Screw
2. Lens
3. Lens rim
4. Gasket
5. Clamp bolt
6. Bulb
7. Turn signal housing
8. Clamp nut
9. Damper
10. Blind plug
11. Turn signal bracket
12. Bolt
13. Bracket cover

ELECTRICAL SYSTEM

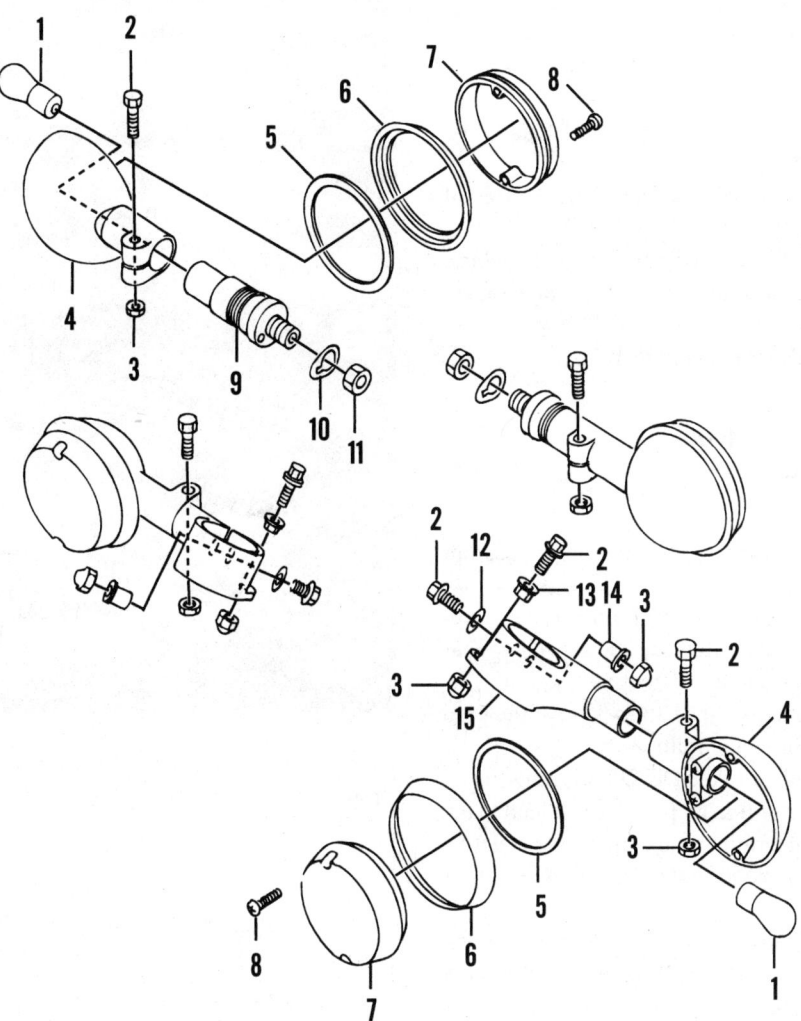

TURN SIGNAL ASSEMBLY (V-STAR CUSTOM)

1. Bulb
2. Clamp bolt
3. Clamp nut
4. Turn signal housing
5. Gasket
6. Lens rim
7. Lens
8. Screw
9. Turn signal bracket (rear)
10. Washer
11. Nut
12. Washer
13. Spacer
14. Collar
15. Turn signal bracket (front)

CHAPTER NINE

b. Locate and disconnect the bullet connectors (**Figure 65**, V-Star Classic) for the turn signal.
c. Loosen and remove the nuts from the turn signal assembly bolt.
d. Remove the turn signal housing from the mounting bracket.

2. Install by reversing these removal steps while noting the following:
   a. Make sure the electrical terminals are free of corrosion.
   b. To help seal out moisture, pack dielectric grease into the connector and reconnect it securely.
   c. Tighten the clamp nuts securely.

HORN

Horn Circuit Test

Perform the following test if the horn does not sound.

1. Check the continuity of the horn switch as described in this chapter. Replace the left handlebar switch if the horn switch is defective.
2. Check the voltage on the battery side of the horn circuit by performing the following:
   a. Set a voltmeter to the DC 20 volt range.
   b. Connect the voltmeter positive test lead to the brown horn terminal and connect the negative test lead to a good frame ground. See **Figure 66**.
   c. Turn the main switch to ON and check the voltage on the meter. It should read battery voltage.
   d. If the reading is less than 12 volts, the wiring between the main switch and the horn is defective.
3. Check the voltage from the horn to ground by performing the following:
   a. Set a voltmeter to the DC 20 volt range.
   b. Connect the voltmeter positive test lead to the pink horn terminal and connect the negative test lead to a good frame ground. See **Figure 67**.
   c. Turn the main switch to ON and check the voltage on the meter. It should read battery voltage.
   d. If the reading is less than 12 volts, replace the horn.

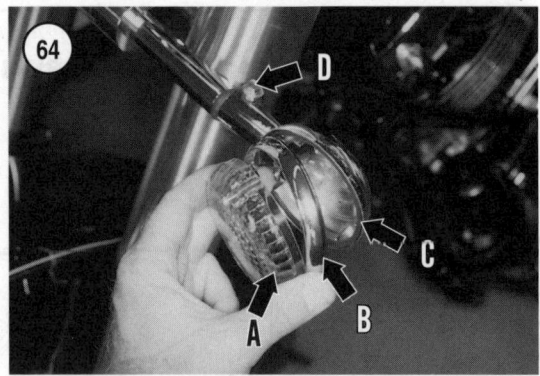

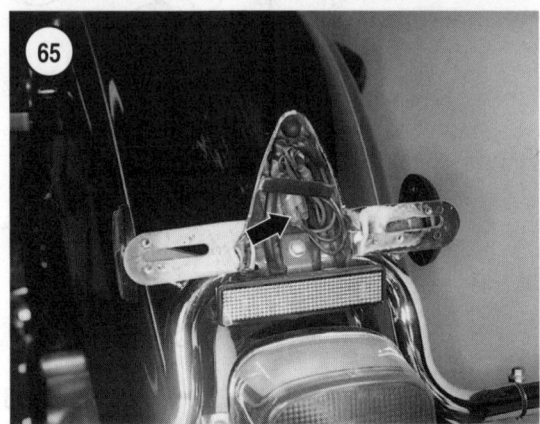

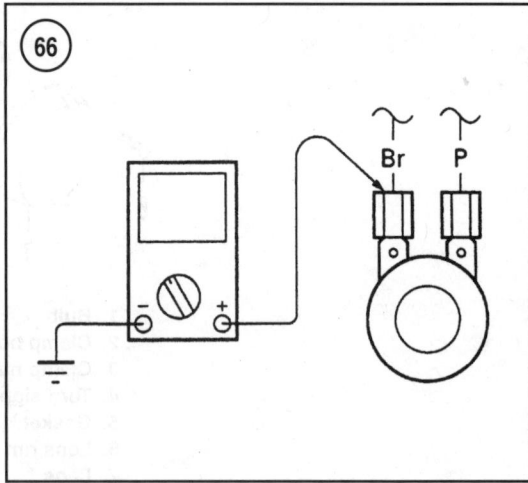

Horn Removal/Installation

1. Remove the horn mounting bolt (**Figure 68**) and lower the horn from the frame.
2. Disconnect the connectors from the two spade terminals on the back of the horn.
3. Installation is the reverse of removal.

ELECTRICAL SYSTEM 263

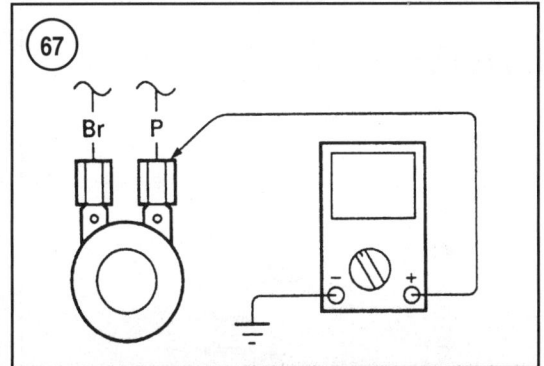

FUEL PUMP SYSTEM

Whenever there is a problem with the fuel pump, first perform the fuel pump operation test described below. If the fuel pump is operational, the problem is in the fuel pump system circuit. Troubleshoot the circuit by following the fuel pump circuit troubleshooting procedures listed below. Refer to **Figure 69** for the fuel pump system circuit diagram.

Fuel Pump Operation Test

Check the operation of the fuel pump by applying battery voltage directly to the fuel pump.
1. Remove the fuel tank and surge tank as described in Chapter Eight.
2. Disconnect the black 2-pin fuel pump connector (**Figure 70**). This connector has a blue/black and a black wire on each side of the connector.
3. Disconnect the fuel pump outlet hose (**Figure 71**) from the fitting on the carburetor, and feed the hose into a container.
4. Add fuel to an auxiliary fuel tank, and connect the fuel pump inlet hose to the auxiliary tank.
5. Use jumper wires and connect a battery to the fuel pump side of the connector as shown in **Figure 72**. Fuel should flow from the fuel pump outlet hose.
6. The fuel pump is defective if fuel does not flow from the fuel pump outlet hose. Replace the fuel pump.

Fuel Pump Circuit Troubleshooting

When there is a problem with the fuel pump circuit, follow the troubleshooting procedures listed below. Start with the first inspection, and perform the indicated checks. If a test indicates that a component is working properly, reconnect the electrical connections and proceed to the next step. Systematically work through the troubleshooting checklist until the problem is found. Repair or replace the defective part as described in the appropriate section of the manual.

Perform these procedures in the listed sequence. Each test presumes that the components tested in the earlier steps are working properly. The tests can yield invalid results if they are performed out of sequence.

1. Inspect the main fuse and the ignition fuse as described in this chapter.
2. Check the battery as described in Chapter Three.
3. Check the continuity of the main switch as described in this chapter.
4. Check the continuity of the engine stop switch as described in this chapter.
5. Check the fuel pump relay in the relay unit as described below.
6. Check the resistance of the fuel pump as described below.
7. Check the fuel system wiring and all connectors. Repair as necessary.

Fuel Pump Relay (Relay Unit) Test

1. Remove the battery box cover as described in Chapter Thirteen.
2. Remove the relay unit from the bracket on the rear of the battery box, and disconnect the connector from the relay unit.
3. Check the continuity of the fuel pump relay by performing the following:
   a. Set an ohmmeter to the R × 1 range.

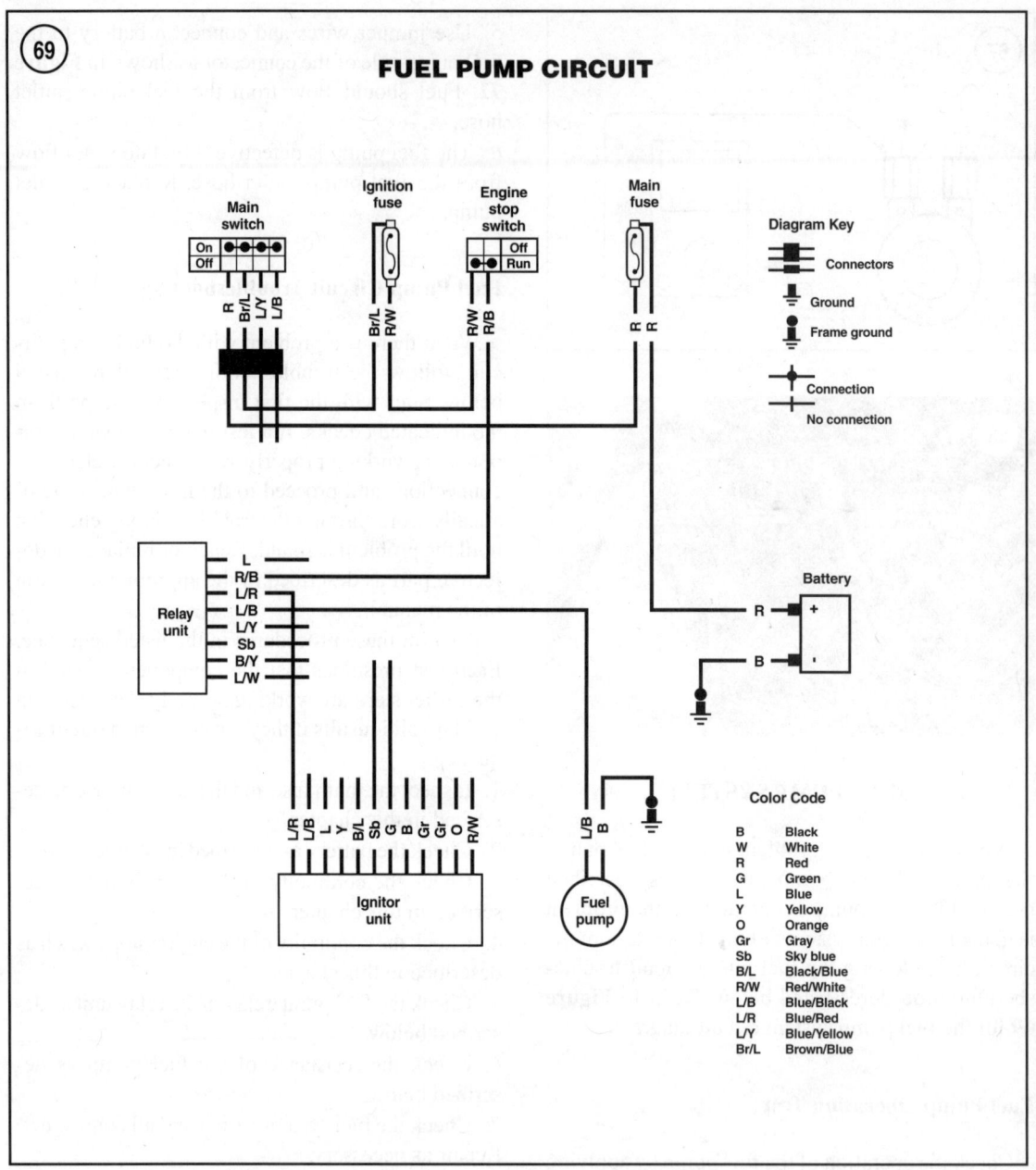

b. Use a jumper wire to connect the positive battery terminal to the red/black terminal (A, **Figure 73**) on the relay unit and to connect the negative battery terminal to the blue/red terminal (B, **Figure 73**) on the relay unit.

c. Connect the ohmmeter positive test lead to the red/black terminal (A, **Figure 73**) on the relay unit and connect the negative test lead to the blue/black terminal (C, **Figure 73**) on the relay unit.

d. The fuel pump relay should have continuity during this test. Replace the relay if there is no continuity.

Fuel Pump Resistance Test

1. Check the resistance of the fuel pump by performing the following:
   a. Remove the fuel tank as described in Chapter Eight.

ELECTRICAL SYSTEM

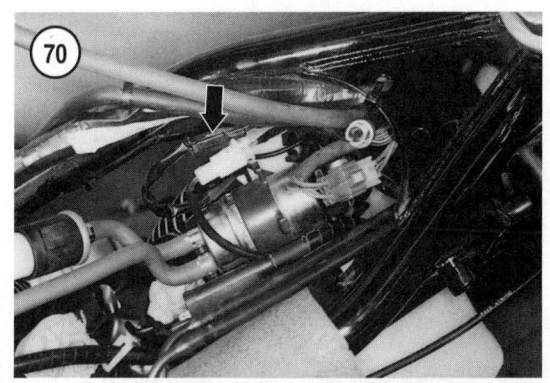

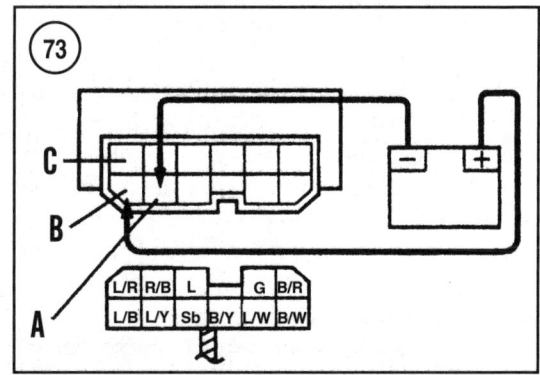

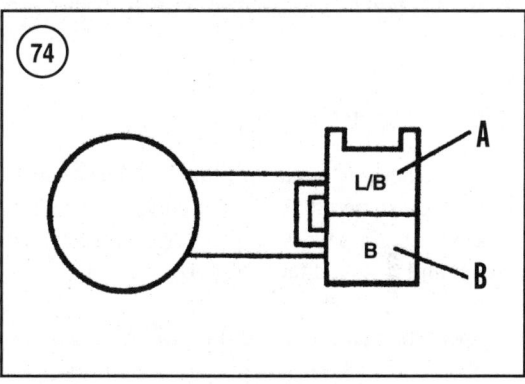

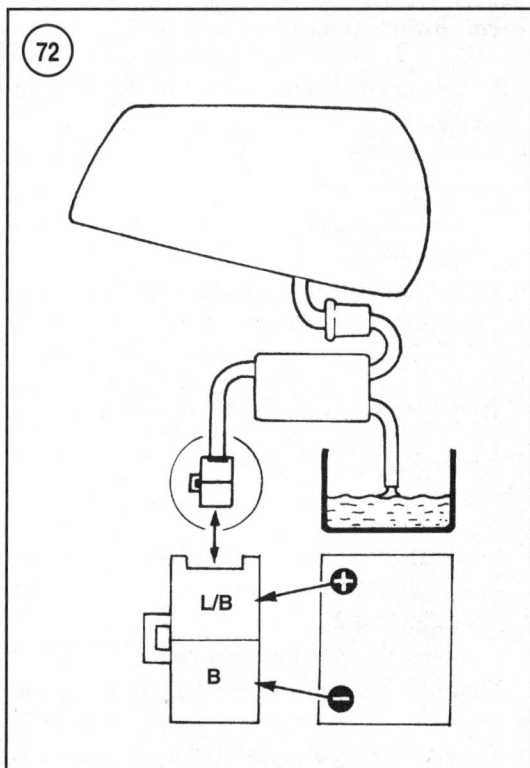

b. Disconnect the 2-pin fuel pump connector.

c. Set an ohmmeter to the R × 1 scale.

d. Connect the ohmmeter positive test lead to the blue/black terminal (A, **Figure 74**) in the pump side of the connector and connect the negative test lead to the black terminal (B, **Figure 74**).

e. Measure the fuel pump resistance. Replace the fuel pump if its resistance is outside the range specified in **Table 1**.

Fuel Pump Removal/Installation

1. Remove the fuel pump bracket as described in Chapter Eight.

2. Pull the fuel pump from the rubber mount (A, **Figure 75**) on the fuel pump bracket.

3. Disconnect the fuel pump inlet hose (B, **Figure 75**) and outlet the hose (C, **Figure 75**) and remove the fuel pump.

4. Installation is the reverse of removal.

CARBURETOR HEATER SYSTEM

Whenever there is a problem with the carburetor heater system, follow the carburetor heater troubleshooting procedures listed below. Start with the first inspection, and perform the indicated checks. If a test indicates that a component is working properly, reconnect the electrical connections and proceed to the next step. Systematically work through the troubleshooting checklist until the problem is found. Repair or replace the defective part as described in the appropriate section of the manual.

Refer to **Figure 76** for the carburetor heater circuit diagram.

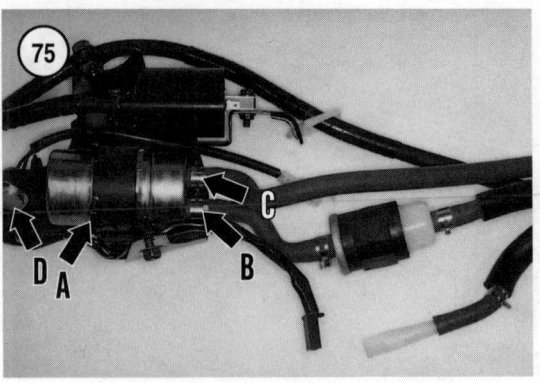

Carburetor Heater Troubleshooting

Perform these procedures in the listed sequence. Each test presumes that the components tested in the earlier steps are working properly. The tests can yield invalid results if they are performed out of sequence.

1. Inspect the main fuse and the carburetor fuse as described in this chapter.
2. Check the battery as described in Chapter Three.
3. Check the continuity of the main switch as described in this chapter.
4. Check the continuity of the neutral switch as described in this chapter.
5. Test the carburetor heater relay as described below.
6. Test the thermo switch as described below.
7. Test the carburetor heater as described below.
8. Check the carburetor heating system wiring and connectors. Repair as necessary.

Carburetor Heater Relay Test

1. Remove the carburetor heater relay as described below.
2. Use a jumper wire to connect the battery positive terminal to the brown/yellow terminal (A, **Figure 77**) at the relay and the battery negative terminal to the sky blue relay terminal (B, **Figure 77**).
3. Set an ohmmeter to the R × 1 scale.
4. Connect the ohmmeter positive test lead to the brown/black relay terminal (D, **Figure 77**) and the negative test lead to the black/yellow relay terminal (C, **Figure 77**).

5. The ohmmeter should show no continuity. If there is continuity, replace the heater relay.

Carburetor Heater Removal/Installation

1. Remove the battery box cover as described in Chapter Thirteen.
2. Disconnect the harness connector from the carburetor heater relay (**Figure 78**) and remove the relay.
3. Installation is the reverse of removal.

Thermo Switch Test

1. Remove the fuel pump bracket as described in Chapter Eight.
2. Remove the thermo switch (D, **Figure 75**) from the end of the bracket.
3. Fill a beaker or pan with water and place it on a stove or hot plate.
4. Suspend the thermo switch so it is immersed in the water as shown in **Figure 79**.

NOTE
The thermometer and the thermo switch must not touch the side or bottom of the container during this test. If either does, test results will be inaccurate.

5. Suspend a thermometer in the water. Use a cooking or candy thermometer that is rated higher than the test temperatures.
6. Set an ohmmeter to the R × 1 range.
7. Connect the ohmmeter positive test lead to the brown/yellow terminal at the thermo sensor connector. Connect the negative test lead to the black/yellow terminal (**Figure 79**).

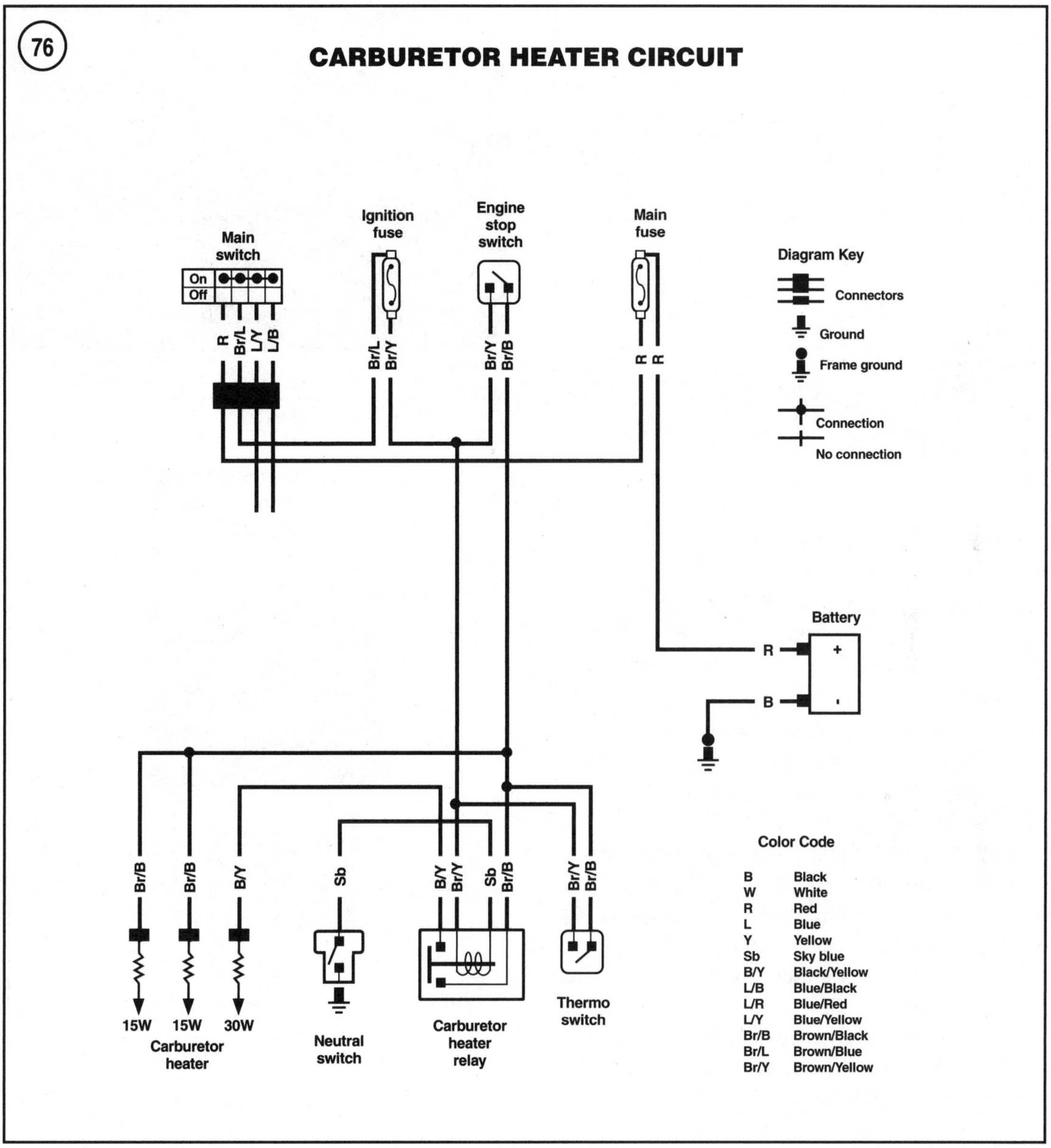

ELECTRICAL SYSTEM

76

CARBURETOR HEATER CIRCUIT

Color Code

B	Black
W	White
R	Red
L	Blue
Y	Yellow
Sb	Sky blue
B/Y	Black/Yellow
L/B	Blue/Black
L/R	Blue/Red
L/Y	Blue/Yellow
Br/B	Brown/Black
Br/L	Brown/Blue
Br/Y	Brown/Yellow

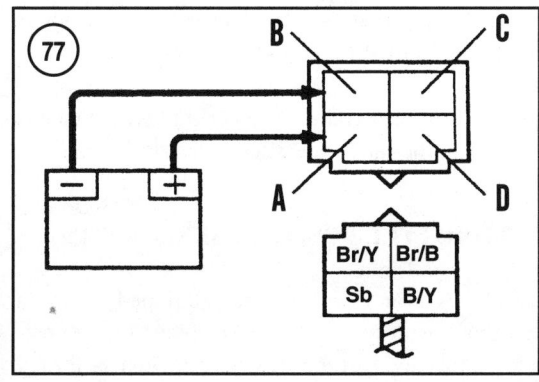

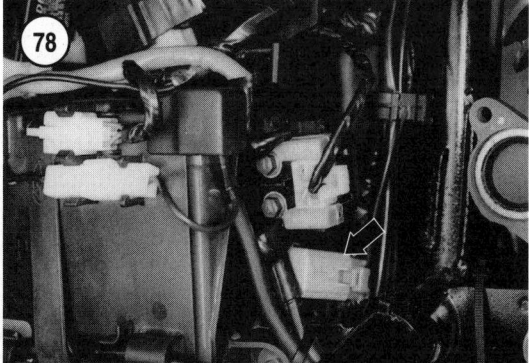

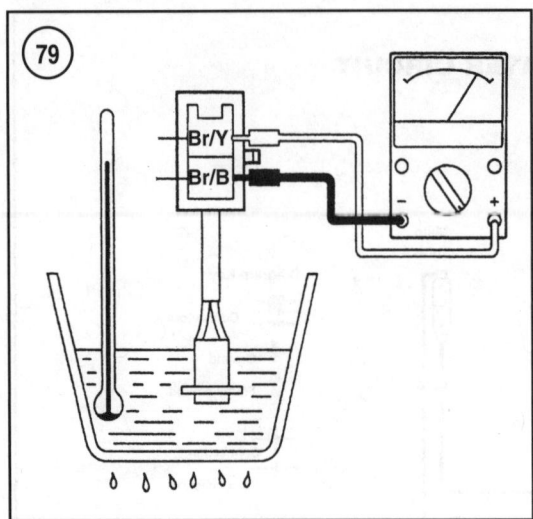

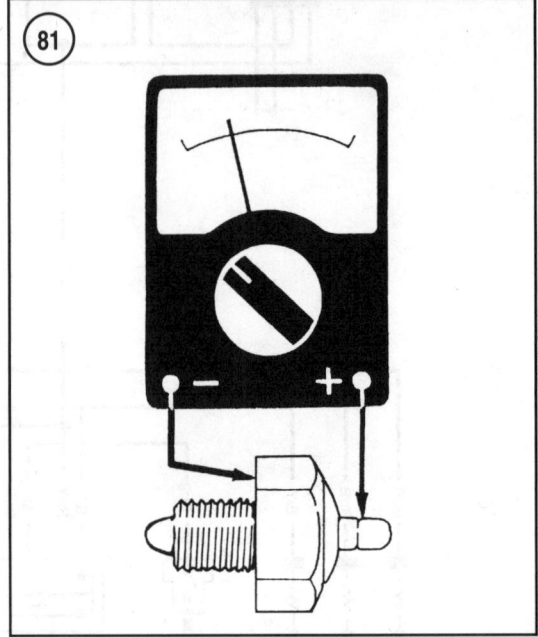

carburetor heater with the black/yellow lead is a 30 watt heater; the two with the brown/black leads are 15 watt heaters.

8. Gradually heat the water and observe the continuity as the temperature rises.
   a. With a temperature of less than 68-78° F (20-26° C), the thermo switch should be ON. There should be continuity between the switch terminals.
   b. When the temperature reaches 68-78° F (20-26° C), the switch should turn OFF. There should be no continuity between the switch terminals.
9. Turn the heat off and observe the continuity as the temperature decreases.
   a. With a temperature above 46-60° F (8-16° C), the thermo switch should be OFF. There should be no continuity between the switch terminals.
   b. When the temperature drops to 46-60° F (8-16° C), the thermo switch should turn ON. There should be continuity between the switch terminals.
10. Replace the thermo switch if the test results are not within the above specifications.

Carburetor Heater Test

1. Remove the electrical lead from the carburetor heater and remove the heater from the carburetor.
2. Set an ohmmeter to the R × 1 scale.

NOTE
Three carburetor heaters (A, Figure 80) are used on these models. Two are rated at 15 watts; one at 30 watts. The

3. Connect an ohmmeter to the carburetor heater as shown in **Figure 81** and check the heater's resistance.
4. Replace the carburetor heater if the resistance is not within the range specified in **Table 1**.

THROTTLE POSITION SENSOR (TPS)

Both V-Star models are equipped with a self-diagnostic system that checks the throttle position sensor every time the main switch is turned

ELECTRICAL SYSTEM

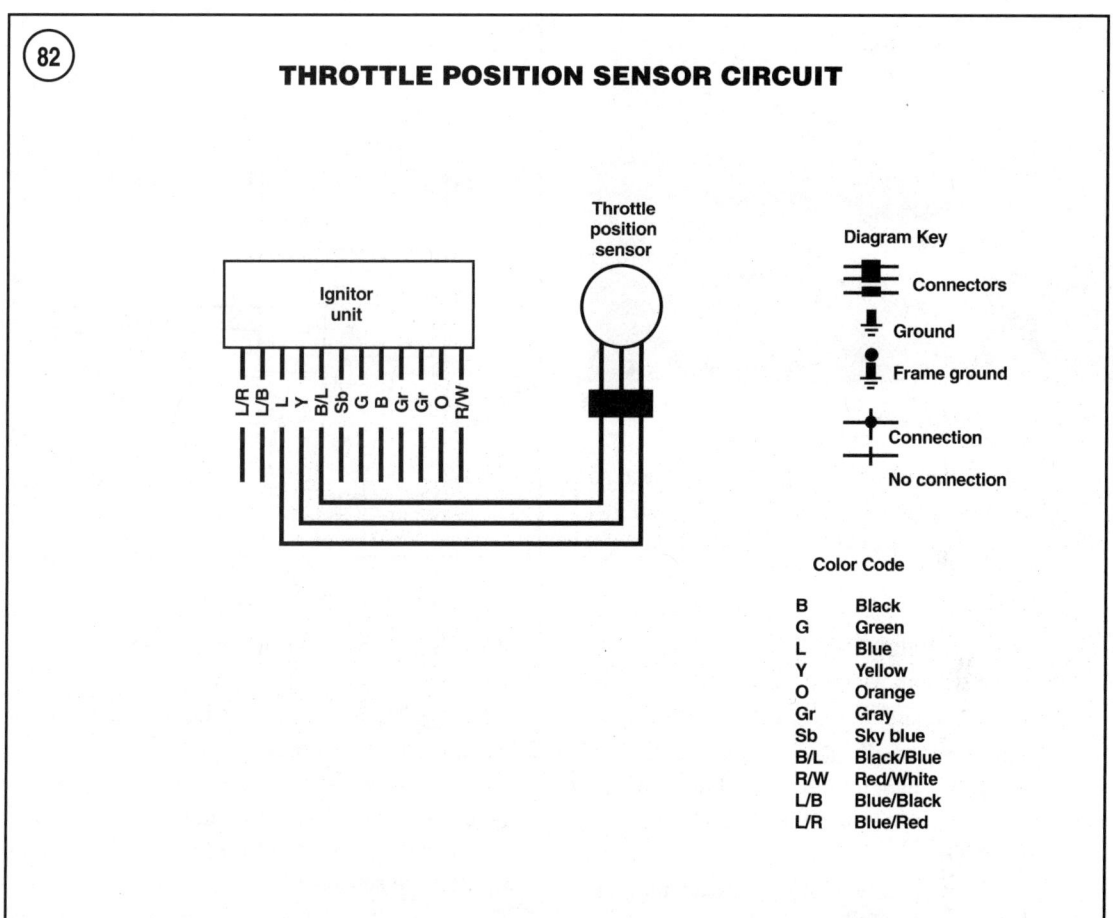

82 THROTTLE POSITION SENSOR CIRCUIT

ON. During normal operation, the engine indicator light on the meter assembly turns on and the system runs a series of checks whenever the main switch is turned ON. If the throttle position sensor is operating properly, the engine indicator light goes out after approximately 1.4 seconds or when the engine is started.

If the self-diagnostic system detects an error in the throttle position sensor, the engine indicator light flashes after the initial 1.4 second period or it remains on once the engine has started.

If the self-diagnostic system indicates a TPS error, perform the TPS troubleshooting procedure listed below.

TPS Troubleshooting

Perform these procedures in the listed sequence. Each test presumes that the components tested in the earlier steps are working properly. The tests can yield invalid results if they are performed out of sequence.

Refer to **Figure 82** for the throttle position sensor circuit diagram.

1. Refer to the circuit diagram and check the continuity of the circuit wiring. Make any necessary repairs.
2. Test the throttle position sensor as described below.
3. Replace the igniter unit.

Throttle Position Sensor Test

1. Remove the fuel tank and surge tank as described in Chapter Eight.
2. Press the tab on the throttle position sensor connector (**Figure 83**) and disconnect the connector from the sensor.
3. Check the sensors internal resistance by performing the following:

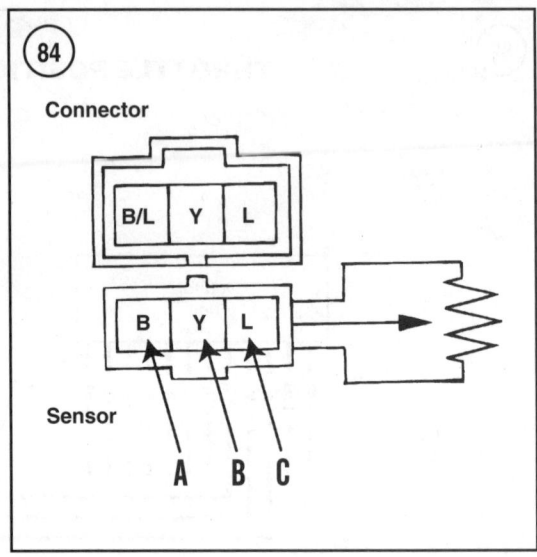

a. Set an ohmmeter to the R × 1,000 scale.
b. Connect the ohmmeter positive test lead to the black sensor terminal (A, **Figure 84**) and the negative test lead to the blue terminal (C, **Figure 84**).
c. Replace the sensor if the internal resistance is outside the range specified in **Table 1**.

4. Check the sensors wide-open resistance.
   a. Set an ohmmeter to the R × 1,000 scale.
   b. Connect the ohmmeter positive test lead to the yellow sensor terminal (B, **Figure 84**) and the negative test lead to the black terminal (A, **Figure 84**).
   c. Note the resistance while slowly opening the throttle from the fully closed to the wide-open position.
   d. Replace the sensor if the resistance is outside the wide-open range specified in **Table 1**.

Throttle Position Sensor Adjustment

Adjust the throttle position sensor by turning the sensor until its resistance is within the adjustment range, which differs for each sensor. The following procedure describes how to calculate the adjustment range.

NOTE
The throttle position sensor is mounted on the side of the rear carburetor.

1. Properly adjust the idle speed as described in Chapter Three.
2. Remove the fuel tank and the surge tank as described in Chapter Eight.
3. Press the tab on the throttle position sensor connector (**Figure 83**) and disconnect the connector from the sensor.
4. Set an ohmmeter to the R × 1,000 scale.
5. With the throttle fully-closed, measure the sensor resistance (R) by performing the following:
   a. Connect the positive ohmmeter lead to the black terminal (A, **Figure 84**) on the throttle position sensor.
   b. Connect the negative ohmmeter lead to the blue terminal (C, **Figure 84**) of the sensor.
   c. Record the resistance value when the throttle is fully closed.
6. Determine the adjustment range using the following formula: R × 0.13 and R × 0.15. The two resultant values are the adjustment range. For example:
   a. If the measured fully-closed resistance (R) in Step 5 was 5k, then 5 × 0.13 = 650 and 5 × 0.15 = 750.
   b. The adjustment range would be 650-750 ohms.
7. With the throttle still fully closed, adjust the throttle position sensor by performing the following:
   a. Loosen the throttle position sensor mounting screws.
   b. Connect the positive ohmmeter lead to the black terminal (A, **Figure 84**) on the throttle position sensor, and connect the negative lead to the blue terminal (C, **Figure 84**).

ELECTRICAL SYSTEM

85 HORN SWITCH

Button position	Wire color	
	P	B
Push	●——————●	
Off		

c. Rotate the sensor body until the resistance is within the adjustment range calculated in Step 6.

d. Tighten the throttle position sensor screws securely.

SWITCHES

Test switches for continuity with an ohmmeter (see Chapter One) or a test light. Disconnect the switch connector and check continuity at the terminals on the switch side of the connector. If a connector connects directly to the switch (the clutch and brake switches, for example), check for continuity at the switch. Operate a switch in each of its operating positions and compare the results with the switch continuity diagram.

For example, **Figure 85** shows a continuity diagram for a horn switch. It illustrates which terminals should have continuity when the horn switch is in that position. The line on the continuity diagram indicates there should be continuity between the pink and black terminals when the horn button is pressed and there should be no continuity between these terminals when the button is released. When the horn button is pressed, an ohmmeter connected between these terminals should indicate little or no resistance (a test lamp should light). When the horn button is released, there should be no continuity between the same terminals. An ohmmeter should indicate infinite resistance (a test lamp should not light).

Precautions

When testing switches, note the following:
1. First check the fuses as described in this chapter.
2. Check the battery as described in Chapter Three. Correct the state of charge, if required.
3. Disconnect the negative battery cable if the switch is not disconnected from the circuit.

CAUTION
Do not attempt to start the engine with the negative battery cable disconnected or the wiring harness will be damaged.

4. When separating two connectors, pull on the connector housings and not the wires.
5. After locating a defective circuit, check the connectors to make sure they are clean and properly connected. Check all wires going into a connector housing to make sure each wire is properly positioned and that the wire end is not loose.
6. To properly connect connectors, push them together until they click into place.
7. When replacing handlebar switch assemblies, make sure the cables are routed correctly so they are not crimped when the handlebar is turned from side to side.

Testing

If a switch or button does not perform properly, replace it. Refer to the following figures when testing the continuity of switches:
1. Horn switch: **Figure 85**.
2. Main switch: **Figure 86**.
3. Engine stop switch: **Figure 87**.
4. Neutral switch: **Figure 88**.
5. Sidestand switch: **Figure 89**.
6. Clutch switch: **Figure 90**.
7. Starter switch: **Figure 91**.
8. Headlight dimmer switch: **Figure 92**.
9. Front brake switch: **Figure 93**.
10. Rear brake switch: **Figure 94**.
11. Turn signal switch: **Figure 95**.

Left Handlebar Switch Replacement

The left handlebar switch housing includes the headlight dimmer, turn signal, horn and clutch switches:
1. Remove the fuel tank and surge tank as described in Chapter Eight.

CHAPTER NINE

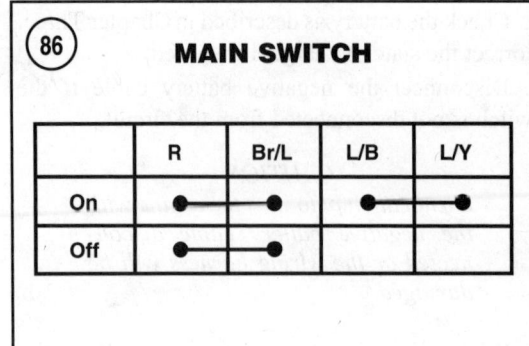

86 MAIN SWITCH

	R	Br/L	L/B	L/Y
On	●—	—●	●—	—●
Off	●—	—●		

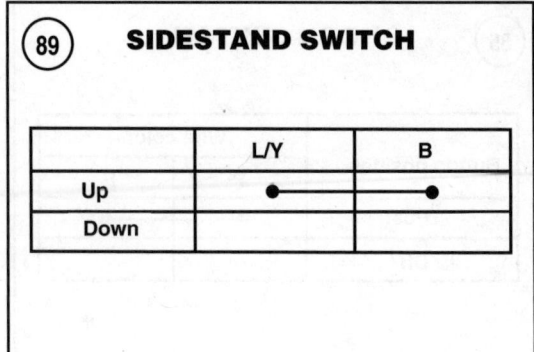

89 SIDESTAND SWITCH

	L/Y	B
Up	●——	—●
Down		

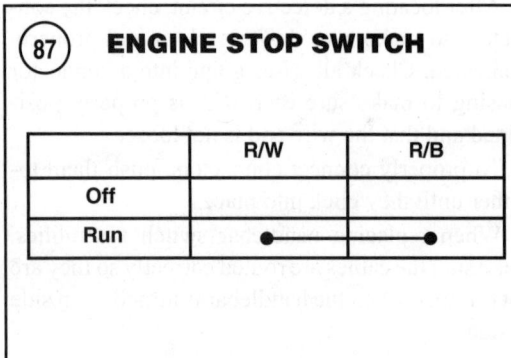

87 ENGINE STOP SWITCH

	R/W	R/B
Off		
Run	●———	———●

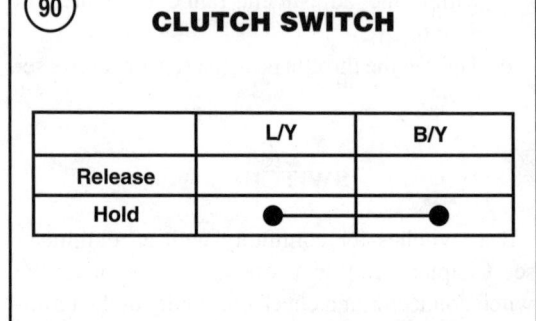

90 CLUTCH SWITCH

	L/Y	B/Y
Release		
Hold	●———	———●

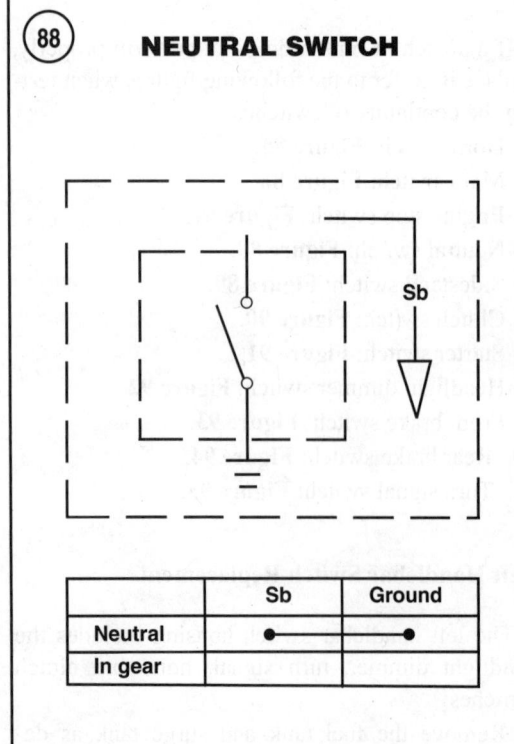

88 NEUTRAL SWITCH

	Sb	Ground
Neutral	●——	———●
In gear		

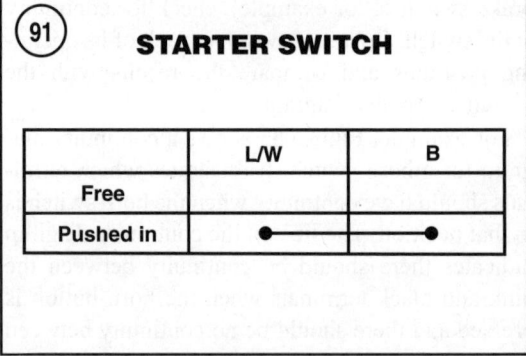

91 STARTER SWITCH

	L/W	B
Free		
Pushed in	●———	—●

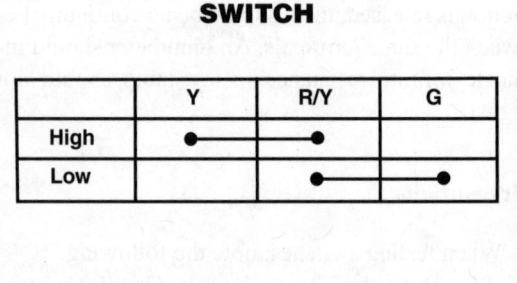

92 HEADLIGHT DIMMER SWITCH

	Y	R/Y	G
High	●—	—●	
Low		●———	—●

ELECTRICAL SYSTEM

93 FRONT BRAKE SWITCH

	Br	G/Y
Off		
On	●——	——●

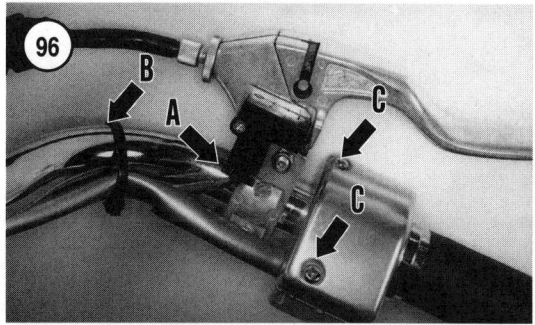

94 REAR BRAKE SWITCH

	Br	Y
On	●——	——●
Off		

95 TURN SIGNAL SWITCH

	Br	Br/W	Dg	B	Y/R
L	●——	——●		●——	——●
(L)	●——	——●			
N					
(R)			●——	——●	
R			●——	——● ●—	——●

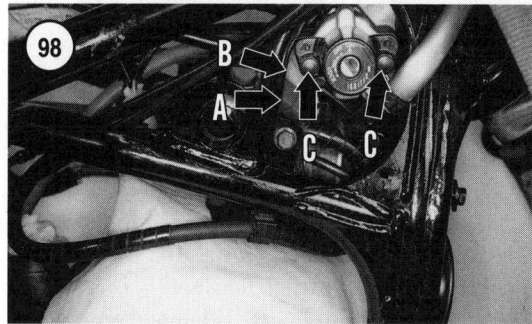

2. Remove the frame neck cover as described in Chapter Thirteen.

3. Disconnect the clutch switch connector (A, **Figure 96**).

4. Remove the cable tie that secures the switch cable to the handlebar (B, **Figure 96**) and the tie (**Figure 97**) that secures it to the upper fork bridge.

5. Follow the left handlebar switch cable behind the headlight and disconnect the blue 6-pin connector (A, **Figure 98**) and the white 6-pin connector (B, **Figure 98**) from their mates on the wiring harness.

6. Remove the screws (C, **Figure 96**) and separate the housing halves from the handlebar.

7. Remove the switch housing and wiring cable.

8. Installation is the reverse of these steps. Note the following:

   a. Position the switch assembly so the edge of the switch half mating surface (A, **Figure 99**) aligns with the index mark (B, **Figure 99**) on the handlebar.

   b. Make sure the electrical terminals are free of corrosion.

   c. To help seal out moisture, pack dielectric grease into the connector and reconnect it securely.

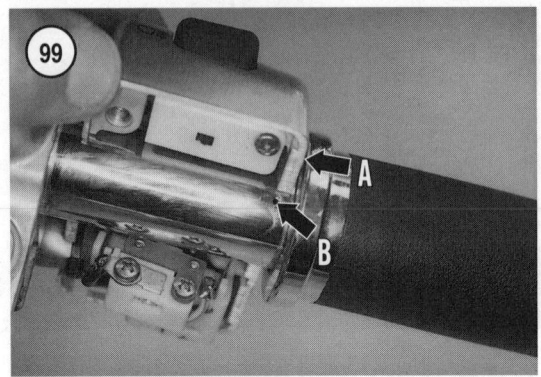

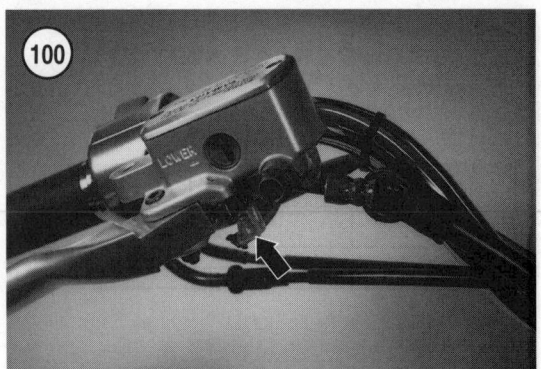

d. Install all removed items.

Right Handlebar Switch Replacement

1. Remove the fuel tank and surge tank as described in Chapter Eight.
2. Remove the frame neck cover as described in Chapter Thirteen.
3. Disconnect the two electrical connectors (**Figure 100**) from the front brake switch.
4. Remove the cable ties that secure the switch cable to the handlebar (A, **Figure 101**) and the tie that secures the cable to the upper fork bridge.
5. Follow the right handlebar switch cable behind the headlight and disconnect the black 6-pin connector and 3-pin connector from their mates on the wiring harness.
6. Remove the screw (A, **Figure 102**) that secures the pull cable to the switch housing.
7. Remove the two switch assembly screws (B, **Figure 102**), and separate the halves of the switch assembly (B, **Figure 101**) from the handlebar.
8. Installation is the reverse of removal. Note the following:
   a. Make sure the projection on the switch assembly (**Figure 103**) engages the hole in the handlebar.
   b. Make sure the electrical terminals are free of corrosion.
   c. To help seal out moisture, pack dielectric grease into the connector and reconnect it securely.
   d. Use cable ties to secure the switch cable to the upper fork bridge and to the handlebar (A, **Figure 101**).
   e. Securely tighten the pull cable mounting screw (A, **Figure 102**).

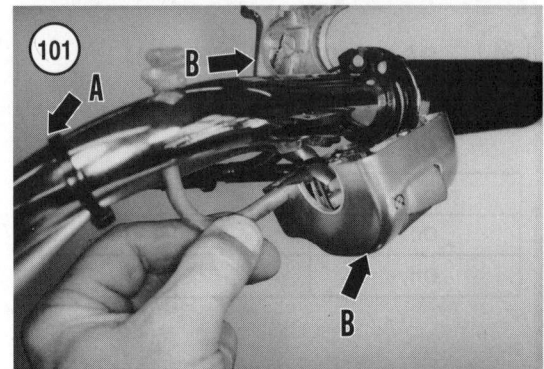

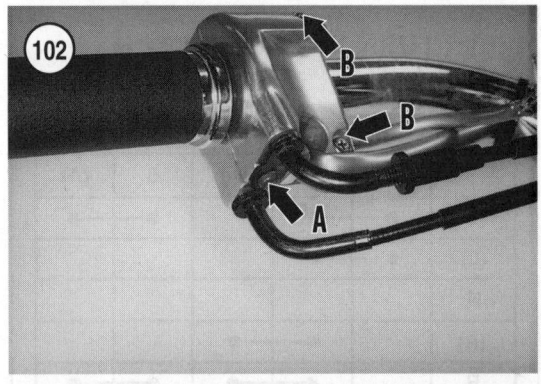

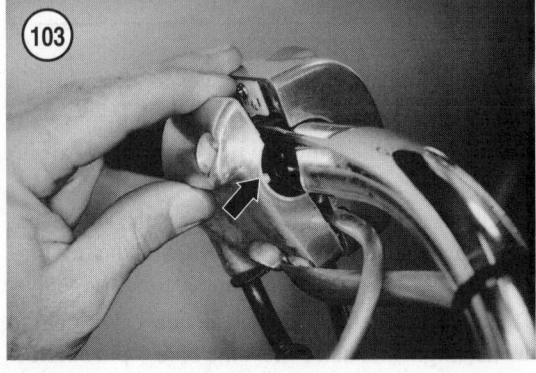

ELECTRICAL SYSTEM

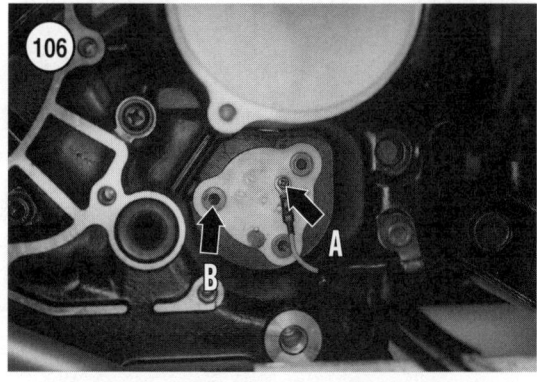

f. Adjust the throttle cable as described in Chapter Three.

Main Switch Replacement

1. Remove the fuel tank and surge tank as described in Chapter Eight.
2. Remove the frame neck cover as described in Chapter Thirteen.
3. Follow the main switch wire, and disconnect the red 4-pin connector (**Figure 104**) from its white mate on the wiring harness.
4. Remove the plug (C, **Figure 98**) from each mounting bolt and the two main-switch mounting bolts. Remove the switch from the frame.
5. Installation is the reverse of these steps. Note the following:
   a. Make sure the electrical terminals are free of corrosion.
   b. To help seal out moisture, pack dielectric grease into the connector and reconnect it securely.
   c. Install all removed items.
   d. When installing a shear bolt, tighten the bolt until the head twists off.

Neutral Switch Replacement

1. Remove the left side cover as described in Chapter Thirteen.
2. Remove the two mounting bolts (**Figure 105**) and the middle gearcase cover.
3. Disconnect the electrical lead (A, **Figure 106**) from the neutral switch.
4. Remove the three mounting bolts (B, **Figure 106**). Remove the neutral switch and its O-ring (**Figure 107**).
5. Install by reversing these removal steps while noting the following:
   a. Make sure the electrical connector is free of corrosion and secure.
   b. Install a new neutral switch O-ring.

Sidestand Switch Replacement

1. Use jack stands or a scissor jack to securely support the bike on level ground.
2. Remove the fuel tank and surge tank as described in Chapter Eight.

3. Remove the frame neck cover as described in Chapter Thirteen.

4. Follow the sidestand switch wire to the 2-pin connector at the frame neck. Release the wire from the cable holders (A, **Figure 108**) and ties that secure it to the frame. Note how the wire is routed along the frame and where the wire is secured to the frame. The new switch wire must be routed in the same manner.

5. Disconnect the blue 2-pin connector at the switch.

6. Remove the two screws securing the sidestand switch to the sidestand bracket, and remove the switch (B, **Figure 108**).

7. Installation is the reverse of these steps. Note the following:
   a. Make sure the electrical terminals are free of corrosion.
   b. To help seal out moisture, pack dielectric grease into the connector and reconnect it securely.
   c. Make sure the sidestand switch electrical wire is routed along the same path noted during removal.
   d. Secure the switch wire at the same locations noted during removal.
   e. Install all removed items.

Clutch Switch

The clutch switch is mounted underneath the clutch lever mounting bracket. Disconnect the electrical connector (A, **Figure 96**), remove the switch screw and the switch. Install by reversing this procedure.

Front Brake Switch Replacement

The front brake light switch is mounted underneath the front brake master cylinder.

1. Disconnect the spade connectors (A, **Figure 109**) from the front brake switch.

2. Remove the switch mounting screw (B, **Figure 109**) and the switch.

3. Install by reversing this procedure. Check switch operation. The rear brake light should come on when the front brake lever is applied.

Rear Brake Switch Replacement

The rear brake switch is mounted on the right frame just inside of the brake pedal.

NOTE
Figure 110 is shown with the brake pedal/footpeg assembly removed for clarity. It is not necessary to remove this assembly to replace the rear brake light switch.

ELECTRICAL SYSTEM

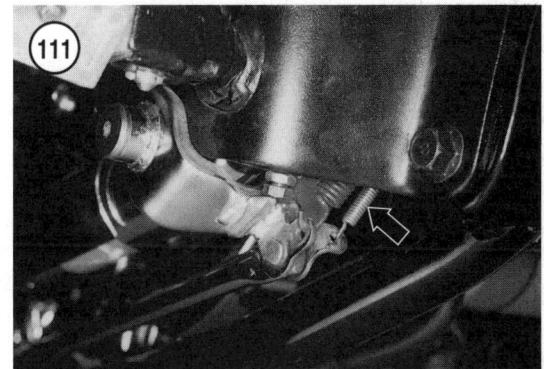

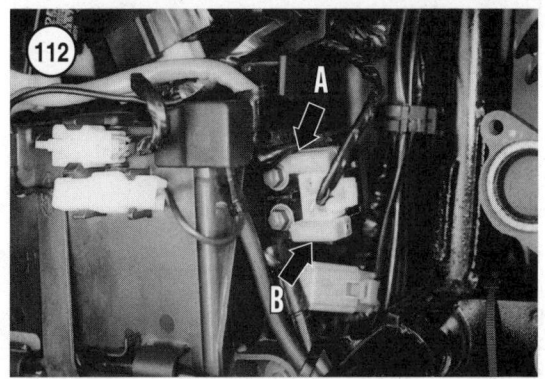

WIRING CONNECTORS

Many electrical troubles can be traced to damaged wiring or contaminated connectors. Service connectors by disconnecting them and cleaning them with electrical contact cleaner. Pack multiple pin connectors with a dielectric compound (available at most automotive and motorcycle supply stores).

FUSES

Whenever a fuse blows, determine the reason before replacing the fuse. Usually, the trouble is a short in the wiring. This may be caused by worn-through insulation or a disconnected wire shorting to ground.

> *CAUTION*
> *Never substitute metal foil or wire for a fuse. Never use a higher amperage fuse than specified. An overload may cause a fire and complete loss of the bike.*

1. Follow the switch electrical wire up the right side of the frame. Locate the 2-pin electrical connector and disconnect it.

2. Disconnect the spring (**Figure 111**) from the boss on the brake pedal.

3. Lift the switch assembly (**Figure 110**) from the frame bracket.

4. Install a new switch into the switch mount. Attach the spring and plug in the electrical connector.

5. Adjust the rear brake switch as described in Chapter Three.

Five fuses are used in these models.
1. Main fuse: 30 amp (A, **Figure 112**).
2. Ignition: 10 amp (A, **Figure 113**).
3. Signal system: 10 amp (B, **Figure 113**).
4. Headlight: 15 amp (C, **Figure 113**).
5. Carburetor heater fuse: 15 amp (D, **Figure 113**).

The 30-amp main fuse (A, **Figure 112**) and a spare 30-amp fuse (B, **Figure 112**) are located on the starter relay. The remaining fuses, along with a spare 10- and 15-amp fuse, are in the fuse holder above the battery (**Figure 114**).

Testing

1. Remove the battery box cover as described in Chapter Thirteen.
2. Remove the fuse holder (**Figure 114**) and open the cover.
3. Remove the fuse by pulling it out of the holder with needlenose pliers.
4. Visually inspect the fuse (**Figure 115**). Replace it if it is blown or cracked.
5. If necessary, check the continuity across the two spade connectors. Replace a fuse that does not have continuity (low resistance).
6. A replacement fuse must have the same amperage rating as the original.

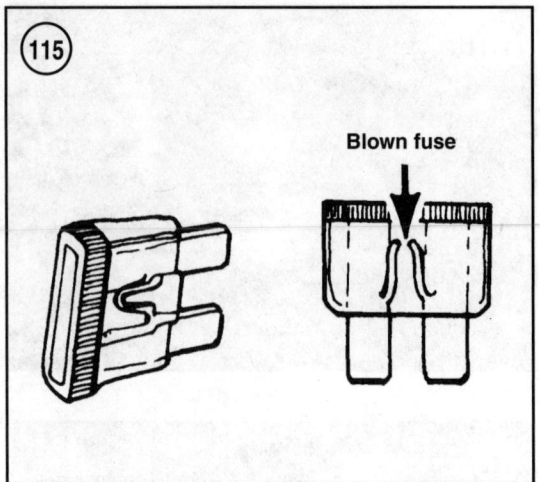

Table 1 ELECTRICAL SYSTEM SPECIFICATIONS

Battery	
Type	Maintenance free (sealed)
Capacity	12 V 10 AH
Open-circuit voltage	12.8 V at 68° F (20° C)
Charging voltage (output voltage)	14 volts, 20 amps at 5000 rpm
Stator coil resistance	0.50-62 ohms at 68° F (20° C)
Voltage regulator no-load output	14.1-14.9 volts
Rectifier	
Capacity	18 A
Withstand voltage	200 V
Pickup coil resistance	182-222 ohms at 68° F (20° C)
Ignition minimum spark gap (air gap)	6 mm (0.24 in.)
Ignition coil	
Primary coil resistance	3.8-4.6 ohms at 68° F (20° C)
Secondary coil resistance	10.1-15.1 k ohms at 68° F (20° C)
Ignition timing	12 degrees BTDC at 1200 rpm
Advancer type	TPS and electrical
Recommended spark plug	NGK DPR7EA-9, Denso X22EPR-U9
Spark plug gap	0.8-0.9 mm (0.031-0.035 in.)
Spark plug cap resistance	10 K ohms at 68° F (20° C)
Starter motor	
Brush length	12.5 mm (0.49 in.)
Brush length wear limit	4 mm (0.157 in.)
Commutator diameter	28 mm (1.102 in.)
Commutator diameter wear limit	27 mm (1.063 in.)
Mica undercut	0.7 mm (0.028 in.)
Carburetor heater resistance	
12 volt, 15 watt	6-12 ohms at 68° F (20° C)
12 volt, 30 watt	6-10 ohms at 68° F (20° C)
Throttle position sensor	
Internal resistance	4.0-6.0 K ohms at 68° F (20° C)
Wide-open resistance	0-5 ± 1.0 K ohms at 68° F (20° C)
Fuel pump output pressure	12 kPa (1.7 psi)
Fuel pump amperage	0.8
Fuel pump resistance	1.6-2.2 ohms at 68° F (20° C)

ELECTRICAL SYSTEM

Table 2 REPLACEMENT BULBS

Item	Voltage/wattage
Headlight (high/low beam)	12 V 60/55 W
Tail/brake light	12 V 8/27 W
Turn signal	12 V 27 W
License light	12 V 5 W
Meter light	12 V 1.7 W
Neutral indicator light	12 V 1.7 W
High beam indicator light	12 V 1.7 W
Turn signal indicator light	12 V 1.7 W

Table 3 ELECTRICAL SYSTEM TIGHTENING TORQUES

Item	N•m	ft.-lb.	in.-lb.
Alternator cover bolts	10	–	88
Alternator rotor bolt	80	59	
Pickup coil screws	7	–	62
Rectifier/regulator bracket bolts	13	–	115
Spark plug	18	13	–
Stator mounting screws	7	–	62
Starter motor mounting bolt	10	–	88
Starter relay terminals	7	–	62

CHAPTER TEN

FRONT SUSPENSION AND STEERING

This chapter describes service operations for the front wheel, fork, steering components, and tires.

Tables 1-4 are at the end of the chapter. Tire specifications are listed in **Table 1**, tire inflation pressures in **Table 2**, front suspension specifications in **Table 3**, and front suspension and steering torque specifications are in **Table 4**.

BIKE STAND

Many procedures in this chapter require the bike to be supported with a wheel off the ground. A quality motorcycle front end stand (**Figure 1**) or swing arm stand does this safely and effectively. Before purchasing or using a stand, check the manufacturer's instructions to make sure the stand will work on the motorcycle. If the bike or stand requires any adjustment or the installation of accessories, perform the required modification(s) before lifting the bike. When using a bike stand, have an assistant stand by.

An adjustable centerstand can also support the bike with a wheel off the ground. Again, check the manufacturer's instructions and perform any necessary modifications before using an adjustable centerstand on the V-Star. It may also be necessary to tie down one end of the bike.

Regardless of the method used to lift the bike, make sure it is properly supported before walking away from it.

FRONT WHEEL

Removal/Installation

CAUTION
*Take care when removing, handling and installing a wheel with a disc brake rotor. The rotor is relatively thin in order to dissipate heat and to minimize unsprung weight. Brake rotors are designed to withstand tremendous rotational loads but can be damage when subjected to side impact loads. If the rotor is knocked out of true by a side impact, a pulsation will be felt in the front brake lever when braking. The rotor is too thin to be turned and must be replaced. Protect the rotor when taking a wheel to a dealership or tire specialist. Do **not** place a wheel in a car trunk or truck bed without protecting the rotor from side impact.*

1. Support the bike securely with the front wheel off the ground.

FRONT SUSPENSION AND STEERING

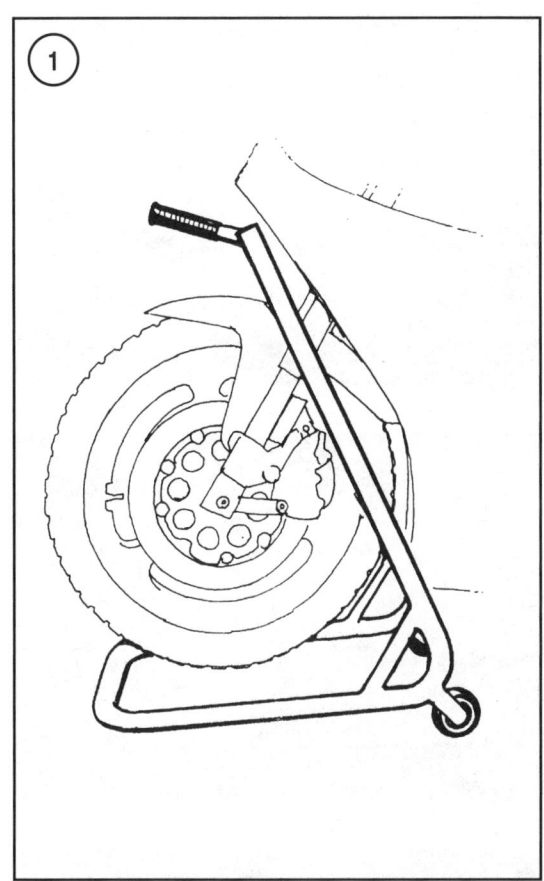

NOTE
Insert a piece of vinyl tubing or wood into the caliper in place of the brake disc. With the spacer in place, the pistons will not be forced out of the cylinders if the brake lever is inadvertently squeezed. If this does occur, the caliper will have to be disassembled to reseat the pistons and the system bled.

5. Carefully lower the front wheel and disengage the disc from the brake caliper assembly.

6. Pull the wheel forward and remove it from the fork.

CAUTION
Do not set the wheel down on the disc surface. Place the tire sidewalls on two wooden blocks.

2. Unscrew the speedometer cable (**Figure 2**) and pull the cable out of the speedometer housing.

3. Loosen the front axle clamp bolt (A, **Figure 3**) on the right fork slider.

4. Loosen the axle (B, **Figure 3**), and withdraw it from the right side.

7. Remove the speedometer housing (A, **Figure 4**) from the left side of the hub.

8. Remove the collar (**Figure 5**) from the right side of the hub.

Installation

1. Make sure the axle and the axle bearing surfaces of the fork sliders are free from burrs and nicks.
2. Lubricate the axle with lithium grease.
3. Apply a light coat of lithium grease to the lips of the seals in the hub and in the speedometer housing.
4. Install the collar (**Figure 5**) into the right side of the hub.

NOTE
Make sure the speedometer housing seats completely within the hub. If the speedometer components do not mesh properly, the wheel will not fit into the fork.

5. Apply lithium grease to the speedometer drive and driven gears.
6. Align the two slots (B, **Figure 4**) in the speedometer housing with the two drive tabs (C, **Figure 4**) on the speedometer clutch inside the front wheel hub, and then install the speedometer. Push the housing until it is completely seated in the hub.
7. Remove the spacer from the brake caliper.
8. Position the wheel into place between the fork legs and guide the brake disc between the brake pads. Make sure the speedometer gear housing engages the locating boss on the left fork slider. See **Figure 6**.
9. Insert the front axle (B, **Figure 3**) through the right fork slider, the hub, and the speedometer housing. Screw the axle into the left fork slider but do not tighten it to the final torque at this time.
10. Slowly rotate the wheel and install the speedometer cable (**Figure 2**) into the speedometer housing.
11. Tighten the front axle to the torque specification listed in **Table 4**.
12. After the wheel is completely installed, rotate it several times to make sure that it rotates freely. Apply the front brake as many times as necessary to make sure the brake pads properly engage the brake disc.
13. Tighten the front axle clamp bolt (A, **Figure 3**) to the torque specification in **Table 4**.

Inspection

1. Inspect the speedometer housing for wear or damage, and replace it if necessary.

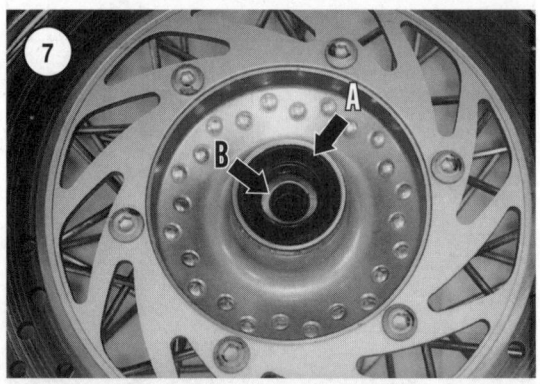

2. Inspect the seals (A, **Figure 7**) for excessive wear, hardness, cracks or other damage. If necessary, replace the seals as described below in *Front Hub*.

3. Turn each bearing inner race (B, **Figure 7**) by hand. Each bearing must turn smoothly with no trace of roughness, binding or excessive noise. Some axial play (side-to-side) is normal, but radial play (up and down) must be negligible. See **Figure 8**. If either bearing is damaged, replace them both as described in *Front Hub*.

FRONT SUSPENSION AND STEERING

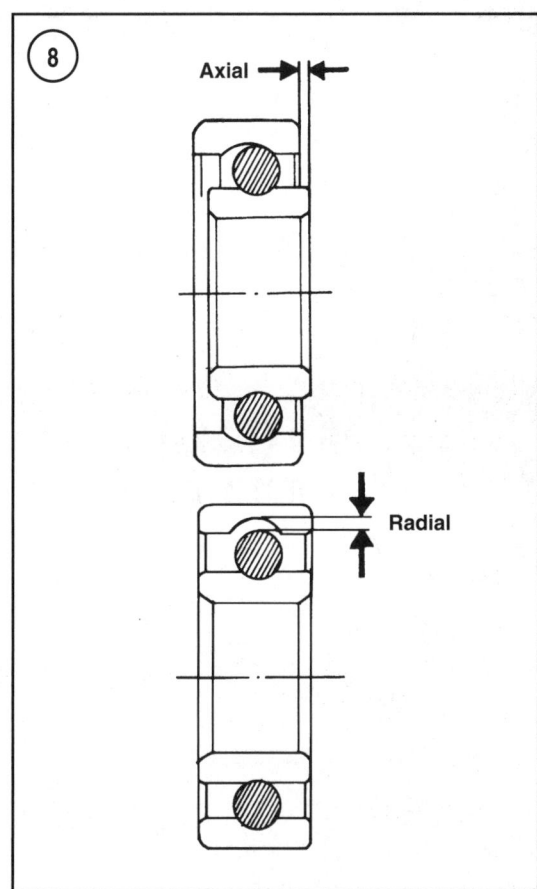

4. Remove any corrosion from the front axle with a piece of fine emery cloth.

WARNING
Do not attempt to straighten a bent axle.

5. Check axle runout by rolling the axle along a surface plate or a piece of glass. If the axle is not flat, replace it.

6. Inspect the wheel rim for dents, bending or cracks. Check the rim and rim sealing surface for scratches that are deeper than 0.5 mm (0.01 in.). If any of these conditions are present, replace the wheel.

7. Check the tightness of the brake disc bolts and inspect the brake disc as described in Chapter Twelve.

8. Inspect the rim and spoke tension as described in this chapter.

FRONT HUB

Disassembly

Refer to **Figure 9** when servicing the front hub.
1. Remove the speedometer housing (A, **Figure 4**) from the left side of the hub, and remove the collar (**Figure 5**) from the right side.
2. Pry the seals out of the hub with a wide blade screwdriver (**Figure 10**). Place a rag under the screwdriver to prevent damage to the hub or brake disc.
3. Remove the clutch retainer and the speedometer clutch seated behind the seal on the left side of the hub.
4A. Remove each wheel bearing with a standard bearing puller. Follow the manufacturer's instructions.
4B. If a bearing puller is not available, remove the bearings by performing the following:
   a. Using a long drift, tilt the distance collar away from one side of the right bearing (**Figure 11**). Then drive the right bearing out of the hub.
   b. Working around the perimeter of the bearing's inner race, tap the bearing out of the hub with a hammer.
   c. Remove the distance collar.
   d. Drive out the opposite bearing with an appropriate size socket or bearing driver.
5. Discard the bearings and seals.
6. Clean the distance collar and hub in solvent. Thoroughly dry them with compressed air.

Assembly

1. Blow any dirt or foreign matter out of the hub.
2. If installing unsealed bearings, pack the bearings with a good quality, waterproof bearing grease.
3. Apply a light coat of bearing grease to the bearing seating surfaces of the hub.
4. Place the bearing squarely against the bore opening on the right side of the hub.

CAUTION
*Install sealed bearings with the sealed side facing out of the hub. When installing a bearing, apply force along the bearing's outer race only. See **Figure 12**. Do not apply force to the inner race because it could damage the*

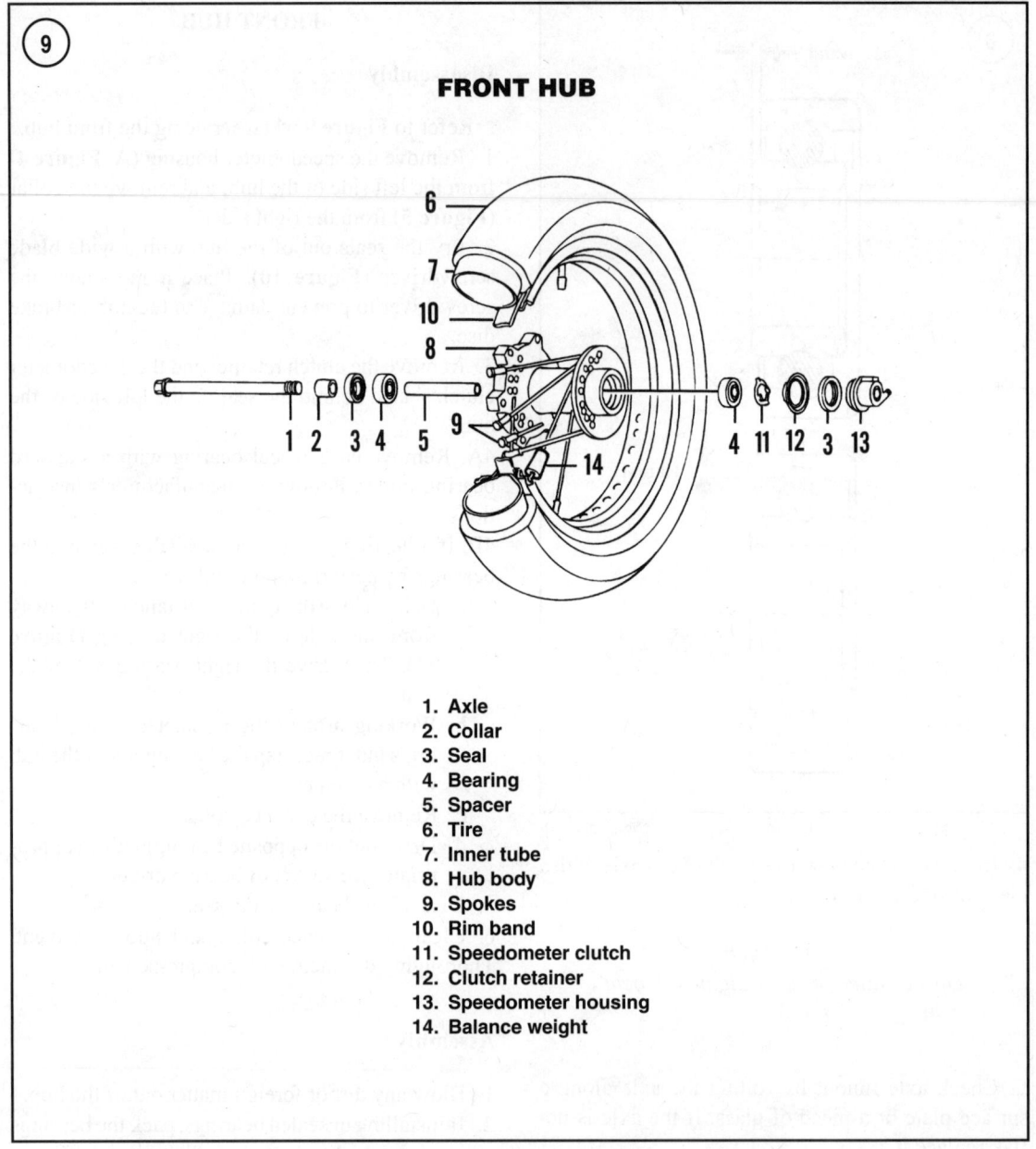

FRONT HUB

1. Axle
2. Collar
3. Seal
4. Bearing
5. Spacer
6. Tire
7. Inner tube
8. Hub body
9. Spokes
10. Rim band
11. Speedometer clutch
12. Clutch retainer
13. Speedometer housing
14. Balance weight

bearing. Make sure the bearing is completely seated in the hub bore.

5. Using a bearing driver or socket that matches the diameter of the bearing's outer race, **(Figure 13)** drive the bearing squarely into the bore until it bottoms.

6. Turn the hub over and install the distance collar. Center the collar in the right bearing's inner race.

7. Place the bearing squarely over the left side bore of the hub. Drive the bearing partially into the bore.

Stop and check the distance collar. It must still be centered within the bearing. If it is not, partially install the axle through the hub and center the distance collar within the bearing. Remove the axle and continue installing the left bearing until it is completely seated in the bore.

8. Install the speedometer clutch and clutch retainer.

9. Install a new left seal. Lubricate the seal with lithium grease, and drive the seal into the hub with a

FRONT SUSPENSION AND STEERING 285

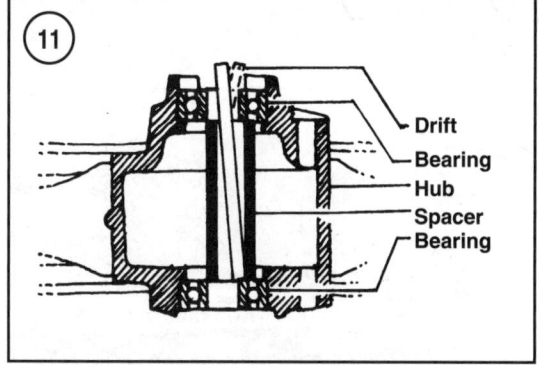

- Drift
- Bearing
- Hub
- Spacer
- Bearing

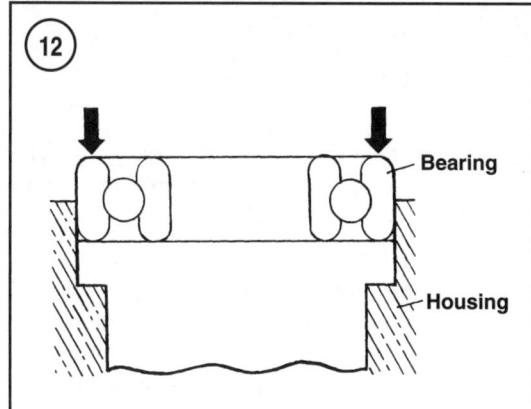

- Bearing
- Housing

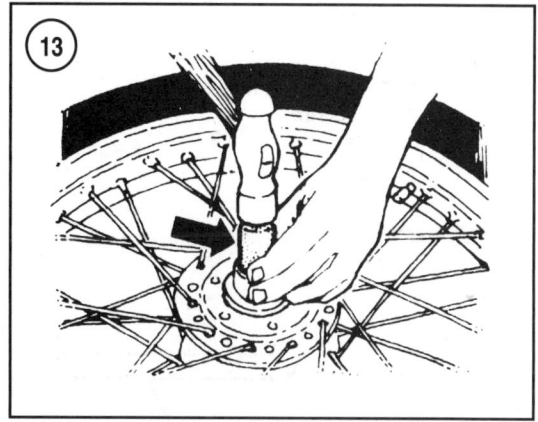

large diameter socket placed on the outer portion of the seal. Drive the seal squarely into the bore until the seal seats against the clutch retainer.

10. Install a new right seal. Lubricate the seal with lithium grease, and drive the seal into the hub with a large diameter socket placed on the outer portion of the seal. Drive the seal squarely into the bore until the seal seats against the bearing or until its outer surface is flush with the hub.

11. Install the wheel as described in this chapter.

RIM AND SPOKE SERVICE

The wheel assembly consists of a rim, spokes, nipples and hub (containing the wheel bearing, distance collars and seals.)

Loose or improperly tightened spokes can cause hub damage. Periodically inspect the wheel assembly for loose, broken or missing spokes, rim damage and runout. Wheel bearing service is described in this chapter.

Spoke Tension

Spokes loosen with use and should be checked periodically. The tuning fork method for checking spoke tightness is simple and works well. Tap each spoke with a spoke wrench or the shank of a screwdriver and listen for a tone. A tightened spoke emits a clear, ringing tone. A loose spoke, on the other hand, sounds dull or flat.

Replace bent, stripped or broken spokes as soon as they are detected. If left in place, they can destroy an expensive hub. Unscrew the nipple from the spoke. Depress the nipple into the rim far enough to free the end of the spoke, taking care not to push the nipple all the way in. Remove the damaged spoke from the hub and use it determine the proper length for the new spoke. If necessary, trim the new spoke to match the original and dress the end of the thread with a thread die.

Install the new spoke into the hub and screw on the nipple. Tighten the spoke to the torque specification in **Table 4**. Once it is tightened, the tone of the new spoke should sound similar to that of the others on the wheel. Periodically check the new

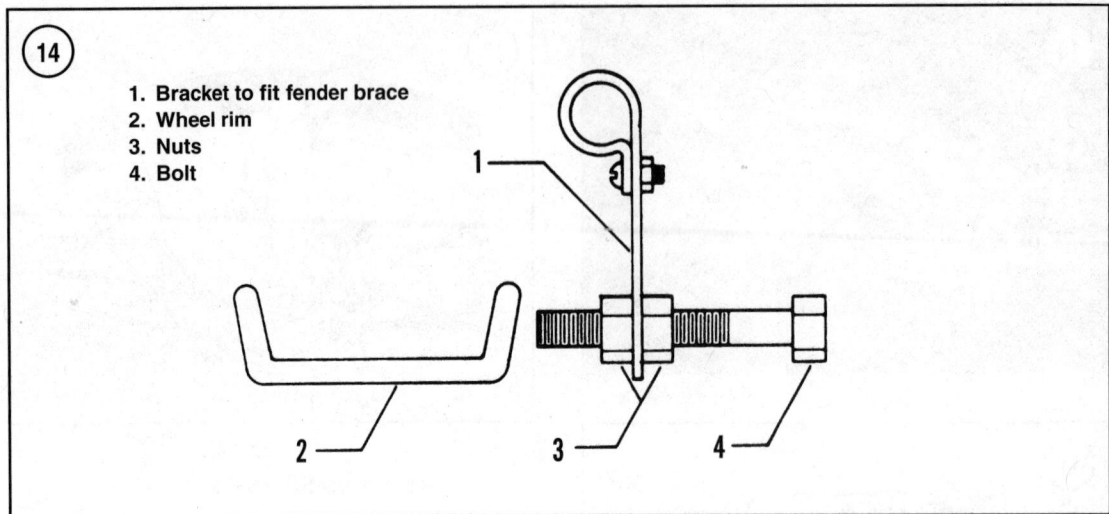

1. Bracket to fit fender brace
2. Wheel rim
3. Nuts
4. Bolt

spoke. It will stretch and must be retightened several times before it takes a final set.

Wheel Truing

When the wheels on the V-Star were new, they ran true. That is, there was no lateral (side-to-side) or radial (up-and-down) play, and the spokes were tightened to the same tension. When a wheel starts to run with a noticeable wobble, it is out of true. This wobble is usually referred to as wheel runout. Runout is normally caused by loose spokes, but it can also be caused by bent or broken spokes or a damaged rim.

Truing a wheel corrects the lateral and radial runout and brings the wheel back into specification. Truing a wheel is a standard procedure that can be learned with patience. When checking runout and truing a wheel, note the following:

a. Spoke condition. It is very difficult to true a wheel with bent or damaged spokes. Before truing a wheel, visually inspect the spokes. Since bent spokes are almost impossible to straighten, always replace any bent spokes. Tightening the nipple on a bent spoke puts excessive tension on the spoke and will eventually crack the hub or enlarge the rim hole. Replace any damaged spokes before truing the wheel.

b. Stuck nipples. The nipple threads into the bottom of the spoke and connects the spoke to the rim. Turning the nipple loosens and tightens the tension on a spoke. When truing a

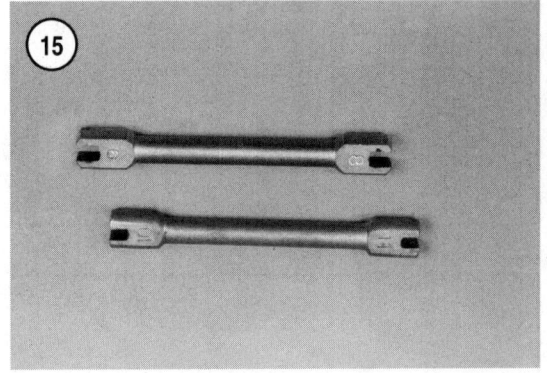

wheel, the nipples must turn freely. Unfortunately, corrosion on the nipple and spoke threads can lead to seizure.

When faced with seized threads on a spoke(s), apply a penetrating lubricant to the nipple(s) threads. Allow sufficient time for the lubricant to penetrate the threads, and then try to turn the nipple. If the nipple still does not turn, remove the tire from the rim and cut the spoke(s) with a wire cutter. Install new spokes and retrue the wheel.

c. Damaged rim. Dings and other damage to the side of a rim make it run out of true. Flat spots across the outer surface of the rim cause excessive radial runout. Trying to true a wheel with these conditions usually causes hub and rim damage due to overtightened spokes. If the damage is not excessive, accept the fact that the wheel will run with some runout. If runout is excessive, replace the rim so it does not cause a loss of control.

FRONT SUSPENSION AND STEERING

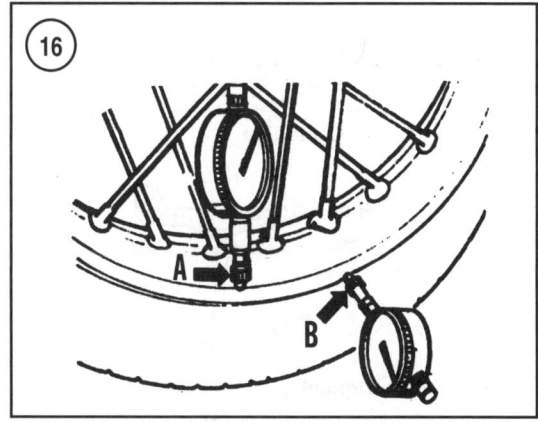

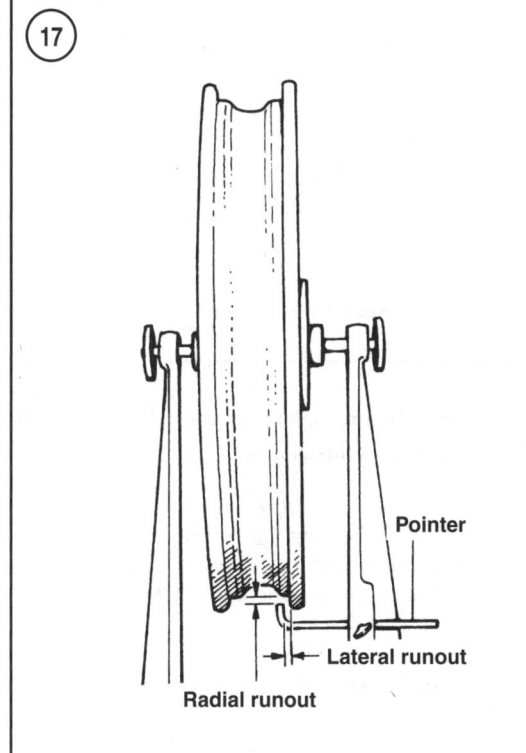

NOTE
Do not try to true the wheel to a perfect zero reading. If this is attempted, the spokes may become overtightened, which puts extreme stress on the spokes, hub and rim. This eventually causes spoke and hub damage. Adjust the spokes to an even tension while getting the wheel to run true. Take the condition of the parts into account when deciding to true a wheel.

d. Lateral runout can be checked quickly with the wheels on the bike. Simply support the wheel on the bike with the wheel off the ground. Mount a pointer (**Figure 14**) on the front fork or swing arm and turn the wheel slowly.

e. Always use the correct size spoke wrench (**Figure 15**) when checking and tightening the spoke nipples. (Motion Pro spoke wrenches are designed with square-end openings that grip all four nipple corners to prevent them from being rounded during tightening.) Turning the nipple with an adjustable wrench or an incorrect-size spoke wrench will round off the corners of the spoke nipple, making further adjustment difficult. And locking pliers will most likely crush the nipple and cause permanent damage.

f. Perform major wheel truing with the tire and tube removed from the rim and the wheel mounted on a truing stand or on the bike. When truing a wheel on the bike, place spacers on either side of the wheel to keep if from sliding along the axle.

g. Make sure the wheel bearings are in good condition.

h. When using a torque wrench to tighten the spoke nipples, torque them to the specification in **Table 4**.

1. Set the wheel in a truing stand.
2A. If there is a dial indicator available, use it to check rim runout by performing the following:
   a. Measure the radial (up and down) runout with a dial indicator positioned as shown in A, **Figure 16**. If radial runout exceeds the wear limit specified in **Table 3**, replace the rim.
   b. Measure lateral (side-to-side) runout with a dial indicator positioned as shown in B, **Figure 16**. If lateral runout exceeds the wear limit specified in **Table 3**, replace the rim.
2B. If a dial indicator is not available, check rim runout by performing the following:
   a. Position a pointer facing toward the rim as shown in **Figure 17**. Spin the wheel slowly and check the lateral runout.
   b. Adjust the position of the pointer and check the radial runout.
3. If the runout is excessive but not beyond the wear limit specified in **Table 3**, continue with Step 4.

4A. If lateral (side-to-side) runout is excessive, move the rim relative to the centerline of the wheel. See **Figure 18**. To move the rim to the left, for example, tighten the spoke(s) on the left of the rim and loosen the opposite spoke(s) on the right.

NOTE
The number of spokes to loosen and tighten depends on the amount of the runout. As a minimum, always adjust two or three spokes in the vicinity of the rim runout. If runout affects a greater area along the rim, adjust a greater number of spokes.

4B. If radial runout is excessive, the hub is not centered within the rim. Move the rim relative to the centerline of the hub. See **Figure 19**. Draw the high point of the rim toward the centerline of the hub by tightening the spokes in the area of the high side of the hub and by loosening the opposite spokes on the point side of the hub. Tighten the spokes in equal amounts to prevent distortion. If tightening two spokes at the high point one-half turn, tighten the adjacent spokes one-quarter turn. Loosen the spokes on the opposite side of the hub in equivalent amounts.

5. Rotate the wheel and check runout. Continue adjusting the spokes until runout is within the specification listed in **Table 3**. Be patient and thorough, adjusting the position of the rim a little at a time.

6. After truing the wheel, seat each spoke in the hub by tapping it with a flat nose punch and hammer. Recheck the spoke tension and wheel runout. Readjust if necessary.

7. Check and grind off any spoke that protrudes from the nipple so it will not puncture the tube.

WHEEL BALANCE

An unbalanced wheel is unsafe. Depending upon the degree of unbalance and the speed of the motorcycle, the rider may experience anything from a mild vibration to a violent shimmy that may result in loss of control.

Before balancing a wheel, thoroughly clean the wheel assembly. Make sure the wheel bearings are in good condition and properly lubricated. The wheel must rotate freely. Also check that the balance mark on the tire (**Figure 20**) is aligned with the valve stem. If not, break the tire loose from the rim

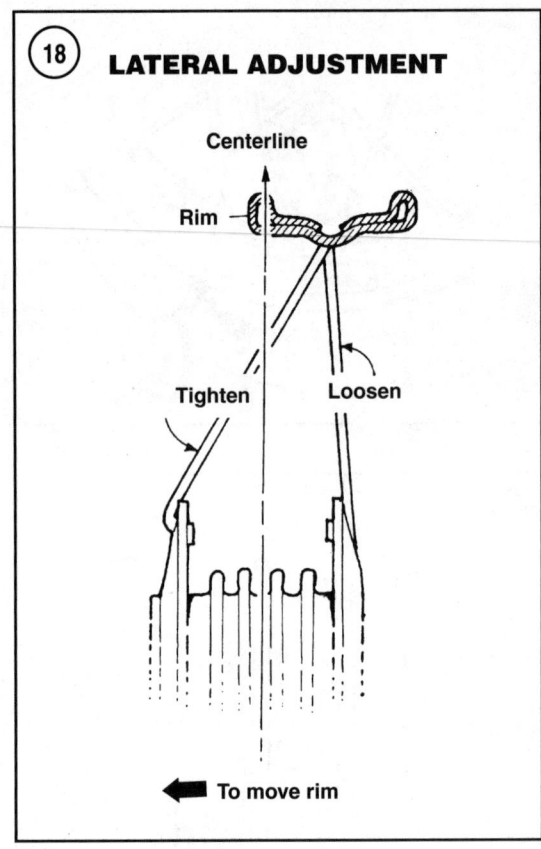

and align it before balancing the wheel. Refer to *Tire Changing* in this chapter.

NOTE
When balancing the wheels, do so with the brake disc attached. The disc rotates with the wheel and affects the balance.

1. Remove the wheel as described in this chapter or in Chapter Eleven.

2. Make sure the valve stem and the valve cap are tight.

3. Mount the wheel on a fixture such as the one shown in **Figure 21** so it can rotate freely.

4. Check the wheel runout as described in this chapter. Do not attempt to balance a wheel with excessive runout.

5. Remove any balance weights mounted on the wheel. If only checking the wheel balance, leave the weights in place.

6. Spin the wheel and let it coast to a stop. Mark the tire at the 12 o'clock position. This is the lightest point.

FRONT SUSPENSION AND STEERING

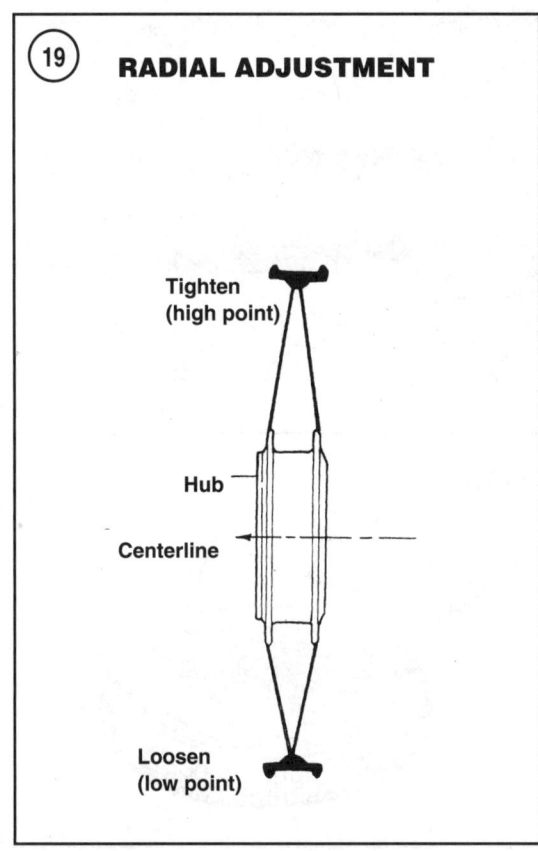

19 RADIAL ADJUSTMENT

20

21

8. Loosely attach a balance weight (or tape a test weight) at the upper or light side of the wheel.

9. Rotate the wheel one-quarter turn. Release the wheel and observe the following:

   a. If the wheel does not rotate, the correct balance weight was installed. The wheel is balanced.

   b. If the wheel rotates and the weighted portion goes up, replace the weight with the next heavier size.

   c. If the wheel rotates and the weighted portion goes down, replace the weight with the next lighter size.

   d. Repeat this step until the wheel remains at rest after being rotated one-quarter turn. Rotate the wheel another one-quarter turn, then another one-quarter turn, and finally another to see if the wheel is correctly balanced.

10. Remove the test weight, and install the correct weight. Firmly crimp the balance weight on the spoke(s) with pliers.

7. Spin the wheel several more times. If the wheel continues to stop at the same point, it is out of balance. If the wheel stops at different points each time, the wheel is balanced.

NOTE
Adhesive test weights are available from motorcycle dealers. These are adhesive-backed weights that can be cut to the desired weight and attached to the rim.

TIRE CHANGING

The wheels can easily be damaged during tire removal. Take special care with tire irons when changing a tire to avoid scratching and gouging the outer rim surface. Insert scraps of leather between the tire iron and the rim to protect the rim from damage.

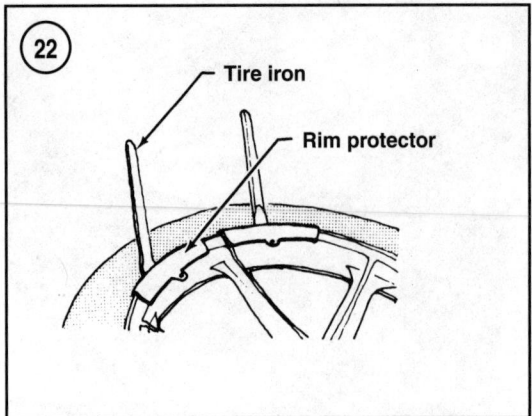

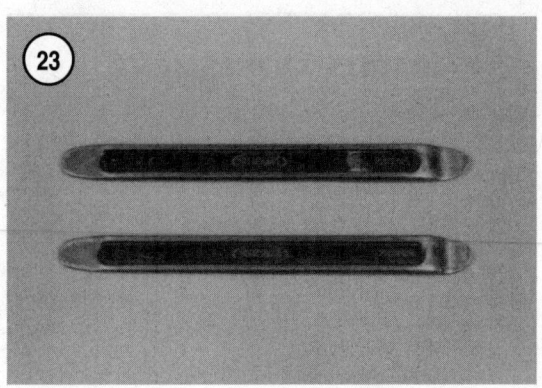

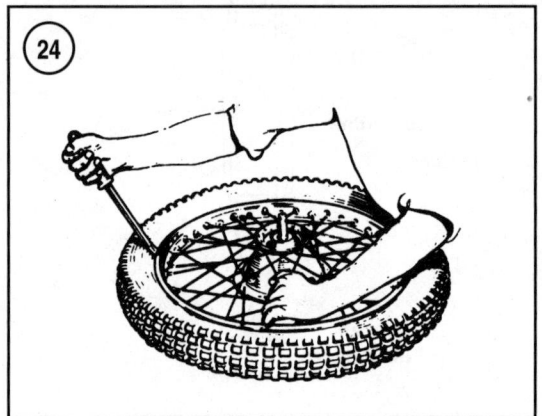

Removal

NOTE
While removing a front tire, support the wheel on two blocks of wood, so the brake disc does not contact the floor.

1. Remove the wheel as described in this chapter or in Chapter Eleven.
2. If reinstalling the tire, mark the valve stem location on the tire (**Figure 20**) so the tire can be reinstalled in the same position for easier balancing.
3. Remove the valve core to deflate the tire.
4. Press the entire bead on both sides of the tire away from the rim and into the center of the rim.
5. Lubricate both beads with soapy water.

NOTE
*Use rim protectors (**Figure 22**) between the tire irons and the rim to protect the rim from damage. Also, use only quality tire irons without sharp edges (**Figure 23**). If necessary, file the ends of the tire irons to remove rough edges.*

6. Insert the tire iron under the upper bead next to the valve stem (**Figure 24**). Press the lower bead into the center of the rim and pry the upper bead over the rim with the tire iron.
7. Insert a second tire iron next to the first to hold the bead over the rim. Then work around the tire, prying the bead over the rim with the first tool. Be careful not to pinch the inner tube with the tire irons.
8. When the upper bead is off the rim, remove the nut from the valve stem. Remove the valve from the hole in the rim and the tube from the tire.

NOTE
Step 9 is required only if it is necessary to completely remove the tire from the rim.

9. Stand the wheel upright. Force the second bead into the center of the rim. Insert the tire iron between the second bead and the side of the rim (**Figure 25**) that the first bead was pried over. Pry the second bead off the rim by working around the wheel with the tire irons.

Inspection

1. Remove and inspect the rubber rim strip. Replace the strip if it is deteriorated or broken.
2. Clean the inner and outer rim surfaces of dirt, rust, corrosion and rubber residue.
3. Inspect the valve stem hole in the rim. Remove any dirt or corrosion from the hole.
4. Inspect the rim profiles for any cracks or other damage.

FRONT SUSPENSION AND STEERING

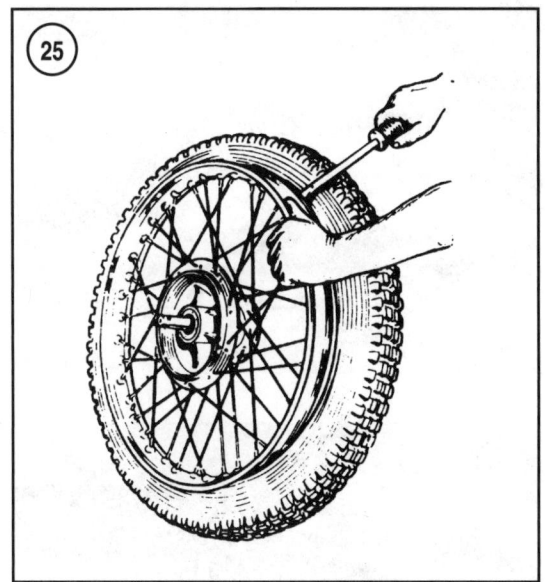

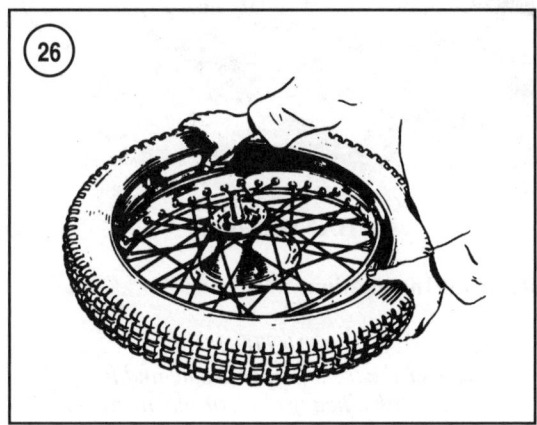

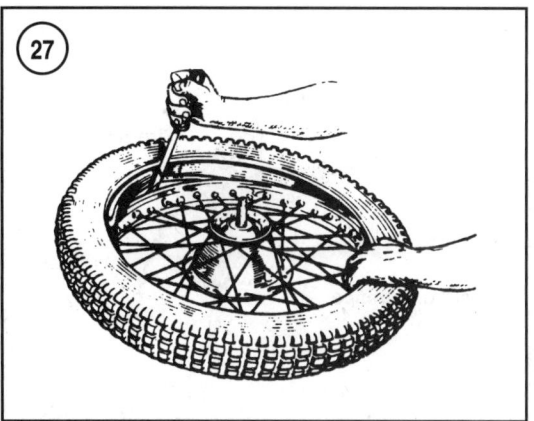

5. If intending to reuse the tube, reinstall the valve core, inflate the tube and check it for any leaks.

6. While the tube is inflated, clean it with water.

7. Carefully check it inside and outside for damage. Replace the tire if any damage is found.

8. Make sure the spoke ends do not protrude from the nipples into the center of the rim.

Installation

NOTE
Before installing the tire, place it in the sun or in a hot, closed car. The heat softens the rubber and eases installation.

1. Reinstall the rubber rim strip. Align the hole in the strip with the valve hole in the rim.
2. Liberally sprinkle the inside of the tire with talcum powder to reduce chafing between the tire and tube and to prevent tube damage.
3. Most tires have directional arrows on the sidewall that indicate the direction of rotation. Install the tire so it rotates in the indicated direction.
4. If remounting the old tire, align the valve stem indexing mark made with the valve stem hole in the rim. If installing a new tire, align the colored valve stem indexing spot with the valve stem hole. See **Figure 20**.
5. Lubricate the lower bead of the tire with soapy water, and place the tire against the rim. Using your hand, push as much of the lower bead past the upper rim surface as possible (**Figure 26**). Work around the tire in both directions. If necessary, use a tire iron and a rim protector for the last few inches of bead (**Figure 27**).
6. If necessary, rotate the tire around the rim to align the valve-stem indexing mark (**Figure 20**) with the valve stem hole.
7. Install the valve core into the valve stem in the inner tube.
8. Place the tube into the tire and insert the valve stem through the hole in the rim. Inflate the tube just enough to round it out. Too much air makes tire installation difficult; too little air increases the change of pinching the tube with the tire irons.
9. Lubricate the upper tire bead and rim with soapy water.
10. Press the upper bead into the rim opposite the valve stem. Pry the bead into the rim on both sides of this initial point by hand and work around the rim to the valve stem. If the tire pulls up on one side, ei-

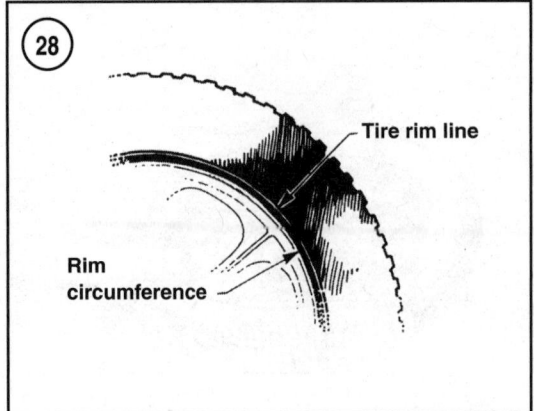

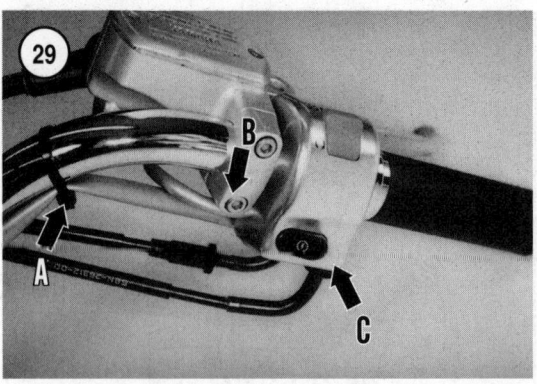

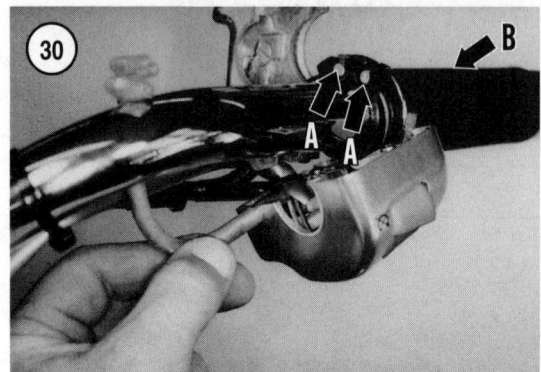

ther use a tire iron or a knee to hold the tire in place. The last few inches are usually the toughest and also the place where most tubes are pinched. Try to continue to push the tire into the rim by hand. Relubricate the bead if necessary. If the tire bead pulls out from under the rim, use both of your knees to hold the tire in place. If necessary, use a tire iron and rim protector for the last few inches.

11. Wiggle the valve stem to make sure the tube is not trapped under the bead. Set the valve squarely in its hole.

WARNING
*In the next step, seat the tire on the rim by inflating the tire approximately 10 percent above the recommended inflation pressure in **Table 2**. Do not exceed 10 percent. Never stand directly over a tire while inflating it. The tire could burst with enough force to cause severe injury.*

12. Check the bead on both sides of the tire for an even fit around the rim, and then relubricate both sides of the tire. Inflate the tube to seat the tire on the rim. Check to see that both beads are fully seated and that the tire rim lines (**Figure 28**) are the same distance from the rim all the way around the tire. If the beads do not seat, release air from the tire. Lubricate the rim and beads with soapy water and then reinflate the tube.

13. Lower the tire pressure to the recommended pressure in **Table 2**. Install the valve stem nut, tighten it against the rim, and install the valve stem cap.

14. Balance the wheel as described in this chapter.

HANDLEBAR

Removal/Installation

CAUTION
Cover the front fender, frame and fuel tank with a heavy cloth or plastic tarp to protect it from accidental brake fluid spills. Immediately wash brake fluid off any painted or plated surface. Brake fluid destroys the finish. Use soapy water and rinse the area thoroughly.

NOTE
If handlebar replacement is not required, proceed to Step 8.

1. Use jack stands or a scissor jack to securely support the motorcycle on level ground.
2. Remove all cable ties (A, **Figure 29**) securing the cables to the handlebar.
3. Remove the master cylinder clamp bolts (B, **Figure 29**) and the master cylinder from the handlebar. Secure the master cylinder to the frame with a bunjee cord. Make sure the master-cylinder reser-

FRONT SUSPENSION AND STEERING 293

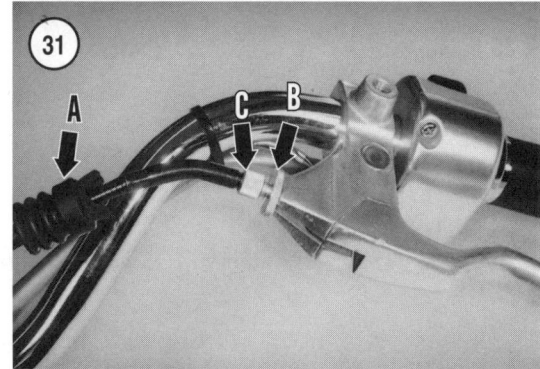

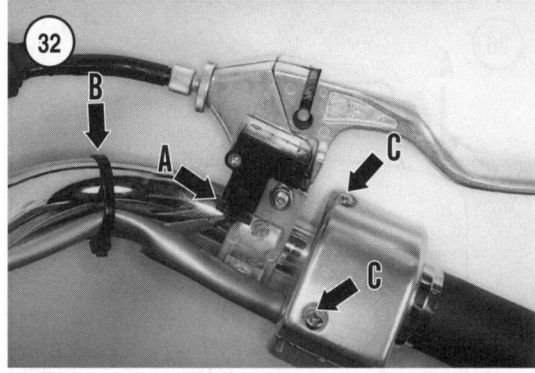

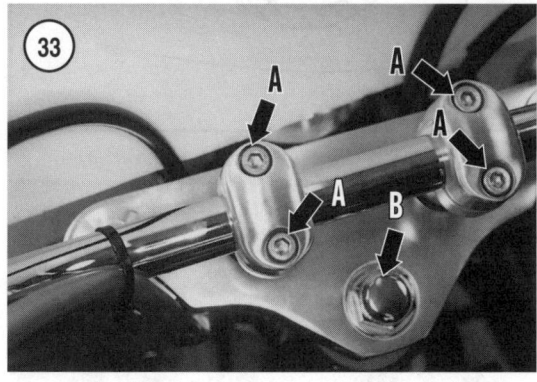

voir remains upright. Do not disconnect the hydraulic brake line.

4. Remove the two mounting screws and separate the halves of the right handlebar switch assembly (C, **Figure 29**) as described in Chapter Nine.

5. Disengage the ends (A, **Figure 30**) of both the pull and push cables from the throttle grip. Remove the throttle grip assembly (B, **Figure 30**) from the handlebar.

6. At the left side of the handlebar, slide the clutch lever boot (A, **Figure 31**) away from the adjuster.

Loosen the clutch cable locknut (B, **Figure 31**) and rotate the adjuster (C, **Figure 31**) to provide maximum slack in the cable.

7. Disconnect the cable end from the clutch hand lever.

8. Disconnect the electrical lead from the clutch switch (A, **Figure 32**).

9. If still attached, remove the cable tie (B, **Figure 32**). Remove the screws (C, **Figure 32**) and separate the halves of the left handlebar switch assembly.

10. Remove the caps, and then loosen the Allen bolts (A, **Figure 33**) on the upper handlebar holders.

11. Remove the upper handlebar holders from the handlebar, and lift the handlebar from the lower handlebar holders.

12. If necessary, replace the hand grips as follows:
   a. Unscrew the handlebar end and remove it from the handlebar.
   b. Insert a thin bladed screwdriver under the hand grip.
   c. Spray electrical contact cleaner under the hand grip and twist it quickly to break its seal and remove it.
   d. Lubricate the throttle grip assembly with lithium grease.
   e. Apply a thin layer of rubber cement to the end of the handlebar when installing a new grip.
   f. Check the hand grip after 10 minutes to make sure it is tight.

WARNING
Do not ride with loose hand grips.
Loss of control is sure to result.

13. Install the handlebar by reversing these removal steps. Note the following:
   a. Replace the handlebar if it is bent.
   b. Make sure the punch mark on the handlebar (A, **Figure 34**) aligns with the top edge of the lower handlebar holder.
   c. Install the upper handlebar holders with the punch mark on the top of each holder (B, **Figure 34**) facing forward.
   d. Tighten the handlebar holder clamp bolts to the specifications in **Table 4**. Tighten the front bolt first, and then tighten the rear bolt for each handlebar holder.
   e. Position the left handlebar switch assembly so the edge of the switch half mating surface

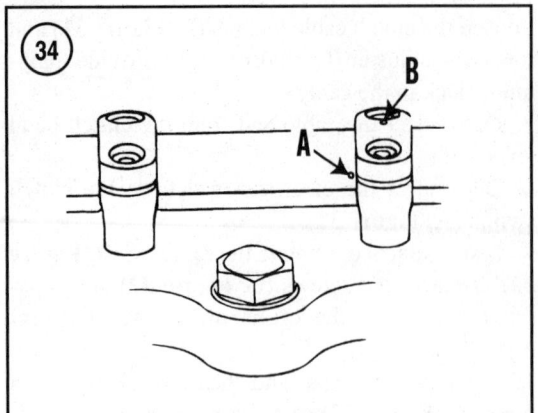

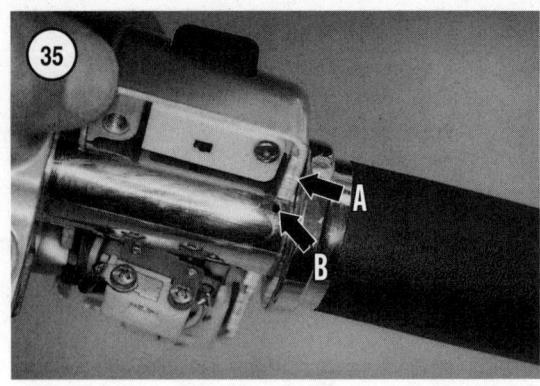

(A, **Figure 35**) aligns with the index mark (B, **Figure 35**) on the handlebar.

f. Position the clutch lever bracket (A, **Figure 36**) so the gap in the bracket clamp aligns with the indexing mark (B, **Figure 36**) on the handlebar.

g. Make sure the projection on the right handlebar switch assembly (**Figure 37**) engages the hole in the handlebar.

h. Lubricate the ends of the clutch and throttle cables with lithium grease.

i. Install the master cylinder as described in Chapter Twelve.

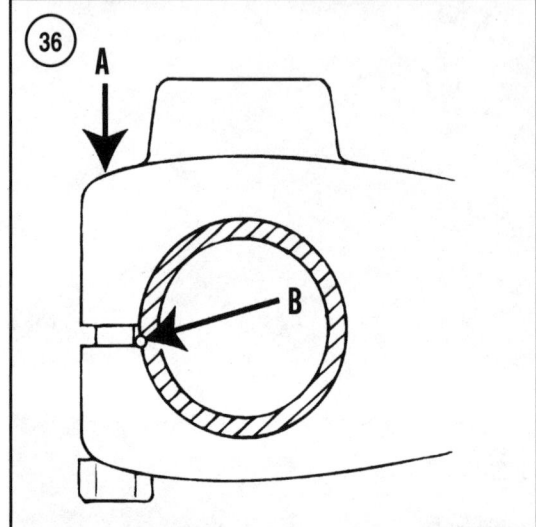

Inspection

Check the handlebar along the entire mounting area for cracks or damage. Replace a bent or damaged handlebar immediately. If the bike is involved in a crash, examine the handlebar, steering stem and front fork carefully.

STEERING HEAD

Disassembly

Refer to **Figure 38** for this procedure.

1. Support the bike securely with the front wheel off the ground.
2. Remove the handlebar as described in this chapter.
3. Remove the headlight housing as described in Chapter Nine.
4A. On V-Star Custom models, remove the turn signal assemblies as described in Chapter Nine.

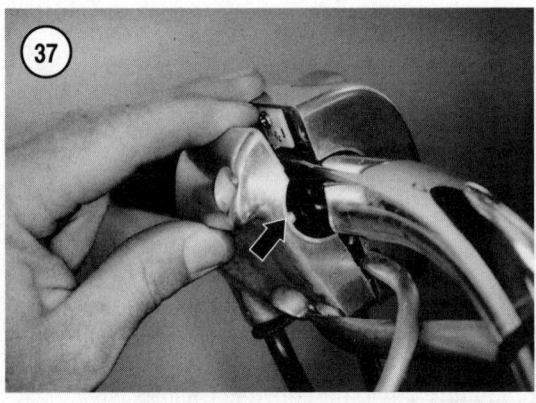

4B. On V-Star Classic models, remove the front flasher bracket and bracket cover from the lower fork bridge. See **Figure 39**.
5. Remove the headlight housing bracket(s). On V-Star Classic models, the front fork cover comes off with the headlight housing bracket.

FRONT SUSPENSION AND STEERING

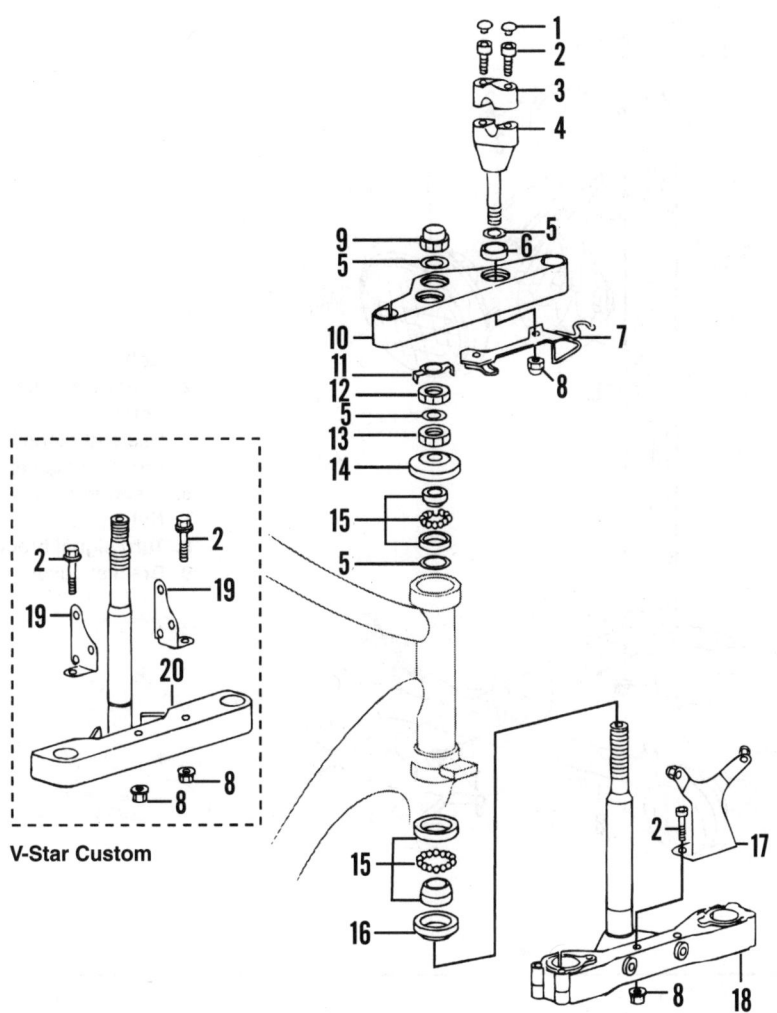

STEERING HEAD

V-Star Custom

1. Cap
2. Bolt
3. Upper handlebar holder
4. Lower handlebar holder
5. Washer
6. Damper
7. Cable holder
8. Nut
9. Steering stem head nut
10. Upper fork bridge
11. Lockwasher
12. Upper ring nut
13. Lower ring nut
14. Bearing cap
15. Bearing
16. Dust seal
17. Headlight housing bracket (V-Star Classic)
18. Steering stem (V-Star Classic)
19. Headlight housing bracket (V-Star Custom)
20. Steering stem (V-Star Custom)

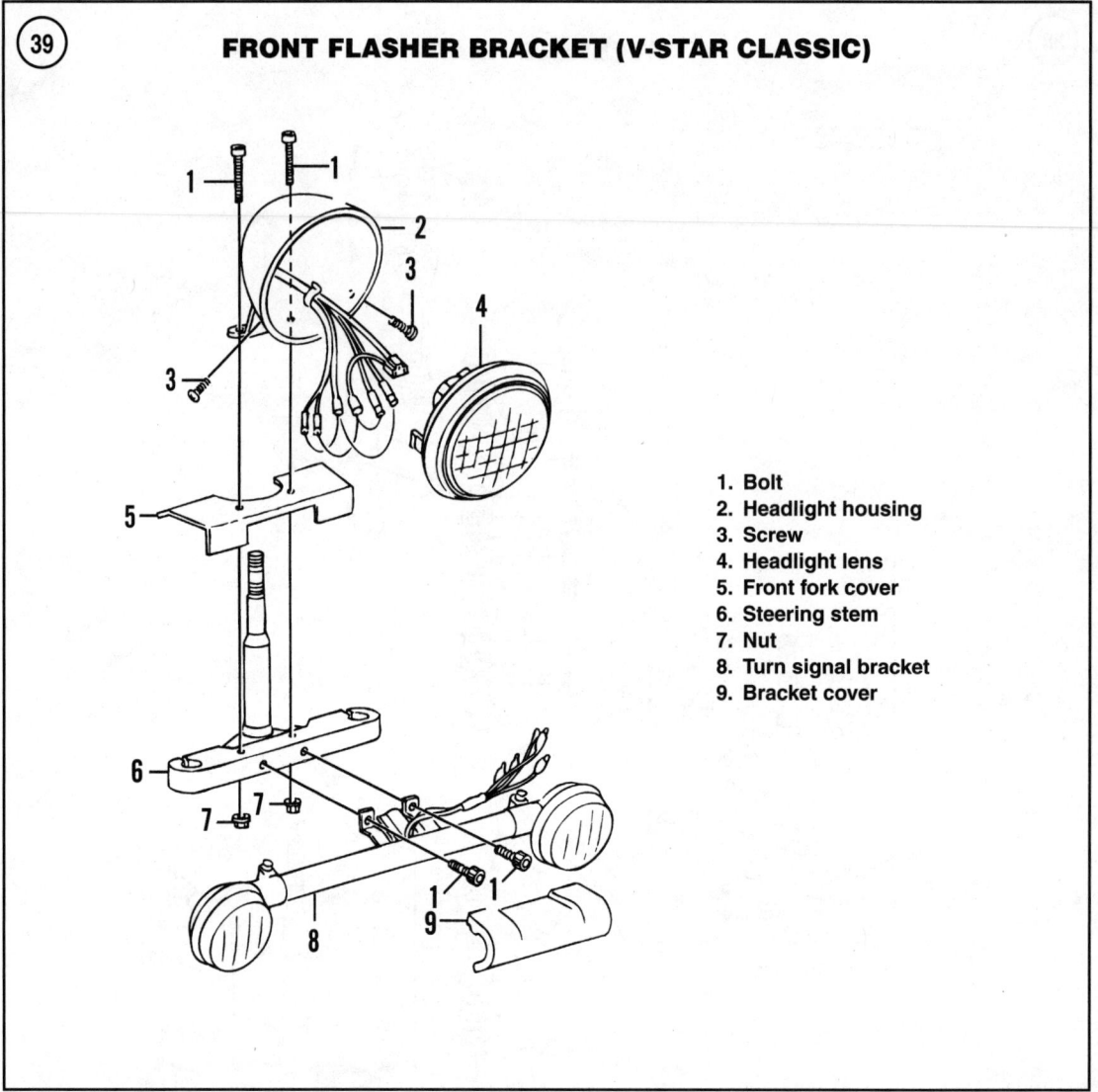

FRONT FLASHER BRACKET (V-STAR CLASSIC)

1. Bolt
2. Headlight housing
3. Screw
4. Headlight lens
5. Front fork cover
6. Steering stem
7. Nut
8. Turn signal bracket
9. Bracket cover

6. Remove the cable holder and the lower handlebar holders from the upper fork bridge. Do not loose the washer and damper that sits beneath each lower handlebar holder.

7. Remove the front wheel as described in this chapter.

8. Remove the front fork as described in this chapter.

9. Remove the steering stem nut (B, **Figure 33**) and washer. Lift the upper fork bridge off of the steering stem shaft.

10. Remove the lockwasher from the top of the steering stem.

11. Loosen the upper ring nut (**Figure 40**). Remove the ring nut and the washer.

12. Hold onto the lower end of the steering stem assembly.

13. Loosen and remove the lower ring nut.

14. Remove the bearing cap, and then remove the upper bearing from the steering head.

15. Lower the steering stem assembly down and out of the steering head.

16. Remove the washer and the lower bearing from the steering stem (**Figure 41**). The lower bearing race and the dust seal will remain on the steering stem.

FRONT SUSPENSION AND STEERING

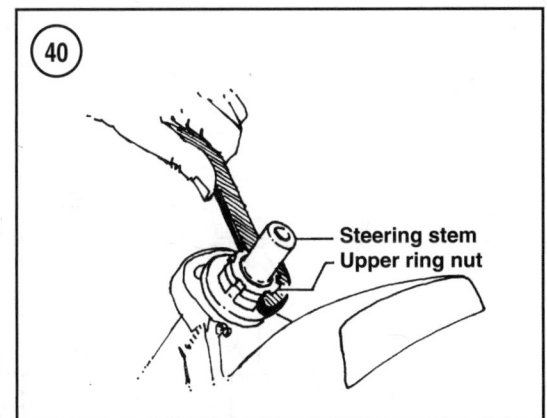

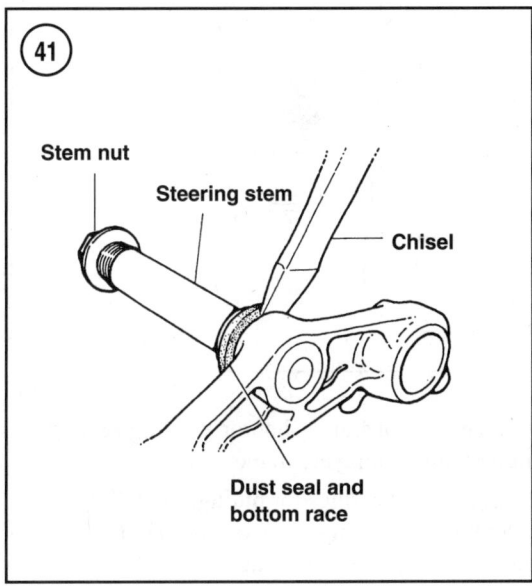

Installation

1. Apply a coat of lithium grease to both bearings.
2. Install a new dust seal and the lower bearing onto the steering stem.
3. Install the washer onto the steering stem.
4. Apply a coat of lithium grease to both bearing races in the steering head.
5. Carefully slide the steering stem up through the steering head.
6. Install the upper bearing and the bearing cap.

NOTE
For accurate steering stem installation and adjustment, use the Yamaha ring nut wrench, part no. YU-33975 (Figure 42).

7. Install the lower ring nut with the tapered side of the nut facing down. Adjust the steering head bearings by performing the following:
   a. Set a torque wrench at a right angle to the ring nut wrench (**Figure 42**).
   b. Seat the bearings within the steering head by tightening the lower ring nut to the first stage torque specification in **Table 4**.
   c. Loosen the lower ring nut one turn.
   d. Tighten the lower ring nut to the second stage torque specification in **Table 4**.

8. Install the washer and the upper ring nut with the tapered side of the nut facing down. Tighten the upper ring nut finger-tight. Check the slots on the upper ring. They should align with those on the lower ring nut. If they do not, tighten the upper ring nut until they are aligned. If necessary, hold the lower ring nut so it does not move while aligning the slots.
9. Install the lockwasher so its fingers are seated in the ring nut slots.
10. Install the upper fork bridge onto the steering stem shaft. Loosely install the washer and the steering stem head nut (B, **Figure 33**).
11. Temporarily insert both fork tubes through the upper fork bridge and tighten the lower bridge pinch bolts to hold the fork tube in position. Then tighten the steering stem head nut to the torque specification listed in **Table 4**.
12. Turn the steering stem by hand to make sure it turns freely and does not bind. If the steering stem is too tight, it may damage the bearings; if the steering stem is too loose, the steering will be unstable. Repeat Steps 7-11 if necessary.
13. Remove the fork tubes, and install them properly as described in this chapter.

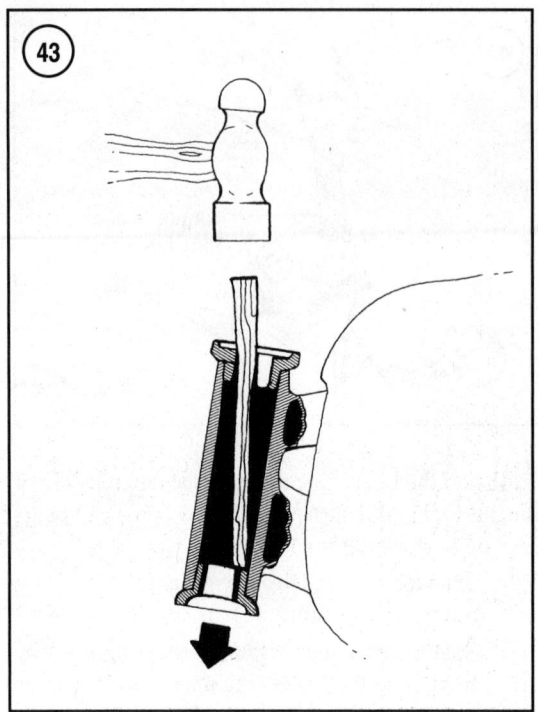

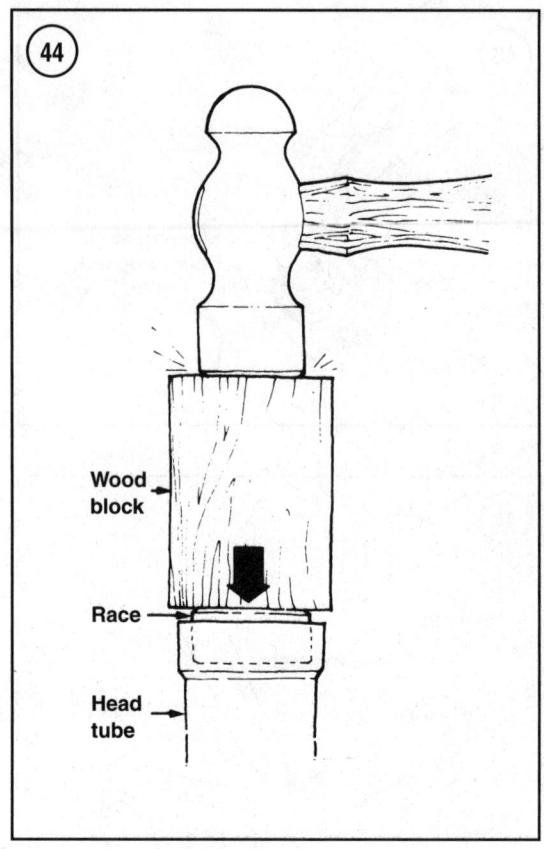

14. Install the front wheel as described in this chapter.
15. Install the cable holder and the lower handlebar holders onto the upper fork bridge. Make sure to install the damper and washer beneath each handlebar holder.
16. Install the headlight housing bracket(s). On V-Star Classic models, also install the front fork cover when installing the headlight housing bracket.
17A. On V-Star Custom models, install the turn signal assemblies as described in Chapter Nine.
17B. On V-Star Classic models, install the front flasher bracket onto the lower fork bridge and install the bracket cover.
18. Install the headlight housing as described in Chapter Nine.
19. Install the handlebar as described in this chapter.

Inspection

1. Clean the bearing races in the steering head and both bearings with solvent.
2. Check for broken welds on the frame around the steering head. If any are found, have them repaired by a competent frame shop or welding service familiar with motorcycle frame repair.
3. Check the bearings for pitting, scratches, or discoloration indicating wear or corrosion. If necessary, replace the bearings races as a set.
4. Check the upper and lower races in the steering head for pitting, galling and corrosion. If any of these conditions exist, replace them as described in this chapter.
5. Check the steering stem for cracks and check its race for damage or wear. Replace it if necessary.

Bearing Race Replacement

NOTE
Always replace the bearings and races as a set.

The headset and steering stem bearing races are pressed into place. Because they are easily bent, do not remove them unless they are worn and require replacement.

FRONT SUSPENSION AND STEERING

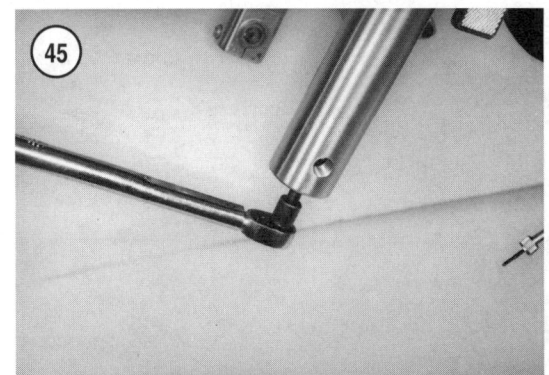

To remove a headset race, insert a hardwood stick or brass drift into the head tube and carefully tap the race out from the inside (**Figure 43**). Tap around the race in different locations to prevent it from binding in the head tube. To install a race, fit it into the end of the head tube. Tap it slowly and squarely with a block of wood (**Figure 44**).

To remove the bearing race from the steering stem, use a chisel to tap between the race and the steering stem(**Figure 41**).

FRONT FORK

Front Fork Service

If the front suspension is exhibiting poor damping, a tendency to bottom or top out, service the fork oil before concluding that major fork repairs are required. Drain the fork oil and refill as described in Chapter Three. If there is still poor front suspension operation, follow the service procedures in this section.

To simplify fork service and to prevent the mixing of parts, remove, service and install each fork leg individually.

Removal

NOTE
The photographs show the front fork removal and installation for a V-Star Classic. Unless otherwise noted, these photographs also apply to the V-Star Custom.

1. Securely support the motorcycle with a front end stand.
2. Remove the front wheel as described in this chapter.

NOTE
Insert vinyl tubing or a piece of wood between the pads in the caliper. If the brake lever is inadvertently squeezed, the pistons will not be forced out of the caliper. If it does occur, the caliper will have to be disassembled to reseat the pistons.

3. Remove the brake caliper as described in Chapter Twelve.
4. Remove the bolt securing the brake hose holder to the fork slider and move the brake hose out of the way. Suspend the brake caliper with a wire or bunjee cord.
5. Remove the front fender as described in Chapter Thirteen.

NOTE
The Allen bolt at the base of the slider has been secured with a locking agent and is often very difficult to remove because the damper rod will turn inside the slider. It sometimes can be removed with an air impact driver. If unable to loosen or remove it, remove the fork and take the fork tubes to a dealership and have the bolts removed.

6. If intending to disassemble the fork(s), loosen the Allen bolt (**Figure 45**) at the bottom of the slider and loosen the fork cap (**Figure 46**). Do not remove the bolt or the cap at this time.

7A. On V-Star Classic models, perform the following:
   a. Loosen the clamp bolt (A, **Figure 47**) on each side of the upper fork bridge.
   b. Remove the steering stem head nut (B, **Figure 47**) and washer.
   c. Cover the tank to protect it from scratches and brake fluid spills. Lift the upper fork bridge from the fork tubes, with the handlebar attached, and lay the fork bridge/handlebar assembly on the tank. See **Figure 48**.
   d. Slide the upper fork cover (**Figure 48**) from the fork tube.
   e. Remove the upper fork cover spacer (A, **Figure 49**) and its washer from the fork tube.
   f. Loosen the two clamp bolts (B, **Figure 49**) on the lower fork bridge. Lower the fork from the lower fork bridge, and remove it from the lower fork cover. See **Figure 50**. Rotating the fork tube slightly may ease removal.
   g. If necessary, remove the three mounting bolts (**Figure 51**) and remove the lower fork cover from the lower fork bridge.

7B. On V-Star Custom models, perform the following:
   a. Loosen the front flasher clamp nut.

   NOTE
   V-Star Customs use only one clamp bolt on the lower fork bridge.

   b. Loosen the upper fork bridge clamp bolt (A, **Figure 47**) and the lower fork bridge clamp bolt (B, **Figure 49**).
   c. Slide the fork tube from the upper and lower fork bridges. Rotating the fork tube slightly may ease removal.
   d. Support the turn signal bracket once the fork is removed.

8. If necessary, repeat for the opposite side.

Installation

1A. On V-Star Custom models, perform the following:
   a. Install the fork tube through the lower fork bridge, through the turn signal bracket, and up through the upper fork bridge.

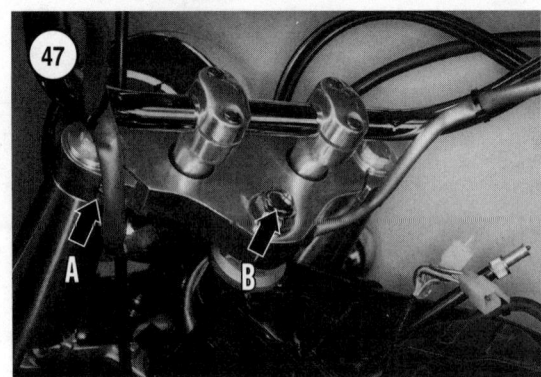

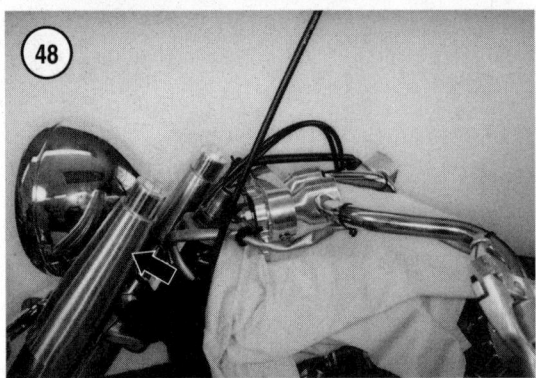

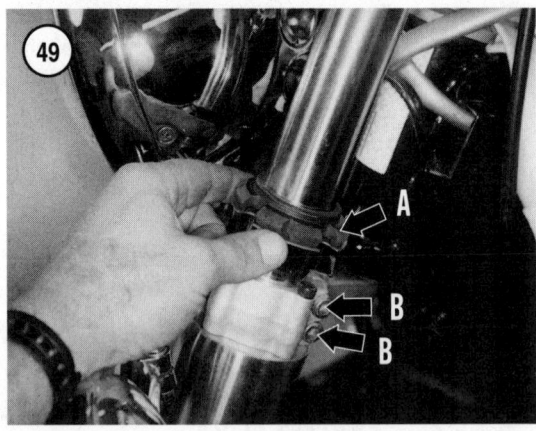

   b. Align the top edge of the fork tube with the top edge of the upper fork bridge as shown in **Figure 52**.
   c. Torque the clamp bolts on the upper and lower fork bridges to the specification in **Table 4**.
   d. Tighten the turn signal clamp bolt securely.
   e. If the front fork tubes were disassembled, torque the cap bolts (**Figure 46**) to the torque specification in **Table 4**.

FRONT SUSPENSION AND STEERING

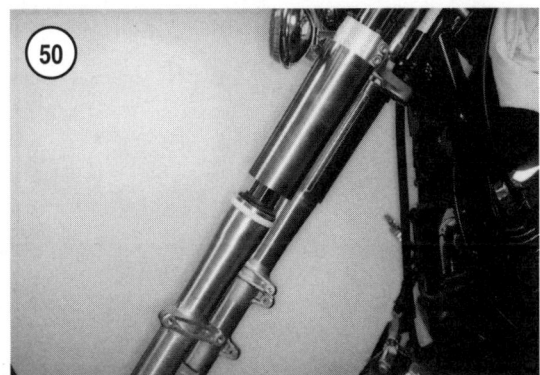

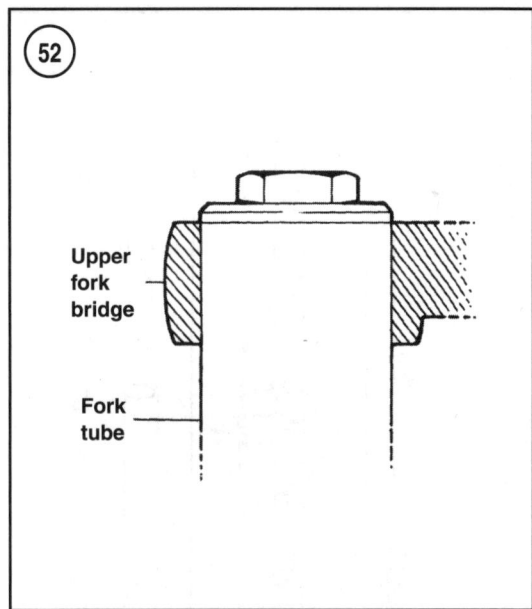

1B. On V-Star Classic models, perform the following:

a. If removed, install the lower fork cover. Secure the cover to the lower fork bridge with the three mounting bolts (**Figure 51**).

b. Install the fork tube through the lower fork cover and up through the lower fork bridge (**Figure 50**).

NOTE
In substeps c-e, the upper fork bridge is temporarily installed so the fork tubes can be properly aligned.

c. Install the upper fork bridge/handlebar assembly onto the fork tubes and the steering stem. Install the steering stem nut and washer (B, **Figure 47**). Torque the steering stem nut to the specification in **Table 4**.

d. Align the fork tubes with the top of the upper fork bridge. The top edge of the fork tubes must be flush with the top edge of the upper fork bridge as shown in **Figure 52**.

e. Tighten the clamp bolts on the lower fork bridge (B, **Figure 49**) to the torque specification in **Table 4**.

f. Remove the steering head nut and washer (B, **Figure 47**), and remove the upper fork bridge/handlebar assembly. Lay the assembly on the fuel tank.

g. Install the upper fork cover spacer (A, **Figure 49**) and its washer onto the fork tubes.

h. Slide the upper fork cover (**Figure 48**) onto the fork tubes.

i. Install the upper fork bridge/handlebar assembly onto the fork and steering stem. Install the steering stem nut and washer. Torque the steering stem nut to the specification in **Table 4**.

j. Check that the upper edge of each fork tube aligns with the upper edge of the upper fork bridge as shown in **Figure 52**. Torque each upper fork bridge clamp bolt to the specification in **Table 4**.

k. If the fork tubes were disassembled, torque the cap bolts (**Figure 46**) to the torque specification in **Table 4**.

2. Complete the installation by reversing Steps 1-5 of the removal procedure. After installing the front wheel, apply the front brake lever several times. If the brake lever feels spongy, bleed the brakes as described in Chapter Twelve.

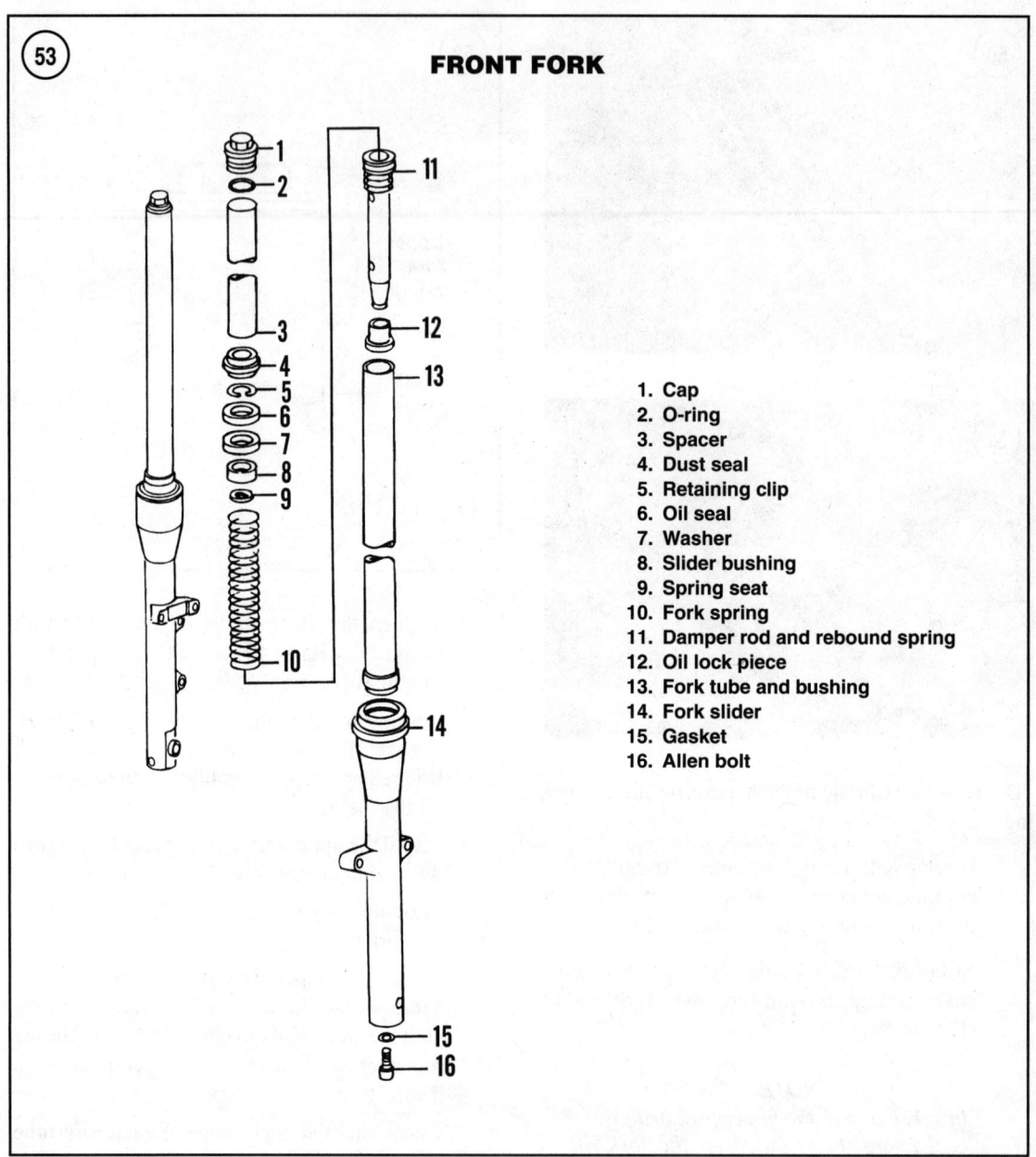

FRONT FORK

1. Cap
2. O-ring
3. Spacer
4. Dust seal
5. Retaining clip
6. Oil seal
7. Washer
8. Slider bushing
9. Spring seat
10. Fork spring
11. Damper rod and rebound spring
12. Oil lock piece
13. Fork tube and bushing
14. Fork slider
15. Gasket
16. Allen bolt

Disassembly

Refer to **Figure 53** for this procedure.

1. To prevent scratching the fork slider in the vise, make a holder out of a piece of flat metal (**Figure 54**).

CAUTION
The fork cap is under spring pressure. Remove the spring cap carefully.

2. Remove the fork cap (D, **Figure 55**) from the fork tube, and then remove the spacer (C), spring seat (B) and fork spring (A) from the fork tube.

3. Pour the fork oil into a drain pan. Pump the fork several times to expel the remaining oil.

4. Remove the Allen bolt (A, **Figure 56**) and gasket (B, **Figure 56**) from the bottom of the fork slider. If the Allen bolt was not loosened during fork removal, temporarily install the fork spring, spring

FRONT SUSPENSION AND STEERING

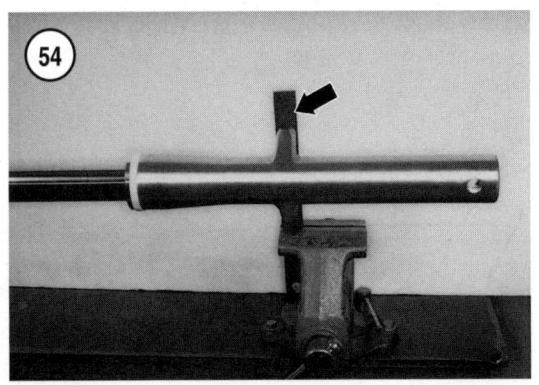

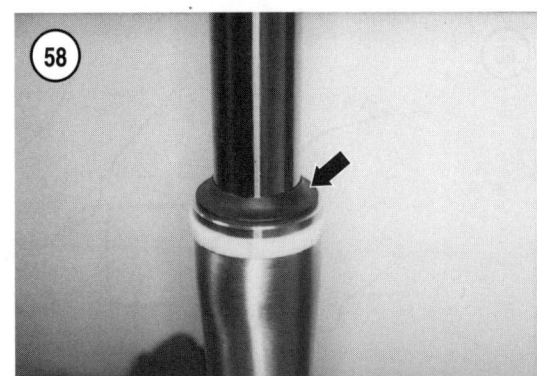

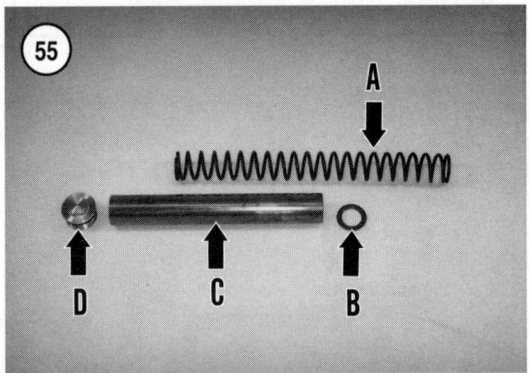

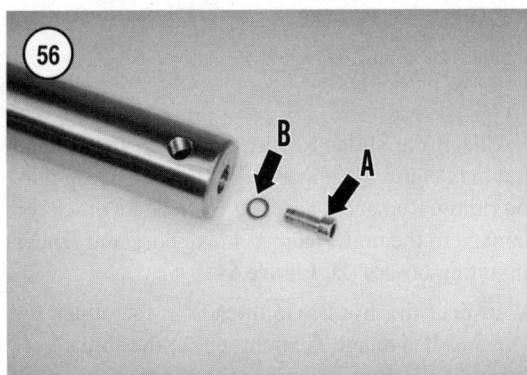

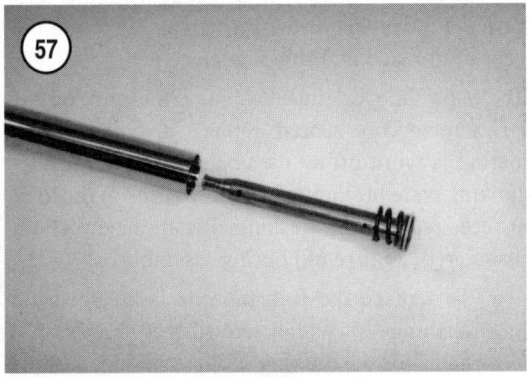

seat, spacer and fork cap to apply pressure against the damper rod and remove the Allen bolt.

5. Turn the fork tube upside down and remove the damper rod and rebound spring (**Figure 57**).
6. Pry the dust seal (**Figure 58**) from the fork slider.
7. Remove the retaining clip (**Figure 59**) from its groove inside the fork slider.
8. Hold the fork tube and slowly move the slider up and down. The slider must move smoothly. If there is any noticeable binding or roughness, check the fork tube for dents or other damage.
9. There is an interference fit between the slider and the fork tube bushings. To remove the fork tube from the slider, pull hard on the slider using quick in and out strokes (**Figure 60**). This action pulls the slider bushing (A, **Figure 61**), washer (B, **Figure 61**), and oil seal (C, **Figure 61**) from the fork slider.
10. If it is still in place, remove the oil lock piece from the slider.
11. Inspect all parts as described in this chapter.

Inspection

1. Thoroughly clean all parts in solvent and dry them with compressed air.

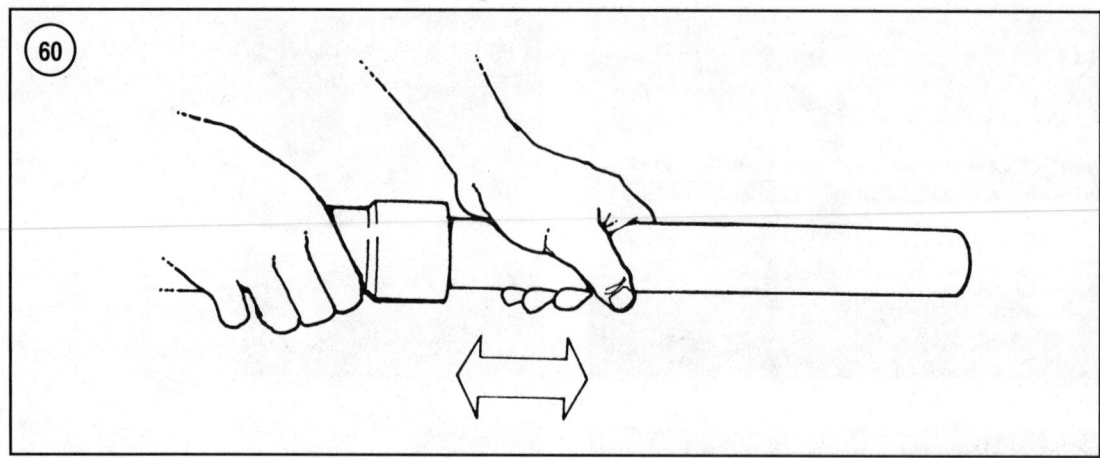

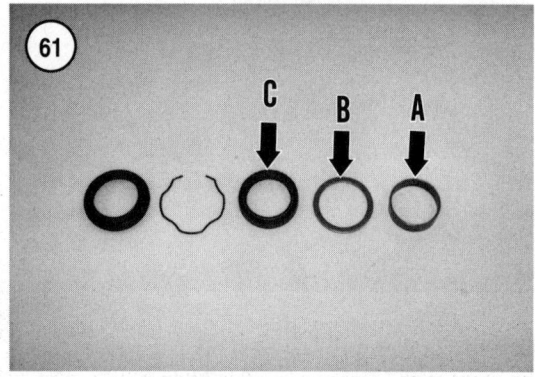

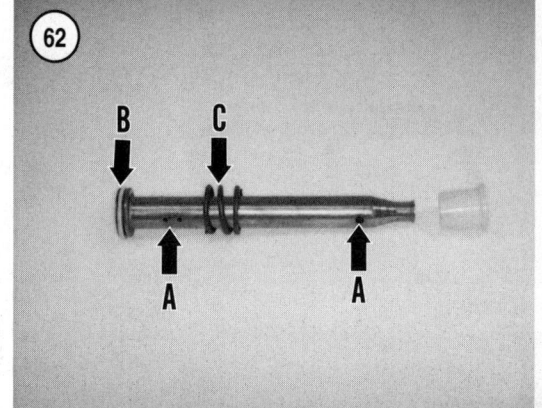

2. Blow out the oil holes (A, **Figure 62**) in the damper rod with compressed air. Clean them if necessary.

3. Check the damper rod assembly for:
   a. Bent, cracked or otherwise damaged damper rod.
   b. Excessively worn rebound spring (C, **Figure 62**).
   c. Damaged oil lock piece (**Figure 63**).
   d. Excessively worn or damaged piston ring (B, **Figure 62**).
   e. Replace any worn part.

4. Check the fork tube for straightness and for wear or scratches. If bent or excessively scratched, replace it.

5. Check the fork tube for chrome flaking or creasing. This condition damages the oil seal. Replace the fork tube if necessary.

6. Check the seal area of the slider bore (A, **Figure 64**) for dents, scratches or other damage that may cause oil leakage. Replace the slider if necessary.

7. Check the slider for dents or exterior damage that may cause the upper fork tube to hang up during riding. Replace if necessary. Check for cracks or damage to the brake caliper, brake hose and fender mounting bosses (B, **Figure 64**).

8. Inspect the front axle threads in the slider for damage. If damage is slight, chase the threads. If damage is excessive, replace the slider.

9. Measure the uncompressed length of the fork spring (**Figure 65**). If the spring has sagged to the wear limit listed in **Table 3**, replace it.

10. Inspect the fork tube bushing (A, **Figure 66**). If it is scratched or scored, replace it. If the Teflon coating is worn off so the copper base material is showing on approximately three-fourths of the total surface, replace the bushing. Install a new slider bushing (B, **Figure 66**) during assembly.
   a. To replace the fork tube bushing, open the bushing slot with a screwdriver (**Figure 67**) and slide the bushing off the fork tube. Lubri-

FRONT SUSPENSION AND STEERING

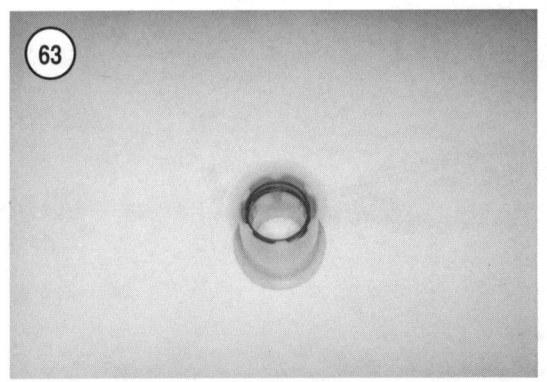

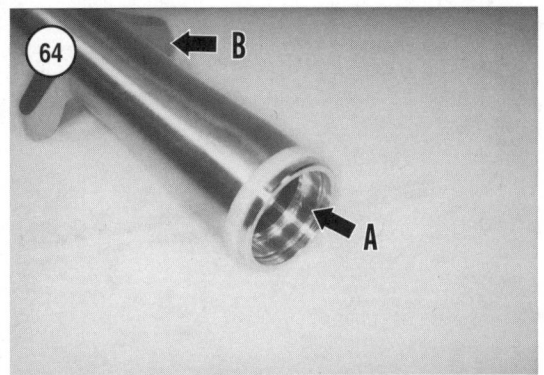

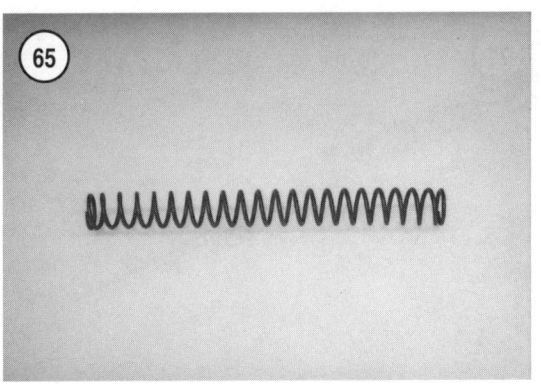

cate the new bushing with fork oil, open its slot and slide the bushing onto the fork tube groove.

11. Replace the fork cap O-ring (**Figure 68**). Lubricate the O-ring with fork oil before installation.

12. Replace any parts that are worn or damaged. Simply cleaning and reinstalling unserviceable fork components does not improve the performance of the front suspension.

Assembly

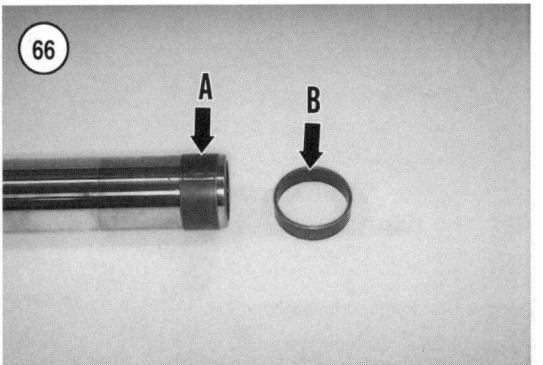

1. Coat all parts with fresh 10W fork oil before installation.

2. Slide the rebound spring onto the damper rod, and insert the damper rod into the fork tube (**Figure 57**).

3. Slide the oil lock piece (**Figure 69**) onto the end of the damper rod.

4. Install the fork tube into the slider until the tube bottoms (**Figure 70**).

5. Mount the slider in a vise (**Figure 54**).

6A. If a Yamaha damper rod holder (part No.: YM-01388) and T-handle (part No: YM-01326) are available, perform the following:
   a. Install the damper rod holder onto the T-handle. Insert the tool into the fork tube so the rod holder engages the damper rod (**Figure 71**).
   b. Install a new gasket (B, **Figure 56**) onto the Allen bolt (A, **Figure 56**).
   c. Apply Loctite 242 (blue) to the threads of the Allen bolt. Install the Allen bolt through the bottom of the slider and thread it into the oil lock piece.
   d. Hold the damper rod with the special tool (**Figure 72**), and tighten the Allen bolt to the torque specification in **Table 4**.
6B. If the Yamaha special tool is not available, perform the following:
   a. Temporarily install the fork spring, spring seat, spacer, and fork cap.
   b. Install a new gasket (B, **Figure 56**) onto the Allen bolt (B, **Figure 56**).
   c. Apply Loctite 242 (blue) to the threads of the Allen bolt. Install the Allen bolt through the bottom of the slider and thread it into the oil lock piece. Tighten the Allen bolt to the torque specification in **Table 4**.
   d. Remove the fork cap, spacer, spring seat and fork spring.
7. Slide a new slider bushing (A, **Figure 73**) and new washer (B, **Figure 73**) onto the fork tube.

> *NOTE*
> *Use a Yamaha fork seal driver (part No. YM-33963) and adapter (part No. YM-01388) to install the slider bushing and washer in the next step. If these tools are not available, use a universal seal driver (**Figure 74**) or a piece of galvanized pipe and a hammer. If both ends of the pipe are threaded, wrap one end with duct tape to prevent the threads from damaging the interior of the slider.*

8. Drive the slider bushing and washer into place (**Figure 74**) until the bushing bottoms in the slider.

> *NOTE*
> *The plastic bag installed in the next step protects the seals so they will not be torn during installation.*

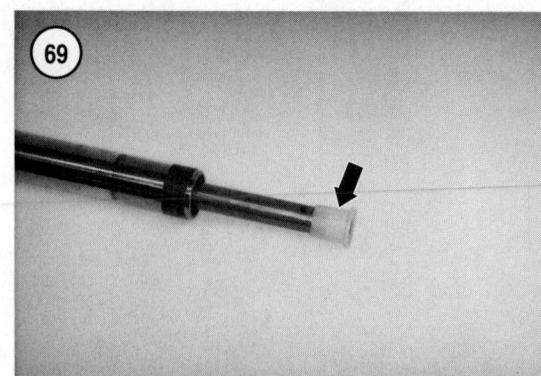

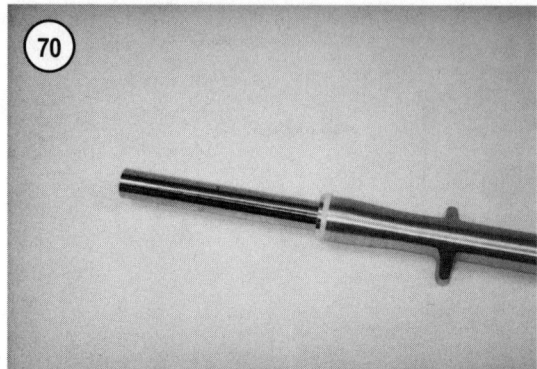

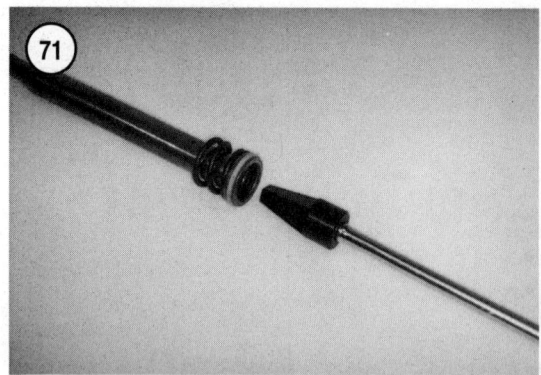

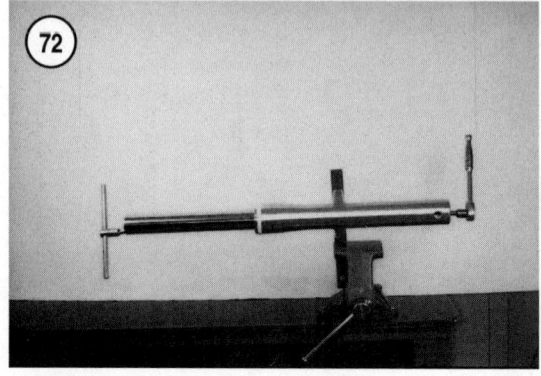

FRONT SUSPENSION AND STEERING

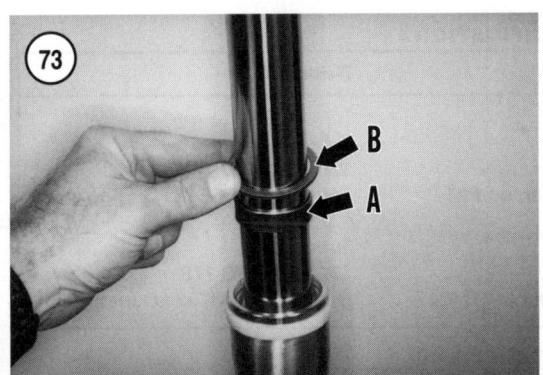

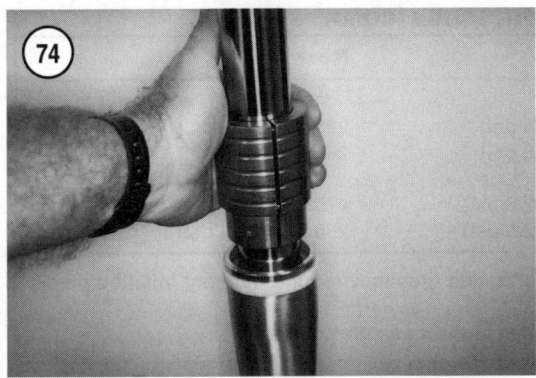

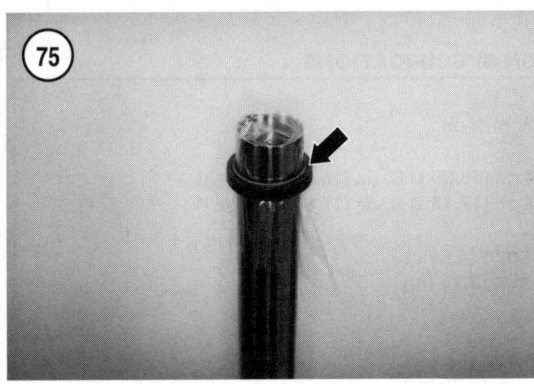

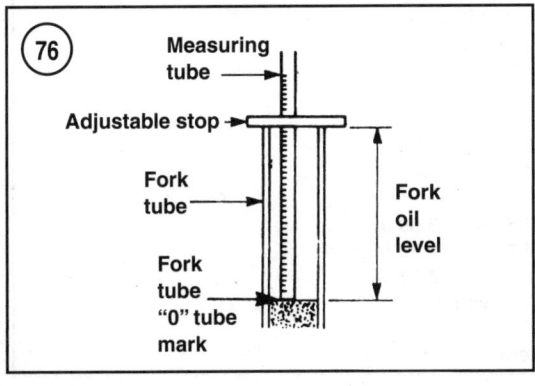

9. Place a plastic bag over the end of the fork tube and lubricate the bag with fork oil.

10. Lubricate the lips of the oil seal with lithium grease, and install the oil seal onto the fork tube (**Figure 75**). Make sure the side with the manufacturer's marks faces up, away from the fork slider.

11. Use the same tool used in Step 8 and drive the oil seal into the slider until the circlip groove in the slider can be seen above the top surface of the oil seal.

12. Install the retaining clip (**Figure 59**) over the fork tube and seat the clip into the groove in the slider. Make sure the clip completely seats in the slider groove.

13. Lubricate a new dust seal with fork oil. Slide the seal down the fork tube, and install it into the fork slider.

14. Carefully tap the dust seal (**Figure 58**) into the slider.

15. Hold the fork assembly upright and fill the fork tube with the correct quantity of 10W fork oil. Refer to **Table 3** for the specified quantity.

16. Hold the fork assembly upright, and slowly pump the fork up and down several times to distribute the fork oil.

17. Compress the fork completely and measure the fluid level after the fork oil settles. Use an oil level gauge to measure the fluid level from the top of the fork tube as shown in **Figure 76**. If necessary, add or remove oil to set the fluid level to the value specified in **Table 3**.

18. Pull the fork tube out of the slider until it is fully extended.

19. Install the fork spring (A, **Figure 55**) into the fork tube.

20. Install the spring seat (B, **Figure 55**) onto the top of the fork spring. Make sure it is seated correctly.

21. Install the spacer (C, **Figure 55**).

22. Lubricate a new O-ring (**Figure 68**) with fork oil and install it onto the fork cap.

23. Install the fork cap (D, **Figure 55**) while pushing down on the spring. Start the bolt slowly, do not cross thread it. Tighten the fork cap as tightly as possible. Once the fork is installed on the motorcycle, tighten the fork cap to the torque specified in **Table 4**.

24. Repeat for the other fork assembly.

25. Install the fork assemblies as described in this chapter.

Table 1 TIRE SPECIFICATIONS

Model	Front	Rear
XVS650		
Tire type	Tube-type	Tube-type
Size	100/90-19 57S	170/80-15M/C 77S
Manufacturer	Bridgestone L309 / Dunlop F24	Bridgestone G546 / Dunlop K555
XVS650A		
Tire type	Tube-type	Tube-type
Size	130/90-16 67S	170/80-15M/C 77S
Manufacturer	Bridgestone G703 / Dunlop D404F	Bridgestone G702 / Dunlop D404

Table 2 TIRE INFLATION PRESSURE (COLD)[1]

Model and Load[2]	Front	Rear
XVS650		
Up to 90 kg (198 lb.) load	200 kPa (29 psi)	225 kPa (32.6 psi)
90 kg (198 lb.) – maximum load	200 kPa (29 psi)	250 kPa (36.3 psi)
XVS650A		
Up to 90 kg (198 lb.) load	225 kPa (32.6 psi)	225 kPa (32.6 psi)
90 kg (198 lb.) – maximum load	225 kPa (32.6 psi)	250 kPa (36.3 psi)

1. Tire inflation pressure for original equipment tires. Aftermarket tires may require different inflation pressures; refer to aftermarket manufacturer's specifications.
2. Load equals the total weight of the cargo, rider, passenger, and accessories.

Table 3 FRONT SUSPENSION SPECIFICATIONS

Fork oil	
Viscosity	10W fork oil
Capacity per leg	
XVS650	454 cc (15.35 U.S. oz [15.98 Imp. oz.])
XV650A	507 cc (17.14 U.S. oz [17.84 Imp. oz.])
Oil level each leg	
XVS650	114 mm (4.49 in.)
XVS650A	95 mm (3.74 in.)
Front wheel travel	
XVS650	
Front	140 mm (5.51 in.)
Rear	86 mm (3.39 in.)
XV650A	
Front	140 mm (5.51 in.)
Rear	98 mm (3.86 in.)
Front fork stroke	0-140 mm (0-5.51 in.)
Fork spring	
XVS650	
Free length	295 mm (11.61 in)
Wear limit	284 mm (11.18 in.)
XVS650A	
Free length	332.5 mm (13.09 in.)
Wear limit	325.9 mm (12.83 in.)
Fork spring rate	3.5 N/mm (19.6 lb./in.)
Front wheel type	Spoke wheel

(continued)

Table 3 FRONT SUSPENSION SPECIFICATIONS (continued)

Rim size	
XVS650	19 x MT2.50
XVS650A	16 x MT3.00
Rim runout	
Radial	
New	1.0 mm (0.04 in)
Limit	2.0 mm (0.08 in.)
Lateral	
New	0.5 mm (0.02 in.)
Limit	2.0 mm (0.08 in.)

Table 4 FRONT SUSPENSION AND STEERING TIGHTENING TORQUES

Item	N•m	ft.-lb.	in.-lb.
Brake disc mounting bolt	23	17	–
Caliper bleed screw	6	–	53
Caliper mounting bolt	40	30	–
Fork bottom Allen bolt	30	22	–
Fork cap bolt	23	17	–
Front axle	59	43.5	–
Front axle clamp bolt	20	15	–
Handlebar holder clamp bolt	23	17	–
Handlebar holder mounting nut	20	15	–
Headlight housing bracket nut	32	24	–
Lower fork bridge clamp bolt			–
XVS650	30	22	–
XVS650A	23	17	–
Master cylinder clamp bolt	10	–	88
Spoke	3	–	26.5
Steering stem head nut	110	81	–
Steering stem ring nut	18	13	–
First stage	52	38	–
Second stage	18	13	–
Upper fork bridge clamp bolt	23	17	–

CHAPTER ELEVEN

REAR SUSPENSION

This chapter includes repair and replacement procedures for the rear wheel, final gear and rear suspension components. Wheel and tire service is covered in Chapter Ten.

Table 1 and **Table 2** appear at the end of this chapter. **Table 1** lists rear suspension and final gear specifications. **Table 2** lists rear suspension and final gear tightening torque specifications.

REAR WHEEL

Refer to **Figure 1** for rear wheel removal and installation.

Removal

1. Securely support the bike on jack stands or a scissor jack so the rear wheel clears the ground.

CAUTION
The rear fender on V-Star Classic models wraps low around the rear wheel, it is necessary to raise the motorcycle very high in order to remove the rear wheel with the rear fender installed. Unless a jack is available that can safely provide the necessary clearance, remove the rear fender before removing the rear wheel.

2. On V-Star Classic models, remove the rear fender as described in Chapter Thirteen.

3. Remove the cotter pin, and the rear torque arm nut (A, **Figure 2**) and washer from the bolt. Disconnect the torque arm from the bolt (**Figure 3**) on the brake panel bracket.

4. Remove the torque arm bolt from the brake panel.

5. Completely unscrew the rear brake adjusting nut (B, **Figure 2**).

6. Depress the brake pedal and remove the brake rod (C, **Figure 2**) from the pivot joint in the brake lever. Remove the pivot joint from the brake lever, and install the pivot joint as well as the adjusting nut onto the brake rod to avoid misplacing them.

7. Loosen the four final gearcase bolts (A, **Figure 4**). Remove each bolt along with its washer.

8. Loosen the axle nut (B, **Figure 4**).

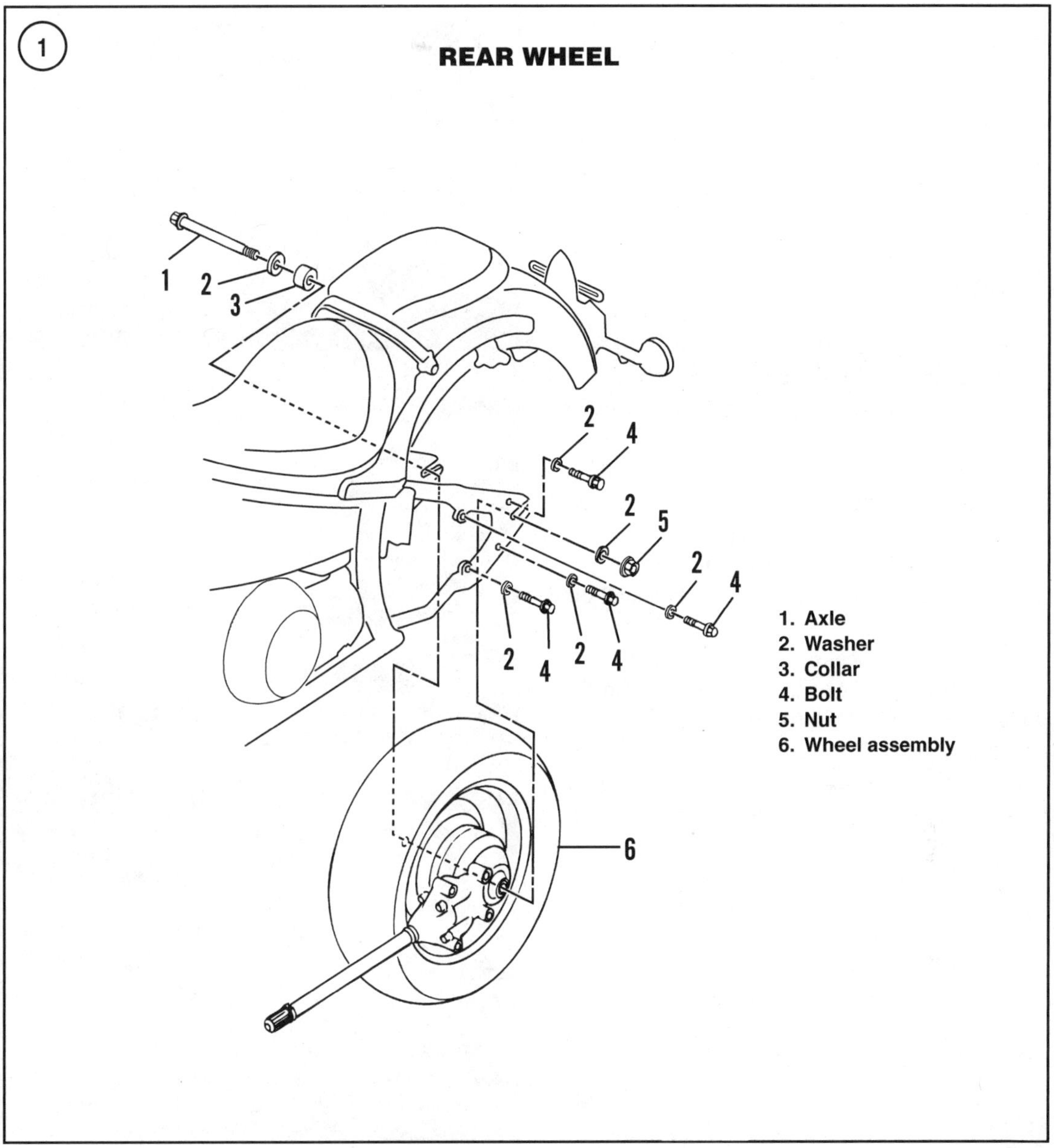

1
REAR WHEEL
1
2
3
2
4
2
5
2
4
2
4
2
4
6
1. Axle
2. Washer
3. Collar
4. Bolt
5. Nut
6. Wheel assembly

2
C
B
A

3

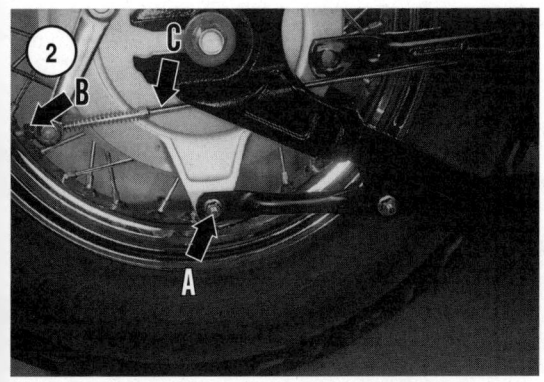

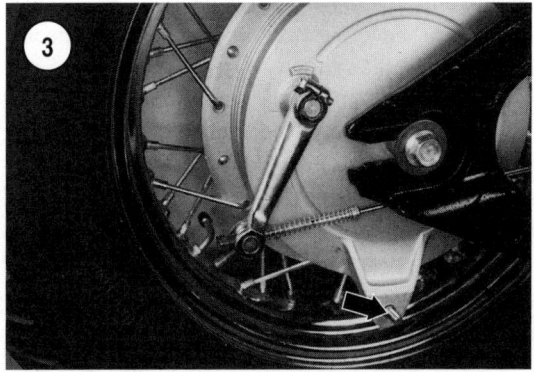

9. Pull the wheel rearward until the drive shaft disengages from the U-joint and clears the bushing in the U-joint housing (**Figure 5**).
10. Remove the axle nut and washer.
11. Remove the axle (A, **Figure 6**), its washer, and the collar (B, **Figure 6**) from the right side of the hub.

Installation

1. Lubricate the splines of the drive shaft and U-joint (**Figure 7**) with lithium grease.
2. To prevent axle seizure, coat the axle with an anti-seize compound.
3. Install a washer onto the axle and then install the collar. From the right side of the wheel, install the axle (A, **Figure 6**) through the hub.
4. Install a washer onto the axle where it emerges from the left side of the hub, and loosely install the axle nut.
5. Move the rear wheel into position in the swing arm. Align the splines of the drive shaft with the splines in the U-joint (**Figure 5**).
6. Push the wheel forward until the splines of the drive axle engage those in the U-joint, and until the axle is properly seated in the boss on each side of the swing arm.
7. Install the four final gearcase bolts (A, **Figure 4**). Install a washer with each bolt and finger-tighten the bolts at this time.
8. Install the torque arm bolt (**Figure 3**) from the inboard side of the brake panel bracket.
9. Install the torque arm onto the bolt. Install the washer and torque arm nut. Finger-tighten the nut.
10. Torque the rear axle nut to the specification in **Table 2**.
11. Torque the final gearcase bolts to the specification in **Table 2**.
12. Tighten the torque arm nut to the torque specification in **Table 2**, and install a new cotter pin.
13. Install the pivot joint into the brake lever.
14. Depress the brake pedal and insert the brake rod (C, **Figure 2**) through the pivot joint in the brake lever. Install the adjusting nut (B, **Figure 2**) onto the brake rod, and turn the nut in until the rear brake can be operated by depressing the brake pedal.
15. Spin the wheel several times to make sure it rotates freely and the rear brake works properly.

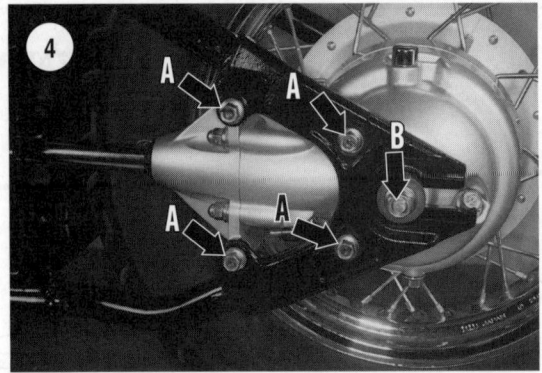

REAR SUSPENSION

REAR HUB

⑧

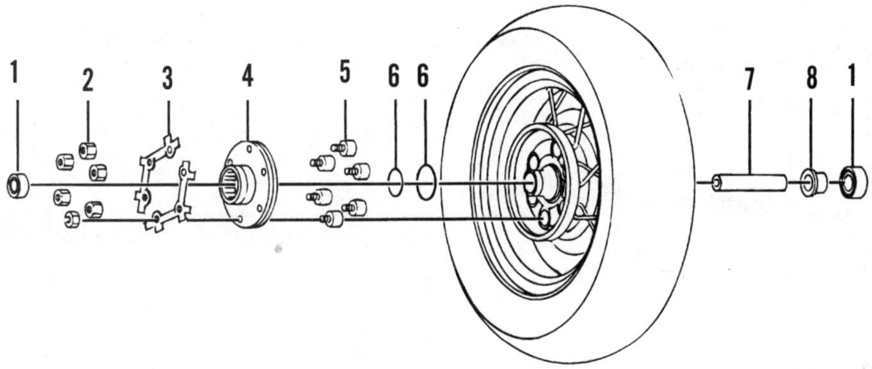

1. Bearing
2. Spacer
3. Lockplate
4. Final-gear clutch hub
5. Damper
6. O-ring
7. Distance spacer
8. Collar

16. Adjust the rear brake free play as described in Chapter Three.

Inspection

1. Remove any corrosion from the rear axle with a piece of fine emery cloth, and wipe the axle clean with solvent.

2. Check axle runout. Roll the axle along a surface plate or a piece of thick glass. If the axle is not straight, replace it. Do not attempt to straighten the axle.

3. Inspect the rim runout as described in Chapter Ten.

4. Inspect the wheel rim for dents, bending or cracks. Check the rim and rim sealing surface for scratches that are deeper than 0.5 mm (0.01 in.). If any of these conditions are present, replace the wheel.

REAR HUB

Disassembly/Assembly

Refer to **Figure 8** when servicing the rear hub.

1. Remove the rear wheel as described in this chapter.
2. If still installed, remove the axle from the hub.
3. Pull the brake panel (**Figure 9**) straight up, and remove it from the hub.

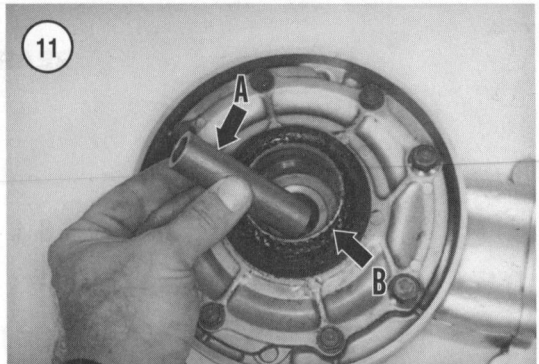

4. Pull the final gearcase assembly (**Figure 10**) straight up and remove it from the hub. Do not lose the distance spacer (A, **Figure 11**). It should come out with the final gearcase.

5. Remove and discard the O-ring (**Figure 12**) from the left side of the hub. Replace the O-ring during assembly.

6. If removing the final-gear clutch hub, perform the following:

   a. Bend the lock tab (A, **Figure 13**) away from the flat of each clutch hub nut.
   b. Loosen and remove the six clutch hub nuts.
   c. Remove and discard the two lockplates (B, **Figure 13**). Install new lockplates during assembly.
   d. Remove the clutch hub from the rear hub.
   e. Remove and discard the O-ring that sits behind the clutch hub. Install a new O-ring during assembly.
   f. Remove the wheel dampers.

7. Inspect the rear hub as described in this chapter.

8. Assembly is the reverse of removal. Note the following:

   a. Install new O-rings. Lubricate each O-ring with lithium grease before installation.
   b. Use two new lockplates when installing the final gear clutch hub.
   c. Apply Loctite 242 (blue) to the threads of each clutch hub nut, and torque the nuts to the specification in **Table 2**.
   d. Bend a locktab against a flat on each clutch-hub nut.
   e. Install the distance spacer (**Figure 14**) into the final gearcase, and then install the final gearcase assembly onto the rear hub.

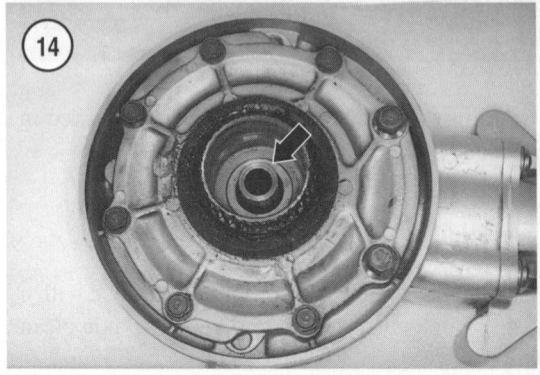

REAR SUSPENSION

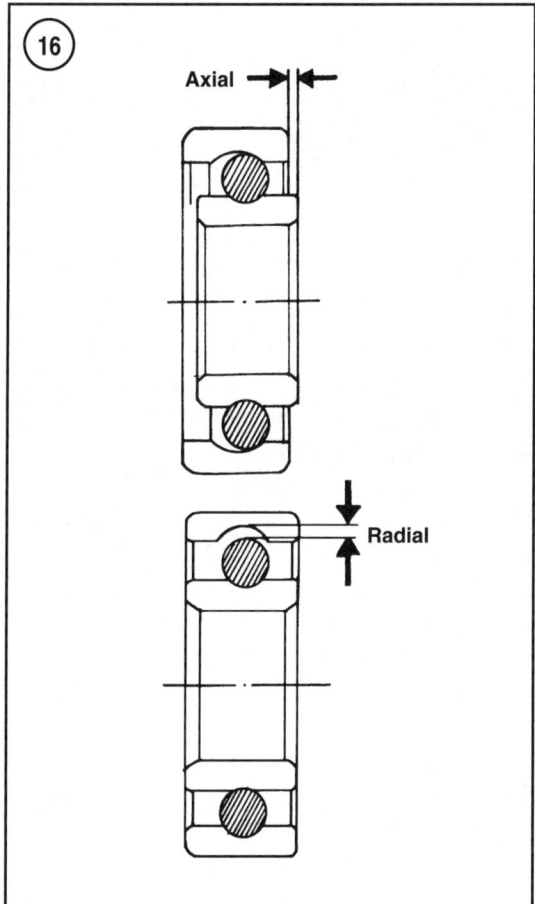

the bearing replacement procedure described in this chapter.

2. Check the bearing seal for damage that might allow dirt to enter. If any seal is damaged, replace both bearings as a set.

3. Inspect the wheel dampers for cracks, wear or deterioration. Replace the dampers as a set.

4. Inspect the splines on the final gear clutch hub. If there is damage, inspect the mating splines on the final gear assembly (B, **Figure 11**).

5. Inspect the brake drum (**Figure 17**) for scoring or other signs of damage. If there is any damage, inspect the drum as described in Chapter Twelve.

Bearing Removal

NOTE
*Use the Kowa Seiki Wheel Bearing Remover shown in **Figure 18** for the following procedure. This set is available from K & L Supply Co., in Santa Clara, CA.*

1. Select the correct size remover head and insert it into the inner race on the right bearing.

Inspection

1. Turn each bearing inner race (**Figure 15**) by hand. The bearing must turn smoothly with no trace of roughness, binding or excessive noise. Some axial play (side-to-side) is normal, but radial play (up and down) must be negligible. See **Figure 16**. If either bearing is damaged, replace them both. Follow

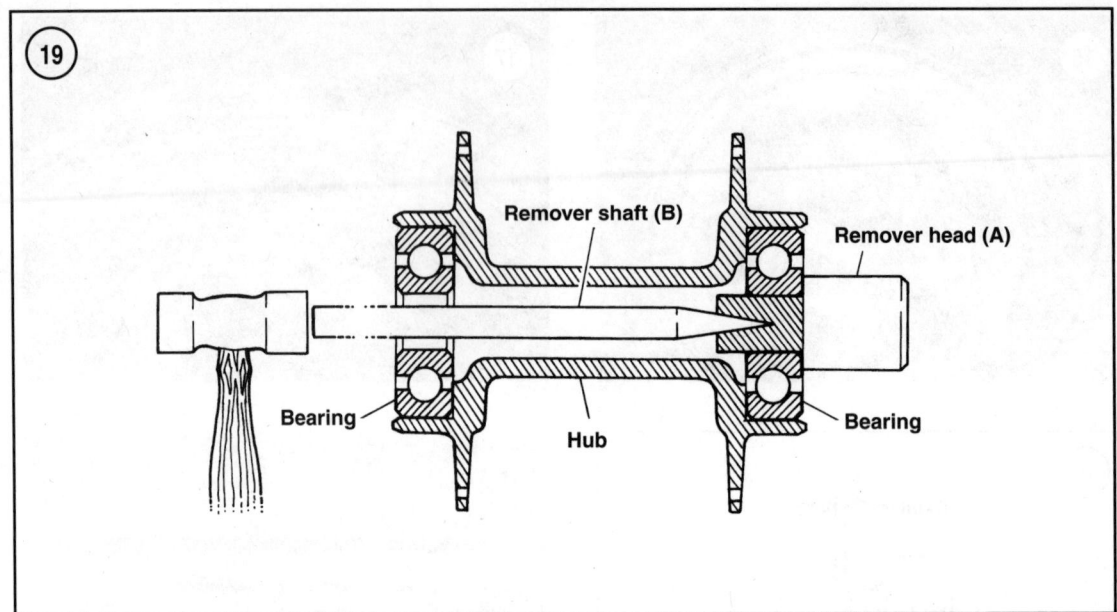

2. From the opposite side of the hub, insert the remover shaft through the hub bore and into the slot in the backside of the remover head. Position the hub with the remover head resting against a solid surface. Strike the remover shaft to force it into the slot in the remover head. This tightens the remover head against the bearing's inner race. (**Figure 19**).

> **NOTE**
> *A collar and distance spacer are installed behind the right bearing. Proceed slowly and watch for the collar. Note how the collar is oriented relative to the hub and the bearing. Reinstall the collar in the same position during assembly.*

3. Support the hub and strike the end of the remover shaft with a hammer and drive the bearing out of the hub.
4. Remove the collar and the distance spacer. Note how the collar is positioned in the hub. Reinstall it with the same orientation during assembly.
5. Repeat this procedure for the left-side bearing.

Bearing Installation

> **NOTE**
> *The left and right bearings are not identical. Make sure to install each bearing into its proper location in the hub.*

1. Place the bearings in a freezer. This eases installation.
2. Blow any dirt or foreign matter out of the hub before installing the bearing.
3. Pack the open side of each bearing with grease.
4. Position the left bearing with the manufacturer's marks facing out, and place the bearing squarely on the bore opening on the left side of the hub. Select a bearing driver or socket with an outside diameter that is slightly smaller than the outside diameter of the bearing. Drive the bearing into the bore until it bottoms (**Figure 20**).
5. Turn the hub over. Install the distance spacer and center it against the left bearing's inner race. Install the collar. Make sure the spacer and collar have the same orientation as before.
6. Place the right bearing (manufacturer's marks facing out) squarely against the bore opening. Select a bearing driver or socket with an outside diameter that is slightly smaller than the outside diameter of the bearing (**Figure 21**), and drive the bearing partially into the bore. Stop and check the distance spacer. It must still be centered within the bearing. If it is not, install the axle partially through the hub and center the spacer. Remove the axle and continue installing the bearing until it bottoms.

REAR SUSPENSION

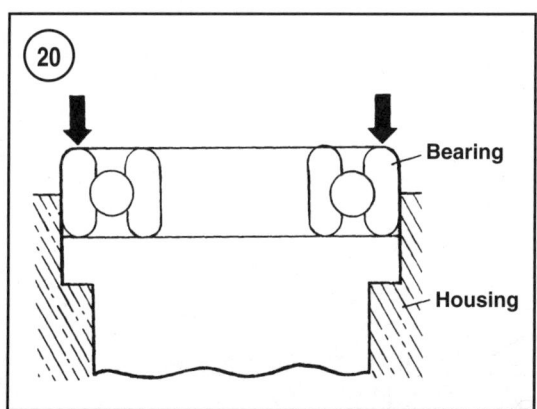

FINAL GEARCASE AND DRIVE SHAFT

Removal/Installation

1. Drain the final gear oil as described in Chapter Three.

2. Remove the rear wheel as described in this chapter.

3. Pull the final gearcase assembly (**Figure 10**) straight up and remove it from the hub. Do not lose the distance spacer (A, **Figure 11**). It should come out with the final gearcase.

4. Installation is the reverse of removal. Note the following:

   a. Install the distance spacer (**Figure 14**) into the final gearcase, and then install the final gearcase assembly onto the rear hub.

   b. Add final gear oil as described in Chapter Three.

Inspection

Inspect the exterior of the unit for signs of wear, cracks, damage or oil leaks. If there is any damage or leakage, have a dealership service the unit.

Disassembling and servicing the final gearcase requires considerable expertise and a number of special tools. If there is any problem with the final gearcase, it is best to remove the unit and have a Yamaha dealership or other qualified shop service it.

SHOCK ABSORBER

The rear shock absorber is spring controlled and hydraulically dampened. Adjust spring preload by performing the procedure described in Chapter Three.

Removal/Installation

Refer to **Figure 22** when servicing the shock absorber.

1. Securely support the bike with the rear wheel off the ground.
2. Remove the rear wheel as described in this chapter.
3. Remove the following items as described in Chapter Thirteen:
   a. Rear fender.
   b. Battery box cover.
   c. Tool box cover.
   d. Tool box.
4. Remove the lower shock absorber pivot nut (A, **Figure 23**) and washer. Remove the pivot bolt. Let the swing arm rotate around its pivot shafts and lower the swing arm to the floor.
5. Remove the upper shock absorber pivot nut (B, **Figure 23**) and washer. Remove the pivot bolt from the right side of the motorcycle, and pull the shock absorber from the frame.

> **WARNING**
> *The shock absorber contains highly compressed nitrogen gas. Do not tamper with or attempt to open the cylinder. Do not place it near an open flame or other extreme heat source. Do not weld the frame with the shock installed. Do not place the shock absorber in household trash. Have a*

318

CHAPTER ELEVEN

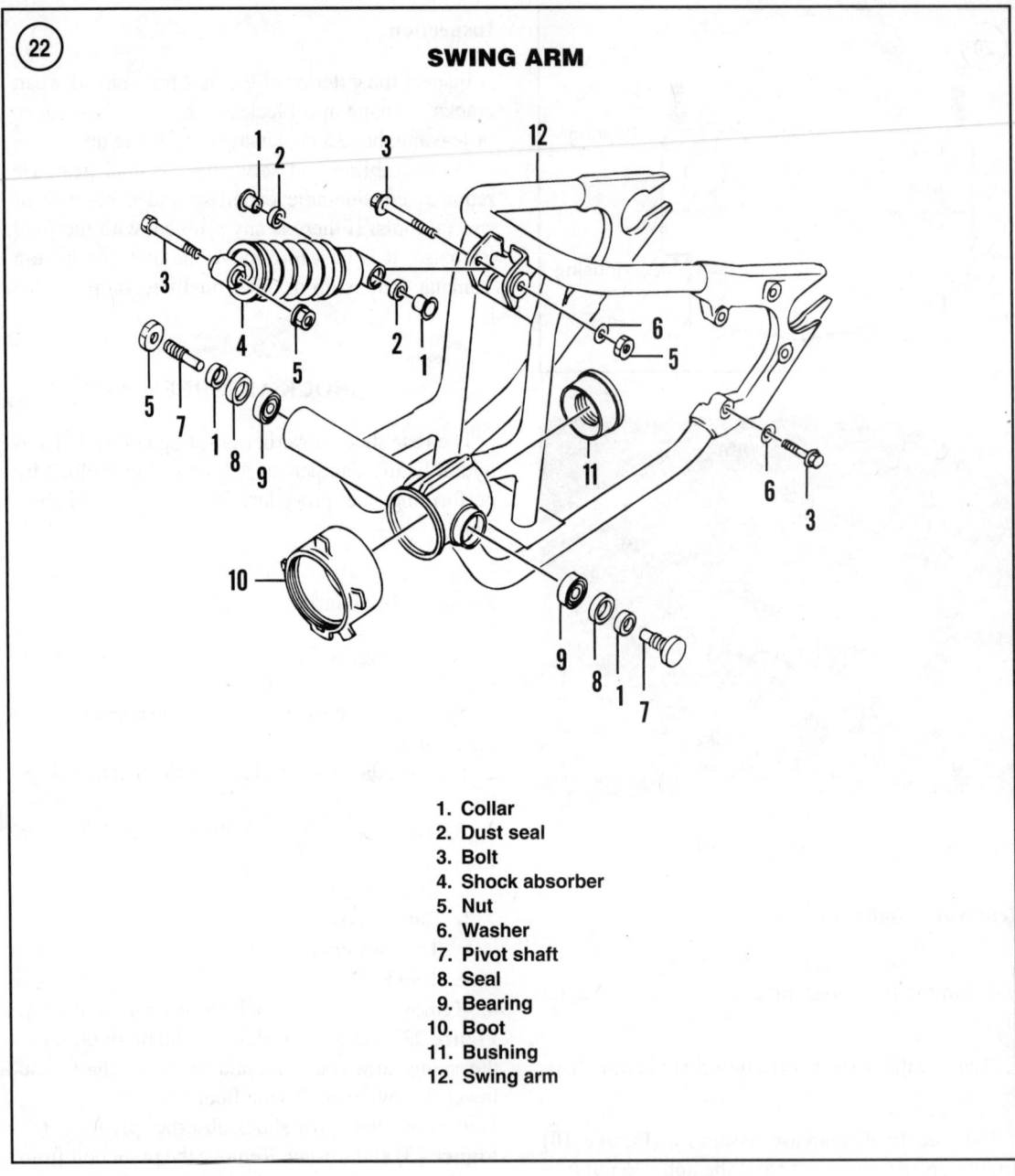

SWING ARM

1. Collar
2. Dust seal
3. Bolt
4. Shock absorber
5. Nut
6. Washer
7. Pivot shaft
8. Seal
9. Bearing
10. Boot
11. Bushing
12. Swing arm

Yamaha dealership deactivate and dispose of the unit.

6. Installation is the reverse of these removal steps. Note the following:
   a. Lubricate the upper shock pivot bolt with lithium grease.
   b. Lubricate each lower shock mount collar with lithium grease, and make sure the collar is in place on each side of the lower shock mount.
   c. Torque the shock absorber pivot nuts to the specification in **Table 2**.

Inspection

NOTE
The shock absorber cannot be disassembled and rebuilt; replace it as an assembly.

REAR SUSPENSION

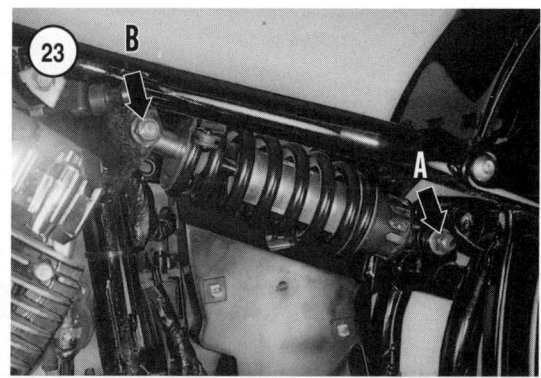

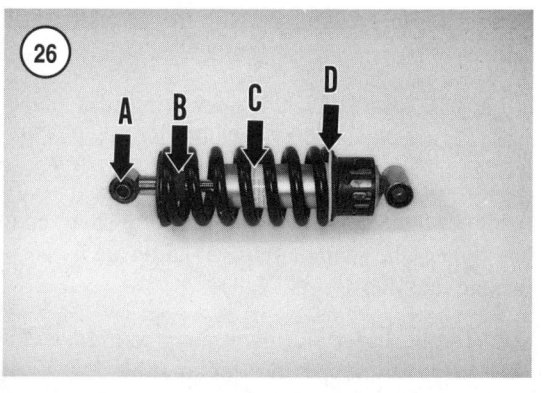

1. Remove each collar (**Figure 24**) from the shock absorber lower mount.
2. Inspect the collar for galling, cracks or other damage and replace if necessary.
3. Inspect the dust seals (**Figure 25**) on each side of the lower shock mount for damage. Replace the seals if necessary.

NOTE
A replacement bushing for the upper shock mount is not available from Yamaha. If the bushing is the only worn component on the shock, consider checking a bearing supplier for a replacement bushing.

4. Inspect the shock absorber upper mount bushing (A, **Figure 26**) for elongation, cracks or other damage. If worn or damaged, replace the shock absorber assembly.
5. Inspect the spring for cracks or damage. If damaged, replace the shock absorber assembly.
6. Check the lower spring seat (D, **Figure 26**) for cracks or looseness. If damaged, replace the shock absorber assembly.
7. Check the damper unit (C, **Figure 26**) for oil leakage. If there are any leaks, replace the shock absorber assembly.
8. Inspect the rubber stopper (B, **Figure 26**) for deterioration or damage. If damaged, replace the shock absorber assembly.

SWING ARM

Removal/Installation

Refer to **Figure 22** when servicing the swing arm.
1. Securely support the bike with the rear wheel off the ground.
2. Remove the exhaust pipes as described in Chapter Eight.
3. Remove the rider and passenger seats as described in Chapter Thirteen.
4. Remove the following items as described in Chapter Thirteen:
   a. Battery box cover.
   b. Right and left lower side covers.
   c. Tool box cover.
   d. Tool box.
5. Remove the rear wheel as described in this chapter.

6. Before removing the lower shock mount, check swing arm side play by performing the following:
   a. Grasp the swing arm at the rear and hold it in a horizontal position.
   b. Check swing arm side play by moving the swing arm from side to side. There should be no noticeable side play.
   c. Check swing arm vertical movement by moving it up and down. The swing arm should move smoothly.
   d. If the swing arm moved abnormally, replace the swing arm bearings as described in this chapter.

7. Remove the lower shock absorber pivot nut (A, **Figure 23**) and washer. Remove the pivot bolt from the right side of the motorcycle, and lower the swing arm from the shock absorber.

8. Remove the swing-arm pivot nut (**Figure 27**) from the right side of the motorcycle. Use an Allen wrench and remove the right side pivot shaft (**Figure 28**).

9. Remove the left side swing arm pivot shaft (A, **Figure 29**).

10. Pull the swing arm rearward until its housing (B, **Figure 29**) clears the U-joint, and remove the swing arm.

Installation

1. Check that a collar is in place on each side of the swing arm pivot, and position the swing arm in the frame. Also make sure the dust boot (C, **Figure 29**) is properly installed on the middle gearcase. The drain hole on the boot must face down.

2. Raise the swing arm so the housing aligns with the U-joint and push the swing arm forward until

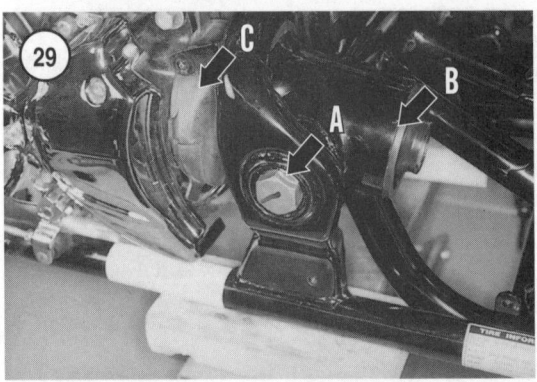

the swing arm pivot aligns with the pivots on the frame.

3. Loosely install the left side swing arm pivot shaft (**Figure 30**) and the right side pivot shaft (**Figure 31**).

4. Finger-tighten each swing arm pivot shaft, and then tighten the swing arm pivot hardware by performing the following:

   a. Torque the left side pivot shaft (A, **Figure 29**) to the torque specification in **Table 2**.

REAR SUSPENSION

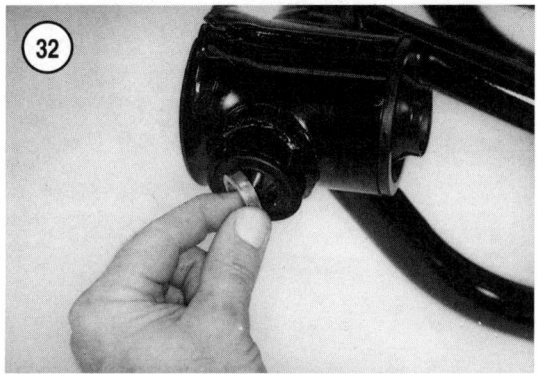

b. Torque the right side pivot shaft (**Figure 28**) to the specification in **Table 2**.
c. Install the swing arm pivot nut (**Figure 27**) onto the right side pivot shaft.
d. Mark the position of the right-side pivot shaft with chalk or a grease pencil. The pivot shaft must not turn when torquing the pivot nut.
e. Torque the swing arm pivot nut to the specification in **Table 2**.
f. Check the mark on the right-side pivot shaft. If the pivot shaft moved when the nut was torqued, loosen the nut and the pivot shaft, and repeat substeps b-e.

5. Fit the dust boot (C, **Figure 29**) over the forward lip of the U-joint housing (B, **Figure 29**).
6. Lubricate each lower shock mount collar with lithium grease, and make sure the collar is in place on each side of the lower shock mount. Raise the swing arm up until the lower shock mount sits between the mounting boss on the swing arm.
7. Install the shock absorber pivot bolt from the right side of the motorcycle, and install the pivot nut. Torque the shock absorber pivot nut to the specification in **Table 2**.
8. Reinstall the removed parts as described in the appropriate chapters.

Swing arm Inspection

1. Remove the collar (**Figure 32**) from the seal on each end of the swing arm pivot. Inspect the collar for wear or damage. Replace it if necessary.
2. Inspect each seal for wear or signs of leakage or deterioration. If either seal is worn, replace both seals.
3. Turn the inner race of each bearing by hand. It should move smoothly. If either bearing is worn, replace both bearings.
4. Inspect the dust boot (**Figure 33**) for wear or deterioration. Replace the boot if there is any wear.
5. Inspect the swing arm (**Figure 34**) for cracks, bends or other signs of damage. Replace the swing arm if damage is noted.
6. Inspect the pivot shafts (**Figure 35**) for worn or damaged threads. Replace the shaft if it is damaged.

Bearing Replacement

1. Chill the new bearings in a freezer.

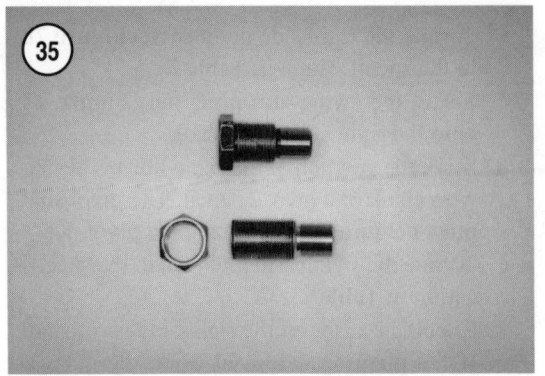

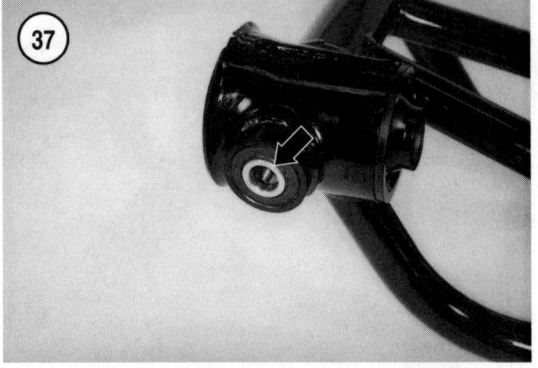

2. Remove the collar (**Figure 32**) from the seal on each end of the swing arm pivot. Inspect the collar for wear or damage. Replace it if necessary.

3. Use a wide blade screwdirver or similar tool and pry the seal (**Figure 36**) from each side of the swing arm. Discard the seals.

4. Use a vernier caliper and measure the depth from the end of the swing arm to the top edge of each bearing. The new bearings must be installed to precisely the same depth.

5. Use a blind bearing puller to remove the bearing from each end of the swing arm pivot.

6. Clean the swing arm bearing bore with solvent, and let it dry.

7. Pack the bearings and lubricate the bore with lithium grease.

CAUTION
Never reinstall a bearing that has been removed. The bearing is damaged during removal and is no longer true. If reinstalled, it will create an unsafe riding condition.

CAUTION
Do not drive the bearings too far into the swing arm or damage to the bearing will result.

8. Use a hydraulic press to install each new bearing to the depth measured in Step 4. If a press is not available, select a socket with an outside diameter that is slightly smaller than the diameter of the bearing. Use the socket to drive the bearing to the depth in Step 4. Install each bearing with the manufacturer's marks facing out.

9. Lubricate new seals with lithium grease and install them into the swing arm bore. Make sure the manufacturer's marks face out.

10. Lubricate the collars with lithium grease and install them into the seals (**Figure 37**).

Table 1 REAR SUSPENSION AND FINAL GEAR SPECIFICATIONS

Item	New	Wear limit
Rear wheel travel		
XVS650	86 mm (3.39 in.)	–
XVS650A	98 mm (3.9 in.)	–
Rear wheel rim runout		
Radial	1.0 mm (0.04 in.)	2.0 mm (0.08 in.)
Lateral	0.5 mm (0.2 in.)	2.0 mm (0.08 in.)
	(continued)	

REAR SUSPENSION

Table 1 REAR SUSPENSION AND FINAL GEAR SPECIFICATIONS (continued)

Item	New	Wear limit
Shock absorber travel		
XV650	37 mm (1.46 in.)	–
XV650A	42 mm (1.65 in.)	–
Shock spring free length		
XVS650	168.5 mm (6.63 in.)	165 mm (6.5 in.)
XVS650A	179.5 mm (7.07 in.)	165 mm (6.5 in.)
Spring rate (K1)		
XVS650	186 N/mm (1041.6 lb./in.)	–
XVS650A	137 N/mm (6.52 lb./in.)	–
Shock stroke (K1)		
XVS650	0-37 mm (0-1.46 in.)	–
XVS650A	0-42 mm (0-1.65 in.)	–
Swing arm free play		
End	–	1.0 mm (0.04 in.)
Side	–	1.0 mm (0.04 in.)
Final gear backlash	0.1-0.2 mm (0.004-0.008 in.)	–

Table 2 REAR SUSPENSION AND FINAL GEAR TIGHTENING TORQUES

Item	N•m	ft.-lb.	in.-lb.
Brake lever pinch bolt	10	–	88
Drive shaft housing nut			
(drive-shaft housing cover			
to final gear case nut)	42	31	–
Final-drive clutch hub nut	62	46	–
Final-drive-pinion bearing retainer			
(left-hand thread)	115	85	–
Final gear bearing housing bolt			
(8 and 10 mm)	23	17	–
Final gear oil drain bolt	23	17	–
Final gear oil filler bolt	23	17	–
Final gearcase housing cover	18	13	–
Final gearcase mounting bolt	70	52	–
Rear axle nut	92	68	–
Shock absorber pivot nut	62	46	–
Swing arm pivot nut	100	74	–
Swing arm pivot shaft			
Left side	100	74	–
Right side	7	–	62
Torque arm nut	20	15	–

CHAPTER TWELVE

BRAKES

All models are equipped with a front disc brake and a rear drum brake. This chapter describes repair and replacement procedures for all brake components.

Refer to **Table 1** for brake specifications; **Table 2** for brake torque specifications. **Table 1** and **Table 2** are at the end of the chapter.

DISC BRAKES

The disc brake unit is actuated by hydraulic fluid controlled by the front brake hand lever. As the front brake pads wear, the caliper pistons move outward to compensate for the pad wear, and the brake fluid level in the master cylinder reservoir will drop as the pads wear.

When working on a hydraulic brake system, the work area and all tools must be absolutely clean. Tiny particles of debris can damage caliper or master cylinder components. Also, do not use sharp tools inside a caliper or on a caliper piston. If there is any doubt about completing major brake service correctly and safely, have a Yamaha dealership or a brake specialist perform the service.

NOTE
Never add used brake fluid to oil that is intended for recycling. Most oil recyclers will not accept used oil if other fluids (fork oil, brake fluid, etc.) have been combined with it.

Consider the following when servicing the front brake system:

1. Disc brake components rarely require disassembly, so do not disassemble them unless necessary.

2. When adding brake fluid, only use DOT 4 brake fluid from a sealed container. Other types may cause brake failure.

BRAKES

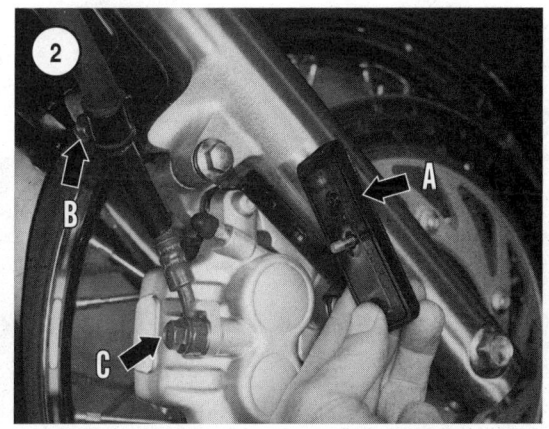

3. Brake fluid absorbs moisture, which greatly reduces its ability to perform correctly. It is recommended to purchase brake fluid in small containers and discard any small leftover quantities. Do not store a container of brake fluid with less than a quarter of the fluid remaining in the container. This small amount will quickly absorb the moisture in the container.

4. Do not allow brake fluid to contact any plastic parts or painted surfaces. They will be damaged.

5. Always keep the master cylinder reservoir cover installed to prevent dust or moisture from entering the system.

6. Use only DOT 4 brake fluid to wash parts. Never use petroleum-based solvents on internal brake system components. These solvents swell and distort the seals. These parts will have to be replaced.

7. Whenever *any* component has been removed from the brake system, the system is considered opened. Bleed the system to remove air. A spongy brake lever usually means there are air bubbles in the system, and it must be bled. For safe brake operation, bleed the system as described in this chapter.

WARNING
*When working on the brake system, do **not** inhale brake dust. It may contain asbestos, which can cause lung injury and cancer. Wear a face mask that meets OSHA requirement for trapping asbestos particles, and wash hands and forearms thoroughly after completing the work.*

FRONT BRAKE PAD REPLACEMENT

There is no recommended mileage interval for changing the brake pads. Pad wear depends greatly on riding habits and conditions. Check the pads for wear periodically and replace them when the wear indicator reaches the edge of the brake disc.

To maintain even brake pressure on the disc, always replace both pads in the caliper at the same time. Do not disconnect the hydraulic brake hose from the brake caliper during brake pad replacement. Disconnect the hose only if the caliper is going to be disassembled.

CAUTION
*Check the pad more frequently when the wear limit lines (**Figure 1**) approach the disc. On some pads, the wear lines are very close to the metal backing plate. If pad wear is uneven, the backing plate may contact the disc and cause damage.*

WARNING
Use brake fluid clearly marked DOT 4 from a sealed container. Other types may vaporize and cause brake failure. Always use the same brand of brake fluid. Do not mix brake fluids from different manufacturers. They may not be compatible.

WARNING
Make sure the brakes are operating correctly before riding the motorcycle. If necessary, bleed the brake as described in this chapter.

1. Use jack stands or a jack to securely support the motorcycle on level ground.
2. Remove the reflector (A, **Figure 2**) and the brake hose holder (B, **Figure 2**).
3. Loosen the retaining bolt (A, **Figure 3**), but do not remove it at this time.
4. Remove the two caliper mounting bolts (B, **Figure 3**), and lift the brake caliper from the brake disc.
5. Remove the retaining bolt, and rotate the pad holder (A, **Figure 4**) away from the caliper body. Notice that the outboard pad (B, **Figure 4**) has a caliper shim. A similar shim is not used on the inboard pad.
6. Remove the outboard brake pad (B, **Figure 4**) and the inboard pad from the pad holder.

7. Replace the pad springs (**Figure 5**) in the pad holder whenever the brake pads are being replaced.

8. Check the pad spring (A, **Figure 6**) in the caliper for wear or fatigue. Replace the pad spring if it shows any damage or excessive wear.

9. Check the brake pad friction surfaces (**Figure 7**) for oil contamination or fraying. Check the pad plates for cracks or other damage. If the brake pads are good, measure the thickness of the friction material with a vernier caliper. Replace both brake pads if the thickness on either pad equals or is less than the wear limit listed in **Table 1**.

> *WARNING*
> *The brake pads must be replaced as set.*

10. When new pads are installed in the caliper, the master cylinder brake fluid level will rise as the caliper pistons are repositioned. Perform the following:

    a. Clean all debris from the top of the master cylinder.

    b. Remove the screws securing the master cylinder cover. Remove the cover and the diaphragm from the master cylinder and slowly push the caliper pistons (B, **Figure 6**) into the caliper. Repeatedly check the reservoir to make sure brake fluid does not overflow. Remove fluid if necessary.

    c. The pistons should move freely. If they do not move smoothly without sticking, remove the caliper and service it as described in this chapter.

11. Push the caliper pistons in until they bottom in the bore to allow room for the new pads.

> *NOTE*
> *When purchasing new pads, check with the dealership to make sure the friction compound of the new pads is compatible with the disc material. Remove any roughness from the backs of the new pads with a fine-cut file.*

> *NOTE*
> *Position each brake pad so the friction material faces the brake disc.*

12. If removed, install the pad spring (A, **Figure 6**) into the caliper.

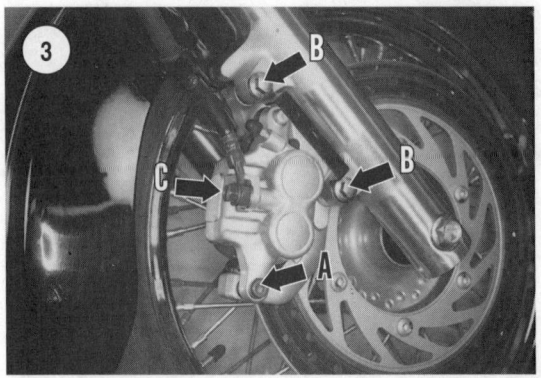

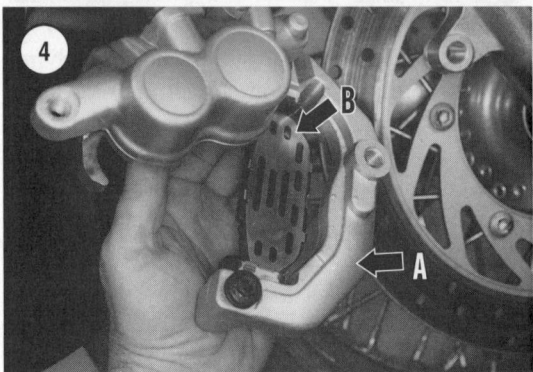

13. If removed, install the pad springs (**Figure 5**) onto the pad holder. Always use new pad springs when installing new brake pads.

14. Install the inboard and then outboard pad into the pad holder. The ears on each pad must engage the pad springs in the holder. Also, make sure that the shim is on the outboard pad (B, **Figure 4**).

> *WARNING*
> *Use just enough grease to lubricate the retaining bolt in the next step. Excess grease could contaminate the*

BRAKES

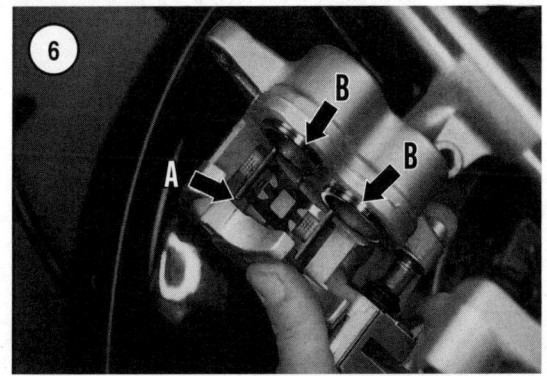

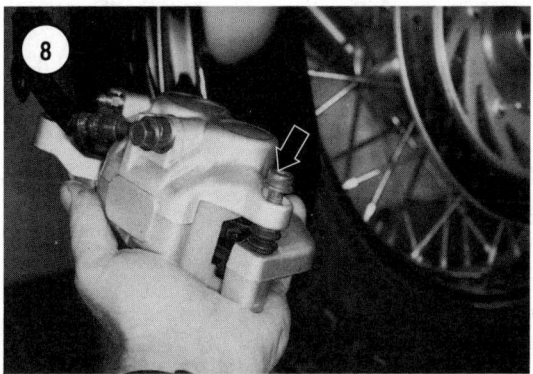

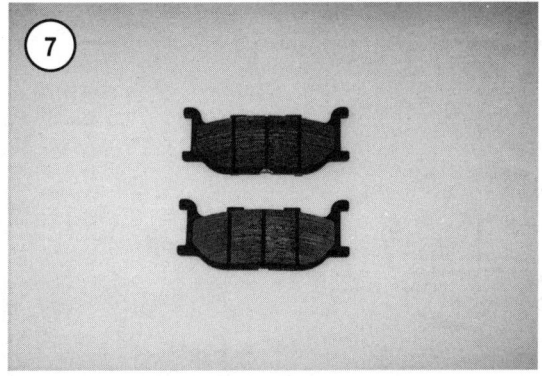

brake pads. Do not get any grease on the brake pads.

15. Lubricate the retaining bolt with lithium grease. Rotate the pad holder into place in the caliper. Install and finger-tighten the retaining bolt (**Figure 8**).
16. Rotate the caliper, and separate the brake pads.
17. Lower the caliper onto the brake disc. Carefully fit the brake disc between the pads to avoid damaging the edges of the brake pads.
18. Install the two caliper mounting bolts (B, **Figure 3**). Apply blue Loctite (No. 242) to the threads of each bolt, and torque them to the specification in **Table 2**.
19. Torque the retaining bolt (A, **Figure 3**) to the specification in **Table 2**.
20. Reinstall the brake hose holder (B, **Figure 2**) and the reflector (A, **Figure 2**). Torque the brake hose holder bolt to the specification in **Table 2**.
21. Support the motorcycle with the front wheel off the ground. Spin the wheel and operate the brake lever until the pads are seated against the disc.
22. Refill the master cylinder reservoir, if necessary, to maintain the correct fluid level. Install the diaphragm and top cover. Tighten the cover screws securely.

> **WARNING**
> *Use brake fluid clearly marked DOT 4 from a sealed container. Other types may vaporize and cause brake failure. Always use the same brand of brake fluid. Do not intermix brake fluids. Many brands are not compatible with one another.*

> **WARNING**
> *Make sure the brakes are operating correctly with full hydraulic advantage before riding the motorcycle. If necessary, bleed the brake as described in this chapter.*

23. Bed the pads in gradually by using only light pressure as much as possible. Immediate hard application glazes the new pads and greatly reduces the effectiveness of the brake.

FRONT CALIPER

Removal/Installation

1. Use jack stands or a scissor jack to securely support the motorcycle on level ground.
2. Remove the reflector (A, **Figure 2**) and the brake hose holder (B, **Figure 2**).
3. Remove the banjo bolt (C, **Figure 2**). Remove the brake hose and the two copper washers from the caliper.

> **NOTE**
> *Brake fluid destroys paint and finish. Immediately wash any spilled brake*

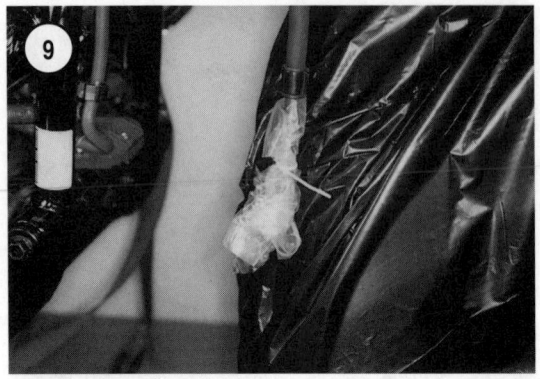

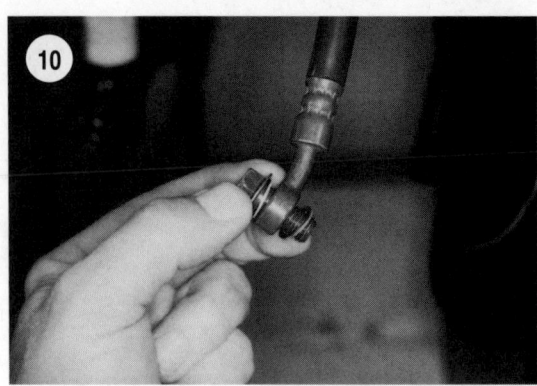

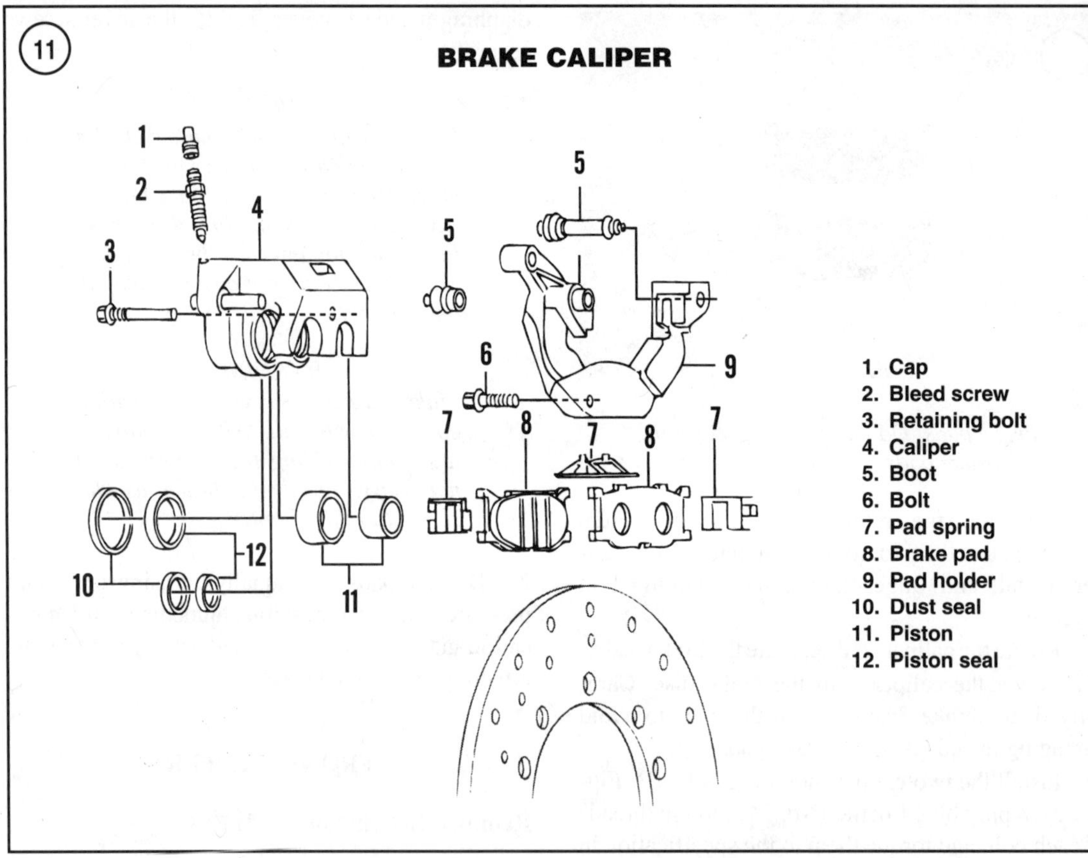

9

10

11
BRAKE CALIPER
1
2
3
4
5
5
6
7
8
7
8
7
9
10
11
12
1. Cap
2. Bleed screw
3. Retaining bolt
4. Caliper
5. Boot
6. Bolt
7. Pad spring
8. Brake pad
9. Pad holder
10. Dust seal
11. Piston
12. Piston seal

fluid from the motorcycle. Use soapy water, and rinse the area completely.

4. Place the loose end of the brake hose into a recloseable plastic bag (**Figure 9**) to keep debris out of the system and to protect the motorcycle from brake fluid.

5. Loosen but do not remove the retaining bolt (A, **Figure 3**) at this time.

6. Remove the two caliper mounting bolts (B, **Figure 3**), and lift the brake caliper from the brake disc.

7. Remove the retaining bolt (**Figure 8**), and rotate the pad holder (A, **Figure 4**) away from the caliper body. Notice that the outboard pad (B, **Figure 4**) has a caliper shim. A shim is not used on the inboard pad.

8. Remove the outboard brake pad (B, **Figure 4**) and the inboard pad from the pad holder.

BRAKES

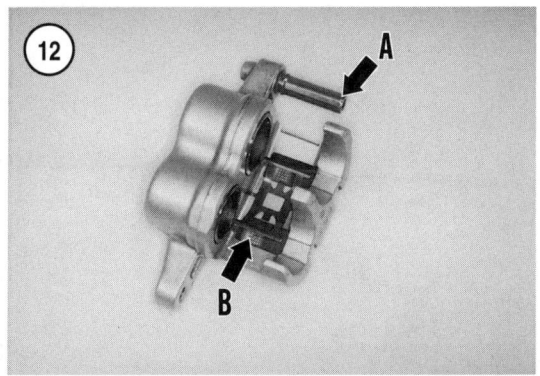

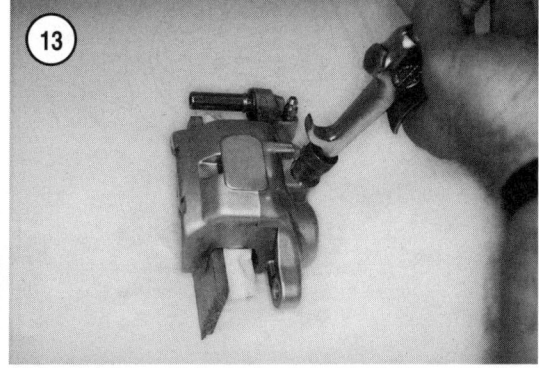

9. Installation is the reverse of removal.
   a. Make sure the ears of each brake pad engage the brake pad spring (**Figure 5**) on the pad holder. Also, make sure the shim is on the outboard pad (B, **Figure 4**).

   WARNING
   Use just enough grease to lubricate the retaining bolt in the next step. Excess grease could contaminate the brake pads. Do not get any grease on the brake pads.

   b. Lubricate the retaining bolt with lithium grease. Rotate the pad holder into place in the caliper. Install and finger-tighten the retaining bolt (**Figure 8**).
   c. Spread the brake pads apart (**Figure 1**), and lower the caliper onto the brake disc. Carefully insert the disc between the brake pads to avoid damaging the edges of the pads.
   d. Apply blue Loctite (No. 242) to the threads of the two caliper mounting bolts (B, **Figure 3**), and torque the bolts to the specification in **Table 2**.
   e. Torque the retaining bolt (A, **Figure 3**) to the specification in **Table 2**.
   f. Install new copper washers on each side of the brake hose fitting (**Figure 10**), and install the banjo bolt (C, **Figure 3**). Torque the banjo bolt to the specification in **Table 2**.
   g. Bleed the brakes as described in this chapter.

Disassembly/Assembly

Refer to **Figure 11** for this procedure.
1. Remove the brake caliper and brake pads as described in this chapter.
2. Lift the pad holder from the pivot post (A, **Figure 12**) on the caliper.
3. Remove the pad spring (B, **Figure 12**) from the caliper body.

WARNING
*In the next step, the pistons may shoot out of the caliper body forcefully. Keep hands out of the way. Wear shop gloves, and apply air pressure gradually. Do **not** use high pressure air or place the air hose nozzle directly against the hydraulic line fitting in the caliper body. Hold the air nozzle away from the inlet, allowing some of the air to escape.*

4. Pad the pistons with shop rags or wooden blocks as shown in **Figure 13**. Block the exposed housing fluid port holes on the back of the caliper housing. Then apply compressed air through the caliper hose joint and force the pistons out of the caliper. Remove the pistons from the caliper cylinders. See **Figure 14**.

CAUTION
Do not use a sharp tool to remove the dust and piston seals from the caliper

330

cylinder. Sharp tools could damage the cylinder surface. Replace the caliper if the cylinder surface is damaged.

5. Use a piece of plastic or wood to carefully remove the dust seal (A, **Figure 15**) and the piston seal (B, **Figure 15**) from their grooves in each caliper cylinder. Discard both seals.

6. Clean all caliper parts, and inspect them as described in this chapter.

NOTE
Never reuse the old dust seals or piston seals. Very minor damage or age deterioration can make the seals useless.

7. Coat the new dust seal and piston seal with fresh DOT 4 brake fluid.

8. Carefully install the new piston seal (B, **Figure 15**) and dust seal (A, **Figure 15**) into the grooves in the caliper cylinders. Make sure the seals are properly seated in their respective grooves.

9. Coat the pistons, the seals and caliper cylinders with fresh DOT 4 brake fluid.

10. Position each piston with the open end facing out toward the brake pads (**Figure 14**), and slide the pistons into the caliper cylinders. Push the pistons in until they bottom in the cylinders.

11. Install the pad spring. Make sure the spring is completely seated in the bottom of the caliper body as shown in B, **Figure 12**.

WARNING
Use just enough grease to lubricate the pivot post in the next step. Excess grease could contaminate the brake pads.

12. Lubricate the caliper pivot post (A, **Figure 12**) and the boots with lithium grease. Slide the pad holder onto the post. Remove any excess grease to prevent brake pad contamination.

13. Install the brake pads and caliper as described in this chapter.

Inspection

1. Clean all parts (except brake pads) with clean DOT 4 brake fluid. Place the cleaned parts on a lint-free cloth while performing the following inspection procedures.

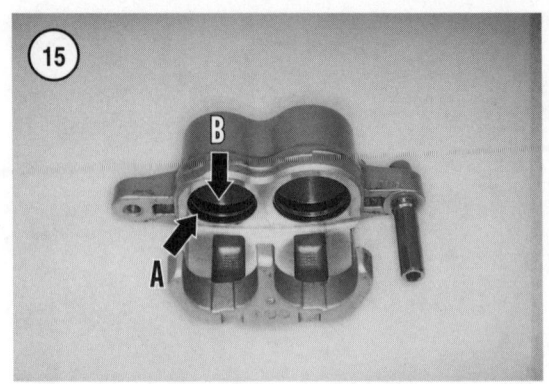

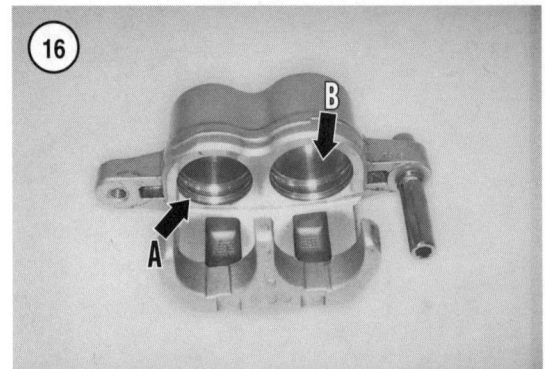

2. Inspect the seal grooves (A, **Figure 16**) in both cylinders for damage. If damaged or corroded, replace the caliper assembly.

3. Inspect the walls (B, **Figure 16**) in both cylinders for scratches, scoring or other damage. If corroded, replace the caliper assembly.

4. Measure the inside diameter of each cylinder bore with a bore gauge (**Figure 17**). Replace the brake caliper if the inside diameter of either bore exceeds the specification listed in **Table 1**.

BRAKES

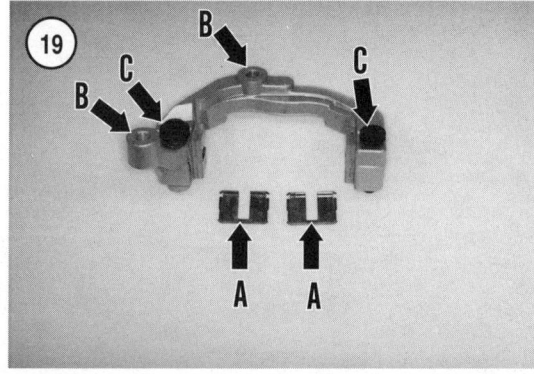

5. Inspect the pistons (**Figure 18**) for scratches, scoring or other damage. If corroded, replace the pistons.

6. Inspect the caliper body for scratches or damage. Replace the caliper assembly if necessary.

7. Inspect the pad spring. Replace the spring if it is cracked, worn or shows signs of fatigue.

8. Remove the pad springs (A, **Figure 19**) from the pad holder if they are not removed already, and inspect the springs. Replace both pad springs if either one is cracked, worn or shows signs of fatigue.

9. Inspect the pad holder for cracks or other signs of damage. Replace the caliper assembly if necessary.

10. Inspect the caliper mounting bolt holes (B, **Figure 19**) on the pad holder. If worn or damaged, replace the caliper assembly and inspect the bolt holes on the fork leg.

11. Inspect the boots (C, **Figure 19**) in the pad holder. Replace a boot that is torn or becoming hard.

12. Remove the bleed screw from caliper body. Apply compressed air to the opening and make sure it is clear. If necessary, clean out the bleed screw.

13. Inspect the fluid opening in the base of each cylinder bore. Apply compressed air to the opening and make sure it is clear. Clean out the opening if necessary.

14. Inspect the threads of the banjo bolt (**Figure 20**) and the retaining bolt for wear or damage. Clean up any minor thread damage. Replace the bolts and the caliper assembly if necessary.

FRONT MASTER CYLINDER

Removal/Installation

CAUTION
Cover the fuel tank and front fender to protect them from brake fluid spills. Wash spilled brake fluid off any painted or plated surfaces immediately. Brake fluid destroys the finish. Use soapy water and rinse the area completely.

1. Drain the master cylinder as follows:
   a. Attach a hose to the brake caliper bleed screw (**Figure 21**).
   b. Place the end of the hose in a clean container.

332

c. Open the bleed screw, and operate the brake lever to drain all brake fluid from the master cylinder reservoir.

d. Close the bleed screw, and disconnect the hose.

e. Discard the brake fluid.

2. Remove the electrical connector from the brake switch (A, **Figure 22**) on the master cylinder.

3. Pull back the boot, and remove the banjo bolt (B, **Figure 22**) securing the brake hose to the master cylinder. Remove the brake hose and both copper washers.

NOTE
Brake fluid destroys paint and finish. Immediately wash any spilled brake fluid from the motorcycle. Use soapy water, and rinse the area completely.

4. Place the loose end of the brake hose into a recloseable plastic bag to prevent debris from entering the system and to protect the motorcycle.

5. Remove the two clamp bolts (A, **Figure 23**) securing the master cylinder to the handlebar, and remove the master cylinder.

6. Remove the screws securing the reservoir cap and diaphragm. Pour out and discard any the remaining brake fluid. *Never* reuse brake fluid.

7. Install by reversing these removal steps. Note the following:

  a. Position the master cylinder so the face of the clamp mating surface aligns with the mark on the handlebar. See A, **Figure 24**.

  b. Install the master cylinder clamp (B, **Figure 24**) so the UP stamped on the clamp faces up.

  c. Tighten the upper clamp bolt first, then the lower bolt (A, **Figure 23**) to the torque specification in **Table 2**. Make sure there is a gap at the lower part of the clamp after tightening.

  d. Install the brake hose onto the master cylinder. Make sure to place a new copper washer on each side of the hose fitting, and tighten the banjo bolt (B, **Figure 22**) to the specification in **Table 2**.

  e. Reconnect the brake switch electrical connector (A, **Figure 22**).

  f. Add fresh DOT 4 brake fluid to the master cylinder, and bleed the brake system as described in this chapter.

CHAPTER TWELVE

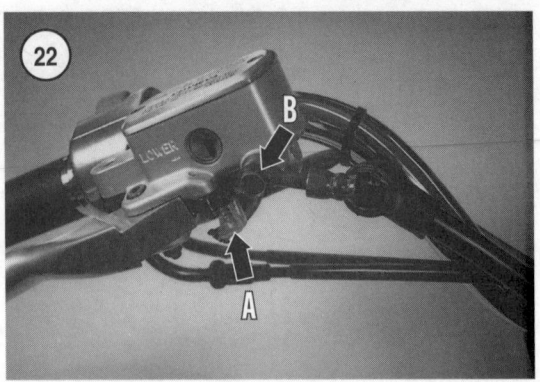

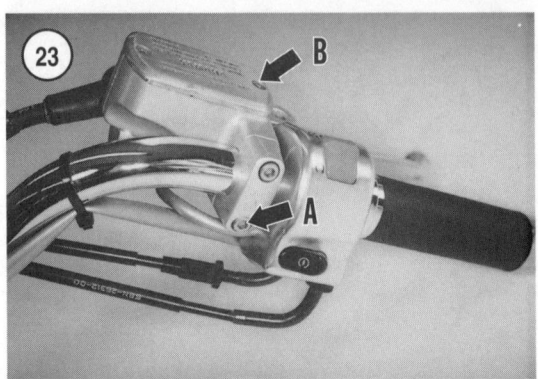

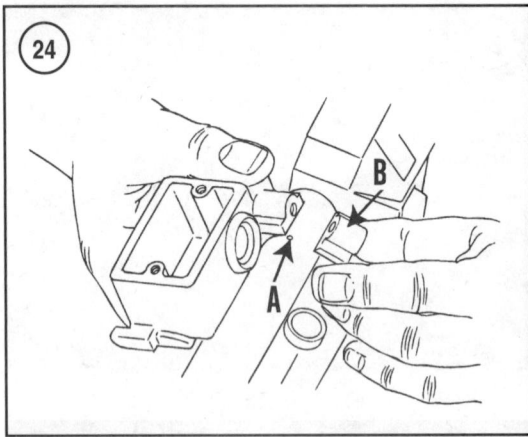

  g. Install the diaphragm into the reservoir. Secure the reservoir cap in place with the two mounting screws (B, **Figure 23**).

WARNING
Make sure the brakes are operating correctly with full hydraulic advantage before riding the motorcycle. If necessary, bleed the brakes as described in this chapter.

BRAKES

25 MASTER CYLINDER

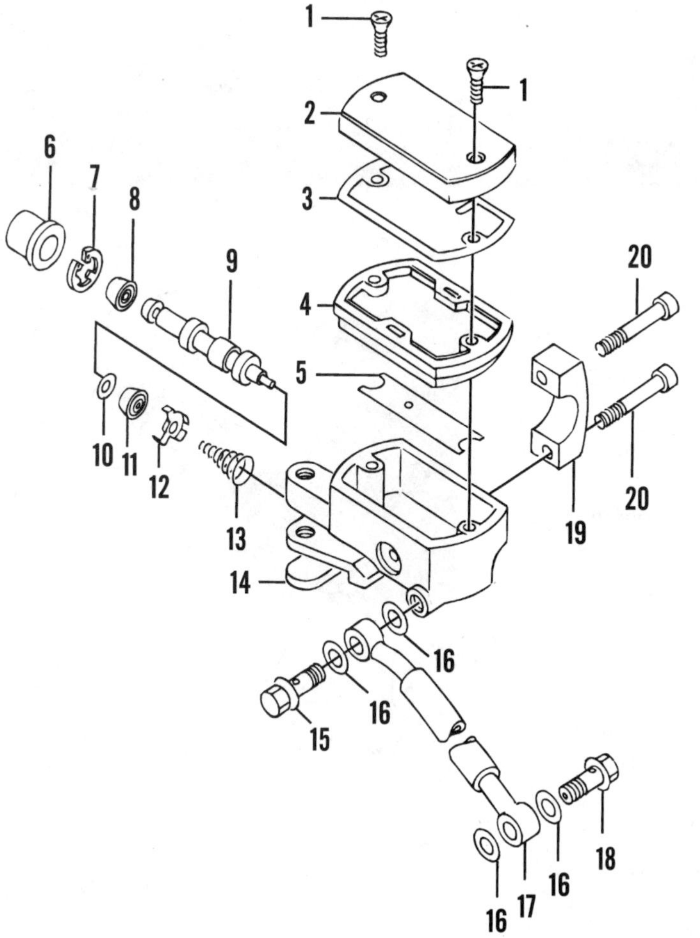

1. Screw
2. Reservoir cap
3. Gasket
4. Diaphragm
5. Blow-back baffle
6. Boot
7. Circlip
8. Secondary cup
9. Piston
10. Washer
11. Primary cup
12. Spring seat
13. Spring
14. Reservoir body
15. Banjo bolt
16. Copper washer
17. Brake hose
18. Banjo bolt
19. Clamp
20. Clamp bolt

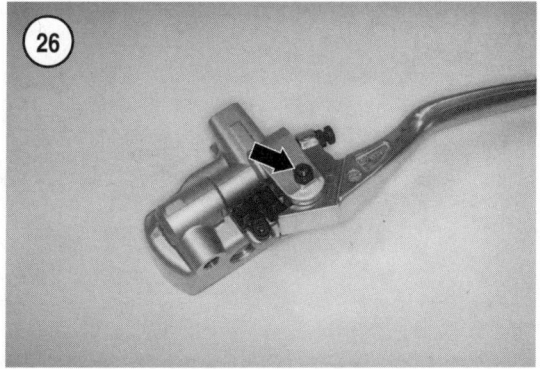

Disassembly

Refer to **Figure 25** when servicing the front brake master cylinder.

1. Remove the master cylinder as described in this chapter.

2. Remove the screws securing the reservoir cap and diaphragm. Pour out and discard any remaining brake fluid. *Never* reuse brake fluid.

3. Remove the nut (**Figure 26**) from the lever bolt and remove the bolt.

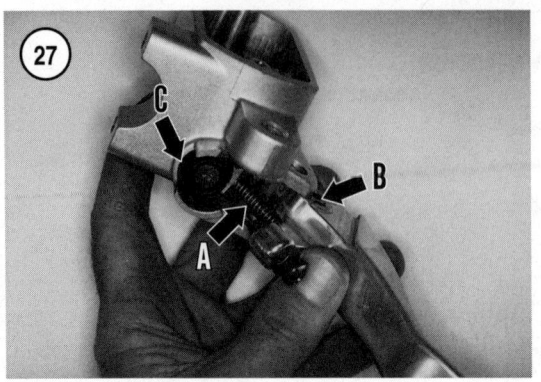

4. Carefully pull the brake lever from the master cylinder. Do not lose the compression spring (A, **Figure 27**) or the bushing (B, **Figure 27**) from the lever.

5. Remove the blow-back baffle (**Figure 28**) from the master cylinder.

6. Remove the boot (C, **Figure 27**) from the master cylinder bore.

7. Remove the circlip (**Figure 29**) from its groove in the cylinder bore, and then remove the piston assembly (A, **Figure 30**).

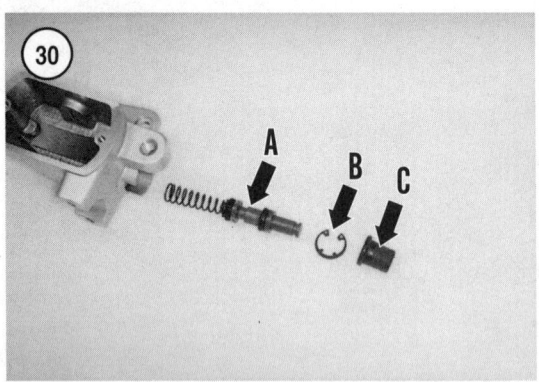

Inspection

1. Clean all parts in fresh DOT 4 brake fluid. Place the master cylinder components on a clean lint-free cloth when performing the following inspection procedures.

2. Inspect the cylinder bore (**Figure 31**) and piston contact surfaces for scratches, wear or other signs of damage. Replace the master cylinder body if necessary.

3. Inspect the inside of the reservoir (see **Figure 32**) for scratches, wear or other signs of damage. Replace the master cylinder body if necessary.

4. Make sure the passage in the bottom of the brake fluid reservoir (A, **Figure 32**) is clear.

NOTE
*The spring (A, **Figure 33**), spring seat (B,) primary cup (C,) secondary cup (D) and piston (E) as well as the circlip (B, **Figure 30**) and boot (C, **Figure 30**) are not available separately. If any part is worn or damaged, replace the complete assembly with a master cylinder kit.*

BRAKES

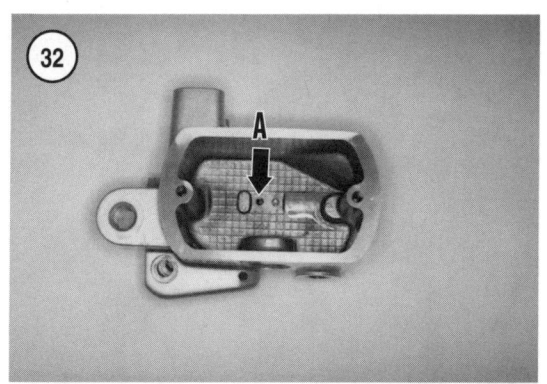

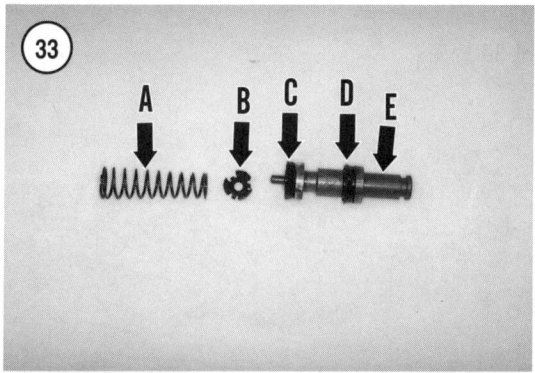

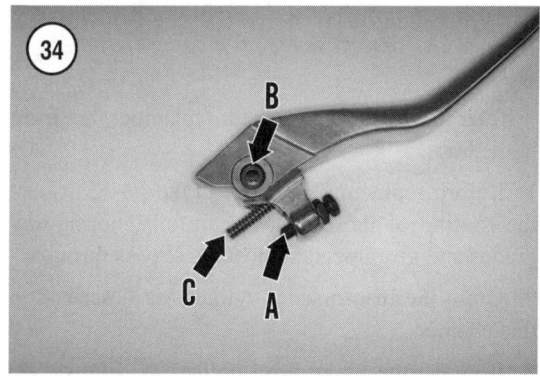

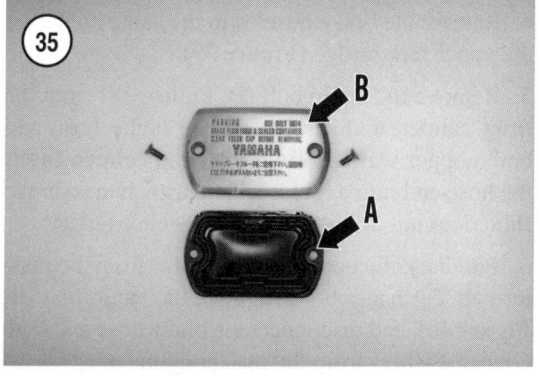

5. Check the end of the piston (E, **Figure 33**) for wear.

6. Check the primary cup (C, **Figure 33**) and secondary cup (D, **Figure 33**) on the piston for damage, softness or for swollen conditions.

7. Check the end of the adjuster screw (A, **Figure 34**) for wear. Replace the spring if necessary.

8. Remove and inspect the brake lever bushing (B, **Figure 34**). Replace the bushing if it is worn or elongated.

9. Remove the compression spring (C, **Figure 34**) from the hand lever. Replace the spring if it is worn or shows signs of fatigue.

10. Check the reservoir diaphragm (A, **Figure 35**) and cover (B, **Figure 35**) for damage and deterioration. Replace if necessary.

11. Inspect the threads in the master cylinder brake port. If the threads are damaged or partially stripped, replace the master cylinder body.

12. Measure the inside diameter of the master cylinder bore with a bore gauge (**Figure 36**). Replace the master cylinder if the inside diameter equals or exceeds the service limit listed in **Table 1**.

Assembly

Refer to **Figure 25** when servicing the front master cylinder.

1. If removed, install the spring seat (B, **Figure 33**) onto the piston (E, **Figure 33**), and fit the small end of the spring (A, **Figure 33**) onto the spring seat.

2. Lubricate the piston assembly (A, **Figure 30**) with fresh brake fluid, and install the assembly into the cylinder bore. Make sure the piston assembly is oriented as shown in **Figure 30**.

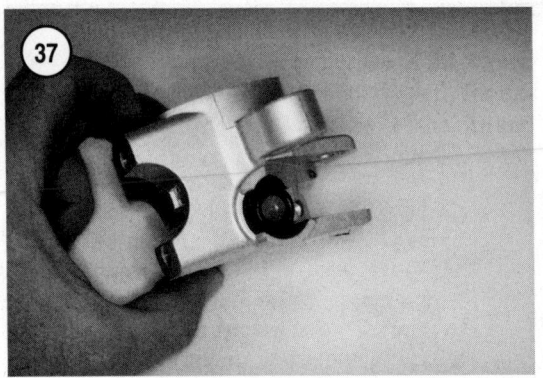

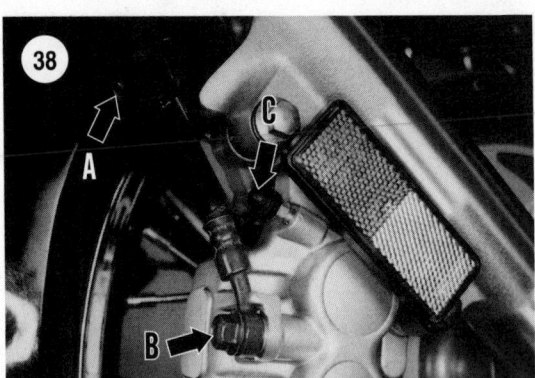

3. Press the piston into the bore, and secure it in place with a new circlip (B, **Figure 30**). Make sure the circlip is seated in the groove inside the cylinder bore as shown in **Figure 29**.

4. Lubricate the boot with fresh brake fluid. Position the boot so the end with the lip faces into the master
cylinder bore, and carefully roll the boot over the piston so the boot seals the master cylinder bore. See **Figure 37**.

5. If removed, install the compression spring (A, **Figure 27**) and the bushing (B, **Figure 27**) into place on the brake lever.

6. Slide the brake lever into place on the master cylinder body. Make sure the compression spring (A, **Figure 27**) engages the boss on the master cylinder body.

7. Lubricate the lever pivot bolt with lithium grease, and secure the brake lever to the body with the pivot bolt and nut (**Figure 26**).

8. Install the blow-back baffle (**Figure 28**) into the master cylinder reservoir.

9. Install the diaphragm and cover after the master cylinder has been installed onto the handlebar.

FRONT BRAKE HOSE REPLACEMENT

Replace a brake hose whenever it shows cracks, bulges or other damage. The deterioration of rubber by ozone and other atmospheric elements may require hose replacement every four years.

CAUTION
Cover components to protect them from brake fluid spills. Brake fluid destroys the finish on any plastic, painted or plated surface. Immediately wash any spilled brake fluid off

the motorcycle. Use plenty of soapy water and rinse the area completely.

Refer to **Figure 25** when replacing the front brake hose.

1. Before replacing the front brake hose, inspect the routing of the old hose carefully, noting any guides and grommets the hose must pass through.

2. Drain the front master cylinder as described in this chapter.

3. Remove the brake hose holder (A, **Figure 38**) from the front fork.

4. Release the brake hose from the cable holder on the upper fork bridge (**Figure 39**).

5. Remove the banjo bolt (B, **Figure 38**) from the front caliper, and disconnect the brake hose and both copper washers from the front caliper. Insert the hose end into a recloseable plastic bag so brake fluid does not dribble onto the wheel or fender.

6. Pull back the boot (A, **Figure 40**) from the master cylinder banjo bolt. Remove the banjo bolt (B, **Figure 40**), and disconnect the brake hose and both copper washers from the master cylinder.

BRAKES

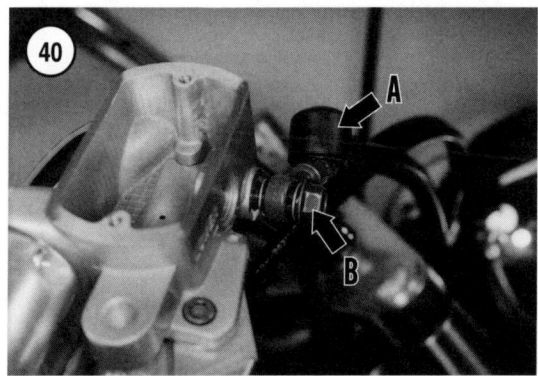

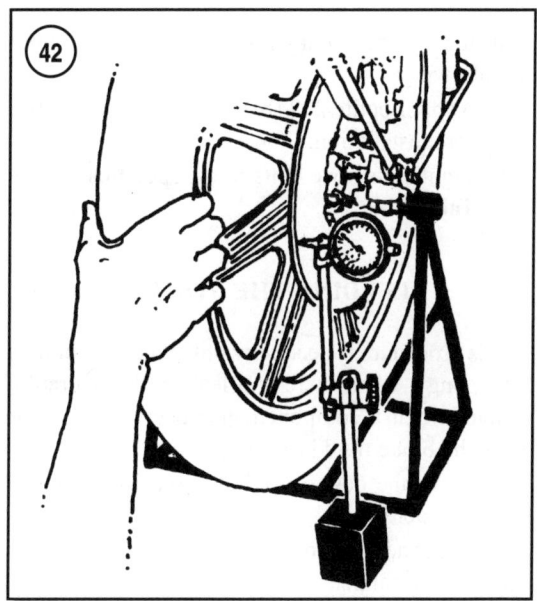

7. Carefully pull the old brake hose from the cable holder on the fork bridge so brake fluid does not leak onto the motorcycle.

8. Install a new brake hose, new copper washers and banjo bolts in the reverse order of removal. Make sure to install the new copper washers on each side of the brake hose fittings.

9. Tighten both banjo bolts and the brake holder bolt to the torque specifications listed in **Table 2**.

10. Refill the front master cylinder with fresh brake fluid clearly marked DOT 4.

11. Bleed the front brake as described in this chapter.

BRAKE DISC

Inspection

The brake disc can be inspected while it is still installed on the wheel. Small marks on the disc are not important, but radial scratches deep enough to snag a fingernail reduce braking effectiveness and increase brake pad wear. If these grooves are evident, replace the disc.

1. Measure the thickness around the disc at several locations with a vernier caliper or a micrometer (see **Figure 41**). Replace the disc if the thickness at any point is less than the wear limit specified in **Table 1**.

2. Make sure all the disc mounting bolts are tight.

3. Mount a dial indicator to the fork leg or to a stand as shown in **Figure 42**.

4. Slowly rotate the wheel and observe the dial indicator. If the runout exceeds the wear limit in **Table 2**, replace the disc.

5. Clean any rust or corrosion from the disc, and wipe the disc clean with brake parts cleaner. Never use an oil-based solvent. It will leave an oil residue on the disc.

Removal/Installation

1. Remove the front wheel as described in Chapter Ten.

NOTE
Place a piece of wood in the caliper in place of the disc. If the brake lever is inadvertently squeezed, the pistons will not be forced out of the cylinders. If this does occur, the caliper will have to be disassembled to reseat the piston and the system will have to be bled.

2. Remove the bolts securing the disc to the wheel, and remove the disc. Refer to **Figure 41**.

3. Install by reversing these removal steps. Note the following:
   a. Apply Loctite 242 (blue) to the disc bolts before installation.
   b. Tighten the disc bolts to the specifications in **Table 2**.

BLEEDING THE SYSTEM

This procedure is necessary only when the brakes feel spongy, when there is a leak in the hydraulic system, when a component has been replaced or when the brake fluid has been changed.

1. Remove the dust cap (C, **Figure 38**) from the brake bleeder valve.
2. Connect a length of clear tubing to the bleeder valve on the caliper.

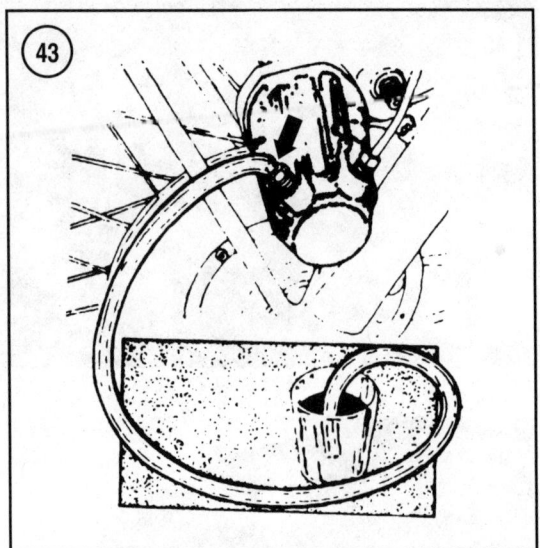

3. Place the other end of the tube into a clean container. Fill the container with enough fresh brake fluid to keep the end submerged. The tube should be long enough so that a loop can be made higher than the bleeder valve to prevent air from being drawn into the caliper during bleeding. See **Figure 43**.

CAUTION
Cover surrounding parts to protect them from brake fluid spills. Immediately wash spilled brake fluid from any painted or plated surface. Brake fluid destroys the finish. Use soapy water and rinse the area completely.

4. Clean all debris from the top of the master cylinder.
5. Remove the cover and diaphragm.
6. Fill the reservoir to about 10 mm (3/8 in.) from the top. Install the diaphragm to prevent the entry of dirt and moisture.

WARNING
Use brake fluid clearly marked DOT 4 only. Others may vaporize and cause brake failure. Always use the same brand name, some brands may not be compatible.

7. Slowly apply the front brake lever several times. Hold the lever in the applied position, and open the bleeder valve with a wrench about a half turn. This forces air and brake fluid from the brake system. Squeeze the lever to its limit, and then tighten the bleeder valve. Do not release the brake lever while the bleeder valve is open.

Maintain the brake fluid level at about 10 mm (3/8 in.) from the top of the reservoir to prevent air from being drawn into the system.

8. Continue to apply the front brake lever and fill the reservoir until the fluid emerging from the hose is clean and free of air bubbles. The system is bled when the brake lever feels firm and when no air bubbles emerge from the hose. If the system is difficult to bleed, light tap the master cylinder with a plastic mallet to release air trapped in the system.

9. Hold the front brake lever in the applied position, and tighten the bleeder valve. Remove the bleeder tube, and install the bleeder valve dust cap.

10. If necessary, add fluid to correct the level in the master cylinder reservoir.

11. Install the cover. Tighten the screws on the front master cylinder securely.

12. Test the feel of the brake lever. It should feel firm and offer the same resistance each time it is operated. If it feels spongy, air is probably still in the system. Bleed the system again. When all air has been bled from the system and the brake fluid level is correct in the reservoir, double-check for leaks, and tighten all fittings and connections.

WARNING
Before riding the motorcycle, make sure the brake is operating correctly with full hydraulic advantage.

BRAKES

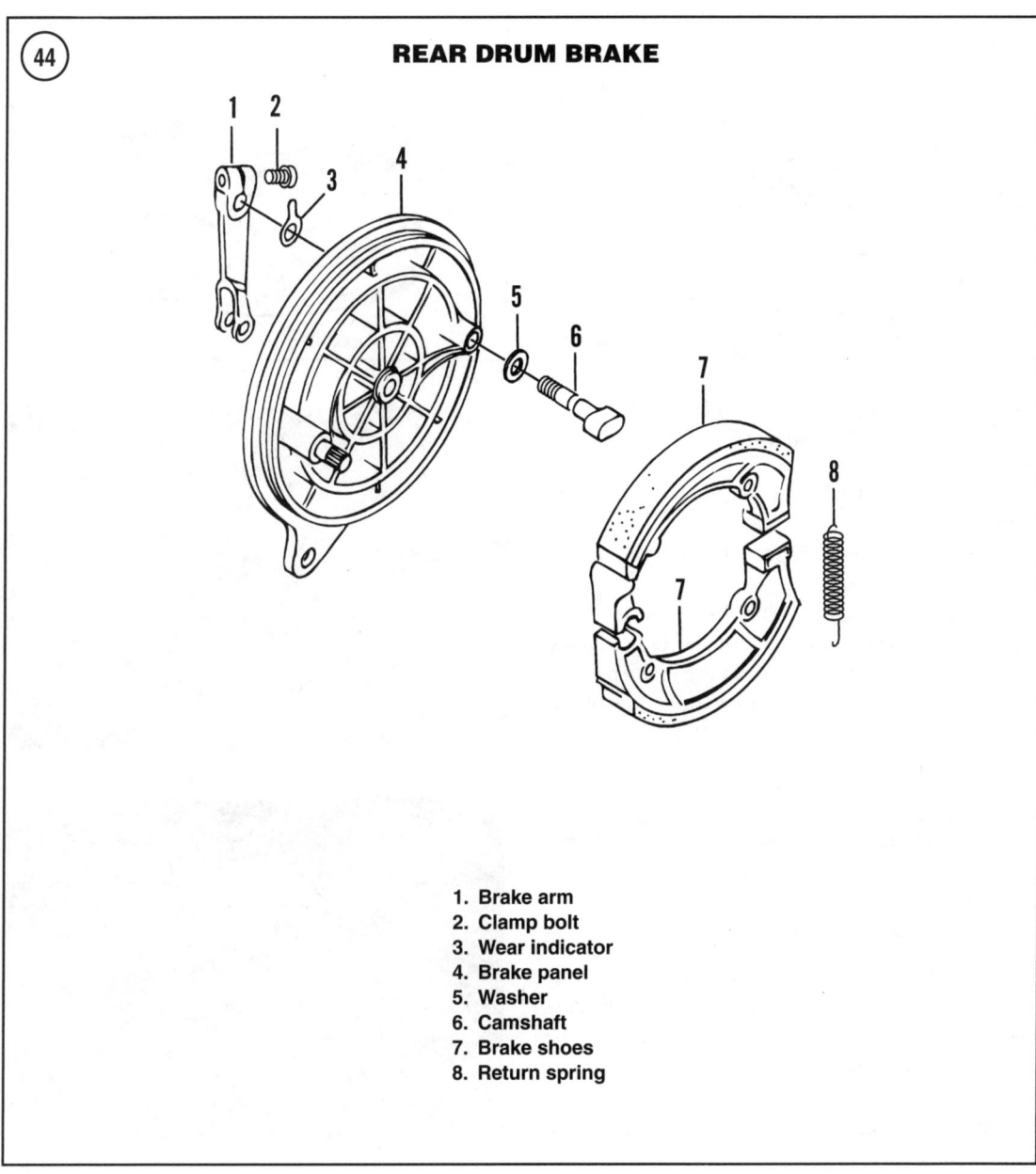

REAR DRUM BRAKE

1. Brake arm
2. Clamp bolt
3. Wear indicator
4. Brake panel
5. Washer
6. Camshaft
7. Brake shoes
8. Return spring

REAR DRUM BRAKE

Pushing down on the brake pedal pulls the rod assembly which moves the brake arm and rotates the camshaft. The rotating camshaft forces the brake shoes out into contact with the brake drum.

Pedal free play must be maintained to minimize brake drag and premature brake wear and to maximize braking effectiveness. Refer to Chapter Three for complete drum brake adjustment procedures.

Disassembly

Refer to **Figure 44** for this procedure.

WARNING
*When working on the brake system, do **not** inhale brake dust. It may contain asbestos, which can cause lung injury and cancer. Wear a face mask that meets OSHA requirements for trapping asbestos particles. Always*

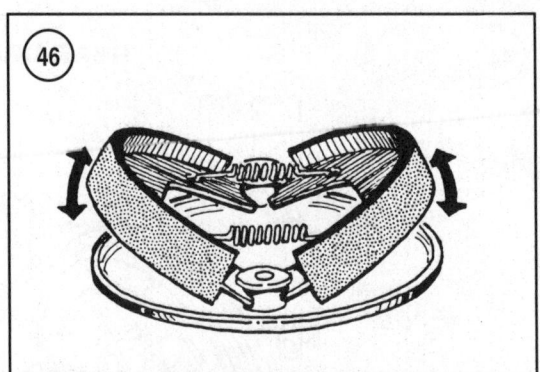

wash hands and forearms thoroughly after completing the work.

1. Remove the rear wheel as described in Chapter Twelve.
2. Pull the brake panel (**Figure 45**) straight up and out of the brake drum.
3. Carefully pull up on both brake shoes in a V-formation (**Figure 46**) and lift the brake shoes and return springs assembly from the brake panel.
4. Disconnect the return springs from the brake shoes.

NOTE
Before removing the brake arm, place a chalk mark on the arm opposite the indexing mark on the end of the camshaft (A, Figure 47). Use this reference during installation.

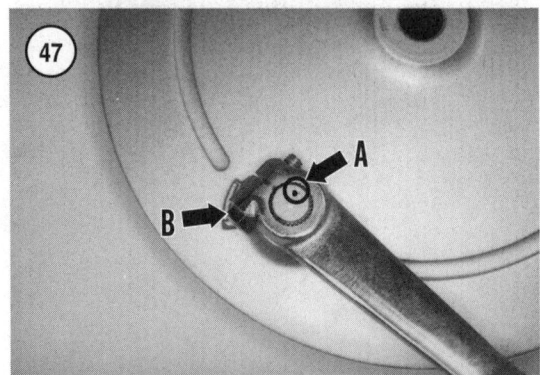

5. If necessary, remove the brake arm clamp bolt (B, **Figure 47**) and lift the brake arm from the camshaft.
6. Remove the wear indicator that sits behind the brake arm.
7. Withdraw the camshaft from the brake panel and remove the washer.

Inspection

1. Thoroughly clean and dry all parts except the brake linings.
2. Check the contact surface of the drum for scoring (**Figure 48**). If there is any groove deep enough to snag a fingernail, resurface the drum. Also, if oil is found on the drum, remove it with brake parts cleaner.
3. Measure the inside diameter of the brake drum (**Figure 49**). If the measurement is greater than the

BRAKES

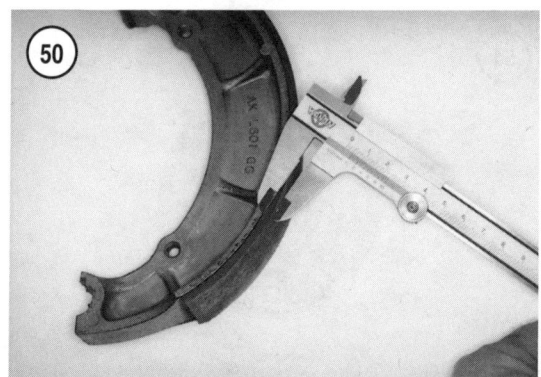

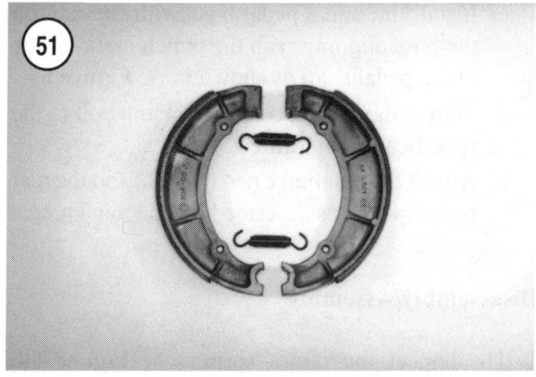

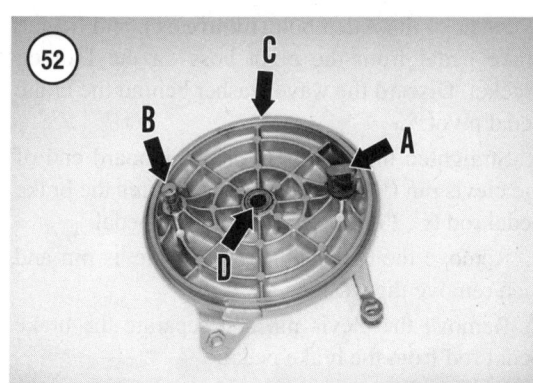

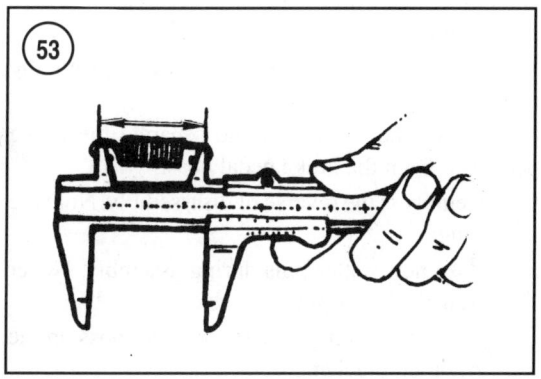

service limit listed in **Table 2**, replace the rear wheel hub.

4. If the drum can be machined oversize (turned) and still be within the maximum service limit diameter, replace the brake shoes and arc the linings to conform to the new drum contour.
5. Measure the brake lining thickness with a vernier caliper (**Figure 50**). Replace both shoes if any portion of either lining is worn to the service limit in **Table 2**.
6. Inspect the linings for imbedded foreign material. Remove dirt with a stiff wire brush. Check for traces of oil or grease. If the linings are contaminated, replace them.
7. Inspect the brake shoe assemblies (**Figure 51**) for wear, cracks or other damage. Replace the shoes as a set if necessary.
8. Inspect both faces of the camshaft (A, **Figure 52**) and inspect the pivot pin (B, **Figure 52**). Remove minor wear or roughness with fine emery cloth. If there is excessive wear or corrosion, replace the camshaft or the brake panel.
9. Inspect the brake panel (C, **Figure 52**) for wear, cracks or other damage. Replace the brake panel if necessary.
10. Inspect the rear axle bushing (D, **Figure 52**) in the brake panel for wear, scoring or other damage. Replace the brake panel if the bushing is worn or damaged.
11. Inspect the two brake shoe return springs (**Figure 51**) for wear. If they are stretched, they will not fully retract the brake shoes. Replace them as necessary.
12. Measure the free length of each brake shoe return spring (**Figure 53**). Replace both springs if the free length of either spring exceeds the specification in **Table 2**.

Assembly

1. Lubricate the camshaft and pivot pin with a small amount of lithium grease. Make sure to apply grease to the shaft and both faces of the camshaft.
2. Slip the washer onto the camshaft, and install the camshaft into the brake panel. Make sure the camshaft is installed from the inboard side of the brake panel.
3. Install the wear indicator onto the camshaft where it emerges from the outside of the brake panel.

4. Align the mark made on the brake arm with the indexing mark made on the end of the camshaft (A, **Figure 47**), and install the brake arm onto the camshaft.
5. Tighten the brake arm clamp bolt (B, **Figure 47**) to the specification in **Table 2**.
6. Lightly lubricate the brake shoe pivots. Do not get any grease on the brake shoes.
7. Place the brake shoes opposite each other, and install the return springs onto the shoes.
8. Hold the brake shoes in a V-formation (**Figure 46**) with the return springs attached and snap them into place so both shoes are firmly seated on the brake panel. When properly installed, the flat end of each shoe should sit against a face of the camshaft (**Figure 54**).
9. Install the brake panel assembly into the brake drum.
10. Install the rear wheel as described in Chapter Eleven.
11. Adjust the rear brake free play as described in Chapter Three.

BRAKE PEDAL/FOOTPEG ASSEMBLY

Removal/Installation

Refer to **Figure 55** when servicing the brake pedal/footpeg assembly.
1. Disconnect the rear brake switch spring (**Figure 56**) from the boss on the brake pedal.
2. Note how the line on the brake pedal boss aligns with the punch mark on the brake pedal shaft. See A, **Figure 57**. If necessary, highlight these marks so the parts can be properly aligned during installation.
3. Loosen the clamp bolt (B, **Figure 57**) on the brake pedal boss, and remove the boss from the brake pedal shaft.
4. Remove the two footpeg mounting bolts (**Figure 58**), and lower the brake pedal/footpeg assembly from the motorcycle.
5. If necessary, disassemble the brake pedal/footpeg assembly as described below.
6. Installation is the reverse of removal. Note the following:
   a. Make sure the circlip (A, **Figure 59**) is properly seated in the groove on the brake pedal shaft (B, **Figure 59**).
   b. Torque the footpeg mounting bolts to the specification in **Table 2**.

   c. Install the brake pedal boss with the line on the boss aligning with the punch mark on the brake pedal shaft as shown in A, **Figure 57**.
   d. Torque the brake pedal boss clamp bolt to the specification in **Table 2**.
   e. Adjust the rear brake pedal height and the rear brake switch as described in Chapter Three.

Disassembly/Assembly

1. Disconnect the return spring (A, **Figure 60**) from the footpeg bracket and from the brake pedal.
2. Remove the Allen bolt (**Figure 61**), and lift the brake pedal from the pivot boss on the footpeg bracket. Discard the wave washer behind the brake pedal pivot.
3. Straighten the cotter pin on the inboard end of the clevis pin (B, **Figure 60**) that secures the brake pedal rod (C, **Figure 60**) to the brake pedal.
4. Remove the cotter pin from the clevis pin and then remove the washer.
5. Remove the clevis pin and separate the brake pedal rod from the brake pedal.
6. Straighten the cotter pin and remove it from the clevis pin (A, **Figure 62**) that secures the brake pedal rod to the brake pedal boss (B, **Figure 62**).
7. Remove the cotter pin and washer from the clevis pin.
8. Remove the clevis pin and separate the brake pedal rod from the brake pedal boss.
9. Assembly is the reverse of disassembly. Note the following:
   a. Use new cotter pins during assembly. Never reuse a cotter pin.
   b. Apply lithium grease to the pivot boss on the footpeg bracket.

BRAKES

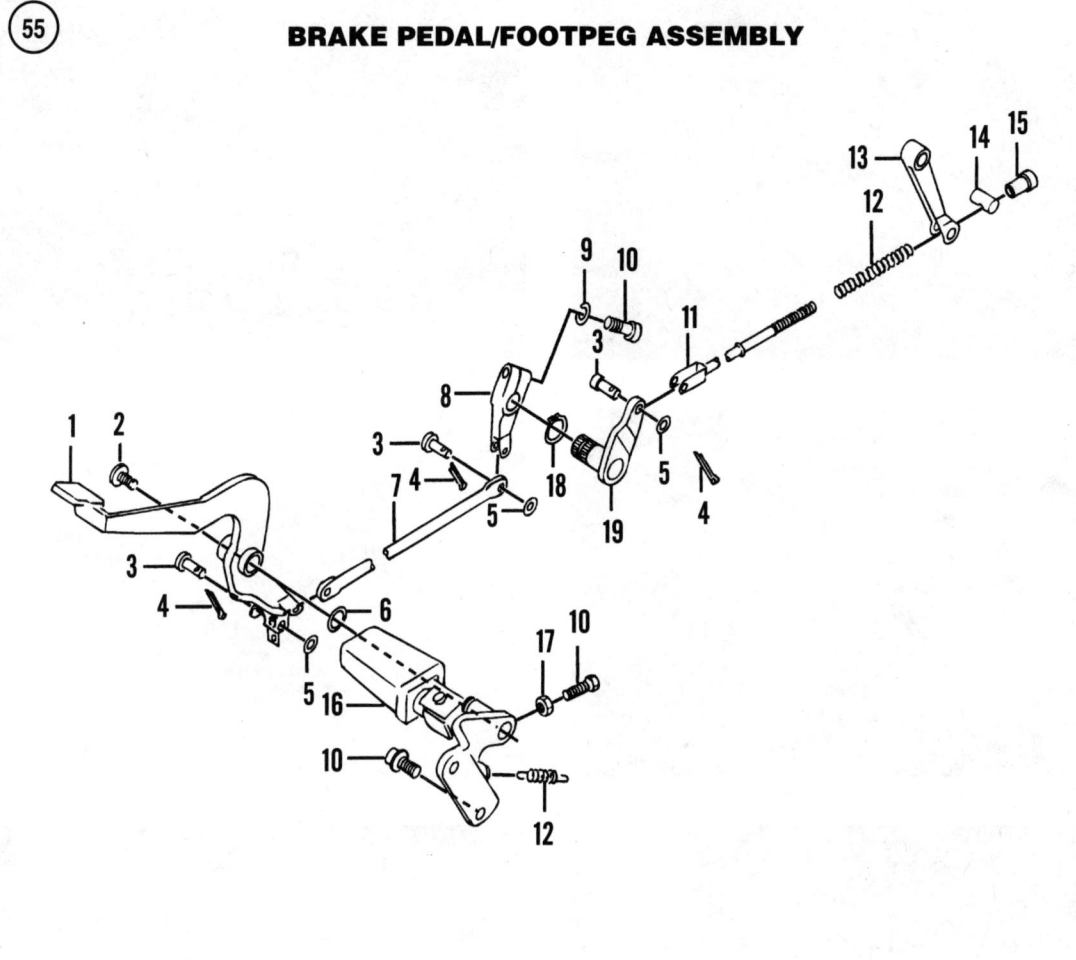

BRAKE PEDAL/FOOTPEG ASSEMBLY

1. Brake pedal
2. Allen bolt
3. Clevis pin
4. Cotter pin
5. Washer
6. Wave washer
7. Brake pedal rod
8. Brake pedal boss
9. Lockwasher
10. Bolt
11. Brake rod
12. Spring
13. Brake arm
14. Pivot
15. Nut
16. Footpeg
17. Locknut
18. Circlip
19. Brake pedal shaft

CHAPTER TWELVE

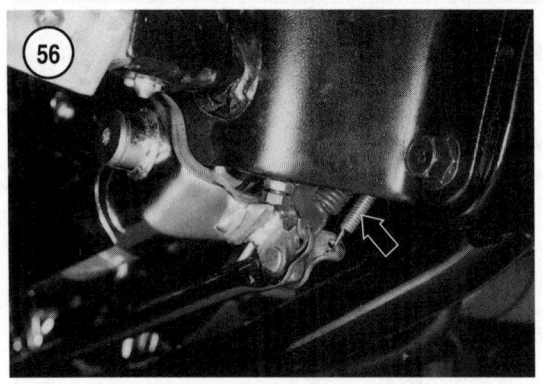

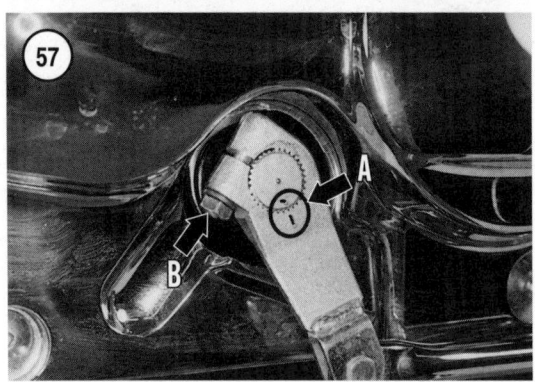

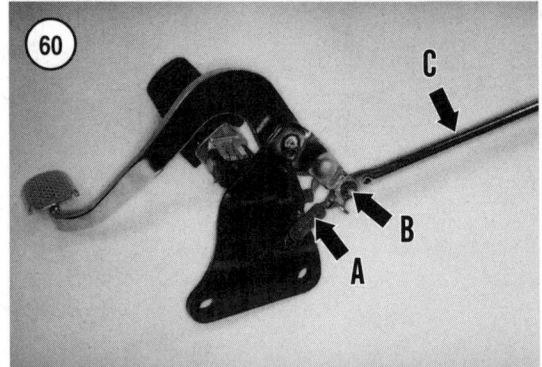

c. Replace the wave washer when installing the brake pedal onto the pivot boss. Tighten the brake pedal Allen bolt securely.

BRAKE ROD ASSEMBLY

Removal/Installation

1. Completely unscrew the rear brake adjusting nut (A, **Figure 63**).

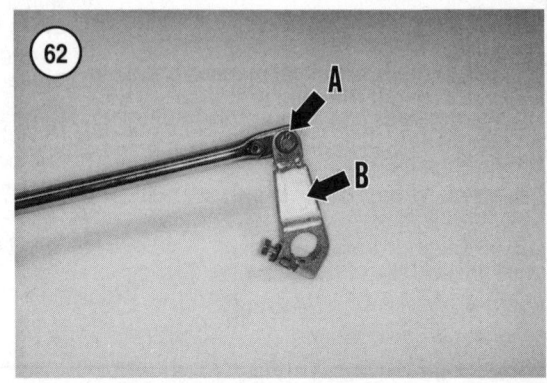

BRAKES

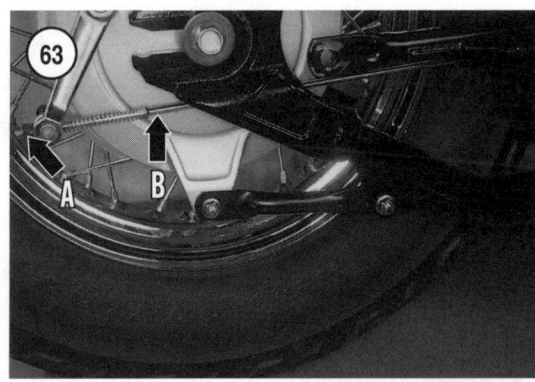

2. Depress the brake pedal and remove the brake rod (B, **Figure 63**) from the pivot joint in the brake arm. Remove the pivot joint from the brake lever, and install the pivot joint and the adjusting nut onto the brake rod to avoid misplacing them.

3. Note how the line on the brake pedal boss aligns with the punch mark on the brake pedal shaft. See A, **Figure 57**. If necessary, highlight these marks so the parts can be properly aligned during installation.

4. Loosen the clamp bolt (B, **Figure 57**) on the brake pedal boss, and remove the boss from the brake pedal shaft.

5. Remove the circlip (A, **Figure 59**) from the brake pedal shaft.

6. Push the brake pedal shaft from the boss in the frame, and carefully pull the brake rod assembly forward and remove it.

7. Installation is the reverse of removal. Note the following:

   a. Apply lithium grease to the brake pedal shaft before installing it in the frame boss.

   b. Use a new circlip (A, **Figure 59**), and properly seat it in the groove in the brake pedal shaft (B, **Figure 59**).

   c. Install the brake pedal boss so the line on the boss aligns with the punch mark on the brake pedal shaft as shown in A, **Figure 57**.

   d. Torque the brake-pedal-boss clamp bolt to the specification in **Table 2**.

   e. Depress the brake pedal and insert the brake rod (B, **Figure 63**) through the pivot joint in the brake arm. Install the adjusting nut (A, **Figure 63**) onto the brake rod, and turn the nut in until the brake can be operated by depressing the brake pedal.

   f. Adjust the rear brake free play as described in Chapter Three.

Table 1 BRAKE SYSTEM SPECIFICATIONS

Item	Specification	Wear limit
Front brake		
Brake fluid	DOT 4	–
Brake pad thickness		
XVS650	6.2 mm (0.24 in.)	0.8 mm (0.03 in.)
XVS650A	6.0 mm (0.23 in)	0.8 mm (0.03 in.)
Brake disc thickness	5 mm (0.2 in.)	4.5 mm (0.17 in.)
Brake disc outside diameter	298 mm (11.73 in.)	–
Brake disc runout		0.15 mm (0.0059 in.)
Caliper cylinder bore		
inside diameter	30.2 and 33.3 mm	
	(1.19 and 1.31 in.)	–
Master cylinder bore		
inside diameter		
XVS650	12.7 mm (0.5 in.)	–
XVS650A	14 mm (0.55 in.)	–
Brake lever free play		
At pivot	2-3 mm (0.08- 0.12 in.)	–
At lever end	10-15 mm (0.39-0.59 in.)	–
	(continued)	

Table 1 BRAKE SYSTEM SPECIFICATIONS (continued)

Item	Specification	Wear limit
Rear brake		
Brake pedal position (above top of the footpeg)	85 mm (3.35 in.)	–
Brake pedal free play	20-30 mm (0.79-1.18 in.)	–
Brake drum inside diameter	200 mm (7.87 in.)	201 mm (7.9 in.)
Brake lining thickness	4 mm (0.16 in.)	2 mm (0.08 in.)
Return spring free length	68 mm (2.68 in.)	–

Table 2 BRAKE SYSTEM TIGHTENING TORQUES

Item	N•m	ft.-lb.	in.-lb.
Brake hose banjo bolt	30	22	–
Brake hose holder bolt	7	–	62
Brake caliper bleed screw	6	–	53
Brake disc mounting bolt	23	17	–
Caliper mounting bolt	40	29.5	–
Retaining bolt	23	17	–
Brake pedal/footpeg mounting bolt	64	47	–
Torque arm nuts	20	15	–
Brake arm clamp bolt	10	–	88
Master cylinder clamp bolt	10	–	88
Brake-pedal-boss clamp bolt	10	–	88
Footpeg mounting bolt	64	47	–

CHAPTER THIRTEEN

FRAME

This chapter contains removal and installation procedures for the front and rear fenders, passenger footpegs, various side covers and other frame items. The shift pedal/footpeg assembly is covered in Chapter Seven; brake pedal/footpeg assembly in Chapter Twelve.

When removing a body component, reinstall all mounting hardware onto the component as soon as it is removed from the motorcycle. After removal, place body components away from the service area to prevent accidental damage.

Table 1, which lists frame component tightening torques, appears at the end of this chapter.

SEAT

Removal/Installation (V-Star Classic)

Refer to **Figure 1** for this procedure.
1. Remove the passenger seat mounting bolt.
2. Lift the back of the passenger seat. Pull the seat rearward until the tabs on the front of the seat disengage from the seat bracket, and remove the seat from the rear fender.
3. Remove the rider's seat mounting bolt.
4. Lift the back of the rider's seat. Pull the seat rearward until the projection at the front of the seat disengages from the seat holder on the frame, and remove the seat.
5. Installation is the reverse of removal. Note the following:
   a. Make sure the projection on the front of the rider's seat engages the seat holder on the frame.
   b. Make sure the tabs on the front of the passenger seat engage the seat bracket on the fender.
   c. Torque each seat mounting bolt to the specification in **Table 1**.

Removal/Installation (V-Star Custom)

Refer to **Figure 2** for this procedure.
1. Remove the passenger seat mounting nut.
2. Lift the back of the passenger seat. Pull the seat rearward until the tabs on the front of the seat disengage from the seat bracket, and remove the passenger seat from the rear fender.
3. Remove the two seat bracket bolts, and remove the seat bracket from the fender.
4. Lift the back of the rider's seat. Pull the seat rearward until the projection at the front of the seat disengages from the seat holder on the frame, and remove the seat.
5. Installation is the reverse of removal. Note the following:
   a. Make sure the projection on the front of the rider's seat engages the seat holder on the frame.

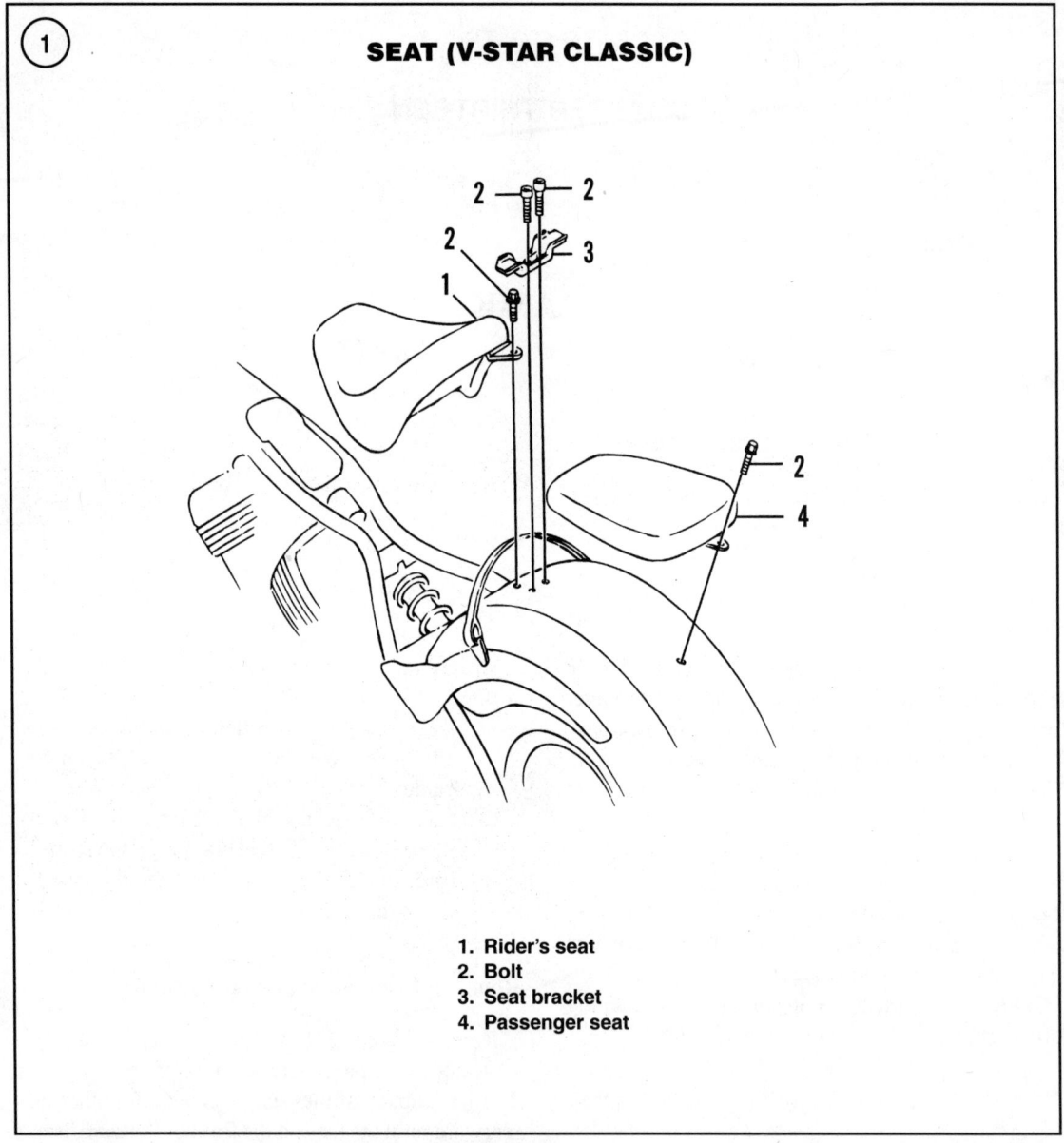

SEAT (V-STAR CLASSIC)

1. Rider's seat
2. Bolt
3. Seat bracket
4. Passenger seat

b. Make sure the tabs on the front of the passenger seat engage the seat bracket on the fender.
c. Torque the mounting hardware to the specification in **Table 1**.

FRONT FENDER

Removal/Installation

Refer to **Figure 3** when servicing the front fender.
1. Remove the front wheel as described in Chapter Ten.
2. Pull the speedometer cable from the cable holder on the left side of the front fender.
3. Remove the mounting bolt (**Figure 4**) and release the brake hose holder from the right side of the fender.
4. Remove the two fender mounting bolts from each side of the fender, and remove the fender from between the front fork.
5. Installation is the reverse of removal. Note the following:
   a. Torque the fender mounting bolts to the specification in **Table 1**.

FRAME

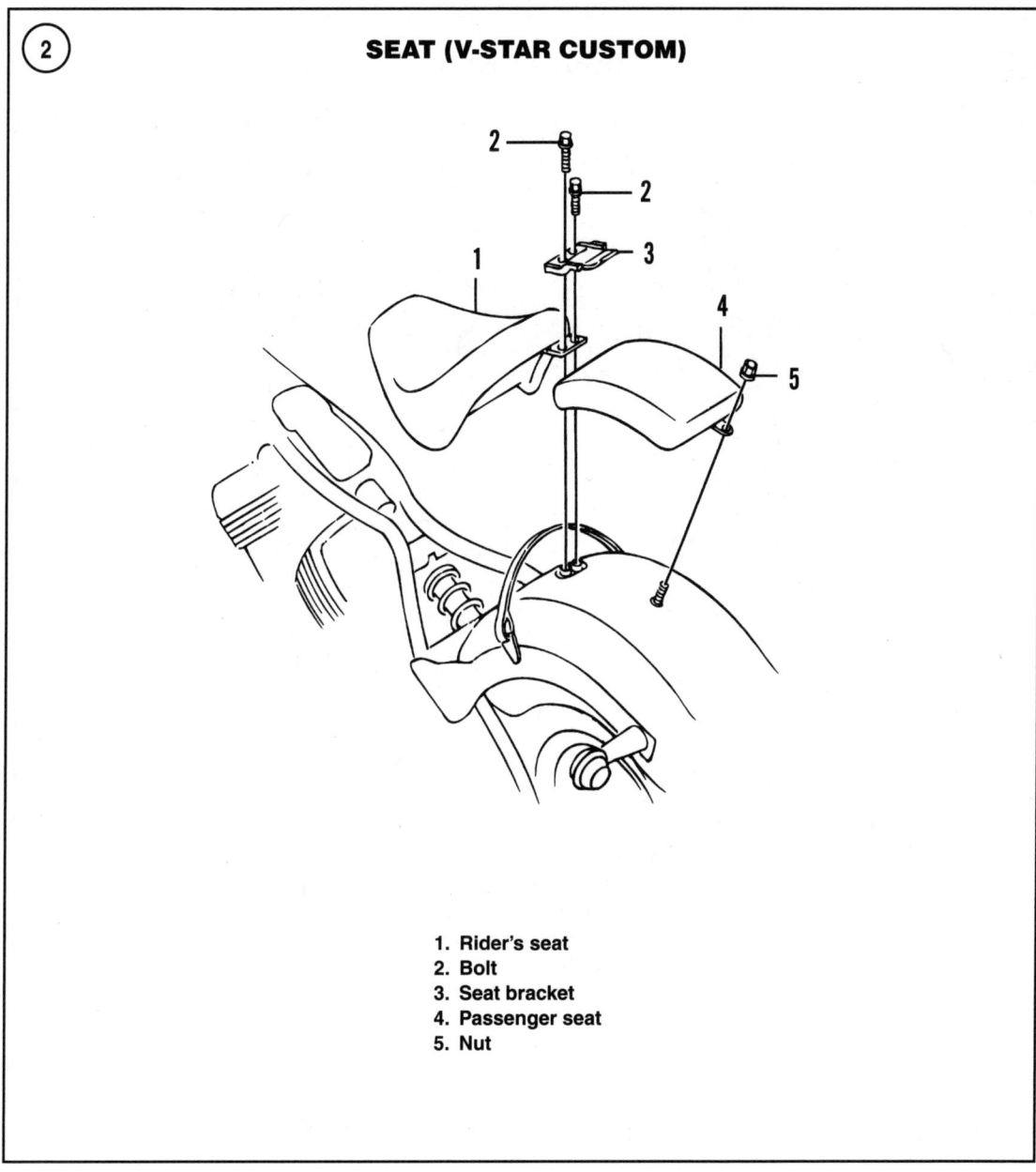

SEAT (V-STAR CUSTOM)

1. Rider's seat
2. Bolt
3. Seat bracket
4. Passenger seat
5. Nut

b. Route the speedometer cable through the cable holder on the left side of the fender.

c. Torque the brake hose holder bolt to the specification in **Table 1**.

REAR FENDER

Removal/Installation

1. Remove the rider and passenger seats as described in this chapter.

2. Remove the battery box cover from the right side of the motorcycle as described in this chapter.

3. Disconnect the taillight/brake light connector (**Figure 5**). Note how the wire is routed through the back of the frame. It must be rerouted along the same path during installation. Release the wire from any cable holders that secure it to the frame.

4. Remove the four fender mounting bolts (**Figure 6**). Do not lose the damper that is installed with each bolt.

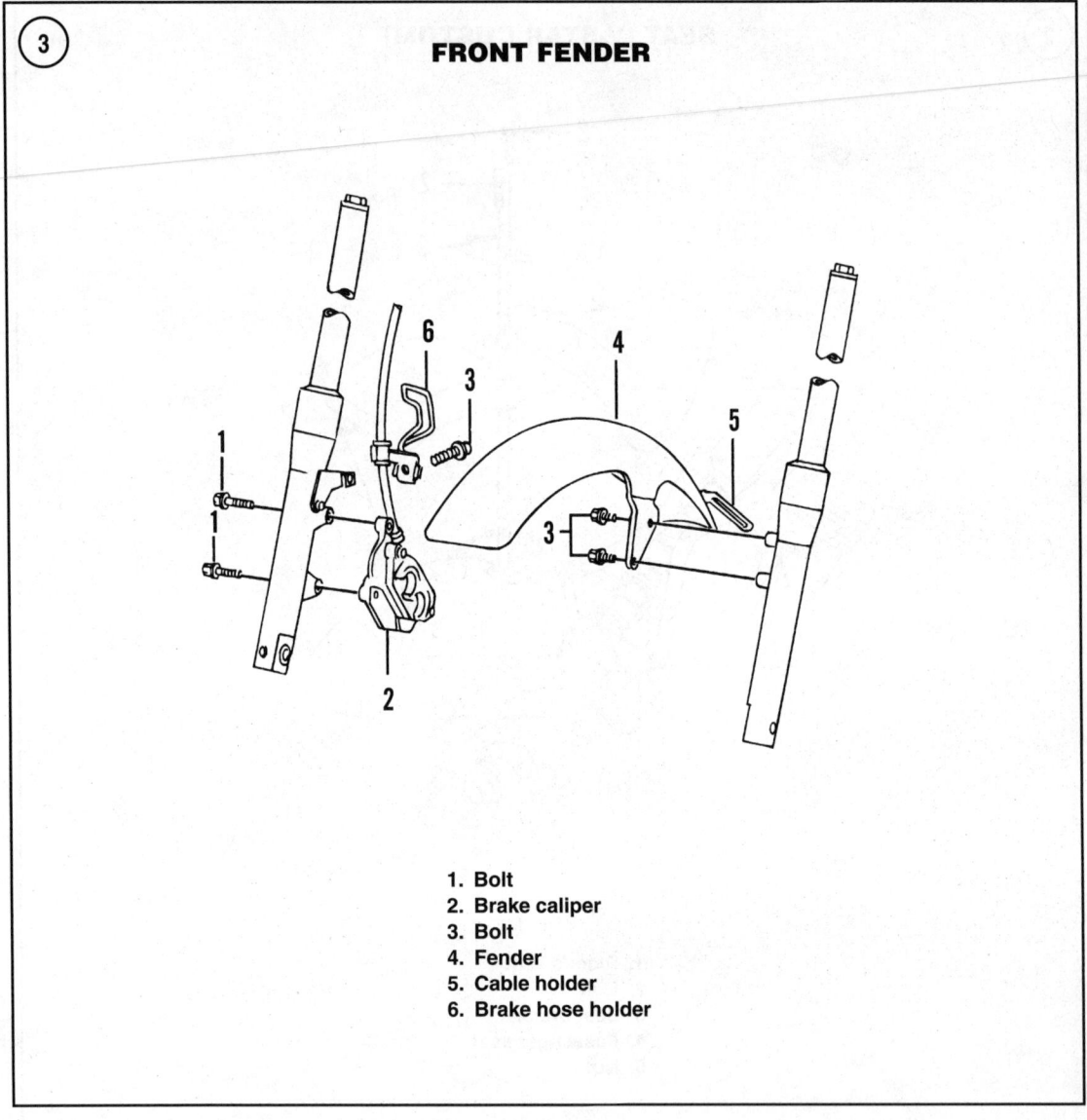

FRONT FENDER

1. Bolt
2. Brake caliper
3. Bolt
4. Fender
5. Cable holder
6. Brake hose holder

5. Pull the fender rearward and lift it from between the frame brackets. On V-Star Custom models, the rear fender stay should come out with the fender. If it does not, remove the stay from the frame. Install the stay on the underside of the fender so the stay will not be misplaced.

6. Installation is the reverse of removal. Note the following:

   a. Torque the fender mounting bolts to the specification in **Table 1**.

   b. Route the taillight/brake light wire as noted in Step 3.

FRAME NECK COVER

Removal/Installation

1. Remove the two fuel tank grommets (A, **Figure 7**) from the post on each side of the frame.

2. Remove each neck cover bolt (B, **Figure 7**) from the front of the frame.

3. Separate the top edges (**Figure 8**) of the left and right covers, and remove each neck cover from the frame.

4. Installation is the reverse of removal. Note the following:

FRAME

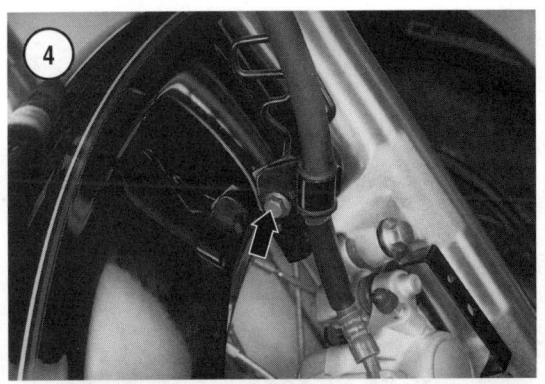

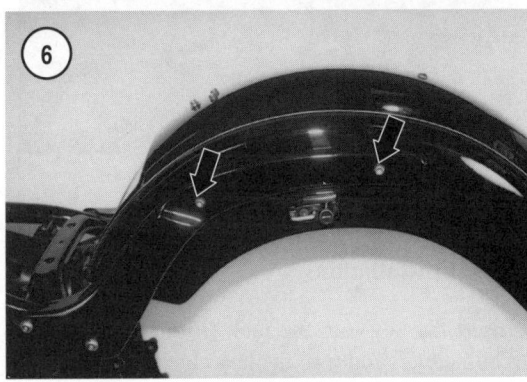

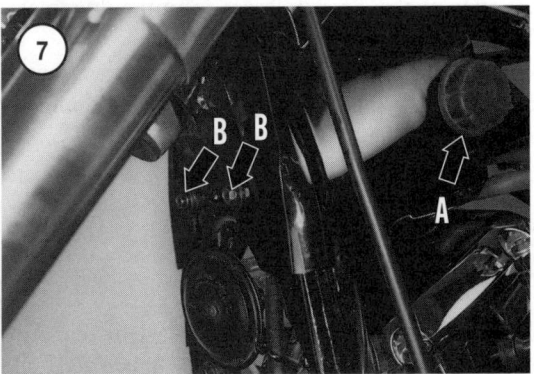

a. Set each neck cover in place on the frame. Make sure the top edges of the cover are properly mated (**Figure 8**).
b. After both covers are in place, install the neck cover bolts (B, **Figure 7**) and the fuel tank grommets (A, **Figure 7**).

BATTERY BOX COVER

Removal/Installation

1. Remove the rider's seat as described in this chapter.
2. Remove the battery box cover bolt (**Figure 9**).
3. Grasp the cover and pull it out from the frame until the post in the upper right corner and the slot on the lower left side are free of their grommets.
4. Remove the cover.
5. When installing the cover, perform the following:
    a. Position the cover so the post and slot align with their respective grommets on the frame.
    b. Press the cover into the frame until the cover securely engages these grommets.

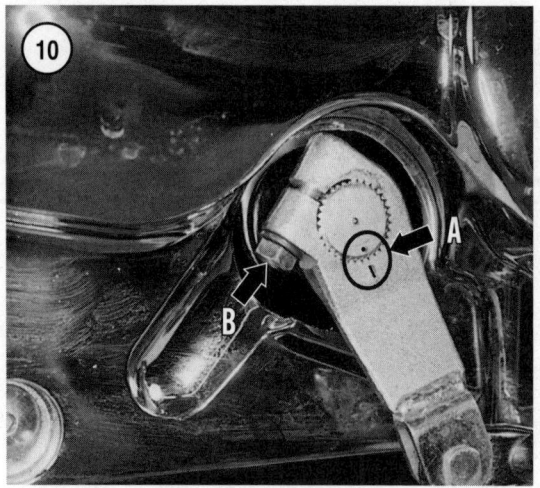

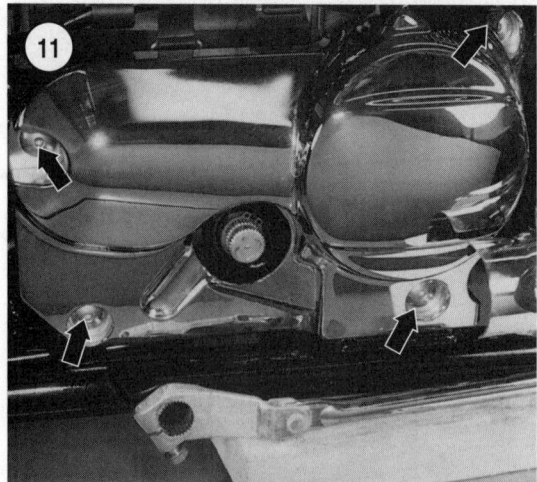

c. Install the battery box cover bolt (**Figure 9**), and torque it to the specification in **Table 1**.

RIGHT SIDE COVER

Removal/Installation

1. Note how the line on the brake pedal boss aligns with the punch mark on the brake pedal shaft. See A, **Figure 10**. If necessary, highlight these marks so the parts can be properly aligned during installation.

2. Loosen the clamp bolt (B, **Figure 10**) on the brake pedal boss, and remove the boss from the brake pedal shaft.

3. Remove the four right side cover bolts (**Figure 11**), and lift the right side cover from the motorcycle.

4. Installation is the reverse of removal. Note the following:

   a. Torque the right side cover bolts (**Figure 11**) to the specification in **Table 1**.

   b. Install the brake pedal boss so the line on the boss aligns with the punch mark on the brake pedal shaft as shown in A, **Figure 10**.

   c. Torque the brake pedal boss clamp bolt (B, **Figure 10**) to the specification in **Table 2**.

   d. Adjust the rear brake pedal height and the rear brake switch as described in Chapter Three.

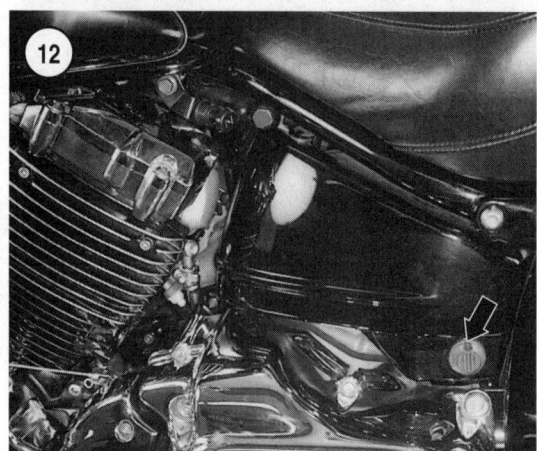

TOOL BOX COVER

Removal/Installation

1. Insert the key into the lock (**Figure 12**) on the tool box cover, and turn the key clockwise.
2. Pull the cover outward until the slot on the top left edge of the cover releases from the grommet. Remove the cover.
3. When installing the cover, press the cover until the slot on the top left edge engages the grommet, and then turn the key counterclockwise.

LEFT SIDE COVER

Removal/Installation

The left side cover is secured in place by four Allen bolts; one 6 × 54 mm bolt (A, **Figure 13**) and

FRAME

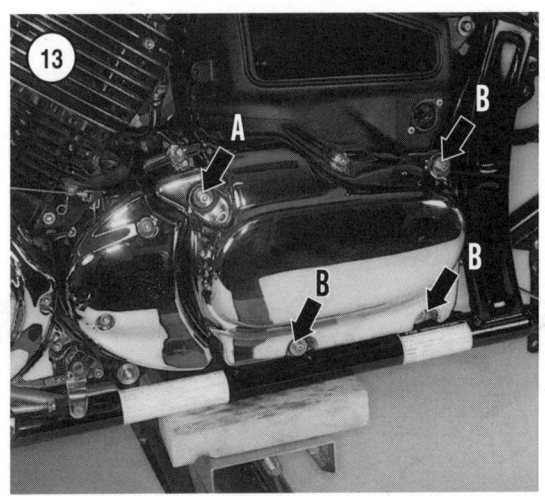

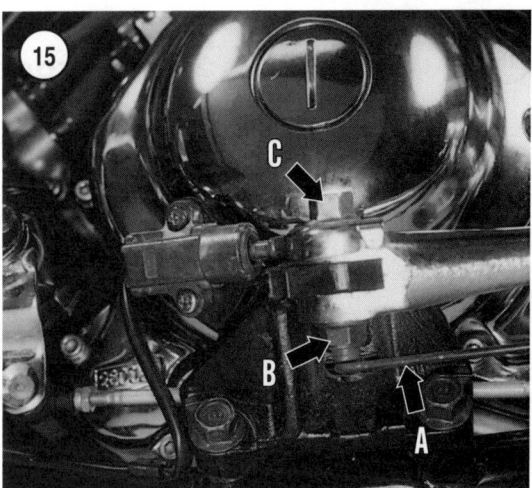

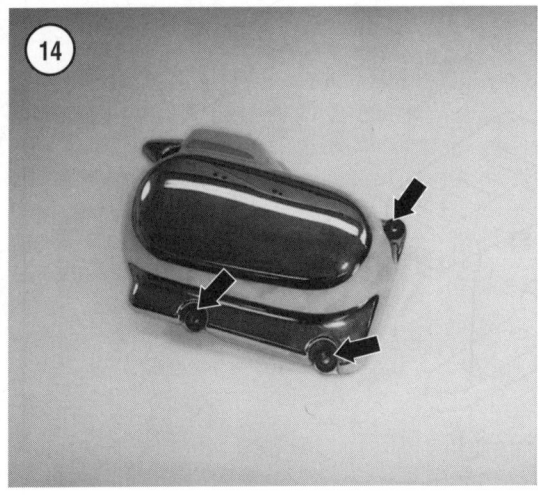

three 6 × 20 mm bolts (B, **Figure 13**). A grommet, collar, and washer are used with the three 6 × 20 mm bolts. Make sure these are in their respective locations during assembly.

1. Remove the shift pedal/footpeg assembly from the motorcycle as described in Chapter Seven.
2. Remove each of the four side cover bolts (A and B, **Figure 13**) along with their washers.
3. Lift the left side cover from the motorcycle.
4. Installation is the reverse of removal. Note the following:
   a. Make sure a grommet and collar are in place at the three locations shown in **Figure 14**.
   b. Install the long bolt (6 × 54 mm) at the upper forward mount on the cover (A, **Figure 13**). Install a short bolt (6 × 20 mm) at the three remaining mounts (B, **Figure 13**).

   c. Install a washer with each right side cover bolt, and torque the bolts to the specification in **Table 1**.

SIDESTAND

Removal/Installation

1. Use a jack and jack stands to securely support the motorcycle in an upright position on level ground.
2. Raise the sidestand, and use locking pliers to disconnect the return spring (A, **Figure 15**) from the sidestand boss.
3. Remove the self-locking nut (B, **Figure 15**) from beneath the sidestand mount.
4. Remove the pivot bolt (C, **Figure 15**), and the sidestand. Do not lose the collar from the mounting tab.
5. Install by reversing these removal steps while noting the following:
   a. Apply a light coat of lithium grease to the pivot surfaces of the mounting bracket and sidestand.
   b. Make sure the collar is in place in the mounting tab.
   c. Install a new self-locking nut, and torque the nut to the specification in **Table 1**.

FOOTPEG

Disassembly/Assembly

Refer to **Figure 16** when servicing a footpeg.

FOOTPEGS

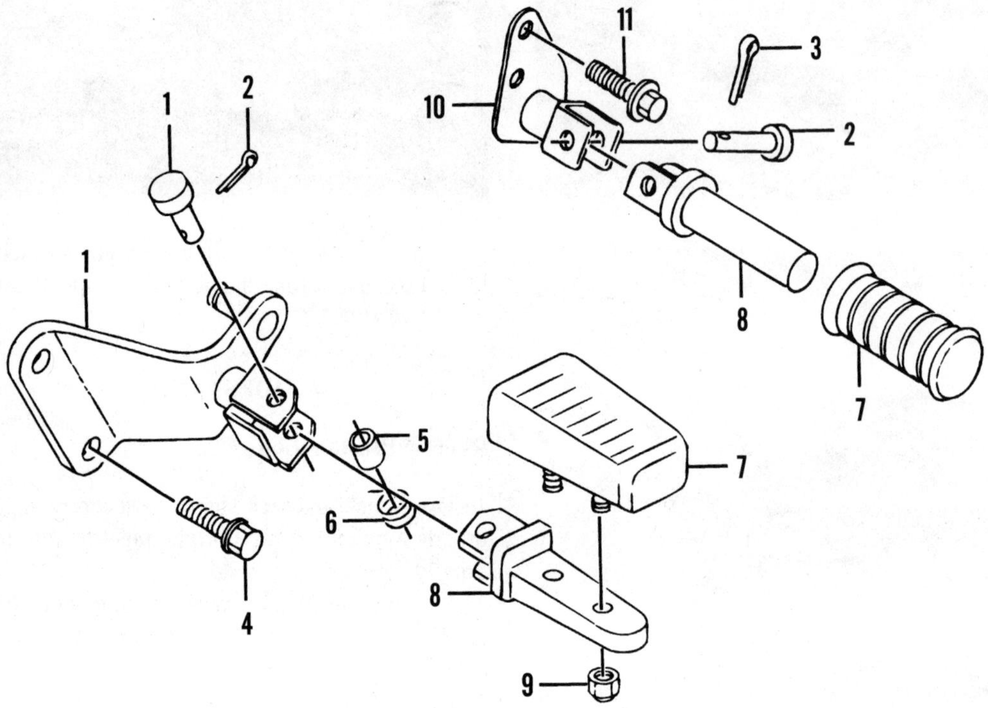

1. Rider's footpeg bracket
2. Clevis
3. Cotter pin
4. Bolt
5. Collar
6. Spring
7. Footpeg pad
8. Footpeg
9. Nut
10. Passenger footpeg bracket
11. Bolt

FRAME

1. Straighten the cotter pin, and remove it from the clevis pin. Discard the cotter pin. Use a new one during assembly.

   NOTE
   When disassembling a front footpeg, carefully separate the footpeg from the bracket so the collar or spring does not get lost.

2. Remove the clevis pin, and remove the footpeg from the bracket.

3. Installation is the reverse of removal. Note the following:

   a. When assembling a front footpeg, install the spring so one tang engages the boss on the footpeg while the other tang engages the footpeg bracket. Make sure the collar is in place in the spring.

   b. Install the clevis pin, and secure it in place with a new cotter pin.

FRAME

The frame does not require routine maintenance. However, inspect it immediately after any accident.

Table 1 FRAME COMPONENT TIGHTENING TORQUES

Item	N•m	ft.-lb.	in.-lb.
Banjo bolt	30	22	–
Battery box cover bolt	7	–	62
Brake hose holder bolt	7	–	62
Brake pedal boss clamp bolt	10	–	88
Front fender mounting bolt	10	–	88
Left side cover bolts	7	–	62
Muffler bolt	30	22	–
Passenger footpeg mounting bolt	26	19	–
Rear fender bracket bolts	26	19	–
Rear fender mounting bolts	26	19	–
Rear flasher mounting nut	23	17	–
Right side cover bolts	7	–	62
Seat bracket bolt	7	–	62
Seat mounting hardware (rider and passenger)	7	–	62
Sidestand nut	56	41	–
Sidestand switch screw	4	–	35
Tail/brake light mounting bolt	6	–	53

INDEX

A

Air
   filter housing 201-202
   induction system 221-223
Alternator
   cover 144-145
   rotor and starter gears............. 145-148

B

Ball bearing replacement............... 32-37
Battery............................... 61-64
   box cover....................... 351-352
   electrical cable connectors 64
   new installation....................... 64
Bike stand............................ 280
Bleeding the system 338
Brakes
   bleeding the system.................. 338
   disc 324-325, 337-338
   front
      caliper 327-331
      hose replacement 336-337
      master cylinder................ 331-336
      pad replacement 325-327
   light................................ 255
   pedal/footpeg assembly 342-344
   problems,
      troubleshooting 58
   rear drum 339-341
   rod assembly 344-345
Break-in 170

C

Caliper
   front............................ 327-331
Cam chain and chain guides............ 113-114
Camshaft 111-113
Carburetor......................... 204-212
   heater system 212, 266-268
   operation........................... 204
   troubleshooting 56-57
Chain guides and cam chain............ 113-114
Charging system 229-231
Choke cable........................ 214-215
Clutch 174-182
   cable replacement 183
   cover 173-174
   external shift mechanism 185-188
   primary drive gear and
      oil pump spur gear 184-185
   release mechanism................ 182-183
   troubleshooting 51-52
Connecting rods 168-170
Cover
   left side 352-353
   right side 352
   tool box............................ 352
Crankcase 158-165
Crankshaft......................... 165-167
Cylinder
   block 124-127
   head covers 94-98
   head............................. 99-108
   leakdown test,
      troubleshooting 50-51

INDEX

D

Disc brakes 324-325
Drive
    gear primary 153
    pinion gear middle 151-153
    shaft and final gearcase 317
Driven gear assembly, middle 149-151
Drum brake, rear 339-341

E

Electrical system
    battery 61-64
        electrical cable connectors 64
        new installation 64
    brake light 255
    carburetor heater system 266-268
    charging system 229-231
    fuel pump system 263-265
    fuses 277-278
    headlight 248-253
    horn 262
    igniter unit 239
    ignition
        coil 236-237
        system 233-236
    lighting system 248
    meter assembly 253
    neutral indicator light 255-258
    pickup coil 237-238
    relay unit 238
    signal system 254-255
    spark plug 238
    starter
        motor 241-246
        relay 247-248
    starting
        circuit cut-off relay 246
        system diode 246-247
        system 239-241
    stator 231-233
    switches 271-277
    taillight 253-254
    throttle position sensor (TPS) 268-271
    troubleshooting, problems 53-54, 56
    turn signals 258-262
    voltage regulator/rectifier 233
    wiring connectors 277
    wiring diagrams 361-363

Emission control
    air induction system 221-223
    evaporative 223-225
    surge tank assembly 202-204
    valve 217-219
Engine 138-144
    lower end 138-144
        alternator
            cover 144-145
            rotor and starter gears 145-148
        break-in 170
        connecting rods 168-170
        crankcase 158-165
        crankshaft 165-167
        middle drive pinion gear 151-153
        middle driven gear assembly 149-151
        oil
            pump 153-157
            strainer 157-158
        primary drive gear 153
        servicing in frame 138
        starter clutch 148-149
        stator and pickup coils 145
    top end
        cam chain and chain guides 113-114
        camshaft 111-113
        cylinder
            block 124-127
            head covers 94-98
            head 99-108
        pistons and piston rings 128-135
        principles 94
        rocker arms 108-111
        servicing in frame 94
        valves and valve components 114-124
    troubleshooting
        lubrication 50
        noises 49-50
        performance 47-49
        starting the 44-47
Evaporative emission control 223-225
Excessive vibration,
    troubleshooting 57
Exhaust system 225-227
Expendable supplies 12-13
External shift mechanism 185-188
    cover 173-174

F

Fasteners 7-11

Fender
- front.............................. 348-349
- rear............................... 349-350

Final gearcase and drive shaft............. 317
Footpeg.............................. 353-355
Front, fork.......................... 299-307
Frame................................... 355
- cover
  - battery box..................... 351-352
  - left side....................... 352-353
  - tool box........................... 352
- fender
  - front.......................... 348-349
  - rear........................... 349-350
- footpeg.......................... 353-355
- neck cover...................... 350-351
- right side cover.................... 352
- seat............................ 347-348
- sidestand........................... 353

Fuel
- air filter housing............... 201-202
- carburetor
  - heater system..................... 212
  - operation......................... 204
- choke cable..................... 214-215
- filter.............................. 219
- level........................... 212-213
- pump bracket.................... 219-221
- pump system..................... 263-265
- tank............................ 215-216
- throttle cable.................. 213-214
- throttle position sensor............ 212

Fuses.............................. 277-278

G

Gasket remover........................... 12
Gearshift linkage
- troubleshooting....................... 52

General information
- ball bearing replacement........... 32-37
- expendable supplies............... 12-13
- fasteners......................... 7-11
- gasket remover....................... 12
- lubricants........................... 11
- mechanic's tips...................... 32
- riding safety..................... 37-38
- RTV gasket sealant................ 11-12
- seals................................ 37
- serial numbers....................... 13
- special tips.......................... 6

- storage............................... 38
- threadlocking compound................ 12
- tools
  - basic hand..................... 13-18
  - fabricating........................ 32
  - precision measuring............ 18-31
  - special........................... 31
- torque specifications............... 6-7
- warning and information labels....... 13
- washing the bike.................... 5-6

H

Handlebar.......................... 292-294
Headlight.......................... 248-253
Horn................................... 262
Hub
- front............................ 283-285
- rear............................. 313-316

I

Igniter unit........................... 239
Ignition
- coil............................. 236-237
- system........................... 233-236
Internal shift mechanism........... 196-198
- shift pedal/footpeg assembly......... 199

L

Lighting system........................ 248
Lubricants.............................. 11
Lubrication
- periodic.......................... 64-71

M

Maintenance
- battery........................... 61-64
  - electrical cable connectors........ 64
  - new installation................... 64
- intervals............................ 60
- periodic.......................... 71-80
- pre-ride checks................... 59-60
- tires............................. 60-61
Master cylinder
- front............................ 331-336
Mechanic's tips......................... 32

INDEX

Meter assembly 253

N
Neutral indicator light 255-258

O
Oil
  pump 153-157
  spur gear and
    primary drive gear 184-185
  strainer 157-158
Operating requirements, troubleshooting 44

P
Periodic lubrication 64-71
Periodic maintenance 71-80
Pickup coil 237-238
  and stator 145
Pistons and piston rings 128-135
Pre-ride checks 59-60
Primary drive gear and
  oil pump spur gear 184-185
Procedures,
  basic test, troubleshooting 54-56

R
Relay unit 238
Riding safety 37-38
Rim and spoke service 285-288
Rocker arms 108-111
RTV gasket sealant 11-12

S
Seals 37
Seat 347-348
Serial numbers 13
Servicing engine in the frame
  lower end 138
  top end 94
Shift mechanism
  external 185-188
  cover 173-174
  internal 196-198
    shift pedal/footpeg assembly 199
Shift pedal/footpeg assembly 199
Shock absorber 317-319
Sidestand 353

Signal system 254-255
Spark plug 238
Special tips 6
Starter
  clutch 148-149
  motor 241-246
  relay 247-248
Starting
  circuit cut-off relay 246
  difficulties,
    troubleshooting 46
  system diode 246-247
  system 239-241
  the engine, troubleshooting 44-46
Stator 231-233
  and pickup coils 145
Steering
  and suspension,
    front, troubleshooting 57-58
  bike stand 280
  front
    fork 299-307
    hub 283-285
    wheel 280-283
  handlebar 292-294
  head 294-299
  rim and spoke service 285-288
  tire changing 289-292
  wheel
    balance 288-289
Storage 38
Surge tank assembly 202-204
Suspension
  front
    bike stand 280
    fork 299-307
    handlebar 292-294
    hub 283-285
    rim and spoke service 285-288
    steering head 294-299
    tire changing 289-292
    troubleshooting 57-58
    wheel 280-283
      balance 288-289
  rear
    final gearcase and drive shaft 317
    hub 313-316
    shock absorber 317-319
    swing arm 319-322
    wheel 310-313

14

Swing arm 319-322
Switches 271-277

T

Taillight 253-254
Test equipment
    troubleshooting 54
Threadlocking compound 12
Throttle
    cable 213-214
    position sensor (TPS) 212, 268-271
Tires 60-61
    changing 289-292
Tools
    basic hand 13-18
    fabricating 32
    precision measuring 18-31
    special 31
Torque specifications
    brake 346
    electrical 279
    engine 137, 171
    exhaust 227
    frame 335
    fuel 227
    maintenance 93
    suspension
        front 309
        rear 323
    transmission 200
Transmission 190-196
    troubleshooting 52-53
Troubleshooting
    basic test procedures 54-56
    brake problems 58
    carburetor 56-57
    clutch 51-52
    cylinder leakdown test 50-51
    electrical 53-54
        problems 56
    engine
        lubrication 50
        noises 49-50
        performance 47-49
        starting the 44-47
    excessive vibration 57
    front suspension and steering 57-58
    gearshift linkage 52
    instruments 44
    operating requirements 44
    starting difficulties 46
    test equipment 54
    transmission 52-53
Tune-up 80-89
Turn signals 258-262

V

Valves and valve components 114-124
Voltage regulator/rectifier 233

W

Warning and information labels 13
Washing the bike 5-6
Wheel
    balance 288-289
    front 280-283
    hub
        front 283-285
        rear
    rear 310-313
Wiring
    connectors 277
    diagrams 361-363

WIRING DIAGRAMS

CHAPTER NINETEEN

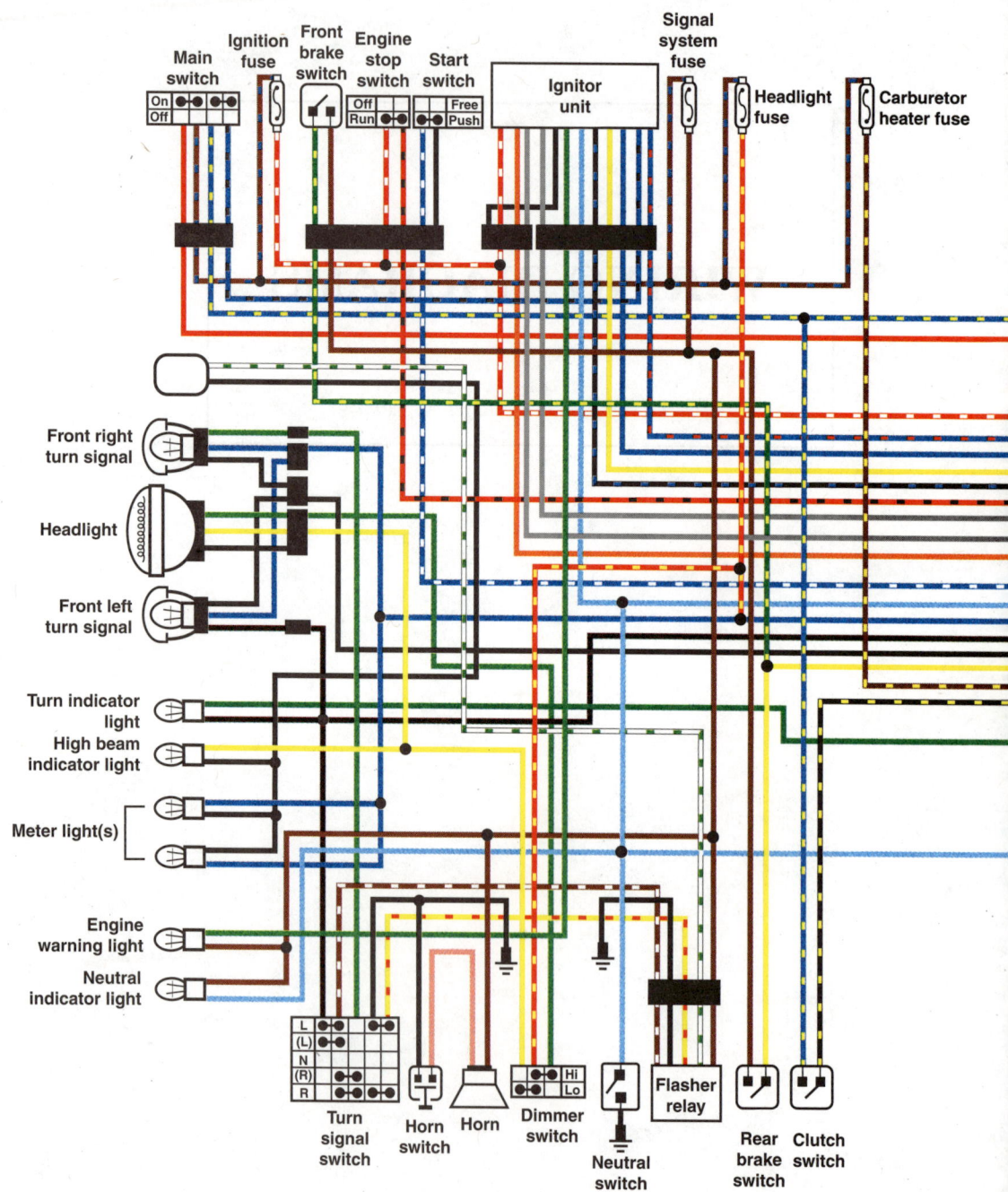

1998-2004 V-STAR 650

WIRING DIAGRAMS

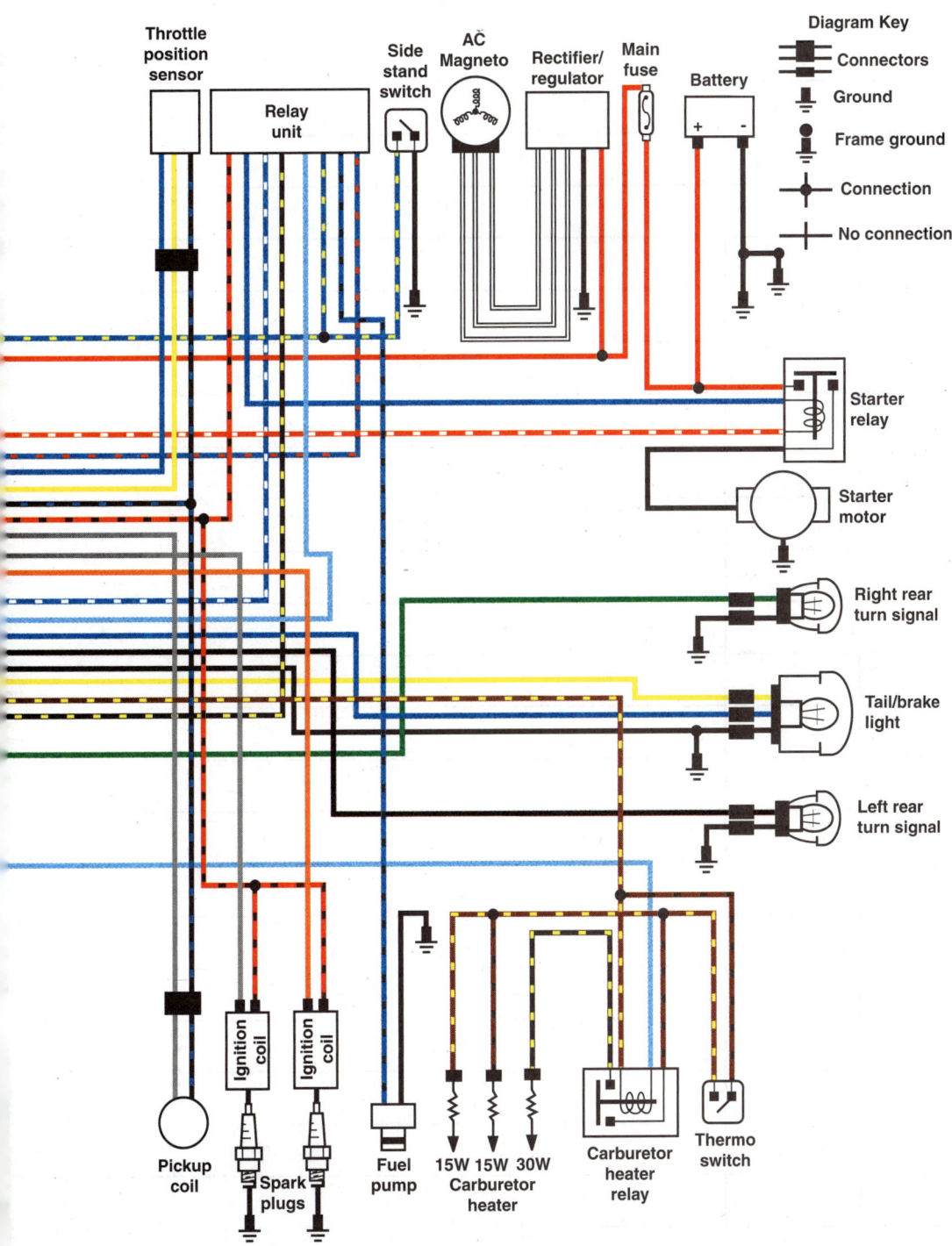

MAINTENANCE LOG

Date	Miles	Type of Service